HISTORY
OF
WALKER COUNTY
GEORGIA

BY

JAMES ALFRED SARTAIN

VOLUME I

Southern Historical Press, Inc.
Greenville, South Carolina

This volume was reproduced from
An 1932 edition located in the
Publisher's private Library

All rights reserved. No part of this publication may be reproduced,
stored in a retrieval system, transmitted in any form, posted
on to the web in any form or by any means without
the prior written permission of the publisher.

Please direct all correspondence and orders to:

www.southernhistoricalpress.com
or
SOUTHERN HISTORICAL PRESS, Inc.
PO Box 1267
375 West Broad Street
Greenville, SC   29601
southernhistoricalpress@gmail.com

Originally published: Dalton, GA. 1932
ISBN #0-89308-887-0
All rights Reserved.
Printed in the United States of America

Dedication

To the Mound Builders, whoever they were, who were the primitive occupants of Walker County, living here hundreds, perhaps thousands of years, who left numerous monuments to their ingenuity, intelligence and progress in civilization, as a memorial to their existence and claim to the territory, a great many of which mounds are still scattered over the county notwithstanding the ravages of time and man; and,

To the Cherokee Indians, their successors, who lived among its hills and mountains, roamed through its woodlands, hunted throughout its beautiful valleys, fished in its limpid waters, and made war on adjoining hostile tribes; who, next to the Mound Builders, were indigenous to the soil, and who, altho holding the territory by an ancient title, if not by divine right, were, nevertheless, expelled from its borders by an alien race, and sent, horrified and grief-stricken, to make their home in a strange land.

To the early pioneers of the county, who came into its uninviting wilds and fastnesses to make their homes—to build log cabins, to fell the forests and plant the fields, build roads and carry on commerce, establish churches and schools and bring a superior civilization within its bounds.

To the old time Gospel preachers, who braved the inconveniences of those early days, enduring hardships as good soldiers, and planting churches in every community in the county; traveling from church to church and preaching the Gospel seven days in the week; and,

To the old-time teacher, who labored in the old-field school, going the rounds of the community with his "Articles of Agreement," making his school, teaching from sun to sun, boarding among his pupils, his principal working materials being the goose-quill, Smiley's arithmetic, and the old Blue Back Speller.

To the later—the present-day citizens of the county, who have contributed, and are contributing their time and energies to the progress, improvement and advancement of the greatest county in Georgia; and lastly,

To the future citizens of the county—the citizens of to-morrow —children now, or yet unborn, who must in future wield the helm and guide the ship and shape the destiny of the county,

"To you from failing hands we throw
The torch; be yours to lift it high;"

this history is reverently dedicated.

Introduction

Youth looks toward the future. Age cons the pages of the past. Walker county, young enough to look confidently towards the future, is yet old enough to claim a worthy past. Heretofore, there has been no published history of the county. Its past has been recorded only in articles published from time to time, and in the memories of its citizens.

The grand jury wisely selected the author of this history, Mr. J. A. Sartain, as the official historian of the county. With unselfish fidelity to the duty imposed upon him, he has undertaken the laborious task of gathering and recording the history of the area now within the confines of Walker county. This history has, with much labor, been assembled only after careful search of historical works, Government, State, County and family records, and numerous interviews with the living descendants of pioneer families. Within its pages are recorded the trials of hardy pioneers and the life of their simple but happy homes, the bravery of her soldiers, the fortitude of her women in peace and in war, the hardships of reconstruction, and the industrial and social life down to the present time. It is—the history of Walker county.

The work has been faithfully done by one devoted to the task, and those who now claim Walker county as home, or whose ancestors contributed to the making of this history, will find, I am sure, as I have found, an absorbing interest in these pages—the record of a hardy, brave and patriotic citizenry.

Walter B. Shaw.

J. A. Sartain
The Author.

Foreword

In compiling a history of the county I have proceeded on the idea that a county history is much like a family history,—is, in fact, history of a very large family where every one is more or less acquainted with the others. This theory eliminates much of dignity and formality and permits the writer to express his views on certain matters and events, which, in other histories, might be of questionable propriety. The reader must accept the facts of history whether they are palatable or not; but in all mere individual whims of the author he has the privilege of taking the other side of the argument.

Too, in a county history it is possible to deal in details to a much larger extent than is possible in other histories, and my readers will discover that I have taken advantage of this possibility; they will find also, that I have occasionally introduced an article with no special historical value, this being done because of its general interest.

This has been a work of love. I have never engaged in an undertaking that appealed to me with greater interest. If my readers shall feel a fraction of the pleasure in reading it that I have experienced in its preparation, I shall be content. No one is more keenly conscious of its limitations than the writer. Practically all of it has been written, re-written and revised at least three times; and still there is room for revision. Aside from its spiritual shortcomings, I am sensible of mechanical errors—errors in paragraphing, punctuation and in arrangement of material. I wish that my readers may cast over my mistakes the broad mantle of charity.

I desire to express my sincere thanks to every one who has so willingly and freely, often at considerable labor, contributed in any way toward the success, if it is such, of this work. If I should undertake to name them I would hardly know where to begin or end. I thank you.

This book is now out of print, only a limited number of copies being published. Naturally it will become more valuable as time passes. I hope that every copy may be carefully preserved and cared for and passed on to the next generation. A century hence your copy may be highly prized by your descendants.

With much trepidation, fear and hesitation, but with infinite relief, I now send it forth.

J. A. S.

LaFayette, Ga., July, 1932.

Table of Contents

CHAPTER		PAGE
I	Geological History — Mound Builders — Indian History	1
II	Indian History, Continued	5
III	Indian History Continued — John Ross—John Howard Payne	10
IV	Indian History Continued — Their Removal — Sequoya—Hardships of the Voyage	14
V	Indian Lore and Legends—First Court House at Crawfish Spring	22
VI	Indian Trails — Farming — Graves — the First Roads	27
VII	Indian Romances and Stories	33
VIII	County Organized—Its Name—Early Settlers	41
IX	Militia Districts—Boundaries—"Wax and Tallow" Deeds	47
X	Fort Cummings—Echo from 1838	51
XI	Chickamauga Battle — Bragg at LaFayette — Skirmishes	55
XII	Chickamauga Battle Continued—General Gordon's Description	60
XIII	Chickamauga Battle Continued — Confederates Win	66
XIV	Chickamauga Battle Continued—Official Reports, Confederate	68
XV	Chickamauga Battle Continued—Official Reports, Union	73
XVI	Chickamauga Battle Continued—Hill's Report	80
XVII	Chickamauga Battle Continued—Bragg's Report	86
XVIII	Chickamauga Battle Continued — Judge Lusk's Article	98
XIX	Battle of LaFayette	111
XX	Civil War Terrorists	120
XXI	The Negro—Bills of Sale	125
XXII	Muster Rolls, Confederate Soldiers	134
XXIII	Camp Chickamauga—Pension Rolls—Confederate Monument—Revolutionary Soldiers	149

Table of Contents—Continued

CHAPTER		PAGE
XXIV	Schools — Poor School Fund — Other Schools — Earliest School Records—Current School History, 1931	160
XXV	"The Old Field School"—Early Teachers—Recent Teachers—Roster County School Superintendents Roster Members Board of Education	170
XXVI	Walker County, Position—Topography—Drainage Climate	180
XXVII	Mineral and Economical. Coal—Iron Ore—Furnaces—Wealth—Autos—Bonds—Miscellaneous	185
XXVIII	Early Customs and Living in Walker County—Country Young People a Generation Ago	189
XXIX	Country Social Life Sixty Years Ago—Clothes—Amusements and Entertainments—Conveniences	196
XXX	Contributions,—White's Historical Collections—T. A. Cooper's Article—Captain Wood's—John Ross House—Early Days Around Crawfish Spring Reminiscences of a Refugee—Mother's Gift to a Soldier Boy—History of a Refugeeing Family	204
XXXI	Contributions, Continued—LaFayette Volunteers—Note of a Partridge—LaFayette Before the War Skirmish at LaFayette—Walker's Quota of Soldiers—When Husband Went to War—A Heroine as Guard—Murder of the McSpaddens—An Ante-Bellum Picture	225
XXXII	Miscellaneous,—Wool Rolls—Hat Factory—Shooting Match—Sunnyside—Ante-Bellum Homestead—Irregular Southern Boundary Line—Menu in Revolutionary War—A Pottery Plant	239
XXXIII	Miscellaneous, Continued — Andrews' Raiders—Indian Rock Mound — Blackwell Ledger — Lane Home—Thomas Pattan "Secesh"—Old Singers—Bryan Family — Hixon-Miller Family — Schmitt Family — Filched a Church — T. A. Cooper — White's Sattistics — Horse Swapping — Gander Pulling	246
XXXIV	Miscellaneous Continued — Anderson Spring — A "Witch" Spring—James R. Jones Ledger—Signal Point—Whipping Post—Augustus McCutchen—	

Table of Contents—Continued

CHAPTER		PAGE
	Declaration—Born at Sea—Hunter's Paradise—Records from 1883—Indian Doctor—"Home Sweet Home"—Indian's Valedictory	254
XXXV	Miscellaneous, Continued—Allgood Wagons—Judicial Community—Yankee Bullets—Singing Convention—Public Square—Treasure Trove—Blacksmith Shop—Secession Convention—Fish Trap—Family Reunions—Clements vs. Felton	260
XXXVI	Miscellaneous, Continued—Straight Gut Valley—Tan Yard—Old Tax Receipts—Record Births of Negroes—A Fight—General Assembly, 1835—Rare Old Teacher—Civil War Incident—Lost in the Mountains—LaFayette Baptist Church—Hog Rifle—Bugle Call—Other Tax Receipts—First Court House at Crayfish Spring—Unique School Collection—Hurricane—Recalling Solomon's Temple—Autograph Album—John Ingraham—Mr. Freeman—Indian Hominy	267
XXXVII	County Names, Their Meaning	277
XXXVIII	Soldiers in the World War—Roster of County Officers—Ulster County Gazette	286
XXXIX	Recollections of: Frank Copeland; T. B. Simmons; Old Documents—LaFayette's Early History—Legal Executions—Longevity—Golden Weddings—Ante-Bellum Houses—Heirlooms—Sentences—Large Families	306
XL	"Bill Arp's" Humor—Walker County Messenger—Rossville New Age—Rossville Open Gate—Medical Profession—Legal Profession	319
XLI	Post Office Records—Masonic Lodges	327
XLII	Some Efforts at Composition by Walker County Citizens	335
XLIII	Church Records and History	356
XLIV	Family Reviews	395
XLV	Blank Pages for Current History	508
XLVI	Graveyards—Tombstone Inscriptions	520
APPENDIX		546
Index		551

BOARD OF ROADS AND REVENUES, 1929-32.

L. P. Keith J. H. Kilgore W. R. Morgan
F. M. Shaw   C. A. Chambers

Chapter One

GEOLOGICAL HISTORY—MOUND BUILDERS—INDIAN HISTORY.

THERE is a natural desire in most intelligent people, especially those advanced in years, to know something about their ancestors. That homely adage, "distance lends enchantment," is true both as to time and place. We take an especial pleasure in picturing to ourselves the conditions prevailing among our forbears a century or more ago. Enraptured we read about, or contemplate the actions, scenes, activities, movements and expressions of those who went before us; we take delight in contemplating our hardy pioneer forefathers. With an adoration bordering on reverence, we examine an ancient log cabin in which our ancestors were domiciled; or the old log school house where they got a smattering knowledge of the three R's; the old spinning wheel or loom or the hand cards for making rolls, that our grandmothers used, we esteem almost with veneration. Any old heirloom, handed down from the days of the pioneer settlers, we regard with a peculiar pleasure. Truly, distance lends enchantment.

The ravages of time, of man, and of animals unite to destroy the records of the human race. The dearth of reliable information concerning the early days of our county is a matter to be greatly deplored. The hand of man—no less than the hand of time—has been a potent agent in effacing—destroying—that early record. There are numerous descendants of the early settlers of the county still residing among us, some, maybe, on the ancestral patrimony left by those settlers; and yet, unhappily, there has been little or nothing preserved from those early days. Occasionally an ancient deed or a bill of sale for negroes, or more rarely still, an old letter, written, maybe, by a grandsire during some of the Indian wars, or more recently, during the Civil War, is unearthed, showing how letters were sent in those historic days, without envelopes, with a wax impression, postage collect. Not only is there scant information of the pioneers of the county—of their business, social, religious and educational affairs—but there is no record whatever of their legal transactions in the courts, the court house having been destroyed by fire, together with all court records, in the year of our Lord eighteen hundred and eighty-three. It has been a rather heroic undertaking, therefore—this attempt to chronicle some account of our great county.

GEOLOGICAL HISTORY. The geologist—with hammer and glass—probing along the valleys and among the mountains of Walker county, tells us that he finds evidence that the surface of our county was once a part of the ocean bed. Even the topmost rocks on Lookout mountain carry a tell-tale evidence that they were formed under water. There are, he says, to be seen innumerable fossils of sea animals in the form of shells —sea shells—such as may be seen to-day in the ocean. These living animals, minute and quite invisible to the unaided eye, died as all things must, and falling, sank into and were imbedded in the ooze which covered the ocean floor and which was by slow degrees metamorphosed and became rock. This condition prevailed for ages during which time old ocean's waves and breakers washed and tumbled as we seen them do to-day.

In many parts of the county, especially at the bases of the mountains and ridges, are to be seen scattered over the ground numerous stones varying in size from boulders weighing many tons to small gravels. These stones are often worn quite smooth and round which was caused, according to geologists, by the action of the waves of the sea as they were tossed and pushed about and rolled together. These stones are prolific along the base of Lookout and Pigeon mountains near Harrisburg and further up the valley toward Bronco, as well as in many other parts of the county.

Another geologic wonder of the county is the scene just west of the top of Pigeon mountain on the Dug Gap road where the rock may be seen in many folds, showing in language intelligible that the forces of Nature were active at that place many millenniums ago. These twistings and contortions of the earth's surface tell of the immense pressure to which they were subjected in the ages of the early history of the county.

In the course of time the ocean's bed was elevated above the water and in time vegetation appeared and prepared the way for the appearance of animals. It was during this period that the vast beds of coal that have been such a source of wealth and means of activity to the county were deposited. These coal-beds, the iron ore and other minerals all have an historical connection with the aeons of time while our county was in the making. Such, according to the geologist, is an epitome of the earliest history of our county.

"Walker county has a vast store of the signs of Nature's forces and the contacts of earths' agencies in presenting a surface and soil which must carry more than ordinary interest to one of geologic inquiry."

MOUND BUILDERS. It is believed by historians and others who have given the subject serious investigation that a race of men inhabited Walker county prior to the Indians. The principal reason advanced for this belief is the prevalence of the so-called Indian Mounds scattered throughout the county. The mounds, they say, were not of Indian origin. The Indians themselves disowned their construction. They claimed they were erected by a people who had occupied this territory before them, and of whom they had not even a tradition. There are, according to some investigators, two distinct classes of mounds; one of these is very ancient and has no Indian characteristics, while the other class is more modern and bears the earmarks of Indian origin.

Not only in our county but in most of the adjoining counties are numerous mounds. Along the stretches of Chickamauga creek they may be seen, sometimes isolated and sometimes arranged in groups. Others may be seen in other parts of the county. Near Rome, in Floyd county, and near Cartersville, in Bartow county, are large numbers of them, some of immense size. One of these is eighty feet in height and 225 feet in diameter. Another one near Cartersville was explored by some scientists from the Smithsonian and found to contain the skeleton of a giant which measured seven feet and two inches. The skeleton was intact with black hair reaching to the waist. Other smaller skeletons, as of children, were also found. These people left no record of themselves—save the mounds—by which they could be named, hence they have been called the Mound Builders.

USING INDIAN HISTORY AS A BACKGROUND. The first recorded history of North Georgia is the very scant and obscure records left by De Soto's followers as it pertains to his march through what was afterward the state of Georgia and the states westward. De Soto passed through this part of the state, although his precise route is, in many parts, not exactly known. It is generally agreed that he passed by and was encamped for a while at the head of the Coosa river near Rome. Some Tennessee historians claim that he penetrated as far as the southern boundary of that state. If this be true it is likely that he passed through Walker county. According to other authorities, De Soto sent some of his soldiers as spies to explore the more northern lands and that these penetrated as far as the Tennessee River. This was about the year 1540, and from that date for nearly 200 years nothing more is recorded concerning the regions in this part of the state. "The next record of visitors to this section is that of a small band of hunters and trappers, clad in buckskin, who ventured as far south as Walden's Ridge and Lookout Mountain. The leader of this band was named Wallen, for whom Wallen's Ridge was named; afterward corrupted into 'Walden's.' This was about the year 1765."* This band of hunters and trappers was probably from the newly established settlements of Boone and his followers in Kentucky and Tennessee.

About the middle of the eighteenth century, certainly as early as 1760, many pioneers from Virginia and North Carolina began to venture beyond the Allegheny Mountains and make settlements in what is now Kentucky and Tennessee. Daniel Boone was one of these early settlers. Soon others followed and the settlements were pushed gradually westward. These early immigrants followed, in the main, the water courses as highways. The Tennessee River thus became one of the principal thoroughfares of travel for these hardy folk. They were lured by the rich valley lands and the abundance of game to be found along the western waters. As reports of these rich lands spread, more and more settlers ventured across the Blue Ridge in search of this Eldorado. The Cherokees looked upon this westward movement of the whites with suspicion and great displeasure. They opposed the settlement of the whites in their "happy

---

*"Walker's History of Chattanooga."

hunting ground." A large body of these Cherokees lived on the south bank of the Tennessee River near the Chickamauga Creek. This band of Indians had isolated themselves from the main body of the Cherokees and became a distinct group, called the Chickamaugas, from the name of that stream. They were more warlike than the Cherokees proper, probably because of their more warlike chiefs and the British agents residing among them. They constantly preyed on the settlers and travelers passing down the river at this point, whom they robbed or killed. This continued so long that it became a much dreaded place by travelers. Also, later, when the Colonies were at war with Great Britain, British emissaries were kept at this place to encourage the Chickamaugas in their nefarious practices. This was about the year 1778 while the War of the Revolution was in progress. The city of Chattanooga had not yet been dreamed of. Indeed, the State of Tennessee had not been established.

Quoting from Ramsey's Annals of Tennessee: "At the Great Look Out or Chatanuga Mountain, commences a series of rapids, where, in its tortuous passages along the base of several mountain ranges, the Tennessee River, contracted into a narrow channel, hemmed in by projecting cliffs and towering precipes of solid stone, dashes with tumultuous violence from shore to shore, creating, in its rapid descent over immense boulders and masses of rock, a succession of cataracts and vortices. Beautiful and interesting in the extreme to the beholder, these rapids constitute a formidable obstacle to navigation, which, even yet, is not entirely over come by the agency of steam. Cherokee tradition is prolific of accident and disaster to the navigation of the aborigines. It is fabled that a fleet of canoes, rowed by Uchee warriors, and destined for an invasion of the Shawnees, at the mouth of the Ohio, was engulfed in the whirlpool, now known as the 'Suck.' Civilization, skill and experience have diminished these obstacles to commerce and navigation, but a century ago it was an achievement of no ordinary kind to pass through them, though at high tide. Even now the voyager must be fearless and vigilant."

Thus the early settlers and voyagers passing down and through these "Narrows" became an easy prey to the Chickamaugas stationed along the overhanging precipices of this dangerous passage. When boats were seen passing the towns of the Chickamaugas some miles above what is now Chattanooga, runners could easily be sent ahead to the Narrows where they were prepared to intercept and destroy any boats or canoes passing down the river and to kill or capture the inmates. It was a matter of the greatest importance, therefore, that some steps be taken to punish the Chickamaugas and put a stop to their ravages on commerce.

It was about this time that General George Rogers Clark was planning his celebrated incursion against Kaskaskia and Vincennes in the Illinois country against the British. The Governor of Virginia sent Major W. B. Smith beyond the Blue Ridge to recruit men for this expedition. It was desired to get these troops from beyond the Blue Ridge so as not to weaken the Atlantic defence. Smith raised four companies in the Holston country in upper East Tennessee. These four companies, with other troops, making about 1,000 altogether, were sent against the Chickamaugas. They were only temporarily withdrawn from the Clark expedition, being expected to return in time to reinforce Clark at Kaskaskia. Having built boats and canoes in which to drop down the rivers, these troops, under command of Cols. Evan Shelby and John Montgomery, descended the Holston and Tennessee Rivers, and on reaching the Chickamauga Creek, turned into that stream. Here they captured an Indian whom they forced to act as guide. They soon came to the town of Chickamauga which was about a mile in length. Approaching the town through the canebrake they took the inhabitants completely by surprise who fled precipitately without offering to fight. This town was governed by two chiefs called Dragging Canoe and Big Fool. They were pursued to the hills and mountains and about forty warriors were slain and the whole band scattered. Large quantities of stores and goods were captured and destroyed or sold as well as 20,000 bushels of corn, 150 head of horses, 100 cattle, and $100,000 worth of other goods. Also great quantities of deer skins. The town was completely destroyed as well as other towns in the vicinity. Having accomplished their mission, these troops after sinking their boats and canoes returned to their homes by land, enduring great privations en route.

Thus, it is seen, that at the very door of what was afterward Walker County, and most probably in the county, some of the most important and exciting scenes and battles of the American Revolution were enacted. (A British emissary and agent, Colonel Brown, and numerous Tories—refugees—lived at Chickamauga with the Indians, and regularly kept them stirred up and committing raids against the immigrants and nearest settlers.)

Chapter Two

INDIAN HISTORY—Continued.

AFTER the famous capture of Kaskaskia and Vincines by George Rogers Clark, Governor Hamilton, a British officer, laid plans to recapture those places. He arranged a grand coalition between the northern and southern Indians, aided by the British regulars, to effect a recapture of the Illinois country. He advanced from Detroit and succeeded in recapturing Vincines, and, expecting to be reinforced by 1,000 warriors from Chickamauga, was planning an expedition against Kaskaskia. But Shelby and Montgomery had destroyed the towns and killed and dispersed the warriors of his allies at Chickamauga, and thus prevented the coalition above referred to.

Thus are we able to perceive the possible far-reaching results of Shelby's victory against the Chickamaugas. Had he failed in his campaign against that hostile tribe, they might, and probably would, have joined with Hamilton's troops and the recapture of the Illinois country would have been likely. If this had been accomplished, all that vast region north of the Ohio River, including what is now the great states of Ohio, Indiana, Illinois and Michigan, would have, at the conclusion of peace with Great Britain, remained a part of that country's domain. This action at Chickamauga, therefore, can only be viewed as one of the important battles of the American Revolution. And this action took place in WALKER COUNTY—certainly at its very door.

The Chickamaugas, however, returned to and rebuilt their towns, and, encouraged by the British agents domiciled among them, continued their depredations against the whites. This continued for several years. In 1782 John Sevier, with 200 mounted men, descended upon their town and laid waste the settlements along the Chickamauga Creek. Sevier traveled as far as the present town of Calhoun, Georgia, killing every Indian warrior he found. (From Walker's History of Chattanooga). There can be little doubt that Sevier and his army passed up the Chickamauga Creek, probably as far as Crawfish Spring, fighting and dispersing the Indians. He probably then followed the Indian trail leading thence by way of Rock Spring, Villanow, and on to Calhoun. This was a part of the trail known as the GREAT CHICKAMAUGA PATH.

After these several repulses the Chickamaugas left their abodes on the Chickamauga Creek and moved farther down the Tennessee River and established what was known as the Five Lower Towns, which were Lookout Town (in Lookout valley, afterward Walker, now Dade County), Nickojack, Crow Town, Island Town and Running Water (Hale's Bar). This fierce tribe had two reasons for establishing themselves at these points: First, there was an easy crossing of the river near these towns and most of the important Indian trails of the Southeast converged at that crossing; and second, because of the peculiar formation of the mountain ranges, causing the waters of the river to converge through the "Narrows" and the "Suck" making it a most perilous passage for frail boats to navigate, it was an ideal place to prey upon commerce and immigrants passing down the river. Having established themselves at this place, they continued their nefarious practices of robbing and killing immigrants.

The Lower Chickamauga Towns were situated, as stated above, near the Great Crossing of the Tennessee River where hunting and war parties going north or south always crossed the river. "To this point congregated with fearful rapidity the worst men in all the Indian tribes. Murderers, thieves, pirates, banditti, not of every Indian tribe only, but depraved white men, rendered desperate by crime—hardened by outlawry and rendered remorseless by conscious guilt, fled hither and confederated with barbarian aborigenes in a common assault upon humanity and justice, and in defiance of all laws of earth and heaven. These miscreants constituted for a number of years the Barbary Powers of the West—the Algiers of the American frontier.

"They had become very numerous, composing a banditti of more than a thousand warriors. These had refused the terms of peace proposed by the whites and had perpetrated the greatest outrages upon the whole frontier. The Chickamauga Towns were the central places from which their detachments were sent out for plunder and murder, and where guns, and ammunition, and other supplies were received from their allies, the British, in Florida". (Ramsey's Annals).

To be more explicit it might be said that the Chickamaugas were established first on Chickamauga Creek which enters the Tennessee River some miles above the present site of the City of Chattanooga. This stream has its source in the head of McLemore's Cove and meandering northward traverses some of the most fertile lands in the county. Along this stream are numerous evidences that the Indians once inhabited the county. Near the junction of the Crawfish Spring branch with the stream there are several so-called Indian mounds. Crawfish Spring, originally called Crayfish, was a noted Indian gathering place. This spring being not over six or eight miles from the Chickamauga Towns was most likely one of their principal points of gathering. Here for many years they lived and built many towns and villages. These towns extended for several miles and for this reason we are persuaded that this tribe of Indians occupied at least a part of the present area of Walker county. In any event, it may be confidently asserted that the Chickamaugas were intimately acquainted with the streams, valleys, mountains, and scenery of the county. In their hunting and warlike expeditions they roamed hither and yon and explored every nook and corner of the county's area. Although they were originally Cherokees they had separated themselves from that tribe and had become a distinct branch of that tribe. They were a fierce and warlike branch of the original tribe. They refused to attend the treaties or to be bound by them. They preyed not only on the frontier settlers, especially in East Tennessee and Northwest Georgia, but more especially did they prey on commerce and travelers passing down the Tennessee River. Several expeditions were, at different times, sent against them and they were severely punished. Finally they forsook their towns on the Chickamauga Creek and removed further down the Tennessee River and established themselves at the Five Lower Towns some miles below Chattanooga. Here for many years they ravaged commerce, as they had done at the Upper Towns. The Lower Towns were more favorably situated for their nefarious purposes because of the proximity to the narrows or the Suck where, because of the overhanging cliffs and rocks, they were able more easily to overcome and capture commerce passing along the dangerous vortices.

In 1788, Colonel James Brown—a Revolutionary officer of North Carolina—undertook to migrate from that state to the Cumberland region in Tennessee, near Nashville. He decided to go by boat down the Tennessee River as being less dangerous than the shorter route through the Cumberland Mountains. He constructed several stout boats on the Holston River and with his family consisting of wife, five sons, several daughters, some married, and several negroes, also five other young men, all good marksmen, he descended the Tennessee River. When passing the Chickamauga Towns several Indians came aboard and were kindly treated. They returned to their town and immediately dispatched runners to the Lower Towns, or Running Water, to raise a body of warriors to meet the boats. This was accomplished and when Mr. Brown arrived a force of Indian warriors was ready. The party was attacked and Mr. Brown, three sons, three sons-in-law were killed and others wounded. His wife, two sons, and two daughters were made captives for many years. One small son, Joseph, was at length exchanged and afterward led an expedition against these freebooters and thoroughly chastised them. When this boy was an old man he wrote a full description of this horrible affair which has been preserved. (For a graphic account of this tragic affair the reader is referred to Ramsey's Annals of Tennessee).

Ramsey's Annals of Tennessee, page 557, says: "A few days after signing the treaty (May 1791) a party of Creeks were seen on the Lookout Mountain with fresh scalps which they acknowledged had been taken on Cumberland (across the river from Lookout). It was generally conjectured that most of the mischief mentioned here was perpetrated by the Creeks and banditti at the Five Lower Towns".

Also, in describing an Indian attack against Buchanan's Station in Tennessee (pg. 565,) reference is made to several hundred warriors from the Five Lower Towns, especially Running Water, led by several chiefs, one of whom was John Watts who was severely wounded. These were principally Chickamaugas, but there were also quite a number of Creeks. Again, page 600, in describing the results of the action and giving the wounded, it says: "Of the wounded were John Watts, with a ball through one thigh, which lodged in the other, supposed to be dangerous, the White Man Killer, the Dragging Canoe's brother, The Owl's son, a young man of the Lookout Mountains, a Creek warrior, who died and a young warrior of the Running Waters who died".

And yet again: (pg. 608 and following): Here follows a lengthy account of an expedition against the Five Lower Towns where the fierce Chickamaugas, together with numerous Creeks and half breed outlaws had for some years resided and from whence they waged a constant war against the frontier settlements in all directions. This force was composed of about 200 horsemen, some of whom were from Kentucky and was piloted by young Joseph Brown whose father, James

Brown, and several of his family had been killed at this place several years previous. Young Joseph, a mere lad at that time, had been spared, much in opposition to an old Indian squaw, who objected that he would some day live to conduct an expedition against the Indians and bring them to grief. Her prophecy was literally fulfilled. During the space of one day this force of frontiersmen swam the Tennessee River, attacked the Nickojack Town and Running Water, killing, capturing, and dispersing the inhabitants and burning the towns and retreating across the river before night. About 70 or 80 warriors were killed and a large number taken prisoners. Reference is made in this account to a part of this battle being fought on the side of Lookout Mountain.

Still another reference to Ramsey, (pg. 585), gives a lengthy account of a force of soldiers under General Sevier marching against the Indians, during which they visited the head of the Coosa River where the city of Rome now stands and where an important battle was fought in which several warriors were killed. Some of these were from the Five Lower Towns.

In the various incursions against the Five Lower Towns by the frontier soldiers of Tennessee reference is made on one occasion to William and Gideon Pillow, brothers, who swam the Tennessee River, one with a rope in his teeth pulling a raft on which was placed the powder of the army to protect it from the water, the other swimming behind and pushing. The Gideon Pillow mentioned was the father of Gideon J. Pillow, afterward a general in the U. S. Army, and later in the Confederate Army and with his little army fought the battle of LaFayette on June 24, 1864. The other brother, William, was made a Colonel and is often mentioned in the Annals of Tennessee as a brave and gallant Indian fighter. He was also with General Andrew Jackson on his expedition against the Indians in Alabama and against the British at New Orleans, passing through Walker county en route.

As noted elsewhere, the expedition against the Chickamaugas by Colonels Shelby and Montgomery with a force of about 1,000 soldiers from Western Virginia and Tennessee and the defeat of that fierce tribe of hostile Indians should be classed as one of the important battles of the American Revolution. The Chickamaugas were allies of Great Britain. There were at that time, domiciled at Chickamauga British agents who kept them supplied with arms, ammunition and other necessities with which to fight the Americans. They were a serious menace to the Americans, especially at this particular time, when every effort was being put forth to establish independence. This regiment of soldiers was raised for service in the war of the Revolution (Annals pg. 186), being expected to reinforce Clark in the Illinois country. Being diverted temporarily against the Chickamaugas that body of 1,000 warriors were severely punished which prevented them from further service to Great Britain as planned by Governor Hamilton as noted elsewhere.

THIS FACT, SO FAR AS THIS CHRONICLER IS AWARE, HAS ESCAPED THE ATTENTION OF HISTORIANS ENIRELY AND HE HERE AND NOW VENTURES TO SUGGEST THAT THE PROPER AUTHORITIES TAKE COGNIZANCE OF THIS IMPORTANT FACT AND SEE THAT PLANS ARE MADE TO HAVE MARKERS PLACED ON THIS BATTLEGROUND OF THE AMERICAN REVOLUTION.

Chapter Three

INDIAN HISTORY CONTINUED. JOHN ROSS—JOHN HOWARD PAYNE.

JOHN McDONALD was a Scotch-English trader who lived among the Chickamaugas following the Revolution. He had married an Indian woman and established himself at Rossville where he built what is now called the "Ross House." Here he lived and traded with the Indians and with the whites who passed down the Tennessee River. Daniel Ross, also a Scotchman, who, together with a party of traders was passing down the Tennessee River, was captured by the Chickamaugas, who, as was their custom, planned to kill him with all the party. John McDonald, however, interceded for Ross, probably because he was a Scotchman, and thus saved his life, the others being killed. Ross afterward married his benefactor's daughter—Mollie McDonald—and to them was born the illustrious John Ross, afterward head chief of the Cherokee Nation. He was born October 3, 1790. He was, therefore, one-fourth Indian, and three-fourths white.

When he reached his majority, John Ross fell heir to his father's patrimony and lived in the house his grandfather had built, still standing at Rossville. This he improved and enlarged and made it his home till his people were driven from their fatherland and sent west of the Great River. He was given as complete an education as conditions permitted. Several mission schools had been established throughout northwest Georgia and in Tennessee; one, the first, being established at Spring Place, in Murray county, about 1802; another, later, at Brainerd near Rossville just across the Tennessee line. No doubt the future chief of the tribe attended some of these schools. At any rate he is found at a remarkably early age taking part in the councils of his people, and his name appears as a signer on many important treaties and other papers. He seems to have been promoted to the position of leader by the time he reached his majority, and soon after was made chief, and finally, head chief.

Ross was not only a man of influence and power, but he was a man of wealth. He had, besides his home at Rossville, one also at Spring Place,

JOHN ROSS

where he spent part of his time. He had another home at the head of the Coosa river, near Rome, where he spent some time. Being a man of wealth, education and refinement, he was at home in any company. On several occasions he made journeys to Washington in the interest of his people and there conferred with the President and other great leaders, all of whom speak of him in warmest terms.

The great question agitating the Cherokee nation during the early part of the 19th century was that of their proposed removal to the Indian

JOHN ROSS HOME AT ROSSVILLE

Territory. On this question there was a division of opinion. John Ross headed the faction opposed to the removal, while Major Ridge and his son John Ridge favored it.

It was during this period that not only the people of Georgia and Tennessee were greatly agitated concerning the removal of the Indians to the West, but the whole nation was greatly excited by the discussion of the proposed removal. The press was full of the discussion during the second and third decades of the 19th century. Because of this general discussion and excitement many people came into the Cherokee country in order to secure first hand information on the subject, and thus be able to judge as to the merits of the situation. The immortal John Howard Payne, author of "Home, Sweet Home," was one such person who came to Georgia for this purpose. At the time of his visit the State of Georgia had troops patrolling the Cherokee nation to preserve the peace. These troops, suspecting Payne of some ulterior purpose, if not sedition, arrested him on suspicion. He was domiciled at the time of his arrest at the home of John Ross. It has been supposed that this was at the Ross home at Spring Place, but the Chattanooga Times (Dec. 1, 1930) is authority for the statement that it occurred at the Ross home at Rossville. Mr. Payne and John Ross were both arrested, but after a few days were released, there being no specific charges against either. There can be little doubt that Mr. Payne was a visitor at the Ross home at Rossville, during his visit to Cherokee, Georgia. The pathetic story of John Howard Payne's visit to Georgia and the sad romance with Miss Harden, of Athens, as well as his whole life, is one calculated to produce songs in the minor key—sad and plaintive.

"In 1780, Lookout Mountain (then without a name) was included in a claim by Spain, whose ruler declared that all the Indians living within the region were free and under Spanish protection. Whatever title Spain had to this vast wilderness on being transferred, it was simply referred to as "a part of the territory of the great Southwest." Two years afterwards Lookout Mountain was included in a tract of 3,500,000 acres granted by the State of Georgia to the Tennessee Company. The vast wilderness was soon divided, and as a means of inducing settlers to come in and establish homes a half thousand acres was offered free to each family, and half that amount was offered to each unmarried pioneer who was willing to settle in this region.

"This part of the country was considered so remote from civilization that the President of the United States issued a proclamation of warning to all settlers that since the territory was not within reach of government protection the people who chose to settle in it did so at risk of life and property.

"As usual, possible dangers held out a challenge to the daring settlers, for the spirit of adventure is a part of the history of the human race, and pioneers began to accept the large tracts of land offered them. However, in 1791, when a report was broadcast of a band of Creek Indians holding a powwow on top of Lookout Mountain the news had a chilling effect, at least for a short while, on the popularity of the tempting offer of free lands."*

Thus it is seen that the territory out of which Walker county was carved was intimately connected with the celebrated YAZOO FRAUD. At the close of the Revolutionary War Georgia's territory reached to the Mississippi River on the west, and included almost the whole of what is now the states of Alabama and Mississippi. In fact, in 1785, the Legislature of Georgia, by an act, created a county near Natches on the Mississippi River and appointed officers for the same. This county was

---
*From "History of Chattanooga," by Robert Sparks Walker.

named BOURBON. However, three years later this act was repealed because of some confusion about settlers and foreigners. In 1789, the Legislature granted to certain parties, known as the South Carolina Yazoo Company, the Georgia Company, and the Tennessee Company, vast tracts of land lying along the Yazoo River, a tributary of the Mississippi. Altogether, there were approximately 20,000,000 acres in this grant—an area more than half as large as the present area of the state. The price to be paid was less than two cents per acre. There was great dissatisfaction about this sale and after much confusion and excitement the legislature next following, rescinded the act, and so saved these valuable lands to the State and the people. For a quarter of a century or more the matter was one that greatly agitated the public mind, not only of the people of the State but of the nation as well. The reader is referred to Stevens' History of Georgia for a full and complete account of this exciting episode. Some years later all these western lands were ceded to the general government, and in return the government agreed to extinguish all Indian titles to lands within the present limits of the State.

These stirring events occurred soon after the War of the Revolution and almost a half century before Walker county was organized. Although we may not be able to see that dim and distant half-century with its actors and passing scenes, however much we may desire to do so, we may, nevertheless, with reasonable accuracy, because of adjacent contemporaneous history, picture to ourselves something of the people who were moving upon the scene and filling a part in the great drama of life. That inborn, innate desire to know something of our forbears and the country which they occupied spurs our immagination and p'ctures to us the possible scenes and actions of those who went before us. From the occasional fragments of history, accidentally preserved from the wreck of time, we may catch a glimpse of the half-century immediately following the War of the Revolution as it pertained to the territory from which our country was formed.

Chapter Four

Indian History Continued. Their Removal—Sequoia— Hardships of the Exodus.

SOME years before the War of the Revolution, that great pioneer hunter and frontiersman, Daniel Boone, brought civilization into the fertile valleys of Kentucky and Tennessee. Having blazed a trail from Virginia and the Carolinas, other settlers soon followed, and with Boone as a leader, these early settlers soon showed the Indians inhabiting those wildernesses that they were as sagacious and as brave as the

Indians themselves. Boone and his followers, with their superior knowledge of the use of fire-arms and the arts of civilization, made themselves a power among the Indian tribes of those regions. These Cherokee Indians had occupied these regions from time immemorial, and who held these lands by an ancient title, if not by Divine right, had shifted by slow degrees southward toward the mountains of North-West Georgia. There were still scattered tribes in the Carolinas, in Tennessee and in Alabama, but they were no longer numerous except in North-West Georgia. The seat of government had for many years been in Tennessee where their principal chiefs lived and where they held their war councils and pow-wows. Now, however, because of the migrations of the whites into their fertile valleys, they were forced toward the south, and New Echota, in Gordon county, became the seat of government for the nation.

"It was about this time that the famous mixed-breed, Sequoia,* invented his great alphabet, an achievement which has been the wonder of scholars in both hemispheres. This invention had a profound effect upon the nation. It gave them a written language which soon produced a formal code of laws.

SEQUOIA

They at once organized themselves into a nation modeled after that of the United States. They possessed a written constitution; they adopted wise and prudent measures; they organized courts; they built schools; they encouraged domestic arts and manufactures; and they embraced the Christian religion. The invention of this alphabet put them at once in the forefront of any Indian tribe in North America. But this intellectual

---

*Sequoia, whose English name was George Guess, was an illiterate Indian of mixed-breed, his grandfather being a Scotchman. He had noted that the whites could send a piece of paper to each other that would talk, and he determined to make the Cherokee language do the same. He went to work and after some two or three years succeeded in formulating an alphabet for the Cherokee language that was not only workable and intelligible, but was extremely simple. By this means one was able to learn to read and write within a few days. There were about 60 symbols used by the inventor, one for every syllabic sound in the language, and is called a syllabic alphabet—possibly the only one of the kind in the world. Every one has read of the colossal trees of California, called Sequoias, which are the largest trees in the world, being in some instances 80 or 90 feet in circumference, and are said by competent authority to be as old as the time of Abraham. These trees were named in honor of George Guess, or Sequoia.

life came too late to save their patrimony. Other matters were operating to seal their fate.

"In 1802 an agreement was made between the State of Georgia and the United States by which the remaining lands of the State were to be cleared of Indian titles. The Creek nation occupied at that time the lower part of the state, while the Cherokees were in the northern part. In consideration of this agreement, the State of Georgia agreed to transfer to the United States all the territory occupied by the states of Alabama and Mississippi. In 1819, in endeavoring to carry out this agreement, the Federal authorities persuaded a number of Cherokees to remove to the West where they were given possession, acre for acre, by way of fair exchange of land. After this, for several years, nothing more was done and the Indians expected no further molestation. They were making great improvement because of the invention of writing."

The Cherokees might have continued to occupy for some time longer, in more or less peaceable possession, their homeland, but for another circumstance which happened about this time. This was the discovery of gold in the vicinity of Dahlonega. Civilized man, even more so than the savage, has ever been willing to risk life, limb, and happiness for possession of the yellow metal. And so, this discovery brought many prospectors, traders, and others into the territory of the Cherokee country, which, of course, brought the two races in contact, and which resulted in many disagreements and conflicts.

Here might follow an extended account of the conflicts between the two races. These disagreements lasted for some years and became so serious at last that the whole state was very much excited and disturbed about the Indian situation. Many atrocities were committed by the Indians, and no doubt by the whites, in retaliation.

At first the Cherokees were a unit in opposition to removal from the state or of surrendering their lands to the whites. But these various events caused a division of opinion, and thus it was that two parties were formed, one headed by Major Ridge, and his son, John Ridge, and a half-breed, Elias Boudinot, an interpreter, who favored removal. The other faction was headed by John Ross, the principal chief of the nation, who opposed removal. There was much enmity between these two factions. Both sent delegations to Washington, but eventually the advocates of removal won. There was much restlessness and excitement among both races. The most thoughtful of the Indians, seeing the futility of the struggle, by degrees, went over to the Ridge faction. A new treaty was signed at New Echota in December, 1835, by which the Indians agreed to exchange their patrimony for $5,000,000 and a joint interest in the lands occupied by some of the tribe already settled beyond the Great River.

After the signing of this treaty the Indians who were opposed to the removal became more troublesome than ever. They waylaid and murdered many of those Indians who were favorable to the removal. White families who lived along the border were in great terror because of the situation, and troops were stationed among them to preserve the peace. Numbers of Indians committed many murders along the rivers where most of the whites lived at that time. Their presence caused great alarm along the borders and the settlers fled to the towns for protection, the Indians pursuing and killing many of them. During the night of May 15, 1836, in Stewart County, a party of them, several hundred in number, made an attack on a small town on the Chattahoochee River and slew nine whites and three blacks. They afterward burned the town and attacked the boat GEORGIAN and killed all except the engineer.

This party of Indians, about 300 strong, undertook to join the Seminoles, in Florida. They passed on through Baker County and murdered several families, and finally hid themselves in the midst of a large swamp. As soon as re-inforcements could arrive, the whites surrounded the swamp and marched into it and engaged them hand to hand. They were completely routed and many of them killed. They surrendered and thus their union with the Florida Indians was prevented. All this shows the desperate character of the Indians and explains why it was necessary to rid the state of such characters. The whole state was greatly alarmed because of the situation, and because of this there was a universal demand that they be removed.

In May, 1838, General Scott, at the head of a force of United States soldiers, was ordered to New Echota where the unpleasant work of carrying out the terms of the treaty was begun, at the point of the bayonet.

It is well, probably, that there has been left to us such scant record of this unpleasant work. Enough, however, has been left to show the harshness of the grim task. "However necessary," says Lucian Lamar Knight, "it may have been to the welfare of the Anglo-Saxon civilization to dispossess the Indians—to drive them out under the lash from the graves of ancestors whom they worshiped and from the doorsteps of homes which they loved—it has left an ineffaceable stigma behind." History presents few examples of so harsh and unjust treatment of any people as that shown with reference to the removal of the Cherokee Indian. Longfellow has immortalised the unjustness of the expulsion, by Great Britain, of the Acadians in his Evangeline, but a careful study of the situation will show that the driving away of the Cherokees was the harsher of the two cases.

We shall, then, for a brief space, examine carefully the course of events with reference to this removal. There were at this time, according to the best authorities, about 17,000 Indians in the nation—some 2,000 having been transferred to the western lands two years previous. Stockades were erected throughout the country at convenient places in which to corral the Indians preparatory to the exit. One such stockade was built about one mile north-west of LaFayette near Big Spring. This was called Fort Cummings.

These enclosures were of different sizes, depending on the number to

MAJOR RIDGE

be confined. They were constructed of heavy timbers placed close together and standing upright some 10 or 12 feet high. As the Indians were collected from among the hills and valleys they were brought to these stockades and incarcerated till all were gathered and then were taken to the general assembling place for the final departure, which for this territory was Ross's Landing. Being confined in these stockades, sometimes for weeks, without exercise, exposed to the inclemencies of the weather, without proper shelter, and fed on rations to which they were unaccustomed, is it any wonder that many sickened and died? Above and beyond all this was their mental attitude at being forced to give up their fatherland and their homes, dearer than life itself. And is it strange that many wooed death rather than follow an exile's life toward the land of the setting sun?

At these stockades soldiers were stationed, and from thence were dispatched throughout the country to search out the Indians from their homes among the coves or mountains, or along the streams of the valleys, and at the point of the bayonet drive them to the stockade where they were detained till the time of the departure. An eminent authority, Professor Mooney, of the Bureau of Entomology at Washington, who spent some years among the Indians subsequent to their departure, says:

"Families at dinner were startled by the sudden gleam of the bayonet at the doorway and rose to be driven with blows and oaths along the weary miles of travel leading to the stockade. Men were seized in the fields or along the roads. Women were taken from their wheels and children from their play. In many cases, on turning for one last look, as they crossed the ridge, they beheld their homes in flames, fired by the lawless rabble who followed the heels of the soldiers to loot and pillage. So keen were these outlaws on the scent, that in many cases they were driving off the cattle and other stock of the Indians almost before the soldiers had started their owners in the other direction. Systematic hunts were made by the same men for Indian graves to rob them of the silver pendants and other valuables deposited with the dead. One of the Georgia Volunteers, afterward a colonel in the Confederate service, said: 'I fought through the Civil War. It has been my experience to see men shot to pieces and slaughtered by the thousand. But the Cherokee removal was the cruelest work I ever saw.'

"To prevent escape the soldiers were ordered to surround each house, as far as possible, so as to come upon the occupants without warning. One old patriarch, when thus surprised, calmly called his children and grandchildren around him, and kneeling down, bade them pray with him in their language, while the astonished soldiers looked on in silence. Then rising he led the way into exile. In another instance, a woman, on finding the house surrounded, went to the door and called up the chickens to feed them for the last time, after which, taking her infant on her back and her two older children by the hand she followed her husband with the soldiers.

"All were not thus submissive. One old man named Charles was seized with his wife, his brother, and three sons, together with the families of the latter. Exasperated by the brutality accorded his wife, who, being unable to travel fast, was prodded with bayonets to hasten her steps, he urged the other men to join with him in a dash for liberty. As he spoke in Cherokee, the soldiers understood nothing until each warrior sprang upon the one nearest and endeavored to wrench his gun from him. The attack was so sudden and unexpected that one soldier was killed, while the Indians escaped to the mountains. Hundreds of others, some of them from the stockades, managed to escape from time to time and subsisted on nuts and berries until the hunt was over. Finding it impossible to secure these fugitives, General Scott finally tendered them a proposition, through Coloned W. H. Thomas, their trusted friend, to the effect that if they would surrender Charles for punishment the rest would be allowed to remain until the matter could be arranged by the government. On hearing of this proposition, Charles voluntarily came in with his sons, offering himself a sacrifice for his people. By command of General Scott, Charles, his brother, and his sons, were shot near the mouth of the Tuckaseegee, a detachment of the Cherokee prisoners being forced to do the shooting in order to impress upon the Indians the fact that they were helpless. From these fugitives who were thus permitted to remain, originated the eastern band of the Cherokees. * * *

"When nearly 17,000 Indians had thus been gathered into the stockades, the work of removal began. Early in June several parties aggregating about 5,000 persons, were brought down by the troops from the old agency on the Hiawassee to Ross' Landing, now Chattanooga, Tennessee, and to Gunter's Landing, now Guntersville, Alabama, where they were put upon boats and transported down the Tennessee and the Ohio to the further side of the Mississippi, where the journey was continued by land to the Indian Territory. The removal in the hottest part of the year was attended by such sickness and mortality that, by resolution of the Cherokee National Council, Ross and other chiefs submitted to General Scott a proposition that the Cherokees be allowed to remove themselves in the fall, after the sickly season was ended. This was granted on condition that all should start by October 20th, except the sick and the aged. Accordingly, officers were appointed by the Cherokee Council to take charge of the emigration, the Indians being organized into detachments averaging about 1,000 each, with leaders in charge of each detachment and a sufficient number of wagons and horses for the purpose. In this way the remainder, enrolled at about 13,000 including negro slaves, started on the long march overland in the fall.

"Those who thus migrated under the management of native officers, assembled, and * * * then the long procession of exiles was set in motion. Some went the river route, but most over land. Crossing to the north side by a ferry, they proceeded down the river, the sick, the old, and the infants with the blankets, cooking pots, etc. (in wagons), the rest on foot or on horse. The number of wagons was 645.

"It was like the march of an army, regiment after regiment, the wagons in the center, the officers along the line, the horsemen on the flank and at the rear. After crossing the Tennessee River, * * * they moved toward Nashville, where the Cumberland was crossed. From there they passed through western Kentucky, and it was here that the noted chief, White Path, who was in charge of one of the detachments, sickened and died. His people buried him by the roadside, with a box over the grave and streamers around it, so that others, coming on, might note the spot and remember him. Somewhat further along this march of death—for the exiles died daily by tens and twenties—the devoted wife of John Ross sank down, leaving him to go on with the bitter pang of bereavement added to his heartbreak at the ruin of his nation. The Ohio was reached at a ferry near the mouth of the Cumberland and the army passed through Southern Illinois, until the great Mississippi was reached, opposite Cape Gireardo, Missouri. It was now the middle of winter, with river running full of ice, so that the several detachments were obliged to wait sometime on the eastern bank for the channel to clear.

"On arrival in the Indian Territory, the victorious leaders were destined to enjoy for a brief season only the fruits of triumph. Even-handed justice was not slow in commending the poisoned chalice to each of the prominent actors in the drama. Major Ridge was waylaid and shot close to the Arkansas line; his son John Ridge, was taken from bed and cut to pieces with hatchets; while Elias Boudinot was treacherously killed near his home. These three men suffered death on the same day, June 22, 1839, showing the deliberate care with which the triple homicide was planned. Factional quarrels not only between the two political parties but also between the new and the old settlers continued to menace the peace of the tribe and years elapsed before anything like national unity was restored.

"It is difficult to arrive at any accurate statement of the number of Cherokees who died as a result of the removal. According to official figures those who removed under the direction of Ross lost over 1,600 on the journey. The proportionate mortality among those who previously removed under military supervision was probably greater. Hundreds died in the stockades and in the waiting camps, chiefly by reason of the rations furnished, which were of flour and other provisions to which they were not accustomed. Hundreds of others died on arrival from sickness and exposure. Altogether, it is ascertained, possibly with reason, that over 4,000 Cherokees died as the direct result of the removal."—From Georgia's Landmarks, Memorials, and Legends, by Lucian Lamar Knight.

(At the risk of being somewhat tedious, the author has thus given a short but sufficiently comprehensive review of the removal of the Cherokee Indians from this and adjoining counties. Parts of this review have been copied and other parts paraphrased. The accounts were taken from various sources. Not all of the scenes and actions as described occurred in Walker county, but part did, and other parts in adjoining counties. However, it is eminently proper to record them here as Walker county was a part of the home of the Cherokees prior to their removal.)

Chapter Five

INDIAN LORE AND LEGENDS—FIRST COURT HOUSE AT CRAWFISH SPRING.

IN the eastern part of the county, lying just west of Taylor's Ridge in the Chestnut Flat District, is a lovely, sequestered valley, known as "Wood Station Valley," which is pregnant with ancient Indian history. In the early days the floor of this valley, with the adjacent highlands, abounded in chestnut trees,—large, healthy and fruitful— which yielded, annually, immense quantities of that delightful food; hence the name Chestnut Flat. Old citizens of that section are wont, yet, to recall the days when one could gather, about October, baskets full of those delicious nuts; and how the pigs of the neighborhood would readily fatten on the mast from those trees!

There are a number of Indian Graves scattered along the valley adjacent to Taylor's Ridge. No doubt along this small but beautiful vale, where numerous springs of clear, cold water gush forth, the old Indian chief, Taylor, and his forbears, had their headquarters and gave orders to their followers. An Indian trail once traversed the entire length of the valley, and at convenient distances other trails led across the ridge, communicating with other tribes in what is called Dogwood Valley. Here, too, he showed his prowess as a hunter. With his bow-and-arrow, blowgun, tomahawk and other Indian weapons, he hunted and slew the buffalo, deer, turkey, bears, wolves and other wild animals. When not on the warpath he was idly sauntering among the forests of his happy hunting grounds.

The Indian, unlike his white brother, never took more game than was necessary for his immediate necessities. In this he was wise and provident. Had he been, like the paleface, greedy of everything in sight, he would have soon found his forests void of food, and in consequence would have been unable to secure an easy and convenient subsistence. It is said, too, that the Indian never took the young for food, unless as a last resort. He always killed an old deer in preference to a young one, even if it was not so fat and toothsome. In this, again, he was provident; for, he reasoned, the old animal would soon die or disappear, while the young had a longer lease on life and could be utilized when occasion demanded. The white man on the other hand is greedy for the choicest piece now, little thinking or caring for the future. As an example, see how the white man has annihilated the vast herds of wild buffalos that used to roam throughout the immense territory of the Mississippi Valley, and the Western Plains. Less than a century ago there were hundreds of thousands—perhaps millions—of them roaming at large on the plains east of the Rockies and in the great Mississippi Valley. They have been hunted and killed by the thousand by greedy, grasping palefaces for the sake of their pelts—for money. But, thanks to Uncle Sam, he has taken a hand and has prevented the absolute extinction of the picturesque buffalo by protecting him from the ravages of man—white man.

It is not generally known, perhaps, that the buffalo once inhabited this immediate region. There are numerous references to the buffalo in the early history of Tennesse and North Georgia. Ranging throughout the mountains and valleys of the county, he browsed on the foliage and native grasses in summer, and in fall and winter fed on the numerous canebrakes spreading along the stretches of its various streams. The early hunter and trapper of this section soon annihilate him along with the bear, wolf, and deer.

Wild life was not so wild among the Indians; because the Indian was more careful of their rights. They were not always fighting and killing them for mere pleasure and sport. The paleface, on the other hand, seems to take a delight in annoying wild animals, not to say destroying them. Notice the effect on that beautiful little rodent, the squirrel, when treated kindly around the home. It becomes quite tame and will sit close at hand and look you over as a friend. It even gesticulates and dances for you and maybe take from your fingers a proffered nut or other titbit. Had the deer been treated thus kindly we might—and probably would—have had her graceful presence yet among our mountains and valleys.

INDIAN TRAIL IN BROOMTOWN VALLEY. When the pioneers began to settle in Broomtown Valley, (so-called from an Indian chief, "The Broom", whose headquarters were near Alpine), they found an Indian trail running through its entire length. This trail was sometimes known as the Five Spring trail, from the fact that it passes, in its course, near five beautiful, cold, clear springs of pure water. The first of these springs is on the L. L. Clarkson place. Another is on Arthur Clarkson's place, somewhat back of Trinity church. The others are in Chattooga County, known as the Teloga Spring, the Knox Spring, and the Berry Springs just across the Georgia-Alabama line, near Alpine church. It is quite probable that the first road built through the valley followed exactly this old Indian trail, and that the present Broomtown road follows approximately this same trail.

INDIAN SETTLEMENT IN DUCK CREEK VALLEY. There is an old Indian burying place and settlement on the "Doc" McWhorter old place in Duck Creek Valley. Many years ago some of these were excavated and some skeletons were exhumed, along with many Indian relics, as tomahawks, arrowheads and the like. In fact there seems to have been in this vicinity a kind of stone works where Indian arrowheads were made in quantity. Either this seems to have been true, or, peradventure, there was at this place, in the remote past, some great battle between hostile tribes, contending here for the mastery; or possibly it was here that the neighboring tribes gathered on stated occasions to engage in some of their periodic contests, one of which was the effort to excel in the use of the bow-and-arrow. Whatever the reason for the great abundance of the arrowheads to be found hereabout, the fact of their number remains as a telltale of some unusual Indian activity in this valley in the remote past.

The old Indian chief, Chee-nah-wah, made this place his headquarters. He had here a bathing pool which can still be seen, though, of course, much changed by the ravages of time. It is said, also, that the Indian collected the sap from the numerous sugar-maple trees that grew in this vicinity and made sugar here. No doubt, at some time in the distant past, there was a thriving Indian settlement and mart of trade in this valley. The Indian trail in Broomtown above referred to passed through this vicinity and continued northward.

A few miles north of this Indian settlement in the same valley lived the Indian chief, "Blue Bird". His abode was near a large spring, known as the Blue Bird Spring, at the foot of Pigeon Mountain where the Blue Bird Gap crosses. Nature, in all ages, in all countries, and among all peoples has its barriers, and man, whether savage or civilized, has learned to take advantage of these barriers. Thus we see the Indian no less than the white man, preferring to live in the level lowlands where food and water are more abundant as well as more easily obtained. Also, when necessary to make a passage of the mountains he selects a natural crossing place for his passage, because it requires less exertion and labor at that particular place. This crossing place leads to more or less traffic at this point and in the course of time some one traveling across notes the desirability of the location for a home, and selecting a spot near a water supply, he establishes his abode—whether it be mansion, cottage, or wigwam, and settles down there, the original settler of the place. Soon other travelers passing and noting the desirability of the location settle near, and soon others come, till by and by there is the nucleus of a village.

This with some modification explains the location of a great many towns and cities in our country. There was a potent reason for the location of every home, village, and city in our county—as well as in every county. It is said that the city of Chattanooga, our nearest large market, owes its location to some natural advantages. An easy landing place for boats, on a large natural waterway, was one great advantage. Another, no doubt, was the fertile, fruitful, contiguous territory to be supplied and to offer supplies to boats passing up and down the river.

Every original homebuilder of our county, as well as of every county, and especially the countryman, had a reason for building where he did. The water supply; the drainage; the orientation; the scenery; the nearness to neighbors, church and school all had their influence. And so the Indian, following this same natural law, selected his abode with care. True, in many instances, his home was only a temporary affair, and subject to change. He was nomadic in his habits. But, although he only remained a limited time at a given place, he selected it because of certain advantages. John Ross' home was in a beautiful valley near a large spring of water. John McLemore lived in the beautiful and fruitful valley which bears his name. Chief Blue Bird's home was near a spring of water gushing from out Pigeon Mountain. Men, both savage and civilized, have certain reasons for the location of their abodes.

Probably the most populous Indian settlements within the limits of the county were along the entire length of the Chickamauga Creek. The Upper Towns, situated near the entrance of the Chickamauga into the Tennessee River, extended far up the former, possibly as far as the Crawfish Spring; but there are evidences that Indians once inhabited the region much further south—possibly and probably to the very head of the Cove. However, there are evidences of Indian occupation of practically every section of the county, especially of the lands along, and contiguous to the streams. Chattanooga Valley, Dry Valley, both Armuchees, Cane Creek and the region about LaFayette, as well as other sections in the county, were once, no doubt, teeming with a busy Indian population.

Some 25 years before the removal of the Indians to the West, that nation had experienced a sudden and unexpected uplift, because of the invention of the Cherokee alphabet. Because of this invention, they were able, within a few days, to learn to read. They were now able to reduce to the written page, their laws; a thing unheard of before. This was accordingly done and the nation was divided into suitable districts and courts established with officers, similar to that of the United States. Crawfish Spring was the county site of one of these districts. Here a court house was built and court was held. White's Historical Collections, written in 1853 says that the first court in Walker county was held at that place, presided over by Judge Hooper. This may have been after the organization of the county; or it may have been before, in which event it was probably a purely Indian proceeding.

It is difficult, perhaps, for us, removed, as we are, a century from the exciting scenes immediately preceding the removal of the Indians to the West, to comprehend, fully, the feeling in Georgia in 1833 when Walker County was organized. All of Northwest Georgia, probably a fourth of its area, was inhabited by the Cherokees who claimed jurisdiction over the territory, having adopted a constitution and established courts with judges and officers. The State also claimed jurisdiction over the territory and had extended her authority over it in criminal matters. The general government also claimed authority over the territory. It is seen, therefore, that three distinct authorities claimed the power of Eminent Domain over these lands. Necessarily there would be a conflict of authority. The Indian nation, the State of Georgia and the United States government all had some reason to be dissatisfied. Let it be noted that there were comparatively few Indians in all Northwest Georgia—probably not over ten or twelve thousand, about one-third of the population of Walker County. Many white settlers had moved into the territory and settled on the Indian lands, much to their displeasure.

In 1802, a compact had been entered into by the State of Georgia and the United States government by which the general government agreed to extinguish all Indian titles in the State in return for the lands lying west of the present western boundary, which were at that time a part of the State. It had been nearly thirty years since that agreement had been made and the State was getting restless about having the general government perform its part of the compact, especially in view of the strained relations between the Indians and the inhabitants of the State. The State Legislature of 1831 ordered the Governor to survey the lands in the Cherokee country, which the Governor proceeded to do.

The lands having been surveyed and mapped out, a lottery, or drawing was ordered in which soldiers of the Revolution, of any of the Indian Wars, or of the War of 1812, or their widows and orphans, were permitted to draw, and those who were fortunate to draw lands could settle at once on the land drawn. Many, however, drew blanks as there were not enough lands for all. But many who drew lands never entered their claims. They were unwilling to brave the wilderness and undertake to live on the frontier as Walker county was at that time. Lots of land unclaimed by the drawee were left unsettled for many years and until some settlers came in and entered those lands as "squatters", and finally, after years of residence, secured a title to them by prescription.

Also, during these early years when lands were cheap, many men of means came into the county and bought settler's claims and in this way accumulated large holdings of real estate. Colonel William Dougherty of the Cove was one such fortunate individual who succeeded to vast holdings of fine valley lands. Also, Major Joseph McCollough of Chattanooga valley secured a vast acreage.

The Cherokee Land Lottery, published in 1838, which gives the names of all those fortunate enough to draw lands at that time, as well as the lot drawn, a copy of which this chronicler has been permitted to peruse, is quite interesting. Most of those who drew lots came from the eastern and central counties of the State. It is noted that Benjamin Jones, of Gwinnett County, drew lot 76 in the 8 district and 4th section of the county. This was the father of the late Dr. G. W. Jones, and grandfather of Olmstead Jones of Cane Creek. There are many other citizens of the county who are able to trace their lineage back to an ancestor who was one of the fortunate drawees in the Cherokee Land Lottery.

"June 16, 1821. Mr. Butrick and brother Reece returned this evening. They had a meeting about eleven miles distant from Brainerd, where the Cherokees have lately built a court house. This building makes a very convenient place for public worship, particularly in the warm season. Nearly or quite all the people in that vicinity were present, and gave very good attention. More than a year ago, Mr. Butrick taught some of them a Cherokee hymn. These placed themselves on a seat together and delighted the ears and hearts of our brethren by singing that hymn with great accuracy and melody."

This quotation is from Robert Sparks Walker's, "TORCHLIGHTS TO THE CHEROKEES—The Brainerd Mission", published by The Macmillan Company, New York. The Moravian Missionaries at Brainerd kept a journal, or diary for many years, recording daily the happenings at the mission. If the reader will take a map and measure the distance from Brainerd in all directions, he will be convinced that Crawfish Spring is the only logical place for the court house mentioned. Crawfish Spring is just eleven miles from Brainerd and no other location will satisfy the conditions. This was in 1821, and a reference is made of a visit there a year previous, or 1820. The court house, therefore, at Crawfish Spring dates back to that time. It was built by the Cherokee nation and was used by them till the exodus in 1838. When the county was organized in 1833, and the machinery for the law's enforcement put into operation, it was natural for the old Cherokee court house at that place to be used—there being no other.

Another incident tending to prove that this was an Indian court house is the following: In the Cherokee Land Lottery in the map for the ninth district and fourth section on lot number 281 is an imitation of a large house and the words "Crawfish C. H." Also, near by are the words, "Big Spring." The early surveyors found the court house located there and simply marked it as shown on the map.

Chapter Six

Indian Trails—Farming—Graves—The First Roads.

ALTHOUGH the Indian was partially nomadic in his habits, he, nevertheless, often remained several years in the same location, especially in the more populous communities. When, however, he was disturbed in his locations, as by a scourge of diseases, failure of food supply, an inundation, or being subjugated by a hostile tribe, he hesitated not to forsake his old haunts and seek a new location. Because of the temporary character of his hut or wigwam, this was no serious inconvenience. His new domicile could, in most cases, be constructed overnight, so to speak, and he was at once at home. Another peculiarity of Indian life was the fact that every thing belonged to the tribe. The individual was as nothing. The tribe was everything. No Indian claimed the land on which he lived. It belonged to the tribe. Nor did he set claim to the wild animals near his wigwam, except so much as was necessary to his meager subsistence. He did not, like his white brother, feel that "I am lord of all I survey." He understood well that everything belonged to the tribe, and that he was a very insignificant part of that tribe. This knowledge and feeling had a tendency to make him migratory.

Then he was often on the warpath. Fighting was a part of his life—a large part of it. Once an Indian on being asked why they could not keep the peace, replied: "We must fight; we cannot live without fighting." In times of peace they had communications with each other, and in times of hostilities their warriors were making incursions into the enemies' country. They, like others of the human race were gregarious. At peace or at war they were often traveling through the country. They had no wagons or horses, they traveled afoot. Their routes took the name of trails, or paths.

Their trails usually went in a direct line; however, they took advantage of a high hill, mountain, or stream by surrounding rather than going straight across. Especially did they utilize the passes over mountains for their trails. There were among them, as with us, certain routes more useful or more frequently used than others. Some were principal routes and others less frequently used—much as we have main highways and roads of less importance.

THE GREAT INDIAN WARPATH. This was probably the most important trail of the Indians in the Southeast. It led from the Creek country in Georgia and Alabama through East Tennessee and on northward. It passed by the Chickamauga Towns, where the Chickamauga Creek unites with the Tennessee River. Hence, it is quite certain that this warpath passed through our county. The exact location is problematical. This was one of the principal highways of Indian travel for the Seminoles, Creeks, and Cherokees in the Southeast and of the tribes living further north. Warriors, hunters, runners, and refugees all traveled this route. No doubt it was, in the heyday of Indian prosperity, a much used and frequently traveled highway.

THE CISCA AND ST. AUGUSTINE TRAIL was another Indian highway that passed through the eastern part of the county. This trail was a general thoroughfare from Florida, via Augusta, Chickamauga, Nashville and northward. It crossed the Tennessee River at Running Water. This was another much traveled trail and was used by the aborigines as a medium of communication between the different tribes north and south.

THE CHICKAMAUGA PATH is shown as leading from the Upper Chickamauga Towns around the circle of Lookout Mountain to Running Water and thence northward. Running Water was the point where all the Indians trails crossed the Tennessee River. The extension of this path southward is not shown on the maps, but there can be little doubt that it passed southward from Chickamauga through the county. Mr. Fred Stanell of East Armuchee, tells of an Indian trail that once passed near the old Furnace in that valley, coming from New Echota near Calhoun and passing near Villanow, thence crossing Dick's and Taylor's Ridges it struck and crossed the old Alabama road near where the present Tarvin road leads to Rock Spring, and going thence via Crawfish Spring leads on to Rossville. This trail likely went to the Chickamauga Towns instead of to Rossville; however, the two places are only a few miles apart. It is likely that this trail was the southern extension of the Chickamauga Path.

THE NICKOJACK TRAIL is shown on some of the old maps as leading from Nickojack Town northward toward Nashville. Nickojack Town lies west from Nickojack Cave, and Nickojack Creek is in the northwest corner of Dade County and of the State of Georgia. Immediately east and on the eastern side of Lookout Mountain is Nickojack Pass, near Eagle Cliff, and nearly east of this in the eastern part of the county crossing Taylor's Ridge, is another Nickojack Pass. All these are in a very nearly east and west line. Mr. S. B. Carson, of Ardmore, Oklahoma, now 78 years of age, and whose father was a pioneer of Walker county, writes that he has heard his father say that this was an Indian trail when his father came to this section; that the trail led from Taylor's Ridge via the Leet Spring, Rock Spring, and on to Crawfish Spring and thence westward which would lead to the pass over Lookout Mountain and on to Nickojack Town. Also Mr. Alonzo Cooper of the Chestnut Flat section says that his father, an original settler in that part of the county, claimed that the Nickojack Trail was a well-beaten path in the early days and that it led all the way to North Carolina.

LOCAL TRAILS. In addition to the trails mentioned above, which were general highways for Indian travel, connecting sections of the Southeast hundreds of miles apart, there were many local trails or paths used by the Indians inhabiting what was afterward Walker County. One of these, according to Mrs. W. W. S. Myers, whose husband's father, William Myers, was one of the county's pioneer settlers, passed through the Cane Creek settlement and going via the Tarteechee Pond, passed near the present city of LaFayette, thence via Coldweather Spring and northward through Straight Gut Valley to Crawfish Spring. Here it connected with the Chickamauga Path.

Another important Indian trail, according to Mr. Seab Shaw, and other old settlers, traversed almost the whole length of Duck Creek and Broomtown valleys passing into Chattooga County and on into Alabama. The northern end of this trail joined with the Tarteechee trail above mentioned near the head of Straight Gut Valley. This trail had a branch near the Blue Bird gap that led across Pigeon mountain into the Cove.

There were probably other branches along its route. Along this trail were numerous Indian settlements, especially in Duck Creek valley.

Another trail, according to Mr. B. V. Kell of the Cove, who has heard old settlers talk of it, traversed the entire length of McLemore's Cove northward to the Tennessee River. There was an Indian settlement in the head of the Cove presided over by that famous old chief, John McLemore, for whom that section was named. Another settlement of Indians was located some two miles north of Trickum where there are numerous old graves, and where, Mr. Kell says, there was seen corn, or maize growing, by some white people who visited the Cove in 1820—the only corn seen in that section at that time. This was an important local Indian trail, connecting, as it did, the interior of the country with the main trails passing the Chickamauga Towns, as well as the traffic passing down the Tennessee River. Numerous other trails have been reported in various parts of the county by old settlers. Several in the Armuchees and one in Chestnut Flat have been reported, also one passing through the Allen gap, at Martindale.

Many citizens of the Cove and of Lookout Mountain talk of the "Three Notch Trail." Some contend that it represents the path of Andrew Jackson on his way to fight the Indians in Alabama and Florida in 1812; or at least a part of his army. Others think it was an old Indian trail. Mr. Reed Johnson says that his father often mentioned the Three Notch Trail. Mr. Terrell Brown, an old settler on the mountain, says that this trail passed up the mountain near Harrisburg and going near the High Church led in a north-west direction toward Johnson's Crook in Dade County. This trail passed by the Indian rock pile, mentioned elsewhere. Mr. C. W. Smith, now 78 years of age and who has resided on Lookout Mountain 75 years, tells me that the Three Notch Trail, sometimes called the Soldier's Trail, led from the neighborhood of Rising Fawn in a southeastern direction to near Harrisburg. This is practically the route given by Mr. Brown. This trail, says Mr. Smith, was used by the Union soldiers in 1863 when passing from Taperton's Ferry to the Broomtown valley, thence toward LaFayette and on to the Chickamauga battlefield.

INDIAN NAMES. The greatest and most interesting monuments left by the Indians to their memory are the names of the water courses in the county, as well as throughout the state. We have such beautiful names as Chickamauga, Armuchee, Chattooga, and Chattanooga (valley) creeks. In adjoining counties and sections the names, Coosa, Oostanaula, Etowah, Conasauga, Catoosa, Coosawattee and many others are met with, all having a most delightful, euphonious sound. The Indians rarely gave names to the smaller branches of the main stream, or if they did the early settlers failed to get them. But the white man, when he took possession, applied such prosy names as Duck Creek, Snake Creek, Peavine Creek, and so forth; streams too insignificant, in Indian economy, to bear names.

INDIAN FARMING. The lands of Walker county had been cultivated by the Indians in a very limited way long before the white settlers came into this section. They had, likewise, built some respectable log cabins and had become, to a limited extent, tillers of the soil. They were giving up, more and more, their nomadic habits. They sold or traded, in some cases, their homes to the white settlers. It is said that William Myers, father of the late W. W. S. Myers, offered an old Indian $25 in gold for his house which the Indian refused, but agreed that if Mr. Myers would move his family and effects to a new abode some few miles away, he would let him have the house. This transaction which happened in the Cane Creek section shows how little the Indian knew or cared for the value of money.

White's Historical Collections says that the missionaries located at Brainerd near the Chickamauga Creek bought a piece of land on that creek on which to raise corn, in order to obviate the necessity of hauling corn from the frontier settlements in East Tennessee. This was about 1820.

In their cultivation of corn the Indians had no tools, save, perhaps, a hoe with which the crop was cultivated. They knew nothing about plowing. The women and children did the hoeing, mostly, while the men were hunting, fishing or on the war-path. Many Indians had slaves who did the work of the farm, or, sometimes, they had captured one of the whites, who were made to do the work, especially the women captives or children.

INDIAN GRAVES. Mr. S. W. Puryear who lives near Zone in East Armuchee valley is authority for the statement that there are numerous Indian graves on the side of Horn's Mountain near what is called the Pocket. They were, he says, originally covered or surrounded by stones or boulders, but some years ago these were removed by treasure hunters, and at the present time it is difficult to locate the exact spot.

Mr. Fred Stansell, of the Furnace, says that an old Indian trail once passed near that place, going from New Echota to Rossville, and that in the early days numerous Indian graves were pointed out along this trail. Now, however, most of them have been lost to sight, only a few being positively located.

Some few miles north of Trickum, in the Cove, near the Akins place, is an old Indian graveyard. There seems to have been an Indian settlement here a century ago. Also, there was an Indian settlement at Horseshoe Cave, near Pond Spring, where the Indians had some clearings and cultivated some patches, raising corn, beans, squashes, etc. Mr. Bennie Jones, one of the pioneer settlers in that section, bought some cleared fields from the Indians, and was one of the very first who raised crops in that part of the county. This is the land afterward owned by the late Mr. Nelson Smith. Tradition is current in that section that the Indians had a lead mine in that vicinity where they mined that metal in quantity.

Some years ago, while working the road near Mr. J. A. Ward's home in East Armuchee valley, a complete skeleton was unearthed in the road bed. It is believed that this was an Indian burying ground, and it is probable that other graves are near by. Also, a skeleton was found on the place of Mr. J. C. Young in West Armuchee, which was examined by Dr. J. C. McWilliams, and pronounced to be that of an Indian. Some 25 years ago a skeleton was plowed up near Pond Spring by some plow hands, which was probably that of an Indian. There is an Indian grave on the Murphy place in head of the Cove.

There is another Indian grave yard on Mrs. Jacob Deck's place near Rock Spring. It was discovered many years ago because of the numerous Indian arrow heads to be found in the vicinity. In searching for these some human bones were discovered which led to further examination of the premises and some wisps of human hair were also found. This old burying ground is situated somewhat back of the residence and not far from what is called Crawfish Creek. This is in line with some of the ancient Indian trails and not far removed from one of the most populous Indian settlements known to have existed during the palmy days of Indian supremacy in this section.

BRAINERD ROAD. In the Cherokee Land Lottery published in 1838 by James F. Smith, and which gives in detail the various districts and sections of the land survey by the early surveyors, there are numerous markings showing routes of travel in the early days. Several of these routes of travel are shown as passing through Walker county.

One is the Brainerd road and starts south from the state line a few miles east of Rossville. Brainerd* was an Indian Mission situated near the Chickamauga Creek and not far from the old Upper Towns of the Chickamaugas. This trace as shown on the map passes up the valley on the west side of Chickamauga river and crosses that stream a little north of where Crawfish Spring branch enters it. Thence it follows Crawfish Creek somewhat west of that stream and passes through the entire length of Straight Gut valley, thence into the head waters of Duck Creek valley and passes along the east side of that stream and finally enters the state of Alabama near where the Chattooga River crosses the state line. This was in all probability a general route of travel for the Indians and those few early traders and settlers who ventured into this section long before the county was established. The early surveyors finding this road simply marked it as a trace and named it Brainerd road because it led from that mission.

The Brainerd Mission was established about 1817, and in a few years the teachers at that place established, also, other mission stations for the evangelization and enlightenment of the Indian. One of these was in Will's valley in Alabama, and it is likely that the Brainerd road was made to connect that place with the mother mission at Brainerd. It is

---

*This mission was an effort to evangelize and educate the Indian and to teach him the arts of civilization. It was first named "Chickamauga," but was later changed to "Brainerd" in honor of an early Indian missionary of that name. Many prominent people visited the mission during its life of about 21 years, including the then President of the United States, James Monroe, who spent the night of May 27, 1819, at the mission. It was this mission that gave the name to Missionary Ridge.—From Walker's History of Chattanooga.

claimed by many that the Brainerd road was the route of march of General Andrew Jackson's army on its way to fight the Creek Indians and the British in Alabama and other points.

FEDERAL ROAD. This road is shown on some old Indian maps as leading out from Rossville and passing eastward till it crosses West Chickamauga and Peavine Creek whence it turns southeastwardly and crossing the middle Chickamauga it continues in an easterly direction. A post-office was established at Rossville in 1819, and this road was the mail route from Nashville to Augusta.

ALABAMA ROAD. This is shown as a continuation of the Federal road. It turns southward near the headwaters of the middle Chickamauga, and following along the western side of Taylor's Ridge traverses Wood Station valley, Cane Creek valley and continues on into Alabama. A careful examination of the old maps in the Cherokee Land Lottery shows a trace in Murray county running east and west and marked "Alabama" road. Another in Cass (Bartow) County also running east and west is marked "Alabama" road. These are all different roads and the reasonable supposition is that they were called Alabama roads from the fact that they led to that state. In those early days there was much traveling westward and the roads leading in that direction would likely be called by the name of the state to which they led. Likewise, in Murray county is a trace running north and south and marked "Tennessee" road, which of course led to Tennessee.

It is claimed also that the Alabama road was the line of march for Andrew Jackson's army in 1812. Many old citizens with whom this chronicler has conversed maintain this as the route. The reader is referred to the article of Mr. T. A. Cooper, printed elsewhere, as one authority.

Chapter Seven

INDIAN ROMANCES AND STORIES.
HARRIET GOLD: A ROMANCE OF NEW ECHOTA.

(From Georgia's Landmarks, by permission of Lucian Lamar Knight.)

ON a knoll overlooking the site of New Echota there is still to be seen a lonely wayside grave around which cluster the incidents of a pathetic tale of the wilderness. When Elias Boudinot was attending the Moravian Mission, at Cornwall, Conencticut, he met and loved Harriet Gold. At the expiration of two years they were married, much to the displeasure of her father and brother, who little relished the thought of her alliance to an Indian, even though of mixed breed. But she took the step with her mother's full permission. It was an affair of the heart which the latter could understand, despite the separation from home and life of isolation among an alien people which it necessarily involved. So the happy couple came to Georgia to live, and here in the course of time they were visited by Mrs. Gold, who found her daughter well provided with domestic comforts and little disposed to complain.

With true missionary zeal, the young wife soon became intent upon the task of bettering the condition of life among the Indians. She founded sometime in the early thirties the first Sunday school in Gordon County; and to her husband who was editor of the Phoenix, she was both a companion and a helpmeet. She did much for the uplift of the tribe, and the life which she lived among them, though brief, was one of beautiful unselfishness. When John Howard Payne was imprisoned in the blockhouse, she frequently went to see him, making the bonds less burdensome by her sympathetic attentions. The story goes that he taught her to sing his famous air of "Home, Sweet Home"; and however reconciled she may have been to her lot by reason of the one thing needful to make it rosy there were doubtless minor chords of love in her heart which sounded a sad response when her memory reverted to her old home in far away Connecticut.

But satisfied though she was with the man of her choice, the days of her joyful wedlock were numbered. Stealthily the fingers of disease began to clutch at the vital chords. Perhaps she foresaw the bolt which was destined to descend upon the Cherokees. It was not difficult to read the future at this troublous hour. There was scarcely a moment when her husband's life was not in danger. The nation was divided into rival camps. The anxieties incident to this vexed period may have been too severe for an organism attuned to gentler surroundings. At any rate she faded day by day; and one afternoon in midsummer they bore her to the hillside, where a slab of marble, yellow with age, still marks the spot. It requires no great stretch of the imagination to picture the broken hearted man who survived her bending over the low mound, on the eve of his departure for the West, and reading, through tear-dimmed eyes the following inscription:

"To the memory of Harriet Ruggles, the wife of Thomas Elias Boudinot. She was the daughter of Colonel Benjamin and Eleanor Gold, of Cornwall, Conn. where she was born June 1, 1805, and died at New Echota, Cherokee Nation, August 12, 1836. We seek a rest beyond the skyes".

More About Harriet Ruggles Gold and Others.

In 1810 there was formed in Massachusetts, the American Board for Foreign Missions, which was the first organized effort in this country to evangelize the heathen. This Board not only sent out missionaries to foreign lands, but also made provisions for evangelizing the Indians scattered throughout America. Seven years later Rev. Cyrus Kingsbury was sent to labor among the Cherokees. After some investigation he established a school near the mouth of the Chickamauga creek for the education of the Cherokees. This school was at first called Chickamauga, later changed to Brainerd*. Here for many years the school was operated by Rev. Kingsbury and his successors.

As the school grew and prospered, and as certain of the pupils came to know more of civilization and enlightenment, and of the Gospel and plan of redemption, many of them embraced Christianity, and some expressed a desire to obtain a more thorough education so that they might be able to labor among their own people.

Hence it was that some of the more promising youths were sent to Cornwall, Conn., where a training school had been established for the education of such foreigners as might desire to labor among their own people. Among others who thus went from Brainerd to the Cornwall school was John Ridge, son of Major Ridge an Indian chief, whose headquarters were on the Coosa River near Rome. Also, Elias Boudenot, a cousin of John Ridge, both being half breeds. Having given this explanation, the following is now copied from Mr. Walker's "Torchlights," by permission of the Macmillan Company:

"TWO CHEROKEE ROMANCES. Cornwall citizens became greatly agitated when it was reliably rumored that John Ridge, a Cherokee pupil, was engaged to be married to Sarah B. Northup, a prominent white girl. This excitement was intensified over a second rumor that Elias Boudenot was also engaged to be married to Harriet Ruggles Gold, daughter of Colonel Gold, a prominent Cornwall citizen. There had been about eighty five such marriages reported in the South and little notice taken of the intermarriages of the two races, yet great was the demonstration that was made in the Connecticut town when it became known that the Cherokees were to marry white girls. In expressing their indignation, the citizens burnt Miss Gold, Mrs. Northup and Sarah in effigy.

In a manuscript left by Mrs. Ellen M. Gibbs, a daughter of Eunice Woodworth (Mrs. James Taylor), the following detailed account is given of the two love affairs:

"'A Foreign Mission School was opened in Cornwall, Litchfield County, Connecticut, in 1817. Mr. Northup kept the boarding house. Mrs. Northup had the care of the students in her family. It was a

---

*Mr. Robert Sparks Walker has recently written a history of this mission, "TORCHLIGHTS TO THE CHEROKEES—The Brainerd Mission." (The Macmillan Company). Mr. Walker visited and spent some time in the east searching the records of the Board for Foreign Mission as it pertained to the Cherokees. The result is that he has given to the country for the first time much very interesting history of the outlawed Cherokee Indians; and what especially appeals to us is the fact that it is largely local history. Those interested in local Indian history will find in this work a wealth of interesting information on the subject.

charity school for the Indians and white pupils from foreign countries. Many boxes of clothing were sent to Mrs. Northup to be distributed where they were most needed. Some scholars were rich and defrayed their own expenses. There was a piece of ground containing several acres called "The Garden," where every pupil morning and night worked his piece of ground. Students from several Indian tribes attended the school, and many young white men learned their language and went home with them as missionaries. I do not recollect the names of all the different tribes, but the Cherokees, Choctaws, Oneidas, and the Sandwich Islands were represented.

" 'The month of May every year there was a public exhibition. It was a grand affair. The Indian pupils apeared so graceful and genteel on the stage that the white pupils appeared uncouth beside them. The Indians sang and prayed in their native tongue. When they prayed, they knelt, clasped both hands together and held them up. When they sang, they sat in a row and all waved their hands simultaneously.

"They never were allowed to go beyond a certain limit from the school, never into people's dwellings without an invitation.

"Among the students was a Cherokee, John Ridge, the son of a chief. John was a noble youth, beautiful in appearance, very graceful, a perfect gentleman every where. He was confined in Mrs. Northup's house two years with a hip disease. Mrs. Northup had so much work and care that she would often send her daughter, Sarah, into John's room to care for him. One day, Dr. Gold, my cousin, said to Mrs. Northup, 'John Ridge now has no disease about him, and I do not think it best to give him any more medicine; but he has some deep trouble and you must find out what it is!'

"That afternoon, Sarah spent away from home, and Mrs. Northup, taking her stockings to darn for the students, went in to sit with John. She said to him, 'John you have some trouble and you must tell me; you know you have no mother here, only me, and you have always confided in me as you would your own mother.' He started up in wild amazemen and said, 'I got trouble; no!'

"She says, 'John, I cannot leave you till you tell me all.'

" 'I do not want to tell you,' he replied. She says, 'You must tell me.'

" 'Well,' he replied, 'you must know, I love your Sarah.' She said, 'You must not.'

" 'I know it,' he said, 'and that is the trouble.'

"She said, 'Have you ever mentioned it to her?'

" 'No; we have not said a word to each other; I dare not, but how could I help loving her when she has taken such good care of me these two years?'

"As soon as Sarah came home, Mrs. Northup said to her, 'Sarah, do you love John Ridge?'

" 'Yes, I do love John,' she admitted.

"Mrs. Northup saw there was trouble in camp. Mr. Northup took Sarah to her grandparents in New Haven and told them why he had brought her there; wished them to make parties and introduce her to other gentlemen and try every way to get her mind off of John Ridge. She stayed three months. She would not take notice of any gentleman, or any company. She had no appetite for food. She lost flesh and they thought she would soon be a victim of consumption. They were alarmed about her and brought her home.

"John was dying for Sarah and Sarah was dying for John. Finally, Mrs. Northup told John to go home and stay two years and if he could come back without crutches, he might marry Sarah. He did so, and came back well. His father, Major Ridge, came with him. They came in the most splendid carriage that ever entered town. They had their waiters in great style. Major Ridge's coat was trimmed in gold lace. On the Sabbath he could not be seen by strangers as 'it was the day of worship of the Great Spirit, and if he went to church, they would worship him.' He would see people every day during the two weeks he remained except on the Sabbath.

John and Sarah were married and went to the Cherokee nation in the State of Georgia, there to live in splendor, but not as missionaries. John was sent several times to Washington to transact business for his nation. Sarah remained at home taking care of her servants, for she had thirty living in her back yard. She dressed in silk.

"After the town of Cornwall had become quiet over the marriage of Sarah and John, there arose another tumult, and the social life of the parish, usually so quiet, arose to a fever heat over the announcement that 'Elias Boudenot, John Ridge's cousin, was about to marry Harriet, daughter of Colonel Gold.' She was one of the fairest, most cultured young ladies of the place, a very pious, amiable girl, and the nearest to perfection of any person I ever saw. She was the youngest of fourteen children; the others were all married except two brothers. One brother was a congregational minister. Her sisters all married well, and some of them were rich. One married a lawyer, one a judge, and one a Congregational minister. All of them had married so well that it seemed a dreadful stroke to have Harriet marry an Indian. She was the idol of the family. They tried to persuade her not to marry him, but all in vain. Not only was her own town stirred up, but one minister came from another town to try to persuade her not to marry Elias Boudenot. They talked to her half a day, but she would argue them down. And then they would say, 'She must have him; no other way;' She would say, 'We have vowed and our vows are heard in heaven; color is nothing to me; his soul is as white as mine. He is a Christian, and ever since I embraced religion I have been praying God would open a door for me to be one of them, and this is the way!'

"After it was known that she must and would go with the Cherokee, the 'roughs' in town burned her and Mrs. Northup and Sarah in effigy.

They used a barrel of tar. While they were burning, Harriet's friends carried her one mile away. The house in which she was stationed stood on a hill. She looked out of a window and said, 'Father, forgive them, they know not what they do;' Sure enough, they afterward repented of it; could not forgive themselves.

Six months after the engagement was publicly known, they were married. Excitement ceased and they had a splendid wedding. No young people were invited. My father and mother attended the wedding. As a result of these two weddings the Cornwall School was discontinued.

"After Mr. and Mrs. Elias Boudenot went to the Cherokee country, Colonel Gold and his wife went in a one-horse carriage to Georgia to visit them. They found them living in a two-story house, neatly furnished. Mrs. Gold told us after her return that she never had seen such a store of provisions. In one room up stairs was a barrel of coffee, a barrel of sugar, and everything good they needed. Mr. Boudenot was a kind, good husband, and Mrs. Gold declared that Harriet had married just as well as any of her other children. Sarah had three children. Harriet had six, and died when the sixth child was born."

The Legend of Nacoochee.

Long before the Anglo-Saxon had made his footprints on these western shores—long before even the Genoese visionary had dreamed of a new world beyond the columns of Hercules, there dwelt in this lovely valley a young maiden of wonderful and almost celestial beauty. She was the daughter of a chieftain—a princess. In doing homage to her, her people almost forgot the Great Spirit who made her, and endowed her with such strange beauty. Her name was Nacoochee—'The Evening Star'. A son of the chieftain of a neighboring tribe saw the beautiful Nocoochee, and loved her. He stole her young heart. She loved *him* with an intensity of passion that only the noblest souls knew. They met beneath the holy stars, and sealed their simple vows with kisses. In the valley, where, from the interlocked branches overhead, hung with festoons, in which the white flowers of the climate, and the purple blossoms of the magnificent wild passion-flower, mingled with the dark foliage of the muscadine, they found a trysting place. The song of the mocking-bird, and the murmur of the Chattahoochee's hurrying waters, were marriage hymns and anthems to them. They vowed eternal love. They vowed to live and die with each other. Intelligence of these secret meetings reached the old chief, Nacoochee's father, and his anger was terrible. But love for Laceola was stronger in the heart of Nacoochee than even reverence for her father's commands. One night the maiden was missed from her tent. The old chieftain commanded his warriors to pursue the fugitive. They found her with Laceola, the son of a hated race. In an instant an arrow was aimed at his breast. Nacoochee sprang forward before him and received the barbed shaft in her own heart. Her lover was stupefied. He made no resistance and his blood was mingled with hers. The lovers were buried in the same grave, and a lofty mound was raised to mark the spot. Deep grief seized the old chief and all his people, and the valley was ever after called Nacoochee. The mound which marks the trysting place, and the grave of the maiden and her betrothed, surmounted by a solitary pine, are still to be seen, and form some of the most interesting features of the landscape of this lovely vale*

The following account of a subterranean village is copied from an old newspaper*:— "About twenty years ago, a singular discovery was made of a subterranean village in this county. The houses were disinterred by excavating a canal for the purpose of washing gold. The depth varied from seven to nine feet. Some of the houses were imbedded in the stratum or gravel. The logs were but partially decayed, from six to ten inches in diameter, and from ten to twelve feet long. The walls were from three to six feet in height joined together, forming a straight line upwards of 300 feet in length, comprising 34 buildings or rooms. The logs were hewn at the ends, and notched down, as in ordinary cabins of the present day. In one of the rooms were found three baskets, made of cane splits, and a number of fragments of Indiam ware. From the circumstances of the land having been covered with a heavy growth of timber previous to its cultivation by the whites, twelve years before the time of its discovery, it was inferred that they were built at some remote period. The houses were situated from fifty to one hudred yards from the channel of the creek.

"A great number of curious specimens of workmanship were found in situations which preclude the possibility of their having been moved for more than a thousand years. During the operations of a gentleman, he found, at one time, about one-half of a crucible, of the capacity of near a gallon. It was ten feet below the surface, and immediately beneath a large oak tree, which measured five feet in diameter, and must have been four or five hundred years old. The deposit was alluvial, and what may be termed table land. There was a vessel, or rather, a double mortar, found in Duke's Creek, about five inches in diameter, and the excavation on each side was nearly an inch in depth, and perfectly polished. It was made of quartz, which had been semi-transparent, but had become stained with iron. Some suppose it was used for grinding paint, or for some of their plays or games. The lot of land upon which this discovery was made is in the third district of Habersham, four miles from the Nacoochee valley, on Duke's Creek."

---

*From White's Historical Collections of Georgia, descriptive of one of the North Georgia Counties.

The Legend of the Cherokee Rose.

Once upon a time, a proud young chieftain of the Seminoles was taken prisoner by his enemies, the Cherokees, and doomed to death by torture; but he fell so seriously ill, that it became necessary to wait for his restoration to health before committing him to the flames.

As he was lying, prostrated by disease, in the cabin of a Cherokee warrior, the daughter of the latter, a dark-eyed maiden, became his nurse. She rivaled in grace the bounding fawn, and the young warriors of her tribe said to her that the smile of the Great Spirit was not more beautiful. Is it any wonder then, though death stared the young Seminole in the face, he should be happy in her presence? Was it any wonder that each should love the other

Stern hatred of the Seminoles had stifled every kindly feeling in the hearts of the Cherokees, and they grimly waited the time when their enemy must die. As the color slowly returned to the cheeks of her lover and strength to his limbs, the dark-eyed maiden eagerly urged him to make his escape. How could she see him die? But he would not agree to seek safety in flight unles she went with him; he could better endure death by torture than life without her.

She yielded to his pleading. At the midnight hour, silently they slipped into the dim forest, guided by the pale light of the silvery stars. Yet before they had gone far, impelled by soft regret at leaving her home forever, she asked her lover's permission to return for an instant that she might bear away some memento. So, retracing her footsteps, she broke a sprig from the glossy-leafed vine which climbed upon her father's cabin, and preserving it at her breast during her flight through the wilderness, plated it at the door of her home in the land of the Seminoles.

Here, its milk-white blossoms, with golden centers, often recalled her childhood days in the far-away mountains of Georgia; and from that time this beautiful flower has always been known throughout the Southern States as the Cherokee rose.*

Tamar Escapes from the Indians.

Not long after the Revolution there lived, on the bank of Cody's Creek, in the flat woods of what is now the county of Elbert, a poor but worthy man by the name of Richard Tyner. During his absence one day a party of Indians made an attack upon his home, and Mrs. Tyner was killed, together with her youngest child, whose head was dashed against a tree. Another child was scalped and left for dead, while a third, whose name was Noah, succeeded, amidst the confusion,

---

*From Georgia's Landmarks, by permission of Lucian Lamar Knight.

in escaping the notice of the Indians, and crept into a hollow tree, which for many years afterward was known as Noah's Ark. An elder son of Mr. Tyner fled to the Savannah River and was pursued by some of the savages, but he effected his escape. Mary and Tamar, two daughters, were carried by the Indians to Coweta Town, and here they remained for several years, until an Indian trader named John Manack purchased Mary, who returned with him to the county of Elbert and became his wife. At another time he offered to purchase Tamar, but the Indians refused to sell her. The main employment of Tamar was to bring wood. One day, an old Indian woman informed her that her captors, suspecting her of an effort to escape, had resolved to burn her alive. The feelings of the poor girl can be better imagined than described. She determined, if possible, upon immediate flight. The old woman obtained for her a canoe, well supplied with provisions, and gave her directions how to proceed down the Chattahoochee River. Bidding adieu to her benefactress, Tamar launched her canoe and commenced her perilous voyage down the stream. During the day she secreted herself amidst the thick swamps of the river, and at night pursued her course. She finally reached Appalachicola Bay, embarked on a vessel going eastward around the peninsula of Florida, and at last arrived in Savannah. With the assistance of some of the citizens she was enabled ere long to reach her home in Elbert, where she afterward married a Mr. Hunt, and many of her descendants are still living in Georgia.

Chapter Eight

County Organized—Its Name—Early Settlers.

WALKER COUNTY, when organized. In 1831, the Legislature of Georgia organized all the territory of Northwest Georgia into one large county, called Cherokee, from the fact that the Cherokee Indians were then inhabiting that part of the State. Northwest Georgia was at that time, and is even yet, often referred to as Cherokee Georgia. It was seen at once that this area was entirely too extensive for one county, so one year later, in 1832, the county of Murray was laid out from Cherokee. Murray was composed of all that territory extending into the northwest angle of the state and from which afterward the counties of Walker, Whitfield, Catoosa, Gordon, Dade, and Chattooga were carved. Then passed another year and when the Legislature again assembled the county of Walker was organized. This was in 1833. At this time the territory of Walker included not only its present area, but all of Dade, and large parts of Whitfield, Catoosa, and Chattooga. In

1837 all of Walker's territory west of the top of Lookout Mountain was cut off and the county of Dade was established as the most northwestern county in the state. In 1838 another portion was cut off from Walker and the county of Chattooga was established. Then again in 1853, more territory was extracted and the county of Catoosa was made a unit. Also, in this same year, 1853, and again in 1859, other portions of Walker's territory were dished out to enrich the county of Whitfield.

Walker county was named for Major Freeman Walker of Augusta. He was one of the leading members of the bar in his day and was for some years a Senator from Georgia. So favorably did he impress himself upon the people of the State that our county was named in his honor—a notable monument in itself. The Hon. Richard Henry Wilde, one of Georgia's loved poets, wrote the following epitaph for the tomb of Hon. Freeman Walker, for whom Walker county was named:

CONSECRATED

To the cherished memory and mortal relics of
FREEMAN WALKER

An able and successful advocate,
and a graceful and fluent speaker.
His influence as a Statesman, his reputation as an orator, and
his urbanity as a gentleman were embellished and
endeared by social and domestic virtues.
Long a distinguished member of the Bar,
Often elected to the Legislature of the State,
He at length became
one of her Senators in Congress,
and retired after two years of honorable service,
to resume a profitable profession,
which he practised with untiring industry, and
unblemished character, until shortly before his death.
Generous, Hospitable, and Humane,
of cheerful temper and familiar manners,
he was idolized by his family,
beloved by his friends, and
admired by his countrymen.
Even party spirit, in his favor,
forgot something of its bitterness, and those
who differed from the politician,
did justice to the man.
Born in Virginia, in October 1780,
His brilliant and useful life
was terminated by a pulmonary complaint,
on the 23rd day of September, 1827,
in the 47th year of his age.

An analysis of the counties of the state shows that the smallest county is Clark with 114 square miles. The largest is Burke with 956 square miles. Walker's area is 432 square miles. Walker is considered a large county. There are 47 counties in the state larger and 113 smaller. The average area for the 161 counties is 367 square miles, so that Walker is 65 square miles above the average.

It is to be regretted that there are so many counties in the state. Georgia has more counties than any state in the union except the great state of Texas. Alabama with an area almost equal to that of Georgia has only 66 counties. If Georgia's counties were cut in half, the economical effect could hardly be other than a perceptible lessening of taxes. Happily, there is now a growing sentiment in favor of consolidating some of the smaller counties.

Generally speaking the larger counties are in the central and southern parts of the state, while the smaller are in the north-central and northern parts.

This is attributable, probably, to the influence of the mountains among which the people of this section reside. Living in a wilderness, among wild beasts and hostile Indians, and hemmed in by many mountain ranges, without adequate roads or means of conveyance, the pioneer settlers were unwilling and unable to travel long distances to the county seat to attend court. The fastnesses of the mountains cut them off from free and easy communication with people at a distance. This is why the county of Dade was cut off from Walker in 1837. If the conditions prevailing now, with good roads and quick communication, had prevailed at that time there would not have been the necessity for the county of Dade. No doubt there are many such reasons for other small counties.

ORIGINAL SETTLERS. One of the most difficult as well as the most interesting parts of collecting data for the county history has been that of securing the names of the first settlers in the county. In some sections it was comparatively easy, as well as, I hope, practically correct; while in other parts it was difficult to find any old people who could give the names of the pioneer citizens of their section, with any degree of certainty. In some instances I have secured the names of first settlers from old records, as, for instance, the James R. Jones and the Blackwell registers, mentioned elsewhere.

The author has tried to get names of those who settled in the county during the first fifteen or eighteen years of its history, that is, up to about the year 1848 or 1850. Some of these pioneers settled here as early as 1830, or maybe earlier, but the majority came during the later thirties and in the forties. Numerous others, who came later than 1850, might have been recorded as original settlers, in that they entered and settled land never before occupied, building a home and clearing virgin land and establishing an original homestead thereon. However, I tried to draw the line about 1850.

It has been impossible, also, to determine, in the majority of cases, from whence most of the early settlers originated. It would be interesting to know from whence they came as well as something of their surroundings in their former homes. In a few cases it has been possible to learn this. Many of the first settlers in the Armuchees—probably a majority—hailed originally from South Carolina, some from North Carolina. Some of them came direct from those states, while others had spent one or more years in some of the counties of eastern or middle Georgia before coming to this county.

Probably a majority of the early settlers in the Cove, and in the Rock Spring section and the region further north came from Tennessee. While there are exceptions, it may be said that, in a general way, the first settlers in the southern and eastern parts of the county came originally from the Carolinas, while those in the western and northern parts came from Tennessee. Many of them, however, came from other Georgia counties or from other states.

Practically all the early settlers were farmers and were in search of some of the fine virgin lands lying among the valleys of this section. The Cherokee country had been surveyed by order of the Legislature in 1831. After the survey these lands were disposed of by lottery. According to this plan any soldier of the Revolution, or of any of the Indian wars, or their widows, or orphans were entitled to draw. Since there were not enough lands for all those applying, enough blanks were added to complete the number. Hence, many drew blanks. Many others who drew land did not appear and claim it. Generally speaking, those who drew especially desirable lands entered upon it and settled there. In this way much land was left unclaimed and remained so for years till some one entered it as a squatter and after some years of residence thereon secured a title.

Quite a numbber of the first settlers were men of considerable possessions when they arrived in the county, many of them having slaves and other property. These usually managed to secure valuable lands and gradually extended their possessions in real estate till they had large plantations which were cultivated by slaves. They built old time Southern Colonial mansions with slave quarters near by. There were numbers of these in the Armuchees some of which are still standing. Also, some in the Cove and in other parts of the county. But it is likely that a majority of the pioneers were poor men. Young or middle-aged men, they were, in the main, who were willing to brave the hardships of the frontier for the sake of an opportunity to possess a home and to begin life anew in a new country. From such hardy stock a majority of the citizens of the county have come.

The following list of original settlers has been compiled after careful inquiry in every section of the county. This chronicler does not flatter himself to believe that it is correct in every particular. No doubt numerous names have been left out, and it is probable that some few are included that should not be. They have been arranged according to militia districts and it is likely that some errors are to be found in this grouping. The list follows:

ORIGINAL SETTLERS OF WALKER COUNTY.

ARMUCHEE, EAST—Benjamin Hunt, Sr., Jack Puryear, Wm. Puryear, Jeff Ponder, Dr. Adam Clements, Newton White, James Keown, Newton Keown, Nathan Keown, John A. Tate, Wm. Hammontree, Sr., Jesse Griffin, Riley Stansell, Adam Davis, John Cavender, A. C. Ward, W. M. Underwood, Needham Cannimore, Cornelius Kinsey, Billy Robbs, Wm. Kinsey, Roland Kinsey, John Oxford, Jacob Goodson, Sr., Matthew Keith, Andrew Womack, Billy Rea, Harris Hammontree, Joe Dobson, Starit Dobson, L. D. Vandiver, Harrison Hamilton.

ARMUCHEE, WEST—Constantine Wood, Hugh McClure, John McWilliams, Wm. Burgess, Jacob Cleckler, Mr. Milum, James Young, Wm. Little, Spencer Bomar, Ephraim Little, Artemus Shattuck, George McWilliams, John B. Suttle, Mr. Camp, Abraham Neal, Moses Jackson, Billy Jackson, Wm. Gore, Jackie Chapman, Samuel Maloney, Anthony Story, James Foster, Mr. Stamper, Ira L. Bennett, Wm. Bailey, E. A. Evans, James Lawrence, Henry Lawrence, Malichi Lawrence, James Coulter.

CANE CREEK—Wm. Ramey, Hezekiah Ellenburg, Hugh A. Smith, John Smith, Alex Calhoun, Wm. Myers, Ausie Mills, Colby Wheeler, Davie Jackson, Thomas Bryan.

CEDAR GROVE—James Ransom, Washington Ransom, Reuben Ransom, George W. Reed, Wm. Daugherty, Billy Connally, Billy Andrews, Major Moses Crow, Alex Hunter, James F. Coulter, "Wolf" A. J. McDaniel, H. B. Colquit, John Hise, Henry Hise, George Hise, Reuben Haney, Johnny Crow, James Blaylock, Tom Roland, Joseph Clarkson, James H. Clarkson, Billy Hammonds, Jim Bunch, John Holloway, Robert Hunter, Burl Smith, Ambrose Smith, Charley Holland, Isaac McCarty, Tom Jones, Robert Anderson, Aus Clark, Ephraim Hancock, A. J. McDaniel, Johnny McDaniel, Emory Hancock, E. P. Thompson.

CHESTNUT FLAT—Andrew Cooper, Louis Williams, Edom Moon, Jacob Arnold, Wm. Arnold, Taylor Fuller, Wm. Lowery, Alex Hall, Hugh Rogers, Amos Williams, James H. Lowery, David Hall, Joel Cooper, Tom Cooper, Johnny Gladden, Elias Arnold, H. G. Fuller, Hiram Shaw, Hugh McMullin, David Lowery, Mark Thornton, Martin Camp.

CHICKAMAUGA—Joshua Hearn, James Roark, Henry Blaylock, Billy Mitchel, Noah Meridith, Wm. Burk, David Autry, George Glenn, Sr., Jesse Bagwell, Joseph Osborn, Jimmy Bryan, Marshall McSpadden, R. H. Dyer, Sr., S. D. Dyer, James Gordon, Thomas F. Gordon, Bob Gentry, W. D. West, Wiley Mullis, James Lewis, Allen Thedford, Jeptha Hunt, Sam Hall, Milton Plaster, John Brock, Young Brock.

CHATTANOOGA VALLEY—James Killer, Mr. Hixon, Joseph McCullough, Ed Howard.

KENSINGTON—Martin Fralix, Martin Davis, John Davis, Jesse Wallin, Robert Lindsay Wallin, D. D. Singleterry, Ben Hardin, Jesse

Stephens, Billy Simmons, Hamp Garmany, Billy Cupp, James Campbell, Jim Bonds, Miles Whitlow, Archie Hill, Wm. Hiniard, Jacob R. Brooks, Robert Guthery, Jeptha Carter, Wm. Connally, Bennie Jones, Willis Crumpton, Wm. Shaw, Stephen B. Phillips.

LaFAYETTE—John Caldwell, Andrew Caldwell, Bob Caldwell, Spencer Marsh, Dr. Robert Burton Dickerson, Michael Dickson, Asa Dickson, Joseph Wardlaw, Dr. Albert Clendennon, Robert Patterson, John R. Wardlaw, J. C. Culberson, James H. Culberson, David Stuart, R. M. Aycock, W. A. Moore, Wm. Catlett, Dr. James Barry, Edwin Dyer, B. F. Davis, John Criswell, Billy Jones, A. B. Culberson, John Jones, Eli Goree, Madison Rhodes, Warren Henry, Thomas N. Nash, Jerry Culberson, Abner Mize, Dr. Green Gordon, Alex Shaw, Ben McCutchen, Daniel Hogue, Lindsay Edwards, Wm. H. Johnson, Hugh Boudinot Johnson, Tom Phipps, Judge W. M. Black, Webb Talley, Jim Gambell, Will Gambell, Gray Lassiter, John B. Wheeler, Jim Rogers, Edmon Russell, Wm. Russell, Jacob Srite, Normon Pogue, John B. Pike, Mr. Coulter, Mr. Kelley, Calvin Wheeler, Eli Center.

LISBON—Joshua T. Dickey, Johnny Long, Henry Mitchel, Hiram Malicoat, Mosey Dickey, John Fricks.

LOOKOUT MOUNTAIN—Sam Burton, John Miller, James Massey, Mr. Drennon, Noah Fugatt, Warren Massey, Charles Moore, Thomas Lecroy.

POND SPRING—Toliver Butler, M. C. Butler, Jordan Bruce, James Bruce, Reuben Childress, John Satterfield, Richard Lane, Archie Bonds, Wm. Mathis, Richard Morgan, Isaac Bridgeman, James Moad, Calvin Barnes, Jeff Morgan, Henry Boss, Ave Camp, Judge John Wicker, John Owings, Starling Moad, Buck Bailey, Billy Mitchel, Sr., Mr. Mucklehannon, Richard Childress, Isaac Garrett, Thomas Abercrombie, Reuben Childress, Bolden Whitlow.

ROCK SPRINGS—Andy Hicks, Milton Lawrence, Robert Richard Shields, Major J. M. Shields, James R. Jones, Moses Park, Wm. Conley, Joshua Brigman, Mr. Frazier, Thomas Jones, Sam Brice, J. T. Deck, Hiram T. Gill, Amos Wellborn, John M. Lawrence, Thomas Lawrence, Wm. Glass, J. T. Renfro, Jeff Tipton, Johnny oJnes, Chessley Payne, Richard Harvell, A. E. Rogers, Sr., Thomas Adams, Thomas Glass, Thomas Evatt, Daniel Evans, Wm. Satterfield, Wm. Conley, Solomon Coker, Drewry Fowler, A. H. Johnson, Aaron Lambert, Jason Conley, John Conley, James Willis Dunn, Peter S. Anderson, Mr. Tierce.

ROSSVILLE—Xanders McFarland, Thomas G. McFarland, John Burie McFarland, John Hawkins, John Pearce, Wash Ellis, A. B. S. D. Wilson, Sr., Mike Smith, John Ellis, General Newman.

WILSON and DUCK CREEK—John C. Lumpkin, Joshua McConnell, Lecil Day, Joshua Martin, David Thurman, Ephraim Mabry, Joe Wardlaw, John Williams, Sr., John Day, Wm. McCurdy, Mr. Clarify, Wm. Pogue, Mr. Allgood, George Shaw, Amos Shaw, Ezekiel McWhorter, John McWhorter, James McWhorter, Berry Atwood, Johnathan Miller,

Archie Beaird, Charley Armstrong, Amzi G. Dickson, John Dickson, Tom Blackwell, Andrew McWhorter, Raney Chastain, Gus McCutchen, Mr. Cole, Thomas Sharpe, Milum P. Rogers.

Following the close of the Civil war and for some 25 or 30 years, or till about the year 1890, there was an almost continuous exodus of citizens of the county emigrating westward. During the seventies and eighties, especially, very many people of the county left each fall seeking new homes beyond the Mississippi river. The county paper during the fall and winter months was filled, so to speak, with notices of sales, both of lands and personal property, and of families leaving for the west. Texas, Arkansas and Missouri were the states to which most of them went. Many of those who went during that time bought lands and settled in that section and prospered; many others became dissatisfied and after a year or two returned to old Walker county and decided to remain at home. In this way numerous of the original settlers of the county, and their descendants, disappeared entirely from its history.

Chapter Nine

MILITIA DISTRICTS—BOUNDARIES—"WAX AND TALLOW" DEEDS.

MILITIA DISTRICT. The history of the militia district is an interesting one. The militia district is the ultimate unit in Georgia's political division. The state is divided into counties, and the county into municipalities and militia districts. Georgia is the only state whose last division is called by that name. Others are called Town, Township, Hundred, Precinct, Parish, etc.

In the formation of the government and its operation, a plan was made for defence when needed, and this plan called for defence by the citizens. A group of citizens located in a certain part of the county was called the militia. This group was supposed to number at least 100, but might fall short or exceed that number. A captain was chosen for this group, or company, and the company was known, at first, by the name of the captain; as Captain Smith's company, or Captain Brown's company. But the captain was liable to be changed occasionally and another captain selected. The company then might be Captain Anderson's company, etc. This was liable to cause confusion, so it was decided to number the companies or districts. The first district was in the oldest county in the state—Chatham. This was Number 1. Other districts came in succession, being numbered consecutively in various counties as they were formed. The official designation of districts, then, is by number, but they are known locally by names. Thus we commonly speak of Wilson District, but it is known officially as Militia District, or G. M. Number 943.

The oldest militia district in the county is number 826, known as Crawfish Spring. This means that 825 districts had already been established in other parts of the state when Crawfish Spring was established. (This fact might be used as circumstantial evidence tending to prove that the first court house was at that place). Other districts are as follows: Chestnut Flat, number 869; LaFayette, 871; Pond Spring, 881; Wilson, 943; Peavine, 944; East Armuchee, 953; Cane Creek, 960; West Armuchee, 1053; Lookout Mountain, 1161; Lisbon, 1501 (including Chattanooga Valley, 956); Daugherty, 1800; Cedar Grove, 1808 (old number 971); Kensington, 1809 (old number 1532); Rossville, 1812 (old Dry Valley, 1257); Chickamauga, 1818 (old Crawfish Spring, 826).

Also, the number of the various districts may be taken as a kind of monitor showing what parts of the county were populated first. After Crawfish Spring, Chestnut Flat came as the second district organized, showing that section as being the second oldest in the county. Here the Cooper's, Arnold's, William's, Lowery's and others settled very early. Next came LaFayette as the third oldest part of the county with the Caldwell's, Marsh's, Culberson's, Aycock's, Barry's, Johnston's, Wheeler's and many others. Then came Pond Spring, Wilson, and the others. It would be interesting to know the dates when these districts were established and thus determine the length of time between each.

BOUNDARIES. It sems that there is no official record of the exact boundaries of some parts of the militia districts. Citizens who live along these boundaries know in a general way their location, but officially there seems to be no record, at least this chronicler has been unable to find them. This is probably because of the burning of the court house. It is suggested that steps be taken to re-establish these boundaries and put them on permanent record. Events may occur when it is important to know the exact lines.

ORIGINAL GRANT OR "WAX AND TALLOW" DEEDS.

Many of these old deeds are still to be found among the older citizens of the county, though much worn and discolored. They are now nearly 100 years old, being dated, generally, during the decade 1830 to 1840. The following citizens of the county have these old deeds which have been handed down from their forbears: W. C. McFarland, lot No. 42 in 9th and 4th, dated Jan. 19th, 1836, granted to John Gray of Elbert County; also, lot 101, 9th and 4th, dated Feb. 25, 1836, drawn by James Weatherby of Randolph County; Miss Mary Ellis, lot No. 109, 9th and 4th, dated Feb. 25, 1836, drawn by James Turner, of Appling County; Cleve Roark, lot 285, 9th and 4th, dated Nov. 19, 1845, drawn by B. Malcomb, of Morgan County; H. R. Johnson, lot No. 12, 9th and 4th, dated Nov. 12, 1839, drawn by Robert H. Fretwell of Morgan County; John T. Thurman, lot No. 304, 12th and 4th, dated Nov. 28, 1835, drawn by Robert March of Warren County; also 273, 12th and 4th, dated Dec. 11, 1837, drawn by Barma S. Freeman of Habersham County; J. R. Tyner, lot No. 13, 8th and 4th, dated Jan. 26, 1833, drawn by Zachariah Batson, of Upson County; Martin Lawrence, lot No. 133, 8th and 4th, dated March 14, 1834, drawn by Martin Thomason of Newton County; J. H. Madaris, lot 38, 8th and 4th, dated Jan. 22, 1837, drawn by Mansel Garrett; Mrs. Rebecca Bomar Blackwell, lot No. 40, 26th and 3rd, dated Dec. 21, 1833; J. C. McWilliams, lot No. 215, 26th and 3rd, dated Feb. 15, 1837; Mrs. Emma Bryan, lot 220, 7th and 4th, dated Feb. 3, 1833, drawn by Henry C. Bragg of Green County; J. C. Rogers, lot No. 248, 7th and 4th, dated July 2, 1835, drawn by Paschal Taylor of Heard County; W. O. McCurdy, lot No. 150, 7th and 4th, dated Dec. 11, 1837, drawn by John Stephens, soldier in late war, of Upson County; Miss Jamie McCullough, lot No. 220, 26th and 3rd, drawn by William Henry Grimes, of Richmond County, dated Aug. 23, 1838; also, lot No. 213, 26th and 3rd, drawn by Mary Jackson, widow, dated May 7, 1837; also, lot No. 219, 26th and 3rd, drawn by Matthew Osburn, of Jasper County, dated June 13, 1836.

LAND DISTRICTS AND SECTIONS. The following districts and sections are numbered east and west beginning at the N.W. corner with number one: 7th and 4th; 8th and 4th; 9th and 4th; 10th and 4th; 11th and 4th; 26th and 3rd; and 27th and 3rd. The 12th and 4th is numbered north and south beginning at the N.W. corner with number one.

Thus it is seen that the early surveyors had no fixed rule for surveying and laying off land lots. Later surveyors have found it difficult if not impossible to follow the original lines laid out by the early surveyors. In the 12th and 4th, especially, some confusion has, at different times, resulted because of this. Mr. Tom Simmons of the Cedar Grove section recalls that he once heard the late Captain Wood say that the surveyors only surveyed and measured that district and section one way; that the corners of the lots were marked but never run out in the opposite direction, and that the Legislature refused to accept the map of the surveyors at that time. Later, a map was arranged, largely by guess, which was accepted.

GEORGIA-TENNESSEE BOUNDARY. Quite often we hear some one contending that the Tennessee River is the real boundary line between Georgia and Tennessee; that the city of Chattanooga is in Georgia. This is an interesting question, and dates back to the founding of the State by General Oglethorpe. The territory of the new colony as described by the charter granted by the king of England, comprised all the territory between the Savannah and Altamaha rivers extending to their head waters and running thence in a westerly direction to the "South Seas." If then we begin at the head waters of the Savannah river and run a line westward with a compass we follow the present line between the two states. However, this question caused no little trouble to our forbears more than a century ago. We find the following item in "Georgia and Georgians," by Lucian Lamar Knight, pg. 485, Vol. 1. "Commissioners from Georgia and Tennessee met in 1818 at a point on Nickojack creek in the northwestern angle of the state and after several weeks succeeded in running a boundary line to the satisfaction of all parties."

The following extract bearing on this matter is copied from The Georgia Gazeteer, by Adiel Sherwood, dated 1837:

> Nickojack, it is said, was the residence, during the war, of an old negro named Jack. The Indians used to call him Nicko instead of Negro Jack. His hut was on the creek. This is the origin of the name of the creek and cave.
>
> Nickojack creek issues from the Rackoon Mt. ¼ mi. N. of the 35°, in the N. W. corner of this state, and runs N. one mile into the Tenn. River. Its rise is in Georgia though its passage is subterraneous. This creek was explored in 1818 by the Commissioner who ran the line between Ga. and Tenn. and the substance of their description follows, for which I am indebted to Judge Stocks:
>
> The mouth of the cave, whence the stream issues, is 80 feet wide and 50 feet high and the solid rock above is 45 feet in diameter. The party proceeded south 10°, east for 100 yards, following an uneven channel, but the rock above is perfectly smooth. One hundred yards from the cave, their course was south 45° east. On the left side is an avenue leading north into a large, round room, and from this there is a narrow passage back to the mouth of the cave—hardly passable. Opposite to this room, the cave or channel is 150 ft. wide and several small rooms are around, presenting columns, arches, etc. The creek at this place is sixty feet wide, clear and beautiful. Distant from this spot ¼ mi., the cave closes in upon the edge of the stream, and is about 30 ft. high and 80 ft. wide. Here our adventurers took a canoe and proceeded in it *one mile* farther, till the creek became so shallow that their slender bark was difficult to move. After six hours of excessive fatigue, they returned from their *unearthly* expedition. They carried large torches with them, for the light of heaven does not penetrate that dreary abode.
>
> Rackoon Mountain is in the N. W. corner of the state. One spur of it extends within 30 ft. of the Tenn. River; and being 150 ft. in perpendicular height, frowns awfully on the trembling traveler as he passes along what is called the Narrows, for there is but 30 ft. for the road between the mountain and the river. Nickojack Creek issues from this mountain west of the Narrows.
>
> On the summit of this mountain, one mile and seven chains south of the Tenn. River, is "Camac's Rock," the N. W. corner of the state, marked on the north side, "Tenn., 1st June 1818," and on the south side, "Georgia." The Georgia commissioner who assisted in fixing the rock here and running the line, was Judge Stocks, of Greene, and Gen. Cooke was the other from Tenn. James Camac was mathematician, and Col. Hugh Montgomery, surveyor.

Chapter Ten

FORT CUMMINGS—ECHO FROM 1838.

Contributed by Frances Park Stiles.

ONE of the very interesting historical spots in Walker County is the Big Spring and the hill above, where once stood the old Indian stockade, Fort Cummings, built by the United States forces in 1836 when it was found that force must be used to remove the Indians beyond the Great River. Being bitterly opposed to leaving their homeland, the Indians had made one last effort to retain their ancient abode by sending Chief John Ross to Washington to plead their case before the great White Father. His pleadings were useless and they were ordered West.

This order struck terror to the hearts of the Indians, for news received from their brethren who had previously gone there was unfavorable.

Fort Cummings was a large enclosure of upright logs; the trenches where the logs were placed can still be seen. There was a rifle tower in each corner after the manner of frontier forts. Port holes were formed by sawing flared notches in the logs before they were put in the building. On the inside of the tower the port holes were eight or ten inches across, thus allowing room for changing the course of the rifle fire.

Captain Samuel Farris, grandfather of the late Dr. Samuel Farris, and one of the first citizens of LaFayette, was in command of a company known as the Captain Farris company of Lindsay's regiment, Georgia Mounted Militia. This regiment, consisting of twelve companies, was stationad at Fort Cummings in April, 1938. Also, the second regiment (designation of company not stated) was ordered to proceed to Fort Cummings on May 25, 1838. Captain Farris' regiment consisting of 12 companies was engaged at this time in collecting the Indians and escorting them to Fort Poinsett, Tenn. Captain Cleveland's company of said regiment is specifically shown to have been engaged in collecting Indians here. This information was given by War Department, 2385861, The Adjutant General's Office, Washington, D. C.

Pioneer citizens of Walker County, now living, distinctly remember seeing Fort Cumming before it rotted down. They also recall hearing their fathers tell of the time the Indians lived here—some living peacefully, some destroying property and were dangerous. Before leaving most of the Indians had an opportunity to sell and receive a fair price for the goods they had that were worth anything.

Many of the pioneer citizens of the county went to the stockade to bid the Indians good bye. Their account of the leavetaking is sad. Many of the Indians fell prostrate on the ground and begged the soldiers to shoot them, that they might be spared this grief and be buried in their own happy hunting ground.

The William Marsh Chapter, Daughters of the American Revolution, placed at the site of Fort Cummings, some years ago, a boulder as a marker, but vandals tore away the plate and so far it has not been replaced.

The following clipping was taken from the Walker County Messenger of October 20, 1881, and is so full of early history that it has been decided to incorporate it in this work. It describes events occurring in 1837-38.

NORTH GEORGIA—Forty-three Years Ago.
By Rev. C. D. Smith.

Bro. Price: During my labors on the LaFayette circuit I had frequent opportunities to study the character of the Cherokee Indians. A goodly number of the younger men had been to the mission school or were converts under Rev. David B. Cummings, who had charge of the missionary work among them, as well as the LaFayette district. I attended several of his meetings amongst them. When an Indian professed conversion he was usually guileless and sincere. There was no political promotion held out to him. He had no social or matrimonial ends to serve. There were no ecclesiasticisms or ritualistic visions presented to his mind to bewilder and deceive him. He did not care to run from town to town to inquire which was the most respectable denomination. The simple unadorned question of salvation, and when once converted he recognized Christ as all in all. This is a representation of the Indian as I saw him when about to be removed by the superior force of the United States government from the graves of his fathers and children, from his home and his hunting grounds—the land he loved. I became cognizant of many acts among the Indians, that rebuked in the most pointed manner the boasted civilization—the professed Christianity of the white people, who settled amongst them. I will relate one occurrence that exemplifies this statement. I knew the parties but will suppress the names except that of the Indian.

There lived in Broomtown Valley an Indian whose name was Bill Hawk. He had been at the mission school where he had learned to speak the English language pretty well, and had made a profession of religion, and could read the English Testament. There also lived in the same neighborhood a gentleman—a North Carolinian—who was emphatically a man of the world whom I will call Mr. A. It was considered an advantageous transaction when a new settler could purchase hogs and cattle and ponies from an Indian, on account of their being accustomed to the range. Hawk was a well-to-do Indian and had considerable stock about him. Mr. A. had frequent conversations with Hawk about purchasing some of his stock when he should leave. Finally Hawk promised him some. The order issued to Gen. Scott to collect the Indians to the Forts was executed on Saturday. Col. Farris, who was in command of the Fort at LaFayette, detailed troops to the different neighborhoods. Some of the soldiers who went to Broomtown Valley were known to Hawk. He told them he was not ready to go up to the Fort—that he had not yet sold his stock, some few tools he had, and some household fixtures. He said if they would allow him to remain till he wound up his matters he would go to the Fort the last of the next week. Knowing his character and having the utmost confidence in his honor, the soldiers agreed he should remain. Mr. A. said he concluded to walk over to Hawk's on Sunday morning to see how matters stood—that he had been there but a few minutes when a Methodist exhorter stepped in somewhat surprised. In a short time in came a Baptist deacon who seemed a little frightened at seeing his neighbors there. But little was said and in a little while in walked a Presbyterian elder who seemed a little scared at so formidable an array of neighbors before him. Some little time passed before much was said. At last the exhorter broke the ice by saying: "Well, Bill, you are going up to the Fort in a few days, I suppose?" "Yes," was Hawk's reply. "Have you sold your ponies, cows and hogs yet?" "No," said Bill . "I want some of your stock when you leave." The deacon struck in on this wise: "I don't want you to promise all your stock, for I want some." Now that the rest should not get the start of him, the elder put in: "Bill, you know me—I've been a good neighbor to you, and I want a cow and calf, and sow and pigs, and a pony or two." A pause. Then Hawk replied in this manner: "Men, I won't trade with any of you today—it is Sunday, and my Bible says: Remember the Sabbath day to keep it holy." Mr. A. said the three sat and looked at the floor for a while, and then like the men who accused the woman taken in adultery, they went out one at a time, till they had all left, when Hawk said: "Mr. A., come over tomorrow and I will do what I promised you."

* * * * * *

There lived in the valley of West Chickamauga Rev. Levi Stansel, a local preacher. While I was going home with him from church one day, he proposed, after dinner, we should walk over to the Indian cabins and see a very old Indian. There was at the cabins a young Cherokee who had attended the schools at the mission and could talk English pretty well, so we had an interpreter, to converse with the old man. We learned that he was over ninety years old—that he had lived in that country since he was a boy. The question was asked if he was willing to go to Arkansas. He said he was not. He was asked why unwilling to go. His reply was substantially as follows: "Because I am an old man and contented with my home. My fathers and many of my children are buried here and I want to be buried with them. I love these hunting grounds and don't want to go away from them. This country was given to us for ourselves, our children and our children's children. The great white Chief came down through our country and told us that if we would go with him to New Orleans to fight the British, he would see that we should have this country forever. I went amongst others. When we got to New Orleans, some of us undertook to swim the big river and get behind the British. I swam the river (and here he showed by signs how the bullets threw the water all around him); by that we helped to whip the British. We came to live and die in our country and now the children of the great white Chief have come to drive us from our homes, and make us go to Arkansas. I don't want to go."

There seemed to be no emotion about him, but while he talked the water ran from his eyes and dropped off his chin. There was much in this for the consideration of a statesman. This man, though a savage, had made friendly league for future national amity. He attached the most sacred meanings to the obligations of the contracts. He had periled his life in the performance of his part of the agreement, and now he felt keenly the injustice that would annul that contract without the agreement of all parties. Nations as well as individuals must be just. I cannot, however, dwell on this subject of Indian character; these two are enough to bring the blush of shame to the church and the nation.

I remained on the circuit after my colleague had left in order to assist the local brethren in holding a camp meeting above LaFayette. This threw me behind the preachers going to conference, which met at Wytheville, Va., that fall. After the meeting had closed, I set out, and on reaching Chatata Valley I stopped to spend the night with Brother Charles K. Lewis who took me into the church. He told me I must not go the next day, assigning as a reason that Brother John Henninger's wife was very sick, and that Bro. H., who had traveled a district that year, was very anxious to meet some preacher going to conference, by whom he could send his official papers. Accordingly, the next morning, accompanied by Bro. Lewis, I rode over to Bro. Henninger's, distant about seven miles, and spent the day with him. I received his papers and instructions, and the next morning set out again on my journey to Wytheville. The whole distance had to be made, by the ordinary circuit rider, on horseback, and I made it alone.—*Holston Methodist.*

* * * * * *

NOTE—It is probable that the name of Fort Cummings was given in honor of the Rev. David B. Cummings named above, who was a noted Methodist minister and missionary to the Cherokee Indians, and who had charge of the LaFayette work during those early times. He sowed the seeds of Methodism a century ago and now are seen the fruits of his work in a multitude of Methodist churches dotting this fair land. He was one of those pioneer preachers who paved the way—laid the foundation. We are reaping where he sowed. We honor his memory.

Chapter Eleven

The Chickamauga Battle—Bragg at LaFayette—Skirmishes.

CHICKAMAUGA

By Robert Sparks Walker
(By permission of the author)

A masterpiece of Nature's hand
    That brings its message from the east,
Through Georgia's hills and valley land,
    And ere its waters are released
Into the twisting Tennessee,
    It threads the knolls and greenest vales,
And bathes the roots of shrub and tree,—
    And when the autumn sunset pales,
Its scenic beauty is increased,—
    Chickamauga, Chickamauga!

The wild swine's feet its bed have trod,
    And feline claws have chafed its sides;
The does have rested on its sod,
    Top-minnows rode its silver tides;
And from each glow of sunset beam,
    Through cavern walls and canvas leaves,
The eyes of cunning raccoons gleam,
    And dreamland tents the spider weaves,—
For Nature thus with it abides,—
    Chickamauga, Chickamauga!

No painter on its banks recline,
    Its vernal grandeur can portray.
No human face look more benign,
    No psalmist mock its rippling lay;
Great artery of Nature's heart,
    Each beating throb its creatures feel
When bluebells in the springtime start,
    And trilliums 'mongst the beech trees steal,
Between whose roots fern mosses play,—
    Chickamauga, Chickamauga!

The Blue and Gray for three days faced
    Each other on its western bank;
The cannons roared, war horses paced,
    The thirsty sod the red blood drank;
But Nature has erased the scar
    With densest trees and green grass blades;
She keeps no record long of war,
    For in a day her memory fades,—
'Neath Lethe's waves all hatred sank,—
    Chickamauga, Chickamauga!

Chickamauga Battle—September 19-20, 1863

The heroic and hard-fought battle of Gettysburg which occurred early in July of the year 1863 probably marked the high tide in the existence of the Southern Confederacy. After the defeat of Southern arms in that battle, the prospect for final triumph grew daily dimmer. On the other hand the Federals were more sanguine of eventual success. During this year, also, the Union leaders had gained complete control of the Mississippi river, thus cutting off other state that could, henceforth, give but little aid. In order to hasten the bloody conflict, and, so, bring to an end the fratricidal clash, the plan of the Federals was now to send an army into the very heart of the South, and thus bring to a close the strife.

After the bloody encounter at Murfreesboro, Tennessee, General Bragg, the Southern commander, retreated toward Chattanooga, pursued by General Rosecrans of the Union army. Each of these leaders proved himself a great commander by the consumate skill by which he was able to handle his army and prevent his opponent from gaining his purpose. Bragg, crossing the Cumberland Mountains, soon reached the Tennessee river which he likewise crossed and entrenched himself within the city of Chattanooga, while Rosecrans planned to drive him out or capture him there. To do this Rosecrans divided his army into several parts and covered the country above the city along the Tennessee river for a distance of forty or fifty miles. It was his plan to cross the river both above and below the city with parts of the army and come in from the south, east and west and thus surround the Confederates and capture them in the city. To do this he used much strategy to fool his antagonist. He built camp fires on the summits of the mountains north and east of Chattanooga to create the impression that his troops were encamped there. During the day many troops were marched around back and forth, and much activity was shown as if preparing for bombarding the city across the river. Really, however, large bodies of troops were hurrying both up and down the river and much preparation was being made for crossing. The army was hurrying to Bridgeport where preparations were being made for the crossing. Pontoon bridges and rafts, logs tied together, rude boats or flats, and anything that could be used for crossing was pressed into use; the cavalry, of course, crossing on horseback. Most of the army crossed at Bridgeport and at Caperton's Ferry. Having crossed the river the troops began their march eastward across Raccoon and Lookout Mountains. Bragg, anticipating this movement of the Federals, had sent out troops to contest the passes over the mountains and ridges surrounding Chattanooga. Every pass on Lookout Mountain, as well as Pigeon, was guarded by Confederate soldiers. At practically all these passes there were skirmishes and clashes between the opposing sides. Some of these skirmishes were in reality serious battles between large divisions of the two armies, in which many men were sometimes killed or wounded on either side.

Bragg was too good a tactician to allow his opponent to surround him and cut him off from his base and line of supplies. He must protect his line of communication which in this case was the railroad to Atlanta. Had he remained in Chattanooga he would have soon starved and been compelled to surrender. When, therefore, he was apprised of the Federal's crossing the river he promptly vacated the city of Chattanooga and moved southward to protect his base or line of communication. He left the city on September 8 and marched south by way of Lee and Gordon's Mills to LaFayette where he established his headquarters and where he remained for some days. His army was at that time scattered along a line of probably 30 miles, reaching from LaFayette and Pigeon Mountain to about five miles east of Rossville, occupying in a general way the east bank of the Chickamauga creek. While holding his headquarters at LaFayette, General Bragg is said to have planned the great battle. In the meantime another large division of Rosecrans army had succeeded in crossing Lookout Mountain by way of Stevens' and Daugherty's Gaps. In this way, it is said that probably 15,000 Union soldiers were encamped for some days in McLemore's cove. The reports of officers of Union troops and their activities in the cove during the several days immediately preceding the great battle name almost every pass, road, cross-road, church, village and stream in that valley as well as many homes of citizens. Serious skirmishes were fought at Stevens' Gap, Dug Gap, Davis' Cross Roads and at other points. Many of Rosecrans' soldiers, also, had been detached at Bridgeport and sent by way of Will's Valley and Alpine, Georgia, marching toward the battlefield by way of Broomtown Valley and LaFayette.

As before stated, General Bragg had his headquarters at LaFayette from September 10 to 17. The large oak tree under which he planned the great battle stood in front of the old brick school house (called the Gordon Hall from the fact that General John B. Gordon went to school there) until about 1925 when it was struck by lightning and was cut down. It was known as the General Bragg oak.

While Bragg was located at LaFayette, Confederate troops were sent out in all directions to ascertain the positions and the strength of the enemy. In this way forces of Confederate soldiers occupied every strategic position in the county. Catlett's Gap, Dug Gap, Bluebird and Rape Gaps and others on Pigeon mountain; Nickajack, Stevens' Daugherty and other gaps were guarded on Lookout Mountain. The clashes between the two armies at these places are called shirmishes, although many men were killed at some of them, and but for the great battle of Chickamauga which was to follow, they would have been properly called battles.

The following extract is from the report of a Union officer, pg. 547, Vol. 30, Series 1, War of the Rebellion:

"On Thursday evening, 17th instant, (Sept), I was ordered with my regiment to Bailey's Cross Roads, in McLemore's Cove, which is opposite and 2½ miles from Dug Gap, and 3 miles from Bluebird Gap. About 3 p.m. my regiment was attacked by a brigade of rebel cavalry at Davis' Ford on Chickamauga creek. The fight lasted 2 hours. The field was left in our possession. We had two men slightly wounded; none killed. The enemy had 2 killed, one of whom was Colonel Estes, of the Third Confederate Cavalry, and 8 wounded. On the next day we skirmished at the widow Davis' Cross Roads, retaining the ground without loss. The enemy's loss unknown. On the night of the 18th instant we were ordered to Pond Spring."

On September 13th the outposts of Bragg's army at LaFayette who were guarding the approaches to that place were attacked some 4 or 5 miles below LaFayette and a little north of Center Post by a part of the Yankee forces who had been deployed at Bridgeport and were approaching the scene of the battle by way of Alpine and Broomtown Valley. There was considerable skirmishing at this place, and several were killed and wounded, besides the capturing of a number of Confederate soldiers by the Yankees. From these captives, the Union leaders learned that Bragg had been reinforced by Breckenridge's division. In war these skirmishes are sometimes sources of important information to the commanding general. He may learn the strength, and position of his enemy. He may capture some prisoners and from them gain important information as to re-inforcements or other changes. Having learned in this skirmish that General Bragg had been reinforced by Breckenridge's soldiers, the Yankees knew at once that it would require more of their energy, skill and vigilance to overcome the Confederates in the impending battle. In this skirmish the Yankees lost 2 men killed and 3 wounded. 18 Confederates were captured.

The two armies were thus converging from all directions toward the wooded lowlands of the Chickamauga creek. A large force of Union soldiers were encamped at Cedar Grove Church on the night of the 17th, having come by way of Daugherty's Gap. The following night they bivouaced at Bailey's Cross Roads, and the following day joined the battle near Crawfish Spring. General Bragg left the vicinity of LaFayette on the 17th and moved his army northward toward Lee and Gordon's Mills. At the same time the Confederate forces on and near Pigeon Mountain were moving down the Chickamauga and as they moved there were frequent clashes with the opposing forces along the creek. Mention is made in various reports of commanding officers of several skirmishes along the banks of this famous creek. There were clashes near Owing's Ford, at Pond Spring, at Glass' Mill, and at other points.

J. M. Ransom, an old citizen who lives now as he did then, in the Glass mill community, relates how, as a boy, on the morrow after the skirmish at Glass' Mill, he was sent on the old family horse with a "turn of corn" to the mill, his mother charging him particularly not to cross the creek where the battle had been the day before. His curiosity, however, was so great that he ventured across to where the soldiers were engaged in burying the dead. He recalls most vividly the scene of the dead soldiers with blood marks over their faces and hands. This, of course, was only a skirmish but the scene was so forceful that this old citizen has never forgotten it. Others relate how, several days after the great battle of Chickamauga, they walked over the main battlefield and viewed the dead bodies of soldiers, still unburied. In certain places, it is said, that it was possible, if one cared to do so, to walk for great distances on bodies of dead soldiers without touching the ground. In many places the Yanks and the Rebs were lying side by side, having paid the supreme debt that awaits us all.

> "The muffled drum's sad roll has beat
>   The soldier's last tattoo'
> No more on life's parade shall meet
>   That brave and fallen few;
> On fame's eternal camping ground
>   Their silent tents are spread;
> And Glory guards with silent round
>   The bivouac of the dead."
>
> * * *
>
> "Rest on embalmed and sainted dead'
>   Dear as the blood ye gave—
> No impious footsteps here shall tread
>   The herbage of your grave.
> Nor shall your glory be forgot
>   While fame her record keeps,
> Or Honor points the hallowed spot
>   Where valor proudly sleeps."

But I have digressed and will return to a detail of the events of the great battle as they successfully followed each other. It had been General Bragg's original purpose to fall upon the enemy before he was concentrated at any point and overcome him piecemeal. To this end he had made an effort to crush the forces in the cove while the main army of the enemy was at or near Chattanooga. He sent General Hill and General Hindman with heavy forces to Davis' Cross Roads to meet and crush the force of Union soldiers there, estimated to be about 5,000 strong. General Hindman left Rock Spring at 12 o'clock at night for that point. Hill was ordered to go from LaFayette early the next day, but for some inexplicable reason he failed to go promptly, and so Hindman failing to get the support he anticipated, the plan failed. Had this plan carried, as the commanding general hoped it might, there would have been an important action at that place and it is probable that there would have been no great Chickamauga battle. Other efforts were made to strike isolated sections of the Union army, which, for one reason or another, failed. Finally the two great armies became concentrated along the two banks of the Chickamauga river, extending from near Crawfish Spring to Ried's, or Alexander's Bridges, a distance of 8 or 9 miles. As the battle progressed the two extremes were drawn into the center or vortex of the action some miles north of Lee and Gordon's Mills. The action proper began on the Confederate right at or near the Alexander Bridge. General Bragg, in a circular notice to all his commanders, had given minute instructions as to the method and plan of the battle. The action was to begin on the Confederate's extreme right and gradually be taken up successively by each brigade toward the left until all were engaged. Reserves were placed at certain points to be used in case of necessity, while the cavalry was ordered to be ready anywhere to meet any emergency. It is doubtful if any battle was ever planned with more care and foresight than that of Chickamauga.

Chapter Twelve

CHICKAMAUGA BATTLE, CONTINUED—GENERAL GORDON'S DESCRIPTION.

THE following extract, taken, by permission, from General Gordon's Reminiscences, page 200, describes most graphically the movements of the two armies during the action of the 19th and 20th:

"In order to obtain a comprehensive view of the ever shifting scenes during the prolonged battle, to secure a mental survey of the whole battle as the marshalled forces swayed to and fro, charging and countercharging, assaulting, breaking, retreating, reforming, and again rushing forward in still more desperate assault, let the reader imagine himself in some great elevation from which he could look down on that wooded, undulated and rugged region.

"For forty-eight hours or more the marching columns of Bragg were moving toward Chattanooga and along the south banks of the Chickamauga in order to cross the river and strike the Union forces on the left flank. At the same time Rosecrans summoned his forces from different directions and concentrated them north of the river. Having passed, as was supposed, far below the point where the Union left rested, Bragg's columns, in the early hours of the 19th of September, crossed the fords and bridges, and prepared to sweep by left wheel on the Union flank. During the night, however, George H. Thomas had moved his Union corps from the right to this left flank. Neither army knew of the presence of the other in this portion of the woodland. As Bragg prepared to assail this Union left, Thomas, feeling his way through the woods to ascertain what was in his front, unexpectedly struck the Southern right, held by Forest's cavalry, and thus inaugurated the battle. Forest was forced back; but he quickly dismounted his men, sent the horses to the rear, and on foot stubbornly resisted the advance of the Union infantry. Quickly the Confederates moved to Forest's support. The roar of small arms on this extreme flank in the early morning admonished both commanders to hurry thither their forces. Bragg was forced to check his proposed assault upon another portion of the Union lines and move to the defence of the Confederate right. Rapidly the forces of the two sides were thrown into this unexpected collision, and rapidly swelled the surging current of battle. The divisions of the Union army before whom Forest's cavalry had yielded were now driven back; but other Federals suddenly rushed upon Forests' front. The Southern troops, under Cheatham and Stewart, Polk, Buckner, and Cleburne, hurried forward in a united assault upon Thomas. Walthall's Mississippians were at this moment hurled upon King's flank, and drove his brigade in confusion from the Union lines; and as Govans' gray-clad veterans simultaneously assailed the Union forces under Scribner, that command also yielded. The federal battery was captured, and the tide of success seemed at the moment to be with the Confederates. Fortune, however, always fickle, was especially capricious in this battle. The Union forces further to westward held their ground with desperate tenacity. General Rosecrans, the Federal commander-in-chief, rode amidst his troops as they hurried in converging columns to the point of heaviest fire, and in person hurled them against the steadfast Confederate front. The shouts and yells and the roll of musketry swelled the din of battle to a deafening roar. The fighting was terrific. Walthall's Mississippians at this point contended desperately with attacks in front and on their flank. The 9th Ohio with double quick and with mighty shout, rushed upon the captured Union battery and recovered it. The Confederate gunners were killed by bayonets as they bravely stood at their posts. Hour after hour the battle raged, extending the area of its fire and the volume of its tremendous roar. Here and there along the lines a shattered command, its leading officers dead or wounded, was withdrawn, reorganized, and quickly returned to its bloody work. Still farther toward the Confederate right Forest essayed to turn the Union left. Charging as infantry, he pressed forward through a tempest of shot and neared the Union flank, when the Federal batteries poured upon his entire line rapid charges of grape, canister and shell. Round after round on flank and front, these deadly volleys came until Forest's dissolving lines disappeared, leaving heaps of dead near the mouths of the Union guns. Reforming his broken ranks, Forest with Cheatham's support, again rushed upon the Union left, the impetuous onset bringing portions of the hostile lines to a hand-to-hand struggle. Still there was no decisive break in the stubborn Union ranks. Coming through woods and fields from the other wings, the flapping ensigns marked the rapid concentration of both armies around this vortex of battle. As the converging columns met, bayonet clashed with bayonet and the trampled earth was saturated with blood. Here and there the Union line was broken by the charges of Cheatham, Stewart, and Johnson, but was quickly reformed and re-established by the troops under Reynolds. The Union commands of Carlin and Heg were swept back before the fire at short range from Southern muskets; but as the Confederate lines again advanced and leaped into the Union trenches, they were met and checked by a headlong countercharge.

"The LaFayette road along or near which the broken lines of each army were rallied and reformed, and across which the surging currents of fire had repeatedly rolled, became the "bloody lane" of Chickamauga.

"The remorseless war-god at this hour relaxed his hold on the two armies whose life blood had been flowing since early morning. Gradually the mighty wrestlers grew weary and faint, and silence reigned again in the shell-shivered forest. It was, however, only a lull in the storm. On th extreme Union left the restless Confederates were again moving into line for a last and tremendous effort. The curtain of night slowly descended, and the powder-blackened bayonets and flags over the hostile lines were but dimly seen in the dusky twilight. Wearily the battered ranks in gray moved again through the bullet-scarred woods, over the dead bodies of their brothers who fell in the early hours and whose pale faces told the living of coming fate. Nature mercifully refused to lend her light to guide the unyielding armies to further slaughter. But the blazing muzzles of the rifles now became their guides, and the first hour of darkness was made hideous by resounding small arms and their lurid flashes. Here might follow a whole chapter of profoundly interesting personal incidents. The escape of officers of high rank, who on both sides rode with their troops through the consuming blasts, was most remarkable; but here and there the missiles found them. General Preston Smith, of Tennessee, my friend in boyhood, was among the victims. A Minie ball in search of his heart struck the gold watch which covered it. The watch was shivered, but it only diverted the messenger of death to another vital point. The inverted casing, whirled for a great distance through the air, fell at the feet of a Texan, who afterward sent it to the bereaved family. Nearby was found the Union General Baldwin, his blue uniform reddened with his own blood and the blood of his dead comrades around him. The carnage was appalling and sickening. 'Enough of blood and death for one day' was the language of the bravest hearts which throbbed with anguish at the slaughter of the 19th and with anxiety as to the morrow's work.

"'Night after the battle.' None but a soldier can realize the import of those four words. To have experienced it, felt it, endured it, is to have witnessed a phase of war almost as trying to a sensitive nature as the battle itself. The night after a battle is dreary and doleful enough to a victorious army cheered by triumph. To the two armies, whose blood was still flowing long after the sun went down on the 19th, neither of them victorious, but each so near the other as to hear the groans of the wounded and dying in the opposing ranks, the scene was indescribably oppressive. Cleburne's Confederates had waded the river with the water to their arm-pits. Their clothing was drenched and their bodies shivering in the chill north wind through the weary hours of the night. The noise of ax blows and falling trees along the Union lines in front plainly told that the Confederate assault upon the Union breastworks at the coming dawn was to be over an abatis of felled timber, tangled brush and obstructing tree-tops. The faint moonlight, almost wholly shut out by dense foliage, added to the weird spell of the somber scene. In every direction were dimly burning tapers, carried by nurses and relief corps searching for the wounded. All over the field lay the unburied dead, their pale faces made ghastlier by streaks of blood and clotted hair, and black stains of powder left upon their lips when they tore off with their teeth the ends of deadly cartridges. Such was the night between the 19th and 20th of September at Chickamauga.

"At nine o'clock on that Sabbath morning, September 20, 1863, as the church bells of Chattanooga summoned its children to Sunday school, the signal guns sounding through the forests at Chickamauga called the bleeding armies again to battle. The troops of Longstreet had arrived, and he was assigned to the command of the Confederate left, D. H. Hill to the Confederate right. On this latter wing of Bragg's army were the troops of John C. Breckenridge, W. H. T. Walker, Patrick Cleburne, and A. P. Stewart, with Cheatham in reserve. Confronting them and forming the Union left were the blue-clad veterans under Baird, Johnson, Palmer, and Reynolds, with Gordon Granger in reserve. Beginning on the other end of the line forming the left wing of Bragg's battle array were Preston, Hindman, and Bushrod Johnson, with Law and Kershaw in reserve. Confronting these, beginning on the extreme Union right and forming the right wing of Rosecran's army, were Sheridan, Davis, Wood, Negley and Brannan, with Wilder and Van Cleve in reserve.

"The bloody work was inaugurated by Breckenridge's assault upon the Union left. The Confederates, with a ringing yell, broke through the Federal line. The Confederate General Helm, with his gallant Kentuckians, rushed upon the Union breastworks and was hurled back, his command shattered. He was killed and his colonels shot down. Again rallying, again assaulting, again recoiling, this decimated command temporarily yielded its place in line. The Federals, in furious countercharge, drove back the Confederates under Adams, and his body was also left upon the field.

"The Chickamauga River was behind the Confederates; Missionary Ridge behind the Federals. On its slopes were Union batteries pouring a storm of shell into the forests through which Bragg's forces were bravely charging. As the Confederates under Adams were borne back, the clear ring of Pat Cleburne's 'Forward!' was heard; and forward they moved, their alignment broken by tree-tops and tangled brush and burning shells. His superb troops pressed through the storm, only to recoil under the concentrated fire of artillery and the blazing muzzles of small arms from the Federals behind their breastworks. The whole Confederate right, brigade, after brigade, in successive and repeated charges, now furiously assailed the Union breastworks, only to recoil broken and decimated. Walthall, with his fiery Mississippians, was repulsed, with all his field officers dead or wounded and his command torn into shreds. The gallant Georgians at once rushed into the consuming blasts, and their brilliant leader, Peyton Colquitt, fell, with many of his brave boys around him, close to the Union breastworks. The Confederates under Walker, Cleburne and Stewart with wild shouts charged the works held by the determined forces of Reynolds, Brannan, and Baird. Bravely these Union troops stood to their posts, but the Southern forces at one point broke through their front as Breckenridge swept down upon flank and rear. George H. Thomas, the 'Rock of Chickamauga,' with full appreciation of the crisis, called for help to hold this pivotal position of the Union left. Van Derveer's moving banners indicated the quick step of his troops responding to Thomas' call; and raked by flanking fire, this dashing officer drove Breckenridge back and relieved the Union flank. At doublequick and with ringing shout, the double Union lines pressed forward until, face to face and muzzle to muzzle, the fighting became fierce and desperate. Charging columns of blue and gray at this moment rushed against each other, and both were shivered in the fearful impact. The superb Southern leader, Deshler, fell at the head of his decimated command. Govan's Mississippians and Brown's Tennesseeans were forced back, when Bate, also of Tennessee, pressed furiously forward, captured the Union artillery, and drove the Federals to their breastworks. Again and quickly the scene was changed. Fresh Union batteries and supporting infantry with desperate determination overwhelmed and drove back temporarily the Confederates led by the knightly Stewart. Still further westward, Longstreet drove his column like a wedge into the Union right center, ripping asunder the steady line of the Federal divisions. In this whirlwind of battle, amidst its thunder and blinding flashes, the heroic Hood rode, encouraging his men, and fell desperately wounded. His leading line was shattered into fragments, but his stalwart supports pressed on over his own and the Union dead, capturing the first Union line. Halting only to reform under fearful fire, they started for the second Union position. Swaying, reeling, almost breaking, they nevertheless captured that second line, and drove up the ridge and over it the Federal fighters, who bravely resisted at every step. Whizzing shells from opposing batteries crossed each other as they tore through the forest, rending saplings and tumbling severed limbs and tree tops amidst the surging ranks. Wilder's mounted Union brigade in furious charge swept down upon Manigault's Confederates, flank and rear, and drove them in wild confusion; but the Union horsemen were in turn quickly driven from the field and beyond the ridge. Battery after battery of Union artillery was captured by the advancing Confederates. The roaring tide of battle, with alternate waves of success for both sides, surged around Snodgrass House and Horseshoe Ridge. Before a furious and costly Confederate charge the whole extreme Union right was broken and driven from the field.

Negley's shattered lines of blue abandoned the position and retreated to Rossville with the heavy batteries. Davis, with decimated Union lines under Carlin and Heg, moved into Negley's position; but these were driven to the right and rear. Onward, still onward, swept the Confederate columns; checked here, broken there, they closed the gaps and pressed forward, scattering Van Cleve's veterans in wild disorder. Amidst the shouting Confederates rode their leaders, Stewart, Buckner, Preston, Kershaw, and Johnson. The gallant McCook led in person a portion of Sheridan's troops with headlong fury against the Southern front; and Sheridan himself rode among his troops, rallying his broken lines and endeavoring to check the resistless Southern advance. The brave and brilliant Lytle of the Union army, soldier and poet, at this point paid to valor and duty the tribute of his heart's blood. The Confederate momentum, however, scattered these decimated Union lines and compelled them to joint the retreating columns, filling the road in the rear.

"Rosecrans, McCook, and Crittenden rode to Chattanooga to select another line for defence. In the furious tempest there now came one of those strange unexpected lulls; but the storm was only gathering fresh fury. In the comparative stillness which pervaded the field its mutterings could still be heard. Its lightnings were next to flash and its thunders to roll around Horseshoe summit. Along that crest and around Snodgrass House the remaining troops of Rosecrans' left wing planted themselves for stubborn resistance—one of the most stubborn recorded in history. To meet the assault of Longstreet's wing, the brave Union General Brannan, standing upon this now historic crest, rallied the remnants of Croxton, Wood, Harker, Beatty, Stanley, Van Cleve, and Buel; but up the long slopes the exulting Confederate ranks moved in majestic march. As they neared the summit a sheet of flames from Union rifles and heavy guns blazed into their faces. Before the blast the charging Confederates staggered, bent and broke; reforming at the top of the slope, these dauntless men in gray moved again to still more determined assault upon the no less dauntless Union lines firmly planted on the crest. Through the blinding fires they rushed to a hand-to-hand conflict, breaking here, pushing forward there, in terrible struggle. Through clouds of smoke around the summit the banners and bayonets of Hindman's Confederates were discovered upon the crest; when Gordon Granger and Steedman, with fresh troops, hurried from the Union left and, joining Van Deveer, hurled Hindman and his men from their citadel of strength and held it till the final Union retreat. With bayonets and clubbed muskets the resolute Federals pierced and beat back the charging Confederates, covering the slopes of Snodgrass Hill with Confederate dead. Roaring like a cyclone through the forest, the battle storm raged. Battery answered battery, deepening the unearthly din and belching from their heated throats the consuming iron hail. The woods caught fire from the flaming shells and scorched the bodies of dead and dying. At the close of the day the Union forces had been driven from every portion of the field except Snodgrass Hill, and as the sun sank behind the cliffs of Lookout Mountain, hiding his face from one of the bloodiest scenes enacted by human hands, this heroic remnant of Rosecrans' army withdrew to the rear and then to the works around Chattanooga, leaving the entire field of Chickamauga to the battered but triumphant and shouting Confederates."

Such is the description of the great Chickamauga battle as given by a former citizen of Walker county, himself a great general and tactician, who, although not present and taking part in that momentous struggle himself, being associated with that peerless soldier, General Lee in Virginia, during almost the whole of the great struggle, was, nevertheless, because of his intimate knowledge of all the great battles of the war, as well as his association for half a century with those who fought at Chickamauga, both Southern and Union, eminently qualified to describe and pass judgment—General John B. Gordon.

Chapter Thirteen

CHICKAMAUGA BATTLE, CONTINUED—CONFEDERATES WIN.

It is not the purpose of this chronicler to follow, with any very careful particularity, the movements of the two armies after the Chickamauga battle, except in so far as to show the result of that bloody conflict. The further activities of the armies were largely beyond the limits of the county. General Rosecrans, himself, with most of his staff officers, left the fateful field of battle about the close of the day on Sunday 20, being borne along by his own routed and frightened soldiery, who had now but one thought and that to escape from those "rebel" soldiers. The latter part of the fearful struggle on Snodgrass hill was enacted after Rosecrans left the field. This final struggle extended into the night so that General Bragg was unaware of the flight of the enemy till next morning. Believing the enemy still in his front, he had planned during the night to engage him at early morn, when, to his surprise, on investigation, he discovered he had fled.

Much criticism was heaped upon General Bragg, both at the time and since, for his failure to follow the enemy to Chattanooga and engage him at that place. It was pointed out by his critics that in the enemy's enfeebled and exhausted condition, and being dispirited by the late reverse, it would have been a most opportune time to strike a most decisive blow; especially so, since his own army was exuberant over the late victory. These critics contend that Bragg could have easily captured the enemy in the city or have driven him across the river.

No doubt General Bragg would have done this if he had had a fresh army—such a one as he had on the morning of the 19th; but let it be remembered that his army was worn to a frazzle during the two days frightful struggle. It had, by almost infinite courage and superhuman endurance, led by as gallant officers as ever drew sword, met and overcome one of the best equipped and best disciplined of armies—another army with almost infinite courage and led by equally as brave and gallant officers. General Bragg in his report of the battle says that he had lost two-fifths of his army—rank and file—in the battle. Is it any wonder, then, that he should hesitate to push that other three-fifths, staggering along on the enforced march, many of them falling by the way, to engage the enemy? Most military critics and tacticians who have given the subject serious consideration—who have analyzed carefully the situation both of the Union and Confederate armies are now of the opinion that General Bragg acted wisely in hesitating to at once offer to engage the enemy—General John B. Gordon being one of these.

Having searched very carefully the official reports of the officers in the battle, it is found that the Confederate loss was 16,775 in dead and wounded; the Union loss being 16,170. General Gordon gives the figures about the same. However, authorities differ as to the casualties, some giving more, some less.

Left in charge of the field, the Confederate devoted itself to the alleviation of suffering as far as possible. For some days detachments of soldiers were kept busy assisting the hospital corps care for the wounded. Every available house in the vicinity as well as the surrounding country was pressed into service as a hospital. The most desperate cases were cared for in the houses in the immediate neighborhood, while others were carried to Crawfish Spring on the south and to Cloud Spring on the north of the battlefield. The less seriously wounded were taken by wagons and ambulances to Riggold and to Dalton where they were transferred to trains and transported to Atlanta and other cities along the route and thus distributed among hospitals where they received all possible attention. Many of these, of course, recovered and returned to their commands; many, however, died, and thus the ranks of the army were decimated.

It was days, yes, weeks before the dead were all buried. In certain localities where fighting was fiercest the dead were strewn so close together as to touch each other, and sometimes lying on each other; having expired when they fell. Many old people are wont to relate how they visited the battlefield afterward and viewed the corpses strewn over the ground, saying that it was possible to step from one body to another for long distances. One old citizen, an octogenarian, recalls how, at a certain place, the trees were marked with bullets some five or six feet high—many marks, he said, on all trees. The wonder is that any one escaped. This must have been on Snodgrass hill where the most desperate fighting occurred.

How fearful must have been the sight of that gory field! There were literally thousands of dead men and horses scattered over the terrain a few miles square. How frightful the scene after exposure for some days to the hot September sun! Only those hardened to such scenes could endure the sight. Within the short space of two days the Grim Reaper had done his frightful work. Many of these were mere lads—boys in their teens; torn from a fond mother's embrace to fall and to die as cattle of the field. Many had grown old in war but, at last, had met the warrior's fate. Some were from homes of wealth and refinement, of education and social standing; some—many—were from the cabin and the field, from poverty and ignorance; some, leaders in their communities, men to whom others look for opinions and leadership; some, hewers of wood and drawers of water, but—now—all have met upon a common level. No longer is there distinction.

And then, the battle over, the news begins to trickle back home to the fireside—to mother, sister, friend. Vague and indistinct at first, it is; then suddenly it comes with a rashness that prostrates—"Robert is dead." "Killed in battle." Such heartbreaking news to the family circle, to friends and to the community! Never a word from him,—no good byes, no farewells, no mementos, no keepsakes from his person. Only silence and the vacant chair to cherish. It is all so harsh and unnatural. When will our civilization arrive at the place where war will be outlawed? when they shall beat their swords into plowshares, and their spears into pruning hooks? When will His millennium be?

Chapter Fourteen

CHICKAMAUGA BATTLE, CONTINUED—OFFICIAL REPORTS, CONFEDERATE.

THE "Official Records of the Union and Confederate Armies; War of the Rebellion*," published by the War Department at Washington, devotes a large portion of some eight or ten volumes to an account of the Chickamauga Campaign, from which I have collected the major portion of the information concerning the Chickamauga battle. Almost the whole of these records is composed of subordinate officer's reports, or of orders from superior officers to their subordinates. There are literally thousands of such reports and orders.

---

*Mr. E. L. Culberson, soldier, patriot, gentleman, Christian, now in his Ninety-third Year, has a complete set of this History—the only set in the county. It consists altogether of 125 volumes, many of them containing more than 1000 pages. He has been very gracious in allowing me free access to this vast store of information while studying the great Chickamauga battle, and the battle of LaFayette, for which I return my thanks.

From among these, almost at random, I have selected a few, some from Confederate sources, and some from Union sources. These are given in the following chapter both because of the local history involved and as throwing light on the movements of the armies immediately preceding the great battle itself.

In addition to the reports herewith reproduced, a multitude of other reports are shown mentioning almost every locality in the county, as follows: Lee and Gordon's Mills, Rossville, Thedford's Ford, Reid's Bridge, Alexander Bridge, Taylor's Ridge, LaFayette, Dug Gap, Catlett Gap, Nickajack Gap, Snake Creek Gap, Gordon's Gap, Bluebird Gap, Daugherty Gap, Crow Gap, Stephens Gap, Cooper Gap, Rape Gap, Warthen Gap, Rock Spring Church, Peavine Church, Lookout Church, Cove Church, Trickum (Whitfield County), Buzzard's Roost, (Rocky Face), Villanow, Crawfish Spring, Lee's Tan Yard, Tavern Road, McLemore's Cove, Davis' Cross Roads, Bailey Cross Roads, Davis House, Glass' Mill, Morgan's, Anderson's, Dalton's Ford, Bird's Mill, Pond Spring, Owen's Ford, Andrew's Ford, Signal Point, Pigeon Mountain, Johnson's Crook, and a great many others, many named numerous times by different officers. All this shows how completely the county was covered by the two armies immediately preceding and following the Chickamauga battle.

REPORTS FROM CONFEDERATE OFFICERS.

Headquarters Department of Tennessee,
Chattanooga, Sept. 4, 1863.

General S. Cooper,
Adjutant-General, Richmond.

Sir: The advance of Burnside with a heavy force from Kentucky upon East Tennessee at the same time that Rosecrans moved upon Bridgeport induced General Buckner to draw his forces (except those at Cumberland Gap) to Loudon. At the same time it was utterly impossible for me to assist him here. Before the arrival of the re-inforcements from Mississippi (not all up yet) he was threatened in front, while a move was made to cut his connections in this direction. Unable to sustain him with a sufficient force, I ordered his command to fall back to the Hiwassee, where it is in supporting distance. These dispositions were not made without great regret and reluctance, but the force disposable rendered it impossible to hold a line extending so many hundred miles, assailable at any point, without the certainty almost of being cut up in detail. With our present dispositions we are able to meet the enemy at any point he may assail, either with a portion or with the whole of his forces, and should he present us an opportunity we shall not fail to strike him. My position is to some extent embarrassing in regard to offensive movements. In a country so utterly destitute we cannot for a moment abandon our line of communications, and unable to detach a sufficient force to guard it, we must necessarily maneuver between the enemy and our supplies. The approach of his right column (the heaviest, it will be observed) is directly on our left flank and seriously threatens our railroad. No effort will be spared to bring him to an engagement whenever the chances shall favor us.

I am, sir, very respectfully, your obedient servant,

       Braxton Bragg, General, Commanding.
  (Endorsement)

Read and returned.

The case demands great activity, with which it is hoped the enemy's purpose may be defeated by fighting his two columns separately. If the weakest can be beaten first the strongest will be attacked afterward, with the advantage which success and reinforcements will give. In the meantime, it seems feasible to operate effectively on Rosecran's line of communication by sending out cavalry expeditions.

               J. D (AVIS).

       Fifteen Miles South of Chattanooga,
          Sept. 9, 1863.

The order to General Jones is just what I desired, and renders the evacuation unnecessary at present. Burnside's force is not less than 20,000 but is mostly tending this way. Rosencrans' main force had obtained my left and rear. I followed and endeavored to bring him to action and secure my connections. This may compel the loss of Chattanooga, but is unavoidable.

              Braxton Bragg.

Hon. James A. Seddon,
  Secretary of War.

      Five miles South of Chattanooga, Sept. 10th,
         Via Dalton, Sept. 11, 1863
          (Received 11th)

The enemy entered Chattanooga yesterday in force, driving out the small garison I could leave behind. His main force in Will's Valley still threatens my rear, and compels me to follow on this side of the mountain. The difficulty of supplying the army in this mountainous region is very great, and may compel me to turn east to the railroad.

            Braxton Bragg, General.

General S. Cooper,
  Adjutant and Inspector-General.

          LaFayette, Sept. 16, 1863.
           (Received 16th.)

We have so far failed to encounter the enemy in any force. Whenever we make our appearance he retires before us. His policy seems to be to avoid an engagement. We shall press him as long as able to subsist.

General S. Cooper.   Braxton Bragg.

Ten Miles South of Chattanooga,
Sept. 21, 1863.

The enemy retreated on Chattanooga last night, leaving his dead and wounded in our hands. His loss is very large in men, artillery, small-arms and colors. Our loss is heavy but not yet ascertained. The victory is complete and our cavalry is pursuing. With the blessing of God our troops have accomplished great results against largely superior numbers. We have to mourn the loss of many gallant men and officers. Brigadier-Generals Preston Smith, Helm, and Deshler are killed; Major-General Hood and Brigadier-Generals Adams, Gregg and Brown, wounded.

Braxton Bragg.

(General S. Cooper)

Chickamauga River, Sept. 21, 1863.

After two days' hard fighting we have driven the enemy, after a desperate resistance, from several positions, and now hold the field; but he still confronts us. The losses are heavy on both sides; especially so in our officers. We have taken over 20 pieces of artillery and some 2,500 prisoners.

Braxton Bragg.

General S. Cooper.

Three Miles from Chattanooga,
Via Tunnel Hill, Sept. 23, 1863.

The enemy is confronting us behind strong defences. Our troops are arriving and deploying, but our policy can only be determined after developing him more fully. He is in very heavy force. A regimental color of Burnside's (Ninth) corps was captured on the field of Chickamauga. Half of McClaws' division not yet up.

Braxton Bragg.

General S. Cooper.

Chattanooga, Sept. 24, 1863.

The report from General Hood last night was favorable. Our prisoners will reach 7,000, of which 2,000 are wounded. We have 25 stand of colors and guidons, 36 pieces of artillery, and have already collected 15,000 small arms over and above those lost on the field by our killed and wounded. More are being found. Our movements are much retarded by limited field transportation and the breaks on the road.

Braxton Bragg.

General S. Cooper.

Headquarters Army of the Tennessee,
Three Miles from Chattanooga, Sept. 24, 1863.

Sir: The enemy having thrown the main body of his forces from his depot at Stevenson to the south of Chattanooga, in the direction of our communications, it became necessary for me to meet that movement or suffer an isolation from my supplies, and the probable destruction of our depots and workshops. Major-General Buckner with his forces, entirely too weak to cope with the heavy column approaching from Kentucky, and threatened by a corps in his rear, had been withdrawn from the line of railroad through East Tennessee and united with this army. Unable to divide without great danger to both parts, our opponents having the power to concentrate on either, I marched from Chattanooga on the 8th instant with my whole force, and took position opposite the enemy's center, extending from the crossing of the Chickamauga to LaFayette, Ga. This movement checked the enemy's advance, and, as I expected, he took possession of Chattanooga, and looking upon our movement as a retreat, commenced a concentration and pursuit. As soon as his movements were sufficiently developed I marched on the 17th instant from LaFayette to meet him, throwing my forces along the Chickamauga between him and my supplies at Ringgold.

On the afternoon of the 18th we effected a crossing of the Chickamauga at two points, about 7 miles nearly due east from Ringgold, after considerable resistance and some loss.

These forces moved at daylight up the Chickamauga, and were joined by others, which crossed in succession as their positions were unmasked. About 10 a. m. our right encountered the enemy, and the action soon became hot and extended gradually toward our left. It was most obstinate until dark, and only resulted in a partial success. Our forces were all concentrated that night, and a vigorous assault ordered at daylight on the 20th, to commence on the right and be taken up to the left. By delays, not yet satisfactorily explained, this movement was not made until near 11 o'clock, and after I had visited that part of the field and reiterated my orders to Lieutenant-General Polk. After being commenced it was promptly, vigorously and satisfactorily followed on the left by General Longstreet. We met with the most obstinate resistance, the enemy holding selected positions strengthened by baricades, slight breastworks of timber and abatis, all concealed from us in a dense forest. Though frequently repulsed at points, our troops invariably returned to the charge, and when night suspended the work the whole field was ours.

The next morning the enemy had entirely disappeared from our front, leaving his dead and wounded. A vigorous pursuit followed his rear guard into Chattanooga, where we found him strongly entrenched.

We lost some artillery the first day, but recovered all before the close of the action. Thirty six pieces taken from the enemy have so far been reported and secured. We have also collected about 15,000 stands of small arms over and above what we left on the field from our casualties and have some 25 stand of colors and guidons, and about 7,000 prisoners. These gratifying results were obtained at a heavy sacrifice on our part. Major-General Hood lost a leg on the 20th, when gallantly leading his command. Brigadier-General Preston Smith was killed on the 19th, and Brigadier-Generals B. H. Helm and James Deshler fell on the next day—all gallant soldiers and able commanders. Brigadier-Generals Gregg, McNair and Adams were severely wounded, the first two not dangerously; the latter is missing. The accounts of him are conflicting, but he probably fell into the hands of the enemy. Brigadier-General Brown was slightly wounded, but is again on duty. The loss of inferior officers and men, though known to be large, is not yet sufficiently ascertained to justify an estimate.

The conduct of the troops was admirable. Though often repulsed, they never failed to respond when called on, and finally carried all before them. For two weeks most of them had been without shelter, on short rations, in a country parched by drought, where drinking water was difficult to obtain, yet no murmur was heard, and all was glee and cheerfulness whenever the enemy was found. During the action, and for a day or two before, and up to this time, all were on short rations and without cooking utensils.

The enemy had concentrated against us four corps, being all of Rosecrans' army, and one infantry standard was captured from a regiment of Burnsides' old army corps—the Ninth. But three small infantry brigades of General Longstreet's command had joined us. Under all the circumstances we could not have anticipated more favorable results, and feel that the protection of a merciful Providence has been extended to us at a time when the safety of our cause was involved.

I am, sir, very respectfully, your obedient servant,
Braxton Bragg, General, Commanding.
General S. Cooper,
 Adjt. and Insp. Gen. C. S. Army, Richmond, Va.

Chapter Fifteen

CHICKAMAUGA BATTLE, CONTINUED—OFFICIAL REPORTS, UNION.
REPORTS FROM UNION OFFICERS.

Hdqrs. 14th Army Corps,
Stevens' Gap, Sept. 14, 1863—6:30 a.m.
Maj.-Gen. McCook,
 Near Alpine:
General: Your dispatch of 5 p.m. yesterday was received at 6 a.m. to-

day.

The route by Winston's Gap, I should think, is the only practicable one for you, but you will have to leave your train to follow you up the mountain at the head of Johnson's Crook, as it will take one day for them to get to the top. Colonel Harrison has not yet reported to me. I do not think he will be in any great danger, as the enemy appears to be afraid to remain in the upper part of the cove. They have all the gaps leading through Pigeon Ridge, but have not come into the cove except to attack Negley Friday.

The want of cavalry prevented us from seizing Dug Gap and Catlett's Gap on Wednesday. Once in our possession, I think we could have held them. General Rosecrans is here.

>Very respectfully,
>Geo. H. Thomas,
>Maj.-Gen. U. S. Vol., Commanding.

Near Bailey's Cross Roads, Sept. 14—8 p.m.

Colonel: I have the honor to report the following information:

The wife of Mr. Roberts passed over the mountain to the point where the rebel signal station is located. She saw a considerable force of the enemy in the neighborhood of Dug Gap. Could make no estimate of the number. Saw several small trains passing to and from LaFayette. Made a second trip later in the day and observed quite a cloud of dust between Catlett's Gap and LaFayette, as though a long train of troops were moving along that road. * * *

My scout, Starr, reports having seen a negro girl near Lee's Mill, who came last night from LaFayette. She says she "seen heaps of rebels between the gap and LaFayette;" that there was a very large army there. * * *

>Yours,
>Jas. S. Negley, Maj-Gen.

At Signal Station on Top of Mountain.

Sept. 14, 4.20 a.m.

Brig.-Gen. J. A. Garfield: Two of my divisions are now marching with all haste to join General Thomas. * * * I intended to march by Dougherty's Gap into McLemore's Cove, with a portion of my infantry, to clear Pigeon Mountain of the enemy to Blue Bird Gap, if not to Dug Gap, but instructions * * * led me to believe that McLemore's cove is in possession of the enemy. * * * I will join Thomas myself this evening. Myself and troops have done and will do every thing that mortal men can do.

>Yours,
>A. McD. McCook.

SKIRMISH AT LaFAYETTE—DEC. 12, 1863.
Hdqrs. 3rd Brig. 1st Div. Cavalry.

Rossville, Ga., Dec. 14, 1863.

General: I have the honor to report that on Saturday morning, Dec. 12th, at 8 a.m., with a force of 200 men from the Fourth and Sixth Kentucky Cavalry, I left this post on a scout in the direction of Dalton. At 4 p.m., 12th inst., I charged into the town of LaFayette, capturing 18 prisoners, 6 of whom were officers of the rebel signal corps, and some 30 animals. Two hours before we arrived at LaFayette the Second Kentucky (rebel) Cavalry had left the town, greatly to the regret of myself and all my command.

After camping for the night on Pigeon Ridge, 5 miles from LaFayette, we crossed the Chickamauga at a bridge 3 miles above Crawfish Spring, and scouting through McLemore's Cove without discovering any enemy we returned to camp.

We found on the route forage only sufficient for the use of the command while out.

I am, sir, etc.,

Louis D. Watkins, Col. Commanding Brigade.

SCOUT FROM ROSSVILLE TO LAFAYETTE, DEC. 21-23, 1863.
Hdqrs. 3rd Brig. 1st Div. Cavalry.

Rossville, Ga., Dec. 23, 1863.

General: I have the honor to report that a scouting party of 150 men, from the 4th and 6th Kentucky Cavalry, left this post under command of Major Welling, of the 4th Kentucky Cavalry, with orders to scout through McLemore's Cove, cross at Blue Bird Gap, and enter LaFayette from the west and then return to camp on the morning of the 21st instant.

These instructions were obeyed and the command returned at 9 this morning, bringing with them 1 commissioned and 4 non-commissioned officers and 12 privates, prisoners of war, 10 citizens, said to be violent rebels, and 38 horses and mules.

The command report forage in abundance on the other side of Bluebird Gap.

Lieutenant Edwards, of the 8th Georgia Battalion, while attempting to escape, was shot by Major Welling, inflicting a severe flesh wound in the thigh.

One of the prisoners, Corp. J. J. Cutler, was captured in a Federal uniform, and, although he claims to be a courier, doubtless is a rebel scout. I transmit for your inspection, papers, found upon his person.

I have the honor to be, general, very respectfully, your obedient servant,

Louis D. Watkins, Col. Commanding Brigade.

P. S. The scout, Lawton, has the papers above referred to.

Hdqrs. 4th Ky. Vet. In. (Mounted).
Sugar Valley (Ga.), June 30, 1864.

Capt. S. B. Moe,
Assist. Adj.-Gen., Chattanooga, Tenn.

Captain: I have the honor to submit the following report of the operations of my command since leaving Chattanooga:

On the 23rd, we left Chattanooga with orders, from the major-general commanding, to proceed to Resaca, via Ship's and Snake Creek Gaps, patrolling the country en route. Being advised that a force of several hundred rebels were annoying the railroad and supposed to have their headquarters at Villanow, I was instructed to get in rear of them, in order to relieve our line of communication to the front from the serious annoyance they were inflicting. On the night of the 23rd, we encamped at Rock Spring Church, intending to move directly to Ship's Gap on the following morning at which time Colonel Watkins had, as I learned, determined to move to Rome. Between 5 and 6 o'clock on the morning of the 24th a half dozen men belonging to Colonel Watkin's camp galloped into my camp, reporting that their camp had been surrounded and surprised at daybreak, and, as they supposed had been captured. These men belonged to the force on picket north of the place, and the enemy had succeeded in getting between them and the town. I immediately mounted my command, and, leaving one company to load and guard the train, galloped at full speed toward LaFayette. On the way I met a citizen scout of Colonel Watkins', and several soldiers, all of whom confirmed the impression that the whole command had been captured. When within a mile of the town I met Captain McNeely, of the seventh Kentucky Cavalry, who had charge of a small squad, who had either been on picket or succeeded in escaping from the town. He also supposed the place had been surrendered. I immediately sent Captain Hudnall with his company to the right of the road, to look out for the enemy in that direction, and galloped on in toward the town. Captain McNeely agreed to dash ahead with his squad and determine the position of the enemy. When in the outskirts of the town he came upon a line, dismounted, who poured a volley into his little band, wounding several men and horses and forcing him to retire. We were a few hundred yards in the rear and I immediately turned from the road to the right. As soon as two companies had cleared the road sufficiently, I halted, dismounted, and deployed them and ordered them to move forward and engage the enemy, while five companies were moved rapidly to the right (aiming as I did to strike the Dug Gap road, having learned the enemy came by that road), and attack him on his flank. Lieutenant-Colonel Kelley, with the two remaining companies, was directed to remain on the road and look out for matters there, as I deemed it important to hold that road, as it led to my train. In the mean time Captain Hudnall, hearing the firing of the enemy on Captain McNeely, immediately moved down a valley half a mile from the road he had left in the direction of the town. His approach was concealed from the enemy by the timber. As he emerged from this he saw in his front, not 200 yards distant, the rebel line of battle. Immediately dismounting and forming, he moved forward to the open ground and opened on the enemy. About the same time the two companies of the right (Captains Jacob and Harrington) came up on Hudnall's left. The surprise was so complete and the firing so vigorous that the enemy immediately broke and fled in confusion before the town, leaving their dead and wounded. Fourteen prisoners were captured by Captain Harrington, including a Lieutenant-Colonel and a Captain of the ninth Alabama. Captain Hudnall captured several prisoners, including the adjutant of the Twelfth Tennessee, also captured an ambulance belonging to Colonel Watkins' command, and the colors of his brigade, which the rebels had taken from his headquarters in the town. Just as I reached the Dug Gap road, in sight of the town, I received word from Colonel Kelly that our forces were in possession. I at once ordered the companies of Captains Jacob and Harrington to remount and join me, intending to push on for the next road leading south. At the same time I threw a force out on the Blue Bird Gap road, who learned that about 200 of the enemy had passed there nearly 2 hours previous, having in charge about 40 prisoners, whom I supposed were captured early that morning.

* * * * * *

Colonel Watkins lost, he informed me, so many horses killed and captured that half of his command were dismounted, and that the whole was well nigh out of ammunition. In view of these facts and of the uncertainty of the nature of Pillow's mission, whether independent or the advance of a large force, together with the pressing necessity of having the railroad communications to the front open and protected, which was my special mission, induced me to abandon a pursuit which could have accomplished little at best, and which might prove hazardous. I therefore withdrew to the east of LaFayette, and halted on the Resaca road, until we could learn something more definite as to the situation. During the afternoon Colonel Watkins determined to move on the following morning back to Gordon's Mills for ammunition and supplies, and requested that I should cover his rear as far as Rock Spring Church, which I promised to do. Just as he moved out of town, however, he received your dispatch, notifying him that the Third Kentucky had been ordered here. He determined to remain. The Third arrived before noon, and that evening we moved through Ship's Gap. Colonel Watkins and his command deserve great credit for the gallantry of their defense against such overwhelming numbers, and in the face of such a complete surprise. As far as I was able to learn, all the out posts were captured or driven off by the enemy getting between them and the town, and the first notice the command had was the presence of the enemy in the streets. On the 25th, I moved by way of Villanow and Snake Creek Gap, to Sugar Valley, in order to get near the railroad to obtain supplies. On the 26th, we returned to Villanow and scoured the valley during that day and the succeeding, but found nothing save a few scouting squads which we chased to the hills. On the 27th, we again returned to Sugar Valley for supplies, where I now await your order. I find no influential rebels in the country. They have left. I have found on the contrary, a number of very reliable loyal men who can be trusted to give us information of matters in that quarter. To day I have sent a company toward Subligna and another toward Floyd's Spring. My scout from the latter place yesterday reports a small force of rebels this side. Your dispatch of the 28th seemed based on the understanding that I was at LaFayette, and had some command in addition of my own regiment. I think, likely, some order sent me has not been received. I expected something the night of the 27th, at Villanow, but nothing came. Newtown (which in the original dispatch was Estontown) is east of Resaca; and one regiment, in my opinion, is not sufficient to guard the line from there to the head of McLemore's Cove. The Fifth Kentucky Cavalry is at Resaca. Capron's brigade left for front. The Third Kentucky is, I presume, still at LaFayette, with Colonel Watkins.

I remain, etc.,

John T. Croxton, Col. 4th Ky. Inf. Mounted.

Hdqrs. Dist. of the Etowah,
Chattanooga, June 24, 1864.

Capt. L. M. Dayton, Aide-de-Camp:

I have just received the following from Colonel Watkins, at LaFayette, Ga.:

> The rebels under Brig. Gen. G. J. Pillow, with 2 brigades, attacked this place at 2 o'clock this morning, and were handsomely repulsed. We have 70 prisoners and over 100 dead bodies, and many wounded. My loss is severe. The 4th Kentucky Mounted Infantry has just arrived and will pursue them. I fear Colonel Faulkner, of the 7th Kentucky Cavalry is captured. Prisoners continually being brought in. Pillow had 3000 men in his command.

I have ordered a cautious pursuit and an additional force to within supporting distance of LaFayette.

James B. Steedman, Maj.-Gen. Commanding.

Hdqrs. Mil. Div. of the Mississippi.
Near Kennesaw Mountain, June 24, 1864.

General Steedman, Chattanooga:

Good for Watkins. If he has force enough let him follow Pillow as far as he pleases. He always had Resaca and Rome to fall back on.

W. T. Sherman, Maj.-Gen. Commanding.

Hdqrs. Dist. of the Etowah.
Chattanooga, June 25, 1864.

Col. L. D. Watkins, Commanding at LaFayette, Ga.:

Colonel: The general directs me to say that the Third and Fourth

Kentucky (mounted men) having fresh horses, he has ordered these two regiments to follow in the track of Pillow, as far as prudent, inflicting such punishment as he can, and then your force in the mean time will remain at LaFayette, scouting in the direction of Trenton, Summerville, and Villanow. The general is inclined to the belief that the rebel forces will not move in the direction of your forces even when joined by Forest, but that they will endeavor to cut the road between here and Bridgeport; but of this you can best inform yourself from reports that Colonel Croxton will send you when he moves.

General Sherman telegraphs: "Good for Watkins."

I am, Colonel, etc.,

S. B. Moe, Capt. and Asst. Adj.-General.

Talladega, Alabama, June 26, 1864—9 p.m.

Assistant Adj.-Gen.,
Meridian, Miss.

Sir: After my letter of this date was closed and mailed I received the news contained in the enclosed duplicate of telegram just prepared. It is thought by several men of General Pillow's command who represent themselves to have been engaged in the attack, and of course is to be received with the allowance always due to the statements of fugitives from a battle. These men state that the attack was made about daybreak on Friday morning, the men having dismounted and left their horses about a mile in the rear; that the streets were barricaded with corn sacks; that the enemy were in the court-house, jail, and other buildings from which they fired upon our troops with comparative safety; that after three unsuccessful efforts to dislodge them, General Pillow was attacked by a large force of cavalry, just then arriving, and his troops thrown into utter confusion, and that the order was given that each man should "take care of himself." They report a heavy loss of officers, among them Colonel Armistead mortally wounded, Majors Lewis and Redwood killed, and Lieutenant-Colonel Hatch wounded.

As LaFayette is at least 125 miles from this place these men must have left the field early and retired with great precipitancy. It is, therefore, to be hoped that further accounts will be more favorable. Two of the fugitives are slightly wounded.

Very respectfully, your obedient servant,

W. T. Walthall, Maj. Commanding Post.

(Inclosure)

Talladega, Ala., June 26, 1864—9 p.m.

Maj.Gen. S. D. Lee, Meridian, Miss.: Fugitives arrived this evening report Gen. Pillow defeated with heavy loss in an attack at LaFayette, Ga., at daybreak on 24th inst.

W. T. Walthall, Maj. Commanding Post.

Talladega, Alabama, June 27, 1864.—8-30 p.m.
Maj.-Gen. S. D. Lee,
Commanding, etc., Meridian, Miss.:
Official news of General Pillow's repulse received: supposed loss about 100 men; Majors Lewis and Redwood killed. General Pillow will be at Blue Mountain to day; he brings off some prisoners estimated about 80.
W. T. Walthall, Maj. Commanding Post.

Meridian, Miss., June 27, 1864.
(Via Mobile. Received Marietta, Ga., 28th).
General J. E. Johnson:
General Pillow has returned to Blue Mountain. He fought the enemy at LaFayette, capturing 100 prisoners and considerable property. He could not dislodge the enemy from the court-house before re-inforcements arrived, when he deemed it prudent withdraw. He was much impeded by high water.
S. D. Lee, Major-General.

Hdqrs. Dept. Cumberland.
Chattanooga, Jan. 15, 1864.
General: I have the honor to report the operations of my command from Dec. 1st to 31, 1863, as follows:
Col. L. D. Watkins, commanding Third Brigade, First Division, from his position at Rossville, has made several successful raids into the enemy's lines. * * * Again on the 14th, with detachments of the Fourth and Sixth Kentucky Cavalry, numbering about 250 men, he made a reconnaisance toward LaFayette, surprised that town, capturing a colonel of the Georgia Home Guards, 6 officers of the rebel signal corps, and about 38 horses and mules; our loss, none. On the 23rd he sent out a scout of 150 men from Fourth and Sixth Kentucky Regiments, under command of Major Welling, of the Fourth Kentucky, which proceeded as far as LaFayette, capturing at that place 1 commissioned officer, 16 non-commissioned and privates, 10 citizens (said to be violent rebels), and 38 horses and mules.
Geo. H. Thomas,
Maj.-Gen. U. S. Vol. Commanding.

Chapter Sixteen

CHICKAMAUGA BATTLE, CONTINUED—HILL'S REPORT.

Report of Lieut. Gen. Daniel H. Hill, C. S. Army, commanding corps.

(COLONEL) I have the honor to report the part taken by my command in the operations around Chattanooga, terminating in the battle of Chickamauga, on September 19 and 20, 1863:

I reached Chattanooga on July 19, and was assigned to Hardee's old corps, consisting of Cleburne's and Stewart's divisions. These were encamped on the Chickamauga about Tyner's station. The Yankees soon made their appearance at Bridgeport, and I made arrangements to guard the crossings of the Tennessee. A regiment was posted at Silvey's Ford, another at Blythe's Ferry, and Wood's brigade at Harrison.

On fast day (August), while religious services were being held in Chattanooga, the Yankees appeared on the opposite side of the river, and commenced shelling the town without giving notice. Our pickets and scouts, if any were out, had given no warning of the Yankee approach. Some women and children were killed and wounded by this not unusual act of atrocity of our savage foe.

A few nights before, Clayton's brigade had been moved up to Birchwood, 3 miles from the mouth of the Hiawassee, and General Clayton was instructed to send an officer up the river until he met our cavalry pickets and endeavor to effect a connection with them. General Clayton reported to me that he found no pickets for 40 miles, the great mass of our cavalry being at Kingston. This report was communicated to the commander-in-chief, and the cavalry pickets were moved down, so as to connect with Clayton.

The shelling of Chattanooga revealed the fact that the Yankees were in our immediate front, and I ordered Cleburne's division to Harrison, and had it distributed so that every ford and ferry from the mouth of the Chickamauga to the mouth of the Hiawassee was guarded and covered by rifle-pits and batteries. It had been the design of the Yankees to interpose a column between Knoxville and Chattanooga and thus isolate Buckner, while Burnside should appear on his flank. But the Yankees, after trying all the crossings and finding them guarded by vigilant and determined men, were constrained to abandon their original plan.

Breckenridge's division, having come up from Mississippi, was assigned to my corps, and Stewart's division was soon after sent up toward Knoxville to join Buckner. Stovall's brigade, of Breckenridge's division, was posted at Sivley's Ford, and as the Yankees still threatened a crossing, Hindman's division of Polk's corps, was sent to our support.

On Sunday, August 31, we learned almost accidentally through a citizen that the Yankee corps of Thomas and McCook had crossed at Caperton's Ferry, beginning the movement the Thursday before. This was the natural point of crossing for the Yankees, as it was near their depot at Stevenson and gave a good road on our flank and rear. Buckner's command was brought down from Knoxville and the commander-in-chief resolved to abandon Chattanooga. The reason given by him for the evacuation was that the Yankees were getting in his rear, and that they might sieze the crossings of the Oostenaula and starve his army, as he had no movable pontoon train.

The movement began on the night of September 7, my corps taking the lead on the LaFayette road. The mass of the Yankee army was supposed to be at Trenton, in Will's Valley; but as our cavalry soon lost the almost impregnable position of Lookout Mountain, with but few casualties on either side, the Yankees began to pour down into McLemore's Cove. I was accordingly ordered by the commanding general to picket the gaps on Pigeon Mountain. This duty was entrusted to General Cleburne' while Breckenridge was left at LaFayette in charge of the trains of the army.

About daylight on the morning of September 10, I received the following order from the general commanding:

      Headquarters Army of Tennessee,
        Gordon Mills, Sept. 9, 1863—11:45 p.m.
General Hill:

I enclose orders given to General Hindman. General Bragg directs that you send or take, as your judgement dictates, Cleburne's division to re-unite with Hindman at Davis' Cross-Roads to-morrow morning. Hindman starts at 12 o'clock tonight, and has 13 miles to make. The commander of the columns thus united will move upon the enemy at the foot of Stephen's Gap, said to be 4,000 or 5,000. If Unforseen circumstances should prevent your movement, notify Hindman. A cavalry force should accompany your column. Hindman has none. Open communication with Hindman by your cavalry in advance of the junction. He marches on the road from Dr. Anderson's to Davis' Criss-Roads.

        W. W. Mascall, Chief of Staff.

I immediately replied to this note, notifying the commanding general of the late hour at which it had been received, and stating that General Cleburne had been sick in bad all day; that two of his regiments which had been picketing above Harrison had not yet joined him; that one of his brigades had to be relieved from picketing at the gaps, and that these gaps had been heavily obstructed by our cavalry and some hours would be required to open them up. Inasmuch, too, as Cleburne would have nearly, if not quite, as long a march as Hindman, I believed that the intended junction would be impossible, and certainly no surprise could be effected. These reasons appeared satisfactory to the commanding general, as he made no complaint in regard to my not making the movement, and met me next day with his usual cordiality. General Buckner, at Gordon's Mills, was directed to make the movement instead of General Cleburne, and the language of the order to Buckner recognized the impractibility of the order issued to me—"General Hill has found it impossible to carry out the part assigned to Cleburne's division." In fact, General Hindman had made his night march and reached the neighborhood of the Yankees almost by the time I received the order to move to effect a junction. As there could be no direct communication with him, the following note reached me from him in the afternoon:

Hdqrs. etc. at Morgan's on Cove Road,
Four Miles from Davis' Cross-Roads, Sept. 10, 1863, 6 a.m.

General: I expected you would open communication with me by the time I reached this place, but as yet hear nothing from you. If it be true, as I learn it is, that the road from LaFayette to Davis' Cross-Roads is blocked at Dug Gap and the Catlett's Gap also blockaded, I fear it will be impossible to effect the intended junction. Your better information will enable you to decide as to that. There are rumors here that a Federal division is at and near Davis' Cross Roads and another at Bailey's Cross Roads. Colonel Russell commanding a cavalry regiment of Martin's brigade, has gone forward to ascertain the facts. I deem it inexpedient to move beyond this place till I learn that you are in motion and that we can safely unite.

Very respectfully, your obedient servant,

T. C. Hindman, Major-General.

On the morning of the 11th, Cleburne's division, followed by Walker's, marched to Dug Gap. It was understood that Hindman and Buckner would attack at daylight and these other divisions were to co-operate with them. The attack, however, did not begin at the hour designated, and so imperfect was the communication with Hindman that it was noon before he could be heard from. I was then directed to move with the divisions of Cleburne and Walker and make a front attack upon the Yankees. The sharpshooters of Wood's brigade, under the gallant Major Hawkins, advanced in handsome style, driving the yankee pickets and skirmishers and Cleburne's whole force was advancing on their line of battle, when I was halted by an order from General Bragg. The object was, as supposed, to wait until Hindman got in the Yankee's rear. About an hour before sundown, I was ordered once more to advance, but the Yankees now rapidly retired. Their rear was gallantly attacked by a company of our cavalry, but made a stand on the other side of Chickamauga Creek under a cover of a battery of artillery. Semple's magnificent battery was ordered up, and in a short time silenced the Yankee fire with heavy loss, and the Yankee rout was complete.

I had in the meantime communicated with General Buckner in person, and by an aide with General Hindman, and had arranged to connect my line of skirmishers and battle with theirs, so as to sweep everything before us. The prompt flight of the Yankees and the approaching darkness saved them from destruction. This force proved to be the advance of Thomas' corps, the main body being opposite Stephens' Gap, in Lookout Mountain.

This day and the following my signal corps and scouts on Pigeon Mountain reported the march of a heavy column up the cove to our left.

These reports were communicated to the commanding general, but were discredited by him.

On the morning of the 13th, all the troops except my two divisions were moved up to Lee and Gordon's Mills to attack Crittenden's corps, isolated at that point. The attack, however, was not made.

At 8 a.m. Lieut. Baylor, of the cavalry, reported to me with a note from General Whorton vouching for his entire reliability. Lieut. Baylor stated that McCook, with his corps, had encamped at Alpine the night before, and that his column was moving on to LaFayette. Our cavalry pickets had been driven in on the Alpine road, the evening before, a few miles from town, and I had directed General Breckenridge to supply their place with infantry pickets. Soon after the report of Lieut. Baylor, a brisk fire opened on the Alpine road about 2 miles from LaFayette. Upon reaching the point I found that 2 regiments of cavalry had attacked the skirmishers of Adam's brigade, and had been repulsed with considerable loss. General Adams was satisfied from the manner of the advance that this force was the vanguard of a heavy column. I therefore brought down a brigade (Polk's) from Cleburne, on Pigeon Mountain, and prepared for battle. The Yankee cavalry had, however, captured the infantry pickets, and upon McCook learning that the men belonged to Breckenridge's division, he became aware that Bragg had been reinforced, and began a precipitate retreat. The report of Lieut. Baylor and the advance upon LaFayette did not satisfy the commanding general that McCook had been in our vicinity. He emphatically denied, on the night of the 13th, that a single Yankee foot soldier had crossed Pigeon Mountain. He stated, however, in the council next morning, that McCook was in Alpine, Thomas in McLemore's Cove, and Crittenden at Lee and Gordon's Mill. The Yankee right was, therefore, separated from the left by some 60 miles, with a difficult mountain to cross, and the center was more than a day's march from each wing. Our own force was concentrated at LaFayette, and could have been thrown upon either corps without the remotest possibility of being molested by the other two. The attack, however, was delayed for 6 days.

The withdrawal of McCook from Alpine and the appearance of a heavy force in front of Catlett's Gap, on the 16th, induced me to reinforce Deshler's brigade at the gap, by the whole of Breckenridge's division.

I was directed, on the 17th, to move my corps at daylight the next morning in the rear of General Polk's corps toward Lee and Gordon's Mills. A demonstration was to be made at that point by General Polk, while the rest of the army should cross lower down on the Chickamauga.

Cleburne's division was drawn up in line of battle at Anderson's house on the 18th, and Breckenridge was sent to guard the pass at Glass' Mill. Just before sundown our cavalry pickets were driven away from Owens' Ford, some miles above the mill, and the Yankees crossed over a considerable force. I hastened there in person with Adams' brigade, but the Yankees did not advance beyond Childress'.

The next morning Adams' brigade was withdrawn to Glass' Mill, and I determined to make a diversion at that point. Helms' brigade was crossed over and opened with ten guns upon the Yankees. An examination of the ground subsequently showed that our fire was unusually accurate and fatal. The ground was still strewed with unburied men, and 11 horses lay near the position of the Yankee battery. Our loss was slight.

In the afternoon I received an order to report in person to the commanding general at Thedford's Ford, and to hurry forward Cleburne's division to the same point. Soon after Breckenridge was ordered to relieve Hindman at Lee and Gordon's Mills. I found upon reporting to the commanding general, that while our troops had been moving up the Chickamauga, the Yankees had been moving down, and thus outflanked us and had driven back our right wing. Cleburne was ordered to take position on the extreme right and begin an attack. We did not get into position until after sundown, but then advanced in magnificent style, driving the Yankees back some three-fourths of a mile.

We captured three pieces of artillery, a number of caissons, two stand of colors and upward of 300 prisoners. His (our) own loss was small, and fell chiefly upon Woods' brigade, which had to cross an open field and encounter log breastworks upon the opposite side of it.

Captain Semple and Lieut. Key ran their batteries, under cover of darkness, to within 60 yards of the Yankee line and opened with happy effect. The other batteries of the division were placed, by my direction, on the right flank, so as to enfilade the Yankee line. I have never seen troops behave more gallantly than did this noble division, and certainly I never saw so little straggling from the field.

The action closed between 9 and 10 o'clock at night. Further pursuit in the darkness was not thought advisable. After readjusting our line (considerably deranged by the fight), and conferring with General Cleburne, and each of the brigade commanders individually, I left at 11 o'clock to find General Bragg at Thedford's Ford, where the orders for the day stated where his headquarters would be. It was near five miles to the Ford, but as I had no orders for the next day, I deemed it necessary to find the commanding general. On my way I learned from some soldiers that General Breckenridge had come up from Lee and Gordon's Mills. I dispatched Lieutenant Ried, of my staff, to find and conduct his division at once to Cleburne's right.

About mid-night, Lieutenant-Colonel Anderson, adjutant-general, reported that my corps had been placed under command of Lieutenant-General Polk as wing commander, and that the general wished to see me that night at Alexander's Bridge 3 miles distant. I was much exhausted, having been in the saddle from dawn to midnight, and therefore resolved to rest till three o'clock. At that hour I went to Alexander's Bridge, but failing to find the courier that General Polk had placed there to conduct me to his tent, I rode forward to the line of battle, which I reached a little after daylight. General Breckenridge had not yet got into position, as General Polk had permitted him to rest the night before on account of the wearied condition of the men. Repeated and urgent orders had been issued from the corps headquarters in regard to keeping rations for three days constantly on hand, but owing to difficulties, and possibly to want of attention, some of the men had been without food the day before, and a division had its rations for the day unissued, but cooked and on hand. Orders were given for their prompt issue.

* * * * * * * * * * *

(Here follows a lengthy account of the second day's operations of the battle)

D. H. Hill, Lieutenant-General.

Chapter Seventeen

CHICKAMAUGA BATTLE, CONTINUED—BRAGG'S REPORT.

Warm Springs, Ga., Dec. 28, 1863.

Sir: Most of the subordinate reports of the operations of our troops at the battle of Chickamauga having been received are herewith forwarded, and for the better understanding of the movements preceding and following that important event the following narative is submitted:

On August 20th it was ascertained certainly that the Federal army from Tennessee, under General Rosecrans, had crossed the mountains to Stevenson and Bridgeport. His forces of effective infantry and artillery amounted to fully 70,000, divided into four corps. About the same time General Burnside advanced from Kentucky toward Knoxville, East Tennessee, with a force estimated by the general commanding that department at over 25,000.

In view of the great superiority of numbers brought against him General Buckner concluded to evacuate Knoxville, and with a force of about 5,000 infantry and artillery and his cavalry took position in the vicinity of Loudon. The two brigades of his command (Frazier's at Cumberland Gap, and Jackson's in Northeast Tennessee) were thus severed from us.

The enemy having obtained lodgement in East Tennessee by another route, the continued occupation of Cumberland Gap became very hazardous to the garrison and comparatively unimportant to us. Its evacuation was accordingly ordered, but on the appeal of its commander, stating his resources and ability for defense, favorably indorsed by Major-General Buckner, the orders were suspended on August 31. The main body of our army was encamped near Chattanooga, while the cavalry force, much reduced and enfeebled by long service on short rations, was recruiting in the vicinity of Rome, Ga.

Immediately after crossing the mountains to the Tennessee the enemy threw a corps by way of Sequtchie Valley, to strike the rear of General Buckner's command, while Burnside occupied him in front. One division already ordered to his assistance proving insufficient to meet the force concentrating on him, Buckner was directed to withdraw to the Hiawassee with his infantry, artillery and supplies, and hold his cavalry in front to check the enemy's advance. As soon as this change was made the corps threatening his rear was withdrawn, and the enemy commenced a movement in force against our left rear.

On the last of August, it became known that he had crossed his main force over the Tennessee River at and near Caperton's Ferry, the most accessible point from Stevenson. By a direct route he was as near our main depot of supplies as we were, and our whole line of communication was exposed, while his was partially secured by the mountains and the river. By the timely arrival of two small divisions from Mississippi our effective force exclusive of cavalry, was now a little over 35,000, with which it was determined to strike on the first favorable opportunity.

Closely watched by our cavalry, which had been brought forward, it was soon ascertained that the enemy's general movement was toward our left and rear in the direction of Dalton and Rome, keeping Lookout mountain between us. The nature of the country and the want of supplies in it, with the presence of Burnside's force on our right, rendered a movement on the enemy's rear with our inferior force extremely hazardous, if not impracticable. It was therefore determined to meet him in front whenever he should emerge from the mountain gorges. To do this and hold Chattanooga was impossible without such a division of our small force as to endanger both parties.

Accordingly our troops were put in motion on September 7 and 8, and took position from Lee and Gordon's Mills to LaFayette, on the road leading south from Chattanooga and fronting the east slope of Lookout Mountain. The forces on the Hiawassee and at Chickamauga Station took the route by Ringgold. A small cavalry force was left in observation at Chattanooga, and one brigade of infantry, strongly supported by cavalry, was left at Ringgold to hold the railroad and protect it from raids.

As soon as our movement was known to the enemy his corps nearest Chattanooga and which had been threatening Buckner's rear, was thrown into that place, and shortly thereafter commenced to move on our rear by the two roads to LaFayette and Ringgold. Two other corps were now in Will's Valley—one nearly opposite the head of McClemore's Cove (a valley formed by Lookout Mountain and a spur of the main range, called Pigeon Mountain) and the other at or near Colonel Winston's, opposite Alpine.

During the 9th it was ascertained that a column, estimated at from 4,000 to 8,000; had crossed Lookout Mountain into the Cove by way of Stevens' and Cooper's Gaps. Thrown off his guard by our rapid movement, apparently in retreat, when in reality we had concentrated opposite his center, and deceived by the information from deserters and others sent into his lines, the enemy pressed on his columns to intercept us and thus exposed himself in detail.

Major-General Hindman received verbal instructions on the 9th to prepare his division to move against this force, and was informed that another division from Lieutenant-General Hill's command, at LaFayette, would join him. That evening the following written orders were issued to Generals Hindman and Hill:

Lee and Gordon's Mills, Sept. 9, 1863—11:45 p.m.
Major-General Hindman, Commanding Division:

General: You will move with your division immediately to Davis' Cross Roads on the road from Lafayette to Stevens' Gap. At this point you will put yourself in communication with the column of General Hill, ordered to move to the same point, and take command of the joint forces, or report to the officer commanding Hill's column according to rank. If in command you will move upon the enemy, reported to be 4,000 or 5,000 strong, encamped at the foot of Lookout mountain at Stevens' Gap. Another column of the enemy is reported to be at Cooper's Gap; number unknown.

I am, General, etc.
Kinloch Falconer,
Asst. Adjt-General.

Lee and Gordon's Mills, Sept. 9th, 1863—11:45 p.m.
Lieutenant-General Hill:
Commanding Corps:

General: I enclose orders given to General Hindman. General Bragg directs that you send or take, as your judgment dictates, Cleburne's division to unite with General Hindman at Davis' Cross Roads to-morrow morning. Hindman starts at 12 o'clock to-night, and he has 13 miles to make. The commander of the column thus united will move upon the enemy encamped at the foot of Steven's Gap, said to be 4,000 or 5,000. If unforseen circumstances should prevent your movement, notify Hindman. A cavalry force should accompany your column. Hindman has none. Open communication with Hindman with your cavalry in advance of the junction. He marches on the road from Dr. Anderson's to Davis' Cross Roads.

I am, General, etc.
Kinloch Falconer,
Asst. Adj-Gen.

On receipt of his order during the night, General Hill replied that the movement required by him was impracticable, as General Cleburne was sick, and both the gaps (Dug and Cartlett) had been blocked by felling timber, which would require 24 hours for its removal.

Not to lose this favorable opportunity—Hindman, by a prompt movement, being already in position—the following orders were issued at 8 a.m. on the 10th, for Major-General Buckner to move with his two divisions and report to Hindman:

Lee and Gordon's Mills, Sept. 10, 1863—8 a.m.
Major-General Buckner,
Anderson's:

General: I enclose orders issued last night to Generals Hill and Hindman. General Hill has found it impossible to carry out the part assigned to Cleburne's division. The General Commanding desires that you will execute without delay the order issued to General Hill. You can move to Davis' Cross Roads by the direct route from your present position at Anderson's along which General Hindman has passed.

I am, General, etc.
George M. Brent,
Asst. Adj-General.

And both Hindman and Hill were notified. Hindman had halted his division at Morgans, some 3 or 4 miles from Davis' Cross Roads, in the Cove, and at this point Buckner joined him during the afternoon of the 10th.

Reports fully confirming previous information in regard to the position of the enemy's forces were received during the 10th, and it became certain he was moving his three columns to form a junction upon us at or near LaFayette.

The corps near Colonel Winston's moved on the mountain toward Alpine, point 20 miles south of us. The one opposite the cove continued its movement and threw forward its advance to Davis' Cross Roads, and Crittenden moved from Chattanooga on the roads to Ringgold and to Lee and Gordon's Mills. To strike these isolated commands in succession was our obvious policy. To secure more prompt and decided action in the movement ordered against the enemy's center, my headquarters were removed to LaFayette, where I arrived about 11:30 p.m. on the 10th, and Lieutenant-General Polk was ordered forward with his remaining divisions to Anderson's, so as to cover Hindman's rear during the operations in the cove.

At LaFayette, I met Major Nocquet, engineer officer on General Buckner's staff, sent by General Hindman, after a junction of their commands, to confer with me and suggest a change in the plan of operations. After hearing the report of this officer, and obtaining from the active and energetic cavalry commander in front of our position,

I verbally directed the major to return to General Hindman and say that my plans could not be changed, and that he would carry out his orders. At the same time the following written orders were sent to the general by courier:

Headquarters Army of Tennessee,
LaFayette, Ga. Sept 10, 1863—12 pm.

Major-General Hindman,
      Commanding, etc.:

General: Headquarters are here, and the following is the information: Crittenden's corps is advancing on us from Chattanooga. A large force from the south has advanced to within 7 miles of this point. Polk is left at Anderson's to cover your rear. General Bragg orders you to attack and force your way through the enemy to this point at the earliest hour that you can see him in the morning. Cleburne will attack in front the moment your guns are heard.

I am, General, etc.,
George Wm. Brent, Asst. Adj-Gen.

Orders were also given for Walker's Reserve Corps to move promptly and join Cleburne's division at Dug Gap to unite in the attack. At the same time Cleburne's was directed to remove all obstructions in the road in his front, which was promptly done, and by daylight he was ready to move. The obstructions in Catlett's Gap were ordered to be removed, to clear the road in Hindman's rear. Breckenridge's division (Hill's corps) was kept in position south of LaFayette, to check any movement the enemy might make from that direction.

At daylight I proceeded to join Cleburn at Dug Gap, and found him waiting the opening of Hindman's guns to move on the enemy's flank and rear. Most of the day was spent in this position, waiting in great anxiety for the attack by Hindman's column. Several couriers and two staff officers were dispatched at different times urging him to move with promptness and vigor.

About the middle of the afternoon the first gun was heard, when the advance of Cleburne's division discovered the enemy had taken advantage of our delay and retreated to the mountain passes. The enemy now discovered his error, and commenced to repair it by withdrawing his corps from the direction of Alpine to unite with the one near McLemore's Cove, while that was gradually extended toward Lee and Gordon's Mills.

Our movement having thus failed in its justly anticipated results, it was determined to turn upon the third corps of the enemy, approaching us from the direction of Chattanooga. The forces were accordingly withdrawn to LaFayette, and Polk's and Walker's corps were moved immediately in the direction of Lee and Gordon's Mills. The one corps of the enemy in this direction was known to be divided, one division being sent to Ringgold. Upon learning the disposition of the enemy from our cavalry commander in that direction, on the afternoon of the 12th, Lieutenant-General Polk, commanding the advance forces, was directed in the following note to attack at daylight on the 13th:

Headquarters Army of Tennessee,
LaFayette, Ga., Sept. 12, (1863)—6 p.m.

Lieutenant-General Polk:

General: I enclose a dispatch from General Pegram. This presents you a fine opportunity of striking Crittenden in detail, and I hope you will avail yourself of it at daylight to-morrow. This division crushed and the others are yours. We can then turn again on the force in the cove. Wheeler's cavalry will move on Wilder, so as to cover your right. I shall be delighted to hear of your success.

Very truly, yours,

Braxton Bragg.

Upon further information the order was renewed in two notes at later hours on the same day, as follows:

Headquarters Army of Tennessee,
LaFayette, Sept. 12, 1863—8 p.m.

Lieutenant-General Polk,
   Commanding Corps:

General: I enclose a dispatch, marked A, and I now give you the orders of the commanding general, viz, to attack at day dawn to-morrow. The infantry column reported in said dispatch at three-quarters of a mile beyond Peavine Church, on the road to Graysville from LaFayette.

I am, General, etc.

George Wm. Brent, Asst. Adjt-Gen.

Headquarters Army of Tennessee,
LaFayette, Ga. Sept. 12, 1863.

Lieutenant-General Polk,
   Commanding Corps:

General: The enemy is approaching from the south, and it is highly important that your attack in the morning should be quick and decided. Let no time be lost.

I am, General, etc.

George Wm. Brent, Asst. Adyt-Gen.

At 11 p.m. a dispatch was received from the general, stating that he had taken a strong position for defense, and requesting that he should be heavily re-inforced. He was promptly ordered not to defer his attack, his force being already numerically superior to the enemy, and was reminded that his success depended upon the promptness and rapidity of his movements. He was further ordered that Buckner's corps would be moved within supporting distance the next morning.

Early on the 13th, I proceeded to the front, ahead of Buckner's command, to find that no advance had been made on the enemy, and that his forces had formed a junction and recrossed the Chickamauga. Again disappointed, immediate measures were taken to place our trains and limited supplies in safe positions, when all our forces were concentrated along the Chickamauga, threatening the enemy in front. Major-General Wheeler, with two divisions of cavalry, occupied the positions on the extreme left, vacated by Hill's corps, and was directed to press the enemy in McLemore's Cove, to divert his attention to our real movement. Brigadier-General Forest, with his own and Pegram's division of cavalry, covered the movement on our front and right. Brig. Gen. B. R. Johnson, whose brigade had been at Ringgold, holding the railroad, was moved toward Reed's bridge, which brought him on the extreme right of the line. Walker's corps formed on his left opposite Alexander's Bridge, Buckner's next Thedford's Ford, Polk's opposite Lee and Gordon's Mills, and Hill's on the extreme left. With Johnson moved two brigades just arrived from Mississippi, and three of Longstreet's corps, all without artillery and transportation.

The following orders were issued on the night of the 17th, for the forces to cross the Chickamauga, commencing the movement at 6 a.m. on the 18th by the extreme right, at Reed's Bridge:

(CIRCULAR)   Headquarters Army of Tennessee.
In the Field, Leet's Tan-yard, Sept. 18, 1863.

1. Johnson's column (Hood's), on crossing at or near Reed's Bridge, will turn to the left by the most practicable route and sweep up the Chickamauga, toward Lee and Gordon's Mills.

2. Walker, crossing at Alexander's Bridge, will unite in this move and push vigorously on the enemy's flank and rear in the same direction.

3. Buckner, crossing at Thedford's Ford, will join in the movement to the left, and press the enemy up the stream from Polk's front at Lee and Gordon's Mills.

4. Polk will press his forces to the front of Lee and Gordon's Mills, and if met by too much resistance to cross will bear to the right and cross at Dalton's Ford, or Thedford's as may be necessary, and join in the attack wherever the enemy may be.

5. Hill will cover our flank from an advance of the enemy from the cove, and by pressing the cavalry in his front ascertain if the enemy is re-inforcing at Lee and Gordon's Mills, in which event he will attack them in flank.

6. Wheeler's cavalry will hold the gaps in Pigeon Mountain and cover our rear and left and bring up stragglers.

7. All teams, &c., not with troops should go toward Ringgold and Dalton, beyond Taylor's Ridge. All cooking should be done at the trains. Rations, when cooked, will be forwarded to the troops.

8. The above movements will be executed with the utmost promptness, vigor, and persistence.

By command of General Bragg.;
George Wm. Brent,
Assistant Adjutant-General.

The resistance offered by the enemy's cavalry and the difficulties arising from the bad and narrow country roads caused unexpected delays in the execution of these movements. Though the commander of the right column was several times urged to press forward, his crossing was not effected till late in the afternoon. At this time Major-General Hood, of Longstreet's corps, arrived and assumed command of the column, Brigadier-General Johnson resuming his improvised division of three brigades.

Alexander's Brigade was hotly contested and finally broken up by the enemy just as General Walker secured possession. He moved down stream, however, a short distance, and crossed, as directed at Byram's Ford, and thus secured a junction with Hood after night.

The movement was resumed at daylight on the 19th, and Buckner's corps with Cheatham's division, of Polks, had crossed and formed, when a brisk engagement commenced with our cavalry under Forest on the extreme right about 9 o'clock. A brigade from Walker was ordered to Forest's support, and soon after Walker was ordered to attack with his whole force. Our line was now formed, with Buckner's left resting on the Chickamauga about 1 mile below Lee and Gordon's Mills. On his right came Hood with his own and Johnson's divisions, with Walker on the extreme right, Cheatham's division being in reserve, the general direction being a little east of north. The attack ordered by our right was made by General Walker in his usual gallant style, and soon developed a largely superior force opposed. He drove them handsomely, however, and captured several batteries of artillery in the gallant charge. Before Cheatham's division, ordered to his support, could reach him, he had been pressed back to his first position by the extended lines of the enemy assailing him on both flanks. The two commands united were soon enabled to force the enemy back again and recover our advantage, though we were yet greatly outnumbered.

These movements on our right were in a direction to leave an opening in our line between Cheatham and Hood. Stewart's division, forming Buckner's second line, was thrown to the right to fill this, and it soon became hotly engaged, as did Hood's whole front.

The enemy, whose left was at Lee and Gordon's Mills when our movement commenced, had rapidly transferred forces from his extreme right, changing his entire line, and seemed disposed to dispute with all his ability our effort to gain the main road to Chattanooga, in his rear. Lieutenant-General Polk was ordered to move his remaining division across at the nearest ford, and to assume the command in person on our right. Hill's corps was also ordered to cross below Lee and Gordon's Mills and join the line on the right. While these movements were being made, our right and center were heavily and almost constantly engaged. Stewart, by a vigorous assault, broke the enemy's center and penetrated far into his lines, but was obliged to retire for want of sufficient force to meet the heavy enfilade fire which he encountered from the right. Hood, later engaged, advanced from the first fire, and continued to drive the force in his front until night. Cleburne's division, of Hill's corps, which first reached the right, was ordered to attack immediately in conjunction with the force already engaged. This veteran command, under its gallant chief, moved to its work after sunset, taking the enemy completely by surprise, driving him in great disorder for nearly a mile, and inflicting a very heavy loss.

Night found us masters of the ground, after a series of very obstinate contests with largely superior numbers. From captured prisoners and others we learned with certainty that we had encountered the enemy's whole force, which had been moving day and night since they first ascertained the direction of our march. Orders had been given for the rapid march to the field of all re-enforcements arriving by railroad, and three additional brigades from this source joined us next morning. The remaining forces on our extreme left, east of the Chickamauga, had been ordered up early in the afternoon, but reached the field too late to participate in the engagement of that day. They were ordered into line on their arrival, and disposed for a renewal of the action early the next morning. Information was received from Lieutenant-General Longstreet of his arrival at Ringgold and departure for the field. Five small brigades of his corps (about 5,000 effective infantry, no artillery) reached us in time to participate in the action, three of them on the 19th and two more on the 20th.

Upon the close of the engagement on the evening of the 18th, the proper commanders were summoned to my camp fire, and there received specific information and instructions touching the dispositions of the troops and for the operations for the next morning. The whole force was divided for the next morning into two commands and assigned to two senior Lieutenant-Generals, Longstreet and Polk—the former to the left, where all his own troops were stationed, the latter continuing his command of the right. Lieutenant-General Longstreet reached my headquarters about 11 p.m. and immediately received his instructions. After a few hours at my camp fire he moved at daylight to his line, just in front of my position.

Lieutenant-General Polk was ordered to assail the enemy on our extreme right at day dawn on the 20th, and to take up the attack in succession rapidly to the left. The left wing was to await the attack by the right, take it up promptly when made, and the whole line was to be pushed vigorously and persistently against the enemy throughout its extent.

Before the dawn of day myself and staff were ready for the saddle, occupying a position immediately in rear of and accessible to all parts of the line. With increasing anxiety and disappointment I waited until after sunrise without hearing a gun, and at length dispatched a staff officer to Lieutenant-General Polk to ascertain the cause of the delay and urge him to prompt and speedy movement. This officer, not finding the general with his troops, and learning where he had spent the night, proceeded across Alexander's Bridge to the east side of the Chickamauga and there delivered my message.

Proceeding in person to the right wing, I found the troops not even prepared for the movement. Messengers were immediately dispatched for Lieutenant-General Polk, and he shortly joined me. My orders were renewed, and the general was urged to their prompt execution, the more important as the ear was saluted throughout the night with the sound of the ax and falling timber as the enemy industriolsly labored to strengthen his position by hastily constructed barricades and breastworks. A reconnaisance made in the front of our extreme right during this delay crossed the main road to Chattanooga and proved the important fact that this greatly desired position was open to our possession.

The reasons assigned for this unfortunate delay by the wing commander appear in part in the reports of his subordinates. It is sufficient to say they are entirely unsatisfactory. It also appears from these reports that when the action was opened on the right about 10 o'clock a.m. the troops were moved to the assault in detail and by detachments, unsupported, until nearly all parts of the right wing were in turn repulsed with heavy loss.

Our troops were led with the greatest gallantry and exhibited great coolness, bravery and heroic devotion. In no instance did they fail when called on to rally and return the charge. But though invariably driving the enemy with slaughter at the points assailed, they were compelled in turn to yield to the greatly superior numbers constantly brought against them. The attack on the left, promptly made as ordered, met with less resistance, much of the enemy's strength having been transferred to our right, and was successfully and vigorously followed up.

About 2 p.m., passing along the line to our left, I found we had been checked in our progress by encountering a strong position strengthened by works and obstinately defended. Unable to afford assistance from any other part of the field, written orders were immediately dispatched to Lieutenant-General Polk to again assault the enemy in his front with his whole force and to persist until he should dislodge him from his position. Directing the operations on our left to be continued, I moved again to the right and soon dispatched a staff officer to General Polk, urging a prompt and vigorous execution of my written orders. About 4 p.m., this general assault was made and the attack was continued from right to left until the enemy gave way at different points, and finally, about dark, yielded us his line. The contest was severe, but the impetuous charge of our troops could not be resisted when they were brought to bear in full force, even where the enemy possessed all the advantages of position and breastworks. The troops were halted by their respective commanders when the darkness of the night and the density of the forset rendered further movements uncertain and dangerous, and the army bivouacked on the ground it had so gallantly won.

Both flanks having advanced more rapidly than the center, they were found confronting each other in lines nearly parallel and within artillery range. Any advance by them, especially at night, over ground so thickly wooded, might have resulted in the most serious consequences.

The enemy, though driven from his line, still confronted us, and desultory firing was heard until 8 p.m. Other noises, indicating movements and dispositions for the morrow, continued until a late hour at night.

During the operations by the main forces on the 19th and 20th, the cavalry on the flanks was actively and usefully employed, holding the enemy in observation and threatening or assailing him as occasion offered.

From the report of Major-General Wheeler, commanding on the left, it will be seen what important service was rendered both on the 20th and 21st by his command, especially in the capture of prisoners and property and in the dispersion of the enemy's cavalry.

Brigadier-General Forest's report will show equally gallant and valuable services by his command, on our right. Exhausted by two day's battle, with very limited supply of provisions, and almost destitute of water, sometime in daylight was absolutely essential for our troops to supply these necessaries and replenish their ammunition before renewing the contest.

Availing myself of this necessary delay to inspect and readjust my lines, I moved soon as daylight served on the 21st. On my arrival about sunrise near Lieutenant-General Polk's bivouac, I met the ever vigilent Brigadier-General Liddell, commanding a division in our front line, who was waiting the general to report that his picket this morning discovered the enemy had retreated during the night from his immediate front. Instructions were promptly given to push our whole line of skirmishers to the front, and I moved to the left and extended these orders. All the cavalry at hand, including by personal guard, were ordered to the front.

Members of my staff, in passing through the lines of our left wing with their escort, were warned of danger and told that they were entering on neutral ground between us and the enemy. But this proved to be an error, and our cavalry soon came upon the enemy's rear guard where the main road passes through Missionary Ridge. He had availed himself of the night to withdraw from our front, and his main body was already in position within his lines at Chattanooga.

Any immediate pursuit by our infantry and artillery would have been fruitless, as it was not deemed practicable with our weak and exhausted force to assail the enemy, now more than double our numbers, behind his entrenchments. Though we had defeated him and driven him from the field with heavy loss in men, arms, and artillery, it had been done by heavy sacrifices, in repeated, persistent, and most gallant assaults upon superior numbers strongly posted and protected.

The conduct of our troops was excellent throughout the prolonged contest. Often repulsed where success seemed impossible, they never failed to rally and return to the charge until the last combined and determined effort, in which the spirit of every man seemed to conspire for success, was crowned with the reward due to such gallantry in such a cause.

Our loss was in proportion to the prolonged and obstinate struggle. Two-fifths of our gallant troops had fallen, and the number of general and staff officers stricken down will best show how these troops were led.

Major-General Hood, the model soldier and inspiring leader, fell after contributing largely to our success, and has suffered the irreparable loss of a leg. That his valuable life should be spared to us, however, is a source for thankfulness and gratitude.

Major-General Hindman, highly distinguished for gallantry and good conduct, received a severe contusion, but persisted in keeping the saddle until he witnessed the success in which his command largely participated.

Brig.-Gens. B. H. Helm, Preston Smith, and James Deshler died upon the field in the heroic discharge of duty. They were true patriots and gallant soldiers, and worthy of the high reputation they enjoyed.

Brig. Gens. Adams, Gregg, and McNair fell severely wounded while gallantly leading their commands in the thickest of the fight. It is gratifying to know they are convalescing and will be again at the post of duty and danger.

Judging from appearance in the field, the enemy's losses must have exceeded our own largely, but we have no means of correctly estimating them. We captured over 8,000 prisoners, 51 pieces of artillery, 15,000 stand of small arms, and quantities of ammunition, with wagons, ambulances, and teams, medicines, hospital stores, &c., in large quantities.

* * * * * * * *

For the many deeds of daring and acts of heroic devotion exhibited on this field reference is made to the subordinate reports. It will be remarked that the private soldier is eminently distinguished, as he always will be in an army where the rank and file is made of the best citizens of the country.

* * * * * * *

I am, sir, very respectfully, your obedient servant,

Braxton Bragg,
General.

General S. Cooper,
 Adjutant-General, C. S. Army, Richmond, Va.

Chapter Eighteen

CHICKAMAUGA BATTLE, CONTINUED—JUDGE LUSK'S ARTICLE.

(NOTE—*The following graphic description of events as they successively followed each other during and immediately following the Chickamauga battle, dealing, as it does with the residents of the territory where this sanguinary conflict was enacted, is from the pen of Judge Charles W. Lusk of Chattanooga. When I wrote Judge Lusk asking permission to use this account in the county history, he was careful to grant permission on one condition: "Mr. Robert Sparks Walker," he said, "was indefatigable in assisting to collect the information for the article as well as for making the pictures, some of which are herewith reproduced, and deserves equal credit with myself." The article was published in the Chattanooga Times in September, 1923—just sixty years after the battle.*)

THOSE who visit the battlefield of Chickamauga, as well as those who read the history of that great conflict, frequently encounter such names as McDonald house, Kelly field, Snodgrass house, Dyer field, etc., and doubtless many feel a desire to know something of the people whose names are thus linked for all time with one of the most momentous events in our national history. It is with the hope of supplying in part this desire that this article is written.

It is remarkable that so little on this subject has found its way into print. The history of the battle, its strategy and its tactics, the unexampled ferocity of its fighting, the fearful losses, the personalities and characteristics of its leaders—these have become fairly familiar to the general reader. But there seems to have been very little written designed to preserve from oblivion the annals of the people whose homes and firesides were so tragically invaded, and whose names will forever designate and identify the salient points of the sanguinary contest.

THE POES. One of the most beautiful spots on the battlefield is that known as the Poe field. It lies along the east side of the Chattanooga and LaFayette road, midway between the Kelly house on the north and the Brotherton house on the south. Here occurred some of the most desperate fighting of the whole battle and survivors tell of the heroic charges of the Confederates from the east side of the field, and the equally heroic resistance by the Federals, posted in the edge of the wood on the west side. The majestic Georgia state monument stands near the south end of this field. The site of the Poe house, which was burned during the battle, is just west of the road from the Georgia monument, and is marked by an iron tablet.

On September 19, 1863, this spot was the home of Larkin H. Poe and his wife, Sarah (Brotherton) Poe, and their two little children, Hilliard Bell Poe, 2 years old, and Gussie Poe, aged 10 months. Mr. Poe, now more than 90 years of age, having been born June 17, 1833, is still living, hale and vigorous, at his home near Apison, Tenn. Many of the facts here related were recently received from his own lips.

Poe was not at home during the battle. He was a Confederate soldier, member of company K, 4th Georgia Cavalry. At the beginning of the battle he was with his command at Rome, Georgia. They were ordered forward, but being delayed did not reach the field till September 23, three days after the battle closed. His company bivouacked at Jay's mill on that night, and Poe, who at that time was acting as teamster, turned his wagon over to a trooper, who in turn loaned Poe his horse, and the latter set out to learn, if possible, the fate of his family. Poe's route was along the direct road from Jay's mill to the Brotherton house, and he thus passed over the scene of the fighting around Jay's mill at the opening of the battle, also of the desperate night fight around the Brock field.

"My recollections of that night's ride," said Mr. Poe, "are as fresh in my mind as if it had happened last night. The moon was far down the west and cast a ghostly light over the woods and fields. The stillness of the night was unbroken except for the sound of my horse's hoofs and the hoot of some solitary owl. I had seen an old house near Jay's mill filled with wounded and suffering men, and I had hardly started till I began to see dead soldiers, yet unburied, lying in and near the road. I rode on, turning my horse first to the right and then to the left to avoid the thick-strewn bodies. In places I saw where great trees had been splintered by shells and riddled by bullets. Most of the dead were on the knolls and higher ground; I saw few on the lower ground. Just before reaching the Brotherton house I came upon a scene of death and destruction noteworthy even on that terrible field. I saw a piece of artillery, evidently a Federal piece, which had been knocked from the wheels by a direct hit from our guns, and apparently most all of the horses and men belonging to the gun had perished there, for their bodies lay in grotesque heaps around their piece. The bodies I saw were apparently all Federals.

Their dead were yet unburied, and some of them lay on the field until after the battle of Missionary Ridge, ten weeks later.

George Brotherton, Poe's father-in-law, lived at the Brotherton house. When Poe reached it he found both house and yard filled with wounded men. He made inquiry of one of the nurses as to the Brothertons and his own family, but was told that nothing was known of them. Another spoke and said an old man was inside the house. Going in, Poe found his father-in-law, and together they went up the road to Poe's place where they found the house in ashes and his family gone. The piled up dead, the trampled and blood-stained ground, the torn and splintered timber, bore mute testimony to the terrible struggle that took place there. The Federals had taken shelter in and around the Poe house and the Confederates, to dislodge them, threw shells into it and thus started the fire which consumed it. One soldier who had fallen near the house was found by Poe with both legs burned off near the body.

Poe finally learned that his family were in the woods in a ravine northwest of the Snodgrass house. He went thither and at last found his wife and the little ones with about sixty others, consisting of old men, women and children, clustered about a burning log heap. They had been there since the first day of the battle and remained there eight days in all. Poe, however, after spending the rest of the night with his family, was obliged to go back to his command. He returned, however, the next day, and brought them a two-bushel bag of meal which he took from the supplies which he was hauling with the consent of his commanding officer. Stern duty would not permit him to linger and he marched away, leaving his loved ones under the open sky, with scanty clothing and no food except the meager supply he was able to bring them, and the pitiful gleanings they were able to pick up in the wake of the foragers of both armies.

The Poes never returned to the battlefield to live. After the war they made a home elsewhere. The wife and two children are long dead, and the old man's voice breaks and his eyes grow misty as he tells of the tragedy of sixty years ago.

THE SNODGRASSES. Snodgrass hill, the scene of the last desperate stand of the Federal army, under General Thomas, on Sunday afternoon, September 20, 1863, took its name from the Snodgrass family who owned the property and lived there at the time, and whose house, marked with an iron plate still stands. George Washington Snodgrass, a native of Virginia, was the head of the family. He was about 60 years of age at the time of the battle, and was, of course, too old for military duty. He was living with his third wife. He had two grown up sons, one of whom, Charles Snodgrass, was a Confederate soldier and was in the battle. The other son, John, was a cripple, and was at home. The other children at home were Mary, 16; Virginia, 12; Georgia Ann, 10; William R., 8; Julia Kittie, 6; and Martha Ellen, 4. The only one of these living now is Julia K., who married D. Green Reed in 1879, and now lives with her husband and family near Parker's Gap, in Hamilton County, Tennessee.

Mrs. Reed is an active, energetic and intelligent lady. She was only six years old at the time of the battle, but her recollections are most clear and vivid. When asked recently to tell something of the battle she graciously did so, and talked most interestingly of her experiences during the battle and afterwards.

The first Federal soldiers seen by her and her family were foragers, who first laid tribute upon their sweet potatoes and later on anything else they could find, including eatables and live stock. She remembers the roar of the battle on Friday when Wilder at Alexander's bridge, and Minty at Reed's bridge, were disputing the crossing of the Confederates. Her father refused at that time to leave the home, and the next morning they heard the increasing thunders of the conflict which began first at Jay's mill and then spread southward toward Lee and Gordon's mill, until from the whole five mile front arose the infernal din of battle. About three o'clock on Saturday afternoon, the 19th, bullets began falling around their house, and going through the roof, and their father gave the word to retreat. They went northwest from their house up a ravine, and camped in the woods. As the battle surged nearer, the missiles began again to whistle about them, compelling them to retreat further into the woods. Here they made camp, and as stated elsewhere, remained for eight days and nights. The families represented at this camp were the Poes, the Brothertons, the Snodgrasses, the Kellys, the McDonalds, the Brocks, and the Mullises, and probably others. As already stated they were utterly without shelter, and practically without food. Foragers had been active for days before the battle and their provisions had all been taken. In addition to the meal brought by Larkin H. Poe, they found a few field peas which they roasted and thus appeased the little ones who were crying from hunger and fright. They suffered much from lack of water. The weather had been dry for weeks, the marching armies had ground the roads into dust which hung over the valley like a pall, and many of the springs and wells were dry. The weather grew colder while they were at this camp and they had not sufficient coverings even for the little children, and on some mornings the children's heads would be white with frost. Their long stay at this camp after the battle is explained by the fact that all houses and buildings were filled to overflowing with the wounded and they thus were prevented from returning home.

Late on Sunday afternoon, as the firing gradually died down on Snodgrass hill, the party suddenly heard a band strike up some southern air. They divined that this meant victory for the Confederates, and as their sympathies were for that side, jubilation broke out among them. Som of the women sang and shouted aloud in the excess of their joy.

When the Snodgrasses left camp they went back to their home. The wounded had been removed and nothing remained but broken and bloodstained furniture and other fearful evidences of the agony of the wounded. It was clear that for the time they must seek other quarters. Their father took them to Elis springs, near Ringgold, where they camped for some time. Mrs. Reed carries indelible impressions of the fearful sights which assailed her childish eyes as she rode across the battlefield—splintered and broken timber, arms and accounterments scattered about, bloody and shell shattered breastworks, dead men and dead horses yet unburied, and all the reck and confusion in the wake of war.

The Snodgrass family did not return to their home till the close of the war. They suffered the destitution common to the people of the south. One small source of income was from the picking up of bullets and other relics on the battlefield and selling them in Chattanooga.

The thunder of the guns at Chickamauga made such an impression on Mrs. Reed that ever since she has dreaded the sound of firearms. Their present home is within sound of the rifle range near Ringgold. The echoes of the soldiers' guns, practicing there during the World war, brought to her such painful recollections of Chickamauga that she could hardly endure it.

THE BROTHERTONS. The Brotherton house was one of the pivotal points of the battle. The great charge of Longstreet's veterans which broke the Federal right was formed in the woods a short distance to the east and the gray-clad heroes of Lee's "old war horse" surged around this house as they rushed upon the Federal lines about 100 yards to the west.

At the time of the battle this house was the home of George Brotherton, his wife, Mary (Carter) Brotherton, and seven children. Another daughter, Sarah, had previously married Larkin H. Poe, as above related, and lived a short distance to the north. George Brotherton and his wife were Virginians. They came to this place in January, 1860, nearly four years before the battle. Their children were Thomas, James Lemuel, William, George W., Susan, Sarah, Janie B., and Adaline. Of these the only survivor is Adaline, who married William C. McDonald shortly after the close of the war, and is still living with her husband at their home a mile east of Spring Creek church, in Hamilton County, Tennessee. Mrs. McDonald was born Aug. 11, 1840, and is therefore in her 84th year. While somewhat disabled by rheumatism she retains all her faculties, and her memory of the events of the battle is clear and accurate. She recently related many facts which came under her personal observation during the battle.

George was too old for military service, but his two sons, Thomas and James L., were both in the Confederate army, and fought during the two days at Chickamauga in the vicinity of their home, and much of the time in sight of it. Gen. Longstreet, commanding the left wing of the Confederate army during the second day, finding that Thomas Brotherton was familiar with the roads and the surrounding country, made him his guide, and Thomas spent most of the day under the eye of the great commander. A few years after the war Gen. Longstreet visited the battlefield, and went to the Brotherton house seeking his old guide, who, however, was already dead.

The Brothertons heard the roar of battle on Friday when Wilder and Minty were fighting the Confederates at Reed's and Alexander's bridges. They were within the Federal lines, and according to Mrs. McDonald, the family delayed their departure for a safer place because of confident assurances given them by Federal officers that the Confederates would soon be driven off. They therefore remained at their home till late Saturday afternoon. During the day they were beaten upon by the thunders of the terrific fighting east of the Kelly field to the northeast, and of the equally sanguinary contest to the southward around the Viniard house. As Saturday drew to its close the steady approach of the noise of battle and the dropping of bullets admonished them that they must depart at once.

Their line of retreat took them by the Dyer house to the west. They turned north and reached the refugee camp already referred to. They remained here with the others, sharing the hardships and privations of those doleful eight days.

The Brothertons had four cows which somehow escaped the hunger of the foragers and the fury of the battle. Adaline Brotherton went once each day, after the battle, to their home and milked these cows, and turned the milk over to the nurses to be fed to the wounded soldiers who filled their yard and home. In this simple act may be seen the depth of the devotion of the women of the south for the cause for which their men were fighting. In the conflict in her heart between the desperate need of the helpless ones around that flickering campfire, and the still more desperate need of the stricken soldiers in gray, she made the choice which exemplifies the spirit which merited for the southern women the wonder and admiration of the world. When the wounded were finally removed the Brothertons went back home. They found nine dead Federal soldiers in their yard. Adaline and her father buried these in a single grave in the yard, and so far as she knows they have never been removed.

THE MCDONALDS. At the north end of the battlefield, a few yards south of the present terminus of the trolley line, will be seen a marker indicating the site of the McDonald house. This was the extreme northward point reached by Gen. Thomas' troops early on the morning of Sept. 19th and where they turned to the east and marched to the opening of the battle at Jay's mill. It also marks the starting point of the charge of Breckenridge's troops southward on Sunday afternoon against the left flank of the Federal army, and which came so near being disastrous to the Union line.

At the opening of the battle a two room log house stood on this site, in which lived John McDonald and his family. McDonald and his wife, Pricilla (Bell) McDonald, were natives of Jefferson County, Tennessee. They had lived at this place some seventeen years before the battle. The children living at the time were William C., Amanda L., and Charles. All are now dead except William C. He married Adaline Brotherton as above related, and is still hale and vigorous at the age of 83. He talked most interestingly of his family and himself and their connection with the battle.

On Sept. 19, John McDonald was picked up by Gen. Wilder, who, finding that he was well acquainted with the country, sent him to the headquarters of Gen. Rosecrans, and the latter required him to serve as guide throughout the battle. He took McDonald to Chattanooga with him after the fight, and he was not allowed to return home until after the battle of Missionary ridge, ten weeks later.

McDonald was with Gen. Rosecrans when the Union right was broken at Chickamauga on Sunday morning, and he later told of the efforts of the general to rally the broken troops, and finally despairing of inducing them to stop and turn against the enemy, he turned to those with him, including McDonald, and said, "If you care to live any longer, get away from here."

The McDonald house survived the battle, but was burned some weeks later, the origin of the fire being unknown, but supposed to have been set by campers temporarily occupying it. John McDonald suffered much from exposure while in the hands of the Federals. He soon became seriously ill and died in 1864.

William Calvin McDonald, the only surviving member of the McDonald family, was a Confederate solder. He enlisted at the beginning of the war in the Twenty-sixth Tennessee infantry. He was captured at Fort Donalson, was later exchanged, and was then transferred to the First Georgia infantry. During the Chickamauga battle he was a teamster and was not actually engaged in the fight, but was close at hand. Immediately after the battle he was engaged in hauling the wounded to Dalton, Ringgold and other points, to be sent thence to hospitals further south. A week after the close of the contest he was still engaged in the care of the wounded. Those not already sent away had been collected around the houses and other places and fed and cared for as well as possible. These were then removed, those from the south end of the field to Crawfish Springs, and those from the north end to Cloud Springs. The dead, still unburied, were so thick in places, especially in the Dyer field, that it was difficult to avoid driving over them.

The reader has probably noted already the singular fact that John McDonald and Thomas Brotherton, neighbors, living within two miles of each other, both acted as guides during the battle, one for the commander-in-chief of the Federals, and the other for a wing commander of the Confederates, and that later the son of the one married the sister of the other.

THE KELLYS. The Kelly house and field are famous spots on the battlefield. The first days' fighting on the left was some distance east of the field. During that night, Gen. Thomas, in command here, fell back to a line just inside the edge of the woods on the east side of the field, and during the night substantial breastworks of logs, rails, etc., were thrown up. During the second day this line was the scene of some of the most terrific fighting of modern times. The Confederates charged the line repeatedly but were unable to dislodge the Federals until the general retreat began in the afternoon. Gen. Breckenridge made his famous charge from the north into the northwest corner of the field, and into the rear of the Union troops, and their whole line was saved from probable rout only by the accidental presence of Van Derveer's brigade, which came suddenly out of the woods at the critical moment and pushed the Confederates back.

This house and field were owned at the time by Elijah Kelly, but were occupied at the time by his brother Elisha Kelly, who had them rented from his brother. Elisha Kelly had five or six children, among them being William, Newton, Jr., and George W. The latter was old enough for military duty and was a Confederate soldier in the same company and regiment with William C. McDonald.

So far as learned, all the war-time Kelly family are now dead, with the possible exception of William Kelly, living on Sand Mountain. The Kellys were among the refugees at the camp near Snodgrass hill, so often referred to.

THE BROCKS. About three-quarters of a mile east of the Brotherton house, on the road to Jay's mill, is the Brock field. This was the scene of fierce fighting on the first day, and it was just west of it that Longstreet formed his troops for his decisive charge against the Federal right wing on the second day. This field took its name from John Brock, who cultivated it, but who, it seems, at the time of the battle, lived in a house a short distance west of the McDonald house, on the road to McFarland's gap. Brock was about 65 years old. His two sons, William and John, were in the Confederate army and both fought at Chickamauga. John was wounded, a bullet splitting his scalp all along the top of his head. He seems to have been well supplied with the unquenchable optimism which upheld the Confederate soldier through so many trials. A comrade, referring to the wound, remarked: "If it had been an inch lower, it surely would have got you;" to which John cheerfully replied, "Yes, and if it had gone an inch higher it surely would have missed me." The smaller Brock children were at the Snodgrass refugee camp. The family moved to Alabama shortly after the war.

THE MULLISES. A short distance west of the McDonalds lived the family of William Mullis. Mullis was a Confederate soldier who was captured by the Federals and held in the north for some time and then exchanged. On his way home he was killed in a railway accident. He left a wife and six children. Nothing is known of their future history.

THE DYERS. The Dyer house and field, lying west of Brotherton's and Poe's, and south of Snodgrass hill, were of grim importance during the closing scenes of the great battle. It was across this field that the shattered right wing of the Union army retreated, closely followed by the legions of Longstreet. The Dyer house was the home of Robert Dyer,

EXPLANATION

Top View—Mrs. Julia Snodgrass Reed at the old Snodgrass House, her girlhood home at the time of the battle, which she distinctly remembers. Her daughter, Mrs. Rhea, stands by her side.

Left bottom—Larkin H. Poe, on the site of his old home on the battlefield. Poe's home was burned during the battle. The Georgia Monument stands on the Poe Field.

Right bottom—William McDonald, standing on the site of his old home on the battlefield. Mr. McDonald spent more than a week hauling off the Confederate dead and wounded after the battle. His father was forced to serve as guide for General Rosecrans during the Chickamauga battle.

Photos by Robert Sparks Walker, Chattanooga, Tenn.

his wife, Carrie Dyer, and their children, Spill, John, Jefferson, James, and Alva Dyer. James Dyer, a bachelor brother of Robert Dyer, was also a member of the family. Spill and John Dyer were in the Confederate army and fought at Chickamauga.

Robert Dyer was also picked up by Gen. Rosecrans and used as a guide. It seems to have been the general's intention to take Dyer to Chattanooga as he did John McDonald, but Dyer was much averse of this, and managed to escape after accompanying the general about a mile from the field.

THE VINIARDS. About half a mile south of the Brotherton house, on the main road through the park, stands the Viniard house. It was here that some of the hardest fighting of the first day took place. Little is known of the Viniard family, they having come to the house only a short time before the battle. However, another Viniard family lived at the same time in Chattanooga, and the heads of the two families are said to have been brothers. The one living in Chattanooga was a Confederate soldier, was captured and taken north, and his family never received any definite tidings as to his fate until some five or six years ago, when Miss Zella Armstrong published in a local paper a list of the Confederate dead in some northern cemetery, where during the war was a military prison. The name of Mr. Viniard was in this list, and his surviving daughter, Mrs. Margaret Fitzgerald, thus learned for the first time that her father had died shortly after being taken north. Mrs. Fitzgerald died about a month ago.

THE WINFREYS. On the road from the Kentucky monument to Alexander's bridge the visitor will pass a marker indicating the site of the Winfrey house. Much of the fighting of the first day was near this house and the terrific night battle of the 19th was in its immediate vicinity. This place was the home of George Winfrey and his wife, and a family of five children, Chap, Sampson, Adaline, May and Minnie. These children were also at the Snodgrass refugee camp, to which reference has been made.

THE VITTETOES. Near the railroad, just north of the town of Lytle, is the site of the Vittetoe house. It was within gunshot of the top of Snodgrass hill, and in plain sight of the Confederates forming for their repeated charges on that position during the closing scenes on the last day of the battle. This house was the home of Hiram Vittetoe, of French descent, who lived here with his wife and four children, Wash, Samantha, Laura and Evada. Some of the descendants of this family still live in the vicinity of the battlefield.

THE CLOUDS. A marker near the north end of the Fort Oglethorpe inclosure indicates the location of the Cloud house and Cloud spring. It was here that Gen. Gordon Granger met some opposition from the Confederates as he marched to the relief of Thomas on Snodgrass hill, and it was also here that the large hospitals were located, where the wounded of both armies were cared for.

Col. A. C. Cloud came here from Savannah, Georgia, some years before the war. He first took up lodgings with William Fulcher, the owner of the property. Later, Cloud bought the property from Fulcher and owned it at the time of the battle. Apparently he was a man of some means and owned several slaves. He was between 50 and 60 years of age. His neighbors seem to have known little about him and nothing further has been learned of his movements during and after the war.

THE GLENNS. When Maj.-Gen. William S. Rosecrans, commander-in-chief of the Federal army, reached the battlefield from Crawfish Springs on Saturday morning, September 19, 1863, he established headquarters at the house of Mrs. Eliza Glenn. This house stood on a commanding hill near the Crawfish Spring road, about half a mile west of the Viniard house. Headquarters were maintained here for about twenty-four hours —that is, from 10 a.m., on the 19th, till about the same hour on the 20th. Gen. John T. Wilder's famous brigade of mounted infantry, one of the few organizations at that time armed with repeating rifles, did some of its fiercest fighting at this place, and the Wilder monument stands on the same hill. In the official records of the battle will be found many orders, dispatches and letters dated at "Widow Glenn's" and signed by Gen. Rosecrans, Gen. J. A. Garfield, chief of staff, and by other officers connected with headquarters. Charles A. Dana, at that time assistant secretary of war, and later famous as editor of the New York Sun, was at this house, and some of his most interesting and important messages to the war department were written under its roof.

At the beginning of the war this place was the home of John Glenn, his wife, Eliza (Camp) Glenn, and their one child, Avery C. Glenn, about two years old. John Glenn promptly entered the Confederate army in the spring or early summer of 1861, and his family never saw him again. He died in a Confederate hospital at Mobile, Alabama, some time before the battle of Chickamauga, and Mrs. Glenn was, therefore, appropriately referred to as the "Widow Glenn." The second child of Mr. and Mrs. Glenn, Ella Nora Glenn, was born Dec. 4, 1861, after her father had enlisted, and he never saw his little daughter.

When Gen. Rosecrans and his staff reached the house he promptly told her that she was in great danger and urged her to depart at once. The battle was already roaring around Jay's mill to the northeast, and firing was beginning directly east around the Viniard house.

When John Glenn went to the army Mrs. Glenn's father, Mr. Camp, who lived near Pond Spring, some six miles to the south, sent her one of his slaves, John Camp, to protect the family and take care of the farm. This humble black man had been true to his trust and in her hour of need Mrs. Glenn turned to him. He put Mrs. Glenn and the two little children, and such articles as they could hurriedly snatch up, into a wagon and went toward the northwest, where they spent the rest of the day and night with the Vittetoes. The next day the tide of battle swept round this house also, and they were again compelled to retreat, this time by a circuitous route, to the home of Mrs. Glenn's father, near Pond Spring.

After the close of the fighting on the first day of the battle, Gen. Rosecrans summoned his commanders to headquarters at the Widow Glenn's house for a council of war. It was a memorable meeting. In that council with Gen. Rosecrans, were his chief of staff, Brig.-Gen. James A. Garfield, afterwards president of the United States; Maj.-Gen. George H. Thomas, commander of the 14th army corps, upon whom this battle was to bestow undying fame as the "Rock of Chickamauga;" Maj.-Gen. Alexander McD. McCook, commander of the 20th army corps, and one of the famous "fighting McCooks;" Maj.-Gen. Thomas L. Crittenden, commander of the twenty-first army corps, and one of the noted Crittenden family of Kentucky; Brig.-Gen. Philip H. Sheridan, later commander-in-chief of the army of the United States; Assistant Secretary of War Dana, and several others whose names have been written high on the nation's scroll of fame.

The council ended late in the evening and the assembled officers returned to their troops to prepare for the bloody work all saw must come with the light of another day. Gen. Rosecrans and his staff remained at the Glenn house. They were destined to be the last it would ever shelter; before another nightfall a hostile shell had set it in flames and reduced it to ashes.

After the close of the war Mrs. Glenn remarried, her second husband being W. B. Compton of Chickamauga, Georgia. She died twenty-five years ago.

Avery C. Glenn, her eldest child, grew to manhood and for many years was an honored citizen of Chattanooga. He was a merchant, carrying on a retail clothing business in partnership with James M. Shaw, under the firm name of Glenn and Shaw. He died some ten years ago. The daughter, Ella Nora Glenn, grew to womanhood and married Dr. D. G. Elder of Chickamauga, Georgia. She died Aug. 28, 1895.

The shades of sixty years have fallen between the present and those tragic days of 1863. The great commanders are all dead and all but a few aged and broken heroes of the rank and file have answered the last call. Gone are the charging legions, the fierce war cries, the thunder crash of battle. The little children who shivered about that desolate campfire, cold, hungry and frightened, have grown to maturity and thence into old age; they have scattered to distant parts, and with a lingering exception here and there, have passed altogether from the earth. The simple record of these humble kindly people shows that they acquitted themselves with honor in the work that fell to their hands. By the fortunes of war they stood in the path of the tempest and received its hardest blows; but by a divine compensation their names have been woven in indelible colors into the fabric of history, and so long as men shall journey here to take inspiration from the courage and devotion of those who made this ground immortal, those names will mark the high spots of gallant and deathless endeavor.

Chapter Nineteen

THE BATTLE OF LAFAYETTE, JUNE 24, 1864.

AFTER the defeat of Federal arms at Chickamauga and the flight of that army to Chattanooga where it took up its encampment, General Bragg, after some few days followed and began a siege, hoping to starve the enemy and thus force a surrender. He established his forces on all sides of the city and was making strenuous efforts to cut off all supplies. For two months there was feverish activity on the part of both armies, the one endeavoring to cut off the other's supplies and thus starve him, compelling a surrender; the other exerting every effort to extricate himself from a desperate strait. Bragg had established detachments on all of the mountains and slopes overlooking the city; and being over-confident of his position and strength had sent General Longstreet with 20,000 troops to attack Knoxville.

During the two months' siege by the Confederates the Federal army had suffered greatly for food and supplies. "Starvation faced the Federal troops in Chattanooga and even the civilians suffered dire privations. Authentic reports have been made that tell of rats and other animals being used for food. Sickness followed. The supply of pure fresh water ran low and rations grew so scarce that soldiers stole corn from the shock. At last all efforts to feed the stock were abandoned and 10,000 of them starved to death.*"

This was the situation when on October 23, 1863, General Grant arrived in Chattanooga to assume supreme command of Federal forces, relieving General Rosecrans. Grant was a man of action—of determination. Within a very few days he raised the morale of his troops to such excellence that they were ready to follow him to any extreme. On November 24, General Hooker made his famous attack on Lookout Mountain, which has been picturesquely described as the
"BATTLE ABOVE THE CLOUDS."

"The day was rainy and dense fogs floated low about the mountains. Hooker's troops, commanded by Geary, attacked from the west, coming around the point beneath the palisades, and pitched their efforts against the Confederate forces posted along the shoulder of the mountain at Craven's house. * * In the early morning of November 25, the Union soldiers climbed the bluff and planted the 'Stars and Stripes' on Lookout as a signal of victory to the armies of Chattanooga.*"

---
*From Walker's History of Chattanooga.

Then followed the battle of Missionary Ridge in which the Confederate forces were severely routed. General Bragg then began his slow retreat southward, obstructing at every possible point the progress of the Union army along the general line of the Western and Atlantic railroad toward Atlanta. The retreating Confederates followed by the Federals thus passed again through the northern and eastern parts of the county, and for many days those parts of the county were permeated with soldiers of the two armies—first the Gray and then the Blue. During this passage there were many sharp skirmishes between these antagonistic forces. Large parts of the two armies thus traversed again the fateful battlefield of Chickamauga. Moving southward and eastward these forces passed successively through the Peavine section, Rock Spring, LaFayette, Chestnut Flat, and the two Armuchees.

The Confederate army was forced southward to Atlanta, where during the following year, it again suffered defeat. Because of these reverses the Western and Atlantic railroad, which had previously been the solicitous care of General Bragg, was now in the hands of the Federal army and was being protected by them, since it had become their line of communication and the agency by which they could supply the army at Atlanta. It now became the plan of the Confederate army to interrupt and, if possible, to cripple that road. The undertaking to carry out this plan was responsible for

THE BATTLE OF LAFAYETTE.

As noted elsewhere, the Federal army in Chattanooga was besieged by General Bragg during the fall of 1863 and until after the battle of Missionary Ridge. So severe had been the siege that a large number of horses died for want of food, and many others were well-nigh starved. Some of the Federal officers speak of them as "skin and bone." Many of these starved animals, however, managed to exist during the winter months and when spring came the authorities undertook to recuperate them and put them in shape for service. They were badly needed. Hence, they were sent from the city to different localities for grazing and grooming. One such drove was ordered to LaFayette in June 1864, the main object being to recuperate the starved horses, but another important duty imposed on the command was to scout the country in search of the numerous bands of guerrillas who were infesting the section and giving much trouble.

Colonel Louis D. Watkins, of the sixth Kentucky Cavalry, commanding the Third Brigade was ordered to LaFayette about June 19, his duty being that mentioned above. He had about 450 men and a large number of horses. Reaching LaFayette, he took up his quarters in the town, using tents and vacant houses for his troops, and utilizing the public buildings, including the court-house, jail, hotel and school building for commissary supplies.

About the same date, June 19, Brigadier-General Gideon J. Pillow,

C. S. Army, was ordered to proceed from near Oxford, Alabama, with two small brigades of cavalry to interrupt, if possible, the Federal line of communication between Atlanta and their base of supplies—Chattanooga. He had under his command about 1,600 men, and was making his way into North Georgia, intending to strike the Western and Atlantic Railroad near Ringgold or Tunnel Hill and endeavor to wreck it —one plan was to wreck the tunnel by an explosion inside. Having marched all day on June 23, he expected to bivouac in the vicinity of Alpine, Georgia. On reaching that point he was informed that a force of Federal soldiers was encamped at LaFayette. He at once determined to continue his march during the night and strike that place before day the next morning. His troops had already halted and were unsaddling their mounts when they received orders to continue the march. Although much worn from a hard day's travel they at once proceeded on the long night-march.

With his little army he reached the forks of the road near Chattooga church about one o'clock at night. Here the army was divided, one brigade under Colonel Charles G. Armistead, of the 12th Mississippi Cavalry, commanding the brigade, took the left hand road and proceeded along the less-frequented, but somewhat longer route near the base of Pigeon mountain to near the Burnt Mill section, then he turned eastward along the Blue Bird gap road so as to approach the town from the west. The other brigade under the immediate command of General Pillow himself took the right hand road at the church and followed the Broomtown road passing what is now the County Almshouse. Although Colonel Armistead's route was possibly two miles longer than the other, he reached the town some twenty or thirty minutes in advance of General Pillow's brigade.

Colonel Armistead halted his brigade about a mile west of the town and sent forward a squad of soldiers under command of Lieutenant McLemore to capture, if possible, and at any rate to clear the road to the town of Federal pickets. This was about 3:30 a.m. Dismounting a part of his command and forming them in order they proceeded at the double-quick toward the town. It was now about 4 a.m., and the first streaks of daylight could be seen in the east. Colonel Armistead says that when he reached the branch about a quarter of a mile from the town, he took a left-hand street (this was Culberson Avenue), and proceeded toward the Chattanooga road (North Main), in order to cut off the Yankees who might wish to escape toward Chattanooga. Proceeding along this left-hand street a short distance, he observed some Federal soldiers on his left leaving a building and preparing to offer resistance. He charged this body of soldiers killing and capturing some. It was here that major Redwood was killed. The building mentioned might have been the Female Academy which was standing at that time near where the present high school building stands, and which was torn down by the Federal soldiers soon after the battle.

Then moving forward toward the Chattanooga road, he engaged a force of the enemy formed in that road and a little to the right of where he intersected it. This was probably near the present site of the Baptist church, possibly a little north of that place. A sharp skirmish ensued which sent them toward the court-house. It was at that point and time that Colonel Armistead says he was captured by the enemy and held for a few minutes. Having mistaken them, he says, in the early morning, because of the smoke and fog, for friends, he approached too close to them to escape with safety. However, within a very few minutes, he was able to effect his escape, dashing away in safety to himself and horse.

Rejoining his command and assuming charge, and having now reached the Chattanooga road, he gave orders to extend his left division across and beyond that road, reaching to and beyond Duke street and even beyond the hollow east of Duke street and south of the cemetery. This left wing, therefore extended from the Chattanooga road eastward for about 200 yards. His right wing and center were also deployed and faced southward toward the court-house. While re-arranging his line as herein noted, Captain William V. Harrell tells in his report of attacking the brick school house (John B. Gordon Hall) and driving out the Yankee soldiers and taking possession. (Note—Miss Orpha Center, now (1931), in her ninetieth year, who lives now as she did then, in the next house, but one, from the old brick school house, relates how she, then a young lady, unable to restrain her curiosity, notwithstanding the danger involved, stood on the back porch of her home and observed the Confederate charge on the old brick school house and saw the Yankee soldiers leave along Duke street toward the center of town, the while bullets were zip, zip, zipping against her home). The Yankees in the meantime had retreated toward the center of the town, being pressed by the Confederates.

The sun was now up. All these charges and movements had happened since four o'clock—about one hour. During this time, Colonel James J. Neely, who was commanding, under General Pillow, the brigade that came by the way of the Broomtown road had arrived and approaching the town from the south, or south-west, had placed his troops on the south and west of the public square. In his report he says that his line of advance was about two blocks west of, and nearly parallel to, the west side of the square. Some of his troops were stationed southeast from the square. It is seen, therefore, that the square was practically surrounded by the Confederate forces. Colonel Armistead had made at least one, maybe two, charges on the court-house before Colonel Neely got into position.

Colonel Armistead's line having been formed as noted above, he gave the order to charge the Yankees, who then retreated to the square and entered the Court-house, jail, and Globe hotel which stood then where the Bank of LaFayette now stands. The Confederates then made at least two, maybe three successive charges on these buildings, but found the doors barred and barricaded with sacks of grain; the windows also filled with sacks of grain leaving, here and there, loop-holes through which the Federal soldiers were able to shoot the attackers. Here the Confederates suffered from a galling fire and many men and officers were killed within a few feet of the court-house, some falling within five feet of that building. After Colonel Neely's brigade had come up and assumed position as noted above, other efforts were made to force the doors of the court-house. At this juncture the Confederates were formed in a circle around the court-house, at no time greater than fifty yards from that building. This circle probably extended from near the present postoffice building around by the Presbyterian church, thence eastward in a circle to near the present location of the new Foster House, with Colonel Neely's line going south from the postoffice circling the square around in the direction of the Fortune brick residence, and possibly east of that point.

In his official report, Colonel Watkins says he received the following message from General Pillow, sent under a flag truce:

Headquarters, Cavalry Division.
LaFayette, Ga., June 24, 1864.

To the Commanding Officer of the U. S. Forces, LaFayette, Ga.:

Sir: To prevent any unnecessary shedding of blood I demand of you an immediate surrender of this post and your forces. I have the force to take the place and am determined to do it. If necessary I will resort to the torch as well as to shot and shell to drive you from your present position. An immediate answer is required.   Respectfully,

Gid. J. Pillow,
Brig-Gen. Commanding.

Replying, he says he respectfully declined to comply with the demands. After which fighting was resumed with great fury.

During one of these several charges, Colonel Armistead was seriously wounded and was carried from the field, the command devolving upon Colonel Charles P. Ball. Colonel Ball, in his report, tells of making a charge upon the court-house and jail in which two gallant officers were lost—Captain England and Lieutenant Johnson, the former wounded, the latter killed within twenty steps of the court-house. Lieutenant-Colonel Hatch was also wounded while gallantly leading his regiment. Colonel Ball tells of reaching the court-house at another time and after examining the doors and windows, and noting the way in which they were barricaded, saw the futility of trying to force the doors and after reconnoitering the situation ordered his men to follow him and escaped by the rear end of the house and rejoined his command.*

---

*In reading the account of this hardly contested and desperate engagement as given by those taking part in it, while the conditions are not at all parallel, one is forcibly reminded of the celebrated battle of the Alamo, in which every man of the Texan army was slaughtered by the brutal Mexicans.

Colonel Philip B. Spence in his report tells of making four desperate charges on the court-house and jail and of losing quite a number of his men in killed and wounded. In the last charge, he says, Lieutenant Bradshaw fell mortally wounded.

The report of Captain William V. Harrell, while brief, is quite interesting. It is somewhat poetic and has some literary merit. He says, "When the command, 'Forward March,' was given, we started for LaFayette at a double quick. On entering it loud and repeated volleys of musketry greeted our ears and told us in forcible language that the ball had already opened. Pushing on rapidly in the direction of the sound, we soon found a portion of our men engaged with the enemy, who had taken refuge in a large frame building (probably Female Academy) situated in the northern part of the town. We charged with a yell, captured the building and took some prisoners. We next attacked a spacious brick edifice, formerly appropriated to school purposes, but lately converted by the enemy into a receptacle for commissary stores. Having in a very short time demonstrated our right to the possession of this house, we secured the Yankee occupants and sent them to the rear. * * When nearly opposite the east end of the jail the noble, gallant and chivalrous Lewis fell, mortally wounded while leading his men to the charge, addressing them in language of endearment and encouragement stimulating them by word and example to the performance of deeds worthy of the world-wide reputation of the sons of the South for bravery and heroism. As the spirit of the lamented Lewis was about to bid adieu to its earthly tenement, his feeble voice was heard saying, 'Charge them, boys! Charge them!' and right nobly did his gallant boys respond." Major Lewis was killed, it is believed, near where the jail now stands.

When Colonel Armistead first made his appearance north of the town and had reached the Chattanooga road, he thereby cut off the Federal pickets stationed still further north of where he intersected that road. These pickets, supposing the whole Federal force to have been surrounded and captured, fled northward in an endeavor to escape. Arriving at Rock Spring about five o'clock, they reported to Colonel John T. Croxton, who with a force of ten companies of cavalry on his way to Resaca, had encamped at that place the night before. Colonel Croxton at once mounted nine of his companies, leaving the tenth to guard and convoy his train, and started at the gallop toward LaFayette. Arriving at that place about eight or thereabout, he at once began to engage the Confederates who, at that time, many of them, had withdrawn from the center of the town and were stationed further north, probably near the brick school house. This unexpected reinforcement on the part of the Yankees and the sharp charges produced some confusion among the troops of General Pillow. Accordingly they began to withdraw rapidly from the center of the town, seeing which, the besieged in the court-house and other buildings forsook those retreats and began to follow the retreating Confederates and to offer serious battle. Being thus attacked from both sides, the Confederates now discovered that they were likely to be cut to pieces. Most of the horses had been left in the neighborhood of the Female Academy, many, however, had been left about a mile west of the town. In order to regain their mounts quickly, many of the troops began to run toward them. However, after some delay and a good deal of excitement and some anxiety, all were again mounted and the forces of General Pillow began a hasty retreat. Just such occurrences as this sometimes plays havoc with an army. It requires a cool head and decided orders to hold soldiers in place at such times. General Pillow and his officers deserve credit for the way in which they were able to control the situation and save the little army from a complete route.

The official reports give the Confederate casualties as follows: Killed, Officers, 4; Privates, 20. Captured, Officers, 11; Privates, 42. Total, 77. Colonel Watkins reports four killed including one officer, Captain Cook, and six wounded; also 2 officers and 51 men captured.

General Pillow says in his report that his force numbered about 1,600 effective men, which means, probably that he had that number engaged in the fight. Others may have been left as a detail to care for the horses. Colonel Watkins says he had 450 men. Colonel Croxton had ten companies, one of which he left at Rock Springs to care for the train, so that he had nine companies in the fight. If each company was composed of 100 men he had then 900 men under his command. This would give the Federal forces at about 1,500, making the number engaged in the battle nearly 3,000. It is probable that this estimate is large.

Colonel John T. Croxton's opportune arrival from Rock Springs probably saved the day for the Federals. Had Colonel Armistead cut off the sentinels north of the town, so as to prevent their retreat to Rock Springs, where they informed Croxton of the situation, the probability is that Pillow would have eventually overcome Watkins' force. The Confederates were still charging the court-house when Croxton arrived.

NOTES ON THE BATTLE. Mr. Thomas Phipps, who was too old for military duty during the battle, together with his family and other near-by neighbors, retreated to the basement of his home for safety, re-appeared during a lull in the fighting, and ventured to see what was going on. Thus exposed he was shot in the leg by the Yankees from the court-house and was ever afterward lame in that member.

There is the mark of a Yankee Minnie ball on the door facing of Mr. E. L. Culberson's home, having been shot during the battle from the court-house. The ball was deflected and struck one of the columns of the piazza.

Miss Orpha Center relates that her mother had baked three large loaves of light-bread the day before the battle for the use of the family.

They were such loaves as were common in that day—baked on the fire place in a large oven—round loaves. She had also several jars of milk cooling in a water trough. She says that during the progress of the battle numerous soldiers came to her door and asked for food. She cut for them generous pieces from her loaves and gave them milk to drink, till all was consumed. (These soldiers had traveled all night as well as the day previous, and had gone into action that morning without food. No wonder they were famished).

Miss Orpha Center relates the following story and thinks it ought of the battle, the Yankee soldiers passed her home carrying the dead Confederate soldiers to the cemetery for burial. They were playing a funeral dirge and were very respectful and solemn. Her brother, Doc, a mere lad at that time, followed them and saw a large grave where he says they buried 15 in one place, all together in one grave.

Judge W. M. Henry, in an old issue of the Walker County Messenger, relates in a most interesting manner, his experiences of that frightful day. A mere lad at the time, he nevertheless recalls the circumstances most vividly. He says among other things: "The old courthouse had received on its walls thousands of bullets. Each of these pitted and marked the stucco until, looked at from a distance, each of the walls suggested a human face badly marked by recent small-pox.

"The Presbyterian church, then having an enclosed front yard, had been converted into a field hospital. Just inside its wide double doors were placed a number of long tables. Upon these a number of surgeons were treating the wounded of both armies. Just outside the door on the south side of it, was a great heap of mangled and bloody fragments of humanity. This consisted of hands and feet and arms and legs, which, when amputated, were thrown out there to be afterward buried.

"Where the Federal dead were laid I do not know. But inside the three sides of the church yard fence, each with his head to the fence, and with something thrown over his face, lay the Confederate dead, numbering as I remember it, a few more than twenty.

"Time can never efface from my memory those sights and the events of that day. The men in blue were of course exultant. Everywhere they recounted the history and incidents of the day. Listening with alert ears to them, and from the remarks of the retreating Confederates, as well as from what I saw, and what I then and soon afterwards heard from people who were in the village, I learned what occurred."

Mis Orpha Center relates the following story and thinks it ought to be recorded in honor of the heroine mentioned: Mr. Davis Allen, a citizen of LaFayette, while visiting his family on furlough, was captured by the Yankees who were planning to send him to prison, but offered him in lieu thereof a parole provided he would swear allegiance to the United States.

Turning to his wife he asked her what he should do. "Da-vee," she replied, in that long drawn out and hesitating manner of hers, "you have boys here who will follow your example. Do right so they can follow you in honor. Go on to prison." That settled it. He went.

Mr. Cyrus Edwards who fought in the battle on the Union side, now living in Kentucky, writes the author under the date of April 25, 1932, as follows: "It was a plain straight fight and left with the participants as little bitterness on our side as was exhibited in any of the many actions I participated in during the years 1861 to 1865. Your men fought bravely and left terrible toll in evidence on the ground. I was detailed to head a party to clear the street after the fight was over. We picked up the dead and laid them in rows on the side of the street—leaving the best shaded places for the wounded, who were many, and were as soon as possible moved into buildings. I counted them at the time and found 29 dead, and later six of the wounded died, and so I reported.

"The street, from where it debouched into the square for a distance of fifty yards or more, was covered with wounded and dead men and pools of blood everywhere, and further on those evidences gradually decreased, but extended for quite a distance.

"So many boys among the dead excited our sympathies and all was done for them that could be done under the circumstances. * * * The prisoners, except those wounded were sent at once to Chattanooga and the wounded sent there as soon as it could be done. Several old men came from the country and secured permission to remove a few of the dead whom they recognized, for burial among their friends—I think only two or three. I saw no more of the dead—being busy elsewhere —until just as the last of them were being placed in the burial ditch. Our party remained at LaFayette for about a month, the whole of the brigade joining us in a day or two. We built a fort on a ridge in town —just across the drain from where I slept that night of the ball."

SKIRMISH AT LAFAYETTE, OCTOBER 12, 1864.

On October 12, 1864, a force of some 200 Confederate soldiers were temporarily encamped at LaFayette, occupying the Court-House, when a portion of a company of the Ninth Pennsylvania Cavalry happened into the town. There was an immediate show of hostilities between the two bodies which developed into a sharp skirmish in which 18 of the Pennsylvania's soldiers were captured. This is one of many such skirmishes that occurred in the county during the latter part of the Civil war.

Chapter Twenty

CIVIL WAR TERRORISTS.

DURING the latter part of the Civil War, especially following the Battle of Chickamauga, three separate bands of irregulars, or terrorists operated in Walker county. It is difficult to designate these groups by an adjective sufficiently descriptive. The old citizens of the county in discussing them use such adjectives as Raiders, Guerrillas, Tories, and Bushwhackers; but none of these names exactly suits.

A man named Gatewood was the leader of the most important of these bands. He claimed to be Southern in his sympathies and, of course, his operations were directed mainly against those citizens who were Union in their sympathies. He had no official status. Because of the unsettled condition of the country, and the fact that the civil authorities were weak and unable to cope with such bands—all able-bodied men being at the front, only women and children and aged men were left in the county—he scoured the county time and time again with his band of irresponsibles, pillaging, ravaging, plundering and killing. The number of men attached to this band varied from time to time. At times there are said to have been two or three hundred, but as a rule the number was much smaller, probably as low as 10 to 25.

Gatewood's area of operations was mainly in Northwest Georgia, but he often went into Tennessee and Alabama. Besides the states mentioned, this author has had reports of his operations in Dade, Chattooga, Floyd, Whitfield, Catoosa, Murray and probably other counties, in addition to Walker. They traveled horseback and usually scattered themselves throughout the section in which they happened to be. When in need of a horse, or if they happened to find a horse in better condition than one of their own, they simply took it and went on. At meal time they presented themselves at the homes in the neighborhood 4 or 5 or more at a place and ordered the meal prepared. In the meantime they fed their mounts from whatever could be found about the place.

Mr. J. T. Ashworth, an octogenarian, who lived at that time in Whitfield County, relates an exciting experience he recalls of one of Gatewood's incursions into Dogwood Valley, north of Villanow. On this occasion he is said to have terrorized the countryside and relieved the community of several horses which were needed, besides committing other depredations. Several old citizens of the county tell the following story: Some time after the Chickamauga battle the Yankees had a large bunch of cattle feeding near Rossville and being guarded by Yankee soldiers. Gatewood, with his band, surprised them, taking the cattle, said to have been several hundred, and capturing the soldiers whom he took and killed by cutting their throats. Those who tell this say it has been related to them in this manner for many years and they have no doubt of its correctness. Whatever may be said as to the taking of the cattle, there is no one, surely, who can condone the treatment of the soldiers.

There is no means of knowing, at this late day, just how many men were killed by Gatewood's band. The author, in discussing the matter with many old citizens, has asked for the names of men whom they know of, or have heard of, who were killed by this band. In this way he has recorded the following names: Dan Clarkson, Bill Clarkson, Jim Johnson, Tom Evitt, Jim Cordell, Dave or Green Cordell, Mr. Head, Sam Hixon, Mr. Lumpkin, Henry Blaylock, John Burton, Jake Bird, Joe Hammonds, Bascomb Hendrix, Jack Reed, Theron Poe, Elias Keys, Bill Campbell, Mr. Carlock. These were all citizens of the county or at least were killed in the county. Many others were reported as having been killed in other counties.

It is likely that this is only a small part of the men who met death at the hands of this band. Nor is there any means of knowing just why each man was killed. Some were known to be Union men while others were Southern. Some were killed while at home on furlough; some, it is said, were scouting out to evade service at the front, and were killed for that reason. But what authority had Gatewood to do this, even if that were true? Does this make him any less an outlaw? Many were killed, it is said, because of suspicion. Gatewood feared for his own life and for that of his men, and so, being suspicious of any man would be sufficient cause in such a character to take life.

There is no doubt that Gatewood was a brave man. He was a born fighter. Mr. Seab Shaw tells the following story which he had from an eyewitness: On one occasion, Gatewood, with his band, came into collision with the John Long band of guerrillas at LaFayette. He had Long's band on the run and sitting on his galloping horse in hot pursuit, was holding his horse's reins in his teeth and with a revolver in each hand was shooting at the fleeing men in front. Mr. Lee H. Dyer tells a similar story as follows: Near Ringgold, Gatewood was preparing to storm the town in which were many Yankees. Lining up his men he said, "Boys, if any of you are afraid, fall out". Then with his horse's reins in his teeth, each hand free to use his firearms, they stormed the town. Many such stories as these have been related to the author. The following, related by a citizen now 80 years of age, probably happened at the time of Long's escape at LaFayette, as noted above: After his escape, Long continued toward the Cove where he had his headquarters. Reaching the foothills of Pigeon Mountain and being overtaken by night, he turned aside from the main road and arriving at a farmhouse, went in and as was the custom announced that he with his men would spend the night. So picketing his horses about the porch he set a watch and lay down to sleep. Gatewood, in the meantime, was in hot pursuit, but it happened that in the darkness, he lost trail of Long, and so missed him. My informant relates this with some degree of pride and pleasure, feeling, as well he may, that had Gatewood not missed the trail in the darkness, there would probably have been no John Long's band and no people living in that house the next morning.

The following story was related to me by Mrs. Mary Lowery, 87, of the Chestnut Flat District, who has since died: She knew the victim personally, but says, by the way, that he was a rather worthless character. She remembers well the circumstance: A man named *Burton* was hanged by Gatewood in the eastern part of the county. His body was left hanging to a tree on the road side with a note attached forbidding anyone to take it down under penalty of like treatment. Because of this his body remained suspended for many days and until animals and vermin devoured the lower limbs. Finally, some one cut him down and buried him. Mr. Tom Arnold in discussing this matter gives the following information: The victim above referred to was cut down by George McKensie's 5th Tennessee Cavalry while passing through Georgia. Also, that John Gatewood was a native of Sparta, in White County, Tennessee; that Gatewood married a Miss Cain of Gaylesville, Alabama, and emigrated to Texas after the War. He saw her at the Confederate Reunion at Atlanta in 1898 and that Gatewood was dead then.

In personal appearance, Gatewood was a handsome man. His hair, which was a reddish-brown color, was worn rather long. He was athletic and active with clear blue and piercing eyes.

The "War of the Rebellion, Official Records of the Union and Confederate Armies" has several references to Gatewood's band. Series 1, Vol. 45, page 980 says, "Gatewood and other guerrillas in Broomtown to the number of about 400. Captain Pope of Gatewood's party, a Texan Ranger, had been in McLemore's Cove and carried off a man by name of Wm. Brooks". Again, pg. 990, Gatewood is referred to as unworthy of consideration, "except for the damage inflicted upon loyal citizens". Also, pg. 1193, "My scouting parties have returned, and report that the band of guerrillas who committed the depredation yesterday number about fifty, under command of Gatewood, I have the names of six men who were murdered; others are reported killed or wounded".

The Official Records above referred to, Series 1, Vol. 49, pg. 605, says:

Headquarters Department of the Cumberland.
Nashville, May 4, 1865.

Maj. Gen. G. H. Thomas, U. S. Army,

General: The following is a memorandum of the information communicated to you this morning by myself:

The terms of surrender between Generals Judah and Wofford were handed you, and an omission pointed out in the last article. The date of the actual surrender was fixed for the 12th proximo, and the place, Kingston, in order to give General Wofford time to collect his forces. These consist, nominally, of all the Confederate and State forces in Northwestern Georgia, amounting, on paper, to about 10,000. General Wofford did not expect to be able to collect more than about a third of them; but of those who will not be present, many are deserters from the C. S. Army, who are quietly at home, and many others are men who have avoided the rebel conscription and will remain quietly at home, having never taken up arms. These two classes, General Wofford considers, will comprise by far the larger part of his absentees. The remainder will be guerrillas of the Gatewood class, who have so far successfully *resisted General Wofford's efforts to compel them to submit to his authority*. These latter, he thinks, will number probably 500. * * * My own opinion is that the country would be better without troops for the present, unless the guerrillas render the occupation of it necessary. * *

I am, general, very respectfully, etc.

Louis Merrill, Col. U. S. Vol.

It is seen from the above, not only that Gatewood had no authority from Confederate powers, but that he actually refused to obey those in authority. General Wofford at the time above mentioned had control of the Confederate forces in Northern Georgia. Gatewood refused to obey him; he acknowledged no authority. He could be classed only as an outlaw.

The next band of guerrillas in importance was that headed by John Long and Sam Roberts. These men and their followers were Union in their sympathies. They operated principally in McLemore's Cove, but often crossed the mountain and raided the county round about. This was just about such another gang of outlaws as that of Gatewood, except, perhaps, not so large in numbers. They pretended to offer protection to all Union men and sympathisers, while opposing and persecuting men of opposite opinions. In a general way a description of Gatewood's actions and movements may be applied to that of the Long-Roberts gang. Long was a native of the Cove; he was not, however, related to the Longs in the lower part of Chattanooga Valley.

There was deadly enmity between the bands of Long and Gatewood. When they met there was pretty sure to be some little excitement, and very likely some one to bury. So far as the author has been able to ascertain by inquiry among the old citizens of the county the following men were killed by Long's band: Atlas Andrews, Wm. Stewart, Hiram Cochran, the two McSpadden boys, and sometime after the war Long killed Blevins Taylor on Lookout Mountain and was given a life sentence by the courts of Alabama but after serving 30 years was pardoned and soon afterward died.

The slaying of the two McSpadden boys was a most deplorable as well as most brutal affair. It seems that they were at home on furlough from the Confederate Army. One of them was seriously, perhaps dangerously ill. The other was nursing his brother. Anticipating trouble from the Long-Roberts gang, they left home and were hiding in Dirt Town in Chattooga County. Here they were discovered by Long and Roberts and were brutally murdered, one of them in bed. In the melee Roberts had his thumb shot off by his opponents. (See Miss Orpha Center's account of this elsewhere).

Mr. C. C. Ransom, 85, an eye witness, relates this circumstance: Soon after the war, at old Liberty Church, in the Cove, there was preaching one night, when Long, under the influence of drink, came in. He first sat down along the aisle, then got up and sat in the "Amen" corner. All this time he was muttering about something. Finally he arose and left the house and as he did so was heard to mutter that he cared not a d-m for anyone present, and that they had better not follow him either. No one followed. It was only a short time after this that he killed Blevins Taylor on Lookout Mountain. He escaped and was at large for some time, but as there was a handsome reward for his capture, and knowing that sooner or later he would be apprehended, he decided to surrender. So going to a house near Cassandra, he went in and surrendered to Temperance Kirkes, saying he would rather surrender to a woman than to a man. He was carried to Alabama, tried, convicted, and given a life sentence.

There was a third band of these guerrillas who occasionally visited the county. This was known as the Doc Morse gang. They operated mainly in Tennessee and the counties in Georgia east of Walker; however, upon occasion, they came as far as Rock Spring and adjacent territory. Not much is known by our people about this band; however, the people in the Peavine section remember that they were much to be dreaded. The author has been informed that a band of these Raiders occasionally visited Whitfield county led by a man named Edmonson from Murray county. It was just such another band of irresponsibles as Walker county had to contend with during the Civil War.

It is probable that these bands were present and operated in practically every community in the South during the Civil War. Since the strength of our manhood was at the front fighting, the sheriff, if there was one, and the other civil authorities, were unable to cope with such bands of men, and so the country was left to their mercy.

It is probable, also and it has often been so stated, that in many cases the adherents of Gatewood were not in sympathy with his methods or his purposes, but were attached to him for their own safety, and as soon as possible escaped from him. It is said too that Gatewood was suspicious of his own men—was afraid of them. At night when possible he would slip off to find a sleeping place where no one could find him, probably fearing for his own life.

In discussing these bands of outlaws among the citizens of the county this chronicler has frequently—almost universally heard them remark that Gatewood was just as bad as Long, and Long as bad as Gatewood—six of one and a half dozen of the other.

From the contribution of Judge John W. Maddox, printed elsewhere, it might be inferred that Gatewood had some kind of semi-official standing, at least among the subordinate officials of the Confederate army, that they "winked at", so to speak, some of his acts of irregularity. But it is difficult to believe that the higher authorities of the Southern Confederacy gave him such status, and the official records above quoted show that it did not.

Chapter Twenty-one

THE NEGRO—BILLS OF SALE.

THE negro is a part of the South—a large part. He is therefore a part of every community in the South, is a part of Walker county. A history of the county would be wanting in something if some account of the negro was not included.

If properly understood the negro has many excellent qualities to recommend him, while he doubtless has, like his white brother, some faults. He is agreeable, friendly, jovial, neighborly, and generally intensely religious. His religion may lapse at times (again like his white brother's), but is happily renewed upon occasion and serves him in season and out of season to help make his life of labor bearable.

No class of people takes its religion more seriously than our colored brother. Engage him in conversation at any time, at labor or at play, and he soon diverts your attention to his abiding faith in Deity. The Bible is his Book of Books and he delights to make reference to its teachings. Whether he understands it or not he accepts it as his guide of faith and practice. The negro as we know him has only been out of heathenism—not to say barbarism—some two or three centuries, many of them a much shorter time, and during that time he has quite forgotten the many inherited instincts of his barbaric forbears.

Let us see what the colored man has done and is doing for the nation. He raises the cotton that clothes the nation and the world. It is safe to say that a large majority of the cotton of commerce is produced by the labor of the negro. It is the negro that plows, hoes and picks the cotton. The negro and the mule are boon companions. They know and understand each other. That loud, jovial, spontaneous, sometimes half-inarticulate conversation, among the negroes at work, is well understood by the mule race. They love it, and vice versa, the negro loves the braying of the mule.

He not only grows the cotton that clothes the nation, but he raises the wheat, the corn, the potatoes, the hay and other crops that feed man and beast. He does most of the menial work about the home and farm, and what is more he does it uncomplainingly—and this is no small recommendation.

Then the colored man has built our railroads. It is he, more than others, who, with pick and shovel, has delved in the torrid heat and in the winter's cold to make it possible to operate the great railroad systems of our country. He it is, also, who furnishes the muscle and brawn to operate the great iron and steel furnaces from which the material comes to make our machinery—farming tools, engines, automobiles, radios and the like. He does a large part of that dangerous occupation of mining ores; builds our telegraph and telephone lines; quarries the rock and marble used in our buildings; makes the brick for our houses and pipes used in eliminating the wastes of our great cities. He acts as servant in our homes, furnishes fuel for fire, does the laundry and any other menial work necessary. Is not a race which thus makes itself useful entitled to receive our kindest consideration and praise?

The white race has no prerogative on genius. There are a great many geniuses among negroes. The South has produced many such and a roster of their names would fill many pages. Especially has the race furnished specialists in poetry and music; geniuses as business men, as writers and orators. Perhaps the greatest genius of recent times among the negroes is Roland Hayes, who while not a native of Walker county was born and reared in an adjoining county—Gordon. He is considered the world's greatest tenor to-day. He has filled engagements in all parts of the world where the English language is spoken. Recently in London he captured that great city by his superb voice.

As a young man he lived in Chattanooga and wrought along with others of his race in an iron foundry. The budding genius was beginning to show his powers at that time, and at his daily work he was wont to engage in song as is the custom of his race. The superintendent noticed that when he was singing everything worked better and with less friction. Hence he encouraged his singing and from this time he has made steady progress as an artist. His voice has made him both famous and wealthy.

Many of the early pioneers brought slaves with them when they came to the county. The author has found many "Bills of Sale" for negroes in his search throughout the county for old history. Some of these are reproduced at the end of this chapter. Besides those given he has seen many others.

There are many ante-bellum houses still standing in the county most of which were erected in whole or part by slave labor. Notable among these might be mentioned the Suttle home and slave quarters still standing in West Armuchee. Also, the Lane home in the Cove built by slave labor in 1859.

It is difficult for the young generation to realize that negroes were bought and sold like cattle in this county less than 70 years ago. No doubt there was at the county seat before the war a slave market where they could be purchased and where they were set up for sale to the highest bidder and auctioned off as we often see in the case of other property. This was true of all sections of the South prior to the Civil War.

The following quotation of prices for negroes as prevailed in days of slavery is taken from an ante-bellum newspaper of the state and is a reliable statement of the cost of different classes of negroes:

"No. 1 men, 20 to 26 years old, $1,459 to $1,500.
"Best grown girls, 17 to 20 years old, $1,150 to $1,250.
"Girls 12 to 15 years old, $1,000 to $1,100.
"Best plough boys, 17 to 20 years old, from $1,350 to $1,425.
"Boys, 12 to 15 years old, from $1,000 to $1,100.
"Likely families and also boys and girls command high prices as there are several gentlemen in the market who are purchasing for their plantations in the South."

The number of slaves in the county in 1850—ten years before the Civil war, was 795 males and 869 females, total 1664. There were also 18 free colored males and 19 free colored females. Total 37. Grand total colored population at that time, 1701.

The number of colored people in the county in 1930 was as follows: Male, 1178; female, 1171. Total, 2349, or an increase of 648 in 80 years. Compared with many Georgia counties, especially those further south, Walker contains few colored people. In the days before the war very little cotton was raised in the county and the need for slaves was not so great as in the cotton belt proper. Because slavery had no very great foothold in this county at that time, the majority of our citizens were opposed to secession and so expressed themselves at the polls when the subject was up for consideration.

There were generally, almost universally, the kindest of relations between master and servant. They were well treated by the whole household and that kind treatment was reciprocated. Only in the rarest cases was there harsh treatment of the slaves.

Slaves had no churches of their own. They were members of, and attended the churches of the whites. There was in many churches a gallery at the back of and above the congregation for the use of negroes. The present Presbyterian church at LaFayette once had such a gallery. "Whether they understood it or not, they took their religion very seriously, and to this day enjoy it thoroughly. Out of it have sprung the spirituals which are a unique contribution to the world's music, composed as they are of unconscious humor, rich melody and haunting mystery—the somnolent inheritance of the jungle life which still to a large extent guides their destiny."

The following incident is reproduced from the Upson County History:

"A MIS'ABLE NIGGER."

"My friend asked Anthony Rox, a superb engine driver on the Ohio River, how he came to get free. 'Why, Massa Vincent, my health was berry bad when I was in Kentuck; I couldn't do no kind o' work; I was berry feeble; 'twas jes as much as I could do to hoe my own gyarden and eat de sass. An' de missus what owned me see dat I was a mis'able nigger! So I said to her, "Missus, I'm a mis'able nigger, an' I ain't wof nothin', an' I tink you'd better sell me." Now, Massa Vincent, I such a poor nigger dat missus 'greed to sell me for a hundred dollars, an' I 'greed to try to wok and yern de money to pay her, an' I did, an' my health has been gittin' better eber since, an' I specks I made 'bout nine hundred dollars out ob dat nigger.'"

The following story is re-produced from memory:

"In the days before the war the accepted medical practice among practitioners refused water to a patient suffering from certain fevers, it being the opinion that water was detrimental to the patient. An old ante-bellum gentleman, Mr. Ellington, a slave owner, and man of affairs, fell sick with fever and was so serious that the physician and family despaired of his recovery. After several days and nights of watching— the family being worn out for want of rest, the patient was left one night in the care of an old trusted negro slave while the family retired to get a much needed rest. The servant was strictly charged not to give him water as this would certainly cause his immediate death.

After all had retired, Mr. Ellington began his argument with the old faithful servant to persuade him to give him water. "Sambo," he said, "if you will give me a gourd of water from the spring I'll give you a thousand dollars when I get well." Sambo was adamant. "Sambo, I'll give you your freedom when I get well if you'll give me some water." Sambo replied that his freedom would always haunt him and make him miserable because he would know that he had caused his master's death.

After a pause, Mr. Ellington, falling on another ruse, said: "Sambo, if you don't go and get me some water, I'll give you the worst whipping you ever had when I get up." Sambo, doubting that he would ever get up, and at any rate feeling that his master would have a softer heart at that time, being grateful for his recovery, still refused. After some pause, Mr. Ellington, always astute in gaining his ends, turned and raised himself on his elbow and looking with his gaunt, ghastly and emaciated face at Sambo, said: "Sambo, I'm going to die and it's all because I can't get a drink of water. If you don't go and get me a drink of water from the spring, I'll come back and *hant* you the longest day you live."

"Oh! Lordy! Lordy! massa, you shall hab de wata! You shall hab de wata!" and he hurried away to the spring and brought him a pitcher of water. Mr. Ellington drank and drank to his satisfaction, and the next morning to the surprise of everybody he was better and soon recovered.

Many slaves were carried by their masters to the war as a bodyguard and servant, as well as for companionship. The following incident illustrates the feeling of the old slaves thus employed:

"A GEORGIA NEGRO BOUND FOR THE WAR."

Describing the march of the troops from Georgia northward, a correspondent of the Charleston Courier relates the following: "Several of them brought along their bodyservants, who were likewise armed and uniformed. One of the latter was a mouldy looking darkey so old and dried up that he might have passed for a preserved preparation of an Egyptian mummy. He had but two teeth left out of the usual complement and his head looked not unlike a dingy cotton patch on a small scale. Some one asked if he wasn't afraid to go to the war. "No sah," said he, "wherebber Massa go dis chile go too—follow him to de debbil." "But suppose Abe Lincoln gets after you, what then?" "Massa look out for him, never let dis chile get hurted in de worl. I'se wof a tousand dollars but ole Linkum aint wof a dam cent. You tink I get killed! No sah," and the old shade turned on his heel and marched off as dignified as a Wall Street Bear.

There are many instances of remarkable longevity of negroes in our county. The census of 1850 for Walker county makes record of two negroes at that time living in the county more than 100 years of age. Rose Allgood, who died in 1930, related that she was a grown woman when she came to this county with the Allgoods long before the war. Doubtless she must have seen a century of time. Abe Coulter, a familiar character about LaFayette for many years and who claimed to have assisted in clearing away the trees for laying out the town in 1833, lived to the ripe old age of 111. Bill Force was said to be 109 at his death, Mose Brown 102, Rose Butler 100, Polly Love 108 and Dicey Cole 114. Doc Thrash, still living near Lytle (1932), is said to be 111 years of age. Many other negroes of the county have lived to be 90 to 100 years of age.

It is insisted by some that since many of these examples are more or less uncertain because of a want of proper records that they should be taken with a grain of salt; but the fact remains that the negro race is given to greater longevity in the main than the white race. This may be attributed to his simple life, free from extravagances both in living and eating, especially the eating of rich foods. It tends to prove, at least, that hard work does not shorten man's days, as is sometimes claimed.

The following old time darkies, still in life (1932), are relics of slavery, having been born before the war: Cicero Suttle, Fannie Shropshire, Anna Wyatt, Ben Clements, Dollie Morris, Millard Wheeler, Willis Marsh, John Davis, Charley Brooks, Alfred Goodson, Charley Neal, George Salmon, Sarah Benton, Texas Liles, Ben Young, Harry McDaniel, Clara McClure, Tim Jackson, Doc Thrash, Milus Long, Jim Bruce, John Akins, Warner Lewis who came into the county with Col. Wm. Daugherty about 1843, now over 90.

Doc Thrash, who claims to have been born Dec. 25, 1820, hence 111 years of age, lives in Chickamauga Park. Was born in Richmond, Va., six months after his parents had arrived as slaves from Africa. Married 4 times, father of 29 children, one son now 88 years old; 10 in first family, 12 in second, 7 in third, none in last. Went with his master to the war as a servant; was captured back and forth several times, winding up in the hands of the Yankees which, luckily for him, entitles him to a handsome pension, which he is enjoying in his old days.

THE OLD DARKEY'S PRAYER. Many years ago a noted Methodist divine was invited to preach to a negro congregation. After the sermon an old darkey was called on to pray. After the usual introduction in the prayer, he proceeded as if to compliment the preacher and to call down heaven's blessings on him, as follows. Observe the sublimity of thought:

"O Lo'd, gib him de eye ob de eagle, dat he may spy sin a-fur off. O Lo'd, nail his tongue to de gospel-tree; and O Lo'd, tie his hands to de gospel plow—then, O Lo'd, bend his knees and bow his head away over in de low ground ov sorrow where much prayer is wont to be made. And, O Lo'd, a-nint his head wi' the kerosine ile ov salvation, and den sot him on fire."

STATE OF TENNESSEE, BRADLEY COUNTY. July 31 day 1838. I have this day sold to Thomas Bryan one negro man named Jacob about sixty-five years old, also one negro woman named Ann about forty years old, for the sum of four hundred dollars in hand paid, which I warrent and defend from myself, my eirs (heirs) and all other persons, also to be sound in mind and body. Whereunto I affix my hand and seal, this 31 day of July 1838.

Robert Woody—(Seal).

Test: Joseph Rogers.

STATE OF GEORGIA, } Whereas, by virtue of an order from the
WALKER COUNTY. } Honorable, the Court of Ordinary of Walker
county, and in persuance of the last will and testament of Joshua Brigman, late of Walker county, deceased, after due and legal advertisement in terms of the law, the undersigned put up and offered for sale to the highest bidder, at the Court House door, at LaFayette, in said county, on the first Tuesday in November, Eighteen Hundred and Fifty Five, a certain negro man named Charles, when Mary Brigman, being the highest and best bidder, said negro was knocked off to her at and for the price of One Thousand and Fifty One Dollars.

Now, received of said Mary Brigman One Thousand and Fifty One Dollars in full payment for said negro man, Charles, so sold as aforesaid.

Witness my hand and seal, this 8th day of January, 1856.

George Brigman—(Seal),
Executor of Joshua Brigman, Deceased.

GEORGIA, } Know all men by these presents that I, Tem-
WALKER COUNTY. } perance Brigman, of the said county and state, for
and in consideration of the sum of Two Hundred and Six Dollars, to me in hand paid by Elizabeth Brigman of the county and state aforesaid (the receipt of which I hereby acknowledge), have bargained, sold, and delivered, and by these presents do bargain, sell and deliver unto the said Elizabeth Brigman, a negro girl named Manda, age three years. To have and to hold the aforesaid bargained girl unto the said Elizabeth Brigman, her heirs, executors, administrators and assigns for ever.

And I, the said Temperance Brigman, for myself, my executors and administrators shall and will warrant and defend the same against all persons, unto the said Elizabeth Brigman, her heirs and assigns by these presents. In witness whereof I have hereunto set my hand and affixed my seal. This 1st day of July 1857.

her
Temperance X Brigman—(Seal).
mark

Test:
P. S. Anderson,
Simon Brigman.

GEORGIA, } For and in consideration of James B. Suttle of
WALKER COUNTY. } said county, having signed a bond for the reply
and forthcoming of sundry negroes, to wit, Frances, a woman, and John and George, two boy slaves, this day levied on by virtue of an attachment in favor of Daniel Blackwell against Aaron Camp, returnable to the next Superior Court to be held in and for said county—Now, to secure the said John B. Suttle against his said liability

on said bond, I, the said Aaron Camp, have this day bargained and sold, and by these presents do bargain and sell unto the said John B. Suttle, his heirs and assigns, the following negroes, to wit, Frances, a woman about thirty years old; a boy by the name of John, about three years old; and George, about one year old; and Betsy or Elizabeth, about five years old; and Frances, a girl about six years old,—to have and to hold said negro slaves to him, his heirs and assigns against the said Aaron Camp, his heirs, executors, &c, to the only proper use, benefit and behoof of him the said John B. Suttle, provided he has any part or portion of said bond to pay, and said negroes to be subject to the possession of the said Suttle at any time when demanded by him or his assigns. But this Bill of Sale to be null and void provided the said John B. Suttle is saved harmless against his said liability on said bond. As witness my hand and seal this the 5th day of October 1842.

Aaron Camp—(Seal).

Attest:
C. I. Hooper,
A. A. Anneson.

Recorded in Clerk's Office Jan. 4, 1843
by R. H. Caldwell, D.C.S.C.

STATE OF GEORGIA,
CHATTOOGA COUNTY.

Received of Milum P. Rogers Nine Hundred and Twenty Nine Dollars in full payment for a negro named July, about six years old, of dark (_____) complexion, which negro I warrant to be normal both in body and mind and (_____) for life. I only (warrant) as executor of Harris Sprayberry and no further. This Jan. 13, 1859.

H. S. Sprayberry, Executor of Harris Sprayberry, Dec.

I. B. Leach,
V. Yearby.

The two following Bills of Sale are in possession of J. B. F. Jones, prized mementoes of his ancestors:

GEORGIA,
NEWTON COUNTY.

Know all men by these presents, that I, Joel Jones senr., for the consideration of the good will and affection to my beloved son James Jones, do by this instrument give unto the said James Jones, a negro boy, named Thomas, the right of which boy I do by this deed of gift warrant and defend against all and singular the claims of my heirs forever, with this proviso: That any time the supreme government of the U. S. should provide a release by law for the emancipation of slaves, then, in that case, this instrument shall not be understood, or so construed, as to be any bar to the force and effect of such an excellent provision &c.

In witness whereof I hereunto set my hand and seal, this the fifth day of April, in the Year of Our Lord One Thousand Eight Hundred and Thirty Two.

Joel J. Jones—(Seal).

Subscribed to before us:
Sarah Ann Neal,
McCormack Neal I.I.C.

GEORGIA, \
MORGAN COUNTY. } Know all men by these presents, that I, Young Bohannon, of the county and state aforesaid, have this day bargained, sold and delivered, unto Joel Jones, of the county and state first aforesaid, one negro woman of the name of Judy, about the age of 18 years, for and in consideration of the sum of Seven Hundred and Twenty Five Dollars in hand paid, the receipt whereof is hereby acknowledged. & I, the said Young Bohannon, bind myself, my heirs, &c, to warrant and forever defend the right and title of said negro woman unto said Jones his heirs &c, and also, do warrant the said negro to be a well and sound negro &c. In testimony whereof, I have hereunto set my hand and seal, this 22, October, 1817.

Young Bohannon—(Seal).

Test:
Wm. Gill.

$2250

Received, Atlanta, March 11, 1863, of G. W. & J. M. Blackwell in full payment for slaves Annis & Charles—Annis about 25 Yrs. old and Charles about 6 years. Said slaves hereby warranted sound in body and mind, and the right and title to the above named slaves we do warrant unto the said G. W. & J. M. Blackwell heirs, and assigns against the claims of all persons whomsoever.

In testimony whereof we have hereunto set our hands, seal, day and date above written.

Witness: Robert A. Crawford.

Butingham & Perkinson (Seal).

$625   Russell County: The State of Alabama.

Received of Mr. Thomas Bryan, Six Hundred and Twenty Five Dollars in full for the purchase of a negro girl about 17 years of age by the name of Louisa, which girl we warrent sound in mind and body though she has been raised exclusive in the house and very tenderly and delicately. The wright and title we warrant good unto him the said Bryan, his heirs and assigns against ourselves, our heirs and assigns, and against all other persons whatever. In witness our hands and seals this 3 day of June 1846.

A. D. Abraham & Co. (Seal).

Larkin Allen,
Rev. H. Line.

Chapter Twenty-two

MUSTER ROLLS, CONFEDERATE SOLDIERS.
MUSTER ROLL OF COMPANY "G," 9TH REGIMENT GA. VOL. INF., C.S.A., WALKER COUNTY, GEORGIA.

("LaFayette Vets.")

Greenberry G. Gordon, Surgeon, 9th Reg.
Andrew J. Healan, 1st Lieut.
Isaac D. Allen, 1st Lieut.
Edward F. Hoge, 2nd Lieut.; Elect. Capt., Pro. Lieut.-Col.; Colonel.
Robert H. Baker, 1st Sergt.
William J. Mize, 2nd Sergt.; Elec. Jr. 2nd Lieut.
Edward A. Sharpe, 4th Sergt.; Apptd. 1st Sergt.
Conway O. Calhoun, 1st Corp.
Samuel P. McWhorter, 2nd Corp.
Egbert C. Palmer, 3rd Corp.
James W. Nash, 4th Corp.
Wm. C. Allen, Pri.; Apptd. 3rd Sergt.; Elect. 2nd Lieut.; 1st Lieut.; Capt.
William S. Allen, Pri.; Apptd. 2nd Sergt.

PRIVATES.

Anderson Arnold
James Arnold
William C. Baird
F. M. Bazemore
Edmund S. Beard
Elbert A. Beard
Jackson Beard
B. E. Benning
Green B. Bennett
Miles B. Bennett
W. B. Bennett
Wm. W. Bice
Aeneas L. Brooks
A. J. Brown
James M. Brown
Francis Marion Brownfield
Asa L. Bryan

Wm. L. Jones
Joseph Kelley
Wm. L. Kendall
Doctor F. Kinman
Gray B. Lassiter
John C. Little
Q. Dell Mann
John Miller
John Mills
Wm. H. Mills
James H. Moreland
Hamilton G. More
Isham Moore
Charles J. Morgan
John B. Morgan
Thomas J. Morgan
Joel Morton

Cicero C. Bryan
James M. Caldwell
James McR. Caldwell
John A. Caldwell
James E. Calhoun
Stephen H. Carson
Wm. H. Caruthers
Elbert S. Cassady
Posey M. Catlett
Harmon L. Center
Wm. R. Cole
James A. Connally
W. D. Cook
Augustus L. Culberson
Wm. A. Culberson
Robert N. Dickerson
Wm. B. Dickerson
John H. Duke
Alex R. Durham
Kearney Eubanks
James O. Evans
Wm. Faulkner
Mike Ford
Clinton J. Fuller
W. M. Gains
Wm. T. Goodwin
Noah S. Gordy
George W. Grady
Augustus A. Greathouse
Bryant A. Greathouse
Robert B. Guthrie
Robert H. Harris
Frederick Hart
Jacob C. Hart
George D. Hearn
James J. Hearn
Edmund J. Henry
John C. Higgins
Reuben W. Higgins
Wm. M. Hoge
Rufus B. Halloway
C. Hoyt
James Hubbard
Wm. J. Huff
Robert T. Jennings
George W. Johnson
James B. Johnson

Wm. C. Murdock
Patrick H. McClure
Russell W. McConnell
E. J. McCrary
George W. McGinnis
Robert A. McGinnis
B. W. McGinnis
R. B. McLeroy
Samuel W. McWhorter
Wm. F. Nash
Wm. H. Owens
Wm. R. Owens
Stamper Owensby
Wm. D. Palmer
John Parker
James H. Partain
Wm. H. H. Rogers
Charles B. Rutledge
Edwin M. Satterfield
Milton M. Satterfield
Reuben P. Satterfield
Wm. P. Satterfield
James E. Shaw
Duncan Smith
Wiley E. Smith
Augustus R. Stewart
John C. Stokes
James M. Talley
Nathaniel G. Talley
Wm. J. Talley
Wm. A. Thompson
James Trammel
Hamilton Tripp
Andrew J. Tuttle
John F. Vickery
Wm. D. Walden
James S. Wardlaw
James G. Watson
Larenze White
George W. Whitten
John P. Whitten
B. C. Williams
Harden H. Williams
John C. Wood
M. P. Wood
James W. Young

MUSTER ROLL OF COMPANY "E," 39TH GA. VOL. INF., ARMY OF TENNESSEE, C.S.A., WALKER COUNTY, GEORGIA.

Charles D. Hill, Captain.
H. P. Osborn, Captain.
W. C. Bunch, 1st Lieut.
A. L. Culberson, 1st Lieut.
John P. (or J. T.) Halloway, 2nd Lieut.
T. J. Fricks, Jr. 2nd Lieut.
John T. Bentley, 1st Sergt.; Elect. Capt.
James M. Owens, 2nd Sergt.
Samuel W. Lord, 3rd Sergt.; Apptd. 1st Sergt.
D. C. White, 4th Sergt.
T. T. Cagles, 5th Sergt.
H. Wesley Hobbs, 1st Corp.
C. H. Roark, 2nd Corp.
Wm. Harrison H. Fricks, 4th Sergt.
Thomas J. Meek, 4th Corp.

CONFEDERATE VETERANS OF WALKER COUNTY, 1932

Left to right, back row: T. B. Carroll, J. M. Clarkson, T. B. Arnold, W. P. Jackson, T. P. Norman. Front row: R. B. Stegall, E. L. Culberson, J. P. Phipps, G. W. Patterson, B. J. Huggins.

PRIVATES.

Harvey C. Alley
Albert L. (or A. J.) Allison
John A. P. Bailey
W. M. Bailey
W. W. Ballard
James M. Bankston
W. R. Bankston
Wm. Blaylock
Henry W. Boss
D. P. Bradley
W. T. Brand
John Bridgeman
J. M. Bunch
A. M. Burrows
H. Burrows
Thomas J. Burrows
J. L. Calloway
Archibald R. Campbell
Enos M. Campbell
James A. Campbell
Andrew B. Carnet
  (or Carnott)
John E. Carson (or J. A.)
Jefferson J. Chambers
S. S. M. Chambers
Martin T. Childress
John C. (or John M.)
  Clarkson
Thomas T. Cole
F. D. Collins
J. C. Collins
J. William Collins
Martin L. Crump
G. W. Cummings
Robert B. Cummings
A. J. Disheroon
John H. Dougherty
J. O. Drennon
W. C. Drennon
J. J. Dyer
G. W. Ellis
J. C. Evans
Thomas M. Faucett
Francis M. Fricks
M. H. Gilliam

W. J. Harp
C. W. Herron
Elisha Herron
James B. Hill
Joseph A. Holloway
Henry W. Ketner
Thomas B. Ketner
Joseph Killingsworth
T. W. (or J. W.) Lawrence
B. W. Lively
Moses Long
Charles F. Lumpkin
Sanford Mann
J. W. Mauldan
Benjamin B. Miller
John H. Miller
Sanford H. Mitchel
Thomas Mitchel
Wm. S. Moore
J. J. Morgan
Thomas M. McBride
Jacob McCoy
Phillip McCoy
Andrew J. McDaniel
J. F. Patterson
W. W. Patterson
E. R. Payne
W. R. Payne
John Pearson
John N. (or J. W.) Phillips
Mark S. Phillips
J. M. C. D. Rape
J. Richardson
Z. H. Robinson
L. A. Rogers
Jess Self
Thomas D. Self
W. H. Show
M. L. Siler (or Silen)
Jefferson Sims
Baswell Smith
Burrell Smith
Wiley Smith
Wm. J. Smith
J. W. Snyder

T. N. Glass
Benjamin L. Glenn
Francis Glenn
J. R. Glenn
James P. Graham
F. J. Hall
John A. Hall
G. W. Hammonds
A. J. Haney
Andrew J. Hanson
John F. Harp
M. J. Harp

Robert Sparger
Thomas Sparger
D. H. Stiles
J. D. Strange
W. F. Turner
S. H. Thurman
Monroe Wallin
  (or Wallace)
Wm. Wallin
  (or Wallace)
A. Weathers
S. Williams

MUSTER ROLL OF COMPANY D, 1ST GA. VOL. INF., C.S.A.

This roster was made out by John B. Henderson in 1925. The company was made up of Walker and Catoosa county boys in 1862 and served till the surrender. So far as known John Lyle is the only surviving member at this time (1932).

OFFICERS.

Regimental Captain, E. M. Dodson, Sr., of Chattanooga.
Company Captain, James Whitsit, of Ringgold.
Colonel J. C. Gordon.
Lieutenant B. M. Jarrett.

PRIVATES.

Hunt Akin
Jasper Adkins
Alson Blaylock
Younger Brock
George Blair
Andrews Chambers
Jack Caruthers
C. C. Caruthers
Mevin Cathorn
Davis Clark
William Conley
George Curry
Henry Davis
James Dalton
E. M. Dodson, Jr.
Davis Ellison
Isaac Elrod
Jack Fielding
Marion Fielding

Daniel Johnson
John Jackson
Lias Kenum
Joseph Lyle
John Lyle
Wash Meek
Chappell M. McFarland
Wyley Mullis
Jas. A. Mullis, Sr.
Eli Myers
Newt Nations
Wylie Nichols
Jessie Owens
Jerry Pack
Albert Pack
James Pettigrew
W. T. Park
Lewis Pitts
Bill Pitts

Thomas Gulett
John Glenn
B. M. Garrett
J. S. Glenn
John B. Henderson
Robert A. Henderson
W. H. Hill
Joseph Hill
Joseph Hays
John Howard
Jesse Hinnard
Frank Hinnard
Jack Hinnard
Ruben Hearn
Hiram Hensley
Ben Hensley
Wright Henry
James Hawkins
Ward Harris
Columbus Harrison
Russell Jones
William Jones
Thomas N. Jones
Reese Jones
Robert Jones
Thomas B. Jones
Revis Jones
Jack Johnson

Thomas N. Reed
Charles Reed
Monroe Reed
James Reed
Russell Smith
Sam Smith
Joe Smith
Thomas Smith
George Smith
Nick Smith
Pryer Stanfield
Zeph Sawyer
James Sutton
J. Poke Tedford
William Thedford
James Trimmier
R. B. Trimmier
Robert Vinsant
Wylie Wall
Aullen Wilson
Justin C. Wells
James Ward
Levi Withers
Asbury Withers
Morris Workman
Joel Youngblood
Cleve Yates

MUSTER ROLL OF COMPANY G, 11TH GA. REGT.

Frank Little, Colonel.
J. Y. Wood, Captain.
J. Guthrie, 1st Lieut.
F. H. Little, 2nd Lieut.
J. M. Jackson, Bvt. 2nd Lieut.
W. H. Harrelson, 1st Sergt.
J. H. McWilliams, 2nd Sergt.
J. V. Little, 3rd Sergt.
J. W. Hill, 4th Sergt.
E. L. Easterling, 1st Corp.
W. N. Russell, 2nd Corp.
J. P. Wood, 3rd Corp.
B. M. Clark, 4th Corp.

PRIVATES.

John Akin
R. W. Bailey
J. N. Bell
B. F. Blackburn
B. Boaz
C. L. Burns
D. H. Brooks
V. P. Bomar
E. A. Bomar
M. C. Cantrell
W. P. Cassada
A. J. Cargal
Benjamin Clark
I. L. Cox
G. M. Cox
H. G. Cowan
B. F. Crain
W. S. Dobson
S. M. Dunn
Joshua Dunagan
A. H. Easterling
J. E. Eslinger
H. Findley
J. N. Fry
G. W. Gentry
J. F. Green
S. F. Green
F. L. Head
J. L. Harris
N. L. Harris
E. A. Howell
H. H. Hamilton
M. Hester
M. D. L. Henderson
W. J. Hill
H. H. Hill
B. J. Huggins
Henry Hulsey
J. H. Keeler
S. Kemp
G. A. Keener
M. C. Lawrence
N. V. Lawrence
J. W. Love
E. M. Mayfield

F. A. McWilliams
J. M. A. Miller
H. J. Miller
J. K. Miller
J. L. Miller
W. S. McLain
G. W. McGahaha
W. S. Murray
B. F. Neal
W. H. H. Orr
O. V. Perry
J. W. Pilcher
W. E. Mylam
H. Y. Puryear
M. C. Ramsey
A. J. Reed
Jordan Reed
Abel Richardson
William Richardson
G. W. Richardson
Rufus Richardson
J. H. Roberts
J. A. W. Roberts
Joseph Robinson
N. D. Robinson
G. C. Leatherwood
G. W. Sampson
T. D. Sampson
W. H. Shahan
W. L. Shattuck
Jefferson J. Smith
P. E. Staples
J. A. Story
L. Stoe
S. C. Talley
J. W. Templeton
J. H. Tipton
J. C. Torbett
B. J. Townsend
R. F. Wells
J. D. Wilkinson
J. M. Wilson
J. S. C. Wilson
L. E. Wilson
G. W. Witherspoon

Nealy McCarthur
R. B. McClure
J. T. McConnell
D. P. McConnell
R. T. McConniel
J. M. McNair
John McNair
C. W. McWilliams

J. H. Witherspoon
D. C. White
Ancel Wright
H. A. Russell
A. J. York
A. T. Coryell
J. A. Swinson
B. F. Brown

MUSTER ROLL OF COMPANY "F," 8TH REGIMENT, 3RD BRIGADE, GEORGIA STATE TROOPS, CHATTOOGA AND WALKER COUNTIES.

Robert Cameron, Captain.
George W. Blackwell, 1st Lieut.
Henry D. C. Edmondson, 2nd Lieut.; Pro. Captain.
Thomas B. Cochran, Jr. 2nd Lieut.
Jesse L. Jones, 1st Sergt.
James P. Hendricks, 2nd Sergt.
Oliver N. York, 3rd Sergt.
Wilson M. Lumpkin, 4th Sergt.
Francis M. Failly, 1st Corp.
Joseph Harmons, 2nd Corp.
David F. W. Smith, 3rd Corp.
Robert L. A. Cameron, 4th Corp.

PRIVATES.

John Akins
Joseph L. Boss
Henry C. Carter
Francis M. Castles
Robert D. Douglas
James H. Daniel
Josiah Flournoy
Wm. Fuller
Wm. W. Frost
Wm. Greeson
Charles R. Hood
Henry S. Hancock
Thomas N. Harper
John N. Harper
Robert Harlow
Robert A. Hemphill
Thomas G. Howell
Joseph A. Henley
Marquis D. Henderson
Ethridge J. Jones

Wm. M. Moss
Green A. H. Mallet
Andrew J. Neal
Abraham H. Neal
Joseph A. Neal
Wm. Penn
Coleman L. C. Pitts
George T. Pullen
Perry K. Rogers
Wm. T. Stewart
Wm. B. Strange
Thomas F. Strange
W. F. Stover
Wm. F. Simpson
Wm. H. Strain
Mark H. Stone
James W. Snow
Paul C. Smith
John O. Smith
Frederick L. R. Thomas

James Jones
James A. Johnson
James R. Knox
John M. Lumpkin
Thomas F. Maxey
Matthew A. Meyers

James J. Thomas
James Tucker
Robert N. Thornberry
Thomas B. White
John M. Williams
George W. Winston

MUSTER ROLL OF COMPANY "K," 39TH REGIMENT GA. VOL. INF., ARMY OF TENNESSEE, C.S.A., WALKER COUNTY, GEORGIA.

John W. Brady, Captain; Elec. Regimental Chaplain.
Alonzo J. Pursley, Captain.
Alford C. Ward, 1st Lieut.; Elec. Captain.
W. O. Alexander, 2nd Lieut.
Augustus A. Cooper, Jr. 2nd Lieut.
K. G. Smith, Jr. 2nd Lieut.
James S. McConnell, 1st Sergt.
T. J. Foster, 2nd Sergt.; Elec. 2nd Lieut.
Benjamin W. Castleberry, 3rd Sergt.
P. G. White, 4th Sergt.; Appt. 3rd Sergt.
A. L. Alexander, 5th Sergt.; Apptd. 2nd Sergt.
S. A. Brice, 1st Corp.
W. H. H. Chafin, 2nd Corp.
E. C. Catlett, 3rd Corp.
J. C. Hovis, 4th Corp.

PRIVATES.

Fleming Aikin
J. M. Anderson
Phillip G. Autry
L. Baker
B. M. Bates
J. N. Bird
Robert W. Brice
J. W. (or J. M.) Brock
J. M. Cannon
R. M. A. Catlett
H. J. Chastain
M. G. Clements
W. G. Clement
Pendleton G. Coker
John W. Crawford
W. B. Culberson
James J. Dobson
H. L. Duncan
C. M. Evett

Wesley Lowery
T. E. Madaris
G. W. Mills
Hugh Mills
Wm. K. Mitchel
Wm. L. Moore
W. D. Moore
Joel P. Morton
   (or Martin)
Wm. M. McAlister
D. W. Oxford
J. H. Oxford
H. A. Partain
J. R. Phelps
J. N. J. (or J. A. J.) Pike
S. T. (or S. S.) Poe
A. R. Powell
Henry T. Redwine
J. L. Reese

J. S. H. Evett or Everette
T. M. Evett or Everett
M. S. Garner
H. J. Gill
Jesse T. (or J. J.) Gill
J. B. Gill
T. Monroe (or M. T.) Gill
J. W. Gray
Needham Griffin
G. A. J. Haile
W. B. Haile
A. L. Hamilton
Newton Hamilton
M. J. Harris
John H. Hawks
C. R. Hendrix
E. M. Higgins
R. M. Houston
James M. James
M. C. James
W. H. James
Reuben Jay
L. W. Keeling
J. M. Keith
William Kinsey
Zara A. Little
I. J. Lofton
B. W. Long
Benjamin C. Lowery

J. F. Robertson
S. M. Robertson
Jesse F. Self
J. L. Self
J. L. Self (another)
W. W. Shields
Anson Aaron Tarvin
A. Tarvin
D. Tate
E. Tate
W. W. Tate
J. J. Taylor
J. N. Taylor
Wm. Thomas
S. P. Tipton
R. J. Tucker
Berry B. Turner
J. R. Turner
William Wall
J. R. Wardlaw
E. Warnock
W. A. Weaver
L. M. White
James Williams
T. B. Williams
J. J. C. Wilson
J. L. Wilson
W. W. Wilson

MUSTER ROLL OF COMPANY "H," 23RD REGIMENT GA. VOL. INF., C.S.A., WALKER, COBB AND GORDON COUNTIES.

("Bartow Invincibles," also called "Walker-Bartow Invincibles.")

Francis M. Young, Captain.
Thomas R. A. Haslerig, 1st Lieut.; Pro. Captain.
Reese B. Neal, 2nd Lieut.
John Edge, Jr. 2nd Lieut.
H. G. Fuller, 1st Sergt.
Alexander Arnold, 2nd Sergt.
B. F. Chapman, 3rd Sergt.
Joseph M. Suttle, 4th Sergt.
J. Wilson Clements, 1st Corp.
S. S. Keenum, 2nd Corp.
John Arnold, 3rd Corp.
Harrison H. Davis, 4th Corp.

PRIVATES.

H. E. A. Adcock
J. J. Adcock
Michael Baker
John W. Bennett
J. T. Burgess
Jerry Burns
James McR. Caldwell
Newton Cargle
Perry G. Cargle
Wm. C. Cargle
Samuel H. Chambers
A. P. Chapman
John H. C. Condry
Andrew J. Coulter
James H. Coulter
Abram C. Davis
A. Robert Davis
Jeremiah L. Davis
Thomas Davis
J. M. Dempsey
Seth W. Dempsey
Wm. B. Dickerson
Franklin Ellenberg
Ezekiel Foster
Wm. B. Foster
W. W. Foster
Hiram S. Fuller
M. H. Fuller
W. B. Fuller
Thomas M. Gasaway
Doctor C. Gladden
J. R. Gladden
Nicholas Goodson
Wm. B. Goodson
J. L. Green
Thomas J. Green
Wm. J. Green, Jr.
Wm. P. Green
John Grigsby
George Sanford Harmon
S. H. Harmon
W. C. Huit
Wm. J. Johnson
Burton Kearns
James D. Keown

or Malory
Robert W. Maloney
   or Malory
S. H. Maloney or Malory
John N. Martin
E. Tip Mattox
Houston Mattox
John Mattox
Porter Mattox
J. M. Mizer
Blakely E. Moon
P. D. H. Morgan
Henry C. Partain
H. H. Patterson
J. B. Patterson
Wm. L. Patterson
Thomas W. Pilcher
G. W. Pogue
John Norman Pogue
John T. Pope
Kinchen T. Pope
Patrick W. Pope
Wm. A. Pope
G. Warren Rawls
Jordan Reed
Virgil M. Reed
Joseph W. Richards
James E. Roach
Wm. H. Roberts
J. F. Sailors, or Saylors
J. H. Sailors, or Saylors
Nimrod Sailors
John J. Sanders
James W. Satterfield
McKinney Seabolt
Abner B. Shipp
W. H. Shipp
John Spragin
John W. Stansell
John C. Stokes
Daniel G. Tate
John M. Tate
Riley J. Tate
Van Tate
John W. Thompson

James H. Keown
Wm. J. Keown
A. J. Kilpatrick
C. C. Kilpatrick
Elisha Kilpatrick
Leroy M. Lamb
—. —. Late
Wm. P. Lewis
Moses Terrell Maloney

Alexander Turner
Thomas J. Tweedle
J. M. Underwood
Wm. W. Underwood
W. T. Wade
D. J. Whitley
Philo W. Whitley
L. A. Winkler

MUSTER ROLL OF COMPANY "I," 60TH REGIMENT GA. VOL. INF., ARMY OF NORTHERN VIRGINIA, EVAN'S BRIGADE, GORDON'S DIV., C.S.A. WALKER COUNTY, GEORGIA.

B. F. Fariss, Captain.
Thomas Warthen, 1st Lieut.
J. C. Fariss, 2nd Lieut.
Wm. J. Martin, Jr. 2nd Lieut.
T. C. McSpadden, 1st Sergt.; Pro. Jr. 2nd Lieut.
Wm. Caughron, 2nd Sergt.
P. D. Mathis, 3rd Sergt.
Wm. Hawkins, 4th Sergt.
Wm. Lazenby, 5th Sergt.
G. W. Innman, 1st Corp.
J. F. Hill, 2nd Corp.
Thomas P. Veal, 3rd Corp.

PRIVATES.

L. M. Hawkins
L. P. Allen
M. S. Baker
J. D. Bentley
J. J. Boss
John Baldwin
E. R. Biles
James Bruce
James Bird
Harris Brigman
A. J. Brigman
W. B. Boss (Elec. 2 Lt.)
A. B. Black
E. C. Black (Elec. 2 Lt.)
Hantel Brigham
R. H. Caldwell
Calvin Culberson

Wylie Jenkins
R. T. Jennings
Griffin Keith
A. J. Kelly
James Lambert
Curtis Lazenby
T. P. Lansford
Joseph Morton
Robert Martin
Nathaniel McCullough
T. L. McCall
James McClain
J. M. McClure
E. R. Martin
John Patterson
J. P. Phipps
Jacob Pettyjohn

E. L. Culberson
  (Apt. Ord.-Sgt.)
A. S. Childress
James Coulter
Joseph E. Caldwell
F. M. Cloud
John Couch
Reuben Couch
R. A. Childress, Sr.
R. A. Childress, Jr.
M. O. Couch
R. H. Calhoun
L. W. Dunn
G. B. Ellenberg
T. L. Farnsworth
H. H. Goodwin
G. H. Garrett
W. F. Gillian
W. B. Hearn
J. C. Hearn
Jesse Hargroves
John Howell
A. R. Hill
R. F. Jones
Lewis Jones
Peter Jones
Samuel Jenkins

W. J. Pettyjohn
Ross Payne
Joseph Parker
E. Q. Pierce
Wm. Partain
J. R. Payne
T. A. K. Reed
Moses Ramey
Harvey Richardson
Samuel Saxon
C. W. Shipp
John T. Still
J. C. Smith
J. W. Stewart
Lawrence Shelly
A. G. Stevenson
Jasper Spier
Wm. Saxon
J. D. Thompson
C. C. Thompson
C. S. Tapp
T. E. Tapp
C. C. Tipton
Scott Vickery
John Weaver
J. C. Woods
W. T. Waides

DIARY OF A CONFEDERATE SOLDIER. The diary of W. H. McWhorter, which he kept during the War Between the States, is in possession of Mr. R. L. McWhorter, a relative, and is an interesting memento of those troublous times that tried men's souls. The first paragraph says:

"W. H. McWhorter left home Sept. 17, 1861, and on the night of the same day landed at Dalton, Ga., with Capt. J. C. Wardlaw's company, at which place he was mustered into the service of the Confederate States and put under command of Col. W. H. Stiles. The company named, with others, remained at the above named town till Oct. 2, when all repaired to Savannah, Ga., and drilled till Oct. 19, and then moved our rendezvous to Skidaway Isle."

Mr. McWhorter had charge of commissary supplies for his company and gives numerous notations of supplies consumed by the company for specified periods, one of which is as follows: "Oct. 24 to 31. 163 lbs bacon; 588 lbs flour; 300 lbs meal; 30 qts salt; 76 lbs rice; 45 lbs. coffee; 90 lbs sugar; 5½ lbs candles; 15 lbs soap; 3½ qts vinegar."

In three different places a roster of the company is given, names neatly written with pen and ink. The first roster follows:

"MUSTER ROLL OF THE WALKER INDEPENDANTS."

"Capt. J. C. Wardlaw; Lieut. M. Russell, E. Napier, and D. C. Myers; Serg. W. H. McWhorter, L. R. McWhorter, D. E. Hall, H. Maddux, W. A. Foster; Corp. G. B. Carroll, C. W. Taylor, W. K. Jones, J. W. Blackwell; Musician, J. D. Taylor; Privates: J. A. Alexander, C. P. Allen, James Arnold, Jacob Arnold, J. C. Atkins, John Atwood, J. H. Bird, P. J. Bird, Wm. Butler, G. W. Brewer, H. H. Carroll, Andrew Carson, J. N. Chastain, S. Caudell, M. Caudell, T. A. Cooper, C. C. Caudell, G. B. Collins, J. M. Cooper, J. H. Crutchfield, J. A. Denton, J. F. Dedman, W. F. Dunn, John Edge, C. M. Edwards, R. A. Ellis, G. W. Ellis, R. L. Farnsworth, J. W. Farnsworth, L. R. Fletcher, James Gillean, J. H. Gillean, A. Gillean, J. S. Gant, W. K. Gray, G. H. Hall, S. M. Hall, J. M. Hall, J. E. Hall, G. W. Hall, J. H. Hall, M. C. Harris, L. M. Hendon, T. B. Hendon, J. A. Hendon, Edward Jackson, D. J. Jackson, H. H. Jones, John Lambert, V. S. Lowery, Angus Lively, R. M. Lanier, W. P. Maddux, J. C. McDonald, T. C. McDaniel, J. E. McCutchen, A. E. McKinney, N. W. Moore, J. W. Mack, A. D. Murray, G. B. Myers, W. D. McWhorter, W. F. McWhorter, W. J. McClure, John Partin, S. S. Pendley, M. Pendley, Thomas Poe, Thomas Rutledge, J. H. Rutledge, Wm. Spraggins, W. C. Strickland, H. A. Serrett, C. W. Taylor, G. W. Tipton, B. F. Thurman, W. H. Tucker, H. H. Wilson, W. W. Wilson, G. K. Wilson, E. A. Ward, J. F. Wardlaw, J. A. Williams, W. K. Williams, H. H. Williams.

Then follow these names written with pencil and not arranged alphabetically: W. S. Hall, J. E. Lansford, J. H. Swift, G. W. Hall, Jun., J. A. Self, J. W. Kirkes, J. A. F. Williams, W. J. McCurder, J. A. Swift, W. H. Rutledge, J. B. Day, R. G. Calhoun, Rob Cooper, J. W. Rutherford, W. R. Pain, E. J. Myers, W. F. Hall, S. D. McClure, A. F. Pendley, Thomas Jackson, W. A. Hall, T. G. Howell, J. H. McWhorter, T. M. Day, James Day, G. W. Farnsworth.

Another interesting and unusual reminder of those days, found in this old diary of Mr. McWhorter, is an old envelope with a .Confederate stamp attached. The stamp carries the likeness of Jefferson Davis with the words "Postage Five Cents," and "Confederate States of America." The envelope is addressed to "Mr. A. B. McWhorter, Duck Creek, Geo." It has been cancelled with a rubber stamp the only words of which now legible is the word "PAID."

COMPANY I, FIRST GA. CAV.

J. F. Leak, Capt.
James Gilreath, 1st Lieut.
Abe Fuller, 2nd Lieut.
Wm. Edwards, 3rd Lieut.
Union Glasco, Orderly Sgt.
C. A. Neal, 2nd Sgt.

PRIVATES.

Green Burgess
Lem Dillard
Mark Edwards
John Fuller
Rance Griffin
John Hicks
John Hollis
Frank Hargas
Poss Hargas
Mark Irvin
Jim Jenkins
Bill Jenkins
Bill Johnson
Jim Kinman

James Kenady
John Mumford
Dr. Milan
A. H. Neal
G. W. Patterson
F. M. Patterson
Bill Puckett
Lee Reed
Sam Smith
Lang Smith
Wiley Venible
Bud Wafford
Jasper Warnock
Newton White

COMPANY I, 23RD INF.

John Burgess
W. P. Bomar
Newton Cleckler
Ben Chapman
Andy Coulter
Pink Chapman
Bob Davis
Harrison Davis
Tom Davis
James Eaton
W. B. Foster
William Foster
Ed Gasner
John Grigsby
Coleman Hewet
Richard Haslerig
James Headrick
Jack Huggins
Elisha Killpatrick

Columbus Killpatrick
John McClure
Rube McClure
F. A. McWilliams
Capt. R. B. Neal
Frank Neal
Sam Pilcher
W. L. Patterson
H. H. Patterson
John B. Patterson
John Stansell
Anson Tarvin
Alson Tarvin
Alvin Tarvin
Albert Tarvin
A. C. Ward
Jim Warnock
F. M. Young

COMPANY F, 1ST GA. CAV.

E. A. Bomar
B. F. Hunt
Bill Hunt
Bill McWilliams
E. D. McWilliams
J. P. Jackson

John Puryear
H. C. Puryear
H. Y. Puryear
Bill Puryear
J. T. Suttle

Chapter Twenty-three

CAMP CHICKAMAUGA—PENSION ROLLS—CONFEDERATE MONUMENT.
REVOLUTIONARY SOLDIERS—D. A. R. AND U. D. C. CHAPTERS.

NOTE—Soon after the Civil war the Confederate Veterans of the county organized Camp "Little," later changed to Camp "Chickamauga." This fraternal and patriotic organization has continued to the present, but is now very weak, only a few of the old soldiers of the sixties being left. During its existence of some sixty years most of the old soldiers of the county, who fought for the "Lost Cause," became members. Many of them, however, for various reasons failed to join the organization.

Out of a membership of more than 200 there are now scarcely a dozen left. The old register of members contains the following names giving such data as is appended.

Name	Rank	Co.	Regt.	Serv.	Name	Rank	Co.	Regt.	Serv.
A. R. Adams	Cor	E	8Ga	Bat	E. L. Culberson	Pri		60Ga	"
W. J. Adkins	Pri	D	1Con	Cav	E. C. Cordell	"	C	60Ga	"
John Agnew	"	B	9Ga	Inf	W. C. Cox	"	D	6Ala	"
Albert Allison	"	E	39Ga	"	E. C. Crawford	"	L	Tenn	"
W. F. Allison	Maj	A	3Ga	Cav	J. W. A. Campbell	"	E	3Con	Cav
T. J. Alsob'k	Lt	F	7Fla	Inf	B. L. Chastain	"	F	4Ga	"
M. C. Alexander	Pri	F	4Ga		G. W. Cothran	Sur		3Con	"
A. Arnold	"	H	23Ga	Inf	J. A. Clements	Sgt	I	1Ga	Trps
I. R. Andrews	"	F	Hill	Sts	A. J. Caldwell	"	C	"	"
T. B. Arnold	Sgt	K	4Ga	Cav	D. M. Carroll	Pri	F	34Ga	Inf
R. B. Bagwell	Pri	B	6Ga	Inf	B. F. Cole	"	B	37Tn	"
M. S. Baker	"	I	60Ga	"	W. G. Conley	"	D	1Ga	"
Elisha Baker	"	H	58NC	"	L. A. Conley	Cor		Sta	Tps
T. M. Ballard	"	H	43Tn		V. T. Cameron	Pri	F	39Tn	
A. A. Bearden	"	D	6Ga	Cav	T. H. Cameron	"	K	4Ga	Inf
T. Bean	"	H	8Ga	Inf	G. W. Carlock	"	K	4Ga	
F. A. Bell	Lt	F	23Ga	"	Robt. Daugh'y	"	K	3Ga	Inf
F. L. Bell	Pri	E	1Con	"	John R. Dorsey	"	F	4Ga	"
J. H. Bird	"	C	60Ga	"	H. L. Duncan	"	K	39Ga	"
J. N. Bird	"	K	39Ga	"	H. S. Davis	"	D	1Con	"
W. B. Bird	"	C	60Ga	"	J. L. Davis	"	H	23Ga	"
J. J. Boss	"	G	5Tn		John C. Devoti	"	C	2Ky	Cav
Wm. Bowen	"	D	60Ga	"	R. N. Dickerson	"	G	9Ga	Inf
Jerem'a Burns	Sgt	H	23Ga	"	T. M. Dunwoody	Sgt	H	1Tn	Cav
W. D. Bryan	Pri	C	1Ga	Cav	E. F. Dilbeck	Pri	I	52Ga	Inf
C. W. Brooks	"	C	9Ga		S. Enerage (?)	"	H	2Ga	"
John F. Bonds	"	I	60Ga	Inf	A. S. Evans	"	D	27Ga	"
J. F. Bryan	"	D	39Ga	"	C. W. Evitt	"	B	1Tn	"
S. A. Brice	"	K	39Ga	"	A. P. Ellison	Ens	F	16Ga	"
H. W. Boss	"	E	6Ga	Cav	John Edge	Lt	H	23Ga	Cav
J. L. Brotherton	"	I	Con	Inf	W. A. Ellis	Pri	E	2Ga	"
J. Bohannon	"	H	19Ga	"	A. J. Erwin	"	A	1Tn	"
A. L. Culberson	Lt	E	39Ga	"	T. A. Eubanks	Lt	K	4Ga	"

Name	Rank	Co.	Regt.	Serv.	Name	Rank	Co.	Regt.	Serv.
Wm. Faulkner	Pri	G	9Ga	Inf	W. Mullis	"	D	1Con	Inf
J. W. Fleming	Lt	Y	5Al	"	W. B. Moore	"	B	55Al	"
W. B. Foster	Ens	H	23Ga	"	L. W. Myers	"	H	26Tn	"
T. J. Foster	Lt	K	39Ga	"	W. W. S. Myers	"		Ind.	Co.
W. A. Foster	"	C	60Ga	"	T. J. Manly	"	E	2SC	Inf
A. J. Fielding	Sgt	D	1Ga	"	W. F. McWhorter	"	E	60Ga	"
Wm. Free	Pri	G	52Ga	"	L. A. McWhorter	Sgt	C	60Ga	"
D. M. Gutherie	"	E	3Ga	Cav	A. McBrayer	Pri	H	4Tn	Cav
W. B. Gutherie	"	E	8Ga	"	F. A. McWilliams	Sgt	G	11Ga	Inf
A. Gravely	"	F	1Ga	"	P. H. G. McGuffie	Pri	E	3Con	Cav
J. H. Hanalan (?)	"	H	4Ga	"	R. B. Neal	Cpt	H	23Ga	"
J. B. Hill	Lt	E	39Ga	Inf	R. P. Neal	Lt	C	39Ga	"
Wesley Hobbs	Pri	E	39Ga	"	N. C. Napier	Cpt	K	6Ga	Cav
J. M. Henderson	Ord	A	65Ga	"	S. P. O'Briant	Pri	H	4Ga	"
J. C. Hall	Pri	H	1Ga	Cav	F. M. Osborn	"	C	2Ky	Cav
J. J. Howell	"	K	42Ga	Inf	G. W. Newsome	Sgt	G	20Ga	Inf
T. C. Hackney	"	E	26NC	Inf	James Norten	Pri	K	21Ga	"
A. Hunter	"				J. A. Park	Lt	F	39Ga	"
J. J. Henning	"	A	35Tn	"	John Partain	Pri	C	60Ga	"
J. O. Hitchcock	"	D	20Ga	"	J. P. Phipps	"	I	41Ga	"
G. D. Hearn	Pri	D	1Con	Cav	J. L. Perryman	"	D	20Ga	"
James Horn	"	E	2Mo	Inf	Joseph Patrick	"	A	5Tn	"
E. N. Hagwood	"	F	55Al	"	James Ponder	"	E	6Ga	Cav
J. M. Henry	"	F	4Ga	Cav	G. W. Patterson	"	I	1Ga	"
J. J. Hilburn	"	F	34Ga	Inf	H. Y. Puryear	"	F	1Ga	"
Henry Hood	"	F	28Ga	"	H. C. Puryear	"	F	1Ga	"
W. T. Hill	"	D	24Ga	"	D. N. Pursley	Sgt	K	5Tn	"
J. L. Hood	"	H	6Ga	Cav	Richard Potter	Pri	K	5Tn	"
W. A. Horton	Sgt	K	43Ga	"	A. H. Peppers	"	C	2Ga	Bat
A. M. Higgins	Pri	H	2Ga	Inf	D. C. Payne	"	D	3Eng	
G. W. Innman	Sgt	I	60Ga	"	C. H. Roark	"	E	39Ga	Inf
D. C. Jackson	Pri	I	60Ga	"	D. A. Rice	"			Art
J. M. Jackson	Cpt	G	11Ga	"	Wm. Riley	"	C	1Ga	Cav
W. P. Jackson	Pri	G	6Ga	Cav	Robert Ramey	"	E	6Ga	"
Lewis Jones	"	K	60Ga	Pri	W. D. Rosser	"	E	6Ga	"
Peter Jones	"	I	60Ga	"	J. H. Rhinehart	"	B	50Al	Inf
T. N. Jones	"	D	1Con	"	T. M. Rowland	"	E	3Ga	Cav
J. J. Jones	Ord	H	6Ga	Cav	D. H. Styles	"	E	39Ga	Inf
J. D. Jay	Pri	C	60Ga	Inf	J. W. Stansell	"	H	23Ga	"
T. K. King	"	F	6Ga	Cav	A. F. Smith	"	F	39Ga	"
F. G. Little	"	H	39Ga	Pri	Hiram Smith	"	F	34Ga	"
J. T. Langley	"	B	16SC	"	J. W. Smith	Sgt	F	39Ga	"
A. Littlejohn	"	H	3Ga	Cav	P. H. Shankles				
A. T. Leslie	"				J. D. Strange	Pri	E	39Ga	"
Moses Long	"	E	39Ga	Inf	G. B. Stewart	"	C	4Ga	Cav
T. H. Liner	"	H	1Ga	"	R. F. Shaw	"	F	4Ga	"
A. J. Liner	"	H	43Tn	"	A. F. Shaw	"	F	4Ga	"
H. P. Lumpkin	"	G	9Ga	"	G. W. Shaw	"	A	3Con	"
B. F. Loughridge	"	I	3Con	Cav	J. M. Shaw	"	I	1Con	Inf
J. M. Leming	"	B	21Ga	Pri	J. E. Shaw	"	G	9Ga	"
E. M. Limmons	Sgt	H	37Tn	"	John Shaw	"	K	21Ga	"
John Ledbetter	Pri		18Al	"	D. D. Singletry	"	K	6Ga	Cav
W. R. Lindsay	"	B	9Ga	"	A. R. Steele	"		Aux	Bat
J. J. Morgan	"	E	39Ga	"	F. H. Sims	"	H	1Ga	
J. H. Miller	"	E	39Ga	"	J. T. Suttle	Pri	F	1Ga	Cav
J. C. Martin	"	C	1Ga	"	W. P. Tate	Ord	A	4Ga	"
Robt. Martin	Sgt		1Ga	Trp	E. M. Tate	Pri	K	39Ga	Inf

Name	Rank	Co.	Regt.	Serv.	Name	Rank	Co.	Regt.	Serv.
J. S. Murphree	Pri	C	8Ga	Bat	J. W. Thompson	"	C	46Ga	"
W. H. Talley	"	F	8Ga	"	G. J. Wilson	"	C	18SC	"
John Taylor	"				James Weaver	"	E	59Tn	"
D. D. Thomas	"			Art.	Jesse Williams	"	B	9Ga	"
H. L. Tatum	"	F	34Ga	Inf	J. H. Webb	"	G	14NC	Cav
F. A. C. Thedford	"	H	4Ga	Art	W. M. Wheeler	"	F	3Ga	
B. F. Thurman	"	C	60Ga	Inf	S. A. Withers	"			
A. Underwood	"	B	21Ga	"	S. A. West	"	K	56Ga	Inf
John Y. Wood	Cpt	G	11Ga	"	J. B. Watts	Sgt	B	6Ga	Cav
J. A. Woods	Pri	F	4Ga	Cav	R. M. Ward	Pri	G	18Ga	Inf
Jesse Wallin	"	E	39Ga	Inf	L. H. Wheeler				
W. A. Weaver	Lt	K	39Ga	"	H. C. Weaver	"	D	4Ga	"
M. A. Ware	Pri	E	39Ga	"	W. D. Winston	"	A	4Al	Cav
J. C. Wardlaw	Cpt	C	60Ga	"	G. W. Wimpee	"	G	1Ga	
J. J. Wallraven	Sgt	K	60Ga	"	C. C. Wheeler				
J. A. F. Williams	Pri	C	60Ga	Inf	F. M. Young	Cpt	H	23Ga	Inf

The following roster of names of Confederate veterans with other data attached is taken from the Pension Rolls in the Ordinary's office:

(Note: These old Pension Rolls are greatly worn and are rapidly falling to pieces. Unless something is done to preserve them, they will soon be gone. It is suggested that the county, or more properly, perhaps, some patriotic organization take the matter in hand and see that they are carefully preserved. With what devotion we examine and care for records of Revolutionary soldiers, and who knows but that our posterity will feel similarly about the records of Confederate soldiers. It is only a matter of sentiment, but one that greatly appeals to our patriotism.)

Name	Co.	Regt.	Cause for Pen.	When Enlisted	Died
John Agnew	B	9Ga	Leg Disabled	1862	1900
A. A. Bearden	D	6Ga	Lost Eye		1921
James Burke	B	60Ga	Arm Disabled	1862	
Jeremiah Burns	H	23Ga	Foot Disabled		
J. D. Catlett	G	16Ga	Lost Left Arm	1862	
J. B. Day	C	16Ga	Arm Disabled	1862	
Robert Daugherty	K	3Ga	Lost Arm	1864	
A. P. Ellison	F	16Ga	Lost Arm	1862	
Samuel Ezell	B	6Ga	Body Injury	1863	
Wm. Faulkner	G	9Vol	Lost Leg	1862	
W. B. Foster	H	23Ga	Lost Eye	1862	
W. A. Foster					
J. B. Hill	E	39Ga	Lost Leg	1864	
C. R. Hood	E	6Ga	Invalid	1865	
G. W. Innman	I	60Ga	Lost Arm	1863	
Peter Jones	I	60Ga	Body-Arm Inj.		1931
Lewis Jones	I	60Ga	Wounded	1864	
R. R. Johnson	B	45Ga	Lost Hand	1862	
D. C. Jackson	C	60Ga	Lost Both Eyes	1862	
J. N. King	B	39Ga	Lost 2 Toes	1863	
W. R. Lindsay	B	9Ga	Wounds	1864	
J. A. Lewallen	D	1Con	Lost Right Arm	1863	

Name	Co.	Regmt.	Cause	Date	Died
J. L. Neal	B	9Ga	Left Arm Dis.	1864	
W. S. Owings	E	3Ga	Leg Wound	1862	1914
M. G. O'Bryant	F	2SC	Foot-Leg Wound	1863	
G. W. Patterson	I	1Ga	Body Wound	1864	
J. A. Park, Sr.	F	39Ga	Lost Hand	1864	
J. L. Perryman	D	20Ga	Lost Leg	1863	
C. W. Richster	D	3Ga	Arm Disabled	1863	
J. A. Smith	I	35Ga	Hand Disabled	1862	
G. W. Smith	K	21Ga	Lost Arm	1862	1915
D. H. Styles	E	39Ga	Lost Toe	1862	1914
A. F. Shaw	F	4Ga	Arm Disabled		
Wm. M. Underwood	G	19Ga	Body Wound		1909
S. Venable	A	8Ga	Leg Disabled	1864	1912
H. C. Weaver	D	4Ga	Lost Eye	1862	1900
Jesse Williams	B	9Ga	Leg Disabled	1864	1905
N. C. Napier	K	6Cav	Lost Eye	1862	

Indigent Soldiers' Pension Roll.

Name	Co.	Regmt.	Enlisted	Cause of Pen.	When Dis.	Died
J. J. Adcock	H	23Ga	1861	Age, Inf., Pov.	1864	1900
E. Q. Atkins	B	9Ga	1862	Indigent		
Francis Bean	H	8Ga	1861	Inf., Pov.		1910
M. V. Burns	G	6Cav		Inf., Pov.		1914
C. W. Brooks	C	9Ga	1861	Age-Inf.-Pov.	1865	1905
J. Burrows	E	3Ga	1861	Age-Inf.-Pov.	1865	1905
J. M. Bird	E	3Cav		Inf.-Pov.		
W. H. Buchannon		5Ala	1861	Indigent		1910
Thos. M. Blair	B	39Ga	1862	Age-Pov.	1865	1915
Wm. F. Brown	E	39Ga	1862	Age-Pov.	1865	
J. B. Childs	H		1864	Age-Pov.	1865	
G. W. Couch	I	19Ala	1861	Age-Pov.		1912
W. F. Cromer	H	48Ala	1862	Body Inj.	1862	
Reuben Couch	I	60Ga	1862	Age-Pov.	1865	
H. L. Cambron	A	1Ga	1861	Age, Pov.	1865	1909
V. T. Cameron	F	38Ten	1861	Inf., Pov.	1864	
Daniel Cagle	B	9Ga	1862	Indigent		1916
Wm. Denton	K	1Con	1863	Inf.-Pov.	1865	
H. A. Dorsey				Age, Inf., Pov.	1865	
H. S. Davis	D	1Con	1861	Age-Pov.		1910
J. C. Dyer			1862	Age-Pov.-Inf.		
R. P. Daniel	K	23Ga		Age-Pov.-Inf.		
B. F. Ellsberry	I	4Ga		Age-Pov.		1914
S. H. Frazier	B	11Ga		Pov.-Inf.		
W. A. Goza	C	12Ga		Age-Pov.-Inf.	1865	1908
G. W. Gentry	C	11Ga	1861	Age-Pov.-Inf.	1865	1914
Alonzo Hamilton	K	39Ga		Indigent		
G. M. Higgins	H	2Ga	1862	Age-Pov.	1865	
Wesley Hobbs	E	39Ga	1862	Inf.-Pov.	1863	1914
E. Hamilton	E	3Ga		Age-Pov.		1914
J. E. Howell	G	36Ga		Inf.-Pov.		1905
Henry Hood	F	28Ga				1916
B. J. Huggins	G	11Ga	1861	Infirmity		
Jack Harris	B	1Ga	1861	Pov.		1915
J. M. Ivey	A	1Ga		Inf.-Pov.	1865	1914
W. H. Jackson	C	63Ga	1862	Age-Inf.-Pov.	1865	1914
J. H. Jones	F		1862	Age-Inf.-Pov.	1865	1914

HISTORY OF WALKER COUNTY, GEORGIA 153

Name	Co.	Regmt.	Enlisted	Cause of Pen.	When Dis.	Died
W. H. Johnson	G	1Ga	1862	Age-Inf.-Pov.		
J. Robert Jones	G	18Ga		Indigent		1910
J. N. King	B	26Ga	1862	Age-Inf.-Pov.	1865	1915
Joel M. Knight	C	8Ga	1862	Age-Inf.-Pov.	1865	1910
Wm. Lazenby	I	60Ga	1862	Age-Inf.-Pov.	1865	
A. Littlejohn	H	3Ga	1862	Age-Inf.-Pov.	1865	1914
John T. Lockwood	A	10Ga	1862	Age-Pov.-Bld.	1865	1914
T. J. Manly	E	2SC		Age-Pov.		1913
W. M. McGregor	H	19Ga		Breast Com.		
T. J. Moreland						
J. S. Murphy	C	8Ga	1862	Inf.-Pov.		1903
H. G. Moore	G	9Ga	1862	Age-Pov.		
P. F. Miller	H	Vol	1864	Indigent	1865	
Henry Moreland	H			Indigent		
John McClaim				Indigent		
A. H. Peppers	C	2Ga	1862	Age-Pov.	1865	1915
Thomas Pilcher	H	23Ga				1912
Newton Powell	E	3Ga	1862	Age-Pov.	1865	1910
W. M. Potts	C	24Ga				
D. A. Rice		Bat	1861	Age-Inf.-Pov.	1865	
V. M. Reed	H	23Ga	1861	Inf.-Pov.	1865	
Wm. Riley	C	1Ga	1862	Age-Inf.-Pov.	1865	1915
R. M. Smith	D	1Con	1862	Age-Inf.-Pov.	1865	1910
W. M. Strickland	E	Cav	1863	Inf.	1865	
J. W. Stansell	H	23Ga	1861	Age-Inf.-Pov.	1865	
E. M. Tate	K	39Ga	1861	Age-Pov.-Blind	1865	1916
W. P. Tate	A	4Ga	1862	Age-Pov.-Inf.		1914
Van Tate	H	23Ga	1861	Age-Pov.-Inf.	1865	1915
J. M. Travillian	A	1Ten	1861	Age-Pov.	1865	
Thos. L. Tapp	I	16Ga	1862	Age-Pov.		
J. W. Thompson	H	23Ga	1861	Age-Pov.	1865	
J. C. Varner	G	19Ala	1861	Pov.-Inf.	1865	
Wiley Wall	D	12Ga	1862	Pov.-Inf.	1865	1913
G. W. Wimpee	G	1Ga	1862	Age-Pov.-Inf.	1865	1904
P. G. White	G	1Ga	1862	Age-Inf.-Pov.	1865	1912
W. D. Winston	I	4Ala	1863	Age-Pov.	1865	1910
B. F. Wells	F	39Ga	1862	Age-Pov.	1865	1914
T. J. Willis	I	39Ga	1861	Indigent	1865	1912
J. F. Wardlaw	C	60Ga	1861	Indigent		

APPROVED PENSION ROLL (Under Acts of 1910).

Name	Co.	Regt.	Died	Name	Co.	Regt.	Died
T. B. Arnold	K	4Ga		Wade Kirklin	B	35Ga	1917
A. Arnold*	H	23Ga		W. B. Morrow	C	33Ala	
J. W. Bolt	E	CSCav	1920	J. H. Miller	E	39Ga	
A. M. Borders	H	24Ga	1916	W. W. S. Myers*	K	4Ga	1921
H. W. Boss	E	39Ga	1924	Robert Martin	C	1Ga	1923
M. D. Bryan	C	1Ga		L. M. McWhorter	A	35Ga	
C. C. Bryan	D	9Ga	1923	W. S. Nelson	F	10Ga	
F. L. Bell	F		1921	T. P. Norman	C	40Ga	
J. T. Chafin	E	9Ga	1918	Lowery Partain	C	33Ala	
E. C. Cordell	C	60Ga	1916	David Payne	C	3Con	1917
Andrew H. Coulter	H	23Ga		J. M. Roper	F	8Ga	
A. J. Caldwell	C	1Ga	1931	J. D. Strange	E	39Ga	1922
E. L. Culberson*	I	6Ga		J. T. Suttle*	E	1Ga	

J. M. Clarkson	E	39Ga		N. D. Smith	K	35Ten	1923
W. M. Dyer		1Ark	1924	E. N. Wagnon	A		1923
J. J. Dyer	C	2Ky		J. B. Watts	B	6Ga	1917
J. B. Day	C	60Ga	1924	J. H. White	C	23Ga	1924
J. A. Eaton	C	23Ga	1920	A. D. Wilson*	F	1Ga	-
T. M. Hensley	G	17Tn	1931	G. H. Westbrooks	A	8Ga	1922
Wm. A. Hartswell	G	59Tn		W. A. Weaver	K	39Ga	1917
T. H. Helton	K	1Ga	Age	J. H. Webb	G	14NC	
J. B. Henderson*	D	1Con	1931	W. F. M. Wall*	K	2Ga	1922
J. M. Jackson	G	1Ga	1920	J. A. F. Williams*	C	60Ga	
W. P. Jackson	E	1Ga					

*Service

1861 — 1865

Erected 1909 By the Chickamauga Chapter of the United Daughters of the Confederacy,

To the Confederate Soldiers of Walker County.

"It is a Duty We Owe to Posterity, to See that Our Children Shall Know the Virtues and Become Worthy of Their Sires."

"TO OUR CONFEDERATE SOLDIERS."

"Centuries on Centuries Shall Go Circling By, But They Are Not Dead, Their Memories Can Never Die."
"To those who were and to those that are."
"Many of whom gave all, and all of whom gave much."

(Inscriptions on the Confederate Monument in the LaFayette City Park.)

Unveiling the Confederate Monument at LaFayette.

"The 27th of April, 1909, was an eventful and happy day to the Confederate women of LaFayette. Despite the drizzling rain throughout the morning, that interfered with the memorial day plans, three thousand people gathered to witness the unveiling of the monument and give proof of their love for the soldiers who wore the gray. Work was suspended in the stores, offices, shops and factories and the trains brought in many veterans and visitors. The platform, the court house, all of the business houses and from the humblest cart to the handsomest automobile were resplendent with Confederate flags and bunting. Many private residences were decorated in honor of the occasion. The address of Col. George M. Napier, of Monroe, was a beautiful and inspiring oration. Col. Napier paid a beautiful tribute to the Confederate soldiers; he said, 'That there was no counterpart in history of the constancy and devotion, genuine chivalric sentiment and unflinching courage exhibited by him in war, and the still prouder record of the trying days of reconstruction.'

"After the address, Mrs. Margaret Moore Patton, President of the U. D. C. local chapter, presented the monument to the veterans of the county. In the name of Camp Chickamauga Veterans, the Honorable B. F. Thurman accepted the splendid gift; after which four children, viz., Helen Bale, Margaret Patton, Robert Steele and Robert Glenn, pulled the cords that unveiled the monument revealing the statue of pure Carrara marble, amid the cheering of the crowd."

The Confederate Mounment.

(Greeting "To the Confederate Statue on Court House Square, Charlottesville, Va.," composed by Mr. W. Sam Burnley, was read by the author at the unveiling in May, 1909).

> It is pleasing to see you, brave comrade, up there,
> Picketed here on the old Courthouse Square.
> Your companions here gathered in the dark days of yore
> And nobly went forth to fight and endure—
> Went forth for the State Rights, went forth for the South,
> And undaunted they charged to the cannon's grim mouth.
>
> Yes, when we weigh and consider, we must all declare
> 'Twas proper to place you on the old Courthouse Square,
> For 'twas here that you came at war's first alarms;
> You volunteered here at the first call to arms.
> Here shall you stand while the years wing their flight,
> The Defender of Home and the Champion of Right.
>
> When the rumors of trouble came borne on each breeze,
> Here met the fathers, here under the trees.
> They met here to ponder, to counsel, debate,

O'er the God-given rights that belong to each State;
And 'twas human, 'twas righteous, that anger arose
When our rights were invaded by merciless foes.

You were fashioned by Yankees (thrice happy the thought);
They clothed you in bronze, and well have they wrought—
In the dread days of conflict you taught them to "feel"
By daring and doing and the thrust of your steel.
Though fashioned by Yankees, the work was well done;
You inspired the chosen by the glories you won.

Your designer, God bless him, it behoves us to say,
Loves and reveres the old soldier in gray;
For his father was one, old comrade like you,
Who fought for the cause so noble and true,
And for you and for him we exultingly raise
Our voices reverberant in sounding your praise.

And do you know it, old fellow, your presence up there
Is due to our women so brave and so fair?
Though human, they seem to us beings supernal;
Their infinite love makes remembrance eternal—
Those creatures of goodness, those angels of light,
Who nursed you in sickness, who nerved you in fight.

A health to you, comrade, a wreath to your brow;
You stood by us then, we'll stand by you now.
Your cause will aye live in song and in story,
Sublime in its sadness, immortal in glory.

REVOLUTIONARY SOLDIERS.

The Revolutionary War occupied a space of seven years, or from 1776 to 1783. Exactly 50 years after peace was declared Walker county was erected. Most of the soldiers who took part in that famous conflict had passed away before the county had its birth. Hence it happens that very few of the old soldiers ever lived in the county.

The important action of Colonel Montgomery and Colonel Evans against the Chickamauga Indians on the Chickamauga Creek, as discussed elsewhere, was partly in the county, so that although there were few of the old soldiers who ever lived in the county, it is rich in Revolutionary history. There can be small doubt that all that little army of 1000 patriots fought within the boundary of our county and bivouaced therein. The battle of King's Mountain went down in history as one of the great and decisive battles of that famous struggle, and justly so. The battle with the Chickamaugas should be classed second only to that of King's Mountain, because of its far-reaching results, or other possible contingencies.

So far as this chronicler has been able to ascertain the following Revolutionary soldiers once lived in Walker county: William Fariss, buried at LaFayette; William White, buried at the White cemetery; Robert Story was living in the county in 1840; Isaac B. Nichols, an indigent revolutionary soldier, was living in the county in 1849; Edward Jackson, a Revolutionary soldier, died in 1845 near Waterville and was buried near Trion, Ga.; Samuel Careathers, soldier of the Revolution, spent his last days in Walker county; David Heffner, said to be a revolutionary soldier, died in East Armuchee Valley at the age of 113.

SOLDIERS OF 1812. Robert Anderson, buried at the Anderson family plot in the Cove; George W. Reed, buried at Thurman grave yard in the Cove; Wm. Davis, and Robert Shields, buried at Peavine. There are probably others.

INDIAN WAR. William P. Hixon, Capt. Rabun's Co., Ga. Mil., Creek War.

DAUGHTERS OF THE AMERICAN REVOLUTION.

The William Marsh Chapter, Daughters of the American Revolution, was organized on April 12, 1911, at the home of Mrs. J. F. Wardlaw, who had been appointed Regent by the National Society, and the name William Marsh was chosen for the Chapter. The charter members, all of whom had been favorably passed on by the National Board, were as follows:

Mesdames J. F. Wardlaw, J. E. Patton, N. C. Napier, John W. Bale, D. W. Stiles, Clara Warthen Glenn, Mary March Sparks, Eddie Warthen Enloe, I. H. Holleman, P. D. Wright, John Cleghorn; Misses Mamie and Sara Hackney, Louise Shouford, and Nannie Warthen.

Since its organization the Chapter has been active in educational, patriotic and civic work. A rest room was maintained for a number of years near the center of the city, which was a boon and great convenience to strangers visiting or passing through the city, as well as to home people. In 1924 the D. A. R. Chapter co-operated with the Chickamauga Chapter, U. D. C., and LaFayette Women's Club in repairing the old brick academy, which had been given to these organizations and which was converted into a club room. A marker was placed at Fort Cummings in 1915, and one at the John Ross home at Rossville, in 1922. The Chapter owns a valuable lot in the best business section of LaFayette.

The following are the names of the Regents of the Chapter since its organization: Mrs. J. F. Wardlaw, Miss Sara Hackney, Mrs. P. D. Wright, Mrs. J. E. Patten, Mrs. A. R. Fortune, Mrs. W. A. Enloe, Mrs. I. H. Holleman, and Mrs. Tom W. Lee.

The present officers are: Regent, Mrs. Tom W. Lee; Vice-Regent, Miss Sara Hackney; Recording Secretary, Mrs. R. S. Wheeler; Treasurer, Mrs. J. W. Massey; Corresponding Secretary, Miss Clarintine Knox;

Historian, Mrs. D. W. Stiles; Registrar, Mrs. I. H. Holleman; Chaplain, Mrs. Caroline Arnold; Press Reporter, Miss Nannie Warthen.

CHICKAMAUGA CHAPTER, U. D. C.

On April 26, 1900, the ladies of LaFayette organized a Chapter of the United Daughters of the Confederacy. There were twenty-three ladies in the organization and much enthusiasm prevailed for a time, but gradually the interest lagged and the Chapter was disbanded for two years. In August, 1906, it was reorganized with the following members:

JOHN B. GORDON HALL

where the General attended school as a lad. This hall is now |the prized property of the D. A. R. and U. D. C. organizations of LaFayette. It is one of the historic places of the city.

Mrs. Isabelle Hix Arnold, Mrs. Adele Latimer Bale, Mrs. Armuchee Rosser Deck, Mrs. Eddie Warthen Enloe, Mrs. Lizzie Steele Fortune, Mrs. Clara Warthen Glenn, Mrs. Eula Fortune Hunt, Mrs. Mary Marsh Hackney, Miss Sara Hackney, Miss Mamie Hackney, Mrs. Susie Holland Herndon, Mrs. Addie Hackney Myers, Mrs. Margaret Moore Patton, Miss Emma Pickle, Mrs. Nannie Pursley, Mrs. Mary Warthen Sparks, Mrs. Jewel Foster Stewart, Miss Jennie Lorain Swan, Miss Nannie Warthen, Mrs. Endora Alexander Wright, Mrs. Belle Steele Jackson, Mrs. Laura

Anderson Jackson. Since the organization many other members have been added to the roll.

With this increased membership new energy and fresh zeal were aroused and the membership vied with each other in making many records and improvements of a historical nature. In January, 1907, the order was given for the monument that adorns the public square, and is a pride and joy to every daughter's heart. This beautiful monument of pure Carara marble was unveiled on the 27th of April, 1909. Its cost was $1,633.00.

In 1924 the U. D. C. co-operated with William Marsh Chapter D. A. R. and the LaFayette Woman's Club in repairing the old brick academy, which had been given to these organizations, and which was named John B. Gordon Hall. It is a meeting place for the Chapter. The Chapter has ever been busy in educational, historic and patriotic work and in caring for the veterans of the sixties.

The present officers are: President, Mrs. J. L. Hammond; Vice-President, Mrs. E. P. Hall, Jr.; Recording Secretary, Miss Mamie Hackney; Corresponding Secretary, Mrs. W. A. Wardlaw; Treasurer, Mrs. M. C. Ballard; Registrar, Mrs. O. W. Bledsoe; Historian, Miss Sara Hackney; Press Reporter, Mrs. J. L. Rowland.

The following are the names of the presidents since the organization: Mrs. P. D. Fortune, Mrs. J. E. Patton, Mrs. John W. Bale, Mrs. E. A. Jackson, Mrs. D. W. Stiles, Mrs. J. A. Shaw, Mrs. W. H. F. Rhyne, Mrs. A. R. Fortune, Mrs. I. H. Holleman, Mrs. R. S. Steele, Mrs. J. L. Hammond, Mrs. E. A. Leonard, Mrs. J. L. Hammond.

Chapter Twenty-four

SCHOOLS.

Poor School Fund—Other Schools—Earliest School Records—Current School History, 1931.

POOR SCHOOL FUND. Recognizing in the interest of its own security and safety, the necessity of an enlightened franchise, the state of Georgia, early in its existence, laid plans for the education of the masses of the people. There was more anxiety about the vote of the illiterate than of those enlightened. This is true among all nations and peoples. A government to be stable must be composed of, and supported by an educated, enlightened and prosperous people.

As an example of this it is only necessary to mention our own nation. The large majority of our people are educated. Provision was wisely made by the founders of the government for schools. Every state saw this vital necessity and made plans for its operation. In consequence of this ours is perhaps the most stable government on the earth to-day. We have no periodic convulsions and revolutions such as are common to the south of us where the franchise is largely uneducated. Our government is responsive to the wish of the people expressed at the polls. No presidential administration has had the hardihood to undertake, by force, to perpetuate itself in office as is sometimes done by some of the Latin-American rulers. All this is largely attributable to public sentiment and the enlightenment of our educated citizenship. Great Britain is another example of a nation noted for its stability because of the education of the masses. Many other European nations may also be put in this class.

On the other hand many weak nations may be cited as examples of unstability because of the uneducated condition prevailing among the people. Mexico, our nearest neighbor to the south, is one such. I have not the figures at hand but a very large percentum of the people of that country are illiterate, perhaps a majority. Being uneducated and ignorant they are susceptible to any false reasoning and may be swayed at the will and pleasure of any scheming demagogue who is anxious to become president of the republic. This is true of many other nations of Central and South America. Some European nations, also, are weak because of the illiterate condition of the masses,—nations like Spain and some others. The most out-standing example of this is the great Chinese nation. Here the people are illiterate to the extreme. Very few, comparatively, are able to read and write the language. From time immemorial they have merely existed, living in squalor and ignorance with no adherence, no vision, no hope, China with perhaps a quarter of the inhabitants of the globe, lies like a vast beast shorn of its power, bound by iron bands, unable to rise in her might and assert her strength and all because of her ignorance.

From the founding of the Colony by Oglethorpe in 1733 it was the custom of those able to do so to educate their children at home and when they had reached the proper age they were sent to some of the old established institutions of learning in other colonies, or, perhaps as often, sent abroad to finish their education. This custom continued till long after the revolution. The founders of the commonwealth were not especially concerned about this class of citizens because they were able to take care of themselves, so to speak. But there was another class that caused much anxiety. This was the poor people who were not able to have their children educated, and perhaps did not realize the importance of an education. Knowing the great danger attached to the suffrage of the illiterate, the builders of the commonwealth laid plans for the education of the poor children. This plan found its expression in what was called Poor Schools.

Provision was made for the operation of poor schools in Walker as in all other counties. These schools were just what the name implies. They were for children whose parents were unable to employ a teacher to instruct them, and who, otherwise, would grow up as illiterates, and thus become, possibly, a menace to society and free government. The children of well-to-do people of the county were not supposed to attend these poor schools. They attended other schools where the teacher was paid a salary by their parents. These poor schools were not popular because of the name as well as for other reasons. Only the weakest teachers could be secured for them and these were very poorly paid. These teachers were required to make an annual report during the month of December after which they were paid their meager salary for the year, *as soon as the funds were available.* I am not informed as to when the poor schools were abandoned, but it was probably soon after the Civil war. The schools of Walker county, then, for probably a half-century were operated under the head of Poor Schools. Little record of the operation of these schools is extant to-day. All records were destroyed in the burning of the Court House. The names of some of the teachers who taught these schools are given further in this discussion.

The original document from which the following is taken is on file in the office of the Secretary of State in Atlanta:

-Poor School Fund 1841:
    Received from Executive Department $398.20
    From S. Marsh, former Senator 40.00
                                                                                  $438.20

Disbursements:
    Paid accounts of teachers of Poor Schools for
        1837, 1838, 1839 and 1840 .... $416.29
    Commissions returned for distributing 21.91
                                                                         $438.20

                (Signed)   R. M. Aycock, Sec.-Tr.

It is seen from the above that the poor school fund for the four years mentioned was $104.07 for each year to be used in paying teachers. Remember, too, that our county at that time was perhaps a third larger than at present.

An original school report on file in the State Department gives the number of school children in the county as 857 for the year 1847. This report is signed by three justices of the Inferior Court, viz.: Daniel Gartman, John Catlett, A. L. Barry. Another report (1861) gives the number of school children in the county as 2343, showing how fast the county was being populated at that time.

Still another old report on file says the Ordinary was ordered by the Inferior Court in 1859 to lay off the county into school districts and to call an election in each district for the purpose of electing school trustees. This was done under a state law governing this proceeding. It appears, therefore, that school trustees as pertains to our county, as well as school districts date from 1859. There seems to have been no county school commissioner at thât time.

OTHER SCHOOLS. In addition to Poor Schools the state also encouraged to some extent academic education or high schools. Almost every county in the state had an academy supported partly by the state. Two such schools were located at LaFayette, one for boys and one for girls. The Legislature of 1835 appropriated $815 for the building of an academy for Walker county. This was built at LaFayette. The school for boys was later operated in the old brick academy later known as the John B. Gordon Hall, from the fact of General Gordon attending school there some years prior to the Civil war.

The following is one among the oldest official documents the author has been fortunate enough to bring to light. This was discovered in the office of the Secretary of State:

"To His Excellency, The Governor:

'The annexed is a correct report of Pleasant Green Academy for the year 1837:

Spelling and Reading	19
Gram., Geo., Philosophy	18
Ancient Languages	6
	43

(Signed)　　James Gambel, Rector.

"This Academy was incorporated 1836. This is our first report. The school has been in existence since May 1836. No funds have as yet been received. There is another Academy in this county, the trustees of which received the special appropriation made to the new counties.

(Signed)　　John T. Story
　　　　　　　John Lamar
　　　　　　　Robert McCaw
　　　　　　　Robert Bayle

"This is a duplicate of a report to the Governor and to the Senatus Academicus at the sessions of the year 1837.

"Aug. 10, 1938."

The Female Academy stood near the present high school building and was destroyed by Federal soldiers during the war. We sometimes think of our ancestors as infallible. We rather take a pride in so considering them. And taken altogether, they probably come nearer to infallibility than many of their descendants—we for instance. But according to our modern way of thinking the idea of educating the sexes in separate schools is erroneous. Why two school houses and two faculties when one of each may serve the same purpose? Aside from this pecuniary advantage it is considered highly proper in our day for the sexes to attend school together, as tending to promote respect, manners and civility among all parties.

For perhaps a score of years before the war LaFayette boasted one of the best schools in all Northwest Georgia. Happily the town was able to attract some of the best teachers of that day. The Rev. Mr. Gamble, a Presbyterian minister, at one time, and at another the Baker Brothers —John W. and Richard—also Presbyterian ministers, had charge of the educational interests of the town. Also, Rev. Mr. Seals, who later became a Methodist minister, was for a time in charge of the schools of the town. All these teachers and others gave their best service to the training of the youth of that day. Many young men and women from different parts of the county as well as from other counties were attracted to LaFayette because of superior educational opportunities. Thus it was that John B. Gordon, who afterward earned a national reputation, and whose home was then at Gordon Springs, Walker county, now Whitfield county, was drawn to the town to attend the schools taught by these grand old master teachers. Many of the older citizens of the town, now octogenarians, are wont, even yet, when in reminiscent mood, to refer to the days when LaFayette enjoyed the reputation of being the seat of learning of all Northwest Georgia. White's Historical Collections, published in 1853, refers to the fact that good schools were maintained and supported at LaFayette. Others of the old histories make mention of the educational advantages to be had at that place.

In addition to these two branches of education—the poor schools and academic—the state also fostered higher education. The University of Georgia drew its patronage from all parts of the state, as well as from other states, and Walker county was represented there in those early times by such men as John Puryear who graduated from that institution in 1841, and at the time of his death was the oldest living member of the alumni. Later Captain John Y. Wood received his degree at that seat of learning, returning to his native county where he was teaching when the war opened and in which he promptly enlisted.

EARLIEST SCHOOL RECORDS.

The earliest school records of Walker county are those on file in the office of the State School Superintendent, and I am indebted to County School Commissioner Love for his assistance in securing these records. In the report of State School Commissioner J. R. Lewis, for 1871, the following data is given for Walker county:

No. Sub-dist. 13; No. Sch. Houses: Wh. 34, Col. 3.
No. mixed ungraded sch: Wh. 31, Col. 4, Tot. 35.
Aver. No. das. sch. was operated: Wh. 17, Col. 15.
No. Teachers white sch: Male 25, Female 6, Tot. 31.
No. Teachers col. sch: M. Wh. 1, Col. 2, Tot. 3.
Fem. Wh. 0, Col. 1. Total, M. 3, Fem. 1, Tot. 4.
Av. No. mos. taught by Males: 7/8, Fem. 3/4.
Av. sal. per mo. Males, Wh. $39.25, Col. $33.33.

Av. sal. per mo. Fem. Wh. $35.83, Col. $33.57.

No chdn. 6 to 21: M. Wh. 1412, Col. 252, Tot. 1664.
Fem. Wh. 1357, Col. 228, Tot. 1585.
Total Males, 1664, Females 1585, Grand Tot. 3249.

Whole number pupils in all common schools.
M. Wh. 689, Col. 77, Tot. 763. Fem. Wh. 669, Col. 76, Tot. 745.
Total male 763,, Total Fem. 745, Grand Tot. 1508.

Av. atten. M. Wh. 586, Col. 60, Tot. 646.
Av. atten. Fem. Wh. 518, Col. 68, Tot. 586. Gr. Tot. 1232.
Av. age, Wh. 14, Col. 14.
No. over 16 yrs.: Wh. 365, Col. 16. Tot. 381.

Subjects taught:
No. in Alphabet: Wh. 365, Col. 15, Tot. 381.
No. in Spelling: Wh. 809, Col. 91, Tot. 900.
No. in Reading: Wh. 626, Col. 45, Tot. 671.
No. in Writing: Wh. 614, Col. 39, Tot. 653.
No. Written Arith: Wh. 193, Col. 15, Tot. 208.
No. Mental Arith: Wh. 506, Col. 10, Tot. 516.
No. in Geography: Wh. 289, Col. 3, Tot. 292.
No. in Eng. Grammar: Wh. 421, Col. 8, Tot. 429.
No. in Higher Branches: Wh. 98, Col. 0, Tot. 98.

Private Schools.
No. Priv. sch., Wh. 19, Col. 0, Tot. 19.
No. Priv. sch. teachers, Wh. M. 16, Fem. 3, Tot. 19.
No. Pupils in Priv. sch.: M. 395, Fem. 423, Tot. 818.
Av. months private schools in session, 5.
Av. cost of tuition per month in priv. sch. $1.33.

Official Duties of C. S. Commissioner:
 (a) Examination of teachers:
  Applicants, M. 31, Fem. 7, Tot. 38, Rejected 2.
 (b) School Visitation:
  No. visited, 1. No. visited more than once, 1.
  No. not visited 25. No. hrs. spent in each, 1.
 (c) Certification of teachers:
  1 year, 16. 2 yrs. 9. 3 yrs. 11. Tot. 36.
 (d) No. days in official service:
  In visitation, 1. In examination 3.
  In Institute work 0. In office work 5.
  In other duties 13. Total 21.

Summary: 37 school houses. Average number days taught 17. 1

white teacher in colored school. More male than female teachers. Salaries $39.25. Number of children from 6 to 21 in the county, white and colored, 3249. Average age of pupils 14. Number over 16, 381. Subjects taught in school: Alphabet, Spelling, Reading, Writing, Written Arithmetic, Mental Arithmetic, Geography, English Grammar and Higher Branches. Private schools. Duties of County School Commissioner.

This report exhibits the condition of the schools of the county sixty years ago. It shows that the public schools were operated an average of 17 days in the year. I take this to be the old Poor Schools. They are seen here slowly dying. The private schools for that same year were operated an average of 100 days. It is interesting too to observe the disparity in the number of male teachers as compared with the female teachers at that time, being 25 to 6. Now the reverse is true, and then some. Truly we have passed through a period of evolution in school matters.

Year 1874: No. Children between 6 and 18:
Wh. 1783, Col. 436. Tot. 2219.
Confed. soldiers under 30 yrs. 134.
Total sch. children and soldiers 2353.

Av. No. mos. taught 4½. Branches taught, Elementary. County's quota (apportionment) was $1830.31.

Report of High Schools:
Name, Lookout Church. Location, High Point.
Principal, J. M. Henry. No. teachers 1.
No. pupils 59. No. months taught 5¼.
Grades taught, Elem. Math. Science.
Av. cost tuition per month $1.50.

Summary: Observe that Confederate soldiers under 30 years of age were used in connection with the number of children as a basis for the apportionment of state funds for the schools. Also, the material increase in the length of the school year, being now 90 days. Note, also ,the report of the high school at High Point. This was the only such school reported to the state school commissioner for that year. This was taught, as may be observed, by the late Josiah M. Henry, of fragrant memory. Mr. Henry has numerous descendants throughout the county who will be pleased to read their sire's careful report after sleeping for more than a half century in musty records.

Year 1876: No. schools: Wh. 29, Col. 5. Tot. 34.
Compensation of C. S. Commissioner $212.
Year 1877: No. children, 3176. Confed. soldiers under 30 yrs. 1.
Blind, 4. Over 20 years 6.

Illiterates: No. between 10 and 18 unable to read:
Wh. 154, Col. 83. Total 237. Over 18 and unable to read:
Wh. 204, Col. 262. Total 466. Grand total 703.
C. S. Commissioner's compensation $100.00.

Summary: Observe that the blind and illiterates were reported. Number of illiterates in 1877 was 703. (The number now, census of 1930, white and colored, is 1131).

Year 1882: Return of school population.
Returns of 1878, 3176, of 1882, 3475. Increase 9%.

No. sch. Wh. 55, Col. 10. Tot. 65. No. pupils 2584.
Av. attend. 1490. Av. cost tuition per mo. $1.00.

Compensation C. S. C. $300.00. Poll tax recd. $1578.63.
Amt. from state, $1865.07. Bal. from 1881 $130.02. Tot. $3573.72.
No. priv. sch. 12. Branches taught: Latin, History.

Year 1883: County's pro-rata, $1929.84.
Private sch. 8. Teachers 8. Length of term 3½ mo.
No. pupils, Wh. 259, Col. 31. Tot. 390.

Priv. High Schools, 2. Taught 5 and 8 mos.
  (a). J. Y. Wood, Prin. St. Mary's Institute.
  (b). Walter H. Little, Prin. Sylvan Bower.

Summary: Observe the gradual, if small, increase in state funds for the schools. Also, the increase in the length of the school term. Notice, too, reports from two others of the county's famous teachers, viz.: J. Y. Wood, and "Boog" Little, as he was familiarly known. Although these old teachers have passed "over the river," they left their impress for good in the hearts and lives of many boys and girls, now old men and women. "Their works do follow them."

Year 1890: 1 Priv. High School at LaFayette.
Miss Alice Napier, Prin. Pupils 47. Term 10 mos.

Year 1892: Increase in Population, 353—8%.
Illiteracy, Wh. 19%. Col. 20%.

Year 1895: No. sch.: Wh. 60, Col. 8. Tot. 68.
No. teachers, Wh. 62, Col. 8. Tot. 70.
No. with 1st gr. L. 23, 2nd gr. 20, 3rd gr. 27.
Monthly sal. 1st gr. 30. 2nd gr. $20. 3rd gr. $18.

No. visits made by C. S. C. during the year 6.
School days 100. Salary C. S. C. $474.
Receipts $8825.14. Paid out $8820.35.

Year 1897: No. sch. Wh. 62, Col. 10. Tot. 72.
No. private schools in county 0.
No. teachers 61. No. normal trained 2.
No. Children 3013.

Year 1900: No. sch.: Wh. 50, Col. 11. Tot. 61.
No. teachers, Wh. 72, Col. 11. Tot. 83. No. Normal tr. 4.
Enrollment, Wh. 2930, Col. 690. Tot. 3620.
Av. daily atten. Wh. 1880, Col. 1407. Tot. 2287.
Term 5 mo. Salary C. S. C. $492.75.

Teachers' Inst. held by T. J. Woofter.
Private High Schools:
(a) LaFayette, C. C. Childs, 9 mos. 136 pupils.
(b) Trans, W. J. Moore, 8 mos. 104 pupils.
(c) Eagle Cliff, C. K. Henderson, 8 mos. 90 pupils.

Year 1905: No. Nor. trained teachers, Wh. 15, Col. 4.
Av. sal. 1st gr. $40, 2nd gr. $28, 3rd gr. $22.

No. sch. Wh. 53, Col. 13. Tot. 66. Enrollment, Wh. 3187,
Col. 665. Tot. 3852. Attend. Wh. 2225, Col. 310. Tot. 2535.
Length of term 100 days. Visits by C. S. C. 80.

No. priv. sch. 10. Local Systems 3.
Sub. taught: Reading, Writing, Eng. Grammar, Geography,
Arithmetic, History, Physiology, Agriculture, Civil Government.

Institute at LaFayette June 3-7, conducted by Thomas L. Bryan.

Year 1906: School fund $11286.33.

Review of School Work: "The year 1906 was one of the most prosperous school years we have ever had. The enrollment and attendance was better than we ever had before, more interest taken by pupils and patrons generally. 55 white schools, 13 colored. We have 14 long term schools running from 7 to 9 months. 69 white teachers and 13 colored Five of the long term schools have special charters, two have local tax under the McMichael law and two high schools in the county. About $4500.00 was raised by tax and otherwise to supplement the long term schools.

"We are well supplied with teachers; have more teachers than schools. Three new buildings in 1906. Held monthly teachers' meetings a portion of the year."

Year 1910: Illiteracy: Wh. 254.
No. sch. receiving Municipal Tax 6.
No. rural schools receiving Local Tax 6.
No. teachers 98. Normal teachers 37.
No. 1st gr. L. 52, 2nd gr. 21, 3rd gr. 12.

Enrollment 4229. Av. daily attend. 2475. Term 121 das.
8th gr. pupils 123, 9th, 6.
No. schools giving high school courses 19.

Received from State	$15,978.50
From Local Tax	7,253.00
From Tuition	1,405.00
From Incidentals	1,131.00
Grand Total	$26,119.20

Av. sal. pd. M. Wh. $53.75. Col. $34.00.
Av. sal. pd. Fem. Wh. $36.64. Col. $23.00.

High Schools:

         LaFayette
         Chickamauga
         Kensington
         Warren
         Pond Spring
         Rossville
         Flintstone
         Linwood
         Shady Grove
         Fairview

CURRENT SCHOOL HISTORY—1931.

No. schools, W. 51; C. 10; Tot. 61. No. Teachers, W. 136; C. 15; Tot. 151. No. consolidated schools operating as such, 4, viz., Cedar Grove, Rossville, West Armuchee and Chattanooga Valley. Two other districts have consolidated but as yet have not erected a building as such—Rock Spring and Lookout Mountain. The following high schools are doing excellent work, the first four being accredited: LaFayette, Chickamauga, Rossville, Chattanooga Valley, Cedar Grove and West Armuchee. Eight trucks are used in the transportation of pupils to school. No. children transported 615.

No. school children in the county, W. 6316; C. 712; Tot. 7028. No.

Local Tax districts 21. State funds received $35,000. Local Tax funds, county wide $29,000. Equalization fund (gas tax) $12,000. Total $76,000.00. This does not include funds received from district local tax, tuition and incidentals, which if included would augment the total considerably, approaching, likely, $90,000.00 per annum.

According to latest report there are 28 children in the county over 10 years of age who cannot read and write, 5 blind, 6 deaf and dumb, 9 crippled and 15 feeble minded.

Salaries of teachers range from $50 to $250 per month, depending on ability, preparation, grade of license and enrollment. County School Superintendent's salary $2,400.00 per annum.

Chapter Twenty-five

"THE OLD FIELD SCHOOL"—EARLY TEACHERS—RECENT TEACHERS—
ROSTER COUNTY SCHOOL SUPERINTENDENTS—ROSTER
MEMBERS BOARD OF EDUCATION.

THE OLD FIELD SCHOOL.*

MANY writers have undertaken to describe what is often, by common consent, called the "Old Field School." It is supposed to have been so-called from the fact, probably, that the log house in which the school was kept was usually situated in, or near, a field and usually at a considerable distance from any residence. The house was built of logs, which were notched down at the corners. In some, the cracks between the logs were filled with small poles or pieces of wood, and were then given a liberal coating of a kind of mortar made from red clay and water, being so ingeniously driven in between and among the logs as to completely close up all cracks, thus rendering the house comfortable even in the coldest weather. In others the cracks between the logs were left open entirely, no effort being made to keep out the cold. These latter were usually only used for schools in the summer time. At one end of the house there was an opening left for a fire place which was about eight feet wide and was likewise built up of logs notched down in a similar manner as the main body of the house. These fire-place logs and the entire chimney were then completely covered with a heavy thick coating of mortar and were hammered or beat into or onto the walls to protect them from fire. Often, this mortar, under the influence of heat would drop away and expose the logs to the fire. In this way the walls of the

---

*Partly paraphrased from various sources.

fireplace would often catch on fire and would have to be put out by pouring water on them. The watchful eyes of both teacher and pupils were necessary to keep the school house from burning down. Always, before leaving the house for the day the teacher was careful to examine for fire and give a liberal application of water to any suspicious coal or spark that might be left burning.

These great fireplaces, being about eight feet long and three or four feet deep, when filled with wood were capable of furnishing, even on the coldest days, sufficient warmth for the comfort of pupils and teacher. Especially is this true with those houses which had been carefully "chinked and daubed." There was generally one door to the house. There were no windows as such; but on either side of the house a log was cut out for its entire length and underneath this opening was placed a long shelf held up by wooden pegs which were placed slantingly into the logs below. This shelf was used for writing purposes principally. The children were seated on puncheons, that is, on roughly dressed timbers supported by large pegs inserted in auger holes. This completed the furniture. Often there was no floor except the bare earth which was beaten down and quite hard and smooth, and was, altogether, reasonably comfortable.

The itinerant teacher usually came into the community with his "Articles of Agreement," which were carefully and pompously worded and displayed to best advantage, and going the rounds of the community he had no trouble in securing the signatures of every parent with children of school age. There were few school officials in those days. The only official was that of County School Commissioner, and his duty consisted, in the main, in dispensing with the small amount of money to the teacher about once a year. He rarely visited the schools, or had anything to do or say as to who the teacher should be.

School hours were long. The school ran almost from sun to sun, that is from sun up to sun down. The subjects taught were the three R's—reading, riting, and rithmetic, plus s for spelling. Rarely was anything else taught in the Old Field School. On very rare occasions a class of two or three pupils might be found studying grammar or geography, but this was not often. Many of these schools were what were called "blab" schools, that is, the pupils studied aloud. Whether reading, spelling, or what not, every one talked aloud. Hardly any two pupils were at the same place or page and all blabbing aloud produced a medley of sounds resembling that of bumblebees in a barrel. This chronicler, who has been a teacher for many years, denies the charge of ever having consciously taught a "blab" school, but he has sometimes been painfully aware of a feeling that some of his pupils showed evidence of having evolved from the pupils of those old "blab" schools.

The old "Blueback" speller was the king of text books in those early days. It was used not only as a speller, but as a reader as well. Moreover, it gave instruction in many other subjects. It taught writing, some arithmetic, a smattering of grammar and geography, and was full of philosophy. Although considered out of date in these modern times, it is certain that Webster's Old Blueback served a very real need when in its heyday. In it children learned their A B C's; learned to spell, first on the book, then by heart; and then learned to read. Many boys and girls who never went further than Webster's Blueback in school, thus laid the foundation for a liberal education; and by application and study later became leaders in church and state. Many of our older citizens have a peculiar affection, not to say reverence, for the Old Blueback.

Another book used in the early days, and one much beloved by all who have been familiar with it, was McGuffy's readers, especially the Sixth. Filled with the choicest of literature, it probably affected the lives of more boys and girls for good than any text book ever printed in our country with the possible exception of the Old Blueback. How the boys would make the welkin ring on Friday afternoons as they recited such grand old selections as: "The American Flag;" "The Brave Old Oak;" "Lochiel's Warning;" "Landing of the Pilgrim Fathers;" "Bill and Joe;" "Antony Over Caesar's Body;" "The Barefoot Boy;" "Lochinvar;" "The Bridge;" "A Psalm of Life;" "Battle of Waterloo," and many others.

Then came Davies' arithmetic, or Smiley's arithmetic, or any other that the pupil happened to have; for there was no special book adopted and to be used. Whatever the pupil happened to have as speller, reader, or arithmetic was satisfactory. Scarcely any two pupils were on the same page, unless it were in the spelling lesson, or maybe the reading lesson. In arithmetic, especially, a dozen or twenty pupils would probably be on as many pages. No effort whatever was made to classify the pupils in arithmetic.

The larger boys when studying arithmetic were permitted to leave the house and go out and sit under the shade of the trees, or in the grass, and "cipher." Every one had a slate and when he had "worked" a sum would run in to show it to the teacher. How grand he felt as he went into the house before all those children and showed his sums to the teacher—then out again to join his companions under the trees. The teacher usually allowed his pupils to go as far as the "Rule of Three," or possibly to cube root, then they were turned back to review.

In his spelling classes, the old field school teacher not only taught his pupils to spell and pronounce each syllable separately, but before proceeding further, he must return to the first of the word and pronounce, in succession, each syllable again, thus: a-m am, i ami, t-y ti, amity; j-o-l jol, l-i li, jolli, t-y ti, jollity; n-u-l, nul, l-i, li, nulli, t-y ti, nullity; p-u-b pub, l-i li, publi, c-a ca, publica, t-i-o-n shun, publication; i-n in, c-o-m com, incom, p-r-e-double-s press, incompress, i incompressi, b-i-l bil, incompressibil, i incompressibili, t-y ti, incompressibility; v-a-l val, e vale, t-u tu, valetu, d-i di, valetudi, n-a na, valetudina, r-i ri, valetudinari, a-n an, valetudinarian. And so on, *ad infinitum.* All this would be so amusing and ridiculous to our modern school methods that it would produce a regular horse laugh among the children of our day. And yet, while it was carried to the extreme, it had an educational value and was one of the means of producing the excellent spellers for which our grandmothers were famous.

Every teacher, especially the rural teacher, knows how difficult it is to keep all the children in school and busy till time to dismiss the school for the day. Many children after they have recited the last lesson for the day will ask to be allowed to go home before school is dismissed. They will present a hundred and eight excuses for making the request. Many of "Ye Olde Teachers" knew how to circumvent this daily disturbance. Every pupil in school—barring possibly the very youngest—were required to join in the last lesson of the day, which was "Dictionary." When all other lessons were duly dispatched and when the sun was now nearly ready to sink below the western horizon the teacher called, "Dictionary Class." Instantly, with much hubbub and confusion, every pupil took his place around the walls of the school room, reaching in most cases around at least three sides of the room. The teacher, then, with book in hand began to pronounce the words of a page of "Webster's Dictionary." And since the children of those days were "SPELLERS," it was rare that a word was misspelled. Having assigned another page for the next day's lesson, the teacher called, "number;" whereupon the second in the class began, "One I, one (I), "Two I's, two" (II), said the next pupil, and so on to the foot, sometimes going to XL "forty." The head pupil was given a "headmark," and went foot the next day. After this lesson all were dismissed for the day and left for home amid the cool of the day, happy and contented.

In his search throughout the county for old records and historical data, the author has often requested old citizens to give the names of their teachers, or of the family physician. By this means he has been enabled to secure the names of most of the old teachers of the county. The records in the office of the School Superintendent does not include these old teachers. It is a pleasure to give the following list of names of old teachers, some of whom taught in the "Old Field Schools."

EARLY TEACHERS.

John Arnold, Henry Abercrombie, Davie P. Allen (1865), John Agnew, George Anderson, Marian Atwood, Alexander Andrews, Rocky Brooks, Porter Brinley, Jacob R. Brooks, Hugh Blaylock, Carrie Baker, Richard Baker (1855), Austin Bradley, John W. Baker (1855), R. W. Blackwell, Joseph Bradley, J. M. Blackwell (1858), James Ball, Ollie Catlett, E. I. F. Chaney, Leola Conley, Octavia Conley, Pink Close, Mich Coulter, W. A. Clements, Billy Cobb, John Cavender (1850), Bill Chambers (1860), E. L. Culberson (1866), Charley Clements (1850), Wm. Clements, Frank W. Copeland, Jeptha Carter (1840), Samantha Carter (1858), Billy Clark (1870), Thomas Dickey, Lee H. Dyer, Seab Durham, George Dodson, Mrs. Sarah Evitt, Mark Edwards, Henry Evans (1851),

George S. Fulton, J. W. P. Floyd (1850), Henry Ford (1879), Joe Gardner, Rev. James Gambell (1836-40), Wm. Gambell (1841-45), Alex. Green, Church Goree (1880), Hamp Garmany, Hyram Gill (1867), Jim Hill, Wm. Hatfield, John Huffman, Mr. Humphrey, Charley Holland (1848), Hamp Hunt, John Hardy, Mr. Howard (1858), John Hatfield, Miss Mary Hubbard, Warren Henry, T. R. A. Haslerig, Mr. Herrington, Josiah Henry, George Head, Susan Harden, J. H. Hardy (1852), Mr. Huffakre (1855), Fannie Johnston, Matilda Johnston, Samantha Jones, Casey Jackson, T. W. Jones, G. W. Jones, C. C. Jackson, David P. Jackson, Maggie Jennings, Captain J. M. Jackson, Grace Levitt, John Love, Cortes Lazenvy, Mr. Leet, "Boog" Little, John Lumpkin, M. D. Lansford (1845), Wm. Lowery, "Shick" Little (1882), John Langston, Steve Morgan, Pete Murray, Ed Myers, Miss Merrick, Andy Myers, Sam McWhorter, Ira Moore, Ann Moore, George Mason, Mr. Marooney (1881), Tate Mann (1883), J. A. Mullis, Sr., Annie Moore, Gus McCutcheon, Prof. McMullen, Prof Mathews, N. C. Napier, T. C. Napier, Jonathan Owensby (1860), George Prather, Mary Powell, Mose Park (1840), Wm. Pursley, Mr. Perry, Miss Mat Powell (1862), James Park, W. S. Parker, Mrs. Pursley (1850), Lee Quinn, Rev. J. M. Robertson, Duke Rogers, Alice Rosser, Fannie Rosser, J. H. Ramey, Sam Rogers, Milton Russell, Jeptha Shaw, Tom Simmons, Fannie Shankle, D. T. Scoggins, Susan Shields, Wm. Stephens, Harvey Sprayberry (1851), Tom Seals, Jennie Smith, Arminda Simmons, Mrs. Stansberry (1879), Dan Stout, Captain J. C. Stokes (1863), Julius Sprayberry, Andrew Turner, Wesley Thurman (1862), Mr. Tweedell, Flemming Taylor (1882), Eph Thurman (1880), John Talley, Mr. Valentine, Roxanna Welborn, John Williams, Lucinda Wheeler, Perry Walls, Captain J. Y. Wood, Rabe Williams.

Many of these teachers, no doubt, were masters of "Ye Olde Field Schools" and some few, probably, taught in what were called "Blab" schools.

RECENT TEACHERS.

Below are given names of teachers who took examination during the year 1911, as gleaned from records in the superintendent's office:

Ex. Jan. 7, 1911: Fannie McWhorter, J. M. Orr, Niel Andrews, Mattie Carroll.

Ex. June 17, 1911: State licenses: Margaret Wheeler, Susie Conley, W. E. Mitchel, Nida Williams.

First Grade: Ellen Brigman, Effie Welchel, Bessie Sigler, Rebecca Bomar, Tempie Roberts, Mattie Coulter, Mary Loyd, Nora Conley, Claudie Hall, Lily Morgan. Cora Roberts, Ruth Graham, Willie Freeman, Ella Arnold, Jennie Johnson, Mary Deck, Fannie Loughridge, Q. M. Clemons, Minnie Hammontree, Ludie Haslerig, Udie Lee, Vera Deck Nannie Warrenfels, Annie Johnson, Johnnie L. Saunders, Jessie Hammontree, Lillian Thurman, Gene Boss, J. S. Leamon.

Second Grade: Jessie Stansell, Burton Davis, Eunice White, Mary

White, Jewel Deck, Susie Jones, Mabel Conley, Delia Fisher, Annie Loughridge, Mae Hale, Elsie Andrews, Myrtle Roberts, Mary Coulter.

Third Grade: Herbert Patterson, Willie M. Powell, John Edge, Blanche Chapman, Amanda Bridges, Wilson Keown, Winnie Shankle, Fred Martin.

Names of other county teachers as shown in school records 25 years ago: J. J. Sizemore, Sara Steele, Charles Blaylock, Dora Williams, Ethel Hasty, Clara Srite, Patsy Glenn, Ollie Johnson, Jesse Durham, (Miss) Lee Thurman, Minnie R. Cooper, Rose Peterson, Emma Story, Gertrude Saunders, Maude Peterson, Elizabeth Wheeler, Nelly Iley, J. C. Jones, Wilson Bowman, Jamie Cremer, Ethel Sizemore, Freeman McClure, Dee Rosser, Vera Meridith, J. B. Davis, Susie Charles, Lola Martin, Odessa Fox, Mrs. H. J. Spencer, Evelyn Thurman, Pearl Turney, Georgia Boss, Maggie Wheeler, Lee Abney, Winnie Thurman, Lula Thurman, Lona Fulmer, Sibyl Deck, Gordon Hill, L. P. Keith, Thomas Bryan, Georgia Ward, Mrs. J. A. Moore, W. A. J. Burns, Frank Weaver, Pearl Camp, J. F. Walker, Byrom Glenn, Judson Durham, Luther Sizemore, Mary Moore, Ola Johnson, Deed Bird, Annie Moore Hammond, Lucile Thurman, Mrs. L. P. Keith, Jessie Iley, Rachel Lumpkin, Emma Lumpkin, Sallie Shankle, Beulah Shankle, Grace Mize, Lillie Cook, J. H. Shahan, B. D. Keown, I. S. Flanagan, Sara Hackney, W. N. Morgan, Z. W. Jones, Glenn Tatum, Wilson Alverson, J. F. Agnew, C. L. Veach, Edith McBroom, Billy Neal, Jessie Wyatt, Fannie Smith, Elizabeth Guille, Clara Hice, Ola Patterson, Sam Dunn, Benson Langley, Lucien Crowder, Guild McWhorter, Lena Evitt, Belle Glenn, Lois Martin, Ada Bolt, Gordon Hill, Ray Johnson, L. V. Swanson, Milner Gray, Leland Rogers, Lois Thurman, Margaret Myers, Mrs. W. A. J. Burns, Addie Patterson, Gerthy Smith, Ruth Iley, Ora White, Exa Roper, Fay McWhorter, Jimmie Norton, Odessa Marks, Delia McClure, Hannah Moreland, Mae Carlock, Mrs. Pearl Hill, Herschel Powell, Louise Shuford, Annie Keith, Lilla Keith, Mary Pitman, Floy Pitman, Minta Shahan, E. G. Carroll, Mrs. E. G. Carroll, W. H. McDaniel, W. A. Wiley, Frances Smith, Mrs. J. W. Shoemate, J. E. Ashworth, Maude Dodd, Bess G. Evans, Ella Chapman, Ruth Andrews, Edith Clements, Grace Gilley, Joe Reed, Theressa Williams, Rita Boss, Georgia Boss, Gladys Carlock, Alma Conley, Sallie Camp, Ima Graham, Lucile Hall, Susie Hall, Susie Hise, Annie Justice, Virgie Steverson, Ada Belle Rutledge, Ila Williams, Vera Williams, Minnie Lee Owings, A. M. Mathis, Mabel Mathis, Carter Pitman, R. T. Rives, J. W. Shoemate, Vera Andrews, Gladys Andrews, Grace Bowen, Theressa Crowder, Mae Camp, Eva Hunter, Sadie Martin, Leila O'Neal, Vinnie Parker, Nelle Loughridge, Mrs. Jessie Street, Elizabeth Leonard, Mrs. Cleve Roark, Mahala Parker, J. D. Edwards, Mrs. A. W. Lupo, Mrs. G. W. Atwood, Mary McCurdy, Nellie Chambers, Nancy Ransom, Lena Parish, Rachel Bird, Margaret Agnew, Pearl Wallin, Mrs. T. M. Wallin, Gertrude Hearn, Lydia Myers, Lucile Payne, Harvey Roper, Bernice Sprayberry, Annie Ruth Parker, Mrs. Ella Wood, Mrs. Cecil Buchanan, Arnie Parker, Ella Lane, Grace

Millican, A. Covert, G. O. McBroom, F. M. Reynolds, S. N. Hamic, Hattie Foster, Mrs. H. E. Dailey, Ada Shankle, Irene Gidden, Fannie Loughridge, Ethel Tyner, Amanda Bridges, Emma Evitt, Maude Little, R. L. Powell, Bettie McClure, J. F. Alverson, Mynne Hammontree, Mary Hammontree, Lena Jones, Tula Hammontree, U. E. Spencer, Lillie Taburieux, C. A. Chambers, J. A. Sartain, B. F. Loyd, Alf Reed, R. D. Love, Exa Shahan.

WALKER COUNTY TEACHERS, 1931-32.

ROSSVILLE—H. L. Brotherton, Supt., G. B. Leinbach, Dovie Williams, Nellie Chambers, Carolyn Au, Mrs. D. Hashburger, Mrs. P. Shinpaugh, Ora Stanley, Esther Flegall, Mrs. John Rhyne, Bertha McBrayer, Beulah Shankles, Johnnie Sanders, Myra Skinner, Carol Hashberger, Mrs. J. W. Leak, Mrs. C. P. Morton, Mrs. Kate Elder, Vesta Elkins, Mrs. Cecil Fuller, Mrs. W. V. Costella, Marion Fox.

CHATTANOOGA VALLEY—J. G. Tatum, Supt., Catherine Bailey, Lillian Hamrick, Eula Bolt, Helen Welchel, Adaline Hester, Pearl Welchel, Anna M. Smith, Mildred Royal, Vera B. Veazy, Olin Brotherton.

FAIRYLAND—Mrs. Floy Hillhouse, Winnie Styles.

HINKLES—Grace Gilley, Ovilene Pack.

ASCALON—C. A. Chambers.

PITTSBURG—A. M. Mathews, Janie Lou Baker.

HIGH—Esther Tinker.

CARMEL—Willie Mae Hixon.

CEDAR GROVE—V. L. Joiner, Supt., Mrs. V. L. Joiner, Mrs. A. H. Camp, Lena Hicks, Imogene Patton.

NEW PROSPECT—Louise Joiner, Flo Henry.

KENSINGTON—Ray Bell, Mrs. Lou Wallen.

ESTELLE—Mrs. Eva Hunter.

POND SPRING—Bill Pettigrew.

HIGH POINT—Mrs. Paul Tarvin, Harvey Smith, Laura Johnson.

GARRETT'S CHAPEL—Ruth Rowland.

OLD BETHEL—Mrs. R. T. Goodson.

OAK GROVE—P. E. Moore.

WALLACEVILLE—Tom Crowder, Mrs. Ella Buchanan, Mrs. Walter Hearn.

OSBORN—Earl Crowder, Bernice Crowder, Eugenia Bailey.

MISSION RIDGE—Mrs. C. H. Williams, Thelma Hill, Beulah Perkinson.

ROCK SPRINGS—Douglas Baine, Elwyn Wallace, Cecil Lawrence, Jennie Mae Poarch, Cora Cooper.

LAFAYETTE—C. W. Peacock, Supt., L. D. Caldwell, L. C. Butcher, W. A. Dubberly, James Whitaker, Mrs. Horace Shattuck, Ruth Hammond, Mrs. Jessie Street, Mrs. H. Davidson, Leila Green, Mary Stiles, Anna Padgett, Elizabeth Doriso, Bess Young.

WEST LAFAYETTE—B. D. Keown, Mrs. R. M. Neal, Hattie B. Wil-

liams, Mrs. George Ransom, Mrs. Jess Abney.
  LINWOOD—Mrs. Annie Greene, Bethie Thurman, Mary Lee Rhyne, Evelyn Pickthorn.
  SUNNYSIDE—Mrs. Ray Pledger.
  NEW BETHEL—Delphyn Mason.
  PINE GROVE—Ettie Greene.
  CATLETT—Lois Hegwood, Mary Jones.
  NAOMI—H. M. Hicks, Mrs. Mary Carroll.
  WARREN—Thelma Neal, Claudie Steverson.
  CORINTH—Mrs. R. L. Burns.
  LEE—W. A. Mitchel, Mrs. Lena Rogers.
  WESLEY CHAPEL—Mrs. I. S. Leonard, Sara Loyd.
  BURNT MILL—Mayborn Mathews.
  FAIRVIEW—Mahala Parker.
  MT. CARMEL—Glenn Hunter, Frances Hunter.
  CENTER POST—Duren Crowder, Roberta Hobbs.
  RIDGWAY—Mrs. Thelma Mallicoat.
  WATERVILLE—J. L. Love, Mrs. J. L. Love.
  HARRISBURG—A. M. Sewell.
  CONCORD—Mrs. S. J. Bomar.
  WEST ARMUCHEE—Theodore Hammer, Mrs. T. Hammer, Gertrude Hammer, Doris Hewitt, C. P. Harris.
  TRANS—T. Griffith, Ruth Tate.
  FURNACE—Marguerite Shahan.
  VILLANOW—Mary Hammontree.
  GRIFFIN—Oscar Williams.
  HENDERSON—Rebecca Huggins.

COUNTY SCHOOL COMMISSIONERS.

D. C. Sutton,	1872-1876	C. M. Conley,	1904-1911
W. W. S. Myers,	1876-1896	R. D. Love,	1911-1920
L. C. Rosser,	1896-1899	J. A. Sartain,	1921-1924
J. Y. Wood,	1899-1900	R. D. Love,	1925-1932
J. E. Rosser,	1900-1904	Sara Hackney,	1933-

MEMBERS BOARD OF EDUCATION (Incomplete).

	Date Elec.	Term Exp.	Whom Succeeded
John Puryear	Feb. T. 1872	1876	
H. Wheeler	" " "	1874	
W. M. Walker	" " "	"	
N. C. Napier	" " "	"	
J. A. Clements	" " 1873	1876	John Puryear
Amajah Dickson	" " "	1874	N. C. Napier
A. R. McCutchen	" " 1874	1878	
R. M. Ward	" " "	"	
L. K. Dickey	" " "	"	

	Date Elec.	Term Exp.	Whom Succeeded
John Y. Wood	" " "		Filled McCutchen vacancy
W. W. S. Myers	Filled Wood's Vacancy—did not qualify		
H. P. Lumpkin	Filled Dickey's Vacancy—didid not qualify		
J. M. Jackson	Feb. T. 1876	1880	
D. C. Fariss	" " "	"	J. A. Clements
W. M. Coulter	" " "	"	
W. W. S. Myers	" " "	"	Self
B. M. Garrett	" " "	"	H. P. Lumpkin
B. F. Thurman	" " "	1888	Self
J. H. McWhorter	" " 1886	1890	Self
Wm. Hawkins	" " "	"	Self
N. C. Napier	" " "	"	R. M. W. Glenn
P. B. Little	" " 1888	1892	B. F. Thurman
J. Y. Wood	" " "	"	
B. F. Thurman	" " 1889	"	J. Y. Wood
N. C. Napier	" " 1890	1894	Self
J. H. McWhorter	" " "	"	Self
Wm. Hawkins	" " "	"	Self
B. F. Thurman	" " 1892	1896	Self
A. H. Neal	" " "	"	P. B. Little
J. P. Shattuck	Feb. T. 1894	1898	N. C. Napier
J. T. Suttle	" " "	"	J. H. McWhorter
E. P. Hall	" " "	"	Wm. Hawkins—res.
C. M. Conley	" " "	1896	B. F. Thurman
M. M. Whitlow	" " "	"	A. H. Neal
B. F. Thurman	" " 1895	"	M. M. Whitlow
F. W. Copeland	Aug. T. 1895	"	B. F. Thurman
C. M. Conley	Feb. T. 1896	1900	Self
T. W. Haslerig	" " "	"	F. W. Copeland
J. L. Rowland	" " "	1898	E. P. Hall
Lee H. Dyer	" " 1898	1902	J. T. Suttle
J. P. Shattuck	" " "	"	Self
J. C. McWilliams	" " "	"	J. L. Rowland
J. H. Hammond	Aug. 1900	1902	J. P. Shattuck
J. C. McWilliams	Feb. 1902	1906	Self
C. C. L. Rudicil	" "	"	L. H. Dyer
E. K. Carlock	" "	"	J. H. Hammond
C. M. Conley	" 1900	1904	Self
T. W. Haslerig	" "	"	Self
W. C. McFarland	" 1904	1906	C. C. L. Rudicil
A. J. Wellborn	" "		C. M. Conley
A. J. Wellborn	Aug. "	1908	Self
B. L. Carlock	Nov. 1905		A. J. Wellborn
E. P. Hall	Feb. 1906	1910	E. K. Carlock
W. C. McFarland	" "	"	Self
J. C. McWilliams	" "	"	Self

B. L. Carlock	"	"	1908	Self
T. W. Haslerig	"	1908	1912	Self
C. D. Weaver—did not qualify			1912	B. L. Carlock
E. H. Hice	Oct.	1908	Next Ses.	G. J. Weaver
J. F. Patterson	Feb.	1910	1914	E. P. Hall
W. J. Shattuck	"	"	1912	E. H. Hice
J. C. McWilliams	"	"	1914	Self
W. C. McFarland	"	"	"	Self
W. J. Shattuck	"	1912	1916	Self
E. M. Goodson—Com. not issued—from same dis. Patterson				
Alf Reed	Aug.	1912	1916	W. J. Shattuck
T. W. Haslerig	"	"	"	Self
J. C. McWilliams	Feb.	1914	1918	Self
E. M. Goodson	Feb.	1914	1918	J. F. Patterson
O. P. Andrews	"	"	"	W. C. McFarland
T. W. Haslerig	"	1916	1920	Self
Alf Reed	"	"	"	Self
O. P. Andrews	Aug.	1917	1922	Self
E. M. Goodson	"	1917	1922	Self
J. C. McWilliams	"	"	"	Self
W. B. Shaw	"	1920	1924	T. W. Haslerig
Leo Au	"	"	"	Alf Reed
O. P. Andrews	Feb.	1922	1926	Self
E. M. Goodson	"	"	"	Self
Alf Reed	"	"	"	J. C. McWilliams
W. B. Shaw	Aug.	1924	1928	Self
W. G. Hunter	"	"	"	Leo Au
Alf Reed (Did not qualify)				
J. S. Alsobrook	Feb.	1926	1930	E. M. Goodson
O. P. Andrews	"	"	"	Self
Reece M. Neal	"	"	"	Alf Reed
J. L. Wright	Nov.	1928	1932	W. G. Hunter
W. B. Shaw	Aug.	1928	1932	Self
O. P. Andrews	Feb.	1930	1934	Self
J. S. Alsobrook	"	"	"	Self
S. J. Bomar	"	"	"	R. M. Neal
W. B. Shaw	Aug.	1932	1936	Self
Don Gault	"	"	"	J. L. Wright

Chapter Twenty-six

AGRICULTURE.

"The farm—best home of the family—main source of national wealth—foundation of civilized society—the natural providence."

WALKER COUNTY, POSITION—TOPOGRAPHY—DRAINAGE—CLIMATE, ETC.

POSITION. The county lies a little south of the 35th parallel of north latitude and a little west of the 85th meridian west longitude. The southern boundary reaches for about 27 miles and is straight except for a short offset near Harrisburg. From this line as a base it extends northward on the east by a series of jogs becoming narrower at each jog till the Tennessee line is reached. This line then runs to the top of Lookout mountain and turns southward along the crest of that elevation which it follows to the Alabama line, thence along the Alabama line to the western end of the base line. The northern boundary line is about 5½ miles in length. The distance between the northern and southern boundary lines is about 27 miles. The area of the county is given as 434 square miles, or, 277,760 acres.

The county is bounded on the north by Tennessee; on the east by Catoosa, Whitfield, and Gordon counties; on the south by Gordon and Chattooga counties; on the west by Alabama and Dade county. The county is bounded by original land lines except along the crest of Lookout mountain and for a short distance along the top of Taylor's ridge. The form of the county is very irregular.

TOPOGRAPHY. The surface is broken. It consists of Lookout mountain lying in the western part and running nearly north and south. Pigeon mountain, so-called, is a spur of Lookout, branching out from it near the southwestern border of the county, and running northeastwardly for a distance of some 15 or 18 miles where it dwindles to mere foot hills. Taylor's and Dick's ridges lie in the eastern part and run in the same general direction as Pigeon mountain. In addition to these there are several other ridges all running in a northeastward direction. The most important of these is Missionary ridge which has its beginning in the head of McLemore's cove and runs thence to the Tennessee line, assuming in some places a considerable elevation. The county's greatest elevation is 2392 feet which is on Lookout mountain near High Point.

The numerous valleys lying between these elevations are as follows: McLemore's cove lying between Lookout and Pigeon and extending northward almost to the Tennessee boundary. West of the northern part of Missionary ridge and east of Lookout mountain lies Chattanooga valley. East of Pigeon mountain is Duck creek and Broomtown valleys; also a considerable extent of smaller valleys and ridges reaching as far as

Taylor's ridge. East of Taylor's ridge is the West Armuchee valley and east of Dick's ridge is the East Armuchee valley. Lookout and Pigeon mountain form the eastern rim of the Cumberland Plateau and the region between that rim and Taylor's ridge is a part of the Appalachian valley; while the part east of Taylor's ridge may be said to be a part of the Appalachian mountain region.

DRAINAGE. Pigeon mountain and its foot hills together with a slight east and west elevation near Noble act as a divide in the county. North and west of that divide the drainage is north into the Tennessee river; south and east the drainage is southward into the Coosa. West Chickamauga with its tributaries, Peavine and Middle Chickamauga, together with Chattanooga creek, are the principal streams flowing toward the north. Duck creek, Cane creek and the two Armuchees send their waters to the Coosa southward. Dr. J. H. Hammond, County Health Commissioner, is authority for the statement that the county's drainage is outward at all points—that there is no point where the water flows into our county from other sources.

CLIMATE. Killing frost rarely comes before November and real cold weather is not expected before Christmas. January and February are the only cold weather months in the year and these are rarely severe. March may be windy and chilly but no frigid weather is apt to appear. Then till middle of June the weather is pleasant. In July and August we sometimes have short periods of hot weather, but even then the temperature rarely goes into the upper nineties. The fall months are the most delightful of the year.

The mean annual temperature for the winter months is 41, for the summer months 75 and for the year 59. The average rainfall is about 54 inches well distributed throughout the year, though this amount varies considerably in wet or dry years. The growing season is about seven months which gives time for the maturing of a large variety of crops.

AGRICULTURE.

The three paramount considerations for making any region a prosperous farming section all obtain in our county. These are fertility of soil, climate and moisture. No extensive region in the state can boast greater richness of soil than Walker county. The valley lands, the table lands and even the slopes are naturally impregnated with the necessary growing elements for plant life. The slow disintegration of limestone rock and other shales through the long ages of the past has combined to make ours a most fertile soil. All types of soil present in the county are rich in plant-producing elements. True, in some parts man has abused the soil and allowed it to deteriorate by erosion and otherwise, but these are isolated cases. If one will make a visit to many other sections of the state and other states he will surely become convinced that for fertility of soil, Walker is the garden spot of Georgia.

The climate leaves little or nothing to be desired. We have not the severe sub-zero temperature of more northern parts nor the super-high hectic weather of the far south. Rarely does the temperature fall below zero and that for only a few hours. Both man and animals may generally be exposed to the severest weather for reasonable periods without harm. And yet we have some brisk frosty weather which is necessary to assist in pulverizing the soil and destroying noxious insects. During the summer months and growing season the temperature generally stands during the day in the lower nineties—rarely reaching the hundred mark. And even on the hottest days there may be felt a gentle breeze to mitigate against the otherwise oppressive heat. The mean annual temperature ranges in the lower sixties.

The county has an abundance of rainfall, the average being about 60 inches annually. Most of this, of course, falls during the winter months, but enough and to spare comes during the growing season for the sustenance and growth of crops. Rare indeed is it that a serious drouth visits the county. A space of more than two weeks between copious showers is rare and no crop should suffer materially in that time. So plentiful has been rainfall in our county from time immemorial that our farmers never think seriously of trying to conserve the moisture in the soil, knowing that a fresh supply will come in time. For fertility of soil, delightful climate and an abundance of rainfall, Walker county is unsurpassed.

The history of agriculture in the county lists some twenty types of soils the most important of which are the following: Clarksville gravelly loam, about 70,000 acres; Decalb fine sandy loam, 38,000; rough stony land, 28,000; Clarksville stony loam, 18,000; Hagerstown clay, 17,000; Montevallo shale loam, 13,000; Decatur and Connesaga silt loam, each about 12,000, and so on; other types showing smaller amounts.

These various types of soil are suitable for different crops, a thorough discussion of which is not contemplated in this place. Suffice it to say that the soils of the county run the gamut of requirements of the people of the county. Every thing necessary for home consumption and more, can be easily produced in the county.

KING CORN. Corn is perhaps the most important crop raised in the county. Every farmer, large and small, raises some corn; many raise large amounts. I remember as a boy to have heard the late James M. Lee say that once in the heyday of his farming life on his farms at Crawfish Spring, he estimated his crop of corn for a certain season at 20,000 bushels. Those who, like myself, remember the immense fields planted to corn, the numerous tenants and work hands, the large number of big fine mules, the wagons, plows and other farm implements; and who recall how in work season every one engaged in farm work was abroad early and late; and who remember likewise the great fertility of the soil in those palmy days, cannot doubt that he usually made what he estimated. These large yields of corn and other crops were back in the eighties. Many other farmers made thousands of bushels of corn in those days. It was cheap of course as every thing was at that time. The surplus was fed to hogs and cattle which were sold on the market at a fair price.

CORN CLUBS. During the first decade of the present century the idea of corn clubs began to be emphasized and fostered among the boys of the county. It was proposed to show by this plan that a few acres well-prepared, fertilized, and cultivated would produce a yield of corn equal or exceeding double that acreage according to the old haphazard, hit-or-miss method. The records of these interesting experiments amply prove that they have taught our farmers some important lessons. For a number of years Dr. Crowder's boys in the Cove won considerable notoriety as well as many valuable prizes by producing very fine crops of corn, reaching often above a hundred bushels to the acre. To Ben Leath, however, went the greatest publicity for being officially credited with raising 214 bushels of corn on one acre of land. This was officially declared to be the greatest yield not only in the state but in the South for that year.

GOLDEN WHEAT. Wheat has been one of the principal crops of the county for a hundred years, or until some 20 or 25 years ago when it began to decline. At the present time very little wheat is raised in the county. This is to be regretted. Mr. Lee, referred to above, was also a great wheat farmer, as were many others in the Cove a half century ago. Rotation of crops was much practised at that time. Wheat was cut (cradled) in June. As soon as corn was laid by, or at least by middle August plowing was begun in the wheat stubble. That heavy coat of rag weeds and crap-grass was plowed under, often using a heavy log chain fastened to the doubletree to drag the heavy weeds down so they could be covered, and allowed to rot during the fall and winter. Early in the spring this fallow land was thoroughly harrowed and planted to corn. In many cases, however, clover was sown as a nurse crop in the wheat, in which case there would be a field of clover following the wheat for one or two years. Generally speaking the rotation was about as follows: Corn, wheat, clover, pasture; taking four years for the rotation.

The young generation can hardly appreciate the strenuous activity of harvest time before the invention of the binder and reaper. It was no unusual sight to see a dozen men, maybe, with cradles, following each other around a large wheatfield with as many more coming on behind binding the wheat into bundles, and still others gathering the bundles into shocks. About two good size lads were required to keep a supply of cool water from a near-by well or spring. The best cradler led the way, the rest keeping up if possible. This was trying work on a hot day in June—a day 16 hours long—and many were not able to endure to the end but would often fall out before sunset.

About 11:30 was noon hour. Sometimes the dinner was brought by the women folks to the field, especially if it was some distance from the house. It was important during harvest time to conserve the time. Harvest wages were high—a dollar a day. Hence, if the field was some distance from the home the noon-day meal was brought to the hands in the field. And such dinners! Every thing a fruitful farm, garden and orchard produced was there. It was spread in abundance in the shade of a large tree near a spring of cool water. In those days it was not an uncommon thing to offer each work hand a glass of gin or beer just before the meal. I recall once when a boy to have been offered a beer, the first I ever tasted (and the last). I tasted it and, boy-like, spewed it out amid the laughter of the crowd.

It is related that the late J. J. Jones, during the palmy days of the seventies when the virgin soil in that Red Belt section was at its best, and before erosion had marred the face of the fields, raised on a certain year on his farm nearly 1500 bushels of wheat, and that Jason Conley the same year produced more than 1000 bushels. Such was the fertility of the soil that it was not uncommon to produce from 30 to 40 bushels per acre. At that time, too, there were few insects to interfere with growing crops and fruits as we experience them at this day.

Noxious insects and weeds as we have them to-day are not as a rule indigenous to the soil. They have come in by transportation. Our forbears were not concerned about so many troublesome insects and plant diseases as we experience. Neither were they worried with the many troublesome weeds that vex us to-day. Wheat, corn and other crops grew to perfection. No need to spray fruit trees. Most old people recall the time in their youth when peaches, apples and other fruits were faultless. Likewise many noxious weeds have been brought into our county to distress us. The bitter weed so common everywhere is a comparatively new arrival—probably about 20 years. The boll weevil and bean beetle have been here a dozen years. Other insects and weeds have come in at various times. No doubt others are to arrive by and by. This is one price that we must pay for our civilization. If we had had no railroads or other convenient communication, we might have existed many years without these undesirable pests. It is likely that the Civil war helped to spread these among us.

THE FLECY STAPLE. Cotton of course is one of the principal crops in the county at present. It is to be regretted that our people have taken so seriously to cotton farming. Cotton impoverishes land. Cotton year after year for a few years and hardly anything else will grow there profitably—not even cotton. Examine the fields of the county; observe the bare hills and knolls in every field where cotton is raised. Lack of humus has caused erosion. We endeavor to overcome this by the use of commercial fertilizers, thus further impoverishing the land.

C. H. Ginn, a tenant on the Lee farms at Crawfish Spring planted about 1880, what was probably the first important crop of cotton in that section. Certainly very little cotton had been raised before that time in the Cove. Following this more and more farmers began the cultivation of the fleecy staple, and large commercial gins began to be erected for ginning purposes.

STRAWBERRIES. The strawberry of all the fruits of the year, is one of the most welcome to our table. It is quite extensively grown in many parts of the county. Clarksville gravelly loam, mentioned above, is especially adapted to its growth, and this type is widespread throughout the county. The following bit of strawberry history as I remember it is given at this point: Soon after the Civil war Mr. Hartwell Weathers, who lived near where the Wilder monument stands, grew a few rows in his garden. This was in the seventies. As he had more than his family could consume, he decided to take them to Chattanooga and see if he could sell them. This he did and found a ready market for all he had. He walked all the way to Chattanooga carrying two baskets, one on his head and one on his arm, his team being busy in the crop. This he kept up for some years, but soon other farmers began to see the possibilities and to plant large fields for the market.

Among those who thus were the first to market the berry in quantity were L. W. Myers, S. B. Dyer, Milton Plaster, John Devotie and numerous others. Most of the pioneers in the business made handsome profits for a few years till the field became crowded. The berry raised at that time was known as the Wilson, a small rather sour specimen. Compared to the Klondike and Aroma of the present it was a mere pigmy.

Truck farming and fruit raising are other forms of agriculture in which many farmers have been engaged for many years, especially in the northern part of the county. This produce is marketed in Chattanooga or shipped to other cities.

Chapter Twenty-seven

MINERAL AND ECONOMICAL.

Coal—Iron Ore—Furnaces—Wealth—Autos—Bonds— Miscellaneous.

WALKER is one of the few counties in the state having an extensive coal deposit, Dade and Chattooga being the others. The main coal deposits of the county are on Lookout and Pigeon mountains. Those on Lookout are located in the vicinity of Round Mountain, a small elevation on Lookout, some seven miles south of Lula falls. Here the Durham Coal and Coke company has operated a mine for more than forty years. The coal was discovered by its outcroppings long before the Civil War and was mined to a limited extent principally for the purpose of supplying blacksmith's forges.

In 1892 the Durham railroad was constructed to the coal fields, and the mines were put in operation, a large part of the output being made into coke for smelting iron ore. The coke ovens were located, mainly, at

Chickamauga. During the early years of its operation the mines were worked largely by convict labor. During these years and for many years afterward the output of coal was from 700 to 1,000 tons daily. Although the capacity has dwindled sharply the mines are still in operation (1932). During its palmy days this was a place of much activity, many hundreds of miners and laborers being employed. The coal not converted into coke was used for steam and domestic purposes and was shipped to all parts of the country.

There are other lower seams of coal and some extending further south along the mountain, as well as on Pigeon mountain which have never been developed. These, in the course of time, are sure to be worked, as means of transportation are provided.

IRON ORE. Several counties in Northwest Georgia abound in iron ore, Walker being one of these. A vast deposit of this valuable ore starts at the eastern base of Lookout Mountain near St. Elmo, Tennessee, and following the foothills of that mountain to the head of McLemore's Cove, it turns sharply to the northeast and follows the western foothills of Pigeon Mountain for some 12 or 15 miles when it turns again to the southwest following the eastern side to Harrisburg and on into Alabama. Also, there are extensive deposits on Taylor's Ridge in the eastern part of the county. At many sectors of this extensive line mines have been opened and worked quite extensively. At Estelle, near Kensington, the mines have been in operation for many years. Here hundreds of men have been employed as miners and laborers in excavating this valuable ore for commerce. This was found profitable because of the proximity of the railroad at that point. Other locations are only waiting sufficient transportation facilities. These will come as the demand increases.

Other deposits, either worked or prospected, are the following: The Allgood property south of Flintstone; the Stoner-Caldwell property near the Allgood; then follow in a general way the following: West property; Moses Long's; Wisdom's; Costello's; Parish's; Phillip's; Partain's; Henry's; Bloom's; Stephen's; Coulter's; Morgan's; Andrew's; Evitt's; Glenn-Warthen's; Hall's; Hammond's and others. The iron ores on all these properties were examined many years ago and found to be in commercial quantities and of excellent qualities. This line of valuable mineral ores stretches in a winding line for more than fifty miles, not to mention the ores on Taylor's ridge.

FURNACE.

Some two miles east of Villanow, in East Armuchee Valley, a blast furnace was built and was in operation before the Civil War and afterwards. It was owned by Doah Edmonson, of Murray county, but was operated by a man by name of Andrew Stroup. The furnace was about 20 feet square at the base and about 20 feet high, being constructed of rock which was quarried from the adjacent mountains and hauled to the site by ox teams. It was some two years in building. It was built at the base of a high hill or bluff, and a platform was laid from the top of the bluff to the top of the furnace along which the fuel and ore were carried and dropped into the furnace. A dam was built in the nearby creek from which water was secured for turning a large wheel, which furnished power for running a fan-wheel, thus giving a strong blast to the furnace. A pair of heavy scales was used for weighing the material, thus insuring the right proportion of each.

Ores from the near-by mountains were hauled to the furnace for smelting; brown hematite (soft ore) from Taylor's Ridge, and red hematite (hard ore) from Snake Creek. These were mixed in the proper proportion by weight, and also a certain amount, by weight, of limestone rock was added. Charcoal was used for fuel. Pine trees on the near-by hills and mountains were converted into charcoal and this was then hauled to the furnace for fuel. The ore was converted into pig iron, after which much of it was made into various vessels and tools for home and farm use, as wash pots, kettles for making molasses, cooking kettles, pots, skillets, ovens, and irons, and various utensils of ordinary home use. Mr. Fred Stansell, who lives near the site of the old furnace, has a pair of andirons made at the furnace. Also, Dr. Clements at Subligna has a vessel made at the furnace. Various other old settlers living in that section of the county have one or more articles made at the furnace. The products of the furnace were hauled first to Augusta, and afterward to Resaca for marketing. About two runs were made weekly, and some 8 or 10 men were required at times to operate all parts. A hammer weighing 600 pounds was used to crush the ore.

A FURNACE AT KENSINGTON. Another furnace erected and operated in the county was at or near Kensington. This furnace was owned and operated by a Mr. Strange. There was an abundance of iron ore in the vicinity, as evidenced by the extensive mines at Estelle which were operated many years from which vast quantities of ore have been extracted. The furnace at Kensington was operated by water power as in the case of the one in the eastern part of the county. This plant, however, was not operated on so extensive a scale as the one in Armuchee.

FIRE CLAY. Another mineral that has been extensively produced in a commercial way in the county is fire clay for making brick and for sewerage. At Mission Ridge in the northern part of the county a large plant was operated for many years in the manufacture of fire brick and brick for building purposes. At that place and at numerous other locations are extensive deposits of shales and clays suitable for making a very fine quality of brick.

OTHER MINERALS. Bauxite, Kaolin, and Tripolite are other minerals that have been worked in a commercial way in the county, as well as shales for the manufacture of cement. Mr. W. H. Boss has operated a tripoli mine on his farm near Naomi for some years. The mineral was discovered when the road was being built near his home.

There are three veins overlying each other varying in width from three to eleven feet. There are two of these triple veins, one sloping about 40 degrees, the other almost perpendicular, each of which have been worked to some extent. There is almost an unlimited amount of the material in that region which extends from near Waterville to Catlett some 8 or 10 miles. Mr. Boss has shipped already some fifty car loads which brings him a handsome profit. He employs from three to a dozen men when in full operation.

In the State Capitol in Atlanta are several aluminum vessels on display, labeled as having been made from bauxite which came from J. D. Taylors' place in Walker county. In addition there are large deposits of ochre, manganese ore, barytes, etc., in various parts of the county.

ECONOMICAL.

WEALTH. The wealth of the county is represented by real estate; manufacturing plants; railroads; mineral; mines and equipments; banks; buildings; homes; stock of all kinds; autos, machinery; farming tools; merchandise, money, notes, and bonds; and other property and is distributed as follows as shown by the tax digest for 1930:

Value real estate and improvements	$2,937,687
City or town property	1,569,670
Bank shares	57,233
Money—notes—accounts	84,086
Goods—merchandise—fixtures—fertilizers	176,098
Autos—motorcycles—bicycles	149,879
Manufacturing plants, buildings, etc.	1,875,324
Household goods	164,258
Jewelry $3,153. Horses $94,300. Cattle $95,871. Total	193,324
Sheep and goats $1,015. Unsold products $600. Total	1,615
Hogs $6,804. Dogs $1,858. Total	8,662
Agricultural tools $38,893. Mineral-timber leases $44,768. Total	83,661
Other property not mentioned	29,650
Aggregate Amount	$7,324,976

Amount of tax on polls $3,180. On professions $465.

This digest of the county's wealth does not represent the actual value by any means. Every one knows that the tax value is short of the real value, but just how far short is a matter of conjecture. Some men in making returns approximate the actual value of the property more nearly than others and for this reason it would be difficult to estimate the wealth of the county. Then again land values, which in this digest is the largest single item, fluctuate from time to time, being responsive to the economical condition of the country and especially to the general prosperity of the farming interests. At the present time the value of farming lands is probably lower than at any time since the Civil War. In like manner the value of all other items in this digest is below an average of value for a long period of years.

Viewing the situation thus one is compelled to admit that the wealth of the county now (1931) is lower than it was 12 or 15 years ago when times were more prosperous. It is believed that a conservative estimate of the country's wealth at this time might be placed at something like $40,000,000. A dozen years back it might have been a third more.

The following are the tax returns by decades for the past half century showing how the wealth of the county has steadily increased:

1880, $_____; 1890, $2,302,160; 1900, $2,319,937; 1910, $3,989,861; 1920, $7,675,511; 1930, $7,324,976.

AUTOS. The number of automobiles in 1915 was 380, valued at $18,978. In 1920 there were 3,726 valued at $223,586. In 1925, 2,607 valued at $130,350. In 1930 the number was 2998 valued at $149,873.

BONDS. In 1921 the county issued bonds to the amount of $400,000.00 for the building and improvement of roads. Of this amount $130,000.00 have been retired, leaving the present bonded indebtedness of the county $270,000.00. It is estimated that this indebtedness will have been paid off by 1946.

In addition to this the following school districts have issued bonds for erecting buildings and for other purposes: (Only the present amount of the bonded indebtedness is given in each case, a part having been paid). LaFayette $62,000. Rossville $57,000. Chattanooga Valley $41,500. West Armuchee $2,800. Cedar Grove $8,000. High Point $2,700. Lookout Mountain $29,000. Chickamauga $37,500. City of LaFayette $36,500. City of Rosville $_____.

MISCELLANEOUS. The county Chain Gang was started in 1909. The Chattanooga Valley road was hard-surfaced from Moon's station to the State line in 1922; the Dry Valley road to T. H. Fowler's in 1927; LaFayette to Chattooga county line in 1929; the McFarland Gap road in 1930; LaFayette to Lee and Gordon's mills (concrete) 1931.

Number of acres of land in the county 277,760; number returned in 1930 was 268,856, leaving 9,104 acres unaccounted for. A portion of this is represented in town and city property, leaving, however, a considerable acreage not returned.

Chapter Twenty-eight

EARLY CUSTOMS AND LIVING IN WALKER COUNTY—COUNTRY YOUNG PEOPLE A GENERATION AGO.

EARLY CUSTOMS AND LIVING IN WALKER COUNTY. Most of the pioneers of the county were plain, hardworking, common people —men who had immigrated here for the purpose of settling in the fertile valley lands of the county, which at that time could be had for practically nothing. These lands had been recently opened up for settlement. About the year 1830,—100 years ago,—the lands of the Cherokee Indians were opened up for settlement. They were surveyed and the numbers of the lots, in the various districts and sections, were arranged for a grand drawing. Any soldier who had fought in any of the wars at that time, or widow, or orphan children was permitted to draw. After the drawing, some few who had been lucky enough to secure a valuable tract, came in and settled. Many, however, fearing to brave the wilderness, or for other reasons, preferred not to emigrate. Hence, it was, that much land was left without a claimant. After a time these unclaimed parcels were settled and held by others. This brought many people into the county—men who were anxious to better their condition in life. They came as a rule on horseback, the wife, possibly, riding with an infant in her arms, the husband and children walking and carrying such things as they specially needed, as an ax, a few farm tools, a little salt and meal, and some bed clothes, possibly. There were no roads in those early days. No such things as wagons till some years later. They were men of iron will and nerve, who were willing to brave the wilderness for a home of their own.

There were among them some few men who were wealthy and had slaves to do the work of the farm. Especially in the Armuchees, there were quite a number of slave owners. There are still to be seen in certain parts of the county signs of the old slave quarters, a grim reminder of ante-bellum days and conditions. Also, there is the old fashioned Southern mansion with its broad portico and imposing columns reaching above the second story of the planter's home. There are quite a number of these to be seen yet in the county, notably the Warthen home at LaFayette, the Suttle home in West Armuchee, and the Lane home in the Cove. There are others in the county.

The houses of the first settlers, as a rule, had one room only. The house was built of logs cut from the near-by forest and notched down at the corners. The space between the logs was filled with a kind of mortar made of mud from a claybank near by. If carefully done, this made quite a warm, comfortable house for winter time, as well as cool for hot weather. The floor was made of split logs with one side smoothed with an ax, called puncheons. At first many settlers had no floor—only the bare earth. There was usually one door, which had a latch on the inside. A string was attached to this latch and was extended upward and out at a hole in the door so that one coming into the house had only to pull the latch string to lift the latch and the door would swing open. Hence we have the expression, "the latch string hangs on the outside," meaning, you are welcome. There was one or maybe two small windows, which were usually on each side of the fireplace, and had a shutter to open or close, but no glass. An elevated scaffold in the chimney corner, just outside the window, and underneath it, was used for the night's wood and pine knots. The material on this scaffold was carefully replenished each evening before nightfall, so that the fire could be kept burning till bedtime, which, in the winter, was usually very late, especially with the housewife, who had her knitting, spinning, and weaving to do. There were few lamps used in those days—possibly none at all. Tallow candles were occasionally to be seen, especially among the better-to-do people. Most of the pioneer settlers, however, used pine knots for lighting purposes. Happily, they were to be found in great abundance at that time. As one knot was about consumed, another was cast into the fire; and then another, as needed. Many a boy has learned to read by these old pine-knot fires. After working all day, he would sit or lie down by the family fire and read or write or "cipher." Many of those boys grew up and became men of worth and power in the county. The author recalls that he once heard that prince of teachers, Captain J. Y. Wood, tell how he learned to read and write by a pine knot fire, under the loving instruction of his mother. Also, how, as a young man, he used to take his Latin grammar to the field where he was plowing, and, while his horse was turning round, he would consult a word or sentence in the book, which was kept on the fence corner, and repeat it while he made another round in the field plowing. In this way he mastered much Latin while at work.

There were no cook stoves. Cooking was done in the open fireplace. Ashcake, or corn bread cooked in the hot ashes, was common. Meat was sometimes roasted in or near the fire, or on a spit, which hung before the fire. Then there might be a crane hanging in the chimney over the fire, upon which a pot or kettle could be placed for boiling vegetables or meats. Potatoes were generally roasted in the ashes. There were few sweets on the table of our grandmothers. Cakes were very rarely seen, and pies were as scarce. Sugar, which sold for 12 to 15 cents a pound, was occasionally to be seen. Sorghum, thick and black, was made in big kettles, and was about the only sweet food our grandfathers knew.

Everybody used coffee, or nearly so. It was bought green and roasted in an oven on the fireplace to a bright brown, enough being roasted at a time to do the family several days. While roasting it required constant stirring to prevent it from burning. There was a coffee mill nailed to the wall in the house for grinding coffee. The sound of the coffee mill in the early morning was a signal for getting ready for breakfast. Tea was little known to our parents.

There were certain customs among the early settlers, which, while they were not peculiar to this county, were, nevertheless, a part of their social fabric. These customs were those of "house raising," "log rolling," and "corn shucking." On those occasions the whole community usually turned out to assist. If a house was to be raised, the logs had been previously collected and hauled, or "snaked" to the spot, so that, now, there was nothing to do but to put them in place and notch them down. The custom of the house raising and the log rolling was one of necessity among the early settlers. One man or two or three men could not handle the logs and put them in place, hence the necessity of calling in the neighbors. This was a day's work for the good of the community—for society. No charge was made for this service by any one present. The same was true of the log rolling. The cornshucking was different, but it grew out of the pioneer's need of society and his desire for sociability.

At the log rollings feats of strength were exhibited. The man who could carry the heaviest load was generally the hero of the community. On these various occasions there was, at noon, prepared by the farmer's wife, a big dinner for all. The other ladies of the community were usually present to assist in the preparation of the noon-day meal. These were great social occasions, especially for the younger set. Here, the young men met the young ladies of the community, and while their elders conversed on various matters pertaining to society, politics, or religion the younger folk were enjoying themselves socially. Often, these gatherings were carried into the night and there was a "frolic," or dance for the younger folk, the elders often taking part. At these frolics, there was generally an old darkey with his banjo, who furnished the music for the dance. These meetings were rarely continued longer than about 10 o'clock at night. These were happy occasions among the early settlers, and had their places for good, as they contributed to the enjoyment of the people, by promoting fellowship, good feeling, manly virtues and contentment.

Another social event that should be mentioned, perhaps, and one much patronised, was the "quilting." At these times the ladies of the community gathered to make a quilt. They sometimes ended as the log rolling, with a frolic for the young of the community.

In those early days everybody rode horseback,—or walked. At first there were few roads and they were usually rough and in bad repair. It was a common sight to see both men and women mounted, going to church, or to market, or elsewhere, as occasion dictated. Almost every woman was an expert rider. They rode sideways according to the custom of the times. There was, in front of every farmer's home, a block, cut from a tree-trunk, from which ladies might spring to the horse's back. Likewise, at the church, was a block for the use of ladies in mounting. They wore a riding skirt to protect their clothes from being soiled. These mounting blocks were very useful for most of the ladies, however, many ladies were able to mount without assistance, by simply placing their hands on the back of the horse and springing into the saddle. It was not an unusual thing to see a lady riding behind her husband, or a sister behind her brother or father, or a young man with his best girl riding behind him.

Many early settlers of the poorer class had no means of conveyance and walked wherever they went. Old people often tell of how they have heard their mothers and aunts relate their experiences of the early days. Often, they traveled long distances to church afoot. Sometimes they carried their shoes in their hands almost to the church, then sat down by the roadside and put them on. After leaving church they took them off and went home barefoot. Some of the men of that day, not quite so fastidious as the ladies, hesitated not to go on to the church barefoot. Indeed, as late as 1900 men have been known to attend church without shoes in Walker county.

There were no railroads in the county till the latter eighties. Back in the thirties and forties there was no near market. Chattanooga, Rome, and even Atlanta, had had no beginning, or were too young to furnish an attractive market. The county's early settlers went to market to Augusta, Columbus, or maybe to Charleston or Raleigh. Many settlers who had emigrated from near those far away cities generally returned to that place for market purposes. Later, in the fifties, marketing was done at Resaca, and still a little later at Ringgold. In an old ledger of Bomar and Burgess who sold goods in West Armuchee in 1844, now in possession of Mr. W. P. Blackwell, there is a record of five trips to market during that year. Two trips to Columbus, one to Wetumpky, one to Madison, and one to Jasper county. The total expenses of the five trips as given was $78.59, which seems very reasonable at this day. There is no record of what goods were carried to market, but the goods brought back consisted, almost wholly, of sugar, salt, and coffee. This record shows that sugar was sold at 7 pounds to the dollar, coffee same price, and salt $1.50 per bushel.

These trips were made in canvas-covered wagons, drawn by horses or mules, usually two teams to each wagon. Neighbors who had to make these journeys started at the same time and traveled together for company and protection. Long trains of these wagons might be seen passing along the roads, from time to time, going to market, two or three weeks being required to make the trip. Provisions and utensils for cooking were carried, as a skillet, and coffee pot. Also, bed clothes and blankets for sleeping at night. About night the caravan would stop near a spring or stream of water, a fire built, supper cooked, and the night spent. A logheap fire was made and recruited during the night as needed. The women, if any were along, slept in the wagons, the men rolling themselves in quilts and blankets by the fire.

The drivers of the teams were expert wagoners. They carried a long whip with which they handled the teams. This whip they were able to wield in such a manner as to make a popping or cracking sound, and there being so many in a body driving along the roads, there was a continual cracking of whips, which sounded much like pistol or gun shots. It is said that from this circumstance they were called "Georgia Crackers," which appellation was afterward applied to Georgians in general.

Other explanations of the origin of "Georgia Crackers" are as follows:
From the Century Dictionary—"One of an inferior class of white hill

dwellers in some of the Southern United States, especially in Georgia and Florida. The name is said to have been applied because cracked corn was their chief article of diet: It is as old in Georgia and Florida as the time of the Revolution."

Richard Malcomb Johnson says, that among the followers of General Francis Marion in his guerrilla warfare, during the War of the Revolution, were some Georgians, who were especially expert in the use of the rifle, the "crack" of which got to be much dreaded by the British, who gave these rifle men the name of Georgia Crackers. After the war the name changed from a military to a social significance.

A theory of Charles H. Smith (Bill Arp) is that the hardy and industrious Scotchmen who settled in Georgia, and who came in conflict with the rough and unlettered settlers from other sections, called them "crackers," which is a Scotch term, and means "Boasters," "Idlers," who talk much and work little. Cracked and crack-brained may have the same origin.—From Evan's History of Georgia.

COUNTRY YOUNG PEOPLE A GENERATION AGO.

A generation or so ago, there were very few events—regular or occasional—religious or secular—to attract and draw the young people. The method of conveyance was, of course, necessarily slow and tedious, and for this reason it was not feasible to make trips of longer lengths than 12 to 15 miles and back in a day, having due regard for horses. Many of the modern attractions and inventions were unknown and undreamed of in those days.

The automobile, at once the greatest blessing and curse, possibly, of our modern civilization, began to make its appearance about the end of the nineteenth century. The phonograph preceded the automobile some few years. Then came the airplane and the movies and the radio. All of these have appeared within a generation. If all these were obliterated from our modern life, what effect would it have on our daily life—especially that of the young? The answer is: They would live and act about as we older ones did 40 years ago.

There were community gatherings in which the young always took much interest. These took the form, usually, of sociables and were held at different homes in the community. Occasionally, though rarely, they developed into dances; usually, however, they were simply occasions of general conversation and amusements. The time was passed in story telling, singing, playing pranks and other forms of innocent amusements. These gatherings were popular, especially, during the fall and winter seasons when the nights were long. Most generally the young people would attend these gatherings afoot—traveling sometimes two or three miles and back in this way. Upon occasion, these young people, at certain seasons would inaugurate and have an old fashion 'possum hunt. Attended by one or more elderly matrons as chaperons the young ladies of the community as well as the young men, in large numbers, on a bright moonlight night, would tramp the hills and valleys for miles hunting 'possums. These were most delightful occasions for all parties and were thoroughly enjoyed. Usually they were fully rewarded by the capture of several 'possums, and sometimes a polecat. This latter was certain to inject extra excitement into the chase. But whether they caught a 'possum or not, they had a delightful evening and the experiences furnished a topic for general conversation for weeks to come.

The debating society and the spelling bee came in for a full share of attention in the days of our grandmother's girlhood. These were held at the local school house during the winter months. They were most interesting and sometimes very animated meetings. All the old popular subjects were duly argued and their merits fully exhausted at such times, and many an awkward, bashful, untutored lad, who afterward made his mark as a leading public speaker of the county, made his beginnings at these meetings. Or, maybe it was a spelling bee; and they were spellers in those days—according to Webster. Having selected two captains as leaders, and the audience chosen by the leaders, according to ability, the row of contestants reached around the room, standing against the wall. The community teacher then stepped forth and drew the Old Blueback. In order to break the ice, so to speak, he began at "baker," and played along for some pages in order to give time for all the timid spellers to feel at home. Then skipping over about "botany," or "amity," the spelling began to pick up somewhat. Among these pages some few of the poorer spellers began to drop out, and as the contestants began to settle down to their task, the teacher suddenly turned to "immateriality," and such like words, at which there was a faint smile to be seen on the faces of some of the better spellers. For nearly an hour the contest raged among these difficult words, during which time many were compelled to "yield the palm." However, there was a goodly number still left on either side, when the teacher turned beyond the pictures and began with such words as, blanc-mange, braggadocio, daguerreotype, ennui, caoutchouc, and such like. Here the battle raged till the list was exhausted, during which time most of the spellers acknowledged defeat; however, several were still defiant. The teacher often found it necessary to go over the same words in order to reach a decision. Sometimes, however, it was decided to call it a draw, especialy if the number remaining on each side was about equal. These meetings were largely attended and fully enjoyed by our ancestors, and years afterward furnished a theme for pleasant reminiscences.

In addition to the above, which might be classed as strictly community affairs, and which, with other similar meetings, were common to all communities, and were largely attended and greatly enjoyed, there were what might be termed sectional or county attractions and which most young people sought to attend. One of these was the annual or semi-annual singing convention. These were held in different parts of the county and were largely attended by most of the young people. They attended in wagons, buggies, horseback, on the train, or sometimes walked. These conventions were the subject of general interest before and afterward. Everybody who could sing took part, and many young people would lead in the singing or perform at the organ. In those days the county paper usually carried an exhaustive report of the activities of the convention.

Another event closely allied to the singing convention was that of the Walker County Sunday School Convention. At these there were discussions of Sunday School work—methods, plans, principles, etc., as well as singing; and our young folks usually attended these in large numbers. Uncle Fletcher Smith of the Cove was, for many, many years the head and the life of the County Sunday School Convention.

Another event of general interest was the County Fair. Everybody who could went to the Fair and many young folks generally attended. The Fair was at first held at Chickamauga, being organized there about 1900 or soon after that date and continued there for some ten years, after which it was located at LaFayette.

There was also, the annual circus which came in for its share of popularity. In the early days it was popular to go to the "show" as it was termed. About the year 1850 a circus was held at John Scott Henderson's just across the Walker-Catoosa county line just north of the home of the late Mrs. Tripp. There were no railroads at that time and everything went by wagon train.

Chapter Twenty-nine

COUNTRY SOCIAL LIFE SIXTY YEARS AGO—CLOTHES—AMUSEMENTS AND ENTERTAINMENTS—CONVENIENCES—OTHER INCONVENIENCES.

MAN has a very strongly marked social instinct. Whether at work or at play he enjoys the association of his fellows. Men are gregarious. They are seen in flocks more often than alone. This proclivity has a marked effect on his life and customs. Of necessity his working hours often isolate him, but when occasion permits he will seek his fellow's companionship.

The countryman is necessarily more secluded than his city cousin. His work calls him apart from his fellows. During his working hours he is alone and has his thoughts for his companions. The urbanite, on the other hand, dwells much of his time in company with his fellows with whom he discusses the events of the day and other matters. The ruralist is, therefore, more secluded, distant, non-communicative and inclined to take council with his own thoughts. He lives close to nature; associates with the Great Open; influences and is influenced by, the wild life around him. His activities being circumscribed by the vicissitudes of the weather, he takes note of the movements of the winds and clouds and this becomes one of his main topics of conversation. He is an early riser. Rarely does he fail to be up and doing by four in the morning, winter and summer. His thrifty housewife prepares breakfast by lamplight. The children are all seated about the table to partake of the morning meal. There is, in the average family on the farm, no dearth of children. It is no unusual matter to find from eight to twelve children in a family. Often the number reaches to fifteen.

Some one has said that "mother" is the sweetest, dearest word in our language. Maybe so, but it seems to me that "motherhood" should be ranked at least second. Motherhood, it seems to me, implies not only a willingness to bear and rear children, but indicates an inward feeling of real duty to do so—a sense of duty performed. The word seems to imply a plurality, and not simply a duality. Motherhood seems to carry the idea of a bevy, a group. It implies an obligation and indicates some sacrifices of concrete things, but in the sense of duty well done, it fully repays all sacrifices. "Duty," says Robert E. Lee, "is the sublimest word in the English language. We cannot do more, we should not wish to do less."

Roman history contributes an incident furnishing a striking example of the high esteem in which motherhood was held among the ancients. It relates that, upon a time, a bevy of matrons of the upper class were assembled at the home of one of their number, when, it happened, that they were discussing their jewels, each one, of course, showing with pride some valuable personal ornament and giving its history—all except one, who, sitting somewhat apart from the others, seemed to take little interest in the conversation. At length some one asked her to show her jewels, whereupon she stepped to the door and called into the room two little chubby boys—sun-tanned and dirty, and throwing her arms around them and implanting kisses on their cheeks, "These," she said, "are my jewels."

But pardon this digression and we return to the subject. The morning meal consists, mainly, of hot biscuits, ham or bacon with gravy, eggs, butter and syrup, and coffee. The mother knows from long experience what it takes to feed her family. Ten or twelve growing boys and girls, besides the husband and wife will consume near half a bushel of hot biscuits, and there will be little left over for the farm dog. Occasionally, in season, the morning meal consists of fried chicken, and when this occurs it is necessary to dress two for this hungry brood which will probably be a sufficiency provided there is a generous supply of gravy. Then, again, once in a while, all meats are left off and breakfast is composed entirely of biscuit, butter and syrup, in which case a pound of butter would not suffice for the morning meal.

The noon-day meal, or dinner, which was served on the farm of our forefathers about 11:30 o'clock was composed of one or more vegetables in season, with a generous slice of boiled bacon, an immense "cobbler" pie made from some of the orchard products, corn bread and buttermilk. The buttermilk has been cooling since early morning in the cellar or springhouse and is a most welcome draught to most of the family at the noon-day meal. If there happens to be a visitor at the home for this meal, some extra dish may make its appearance on the table, but ordinarily something like the above may be expected.

No elaborate preparations were made for the evening meal, which was served in the summertime about sundown—certainly before dark. The mother might cook some fresh corn bread, which, together with the left-over vegetables from dinner and the abundance of cold sweet milk from the springhouse, where it has been since early morning, will satisfy the hunger of all the household.

I have said that the farmer was an early riser. He was, likewise, early to bed. He believed with all his heart in Ben Franklin's "Early to bed" doctrine, which he never failed to practice and to preach. Often, especially in summer, he was in bed before dark. The day's work done, horses fed, he, with tired limbs, is glad to seek his rest:

> "Something attempted, something done,
> Has earned a night's repose."

The children, in the meantime, having completed the evening chores, may have engaged in some simple game for pastime for a short while (for what growing boy ever tires?), soon retire for the night's rest. Last of all, the wife and mother, after seeing that all is well with her brood, and with especial attention to the least ones, steals off to her virtuous couch to get a rest from sixteen hours of activity. Is is any wonder if she sleeps soundly? and yet she awakes at the faintest call from any of the family and ready to minister to their needs.

If the next morning happens to be Sunday, which occurs every seven days, there may not be quite so much hurry about the place. The father will probably be up as early as usual, but the wife and children may enjoy an extra half-hour's repose; but, by and by, all are up and the morning meal over, preparations are begun for church attendance.

Everyone will go—not from necessity, but from pleasure. There is a real desire to attend church. The family has been isolated for a week, maybe more, and now there is a hungering to see friends and neighbors, as well as to hear the sermon and to engage in worship. This is man's social instinct. He enjoys the companionship of his fellows. There is a general bustle and hurry to get ready, and to be on time at the church. The mode of conveyance is necessarily slow. The mother, with wise forethought, during the past few days examined all the children's wearing apparel to see that all was in readiness. It is a matter, then, of only a short while till all are ready.

The two-horse wagon, filled with chairs, will accommodate all, except two or three of the larger boys who will go horseback. I said all; it is likely that the elder sister will have a special conveyance furnished by one of the neighboring swains, who happens along about the time the procession is ready to start. Bashful and stammering, he invites her to ride with him (as if there was not already an understanding to that effect). She mounts behind him and all are away. Arrived at the church long before the hour for preaching, the father, mother and the children enjoy the greetings of friends and neighbors which are cordially returned. This half-hour is spent in animated conversation —conversation about the community happenings, the weather, sickness, marriages, deaths, crops, etc.

A song from the church is the signal for all to enter which is promptly done. The service is a spiritual one; the preacher is a man of God. His prayers, exhortations and sermon are convincing and he holds his audience in rapt attention to the last. Although his sermon may last an hour he has the undivided attention of his congregation. The young people and children are all there. There is no thought of their remaining away from church. The crying baby does not interrupt either the preacher or people. It is a common occurrence and no one thinks of it. And, too, this was the day when there were few books—hymn books—the preacher's being the only one present. The hymns were sung by lining, that is the preacher read two lines and the congregation sang those two; after which two more were read out and sung by the people. In all these services the most reverent attention was displayed by the congregation. And afterwards, for a week or a month, the homes of the community were wont to discuss the sermon and the text and the exhortations.

The sermon over, the benediction is reverently pronounced by the pastor, but there is no hurrying out of the house. No one seems ready to leave. Everybody wants to shake everybody's hand. Everybody wants everybody to go home with him. The pastor is pressed by various admirers to go to his house for dinner. If one there should be who was anxious to leave the house at once, he would find it difficult to mill his way through the aisle to the door. The only thing to do is to wait till everybody speaks and talks to everybody and the procession slowly moves toward the door. Eventually everybody gets out and leaves for home, a happy and contented people.

The afternoon is spent in reading, or meditation, or,—especially if some neighbor has dropped in,—in conversation; or mayhap, the wife and husband will call on some of the neighbors for an hour's talk. The children, in the meantime, are enjoying the freedom of the woods, or the "Ol' Swimmin' Hole." The younger set have gathered at some of the neighbor's homes where others have met to sing. Such were the conditions prevailing among our forefathers a half-century or more ago.

CLOTHES. The wearing apparel of our forbears was quite different from that to which we are accustomed. The mode changes from year to year even in our day, especially in feminine clothes; the change then in eighty years is likely to be considerable. There was little machinery and no easy means of transportation before and immediately following the War Between the States. In Walker county it was necessary to wear home made clothing. There was little else worn till some years after the war. Most men wore home-made cotton or jeans pants and coats. Almost every housewife had a spinning wheel and loom by means of which she made at home cloth to clothe her family. For Sunday wear an especially nice piece of cloth was made into a suit for father or big brother. There were few overcoats but most men had a large woolen shawl which they wore on cold or rainy days when traveling away from home. In those days few boys or young men had any kind of neck-wear. A plain homespun shirt with no collar was worn. This writer was not bothered with any kind of neck-wear till he was nearly twenty years old. Men and boys all wore clothes made by wife and mother.

Feminine clothes have undergone the greatest evolution, however, since the sixties. This chronicler has a faint remembrance of the hoop-skirt. I recall once to have seen one of my aunts dressed according to that mode. Necessarily the skirt was made very large at the bottom and narrowed sharply to the waist. When the hoops were placed under the skirt the circumference must have been in extreme cases about eight feet at the bottom. Almost every woman, young and old, wore the hoop-skirt. In an old ledger kept by the father of Mr. W. P. Blackwell of Greenbush are numerous entries of sales of hoop-skirts to his customers. This was during the sixties and seventies. Milady, also at that time, was especially fond of wearing ribbons. Her waist, chest, arms or hair were sure to be adorned with a bunch of fancy-colored ribbons on all proper occasions. Wide-brimmed straw hats decked with ribbons or artificial roses were common.

A little later the "bustle" came into vogue and was worn by all the gentle sex. This was a spring-like arrangement placed at the back near the hips, which caused the skirt to stand out at that point, forming a bustle. Its life as I remember it was of short duration. The next important change in feminine attire was the full sleeve, which was made very full and large, especially near the shoulders. It must have taken a yard or better for each sleeve.

After this came the slitted skirt and finally the short skirt so familiar to us to-day. The evolution from the hoop-skirt to the short skirt takes in the whole gamut of possibilities—a complete evolution.

AMUSEMENTS AND ENTERTAINMENTS. There were few amusements or entertainments in the lives of our forbears. Every day was a workday. There were houses and barns to be built; fields to be cleared; rails to be split and fences built, and a hundred other duties to be performed. After the crops were laid-by, most farmers began clearings in order to extend their fields for another year. There was little time for amusements at first. However, as time went on and conditions began to improve, there began to appear some signs of entertainments.

Besides the race track, shooting match, quilting, and gander-pulling, described elsewhere, most farmers and young men diverted themselves by hunting and fishing. It was nothing uncommon to hear the sound of guns among the valleys and hills of the county during the spring, summer and fall on Saturday afternoons. Almost every farmer "knocked off" on Saturday at noon, certainly by middle of the afternoon, and went hunting or fishing. Those who did not hunt were very apt to be found on the neighboring stream where they often stayed till after dark in an effort to carry home a "mess" of fish for Sunday's breakfast.

On very rare occasions it happened that a "Punch and Judy" show was advertised in the community to be held at the neighboring school house. At these shows everybody—especially the children and young people—were sure to be seen. The cost of admission was usually small. The manager always had a supply of jokes which he managed by his art of ventriloquism to put into the mouths of Punch and Judy and pull off on the more prominent people of the community. These were animated occasions and since they were only rarely to be enjoyed they were like a fertil spot in a desert in the lives of our grandfathers.

CONVENIENCES. There were few conveniences in the homes of our grandparents. Even among the better class, both in town and country, there was little thought of conserving steps and labor about the work of the home. The log house generally consisted of two large rooms with a hall-way between, and with a back room, or "lean-to" which was used for a kitchen and dining room, and maybe contained one or more beds, especially if the family was a large one which was apt to be the case. One of the large front rooms was a kind of parlor where company was entertained. It contained among other furniture two beds, one of which might be a spare used for company. The other large room also contained two beds besides a trundle bed which was pushed under one of the large beds during the day and at night was drawn out to be occupied by two or three of the smaller children. Or, there might be a bed up stairs in the attic, to which the larger boys ascended by means of a ladder nailed to the side of the house and entered through a kind of trap-door or port hole. It was the custom of the father to call these boys down from their perch every morning about four o'clock to build a log fire before the family arose.

At first there was no stove and the cooking was done at the fireplace. It was best for the log fire to burn well-down to coals before the breakfast was started. The oven with biscuits in it was placed on a bed of these red-hot coals and the lid placed on the oven with other hot coals on it. Soon there were hot brown biscuits ready, "cooked to a turn" as Uncle Remus would say. Unless the housewife had two such ovens it would be necessary to repeat the operation, maybe several times in order to satisfy the appetite of her hungry brood. In the meantime the frying pan was placed on a similar bed of coals and the aroma of several generous slices of ham or bacon was permeating the surrounding atmosphere, causing the mouths of the children to "water." Likewise, a big pot of coffee was simmering on other hot coals ready to furnish a welcome draught to wash down the morning meal.

For cooking vegetables or boiling meats there was the crane, a kind of iron hook which could be made to swing back and forth over the fire, on which a pot might be placed for cooking purposes. When not otherwise occupied this crane generally held a pot of hot water to be used upon occasion.

Often the bread for the meal was simply an "ash-cake." This was cooked by placing the dough on a clean-swept hot rock and covered with hot embers. In due time the bread would be thoroughly cooked and was a most welcome food to the hungry family. Or, the weeding hoe might be pressed into service and the dough placed on it and allowed to cook near the hot fire. This was called "hoecake." Or, the dough might be placed on a clean board or piece of plank and allowed to cook near the hot fire. This was called "johnnycake."

Among the poorer class, as well as also many of the middle class, the cooking and eating was all done in the kitchen, as well as in many cases, sleeping by some of the family. While the mother was cooking the meal around the fireplace she would "fix the table," which stood near by. The mother sat at the head of the table the better to look after any late dishes that may still be cooking as well as to distribute to her brood the viands prepared. The father sat next to the mother on that side toward the fireplace. Then followed the oldest boy or girl and so on to the foot of the table. The small children sat on a bench behind the table next to the wall, for as Webster says, "Six small boys can sit on one long bench."

The early settlers built their homes in the vicinity of a natural spring of water, usually at some considerable distance away. The barn and other out-houses were also at some distance from the dwelling. There was little thought of arranging such trifles so as to conserve time and labor. Often the housewife had to go half a mile to the spring or branch to do the family wash. The pot and tubs were left there from week to week and on wash day the mother took her bundle of clothes with buckets and a gourd of lye soap and spent the greater part of the day down at the Big Spring. She knew nothing about a scrub board. She never heard of one. She used a battling stick on the heavy clothes while the lighter ones were washed and scrubbed with her hands. The members of the family expected no elaborate dinners on wash days, and they were rarely disappointed, the wife's time being taken up by the duties and laborious work at the Big Spring.

OTHER INCONVENIENCES. The early settlers had no lamps for light as a rule. Very few had even candles. They used pine knots for light. Happily, these were to be found in great abundance a century ago in almost every part of the county. A generous supply was always on hand for use during the long winter nights. When the light began to wane, a fresh knot was cast into the fire, which soon burst into a blaze sending a ruddy light throughout the large room. By this the sewing, knitting, spinning and weaving were done, as well as the reading, ciphering, games and so forth. Later the tallow candle made its appearance and people began to use that light on special occasions, still however, employing the pine knot for general use. It was not till after the Civil War that many people began to use lamps. The first lamps used were small brass lamps with round wicks and no globes. They could be carried around by a small handle. They smoked terribly and the unpleasant odor from them was sickening. Later the small glass lamps with globes came into use which was a great improvement.

There is more truth than poetry in the old saw, "Man works from sun to sun, a woman's work is never done." This was especially true with our grandmothers. In those days when there were few conveniences about the home the housewife was literally going from early to late. There was always something to do.

Breakfast over and the men folks off to the field she must now lose no time if she would have everything ready for the noon meal. First there were from one to three cows to milk and this in those days when there were calves to care for was no insignificant job. Then the milk must be strained and placed away for cooling. Then the dishes from the morning meal were to do including the many milk vessels. Following this was the daily churning, molding the butter and arranging the milk in a cool place for the mid-day meal. Next came the bed making and the house sweeping and the dusting and the other little niceties that only a woman knows about but without which there would be something wanting about the home. In the midst of all this there were the smaller children and often a nursing baby to be cared for in addition to the young chicks which must be fed and watered.

Before these things are fairly complete she must begin to gather her material for the noon-day meal. A visit to the garden for some vegetables and their preparation takes time and labor; another such trip to the orchard for some fruit for the "cobbler" pie, and various miscellaneous collections to add to the mid-day meal—all these give her many weary steps. Truly, a woman's work is never done. Happy, thrice happy, is that man who has a wife who can do these things without complaining.

The following incident came under this author's observation when but a lad: The husband with his helpers had hurried away after a hasty morning meal to the field where he was very busy trying to put his crop in good shape. The wife—such a one as described above—in the meantime was doing her best to dispatch the various household duties so as to have all ready for his return at the dinner hour. She had reached the churning duty and was busy at the well-house with this work when the husband hurriedly appeared to secure some tool accidentally left in the early morning, and seeing his wife finishing the churning and with a large bowl was washing and salting the fine yellow butter, and noting her flushed face and, as he thought, a rather worried look thereon, he paused a moment and remarked that she looked like a peach and that he knew that she could make the best butter of any woman in all the countryside. That was all—he hurried on; but that was enough. That wife was happy. She forgot her worries; her steps were brisker; her smiles were radiant and her appearance denoted happiness all that day. At the dinner hour she wore a freshly ironed apron and displayed a bouquet of extra nice flowers on the table.

Chapter Thirty

CONTRIBUTIONS—WHITE'S HISTORICAL COLLECTIONS—T. A. COOPER'S ARTICLE—CAPTAIN WOOD'S—JOHN ROSS HOUSE—EARLY DAYS AROUND CRAWFISH SPRING—REMINISCENCES OF A REFUGEE—MOTHER'S GIFT TO SOLDIER BOY— HISTORY OF A REFUGEEING FAMILY.

WALKER COUNTY, FROM WHITE'S HISTORY.

WHITE'S Historical Collections, published in 1854, devotes several pages to Walker County. For showing the changes since that time, and for its general interest, it is copied and reproduced herewith:

WALKER COUNTY.

"Laid out from Murray, and organised in 1833. Named in honor of Major Freeman Walker. LaFayette is the county town, beautifully situated, distant from Milledgeville two hundred and ten miles. Ringgold is a town of recent date, situated on the State Road.

"Extract from the Census of 1850: Dwellings, 1867; families, 1867; white males, 5803; white females, 5605; free colored males, 18; free colored females, 19; Total population, 11445; slaves, 1664; deaths, 139; farms, 600. One manufacturing establishment. Value of real estate $923600, value of personal estate, $1007725.

"No section is favored with a greater variety of springs than this county. The Medicinal Springs, owned by the Gordons, are situated at the base of Taylor's Ridge. There are twenty springs within the space of a half mile; but the main springs are twelve in number, on a beautiful eminence of Taylor's Ridge. The trees have been cut down. From this spot may be seen various mountains. Cherokee Springs are at the base of Taylor's twenty-four miles from Chattanooga. Yate's Spring is five miles from Gordon's Spring. Crayfish Spring is twelve miles from Gordon's. Catoosa Springs are one and a half miles from the State Road. We give the following extracts concerning these springs from an account written by Mr. S. Rose, one of the editors of the Georgia Messenger:

"Imagine to yourself an elevated cove, or basin, in the Blue Ridge, surrounded almost entirely by towering eminences. From the eastern slope a bold, clear brook comes tumbling into the valley, and passes rapidly westward, until it escapes between two abrupt mountain peaks, and dashes for half a mile over rocky barriers into a branch of the Chickamauga. On the borders of this brook, and in the center of this basin, which I shall designate 'The Vale of Springs,' there is a level spot about two acres in extent, within the limits of which I have counted no less than *fifty-two* distinct, bold, and well-defined springs. The waters are strongly mineral.

"All these springs seem to issue either from the mountain side, upon a bed of hard, black slate, or boil up through the slate. They are perennial; the most severe and continued drouths make no perceptible difference in the quantity of water which they discharge. The country around is protected by its native forests. The atmosphere is pure, dry and bracing, and entirely free from disease, or from any cause which could produce it.

"Immediately in the rear of the springs there are two beautiful mountain peaks, from the summits of which visitors might enjoy an extensive prospect of the surrounding country.

"There is a pond in Chattooga valley called the Round Pond. It embraces four or five acres, forty-eight feet deep in the middle, of a sea green color. Tradition says two Indians were drowned in this pond. There is no visible outlet and the water never becomes stagnant. Long Pond is a beautiful sheet of water, famous for excellent fish.

"Among the first settlers of this county were: X. G. McFarland, T. G. McFarland, John Spradlin, Mr. Allman, J. R. Brooks, General Newnan, Mr. Acock, S. Marsh, S. Fariss, Jesse Land, J. T. Story, Robert Boyle, B. McCutchins, A. Hughes, S. Dunn, Lawson Black, Wm. Hardin, James Park, John Caldwell, John Wicker, Joseph P. McCullough.

"Walker has many caves, among which the most remarkabel is Wilson's Cave. We extract from "Sears' Wonders of the World" the description given by some persons of a visit which they made in 18—.

"The company being met, with lighted torches we entered the cave, through a small aperture, descending a flight of natural stairs, almost perpendicularly, some ten or twelve feet. Coming to the most magnificent room we ever beheld, and being desirous of viewing as minutely as we could, from the amplitude of this anomaly of nature, and illuminated the place as far as we were able by the means we had, when we discovered that an almost infinite number of stalactites had been formed by the continual dripping of the water, resembling, in size and appearance, various animal bodies.

"Being somewhat satisfied with our examination of this apartment, with our hearts glowing with wonder, love, and praise to the Architect of Nature, we moved slowly and rather pensively along this solitary and hitherto unexplored mansion, through devious wiles of '*incognita loca*,' in quest of new discoveries.

"Having reached the extreme end of this spacious dome, we found that to proceed further, we had to ascend stupendous and almost inaccessible eminences, over craggy precipices and yawning gulfs, to the height of some fifty or sixty feet, when, by the dim light of our tapers, we discovered through a small opening into another room, less extensive but far more beautiful and picturesque; for there appeared to the astonished beholder not only a representation of a part of the animal creation, but a true delineation of a great number of inanimate objects, such as cones, altars, pyramids, tables, candle-stands, with a *fac-simile* of some of nature's choicest productions; and it really appeared as if she, in her wild and playful moments, had intended to mock the curiosities of art."

"General Daniel Newnan died in this county. He merits the remembrance and respect of the people of Georgia. In the Indian Wars he proved himself a good soldier. Besides holding many high offices in the State, he was a member of Congress from 1831 to 1833.

MISCELLANEOUS.

"A gentleman who resided among the Cherokees for many years has furnished us with the following items:

"Strawberry was a large town, situated on the head waters of Amuchee, ten miles E. of LaFayette. Dogwood was situated on the head waters of Chickamauga. The principal chief was Charlie Hicks, a man of vigorous mind and of ardent piety. He was a member of the Moravian Church. Elijah Hicks was the son of Charles Hicks—a man, it is said, "who would not have disgraced any circle, either in appearance, manner, or conversation." Richard Taylor was a distinguished chief among the Cherokees. His name is affixed to the treaty made at Washington, March 22, 1816. Chestnut Town was on Peavine Creek. The head chief was Partridge. Crayfish Town was situated west of Chestnut. The principal chief was George Lowery. The first court in Walker was held at this place, Judge Hooper presiding.

"We have been favored with the following letter from a gentleman, giving an account of an Indian play-ball which took place in this county, and at which he was present:

"We started one fine morning in the month of August, for the hickory grounds, having learned that two towns, Chattooga and Chickamauga, were to have a grand play-ball at that place. We found the grounds to be a beautiful hickory level, entirely in a state of nature, upon which had been erected several rude tents, containing numerous articles, mostly of Indian manufacture, which were the stakes to be won or lost in the approaching contest. We had been on the ground only a short time when the contending parties, composed of fifty men each, mostly in a state of nudity, and having their faces painted in a fantastical manner, headed by their chiefs, made their appearance. The war-whoop was then sounded by one of the parties, which was immediately answered by the other, and continued alternately, as they advanced slowly in the regular order toward each other to the center of the ground allotted to the combat.

"In order that you may have an idea of the play, imagine two parallel lines of stakes driven into the ground near each other, each extending for about 100 yards, and having a space of about 100 yards between them. In the center of these lines were the contending towns, headed by their chiefs, each having in their hands two wooden spoons, curiously carved, not unlike our large iron spoons. The object of these spoons is to throw up the ball. The ball is made of deer skin wound around a piece of spunk. To carry the ball through one of the lines above mentioned is the purpose to be accomplished. Every time the ball is carried through these lines counts one. The game is commenced by one of the chiefs throwing up the ball to a great height, by means of the wooden spoons. As soon as the ball is thrown up, the contending parties mingle together. If the chief of the opposite side catches the ball as it descends, with his spoon, which he exerts his utmost skill to do, it counts one for his side. The respective parties stand ready to catch the ball if there should be a failure on the part of their chiefs to do so. On this occasion the parties were distinguished from each other by the color of their ribbons; the one being red, the other blue.

"The strife begins. The chief has failed to catch the ball. A stout warrior has caught it, and endeavors with all speed to carry it to his lines, when a faster runner knocks his feet from under him, wrests the ball from him, and triumphantly makes his way with the prize to his own line; but when he almost reaches the goal, he is overtaken by one or more of his opponents, who endeavor to take it from him. The struggle becomes general, and it is frequently the case that serious personal injuries are inflicted. It is very common during the contest to let the ball fall to the ground. The strife now ceases for a time until the chiefs again array their bands. The ball again is thrown up, and the game is continued as above described. Sometimes half an hour elapses before either side succeeds in making one in the game.

"It is usual at these ball-plays for each party to have their own conjurers at work at the time the game is going on; their stations are near the center of each line. In their hands are shells, bones of snakes, &c. These conjurers are sent for from a great distance. They are estimated according to their age, and it is supposed by their charms they can influence the game. On this occasion two conjurers were present; they appeared to be over one hundred years of age. When I spoke to one of them he did not deign even to raise his head; the second time I spoke he gave me a terrific look, and at the same time one of the Indian women came and said, "*Conagatee Unaka*"—"go away, white man."

"I cannot resist the inclination I feel, to give you an account of an individual whom I met on this occasion. He was a Cherokee Indian belonging to a wealthy family, and had received a finished education at one of our Northern colleges. His talents were of a high order, and upon his return home, he was appointed a petty chief. He was dressed in fine calf boots, blue cloth pantaloons, silk velvet vest, fine beaver hat, with a silver band. His gown was made of red flowered calico, reaching nearly to the ground, with a cape over the shoulders trimmed with blue fringe. Judge of my astonishment when I ascertained this individual to be the distinguished Jim Fields."

NORTHWEST GEORGIA.

(The following article was contributed to a Chicago publication in 1892 by T. A. Cooper, a native of Walker county and brother of our county citizen, Alonzo Cooper, of Chestnut Flat. T. A. Cooper died in California about five years ago at the age of 92.)

"Northwest Georgia was the state on which many of the gigantic military scenes were enacted during the war between the States, 1861-65. It was from Chattanooga to Atlanta that every step of the advance by the Federals was so stubbornly resisted by the Confederates. There was no more desperate fighting during that war than on this famous campaign. The one side saw their hopes for destroying the Union hourly fading, which added desperation to their former zeal, while the Federals saw they were day by day forcing the war to a conclusion, which would enable them to return to families and friends, and peaceful avocations. The country through which the armies marched and fought from Chattanooga to Atlanta is worthy of more than passing mention. Those who were engaged in that unpleasant conflict will concur in the opinion that, for picturesque grandeur, beautiful streams and ice-cold rivulets and springs, North Georgia has no superior. The soldiers, marching and fighting through those fertile valleys, and charging the faces and gaps of those picturesque mountains, were astonished that such a country, with such vast and valuable resources, had remained for years comparatively an undeveloped wilderness. Such thoughts would naturally come to those who had been reared in the Northern States where many localities have natural resources far less valuable, yet had been made to bear fruit profitably for the industrious agriculturist, miner, and mechanic. Again, the Federal soldier could not help feeling surprise at the gross ignorance of the masses up to, and including the war. Many, perhaps, did not at the time think of the prime cause of such ignorance and that such a country should then be comparatively a wilderness. They could only wonder how it could be possible that Georgia, one of the thirteen states forming the Federal union in 1787, could have moved so slowly in progress as to contain millions of acres in timber and thousands of uneducated white citizens. The blighting incubus, slavery, had been the hindering cause, the bar to educating the masses, and it is a fact that, as a rule, it requires education to kindle the fire of ambition, and to stimulate a people in an honorable strife to develop the resources of their immediate locality and make it as desirable, or more so, than any other.

"As Northwest Georgia produced at least a few individuals who figured more or less in the history of the State, and one at least, who has made a national reputation, the writer feels it due here to give a few links in the chain of the early history and settlement of that portion of Northwest Georgia, known fifty years ago as Walker county, from which, from time to time, the counties of Catoosa, a portion of Whitfield and a portion of Chattooga have been formed, and in which the battles of Chickamauga, Missionary Ridge, Lookout Mountain, Ringgold, Tunnel Hill, Rocky Face, etc., were fought, as well as many other minor engagements. Hence the writer will confine his narrative to the territory originally comprised in Walker county. In 1830 North Georgia was inhabited by the Cherokee Indians. General Jackson opened a road down the west side of Taylor's Ridge in 1812, for his forces who marched by land to oppose the attempted invasion of the Gulf States by the British. The road opened by General Jackson was known as the Alabama road. It should here be mentioned that several ranges of mountains traverse Walker county from northeast to southwest. Taylor's Ridge derived its name from a prominent Indian by the name of Taylor, who resided near the present village of Ringgold. East of said mountain and west of Rocky Face Ridge is the stream forming East Chickamauga; west of Taylor's Ridge is middle Chickamauga, the two streams united near Ringgold in Catoosa county. On the west border of Walker county is the majestic Lookout Mountain, which tradition says derived its name from a portion of General Jackson's forces in 1812. General Coffee with his command crossed the Tennessee River at Ross' Ferry, better known since as Ross' Landing, and now Chattanooga, Tenn. The first camp after crossing the river was near the foot, and on the west side of, the mountain. General Coffee gave as the countersign for the night, "Lookout," since which time the mountain has borne the name Lookout. East of this mountain is the stream West Chickamauga, east of which is Pigeon Mountain, which is near midway between Lookout and Taylor's Ridge. Pigeon derived its name from the millions of pigeons roosting thereon in early winter, when the whites first settled in the county. The forest produced chestnuts and acorns in abundance. The pigeons after feeding through the day congregated in countless numbers in the trees at night, where thousands were slaughtered by hunters. Hence, the name Pigeon Mountain. East and Middle Chickamauga, uniting at or near Ringgold, joined the west stream before the three jointly entered the Tennessee River. It is proper here to mention a considerable stream, Pea Vine Creek, midway between and parallel with Middle and West Chickamauga. The area having now been briefly outlined, in which the writer proposes to confine the earlier reminiscences of this narrative, it will be well here to remark that he has consulted some of the first settlers now living in Walker county as to facts prior to his own observation and experiences, and the intention is to give facts; but the limit of this article will not permit all the facts which would interest many readers, neither is it possible to enter into individual mention, only so far as to connect important events with individual action. Some will be mentioned, no doubt, who were less prominent than some not spoken of. The writer has no special friends to favor nor foes to slight, but must confine this article to what he knows, and use only enough knowledge to connect his story with passing time; many stirring events must necessarily be omitted. The following chapter will give names and dates of settlement of a few localities, members of some of whom will figure throughout this story.

"As previously stated Walker county was inhabited by the Cherokee Indians until 1838. In 1835 there was one small country store where the city of Atlanta is now located, at that time known as X Roads (meaning Cross Roads). During the year named, 1835, Louis Williams, and Amos Williams, two brothers, with their families, removed from Gwinnett county, Georgia, to Walker county. Louis Williams settled near what is known as Gordon's Gap, on the Alabama road, where he resided until his death which occurred during the late war. He deserves further notice which will be given in its proper place in this story. Amos Williams settled on the Alabama road in what is now Catoosa county, midway between Gordon's and Nickajack Gaps, nearer the latter than the former, where he resided until his death, a few years prior to the war.

"These two brothers are worthy of notice because they differed to extremes both politically and religiously. Louis Williams was an active member of the Baptist church and a local leader and authority in the Democratic party, and the reader and exponent of democratic doctrine among the rank and file of democrats in his township, and it is but just to his memory to remark that he was a man of more than average ability and culture in that community on the Democratic side during this time. Amos Williams was a Whig in politics, not so argumentative as his brother, Louis, but always ready to give good and sufficient reasons for his faith and practice. He was also a devout and active member of the Methodist church. Both of the brothers raised sons and the children followed in the footsteps of their parents, both religiously and politically. In the fall of 1835 or spring of 1836, Joel

Cooper and Thomas Cooper, two brothers, with their families removed from Jasper county, Georgia, to Walker county. They were Whigs, politically, as were their sons. Thomas Cooper was a member of the Baptist church and a local preacher. Joel Cooper and family were also Baptists. The latter located lands adjoining Amos Williams, where he resided till 1857 when he removed to Alabama (Walker county), where he died during the war. These two brothers were of Scotch-Irish ancestry. Their father, Andrew Cooper, came to America at an early day, and fought under General Marion in the war of independence. At the close of the war he married a Miss Cliatt and settled on the then frontier near where Augusta is now located, and represented his county many years in the Georgia Legislature. At the time the Cooper brothers with their families settled in Walker county, Andrew Cooper, son of Thomas Cooper, was serving as a volunteer in the army then operating against the Seminole Indians. After his discharge from service when the forces were disbanded, he followed his relatives to Walker county, where he was married to his cousin, Nancy Cooper, daughter of Joel Cooper, in the year 1837. He will figure more or less conspicuously in passing events in the history of Walker county from the date of his settlement in the county to the present time—now near 76 years of age. About the date named, 1835-36, H. G. Fuller and Hyram Shaw, half brothers, came to, and settled in Walker county, both of whom were Democrats. Fuller became of some local prominence as a preacher of Hard-shell Baptist doctrine, and will be further mentioned in this narrative in his proper place. Hugh McMullin was one of the early settlers, a Whig, and an able local advocate of the Whig cause. Of the early settlers, Amos Williams and sons, David Hall, David Lowery, Cooper brothers and sons, were Whigs, as were also Hugh McMullin, Louis Williams and sons. Fuller and Shaw, Mark Thornton, Thomas Bryant, John Bryant, Jacob Arnold and sons, Martin Camp and sons were Democrats. Andrew Cooper and Hugh McMullin championed the Whig cause in their respective localities, while Louis Williams and H. G. Fuller occupied similar positons for the Democrats. Andrew Cooper and Louis Williams were near neighbors and their controversies were frequent, and animated. The same will apply to McMullin and Fuller. This is speaking of a certain locality. There were other settlements in the county with their local politicians, some of whom will be mentioned in due time. It is well here to mention that the Cherokee Indians were divided as to the question of disposing of their lands in North Georgia. One Ridge, a leading chief, who with his following, removed to the Indian Territory in 1836. The opposition was led by John Ross who resided at Rossville five miles from where he had a ferry across the Tennessee river, for years known as Ross' landing, now the thriving city of Chattanooga. The Ross party had to be removed by the government to the Indian Territory in 1838, at which time Thomas McFarland came into possession of the Ross property at

Rossville, where he has resided in the house built by Ross, with few changes, ever since. Many soldiers will remember McFarland as living there during the war. The town site, LaFayette, county seat of Walker county, was laid out by Benjamin Wheeler in 1835. Wm. Perry opened the first store there in 1836. In 1837, Spencer Marsh, also David Stewart, engaged in the mercantile business there. John Caldwell opened the first hotel at LaFayette and was elected the first clerk of the county. Wm. Fortner was the first sheriff. LaFayette was principally settled by Democrats, of whom Marsh, Stewart, Caldwell and Fortner were the most prominent. Perry, the first merchant, was a Whig.

"Judge Kenyan held the first court in Walker county in a rude log house. He was a stern judge and felt very indignant at the rudeness of some of the natives during his first term of court. There being no jail he had no means of enforcing proper respect for the dignity of the court. The second time he arrived to hold court he came on horseback. He had a coil of new rope which he threw on the floor in the court house. When asked by one of the lawyers what the rope was for, he said that he was going to hog-tie the first man who failed to respect his court. It is useless to say the rope was never used, as it commanded order, among the rude natives. There are some conflicting statements as to the date of settlement in Walker county of one of the most prominent families, a member of which has attained to national popularity. Hon. John B. Gordon made himself famous as a Confederate leader, represented his State in the United States Senate after the war, then governor of the State and again elected to the United States Senate. His military career will appear later in this narrative."

EARLY DAYS IN WALKER.
By Captain J. Y. Wood.

I write without records and may make some mistakes. Late in the year 1836 my father, Constantine Wood, settled in West Armuchee valley. At that time the forest, abounding in trees of immense size, was occasionally broken by a rude log cabin. Deer, wild turkey, pheasants, and almost every variety of birds and small game were abundant. The Cherokee Indian still roamed through the forest and procured a meager support for his family. It has been said that there are two things an Indian could never learn—to fear death or to work. One thing however can be said of him, he was not destructive. With him the tribe was every thing, the individual was nothing. The land and all living things belonged to the tribe. Hence, under their unwritten law, no one would kill more game than satisfied his present wants.

The beauty and fertility of the country soon attracted settlers. Immigrants poured in from middle Georgia and from other states. In a few years the scene was changed. Almost every lot of fertile land in the rich valleys was settled by industrious and intelligent farmers and the whole country was alive with industry and enterprise. At first there were many inconveniences.

The county was organized in 1833. The first mail route in the county ran from Chattanooga to Rome. The first mail carrier was Ab. Wisdom. He made the trip from Chattanooga and return once a week. LaFayette was the first postoffice in the county. My father at that time took a newspaper which he read and loaned to his neighbors among whom it was circulated until it was worn out. Mail matter was five or six weeks old before it reached its destination.

In that early day there was a stage line from Augusta to Knoxville, Tennessee, which carried the mail. About the year 1840 a mail route was established from LaFayette to New Town, a point in Gordon county on the road above named. This route was by Villanow, through a populous community, and though the mail was carried but twice a month, was a great convenience.

Roads were rapidly opened and churches were organized in almost every neighborhood. Humphrey Posey, a missionary appointed by the Philadelphia Association to preach to the Cherokee Indians, organized Shiloh and other Baptist churches in the county. About 1837 or 1838 Shiloh was organized with seven members. Constantine Wood and wife, Thomas Kite and wife, and three negroes belonging to James Young, Abram, Milly and Oney. Antioch and Peavine and some other Baptist churches were organized about the same time, and churches of other denominations were organized at the same time in almost every neighborhood.

The first court after the organization of the county was held in a little log cabin near Chickamauga, at which two Indians, Pocketbook and Cach, were tried for murder and both were convicted and hanged. In 1838 the court house was finished and the first court in that building was presided over by Judge Hooper, who resided in LaFayette at that time.

The old brick academy was also built about the same time and about the first school in the county was taught in it. Spencer Marsh, John Caldwell, Samuel Fariss and some others were prominent in managing the affairs of the county. Spencer Marsh was among the first merchants to open a mercantile business in the new town.

At that time drygoods were bought in northern cities and shipped to Augusta. They were hauled in wagons from that place to almost all parts of the state.

The Indians were carried from the state in 1838. They were all collected in this section and guarded in a fort a short distance northwest of LaFayette near where the Union Cotton Mills now stand. My father and mother had some warm friends among them and took their little family and went to bid them farewell. These poor children of the forest were griefstricken at the thought of leaving their native hills. When the last handshaking took place all parties gave expression to their grief.

Many fell prostrate on the ground and begged the soldiers to shoot them that they might be buried in the land of their births. The line of march to the west was marked by their graves.

HISTORIC HOME OF INDIAN CHIEF—JOHN ROSS.
By T. F. McFarland.

From the most authentic information, part of the John Ross house was built by John McDonald, a Scotch trader among the Cherokee Indians. McDonald's wife was Anna Shorely, a full blooded Indian maiden who belonged to the Bird of Eagle tribe. To them was born a daughter, Mollie McDonald, who became the wife of Daniel Ross. Daniel Ross was from Inverness, Scotland, and was a member of Mayberry's Trading Expedition which went from Baltimore. While passing down the Tennessee river he was captured by Cherokee Indians and his life alone was spared of the expedition by the intercession of John McDonald, his countryman, who took him home as one of his household and he married Mollie McDonald and his father-in-law established him in the mercantile business in a one and a half story artistically hewn log building where the gate stands to-day in front of the John Ross house and where some of the old foundation stones are to be seen intact.

Daniel Ross became a father on Oct. 3, 1790, when John Ross was born. His father being a full-blooded Scotchman and his mother a half breed, John Ross was, therefore, one-fourth Indian, as the Indians say, "a quarteroon." On March 22, 1816, he signed two treaties as chief, or head man, this being his first known official act. Afterward he became "The Great Chief of the Cherokees." He enlarged the house his grandfather had built, adding also a council chamber, 23 feet long, and for years had only one door to it. As a precaution, he after added two more doors, one opening into his bedroom in center of the house and finishing most of the exterior and interior as it stands to-day. The Cherokees moved to Indian Nation in 1835-38.

John Ross established a postoffice at Rossville as early as 1819, which was supplied by semi-weekly mail by stage from Nashville, Tennessee, to Augusta, Georgia, and the old stage line crossed the mountain not far below the Craven's place. They said 12 horses were required to haul the passengers, etc., over the mountain point. One relay of horses, "stage stand," was at west foot of mountain and the next at Rossville. Chattanooga was Ross' Landing and came to Rossville for her mail till 1839. Some of Chattanooga's society "Four Hundred" ancestors were among the brave old pioneer stage drivers of that day and time.

An old bureau here was shipped to X. G. and T. G. McFarland, care of Hooks and McCaulie, Ross' Landing, Tenn.

John Ross died in Washington, D. C., Aug. 1, 1866.

In 1832, Thomas Gordon McFarland, who had been appointed by the state of Georgia as District Surveyor (see Georgia Land Lottery book), came to Rossville, from Mt. Vernon, Ga., and with his brother, Xanders

Gordon McFarland as assistant, surveyed the 9th district—nine miles square. No underbrush was to be seen. The Indians burned the woods every spring and the grass was from knee to waist high and the antlered deer, proudly lifting his head, wild turkeys and nearly all manner of wild game, in abundance, was everywhere to be seen. A beautiful country.

Three years later from survey these McFarland brothers moved to Rossville, merchandised, farmed, kept postoffice until 1841, dissolved partnership, and X. G. McFarland built the best house in this section, settling at McFarland's Gap, where he lived greatly respected, until his death in 1887. Thos. G. McFarland lived at Rossville, except as a refugee from Sept. 9th, 1863, to Feb. 17, 1866. He went to his last home Sept. 12, 1887.

EARLY DAYS AROUND CRAWFISH SPRING.
By Mrs. Ruth M. Lee.

In the early settlement of a country, when people are so dependent on nature for the necessities of life, we would think surely that beautiful Crawfish Springs, with a tremendous flow of water, teeming with fish, so the old settlers tell us, surrounded by forests of a kind that would indicate fertile lands would have been the location of a settlement of some size.

Such was not the case however. The Indians had cleared some land in the fork made by the spring stream and Chickamauga creek, about four or five acres, which was as much as they usually cultivated. In the "Fork-field," as it is known, are a number of mounds, built by some prehistoric people of whom the Indians knew nothing.

There may have been some superstition connected with the locality which caused the pioneer to pass on and settle at a less favorable spot. Some tale told at an Indian camp fire of a nation wiped out; of a dreadful scourge; a displeased and vengeful Great Spirit. Life was hard enough in the early days without taking chances on ghosts.

The three Gordon brothers, Charles, James and Thomas, emigrated from Gwinnett county to Crawfish Springs in 1836. They bought large tracts of land adjoining each other. James Gordon's land included the spring. His first home was located in the fork field. It was not till the latter part of the fifties that he built the brick house above the spring, which is now owned by his grandson, James Gordon Lee. Thomas Gordon's place was across the creek on the present LaFayette pike and is owned by his great grandson, Thomas Gordon Hunt.

It was just above the spring that the Indians had a council cabin— a double loghouse. The first court of Walker county was held in this building, Judge Hooper presiding. A man named Hog Smith was tried and convicted of murdering two Indians; he was hanged on a gallows erected on the north side of the hill above the spring. This was the first legal hanging to occur in the county.

It was near the spring that years later when the Civil War was brewing the young men of the section came together and organized a company of 110 men, with Clark Gordon as captain, William Gordon first lieutenant, Blackstone Hendricks, second lieutenant, and Jerome Henderson orderly sergeant. They served with distinction during the war, their captain being a colonel at the close.

One of the early settlers was Thomas Beaty, who had a blacksmith's shop near Lee and Gordon's mill. His wife was a Henry and her father had a store in Chattooga county which was robbed by two Indians named Pocket Book and Crush. They soon afterward killed an old woman and were hung for the murder in LaFayette. Thomas Beaty had moved to LaFayette in the meantime, so he forged the handcuffs on the prisoners. The Indians confessed to the theft of the goods and told where they were concealed. Mr. Henry recovered them and among the lot were some bright calicoes, which he gave to his daughters to use in making quilts the women of that day were so famous for. The quilt Mrs. Beaty made has been handed down from mother to daughter and now is in the possession of her great-great-granddaughter, Miss Susie Blaylock, of Chickamauga.

The writer is so fortunate as to have as a neighbor one of the pioneer citizens, and to him we are indebted for much of the information we have. Mr. Jack Harris came to this county as a lad in the early thirties. His thoughts dwelt in the past, the present is of no particular interest. And who would wonder at that? Certainly a past with a virgin country, Indian neighbors, with whom he hunted and fished, the Civil War, etc., has more of interest in it than the humdrum, money seeking present.

Mr. Harris' father bought an improved place about six miles east of Crawfish Spring, from an Indian named Ash Hopper. There were two hewn log houses on the place and a splendid orchard of apples and peaches. The Harris family lived in one of these houses for many years and it is only recently that this Indian-built house has fallen into decay.

While en route to the new country they fell in with a four horse wagon in charge of a man named Myers. He had been to Augusta for goods for A. P. Allgood, who had a store in LaFayette. Mr. Allgood met them on horseback, a day's journey from home, having gotten anxious about his outfit. Samuel Caruthers' family were the nearest of the neighbors. He drew the lot of land and after his death his family came from Carolina and settled on it. He had been a Revolutionary soldier and Mr. Harris remembers to have seen his uniform, which his family took great care of.

There was a mill at the present Lee and Gordon mill site run by Leroy Holiway. Going to mill with this pioneer boy was far from monotonous. He would be put on a horse with a sack of grain and in a few minutes' ride from home would be in the midst of exciting experiences. A herd of deer would spring away as the horse and rider jogged into view; a wolf would slink to thick cover; a drove of wild turkeys might be seen in an opening in the forest and an Indian hunter would meet and greet him.

Mr. John Doyle lived at the present Tom Napier place. He had lived there some time and could speak the Indian language. He was quite a sportsman and had built a race track on his place where races were held from time to time. The course was two parallel half mile stretches. Racing was very popular with these settlers; nearly all the young men kept a race horse just for the sport they would have in trying the mettle of their steeds. But the redletter day would be when some stranger from Tennessee or Kentucky would bring a horse in and a purse would be put up on the result of the race. They also fought game chickens at these gatherings. There was a stage line between Dalton and Chickamauga which followed about the same route as the present pike, making the trip once a week. The relay station was near Boynton.

William Garvin, an early settler, was made a cripple as the result of an accident with his wagon and team on the way to the new settlement, and was thus debarred from the active life of the other men, so they built him a log house and he kept school at such times in the year as the children could be spared from home. It was an ill wind that blew for the man but a good one for the children. Two Indian girls who had previously gone to the mission school at Bird's Mill were pupils in this school. Their father was an Indian doctor and it was not unlikely that Adam Simmons, who lived near and began making the well-known Simmons medicine in 1840, got some of his herb lore from this Indian neighbor.

An occasional traveling preacher supplied the religious needs of the community. Mostly they were Hardshell Baptists and Universalists. The seeds those Universalist preachers sowed are still bearing fruit, as there are a number of families, descended of those early settlers, who are Universalists, in communities where every one else are Methodists, Baptists, or Presbyterians.

When they needed a lawyer they must needs go to LaFayette where they put up at John Caldwell's tavern and took their choice of James Culberson, William Wright and Cicero McCutchen.

Jesse Lane lived a mile due east of the spring on the route of the stage line from Jacksonville, Alabama, to Chattanooga via Rome. There was a relay station and sort of inn where the passengers could stay at Mr. Lane's place. He began the erection of the old Henderson home on the pike, John Henderson having bought the property and completed the house. The two Henderson brothers, John and William, bought large tracts of land in what is known as the Red Belt, of which the greater part is still in the possession of their descendants.

Mr. George Glenn was one of the early settlers. First he lived in the Cove and a few years later moved nearer Crawfish Springs where his grandsons still own. James Wicker owned a great deal of land in the Cove in the early days, as old land deeds show. He had one of the best improved places of the section and owned a great many slaves. He sold land to the settlers who came in numbers after the Indians were taken away. His farm was inherited by his nephew Nathaniel Green Warthen, and is still in the possession of his family. The Childresses, Roarks, and Jacksons came into this section in the Indian times.

As is the rule in a newly settled country, the pioneers of this vicinity were greatly troubled with chills and fevers. Whether this was due to the dense forests surrounding their homes, or the felled and decaying timbers, it is hard to say; but the fact remains that this was a foe beside which the wild beasts and Indians were as naught in comparison. They also had to contend with a curious malady called "milk sickness." If the cows were allowed to graze in the forests before the dew had dried during a certain period of the year, fall, I believe, the animals sickened and died in some cases, as did the people who drank the milk. Of course it took time to find what the trouble was; indeed they probably never could understand why it should be. There is still a section on Lookout Mountain, east of High Point that the same condition still exists, says Mr. John Parish, a son of a pioneer.

REMINISCENCES OF A REFUGEE.
By Mrs. N. G. Warthen.

Alarmed at the rumored approach of the enemy and the distant booming of cannons which reached us in our secluded mountain home in McLemore's cove a day or two previous to the memorable and bloody battle of Chickamauga, we made hurried preparations for flight to safer quarters with our little ones.

Court was in session at LaFayette and my husband was in attendance as juror, and impatient to hasten our flight, I determined to begin packing at once, feeling sure of his approval. However, so disturbed and excited were the people that court was adjourned and much to my joy and relief, my husband came home, finding me in the midst of taking up carpets, packing household goods, etc. Incidents of that night are indelibly impressed upon my memory—no one thought of sleep; indeed the only individuals on the place who were quiet and unconcerned, were the two baby girls tucked snugly away in the same cradle. Even the cows and horses seemed to participate in the general unrest, as was evidenced by their lowing and neighing. Wagons were being packed with provisions and other supplies for the negroes, who were to accompany us, and who were greatly excited. One, "Old Abe," who had a short time previous taken French leave, hearing of our flight, returned and begged to be allowed to go with us. The flashing of pine torches over the plantation added a weird touch to the scene.

At an early hour on the following morning we left our dearly loved home, a sad little company. All day we traveled and at nightfall we were disappointed to find we had only reached Maddox Gap, a short distance east of LaFayette, having gone many miles out of the direct route. We passed a very comfortable night in the old brick house, which is doubtless still standing. The following morning we resumed our journey to Calhoun, where we boarded the train for Washington, the negroes and stock and provisions, carriage and horses, making the entire trip through the country in care of one of the overseers. En route to the station at Calhoun we encountered numerous trains of refugees, notable among them was that of the father of Rev. J. J. S. Caloway, the beloved Baptist minister of fragrant memory. Without incident or delay we arrived at Tennille, on the Central road and then drove through the country to my husband's old home at Warthen. Here we rested for a season but am unable to recall just how long we remained in peace.

My husband's immediate family contributed a generous quota to the Confederate cause. Five of the six sons were in the active and continuous service, the sixth, my husband, being commissioned by the government as commissary agent, besides having in charge large plantations and about one hundred and twenty negroes.

I must pause to pay tribute to the devotion and faithfulness of these colored friends. Often a few women and children were left entirely in their charge with the exception of one feeble old gentleman; our plantations were surrounded by others, well-stocked with blacks, but not one time during these trying days, was there whisper of insurrection or insubordination.

The Federals, however, soon disturbed our temporary security. Again came the rumor of the enemy's approach; columns of smoke were seen ascending and disquieting news came to us of the burning of gins, flour mills, and other property of neighboring planters; hourly the enemy's descent on the little village was expected. Negroes, horses and mules and cattle, wagons loaded with provisions, were carried to the wiregrass for hiding. Silverware and other valuables were buried in a deserted graveyard, and the spot carefully strewn with pine needles; other valuables were hidden in mattresses and feather beds, so popular in those days.

One memorable day as the indications of the nearness of the enemy were multiplied in the many ascending columns of smoke, word came to us that we would be the next victims. My husband's mother had a sumptuous supper prepared and spread in the large old-fashioned dining room, hoping in some degree to placate the enemy, as it is a well-known fact that one way of reaching a man's heart is through his stomach.

The women and children terrified and nervous determined to pass the night together in the sitting room; mattresses were brought down for the comfort of those who might find it possible to rest. Never can I forget the anxiety of that night. The nervous strain was intense as we sat awaiting the coming of the enemy. About 12 o'clock the familiar click of the gate latch was heard, startling and preparing us for we knew not what. However, the quiet approach of the stranger was reassuring, indicating the presence of friends, rather than the enemy. On opening the door in response to a rap, we were confronted with a gentlemanly officer, clad in gray, who informed us of the approach of his company of Texas Rangers. Tears were turned to smiles; sadness to rejoicing!

We felt as though we were with old and dear friends, so great was the reaction. What a delight it was to serve those weary, hungry soldiers that bountiful supper! How thoroughly enjoyed the few remaining hours of the night, passed in song and story! Some of the soldiers of the company being accomplished musicians, contributed delightful music on piano and violin. No one thought of sleep. A typical southern planter's breakfast was served this appreciative company of Confederate soldiers next morning, after which they formed in line in front of the old home, to bid farewell to the sorrowful women and children. The old gentleman to whom I have referred carried my little daughter in his arms to the head of the column that she might present some flowers to the captain; in return he took from his coat a silver star and pinned it to her dress, a star emblematic of his beloved "Lone Star State."

With their departure went again our feeling of security, and dread again hovered over us. The family had just taken seats at the breakfast table, when the sound of rapid and continuous firing was heard, and after an interval of suspense, members of the company who had just left came galloping, bearing the tidings that only a few hundred yards up the Sparta road, almost within sight of our home, they had encountered the enemy. A skirmish followed in which several of the Federals were killed and wounded and the others put to flight. In the pocket of one of the officers killed were orders for the burning of the village of Warthen, prevented only by the timely and providential arrival of the Texas Rangers.

Incidents of interest continually recur to me. The carriage containing President Davis and his attendants after his arrest, passed the Warthen homestead, after having stopped at the lower plantation for supplies. My husband's uncle, Gen. Jefferson Warthen, had his home near Sandersville, but of course was in the army, leaving his wife and daughter at the mercy of the enemy, who was especially spiteful to them on account of their husband and father being an officer in the Confederate army, and who by the way, lost his life in the battle of Seven Pines, or Fair Oaks, Va. His cotton was burned, quantities of syrup poured from the barrels, the library destroyed, in fact, "Forest Grove," the home of Gen. Warthen, was devastated. * * * *

The Yankees were much amused at the unnatural and unusual proportions of some of the women of the family. In truth, their appearance was striking, to say the least, for always rather low of stature, they had donned several of their best frocks, which were made very full in those days, hoping thus to save them from the clutches of the enemy. The unusual attention which these daughters of the South gave their knitting was another matter, but was not to be entirely explained on the score of patriotic zeal, in supplying Confederate soldiers hose, for had not each daughter carefully turned her knitting thread around her treasured watch?

As the clouds of war were dispersing, preparations were made for return to our Georgia home. My husband told the negroes for whom he was responsible that he would see all who desired to return to the old home safely there, which he did. We bade farewell to the dear relatives and friends in Washington and boarding the train at Mayfield, on the Georgia railroad, we were soon at Ringgold, where the remaining servants left us, and we made our way through the sad, battle scarred country to Trion unattended. Our home in McLemore's cove was desolated. The furniture and household goods which had been left carefully stored, had been taken and all that remained of a most excellent library was an almanac.

MOTHER'S GIFT TO HER SOLDIER BOY.
By Brantley Hackney

One of Mr. T. C. Hackney's treasured relics of the war is his "army" Bible. It is an odd-looking little volume, but this is due more to age, use and exposure than to anything unique in design or material of the book. At a glance it would hardly be taken for a book at all. It is very much out of shape, and is covered with a kind of strong somber fabric that is faded, splotched and worn. It was given him by his mother when he started to the war. He was then sixteen years old, the youngest of twelve children. One can hardly contemplate, without a stir of emotion, the mingled feelings of pride and fear that must have played upon the love-cords of the mother's heart when she presented this Bible to her boy as he was going away to war.

From the beginning to the end of the war he carried this Bible constantly. Whether on the battlefield when the conflict was raging, or in the camp when hostilities had temporarily abated; whether upon the march or in the trenches, in summer and in winter, in sunshine and rainy weather, every day, this little Bible was in some pocket of the boy-soldier's clothing. Many times the falling rain would soak it through and through, and at night, "by the camp fire's bright light" it would be dried, leaf by leaf. Mr. Hackney prizes this more highly, perhaps, than any article that he possesses, and is it any wonder? It might well be made the theme of a poem or a song or a story.

Here and there between the weather-beaten leaves, the print upon which is dim from age and use, are to be found Confederate stamps, clippings, letters, pieces of flags, etc., about each of which might be told a story of history and patriotism. One of these is a book-mark on which is delicately worked, with threads of gold, the word, "Mother," and another is a furlough, given him about the middle of the war to make a visit home to see his mother. But perhaps the most interesting thing that is kept in this much-prized Bible, to people in general, and from a historical standpoint, is a piece of a Confederate flag. The flag from which it came waved proudly over the battlefield of Big Bethel. This flag was first carried by the First North Carolina Regiment. After the First Regiment, which was composed of six months volunteers, was reorganized this flag became the flag of the Eleventh Regiment. Just after the battle of Chancellorsville this piece of silk was torn by Mr. Hackney from the battered flag.

A WEST ARMUCHEE FAMILY REFUGEES.
(Contributed by Mrs. Dora Suttle Tittle)

As a prelude:—We were a large family, father, mother, eight daughters, Margaret, Mary, Sarah, Sue, Lou, Emma and George, and one son, James T. Suttle. We lived near enough to the battle of Chickamauga to hear the roar of shot and shell. We had loved ones in the battle. Though nerves were not as much talked of then as they are now, we had them; my mother was all nerves. Oh! the bitter anguish of my mother! She feared my father would be taken prisoner and sent to Camp Chase; she persuaded him to refugee. My father, John B. Suttle, was not eligible to military service, because his hearing was impaired. Just after the battle was over we found ourselves in box-cars made just as comfortable as household goods could make them; we took everything—horses, cattle, hogs, and slaves, except one old slave, his wife and one afflicted slave, one horse and a cow—these dear old slaves we left to try to take care of the home premises, which they faithfully did.

To digress for a moment—when Yankee soldiers reached our beautiful old Southern home in North Georgia this faithful old slave, whom we called "Daddy," was trying to take care of all that "Marse Johnnie"—this was what he called my father—had left with him. The soldier said, "Why do you want to do this for this old rebel? We are fighting for your freedom." He said: "Gentlemen, if that is what you are fighting for you may go home. I am as free as I want to be." How sweet my memory of those dear old darkies!

Well, we located in Jackson, Butts county, Georgia. In a short time Sherman's army passed by our door—General Mead and staff rested on our veranda. Instead of meeting my mother's dreaded anticipations, they were so kind! They put a guard around our house, and when twenty-three houses were burning around us wet blankets were stretched over the house to keep it from catching on fire, and everything in the house was moved to a place of safety, and as soon as the fire danger was over everything was put back in place. In the evening the gentlemen asked permission to come into the parlor and listen to piano music. Thus we mingled Rebel female voices with Yankee male voices. The music was magnificent and the evening was passed pleasantly. But, you ask, why this difference? Other families were suffering. A word picture, if you please—let your imagination play.

Seated on the veranda was a most venerable looking old gentleman, with long white beard, and white hair—my father. At his back I stood with my arms around his neck. On either side of his lap sat a beautiful little girl, with black curls (Emma and George). Each pressed an arm around him—his three youngest children. Our whole beings were throbbing with love. How we clung to him! God looked down in mercy and put pity into the hearts of the officers, and my father was given a written permission to visit all over town, and to take relief to the distressed women and children. Readers, we were sure in our young hearts that Sherman's whole army could not take our fathers from us and it could not, for "the angels of God were encamped round about us."

Back to my story. My brother, James T. Suttle, a Cavalier, sixteen years old, had stopped in passing. When the alarm was shouted, "The Yankees are coming!" Brother, with his negro attendant, rushed away without any ceremonies. In a short time the clash and clamor of the approaching army was heard. Sister Mary was very nervous. The approaching army made her frantic. Sleep left her; narcotics had no effect. Physicians decided that travel might help her. My father and sister, Sarah, decided at once to travel. They made a three days' journey which seemed to help her, so they returned home and decided to take part of the slaves and part of the family and start back to the home in North Georgia, from which we had refugeed. In December, 1864, my father got together the best available means for travel—wagons and one-seated buggy, all drawn by worn-out war horses, which were left us by the Yankee soldiers instead of the good ones they had taken from us. My father, with two sisters, Mary, Sarah, myself and some of the slaves, began the journey. We traveled twenty miles the first day. I walked the whole distance. We had to take it by turns riding, for there was not room for all to ride at once; but I chose to walk the whole day, I was so happy, going home!

My father had a pair of shoes made for brother to wear to war but they were too small for him. I could wear them, though they were too large for me—they were made of rawhide—I was tired, heels and toes blistered, so next morning some other arrangements had to be made for the sore-footed little girl. The rickety old two-seated buggy, drawn by a scrawny little black mule, which could scarcely be seen over the dashboard, with harness that well matched, was lined up; I took the driver's place, six little negroes were packed in, one an infant, in my lap, and we started on the second day's journey. The sun shone brightly for three days; in the evening of the third day there were signs of rain; by morning it was coming down, and for the ablance of the three weeks' journey old Sol hid himself. We did not stop for rain. Oh! the mud, the slush, the roads, the swollen creeks, beggar description—just imagine the worst and maybe you can get a faint idea of the conditions. My father would stretch the tents near some pine groves. After the tents were pitched, the ground was covered with branches from the pines; then the beds were made on top of these and a logheap fire was built at either entrance of the tents, then came sweet rest.

We had three meals a day. One I shall never forget—my father paid $30 for a half bushel of corn meal; it was baked without sifting; that, with fried shoulder meat, made our Christmas morning breakfast, 1864, and I think we had rye coffee, too; I don't remember about that. Every day's experience was a repetition of the one before, tinkering with conveyances and patching harness.

In the meantime, one of the slaves developed typhoid fever—an added burden. We took the best care of him we could; we wanted to leave him in some home on the way but he would not consent; he wanted to get back to the home he loved so much. We left him in his grave near Rome, Ga. It was a sad experience. We reached home late in the evening. The old servants, who had been left to care for the home, came to learn why the cattle were bellowing so—the cows which had learned to follow the wagon, like dogs, had entered the old farm gate, and they realized it—Oh! how they bellowed, and bellowed, so glad to get home! It makes me cry to this day when I think of it. The old man and his wife were so happy to have us back, but when they were told that George was left in a grave near Rome, Ga., how they cried! But the old mother was comforted. She said: "Am glad George was buried across water, he cannot come back to *hant* me." He was her son.

Strange to say, I reached my destination with my six little "nigs" safe and sound, and did not have to be helped out of a single ditch and did not over turn a single time. My father pronounced me a good driver, which was enough for me, for I loved his praise above any other earthly joy. We were so glad to be at home, though separated from mother, sisters, and brothers. As long as we traveled, the nervous sister improved, but she was never well any more; the firing of a gun made her frantic.

I cannot tell my story without telling you of the siege of typhoid fever, which came into the family soon after we reached home; my father, two sisters, Mary, Sarah, and myself, fell victims to it, with ten of the slaves. All of us came near death, but only one died, an old negro woman; she was the mother of twenty-two children.

Just a little digression: My father had moved from North Carolina to North Georgia while the Indians were here; this negro woman belonged to him, her husband belonged to one of my father's neighbors; my father would not separate man and wife; he wrote to his neighbor to know if he would sell the man. He answered, "Yes, for fifteen hundred dollars in gold." The wife and children were made happy, and my father was made glad because he had done right.

Dear reader, if you ever pass through the beautiful West Armuchee valley, near Green Bush, Ga., look toward the east, and more than a mile away you will see this old ante-bellum home, with all the improvements still standing; barns, meathouse, slavehouses, and a tall two-story dwelling. Just inside the old farm gate stands a magnificent marble monument; this marks the resting place of the Suttle family. Years ago the nervous sister was the first one laid to rest there. On Nov. 1, 1925, the young cavalier of the sixties, J. T. Suttle, my brother, answered his last roll-call; he received a welcome plaudit: "Well done, good and faithful servant, enter into the joy of the Lord." On November 2, 1925, he was the last one laid to rest there.

Chapter Thirty-one

CONTRIBUTIONS, CONTINUED—THE LAFAYETTE VOLUNTEERS—NOTE OF A PARTRIDGE—BATTLE OF SWEETWATER—LAFAYETTE BEFORE THE WAR —SKIRMISH AT LAFAYETTE—WALKER'S QUOTA OF SOLDIERS— WHEN HUSBAND WENT TO WAR—A HEROINE AS GUARD—MURDER OF THE MCSPADDENS—AN ANTE-BELLUM PICTURE.

WALKER COUNTY'S FIRST COMPANY—THE LAFAYETTE VOLUNTEERS.
By Mrs. M. E. Patton.

IN the early days of 1861 (it was after the Southern States had seceded and the government had been organized) a call was issued for troops. Walker county was among the first to respond. Good men and true, from all parts of the county, responded, and in a short time a full company was formed and went into camp at the Big Spring. That seemed a serious business then, but before the four years' strife ended, this was merely play at soldiering. The next important thing to be considered was a uniform for the company. That was really a matter for serious consideration—an outfit complete for a whole company. But our noble and wholesouled friends, whom very many of us remember, came forward and offered material, which was in texture just what was needed for service, enough to uniform the whole company, but the goods were white. There was another dilemma. In casting about to see how this difficulty could be surmounted, many ways were suggested, for the dyeing of so large a quantity of heavy goods was no light matter. After various plans had been suggested some one hit upon the one that was finally adopted, which was to have the goods immersed in a vat of tan ooze. After lying for some days in the vat, the goods absorbed the tan color, which all the vicissitudes of wind and weather failed to change.

Next it must be decided the style, or make-up of the uniform. It must have a military look. Mr. Rogers, our one tailor, had the not enviable job of measuring the soldiers and cutting out the suits. There were but two sewing machines in the town at the time. Those were crude, compared to the machines we have now. The ladies—young and old—volunteered to make these uniforms.

We met at the home of Mrs. Dickerson, as she had one machine. The work was not easy, as the goods at best were heavy and hard to manage. The dyeing did not make it any softer. Still, we worked with a will and would have been willing to have undergone greater hardships. The coats were swallow tail, or claw hammer. The front was striped with black velvet, which together with the broad stripe of black velvet down the outside leg of the trousers, gave the whole suit a military air. Just here let me say that the whole "get up" of the company made them conspicuous wherever they went. They were the occasion of a great many witticisms. But the boys took all in good part, giving back in like manner as they received.

Then the company must have a flag. Contributions resulted in sufficient funds to purchase silk. The dainty fingers of some of the young ladies stitched the white stars on the blue field. Mr. Cassidy made a very nice polished staff for the flag. Then a meeting was held of citizens, both men and women, in the Presbyterian church, to elect a lady to present the flag to the company. Miss Laura Kelly was selected, but she utterly refused. So Miss Lizzie Hoge was second choice. The day for the presentation was appointed. The place the grove at the old brick academy. A lady was appointed to represent each a Southern state.

The company stood in open ranks with the young lady at the top, Miss Hoge at the head with the flag, the captain of the volunteers, Dr. G. G. Gordon, and the commissioned officers at her right received the flag, responded in a fine speech which called forth applause from the boys, of course, and the entire crowd gathered to witness the ceremony.

It was some days before the LaFayette Volunteers received orders to report in Atlanta. When the orders came, of course everybody in the county came to town. Very many of them had a loved one in the company. Everybody was interested and wanted to give the parting hand to their friends. At whose suggestion it is not known, but the company was formed in line across the square and everybody shook hands, beginning at the end of the line and going through. It was a most harrowing experience. Conveyances were provided and the soldier boys, bag and baggage, had gone on their way before the morning passed. With those left at home with heavy, sorrowing hearts the day was kept in fasting and prayer. The commissioned officers of the company were: Dr. G. G. Gordon, capt.; Mr. Milton Russell, 1st lieut.; Mr. Jack Healan, 2nd lieut.; Mr. E. F. Hoge, 3rd lieut. The company left on the 19th of June, 1861.

The Note of a Partridge.

Among the men of Walker county, in the War Between the States, who served in Co. F., 4th Georgia Cavalry, Wheeler's Brigade, C. D. McCutchen, 1st lieutenant, were Arby Shaw, Melvin Alexander, Joe Nash, Hugh Lumpkin, A. R. (Gus) McCutchen, John Mathis, Ben Chastain, Green Atwood and Jim McWhorter.

Arby Shaw lived in McLemore's Cove, and Melvin Alexander's home was six miles east of LaFayette. Joe Nash lived in town, while the Lumpkin residence was on the Cove road two and one-half miles northwest of the town. One mile south of Lumpkins', in Duck Creek valley, was the McCutchen home on the east side of the creek, and two miles further south was where Mrs. Mathis and her daughter, Sallie, lived. One-half mile across the creek from Mathis', going west through the field, was the Chastain home, and a quarter of a mile to the south, was where Capt. Rogers lived. Farther down the valley, going southwest on the Shin-bone road, was the home of Green Atwood, and, a mile distant, his maiden sisters lived near Wilson's Cave, where Sharpe's trail started over Pigeon Mountain into McLemore's Cove. Jim McWhorter lived two miles farther south. The home of Rainey Chastain, the father of Ben, was a mile north of that of his son, on the same side of the creek and opposite the McCutchen plantation.

The above explanation as to locations and directions, will serve to enable the reader to understand the story which follows:

In 1864, after the battle of Resaca, in which the 4th Georgia Cavalry was engaged, and which ended at Tanner's Ferry, near Calhoun, Gus McCutchen, John Mathis, and Ben Chastain obtained furloughs to visit their homes thirty miles west in Walker county.

The route led through Snake Creek gap, the two Armuchee valleys, thence across Taylor's Ridge. They traveled the by-ways and bridle-paths to avoid the enemy. Late in the afternoon, within two miles of the Mathis home, they crossed Broomtown road and were seen by one Dan Thomas, a Union sympathizer, who lost no time notifying his clan. The soldiers, unaware of danger, sped on toward their respective homes. Gus McCutchen turned to the right, shortly after crossing the public road, and went north to his home where he was welcomed by his father and mother and sister Senecca. Ben Chastain witnessed the greeting given to John Mathis by his dear mother and sister, then galloped across the field to his home and surprised his loved ones. Tallulah and George were seven and five years old respectively, but Gus and Ben, Jr., were so young that they did not remember the visit of their father.

Next morning, at the break of day, seven tories on horseback approached John Mathis' house. Miss Sallie was up and dressed, and, when she heard the draw-bars fall, she ran and awoke John who jumped out of a window and started to run. The enemy fired two shots at him and he surrendered. The shots were heard by Ben Chastain, who said to his wife, "That's pickets firing, ma!" Quickly putting on his pants and shoes, grabbing his coat and hat, saying, "Save my watch and pistol," he ran westward, about a hundred steps, across the yard into the undergrowth, and, just as he reached it, he heard horses knock down the rail fence on the east side of the house. Hastily, Mrs. Chastain put the watch into her bosom and placed the pistol under the feather bed beneath the baby.

The band of tories had separated; four of them took John and his horse over the creek to Capt. Rogers', where they ordered breakfast. As the other three dashed up to the house, Mrs. Chastain was standing in the doorway. "Is Ben Chastain here?" "No," she replied. "You're a liar!" She said nothing. "Has he been here?" "Yes, but he has gone." "How long has he been gone?" "Not long." "If he is here, we'll burn this house!" "Very well, he is not here." Then they proceeded to search the premises, and questioned Maxie, the negro woman, but learned nothing from her. Tallulah and George witnessed the ordeal. Baffled and cursing, the desperadoes rode off toward Capt. Rogers', where they joined their comrades and prisoner.

Going south two and one-half miles on the Shin-bone road to Sharpe's trail, which led over the mountain to the Cove, the captors, unwittingly, led John over familiar ground. Throughout the day, they celebrated their victory by cracking jokes and drinking liquor, but John would not partake of their revelry. It was a carousing bunch that went to the home of one of their kind to spend the night. The cabin was surrounded by a dense woodland where the horses were tied out. The men lay on a pallet on the floor, John in the midst, and one sat up as sentinel.

John had been studying all day how he could make his escape. After awhile, when all got to sleep, he commenced to beg for water, and continued to do so until the sentinel became exasperated, and awoke one of the men to go with him to help guard John. The spring was on the east side of the cabin just outside the yard fence; the men stood, leaning on the fence with pistols in their hands. When John stooped, as if to drink, he ran out into the thicket and, on account of the darkness, their shots went wild.

John knew his bearings. Although barefooted, and only shirt and slips on, he made good his escape by traversing the same route across the valley and over the mountains, a distance of six or seven miles. Before daylight he reached Wilson's cave.

Early in the morning, the Atwood girls went to the spring which was close to the entrance of the cave. John began to call them by name, which frightened them. Presently, they thought of the cave and started toward it. As they drew near he called to them that he had gotten away from his captors, and was in his night clothes and barefooted. He asked them to get a pair of pants and a pair of shoes, and to bring the bundle, with wood on their arms, as though they were preparing to wash.

After delivering the package, they picked up "washwood" while John gave them further instructions from the cave. "One of you go to your brother's and tell his wife to go and tell Mrs. Chastain that I have gotten away from the tories, and for her to go and tell my mother, and have Sallie go and tell Mrs. McCutchen." All these arrangements were made by the women. Among them, they got a hat and a coat for John, and Mrs. Chastain went to her father-in-law's, who procured a horse and saddle. After nightfall, John made his way home, and he told Sallie of the plan and place for the three to meet, the following night to return to their company. Sallie delivered the message to Mrs. Chastain, who told her husband, then she rode up to McCutchens' to tell them.

Gus McCutchen took the horse, which had been delivered by Rainey Chastain to the appointed place, one mile east of the Mathis home, joining Ben Chastain in the woodland, near an old well, the meeting place. At eleven o'clock they answered John's whistle in the same note—that of a partridge.

(Contributed by Nina Oxford—Mrs. G. L. Chastain.)

AT THE BATTLE OF SWEETWATER.

In East Tennessee, during the fall of 1863, Co. F, 4th Georgia Cavalry, commanded by Gen. Joe Wheeler, took part in the Battle of Sweetwater. The brigade was stationed across the ridge that lies about a mile east of the little town which was held by the enemy. Among the scouts that were sent to the top of the ridge to view the situation, were Gus McCutchen, John Bickerstaff, Joe Nash, Ben Chastain and others.

The minnie balls were flying thick and fast, John Bickerstaff was struck on the forehead and fell to the ground. To all appearances he was dead and some of the boys began to dig a grave, when Gus McCutchen ran up and after an examination, said: "Boys, he is not dead, and we must get him away from here." The minnie ball had pierced his forehead, going upward and outward, leaving the lining membrane of the brain exposed, but not lacerated. They had received orders to fall back and carried their wounded comrade to a cabin near by where two old ladies lived, in whose care they left him, with request that they do all that they could to relieve his suffering. Ben Chastain was the last one to leave. He felt that he could not go without one word. Kneeling down by the helpless mate, he said: "John, I'm going down town for a little while."

Ben Chastain surrendered at Raleigh, N. C., and made his way home to the little farm in Duck Creek valley. One day, in October, 1869, just before sundown, as the last load of corn was being brought in for the day, a man on horseback, dressed in a black suit and wearing a large black hat, rode up to the big front gate and asked if Ben Chastain lived there. George, the eldest son, answered in the affirmative. "Is he at home?" "Yes, sir, yonder he comes walking up the road." Whereupon the man dismounted and said: "Buddie, hold my horse, I am an old war-mate of your father's, and want to see if he will recognize me."

The stranger stepped forward to the middle of the roadway, facing Ben Chastain as he approached with a cornstalk staff in his left hand, walking in front of the wagon which was driven by the little boys. The man stood eagerly rubbing his hands together till within ten steps, then called out: "You've been gone down town a long time." A moment later they clasped hands and looked into each other's eyes. "You don't know me!" In another instant, the cornstalk staff fell to the ground, Ben Chastain raised his hand and knocked the big black hat off the stranger's head, saying, "If it isn't John Bickerstaff, I don't know who it is." He said, "Yes"; and they embraced each other.

Mrs. Chastain was standing on the porch a hundred yards away and wondered what it all meant, but surely no trouble for George was holding the horse. There were many explanations made and the conversation was kept up till midnight. Each of the little boys placed his finger in the scar on the forehead of the stranger. John Bickerstaff told his comrade that he could hear but could not see nor speak, and heard the sound of the spade as it was plied in the earth, and could hear the words spoken to him. The ladies tenderly nursed him till he was able to be moved, then conveyed him as far as they could toward his home; others did the same thing using one-horse wagons, or buggies, until he reached his home in Cobb county.

The next morning there were two horses saddled, ready to make the rounds to see the other boys—John Mathis, Gus McCutchen, Hugh Lumpkin and Joe Nash. After two days of delightful comradeship, John Bickerstaff returned to his home near Marietta.

As a matter of local history, we wish to add the fact, to the foregoing narrative, that the first man killed in the Sweetwater fight was a Walker county man, Nimrod Sitton, a brother-in-law of Ben Chastain and the father of the late Mrs. Amanda Burns.

Nina Oxford (Mrs. G. L.) Chastain.

LaFayette Before the War.
By Mrs. Mary Gordon.

I first knew LaFayette in 1844 or 45, but I was only attending school here and remember little of events at that time. I came to live here in 1848, and while names and dates sometimes slip away, I can remember much of the town and many of the people at that time. The town was filled with a class of the most refined, intelligent, Christian people I have ever met in the State of Georgia. Some of the families I recall were Judge Spencer Marsh's family, Judge Hoge's, Alexander Shaw's, Dr. R. B. Dickerson's family (why, Mr. Bob Dickerson's father and my husband were partners for many years, and his mother and I were great friends), the Simmons family, the families of Thomas and James Patton —and Mr. Jack Patton was an old bachelor. These and many others whose names would come to me if I should stop to recall them. All these were hospitable and we mixed and mingled together like children of the same family. There were such splendid dining parties and social affairs, and agreeable church work—no sectarian affairs among us—all worked together in the greatest harmony. Then there was Judge A. P. Allgood's family—his wife was Mary Marsh, a native of this town.

During the summer of 1849, Dr. G. G. Gordon and Dewitt Fariss went into the practice of medicine; the younger generation coming on, you know. The Edwardses and Coulters lived near the edge of the town —out in the country. The people were more united in religion and politics than at present. We had many great revivals of religion and the great sin of dancing as thought by some in these days was not prohibited then and the young people had grand times. The Kellys were living here then—Sister Phoebe Kelly lived to be 95 years old.

When the war came my husband raised a company of 125 young men —the very cream of this section. Of all these splendid young men only about a dozen ever lived to return. Spencer Marsh donated the uniforms for this company. It was the white linsey cloth, but the company would not have them, so it was taken to the old Phipps tannery and dyed a kind of yellowish-tan color, and then the ladies of the town made the uniforms. I, myself, made many of these, working, often till 12 o'clock at night with a lamp on each side of me. When Mr. Gordon's company was ready he went to Atlanta, where he was made surgeon of Company "G," 9th Georgia Regiment, until the conscript laws let out all doctors who were 37 years of age. Dr. Marsh was a physician and surgeon also.

When the Federal troops came through here they tore down our house and the Female Seminary and used the wood for their fortifications. I remember the battle that was fought at that time, for I was right in the midst of it trying to take care of the wounded. When old Tom Phipps was shot in the leg, the Yankee doctors had him on the table ready to cut it off. He protested most vigorously and sent for Dr. Gordon who brought him to our home and so saved his leg. On the morning of the 24 of June, I was awakened by the firing of cannon and when I arose there was a line of Southern soldiers ranged by the academy and that day there was a fight and 80 men were killed and wounded. The Presbyterian Church was converted into a hospital, and took the last sheet and pillow slip in my house for it. All the ladies of the town contributed whatever they had for the wounded and sick soldiers. I kept one six months. They tore out the pulpit and seats and window sash from the Baptist church. The Presbyterian church was also much abused and damaged.

General Pillow was in command of the Confederate forces in this battle. They fought from the court house, the Goree hotel, the Marsh building and from all the larger buildings in the town. The Federal forces were encamped here grazing their horses when the Confederates attacked them. The main part of the fight was from the Baptist church to the town square where the old court house stood at that time. When the battle was at its height about 400 cavalry from the 4th Kentucky arrived from toward Chattanooga, and General Pillow retreated.

During the fight, one of my house servants was shot in the calf of the leg, and my old cook got so scared that she ran under the house and huddled up against the chimney till the fight was over, while my children kept running around calling for "Mammy" as they always called her. I put the children up in the fireplace of the Goree house and hung mattresses in the window to keep out the bullets. My husband was in the thick of the fight caring for the wounded and I was kept mighty busy helping to care for them.

* * * * *

After the war everybody was bankrupt. A great many had refugeed, and a great many, like me, had lost everything except their children and a little piece of land. There was scarcely a whole house in the town, everything torn up, and I moved here to educate my children and to work for a living. Capt. John Y. Wood taught a high school in the academy right after the war. I picked up boards and fixed up three rooms in the hotel, and the first court I made $30.

Since that time people have lived in LaFayette in peace and harmony, and sometimes they have had their ups and downs, but, taken all together, I think LaFayette is the best town in Northwest Georgia and I hope to live the rest of my life and die here.

A Skirmish at LaFayette as Remembered By One Who Participated.

By Judge John W. Maddox

Having been requested by the historical committee of the U. D. C. to relate some of my personal experiences during our late war between the states, I have selected one that happened at LaFayette.

I was a member of the Sixth Georgia Cavalry. In the fall of 1863 it was attached to the command of General Wheeler. As my recollection serves me, it was about the middle of August, 1864, while we were at Atlanta, General Wheeler was ordered to make that long raid in the rear of General Sherman's way up in Tennessee near Nashville, for the purpose of cutting his communications etc. On our return we came out through middle Tennessee, crossed the Tennessee river at Muscle Shoals in Alabama and started on our way back to Georgia to join General Hood. When we arrived in the neighborhood of Cave Spring, Georgia, we were ordered to strike the W. & A. R. R. between Resaca and Dalton, and destroy the track, trains, and bridges.

Our regiment was ordered to LaFayette to guard the left flank of General Wheeler while he was moving on Dalton. We had been marching all day when this order was received. We at once started for LaFayette, crossed the Coosa river at Veal's Ferry, twelve miles south of Rome, and reached the Bouchillon place (now known as Sprite) on the Central Railroad, where we stopped for some hours and fed our horses. We then mounted and resumed our march for LaFayette, going directly to Summerville, and then to LaFayette, arriving there, as I now remember, about 10 o'clock in the morning. In LaFayette we stopped behind the old court house and dismounted. Pickets were thrown out on the roads leading east, west and north. Very soon after our arrival the noted guerrilla, Gatewood, with five or six of his men, came into LaFayette from the east, where it was reported that they had hung a man that day or the day before by the name of Burton. Lieut. Joel Weathers, with two or three men, was sent out on the road north on a scout. The balance of us were soon asleep on the ground. Major John T. Burns was in command and was lying on the porch of the old Caldwell hotel that stood on the west corner of the square. Col. Hart had stopped back at Mr. Patton's on the south side of the creek to prepare some dispatches. While we were so asleep, being completely worn out, the bugel sounded, "mount up." We sprang to our horses immediately. Major Burns rushed from the portico, where he had been asleep, sprang on his horse, and ordered the first and second squadron to form on the north side of the court house and the third and fourth to form where they stood. This order was instantly obeyed, and before we had gotten into line on the north side we heard a number of shots fired in the direction of Chattanooga, at the same time we saw Lieut. Weathers and the pickets coming down the road, about where Mrs. Warthen lives, about as fast as they could. Immediately behind them was a company of Yankee cavalry charging upon us with drawn sabres, and yelling like mad men. Major Burns ordered us to follow him, and he made a dash for them right up the road toward Chattanooga. This was wholly unexpected by the Yankees, as they thought no one was in LaFayette except a few scouts as we afterwards learned. They soon discovered they had a fight on their hands. They turned to run, and it was then a race till they were all killed or captured. It is my recollection now that only one of their men escaped. He was mounted on a white horse and he got away by simply out-running us. We could not catch him on account of the exhausted condition of our horses, although some of our men followed him almost to Rock Springs. Our horses were already exhausted before this chase began. About a mile north of LaFayette, as I now remember, we gathered all of our prisoners together in a field. About that time Col. Hart caught up with us, and Gatewood, who had joined with us in the chase, came up and demanded that the prisoners be turned over to him. Col. Hart had evidently never seen Gatewood before for he at once demanded to know who he was, and when informed, he immediately, in that sharp and decisive manner for which he was noted, informed Gatewood that the prisoners had been captured by his men and that they would be turned over to the regularly constituted authorities authorized to receive them by the Confederacy. Up to this time the prisoners thought they had been captured by the guerrillas and expected to be shot, but when they were informed that they were in the hands of the regular soldiers and would be treated as prisoners of war, this information made them the happiest men I ever saw. We did not need any guard to keep them, for they stuck to us like brothers. We picked up the wounded and carried them back to the old Goree house and left them with Dr. Gordon, who lived there then. Col. Hart detailed one or two of the prisoners to stay and wait on them. These plead with Col. Hart not to leave them, as they were confident the guerrillas would kill them. Col. Hart sent for Gatewood and told him of the fears of these men, said he was going to leave them in Gatewood's charge, telling Gatewood that if a hair of their head was hurt he would hold him personally responsible. What became of them I do not know. That night we camped in a pine thicket just east of Mr. Clemon's house, three miles south of LaFayette. The next morning we joined our brigade at Villanow and moved on to Dalton. This incident about which I have written was in October, 1864.

Anyone interested in this incident and desiring to get fuller particulars as to it can call on my friend and comrade, whom I am glad to say is still alive and lives near LaFayette, Wiltz Boss, who was in this "scrap" and knows all about it.

WALKER COUNTY SENDS FULL QUOTA OF SOLDIERS TO THE CONFEDERATE ARMY.

By Judge H. P. Lumpkin.

Perhaps it would be interesting to have in this issue of the Messenger a brief statement of the different companies organized in Walker county for service in the Confederate Army, as also the different companies and regiments represented by volunteers from Walker county. Believing this, I will, as well as I can from memory, give this information.

The first company organized was headed by Dr. G. G. Gordon, captain. This company was Company G, of the 9th Georgia Vol. Inf. E. F. Hogue, who was brevet 2nd lieutenant at the organization of the company, became the colonel of the regiment before the final surrender. At the time that Dr. Gordon was making up this company, J. Y. Wood organized a company in the Armuchee valleys. This company was Co. G, 11th Ga. Vol. Inf. Frank Little, then a young man, was made 2nd lieutenant of this company, and was, on the organization of the regiment, made major, afterwards by promotion colonel, and finally brevet brigadier general in the Confederate service.

Soon after this Capt. F. M. Young made up a company and his company became Company H, 23rd Ga. Vol. Inf. At this time Capt. J. C. Wardlaw also made up a company which became Co. C, 6th Ga. Vol. Inf. Next that were made entirely of Walker county men and boys were the companies of Capt. J. W. Brady and C. D. Hill, which became companies K and E in the 39th Regiment, Ga. Vol. Samuel Fariss organized a company which became Co. I in the 61st Ga. Inf. Capt. N. C. Napier made up a cavalry company largely from Walker county boys, which became Co. K, 6th Ga. Cav. Also, Co. F, 4th Ga. Cav., was largely from Walker county, Judge C. D. McCutchen being first lientenant of this company.

There were a large number of companies and regiments in which were many Walker county boys, but I can't give the names of the captains of the companies as they were organized, but will as far as I can, give the company and regiment:

Companies D, F, H and I in the First Regiment, Ga. Cav.
Companies A, F, D and H, 3rd regiment Ga. Cav.
Companies A and E in the 3rd Confederate Cavalry.
Companies A and K, 4th Ga. Cav.
Companies I and D, first Confederate Inf.
Companies H and F, 23rd Ga. Inf.
Companies C and K in the 9th Ga. Inf.
Companies C and D, 39th Ga. Inf.

It would be interesting to know what part each man performed in the service, and I hope each survivor will write a history of his acts and acts of his company, as he may now remember them.

WHEN THE HUSBAND WENT TO WAR.
By Nancy Caruthers Shaw, as told by Mrs. Sam Shaw.

In the year 1861 just west of Pigeon mountain in McLemore's cove, there was a little cabin home where I lived with my dear husband, J. E. Shaw, and three children, Sam, aged five, Eugenia, aged three, and Tom, my baby boy, a little over one year old. It was a happy home, filled with love and peace. We had planted roses around the door and the lilacs and snowballs were bursting into bud. The young corn was marking the long rows in the fertile fields and we made many happy plans for the future when we would build a fine house on the hill where our cabin home stood. It was a beautiful Saturday afternoon; the week's work was done; the cakes and pies baked and the hen dressed, all in readiness for the Sunday dinner and my husband had gone to LaFayette. He was to bring his sister, Mrs. Talley, home with him for a visit, so the little ones and I were waiting in happy anticipation for their coming. Rumors of war had reached us but we had supposed it would not amount to very much; if there should be much fighting it would not be very near us.

But my first heartache came that very night when my husband came home and told me that he had volunteered to go. Oh, how my heart ached! I spent the night in prayer and tears and the Sabbath morning, though bright, brought no gladness to me. What was I to do when my dear one went away to war! But the hope that it might not last long kept me up. Ah, had I known that it would be for four long weary years I never could have borne it.

Then came the preparations for his departure and with loving hands I prepared his clothes and by candle light I knitted his socks. Then came the sad parting over which I do not care to linger, for none except those who have experienced it can realize how sad the parting with loved ones with only a faint hope of ever seeing them alive again. He went with the infantry, so that our one horse was left me with which to finish the little crop. I had never plowed but the corn was now needing to be plowed and I decided to try it, but my father sent us an old negro man to do the plowing, and I with the help of little Sam did the hoeing while the other little ones played in the fence corners. Little Sam would start out in the morning with a brave determination to do all the work, but when the sunshine would get hot he would begin to cry and ask when pa would come home and I would tell him it would not be long, while in my heart I prayed that it might be so. The sad days of hard labor, and nights spent in prayers and tears passed by with only the letters from the dear one to brighten them. Each letter gave me renewed hope, because they told me he was alive and the belief that the war would not last long, but another year passed and still no hope of peace.

At about this time some of our neighbors and some supposed friends formed themselves into a band of tories solely for the purpose of looting and destroying their neighbors' property. They came to our home and took anything they could get their hands on—bedding, clothing, knives and forks; took the only pair of scissors I had and my side-saddle. This was in the third year of the war, and my father thinking it was not safe for me and the children to remain in the Cove had moved us back to his home in Duck Creek valley. His negroes had all run away and my brothers were all in the army. One of them, Harry Caruthers, never came home. He was killed in the battle of the Wilderness. We, my sisters Emily and Herpernann, raised the cotton, picked the seed out of it by hand, carded it, spun it into thread and wove it into cloth for clothing our families. As I have already told you the Tories had already taken my only pair of scissors. I took an old case knife and ground it down to a point and cut out my children's clothes with it.

In 1863, just after the Battle of Gettysburg, the glad news came that my husband had been wounded, and that he was coming home, and I prayed that the war might end before he went back. Then began the preparations for his coming. Everything was cleaned up about the house, the children's homespun clothes neatly washed and ironed and laid away to wear when pa got home. My baby, Tom, could scarcely remember his father, but we had talked to him so much about his coming that he was wild with anticipation and would stand in the road for hours looking for him. It was in July and I told him he must not stay in the hot sun bareheaded—his little bonnet laid away to wear on Sunday. He came in and soon I noticed him again in the road with an old ironing rag on his head, for, he said he was waiting for pa. At last we had the pleasure of welcoming our loved one home once more, wounded, dirty and tired, but ours, nevertheless. Only a few short weeks he stayed with us, then he returned to the army and remained till after the surrender.

STOOD GUARD WHILE REBEL SCOUTS DINED.
Mrs. W. A. Foster.

The battle of Chickamauga was fought September 19-20, 1863, which was Saturday and Sunday. My father, Allen Williamson, lived in McLemore's cove, on Cove road. On the 17th scouts from both sides began to pass through looking the country over in getting the nearest way to Chickamauga. Hooker was then coming across Lookout mountain. Some rebel scouts came in at father's; we asked them to eat. They answered, "We haven't time, the Yankees are near." I said, "Let me stand picket." They asked if I could shoot; I answered, "Yes, indeed." Lieut. Camp gave me his pistol; I stood guard and they had a hasty lunch. They came out. I can never forget when they mounted they said, "If we never see you again, may God bless you." They had not been gone five minutes when they came dashing back and said Yankees were just behind. They went south through a narrow lane to the creek, rode up the stream and hid in some bushes and escaped. The Yankees came up at break-neck speed, asking which way the Rebs went. I told them to keep straight road going west, I thought they might overtake them, for the Rebels had gone another direction. On the 18th, the road seemed to have turned blue; you could smell them for miles, the oil clothes were so strong. They came in and robbed and carried off corn, wheat, hogs, horses, chickens, turkeys, etc. One of the negroes came running and said, "Lord, Miss Nancy, they's a-takin' off the bees," but, kind reader, believe me, the bees were victorious and how they rolled on the clover for relief. Picket firing began at Andrew's Ford and the nearer towards Chickamauga, the fiercer, so on Saturday morning it began in earnest and it was continual firing.

THE MURDER OF THE MCSPADDENS.

Miss Orpha Center

The McSpaddens, who during the war lived in the house now occupied by Mr. G. A. Langley, on the Broomtown road, were one of the best known and most highly respected families in Walker county. The two young sons, Earnest and Christopher, were considered two of the most reliable and genteel boys in the whole community. They were scouts during the war, and when Earnest was taken ill near Bethel down in Chattooga county, and Christopher was nursing him, Sam Roberts, a well-known and much feared desperado, together with a band of outlaws, found out their whereabouts, and after a desperate fight on the part of the boys, the one who was sick in bed using his pistol too, they were killed. Mr. Crawford, a neighbor, hearing of their death, sent one of his negroes up to Bethel to dig the graves and bury them, but these men who killed them threatened to kill the darkey if he touched them. Mr. Crawford himself came, and after talking to the men quite a while, finally got them to let him bury them, and with his own hands he dug the grave and buried them both together.

A short while after this terrible murder by these outlaws, Sam Roberts came to my father's house here in LaFayette, early one morning, bringing with him the clothes worn by the McSpadden boys at the time of their death, and told us he was on his way down to the McSpadden place to make Mrs. McSpadden cook his breakfast, and to show her the bullet holes in the clothes worn by her sons. I begged him not to, telling him what a trial such a thing would be to their mother, and finally told him, if I were her, and could get it, I would give him a dose of poison in whatever I prepared. Nothing would stop a man with such a stone heart as he had, and he went on down there and accomplished his purpose.

An Ante-Bellum Picture.

The following, taken from Smith's Story of Georgia and the Georgia People, is descriptive of the average county town of Georgia before the Civil War. It is reproduced here because it gives a vivid picture of scenes and conditions as they existed in Walker county along with other counties at that time:

"These Georgia towns which had sprung up were all laid out on the same plan—a plan like that of the old Virginia county sites. A square was chosen. In the center was the court house, generally a square box house, with a court room up stairs and offices down stairs. On one corner was the village tavern, and around the square the village stores. These country stores aimed to furnish every thing the people needed. They sold dry-goods, groceries, hardware, drugs, saddlery, and in all of them there were bars from which whiskey was retailed. The county towns were generally small. The county doctor, a few lawyers, the teacher and court officers generally made up the families in them. The farmers lived on the farms, and the planters at this period were few, and those few lived on their plantations. The country came in great numbers to the county towns on court days and the days of the general muster.

"There was a superior court twice in the year, and an inferior court which met every month. On court days there was a large attendance of the people, especially when the superior court was in session. At that time the whole county was represented, and those who had business in town as well as those who had business in court, went to town then, and the crowd was increased by those who had no business at all. The most of the people came on horseback. The lawyers from all the country round came in gigs and sulkies. If it was a time of political excitement, a political speech was sandwiched between the morning and the afternoon sessions of the court. The gingercake wagon with its keg of persimmon beer was always on hand, and the motherly dame who sold a cake for a thrip and threw in the beer was always present. On Tuesday of the first week of the court was horse-swapping day. Whiskey flowed freely and nearly every body took a dram. Fisticuffs were the result, and they were common. The village was crowded with people for a week, court then adjourned, and all became quiet again.

"In the early days of the county, the muster was quite an imposing an affair. The people attended the county seat from all the districts of the county. The major-general with his staff, with glittering epaulets and flowery plumes was mounted on a magnificent charger. He wore his brilliant uniform and cocked hat, and his staff was elegantly equipped. He was the center of attraction. The brigadiers and colonels and majors were in full force, all uniformed and mounted. The captains, however, were as a general thing, in citizen's clothes, with perhaps a feather in their hats. The rank and file were armed with old Kentucky rifles, single-barrelled shotguns, sticks and cornstalks. A pretense of drilling and reviewing was made, and after a day of absurdity the mustering militia was discharged until another twelve months was gone.

"After the muster was over there was generally a time of wild revelry; corn whiskey and peach brandy flowed freely, and 'Ransy Sniffle' managed to bring 'Bill Stallings and Bob Durham' together in the ring. As a general rule there was no more serious casualty resulting from these combats than a bitten ear or a gouged eye. Stabbing was not common and shooting was almost unknown. No man carried a pistol in those days, and the old time dirk was regarded as a cowardly weapon."

MISCELLANEOUS ITEMS.

Chapter Thirty-two

WOOL ROLLS—HAT FACTORY—FIRST COTTON GIN—SHOOTING MATCH—
SUNNYSIDE—ANTE-BELLUM HOMESTEAD—IRREGULAR SOUTHERN
BOUNDARY LINE—MENU IN REVOLUTIONARY WAR.
A POTTERY PLANT.

(NOTE.—The author has gathered these items from various sources in every part of the county, principally from the older citizens now living. No record has ever been made of many of these happenings and in that sense they may be said to be traditional.
Just what is tradition? To what extent is it trustworthy? Webster says it is "the transmission of knowledge, opinions, doctrines, customs, practices, etc., from generation to generation, originally by word of mouth and by example. That which is so transmitted; any particular story, belief or usage handed down." It is evident that tradition becomes less reliable the further we are removed from its origin. So, also, the nearer we stand to its beginning the more trustworthy it becomes. Why? Because man's memory is not only fallible but there may be a tendency, either consciously or unconsciously, to exaggerate or minimize a given account or story. Before the art of printing, the only historic information among our forbears was traditional. While this may not have been exact, it was to them most valuable, since, but for this, the past would have been a complete blank. In like manner it appears that while traditional history cannot be invested with the truthfulness attaching to the printed page, it, nevertheless, contains, in many cases, the germs of truth.
A number of items in this county history may be said to belong to tradition. While this may be true, the period or space of separation from the origin of the occurrence is so short that the possibility of error is reduced to a minimum. Many stories told by veterans of the sixties—stories of their experiences in camp, on the march or in battle, are now traditional, since they have not been, many of them, reduced to writing. But the space of separation is so short that no one doubts their veracity. These stories did not become tradition during the lifetime of those veterans, but after their decease those who told them were dealing in tradition.
The story of the Rev. Artemus Shattuck, told elsewhere, is not tradition, since it has

been, many years ago, carefully printed. On the other hand the story of William White, Revolutionary soldier, mentioned elsewhere, is more or less traditional, since no authentic account of it seems ever to have been written. And yet, there is little doubt of the accuracy of the latter because of the short space we are removed from that time.)

WOOL ROLLS. About 1850, or soon thereafter, there was in operation near Hiniard's cross roads, or somewhat further west from that place and nearer the base of Lookout mountain, a plant for the manufacture of wool rolls. Bert Graham was the owner and proprietor of the business, but it was operated principally by a Mr. Lecroy. A house of convenient dimensions was built and a race or channel was constructed to carry water to an overshot wheel which furnished abundant water power for the business. The water was obtained from Frick's cave.

People from all parts of the county as well as from other sections carried wool to this plant to have it made into rolls. Mr. Graham had machinery for the work which consisted mainly of a large carding machine. The wool was first washed and cleaned and after drying was placed on a kind of apron, somewhat resembling that of a cotton gin. It was then allowed to pass through the carders and came out in large bats about 24 inches long. The bats were then allowed to pass through another machine when there came out the wool rolls which were carefully bound into bundles and were ready for spinning into thread.

It was possible also to mix white and black wool in various proportions and thereby obtain rolls which when spun and woven would give a beautiful gray cloth. However, the housewife often dyed her thread and in this way made cloth of various colors.

These wool rolls were used by the housewife in making thread, and the thread in turn was woven into cloth. The wool rolls could, indeed, be made at home by small hand cards, and this was often done; but this was slow and laborious work, so that it was much better to send the wool to the carding plant to be made into rolls. The plant made the rolls for a fixed price per pound; or, if desired, made them for a portion of the wool.

During the summer and autumn months this was a very busy place, as people came from far and near with wool for making rolls. The wool was brought and left for a week or so to give time for the work to be done, then it was necessary to make another trip to get the rolls.

As stated above almost every home had an outfit for the manufacture of cloth. The housewife or her daughter or other female member of the family were almost always busy with the spinning wheel or the loom. The humming and whizzing of the spinning wheel could be heard far into the winter nights of the days of yore, when our grandmothers labored early and late to clothe their families and keep them warm. There were neat Sunday suits to be made for the "guidman" of the house and for the youngsters; there were dresses to be made for the girls; there were blankets to be made for the beds to keep the childrn warm at night; and there were shawls to be made for wear on rainy or cold days when it was

"YARN-MAKING IN OLD FASHIONED WAY."

Mrs. Laura Massey, Rossville, Ga., 82 years of age, shows how her grandmothers made clothes for the family.

(*Courtesy of Chattanooga Times.*)

necessary to make long trips from home. Overcoats were not then in vogue, and it was a common sight to see men traveling about the country on cold or rainy days with a large shawl thrown over their shoulders. All these garments and articles were made of wool. Every farmer kept several sheep for the wool he annually cut from their backs to clothe his family.

It was not possible in those days for people to go to the store and buy clothes as we do today for the reason that there was very little money in the country and few men had money with which to buy. Nor were these articles kept for sale in the stores of that day. The merchant carried only such merchandise in stock as was in demand, just as he does in our day. The farmer raised almost all his food on the farm, and moreover, he made most of his clothes, shoes, furniture and tools.

A HAT FACTORY. About the same time the wool roll factory above described was in operation, there was being operated a hat manufacturing plant on Lookout mountain situated somewhere north of Cooper's gap. This plant was owned and operated by a Mr. Jordan. He made wool hats principally but was able to make other kinds as well. People carried the material to him and he made what was wanted. His wool hats were very durable and would last for years.

The wool was first washed and cleaned and certain ingredients were added after which it was beaten and rolled into a hard cloth, and then spread over hat-blocks and after further rolling and beating and fashioning it was shaped into hats which after drying were ready for use.

Mr. Jordan could make hats and caps from coon skin. He had a machine that operated somewhat like a bow-and-arrow with which he was able to remove the fur from the skins after which he made them into hats or caps. The fur, however, was not always removed from the skins, but left on, many people preferring it that way. His coon-skin hats and caps would last a lifetime.

In his *Reminiscences*, General John B. Gordon, who is peculiarly the idol of all Walker countians because he once was a resident of the county, tells of raising his first company for service in the War Between the States in Northwest Georgia. He says his home was in Alabama, his business in Georgia and his postoffice in Tennessee. This would put him in or near Walker county, at least so near that some of the soldiers composing his famous company were in all probability from Walker county. He relates that his company were equipped with hats or caps of coonskin, this head dress being the only effort at uniformity as to clothing among his men. These caps were just such as were made by Mr. Jordan on Lookout mountain, and there can be little doubt that Mr. Jordan made some and maybe all the caps for this famous company. The company was known as the *Raccoon Roughs* from the peculiar head dress worn by them. General Gordon had selected, he says, another name for his company but had not communicated the name to the men. When on the streets of

Atlanta with his company, every eye was focused on him and his men when some one asked him the name of his company. He replied that this was the *Mountain Rifles*. "Mountain Rifles, hell," shouted one of his men, "we are the Raccoon Roughs." The General says he never heard of Mountain Rifles again.

When the war broke out General Gordon was operating a coal mine in Northwest Georgia. This may have been in Dade county, but it was so near Walker that his men probably got their hats and caps from Mr. Jordan. No doubt, too, that some of his men were recruited from Walker county.

FIRST COTTON GIN. Probably the first cotton gin ever operated in the county was built by an old pioneer citizen, Mr. Jesse Stephens, long before the war on his farm near the base of Lookout mountain about four miles west of Kensington. This gin was built for the public and was run by horsepower. There was in those days little or no cotton raised for market in the county, but people were beginning to use cotton clothes which were made at home. The early settlers of the county separated the lint from the seed by hand, after which the lint was carded into rolls, then spun into thread and woven into cloth as in the case of wool. The cotton gin had been invented by Eli Whitney some years before, and was in general use in most parts of the state. Walker county a hundred years ago was very much on the frontier, and no cotton gin was as yet thought of. Mr. Stephens' gin was a very small affair and was used to gin small amounts of cotton for home use. It was patronized by the public much as was done in the case of the wool roll plant. More cotton clothes could now be worn by people which was cheaper, and moreover was more comfortable for summer wear. Other gins were erected about this time in other parts of the county. There were, however, no gins of importance till during the decade immediately preceding the war. Following the war cotton began to be raised on a larger scale, and during the latter part of the 19th century large commercial gins were established in almost every part of the county.

THE SHOOTING MATCH. During the early years of the county's history and as late as about 1890, the shooting match was a favorite sport and means of diversion among the settlers. As described by an old citizen and one who often took part in this sport, the procedure was about as follows: A distance of 75 yards was measured off and a spot with a cross in it was erected at one end of the course. The participants at the other end with an old fashion hog-rifle, and a laying-down rest, would shoot at the cross in the spot. The prize might be, and usually was, a beef. However, upon occasion, almost anything might be put up for a prize. Three judges were appointed to decide the shooting. In the case of a beef, there were usually five participants, each paying an equal sum, the amount of which was a fair price for the beef. The beef was supposed to be divided into five parts—two hindquarters, two forequarters, and the hide, head, and tallow. When the shooting was over the judges decided winners according to the accuracy of the shots. The beef was then killed and apportioned according to this decision, each taking first, or second, etc., the fifth getting the hide and tallow.

Sometimes the price of the shots were reduced so that the participants each should have five shots, and in this manner it was possible for one man to get the whole beef, which was occasionally done, and this lucky man would drive the beef home on foot. These matches, were usually held on Saturdays, or other convenient occasions, and were always attended by large numbers of people. They were, almost always, quite orderly and friendly and good-naturedly conducted, but one rare occasions, when some turbulent spirit was present, or possibly had imbibed too freely of Bacchus, there might be some disturbance, as a fist-and-skull fight.

The story is told of how, on a certain occasion, two of these old sportsmen were to shoot for a five dollar gold piece. Their names were Wilson Bailey and Bill Hixon. After the shooting was over, Uncle Wilce, who had lost out, was returning home and being met by a neighbor who had not been present at the match and being anxious to know the result of the shooting asked, "Well, Uncle Wilce, how did the shooting match come out?" "Oh, about even," replied the old sport, "Bill got the money and I had the fun."

SUNNYSIDE. In front of the residence of Mr. J. F. Stanfield, some two miles northeast of LaFayette is a most peculiar arrangement of some cedar trees. They were transplanted there many years ago. They are arranged in two parallel rows in the form of an oblong circle. The distance between the rows is about 16 feet as if it had been laid out for a driveway. The distance from end to end of the oblong is about 90 yards and from side to side about 65 yards, giving an area of something like an acre. There was, originally, a smaller circle at the north end of this oblong-like circle, and connecting with it, but some of the trees composing it were cut some years ago to make room for a dwelling. The whole figure was then, originally, in the shape of the figure 8 with the small part at the top.

No one seems to know who set out these trees, or when, or why. Mr. Pike, an old resident in that community, says that Mr. Richard Baker, who was a teacher before the war, and who owned the farm and who lived and died there, built a school house in the center of this larger circle or oblong, and taught there; that during the war his dwelling was burned, probably by the Yankees, and that the school house was then moved to the site of his dwelling and used as such. There are still standing more than 100 of these trees. They have the appearance of being very old—probably a century old. Let us hope that the owner will spare them for another century. Mr. Baker, so the story goes, named his home, "Sunnyside." Hence the name of the school near by.

AN ANTE-BELLUM HOMESTEAD. At the John Puryear old homestead in East Armuchee Valley many old objects are pointed out to the casual visitor, reminding one of antebellum days. After the battle of Missionary Ridge, and while Sherman was pushing the Confederates toward Dalton, a part of his troops were encamped near Villanow, where Mr. Puryear lived. His daughter, still living at the old home place, tells how she saw the yards and fields literally blue with Yankees. They were encamped there for 2 or 3 days and nights. After their departure, a large chain, evidently used for drawing artillery, was found near the home. It was placed over and around a high limb on a white oak tree standing in the yard, and was used for a swing for the boys. This was in 1864. This chain is still there and used for a swing. The part of the chain in contact with the limb has become imbedded in the fiber of the tree—apparently passes through the very center of the limb. That old army chain has hung there for more than 67 years. The tree at that time was a mere sapling, or youngster, but now shows itself to be a monarch of the surrounding woodland. There are other white oak trees standing near by which were there when Mr. Puryear settled at that place when the Indians roamed their happy hunting ground. These trees are probably more than a century old. Some of them are about 15 feet in circumference.

The dwelling house is another object of interest to the antiquarian. It was built by the owner long before the war; is constructed of poplar logs and is to-day, apparently, as sound as when first erected.

WALKER'S IRREGULAR SOUTHERN BOUNDARY LINE. Many years ago, Captain N. C. Napier had large holdings of land near Harrisburg, all of which was in Walker county, except a small tract which was in Chattooga county. As it was somewhat troublesome to have to pay taxes in two counties, he had a bill introduced in the Legislature of Georgia, by the then representative from Walker county, Madison Rhodes, changing the county line so as to include all his holdings in Walker. This bill was passed and it became a law.

MENU IN REVOLUTIONARY WAR. Michael Plaster, senr., an old citizen, who died about 1880, used to relate some of the experiences of his grandfather, a soldier of the Revolution, as he had heard it from him in his early days. The "Bill of Fare," at least on one occasion went one better than that of General Marion when he offered roasted sweet potatoes to the British officer who came to his camp on official duty under a flag of truce. On one occasion, according to this authority, after going about 2 days without food, the soldiers were issued some fresh beef hide for sustenance, each soldier being given a piece as large as a man's hand. After cutting the hair from this skin, they cut it into very small pieces and boiled it several hours before eating it.

A POTTERY PLANT. Soon after the War Between the States Mr. James Hill, facetiously called "Jug" Hill, operated a pottery plant just west of Mr. Will Stokers' place on the Broomtown road. Clay of excellent quality was secured from a near-by pit, which after being mixed with other ingredients in proper proportions was thoroughly kneaded to the right consistency and formed into various household and kitchen vessels. By means of a turning lay or potter's wheel which was operated by the foot, he could take a piece of prepared clay of sufficient size and form it into any desired vessel. While rotating with his foot the wheel on which was placed the clay, and with one hand in the vessel the other outside, he could build it up and form a jug, churn, crock, bowl or vase, as well as various other vessels used by the housewife.

After making these in quantity they were placed in a furnace where they were subjected to great heat for several hours, during which time they were glazed by the addition of certain materials. After cooling they were further polished and were ready for market. This crockery was hauled to Ringgold, Dalton, Rome and other points and placed on the market. Mr. J. B. Parker was at one time connected with Mr. Hill in the operation of the plant. There was a similar plant operated at LaFayette much later than the one above described—probably as late as 1900.

Chapter Thirty-three

MISCELLANEOUS CONTINUED. ANDREWS' RAIDERS—INDIAN ROCK MOUND —BLACKWELL LEDGER—THE LANE HOME—THOMAS PATTON "SECESH" —OLD TIME SINGERS—BRYAN FAMILY—HIXON-MILLER FAMILY— SCHMITT FAMILY—FILCHED A CHURCH—T. A. COOPER IN REMINISCENT MOOD—WHITE'S STATISTICS—HORSE SWAPPING—GANDER PULLING.

ANDREWS' RAIDERS. On April 12, 1862, at Big Shanty, near Marietta, J. J. Andrews, a private citizen, with 21 others (soldiers), captured the engine, "General," and ran it toward Chattanooga in an effort to sever communications between that city and Atlanta. Failing, he abandoned the engine near Ringgold and with his party of soldiers escaped to the woods. Some were captured near Ringgold, while others fled westward through the country hoping to join their commands in Tennessee. They traveled through Walker county, passing north of Chickamauga and into Chattanooga Valley, according to information from old settlers; thence across Lookout Mountain by way of Nickajack Pass and were eventually captured near Trenton, in Dade county. This was one of the most daring exploits enacted during the Civil War, a complete account of which reads like a thrilling detective story. The leader, J. J. Andrews, with some 6 or 7 others were executed as spies; a few of them broke jail and escaped, while the remainder were exchanged as prisoners of war.

INDIAN ROCK MOUND. There is a large pile of rock or stone near High school house on Lookout Mountain which has been there from time immemorial. Nobody knows anything about who, or why, with reference to it. It is supposed to be an Indian accumulation. It is called the Indian grave by the people of the community. They have no tradition concerning it. It is evidently the work of man.

These piles of stone are often met with in various parts of the country. According to some authorities, there is a tradition among certain aborigines that these grew up as follows: The Indians believed that in certain places or stretches along their trails or paths, there were evil spirits which brought bad luck or sickness or other calamity to travelers, but that this might be prevented by casting a stone in a certain place. Hence, in passing that place, the custom grew up of throwing stones together and in this way, in the course of years, an immense pile of stones might accumulate.

Still another explanation is given in Brown's History of Alabama, as follows: In speaking of the death and burial rites of the Indian he says: "Sometimes a heap of stones was raised to commemorate one who had died away from home and whose bones could not be recovered. Each passer-by added a stone to the pile."

THE BLACKWELL LEDGER. Mr. W. P. Blackwell, of Greenbush, has in his possession three old ledgers or account books once used by his ancestor who sold goods at that place many years ago. The dates run well before the Civil War, back into the fifties. Records of purchases for many years are shown in these old ledgers. They are interesting as showing the variety of merchandise kept for sale and in demand 70 and 80 years ago. A few of these accounts are shown herewith as they appear in the ledgers. These accounts are well-kept and accurate in the main:

Year 1860.

Feb. 13, J. M. Easterling, Dr. 1 lb. soda, 15c.

Feb. 25, Frank Little, Dr. 1 bot. C. Brandy $1.

Feb. 25, W. L. Shattuck, Dr. Madder 03c.

Mch. 30, J. Y. Wood, Dr. 5 lbs. nails 40c.

Apr. 4, Alex Calhoun, Dr. 15 lbs. nails 97c.

Apr. 16, W. L. Shattuck, Dr. 1 cravat 75c; 1 hoop skirt, $2.75; 3 yds. black domestic 48c; 5½ yds. prints 77c.

Apr. 16, Jas. Headrick, Dr. ½ lb. tob. 30c; 1 bar lead 10c; ¼ lb. powder 15c.

Apr. 16, Jeremiah Ramey, Dr. To 5 wool hats $4.25; 2 hoop skirts $2.50.

Apr. 18, Wm. Little, Dr. To 10 yds. muslin $3; 3 yds. ribbon $1.05;

1 belt 65c; 8 yds. jackonet $3.00; 4 pr. hose $1; 4 yds. prints 50c; 5 pens and stock 10c.

Apr. 19, S. Bomar, Dr. 1 silk hdhf. 80c.

Apr. 24, Rebecca Neal, Dr. 8 yds. calico, $1.00.

Apr. 24, S. Saxon, Dr. to cow bell 95c.

Apr. 27, S. Bomar, Dr. To 5 yds. calico, 62½c; 1 pr. puff combs 10c.

May 12, S. S. Keenman, Dr. pr. candle moulds 30c.

June 22, Robt. Little, Dr. Doz. marbles 10c.

July 25, A. Shattuck, Dr. 6 yds. drilling 99c.

Dec. 17, Alex. Copeland, Dr. pr. boots, $3.75.

THE LANE HOME. A most interesting antebellum homestead and one around which clusters much that partakes of those early days, is the Lane homestead in McLemore's Cove. The owner of this plantation, Richard Lane, established himself at that place before the war. He owned broad acres of that fine farming land, which in those early days was so fertile that corn, wheat, hay and other crops grew almost spontaneously. Mr. Lane was a man of considerable wealth, having around him numerous slaves, who cultivated his land and did the other work of the plantation.

In the year 1859, he erected the present dwelling which stands as a reminder of those early days. This home was built principally by slave labor. The style is reminiscent of the old Southern plantation in its construction, and yet differs somewhat from most of those old homes. The upper part has never been completely finished and it is possible to examine it quite minutely and observe the peculiar construction of the work. Looking at this unfinished upper portion, one can easily imagine himself in the hull of one of the large Atlantic passenger ships. No such carpenter work done in these days as is shown here.

Mr. Lane refugeed during the war and left the place occupied by a Mr. Evitt. Two Yankees were domiciled here on one occasion, spending the night, when Gatewood learned of the matter. He made a raid on the house, entered and found them in bed where they were shot. Bullet holes are still pointed out in the walls, and the present owner, Mrs. J. D. Strickland, says that when she first came to live there, the blood marks were distinctly discernible but the floor was eventually painted which obliterated all signs.

THOMAS PATTON, "SECESH." The author has received numerous letters from former old citizens of the county now living in other states, giving interesting items of history concerning the county. The following is from Mr. S. B. Carson of Ardmore, Okla., now nearly 80 years of age: There was a man by the name of Tom Patton living in LaFayette. He was one of the finest men who ever saw that town—a perfect old-fashioned Southern gentleman. Never harmed a soul, either by word or deed. They (the Yankees) had nothing against him except he was what they called a "secesh." Well, they came down and arrested Mr. Patton and put him on an old poor mule that was so weak that it could barely stand up and made him ride that old mule bareback. On the way to Chattanooga, they came to a very bad mud hole in the road. They forced the old mule into the mud hole and he fell down. Mr. Patton, all over muddy when he waded out, and they asked him, "Are you a Secesh yet, old man?" Mr. Patton said, "Secesh bred and born."

"YE OLDE" time singers have nearly all passed. There are very few left among us. Half a century ago the old four-note singing had many devotees. The Sacred Harp and the Southern Harmony were the books mostly used; then came the Christian Harmony which had seven notes but the tunes were in the main the same. The meetings were conducted by men who sang the Gospel. One of these was James Wooten, who, although living in Chattooga county, sang the old songs throughout Walker county for many years. He was often called the "Prince of Old Time Singers." His son "Sandy" is following his father's footsteps. Others of the sweet old singers were Edom Moon of Chestnut Flat, Lee Davis, W. A. Foster and Asbury McCall. A few are still with us, as G. W. Brown and J. A. Mullis.

A strange power sometimes pervaded these old singings which was often shown by the tears and trembling voices of those engaged in the service.

SOME REMARKABLE FAMILIES.

THE BRYAN FAMILY (Lookout Mountain). Mrs. J. W. Bryan came from Savannah in the early seventies, and established her home on Lookout mountain, where she erected a handsome house overlooking beautiful McLemore's cove. Her abode, built near the overhanging bluffs, could be seen for many miles up and down the valley. Here she acquired considerable real estate, and lived and died. She was the daughter of Major C. W. Howard, a noted preacher and writer, her husband being Major Bryan, a Confederate veteran. She had three children, Ella, Howard and Virginia, all of whom were given a fine education in her own home, she being their teacher. All the family are now dead except Miss Ella, the eldest. Mrs. Bryan was a scholarly woman of the old school—educated, refined and accomplished—a fine specimen of the Old South. Her eldest daughter, Ella, whose pen name is Clinton Dangerfield, became and is yet, a noted writer and poet, many of her productions being eagerly sought by the leading magazines and publications of the country. Clinton Dangerfield is, perhaps, Walker county's most noted author, especially in poetry and story-writing.

THE HIXON-MILLER FAMILY. These two pioneers came to the county very early in its history. They both hailed from Tennessee. Hixon had six sons besides daughters—all stalwart boys such as it was common to see among the early settlers of the county. On the other hand James Miller had, among other children, six fine daughters. They lived on adjoining farms, in the Dry valley section of the county. In the course of time, as the children, one by one, grew up to maturity, it came to pass that these fine boys, each courted, wooed, won and wedded, one of the girls—all save one of the boys, who looked abroad and found a wife of another name, who, however, was related to the Miller family. There were, then, five boys, brothers, who married five girls, sisters, and all raised large families of children. (Note: Uncle "Billy" Hixon, who lives on Lookout mountain, is a son of the boy who failed to marry one of the Miller girls, he having married a Nave, who was part Indian and was related to John Ross, head chief of the Cherokees).

THE SCHMITT FAMILY. John Schmitt came to this country during the decade immediately preceding the Civil War. He had, among other children, four sons, Philip, Conrad, John and George. In Germany he had heard marvelous stories of the possibilities to be had in this "Land of Promise," and so, gathering together his little family, he emigrated and settled in the northern part of the county about the year 1855 or 56. Philip, however, his eldest son, did not come at this time as he had already married and because of some position he held as a minor officer under the German government, he could not, at that time, leave Germany. In 1861, he was making preparations to come to join his father in America, when, suddenly, he received a cablegram from his father telling him not to come as war had been declared between the North and the South. Accordingly he waited till the close of the war when he joined his father who had settled in the section south of Rossville.

This family bought or leased from the McFarlands some land on Missionary ridge and cleared up the first land ever cultivated on that ridge. He planted a large vineyard on the west side of the ridge and built a wine-press. However, he soon discovered he would not be allowed to make wine and so the grape business fell through. The descendants of this pioneer are scattered throughout the northern part of the county and in other counties and states and are intelligent, reliable and industrious citizens.

FILCHED A CHURCH. The following bit of traditional history was related to this chronicler by an old citizen of the Cove who heard it told by numerous old citizens many years ago. While it may not be retold here just as it came to pass, there can be no doubt that in some such manner it occurred.

There lived almost a century ago, in McLemore's cove, three pioneer citizens, who were also local Methodist preachers, many of whose descendants are still living in the county. They were neighbors, living in the same community and often meeting together in the neighbors' cabins where they were zealous as Christian workers and often held religious services, first one and then another leading or preaching or exhorting. There were quite a number of Methodist people living in the surrounding community and it was discussed and finally decided to undertake to build a church of that persuasion.

With these three local preachers as leaders it soon developed that there was a division as to where the new church should be located. Two of them who lived near each other favored a location near their homes, while the third who lived some distance away wanted it built near his residence. However, before the matter was finally settled all hands got together and went to the woods and cut and hewed the logs for the building. At this stage of the game the single preacher with his adherents, having had an inkling that the other side might outvote him and place the church too far away from his home, gathered together all the available oxen and horses in the community, and during the night went to the woods and snaked all the logs to the place selected by himself.

On the morrow, when the others came to gather up the logs they found them gone. Following the marks they soon came to the new location and found the other preacher and his helpers busily engaged erecting the new church. This location was called Stony Point. The other clan got together and built a church where they had at first intended and called it Thorny Hall; afterward called Liberty.

T. A. COOPER IN REMINISCENT MOOD. In an old copy of the Walker County Messenger, dated back in the early nineties, Mr. T. A. Cooper, whose father was one of the pioneer settlers of the county, and himself born while the Indians still roamed throughout its valleys, a brother of Mr. Alonzo Cooper of the Chestnut Flat section, writes in reminiscent mood of the early days in Walker county. Mr. Cooper, a facile writer, as the following lines amply show, lived to be about 92 years of age, having died some few years since in California.

Writing of early days in Walker, he says: "There were practically no settlers from Taylor's ridge to LaFayette, or from Chickamauga (meaning middle Chickamauga) to Peavine valley. All that region was known as the "ridges." This was a vast grazing region for everybody's stock—and grazing was good. Following the custom of the Indians, the woods were burned over annually in the early spring, thus keeping down much of the undergrowth and allowing the native grasses full sway. One could see turkey, deer, or other wild animals as far as the topography of the country would permit. In spring and summer the jingling and tinkling of the cow bells, as they swung back and forth on the necks of the cattle could be heard in every direction. A crude music you say? but in harmony with other scenes of the early days and in memory to an old sinner's ear is delightfully sweet music. But the cow bells were not the only sweet music. At that time, looking back fifty years, there were more sweet singing birds, of greater variety, and of a more brilliant hue than now.

"Those happy musicians congregated in May seemingly in one grand concert to pay homage in song to the Great Giver of all good, to sing their warbling anthems of thanksgiving that the long winter of discontent had again passed, and the springtime of joy, hope and love again gave cause for all animal life to join in one grand chorus of thanksgiving and songs of praise. Thus I grew up seemingly in an enchanted region.

"The little brooks, rivulets and rills were full of sportive fish. The borders of those streams were ornamented in springtime with flowering shrubbery of many kinds, with flowers of different fragrance blending together and perfuming the atmosphere. These were halcyon days and I knew it not.

"It was the inspiration then derived from my surroundings, that in later years developed the mind panorama so frequently enjoyed by reflections on days in years past. Little did I then think how my environments were daily forging links, that gradually formed a chain that has ever since, in all circumstances, held me in memory dear to the picturesque hills and valleys, brooks and rills, of Walker county." * * * *

WHITE'S STATISTICS. White's Statistics of Georgia written in 1849 devotes several pages to a discussion of Walker county. Among other matters it says: Postoffices in the county were: LaFayette, Medicinal Springs, Chestnut Flat, Ringgold, Frick's Gap, Rock Spring, Rossville, Snow Hill, Villanow, Wood Station and Duck Creek.

Population: 1848: Whites 7023, blacks 1044, total 8067. State tax returned for 1848, $1939.82.

Character of the People: The people are moral and industrious. They are remarkably attached to their homes and consider Walker the garden spot of Georgia. The amusements are hunting and fishing.

Religious Sects and Education: The principal sects are Baptists of both sorts, Methodists, Presbyterians, Reformed Presbyterians, Bible Christians, Universalists, and a few Roman Catholics. There are good schools in this county. The people generally are anxious to have their children educated.

Roads and Bridges: The roads in the valleys are fair but generally not much can be said in favor of the roads. There are two or three bridges over the Chickamauga river. Planters send their produce to Augusta and Macon.

The following land values are quoted in this work as of 1849: First quality alluvial lands of river and creek bottoms, $15 per acre. Second quality valley lands, gray and dark soils, adapted to corn and cotton, $7 per acre. Third quality lands lying between the valleys, called ridges, $1 per acre. The fourth quality embrace the mountain lands valued at 25 cents per acre, fit for grazing and finely timbered.

LaFayette is thus described: LaFayette is the capital, beautifully situated, having a court house built at an expense of $7000.00; a jail, two churches, Baptist and Methodist *each having a bell;* two hotels, six stores, four groceries, three tailors, two blacksmiths, one shoe shop, one saddlery, two cabinette makers, six carpenters, two bricklayers, one tanner, six or seven lawyers, three doctors, and one academy. * * * It is considered a healthy town. The water is excellent, and the scenery around it is grand beyond description. Several intelligent gentlemen reside in this town and take great pleasure in showing visitors the curiosities of the country. This place was formerly called Chattooga but in 1836 was changed to LaFayette.

HORSE SWAPPING. Among the early settlers horses were cheap and plentiful. Everybody had one. They were indispensable among the pioneers. They were necessary not only on the farm but as a means of conveyance about the country. In those days horseswapping was a fine art, and the horse jockey was a regular profession. He prided himself on his ability to palm off a poor animal on his victim, and various ruses were resorted to to accomplish this. Generally when two of these professionals had met and swapped horses, neither of them was seriously hurt.

All the jockies attended the sessions of the Superior Court. Tuesday was the principal jockey day. At first the plan was to attend the last day of court, but since it was uncertain just how long court would last, they adopted Tuesday as a safe day for horse swapping. Those who had business at court were there; those who had business in town were there; those who had business on the jockey yard were there, and the number was swelled by those who had no business at all. Everybody was present on Tuesday which was the big day of court. The jockey-yard was a most animated place and horses were liable to change hands several times during the day. Old-timers tell of occasions when the judge had to suspend court because of the excitement on the jockey-yard. But this old-time excitement, like many other kindred diversions, is now practically obsolete.

THE GANDER PULLING. A gander with the feathers plucked from his head and neck, which were then thoroughly greased, was suspended from a bar supported by two upright poles about 8 or 9 feet high. After paying a small fee, each contestant, mounted, galloped at full speed between the upright poles and endeavored to grasp the gander's head and pluck it from the body. Because of the rapid rate of travel, and the slick head of the animal, this was no easy feat. The fortunate contestant had the gander for his reward. (Note: Possibly this old pastime of our forbears explains the origin of the expression, "All is lovely and the goose hangs high").

THE RACE TRACK. In antebellum days, there was, in almost every community, a race track. There were several of these in various parts of the Cove. The track was, generally, about a quarter of a mile in length. The farm horses were used for racing. The bets at the races were usually small—probably a quart of whiskey or brandy. These were generally community affairs, and were held on various occasions, both stated and special. They were always well-attended and were occasions of merry-making and of having a jolly good time. Rarely was there any serious disturbance, unless some thirsty soul had imbibed too freely of Bacchus, which was rare.

Chapter Thirty-four

MISCELLANEOUS CONTINUED. ANDERSON SPRING—A "WITCH" SPRING—JAMES R. JONES LEDGER—SIGNAL POINT—WHIPPING POST—AUGUSTUS MCCUTCHEN—HARKS BACK TO DECLARATION—BORN AT SEA—THE HUNTER'S PARADISE—RECORDS FROM 1883—DR. TARVIN, INDIAN—"HOME SWEET HOME"—INDIAN'S VALEDICTORY.

ANDERSON SPRING. There is, near Mr. S. R. H. Anderson's residence, in the head of McLemore's Cove, a large, bold spring of clear, cold water gushing out from the side of Pigeon mountain close to the Rape gap road. A peculiar feature of this cave spring is the cold air that continually blows out. On a hot day one can feel, while yet a hundred feet away, the effect of this cool breeze when approaching it. On a hot day in July, 1930, a party examined it and found that when the thermometer was registering 94 in the shade, if carried into the mouth of the cave where the cold air could be felt, it immediately dropped 40 degrees, or down to 54. The water coming from the cave also registered 54. This cold air comes out continually. The bushes and weeds near the cave's mouth are in a continual motion because of the air currents. Whence comes this air? There is likely an opening somewhere in the mountain where the air is drawn in and then passing through the tunnels and crevices—maybe for miles—is cooled and finally makes its exit at the cave spring. Mr. Anderson has installed a ram here which furnishes an abundant water supply to his home and barn. There is another such spring further up in the very head of the cove on the Murphy farm. Then there is a similar one called Blowing Spring near the Tennessee line. No doubt there are others.

A "WITCH" SPRING. Mr. J. G. Tatum describes what seems to be a periodic spring on the side of Lookout mountain near his home in the Cove. This spring, he says, starts and stops without any apparent reason; especially is this true during a prolonged drought. He has noted it on different occasions. This is, in all probability, a periodic, or syphon spring. There is back in the side of the mountain a large opening or basin where the water collects and whose outet is somewhat in the shape of a coffee-pot spout. As long as the basin is kept full there will be a flow of water. When, however, the outflow becomes greater than the inflow, the basin will be emptied and the flow will stop till the basin is refilled which forces a new flow, thus making it a periodic spring.

Before such springs were thoroughly understood there was a notion among many people that these were "witch" springs; that is, they believed that witches had power over them and the superstitious were careful to avoid them.

THE JAMES R. JONES LEDGER. Miss Mary Jones, a granddaughter of the late James R. Jones of the Rock Spring section, has in her possession a highly prized relic of her ancestor in the way of an old ledger which Mr. Jones used for many years in which he kept his records and accounts. Although parts of it have been destroyed by time, and its pages are dim with age, it is, nevertheless, to the seeker after old records, of great interest. The ledger shows that Mr. Jones was a man of considerable wealth, possessing at various times, several slaves, as well as large holdings in farming lands. This old book shows that he had extensive dealings with his community and that he was a man of careful habits. This chronicler has been much interested in examining this old ledger. The oldest date shown is the year 1844, and other matters are dated as late as 1878. The following entries from the ledger are given as showing the prices of various commodities at that time, as well as for their general interest:

"Aug. 1844. Maj. James M. Shields, Dr. to 22 lbs. beef at 1½c per lb." "Spring 1845. James M. Shields, Dr. to 10 lbs. coffee, $1.00." "Jan. 27, 1845. LaFayette Mounds, Dr. to night's lodging, supper and breakfast, and horse fed, 50c." "April 7, 1845. P. A. Knight, Dr. to one night's lodging for himself and sister, and supper 25c." "Oct. 3, 1845. John Gray, Dr. to 97 lbs. beef at 2c per lb., $1.94." "April 11, 1848. Milton Plaster, Dr. to 1 bu. potatoes, 25c." "Aug. 11, 1848. A. E. Rogers, Dr. to 30 lbs. bacon, at 5c lb., $1.50." "Sept. 15, 1848. John Pilgrim, Dr. to 2 lbs. wool rolls 84c." "1849. Jason Cloud, Dr. to 2 bu. Irish potatoes 40c." "Oct. 5, 1846. John Pilgrim, Dr. to 1½ bu. wheat 75c." "Apr. 11, 1846. Wm. S. Doyal, Dr. to 2½ bu. corn 50c bu.; also, to 20c lent at LaFayette, $1.45." "June 1, 1854. Fields left his horse with me to feed $1.50 per week." "W. G. Sparks, Dr. to 100 bundles fodder $1.50." "John Collins, Dr. to 10 bu. of potatoes 25c bu."

SIGNAL POINT. Just west of the upper part of McLemore's Cove, on Lookout Mountain, and overlooking that beautiful valley is an elevation higher than the surrounding peaks called Signal Point. Perched on that towering elevation one can survey the whole valley and observe the movements of any who may be traveling along the roads or about the valley. Armed with a field glass, one may examine minutely, the farm premises with their occupants, for miles up and down that lovely valley. Here, during the Civil War, the Federal authorities established a signal station where messages could be sent and received, giving information as to the movements of the enemy, or other orders. A high flagpole was erected and was used to convey messages to points surrounding that section of the upper Cove.

There is, likewise, on John's Mountain, in East Armuchee valley, near The Furnace, another elevation called Signal Point, where the Federal army erected a flagpole for the same purpose. It is probable, also, that messages were flashed from one of these stations to the other by means of heliograms.

Many old citizens recall how the late Alvin Leslie, who resided in the Cove, celebrated the election of Judson C. Clements to Congress when he defeated Dr. Felton, in 1880. Mr. Leslie, who was a staunch democrat, worked himself up almost to a frenzy during the campaign, and was so sure that Mr. Clements would be elected, that he planned a grand celebration some days in advance. Accordingly, he erected on Signal Point near the head of McLemore's Cove, a high scaffold built of large pine poles. On this scaffold he placed a wagon load of rich pine knots and other inflammable material. Atop of this he placed a ten gallon keg of coal oil. At the end of the day of the election when he was sure that Mr. Clements had been elected, he lighted the fire and going below, fired a rifle ball through the keg of oil. In this way he hoped to keep the fire burning for a considerable time at its maximum height, which he succeeded in doing. This light was seen not only throughout the Cove, but also in other parts of the county, and even in Alabama. In discussing this matter with Mr. Reed Johnson who lives near Signal Point, he relates that his father, the late H. M. C. Johnson, assisted Mr. Leslie in erecting the scaffold and hauled the pine for the fire.

WHIPPING POST. An old citizen tells of having seen Sheriff Connally whip two negroes for some crime, they having been sentenced by the court. They were given 39 lashes, a large crowd of on-lookers being present. Another old citizen recalls a time when the same sheriff had the unpleasant duty of whipping a white man by order of the court. It is said that the sensitive nature of the sheriff was such that he performed this duty with due regard to the motto on the third pillar supporting the CONSTITUTION of the State of Georgia. Having performed the unpleasant duty, he advised the culprit to quit the country and start anew in a new field, which advice was taken and after some years it is said that a report showed that he was making good in the state of Arkansas.

AUGUSTUS McCUTCHEN. In an old copy of the Walker County Messenger Mr. J. B. Hackney relates the following story: A body of Confederates had been taken completely by surprise and before they could escape they were entirely surrounded by a number of Federal solders—in fact they were all around and among them. Some days before this the Confederates had captured some supplies among which were a number of Yankee uniforms. The Confederates being in dire need of warm clothing appropriated these uniforms and many of the soldiers wore them. Among this band of Confederates thus surrounded by the Yankees was that brilliant and unique character of North Georgia, Augustus McCutchen. He took in the situation at once and rising to his full height and assuming a commanding air, began in a stern voice to give orders to the Federal soldiers about him. As they were all in disorder and everything in confusion, and Mr. McCutchen wore a blue uniform they took him for a Federal officer and without question hurried away as he directed.

Due to his presence of mind and tactfulness, he and his companions easily made their escape, hurrying away to safety.

HARKS BACK TO DECLARATION. Mrs. Nancy Middleton Jones, ancestor of Colonel R. M. W. Glenn, who lies buried in the Jones family grave yard near Rock Springs, was the sister of Arthur Middleton of South Carolina, signer of the Declaration of Independence from that state.

LITTLE BOB DICKERSON. Miss Carrie Napier talks most interestingly of the old days in Walker, having heard many matters discussed by her father and others of the older generation. Among other matters she tells of how Mr. Thomas Sharpe, who gave three sons to the Confederacy, was persecuted by the Yankees, and was captured by the Long-Roberts gang and turned over to the Federal authorities in Chattanooga (See "Thomas Patton, Secesh"). He was sent to Camp Chase where he was confined. While there he wrote a letter home one day in which he remarked that, "Yesterday I saw Little Bob Dickerson in here."

BORN AT SEA. Mary J., daughter of John and Elizabeth McWilliams, was born on the Atlantic ocean while her parents were making the voyage to America in 1815. Her parents first settled in South Carolina, where she married Spencer Bomar, later coming to Walker county and setting in West Armuchee valley during the latter thirties, having followed her parents to that valley. They are the ancestors of the numerous Bomars now living in the county. An amusing story is told of her answers to the census enumerator some years after her marriage when that gentleman called and was asking the usual questions, one of which was: "Were you born in the United States?" "No," was the reply. "In what country were you born?" "I wasn't born in any country," came the answer. The enumerator looked puzzled, wondering whether she was crazy or just trying to make a fool of him. In the meantime the sensible old matron was laughing to herself at the discomfiture of the questioner, when her husband, Mr. Bomar, vouchsafed the information that she was born on the high seas, and she was so listed.

THE HUNTER'S PARADISE.

In order to show the abundance of game and wild life in this section a century ago, the following is given from White's Historical Collections, describing an old hunter and trapper among the mountains of North Georgia: "His favorite game is the deer, but he is not particular, and secures the fur of every four-legged creature that happens to cross his path. The largest number of skins that he ever brought home at one time (a season's catch) was 600. He computes the entire number of deer he has killed in his lifetime at 4,000. When spring arrives, and he purposes to return home, he packs his furs upon his old mule, and seating himself upon the pile of plunder, makes a bee line out of the wilderness. The name of the mule is *Devil and Tom Walker*."

"On one occasion he came up to a large gray wolf, at whose head he discharged a ball. The animal did not drop, but made its way into an adjoining cavern and disappeared. Having waited a while at the opening, and not hearing the wolf, he concluded to investigate, thinking it was dead. Crawling into the cave, he reached the bottom and found the wolf alive, when a 'clinch fight' ensued and the wolf was dispatched by the hunters' knife. On dragging it out he found that the wolf's lower jaw was broken, which was probably the reason he had not succeeded in destroying the hunter.

"At one time when he was out of ammunition, his dogs fell upon a large bear, and it so happened that the latter got one of the former in his power, and was about to squeeze it to death. This was a sight the hunter could not endure, so he unsheathed his large hunting knife, and assaulted the black monster. The bear tore off nearly every rag of his clothing, and in making his first plunge with his knife, he completely cut off two of his own fingers, instead of injuring the bear. He was now in a perfect frenzy of pain and rage, and in making another effort, succeeded to his satisfaction, and gained the victory. That bear weighed 350 pounds.

"On another occasion he had fired at a large buck, near the brow of a precipice some 30 feet high. On seeing the buck drop, he took for granted he was about to die, when he approached the animal for the purpose of cutting its throat. To his surprise, however, the buck suddenly sprang to his feet, and made a tremendous rush at the hunter, with a view of throwing him off the ledge.

"But what was more remarkable, the animal succeeded in his effort, though not until the hunter had secured a fair holt on the buck's antlers, when the twain performed a summerset into the pool below. The buck made its escape, the hunter not being seriously injured in any way. Later he killed a buck with a bullet in its throat, whereupon he concluded that it was the animal which had given him the unexpected ducking."

Stephens' History of Georgia, written about 1840, whose author had abundant opportunity to know the Indian nature and Indian History says, page 50, vol. 1: "During the French and Indian war, the Cherokees fought on the side of the English; but on their return home from the capture of Fort Duquesne, they gave such offense by their misconduct in Virginia that several of their warriors were killed; which circumstance lighted a war against the English, that was not extinguished till two expeditions of British troops reduced them to the royal power. Before they were corrupted by the white men, the Cherokees were frank, sincere, industrious; living in the most beautiful region of the Southern States, the "Hill Country" of Carolina and Georgia, secure in their mountain homes, rich in their valley lands, and strong in the arms and prowess of their death-defying warriors."

MINUTES BOARD OF ROAD AND REVENUE for 1883. On April 3 it was ordered that 36 paupers be paid amounts averaging about $3 each per month. Also, at this meeting contractors were invited to make bids for the erection of a Court House built of brick, 57 by 76 and two stories high. At a later meeting the contract was awarded to Joe B. Patton for $12,000.00. At an election called to decide whether bonds should be issued to pay for the new court house, and held on August 15, a majority voted "No Bonds." The tax levy for the years was 95 cents on the hundred dollars, as follows: For Court House 62½ cents; For paupers 10 cents; For jail fee 4½ cents; For jury 3 cents; For other purposes and outstanding debts 14 cents. For the year 1883, R. N. Dickerson was paid for his services as clerk of the Board the sum of $100.00, including stationery for Superior Court and for Board of Roads and Revenue.

DR. TARVIN, INDIAN.

Some of the older citizens of the Armuchees tell of some very interesting traditions among which is the following: There was in this section before the removal of the Indians, and old Indian, or part Indian doctor, named Tarvin, who practiced the art of medicine as he had learned it according to the Indian customs. He was what was known as a botanic doctor. His was a most peculiar method of practice.

Assording to this sage there were only three principal medicines and these were all obtained from the same source, that is, from the same plant. It was a rather unusual plant growing among the mountains and he spent much of his time searching for it. The bark was the active principal in the plant and he was very careful to gather the bark according to a well recognized method or plan as he had been taught it by his forbears. If the bark was stripped from above downward, it was called High-Pop-O-Lorum; if stripped from below upward it was called Low-Pop-O-Hirum; if stripped sideways around the tree, it was called High-low-Bustum. "High-Pop-O-Lorum," he said, "was a cathartic; Low-Pop-O-Hirum was an emetic, while High-Low-Bustum was a rank pizen."

"HOME SWEET HOME."

In 1836, or thereabouts, there was much excitement all over the State of Georgia concerning the Indian situation. Not only in Georgia but throughout the United States there was general excitement and anxiety. This is shown by the fact that John Howard Payne, the author of "Home Sweet Home," and whose home was in far away New York, had come to the Cherokee country to make investigations as to the situation. He seems to have been acting on his own authority. While in the country he was the guest of Chief John Ross, who was at that time located at his home at or near Spring Place in Murray County. John Ross had other places of residence, one of which, as we know, was at Rossville. He also had a residence in Tennessee. While a guest at the home of John Ross, whose friend he was, it is very probable that he visited Walker county in company with Ross upon occasion when visiting his residence at Rossville.

While at Spring Place, Mr. Payne was arrested by the Georgia Guard on suspicion, and was placed in confinement until it was shown that he had done nothing and was released with apologies. The legislature of the State reproved the soldiers for making the arrest. It is said that Mr. Payne, while under confinement, heard some of the soldiers singing his now famous song, and having convinced the officers that he was the author of it, was forthwith released.

THE INDIANS' VALEDICTORY.

When the dusky warriors and maidens were gathered together for removal westward, the assembled chiefs and counselors met at the Council Ground under the spreading oaks and murmuring pines, and after smoking the pipe of peace, in imploring attitudes turned their dark eyes toward heaven, pulled the swinging limbs to them, and in their wild devotion bedewed the sprigs and branches with their tears. When the final departure drew near all arms were taken from the Indians and they were marched between files of soldiers. Tradition says that a chief known as "Big Bear" had but a short time before buried his wife and only child, and that in his deep grief, he implored that he be spared the life of an exile. His prayers were unheeded and he was forced to take up the march. He secured a bayonet and hiding it under his blanket, as he passed by the graves of his loved ones, broke from his companions and threw himself across the mound, and, falling upon the sharp bayonet, he was pierced to the heart, thus dying by those he loved dearer than life. And to-day, "side by side, in their nameless graves the lovers are sleeping," for General Twiggs, in sympathy, ordered a Christian burial. The Indians turned their faces westward, journeying hundreds of miles, through forest and over desert, sometimes drenched with rain, sometimes consumed with thirst, thousands dying on the long march of months and thus began the "exile without an end and without an example in history."

Willie S. White.

Chapter Thirty-five

MIS. CON. THE ALLGOOD WAGONS—JUDICIAL COMMUNITY—ESCAPING YANKEE BULLETS—WALKER COUNTY SINGING CONVENTION—PUBLIC SQUARE—TREASURE TROVE—BLACKSMITH SHOP—SECESSION CONVENTION—FISH TRAP—FAMILY REUNIONS—WHEN CLEMENTS BEAT FELTON.

THE ALLGOOD WAGONS. One of the most exciting incidents of Ante Bellum days, as well as far into the eighties, especially to the children and young people living along the route of travel, was that attending the passage of the Allgood wagons through the county, on their way to market. Rome was the principal market for the products of the factory at

Trion, or Trion Factory, as it was denominated at that time. Once a week, sometimes oftener, Mr. Allgood sent his wagons with the products of his wheels and looms to Rome to be placed on the market there, or to be shipped thence to other points, there being no railroad at Trion. Occasionally, however, (and this happened right often) the wagons were sent to Ringgold or to Chattanooga, in which event the caravan passed through the county.

This consisted of from four to eight covered wagons drawn usually by four mules each. The roads, especially in winter, were horrible affairs at that time, and travel was necessarily slow and tedious. As the long procession wended its way slowly up and down the muddy hills, with frequent halts to allow the teams time to "blow," the children of the adjacent countryside perched themselves on fences or gate posts, or sought other advantageous positions, while they viewed the passing caravan. There was the driver for each wagon astride his leading wheel mule, with long lines to direct his front team and with a long whip which he never failed to use, especially to crack and pop; and the continuous conversation which he kept up with his team—a jargon which none save the team might comprehend, all this gave the young people along the route of travel a kick compared to which the movies of our day pale into insignificance..

In addition to hauling the factory produce to market, these wagons returned laden with supplies for the operatives, so that they were loaded each way. Three days were usually required for this round trip, which gave two nights to be spent in camp. There was always some excitement about the camp fire and the young people of the community where the camp happened to be, as well as the older ones were wont to spend the evening in conversation with the wagoners.

Everything necessary for cooking was carried—skillets, pots, frying pans, coffee pots and so on, as well as a sufficient supply of food stuffs. For breakfast there was always the neverfailing hard brown biscuits, fried bacon and eggs with plenty of black coffee. Dinner and supper were pretty apt to show up about the same bill of fare with, maybe, an occasional change for sake of variety.

These old scenes are now a thing of the past. Both the scenes and the actors have been gone for many years. One of the most picturesque of these actors was James Wooten, sometimes called by his fellows, "Ginger." He was one of the most trusted and reliable of the Allgood drivers. For many years he might be seen at the head of this caravan, directing and controlling the movements along the countryside. Even after this method of marketing the factory's products was discontinued, he was still to be seen in charge of the teams and wagons of the Trion Company. Did I say that they had all passed? One is left. There is one, happily, still with us, and from him I have been fortunate enough to gather these dots about this interesting bit of old county history. Mr. W. M. Ramey of Cane Creek, now in his 86th year. (Died August 1931).

ESCAPING A HAIL OF YANKEE BULLETS. Capt. Sanford Venable tells the following incident of the battle of Chickamauga:

As captain of Company "A," 8th Georgia Battalion, I was in the thickest of the fight in the battle of Chickamauga, and on Sunday morning, September 20th, I fell with a bullet in my left knee. As I lay wounded on the ground I turned my head to the Yankees and tried as best I could to dodge the bullets as they ploughed the ground around me. The cannons were cutting off limbs and tree tops about me, while the roaring of the guns was heard by my family living then at old Cassville, in Cass, (now Bartow) county.

After lying thus for some time, one of my company snatched me up on his back and in the midst of a perfect storm of bullets, as fast as his legs could carry two passengers, he ran with me off the battlefield. My friend said afterward that if I had not been an expert at dodging bullets we would have been killed, but certainly it was his fleetfootedness that saved us.

A JUDICIAL COMMUNITY. One and a half miles west of LaFayette, within the space of a square mile, five lads grew to manhood and later became judges of courts. There were Benjamin R. McCutchen, judge of the county court before and after the war; Madison Rhodes, judge of the Inferior Court; C. D. McCutchen, son of B. R., was for eight years judge of the Cherokee Circuit; W. M. Henry for twelve years judge of the Rome Circuit; H. P. Lumpkin judge of the county court, serving till it was abolished,—a pretty good record for one small community.

HISTORY OF WALKER COUNTY SINGING CONVENTION.

By James H. Madaris.

The Walker County Singing Convention was organized at Chickamauga on the second Sunday and Saturday before in May, 1894, the following officers being elected: W. A. Foster, Pres.; B. A. McCall, V-Pres.; J. E. Rosser, Secy-Treas. Mr. Foster served as president till 1896, after which the following, in order given, served as president: B. A. McCall 1896-97; A. J. Wellborn 1897-98; R. P. McWilliams 1898-99; E. W. Keith 1899-00; C. M. Groover 1900-01; Chas. Robt. Jones 1901-02; James H. Madaris 1902-03; Chas. Robt. Jones 1903-08; James H. Madaris 1908-10; Lee McCall 1910-12.

Then follow without dates the following names of singers who have served as president: Lawson Duncan; E. G. Carroll; Lum Ezell; J. L. Lane; Henry L. Duncan; A. A. Turner; W. A. Mitchel; Homer McClure; J. L. Lane; U. F. Silvers; Henry L. Duncan; B. L. Hampton; J. L. Lane; E. H. Kelley (1932).

On the fourth Sunday in May 1931 the "Rolling Singing Convention" was organized at Bethel church with the following officers; J. H. Madaris, Pres.; Lawson Duncan, Vice Pres.; Frank Brown, Sec.-Treas. This convention meets monthly on the third Sunday, afternoon only, in different parts of the county, with the hope of stimulating sacred music more in the home churches.

LAFAYETTE'S PUBLIC SQUARE. Mr. Spencer Warthen converses interestingly of many matters connected with the early history of LaFayette and the county. Having been associated with many of the early settlers, he recalls many items of interest which otherwise might have been lost to history. Among other matters he says that the first court house was a log structure, built of large hewn timbers and notched down at the corners. There was one large room for holding court and some other rooms for jury and officers. This house was built in the public square and was used for this purpose for several years. During the forties, however, it was decided to erect another building, larger and more commodious. The public square was smaller then than at present, and it was seen that the new and larger house would leave insufficient space on each side for street purposes; in this circumstance the city (if it could be called such at that time), proposed to donate the alleys back of the buildings to property owners, in return for the same number of feet in front of their property, thus giving considerably more space for the square. This was agreed to and in this way the square was enlarged to its present proportions. This may account for the very wide sidewalks on the east and west sides of the square. The court house built at that time was used during the War and until it was destroyed by fire in 1883. It seems, therefore, that the present court house is the fourth house built for court purposes at LaFayette.

TREASURE TROVE. In his search for Indian lore and legends, this chronicler has heard related in almost every community in the county, numerous stories of hidden wealth in the form of gold, silver or lead mines, or maybe of buried money. Numerous old citizens relate stories told by their ancestors of how certain Indians used to mine gold or silver or lead in certain sections or places in the county. It seems, however, that none of these treasures have ever been located. The Indians were careful never to disclose their exact location. One is reminded in this connection of the story of that celebrated Spaniard, Ponce de Leon, the searcher after the Fountain of Youth. The Indians knew there was no such fountain, but in order to humor the old Spaniard and make a fool of him, they continued to urge him forward, saying that the fountain was just ahead. In like manner it is probable that the Cherokees in this section were only fooling our forbears by telling them of hidden wealth to be found buried in the ground.

THE BLACKSMITH SHOP, or Country Store, at the cross roads was famous as a congregating place for the country folk when our grandfathers were boys and young men. Here they loitered for hours on end on rainy days or in idle seasons to swap jokes, tobacco and knives and to whittle on dry goods boxes. The tobacco was home-raised and was wound into a gorgeous twist and carried in the pocket till needed which was quite often. It cost nothing and was free as water. As soon as an old quid had been thoroughly mulched it was discarded and replaced by a fresh one; in the meantime the twist was passed round with a hearty invitation to each one present to take a "chaw". Particles from this twist were often crushed between the palms and smoked in an old strong clay pipe which was lighted from the smith's forge, there being no matches in those days; or the fire might be taken from the sun by means of a burning glass, or even spectacles might be used for this purpose. Another method of lighting the pipe was by means of "flint and steel". To do this a common flint rock, a pocket knife and a small piece of punk were necessary, either of which could generally be found in any crowd of men in those days. Most men chewed or smoked a pipe but knew nothing of the cigarette and only the fastideous or dignified smoked a cigar.

On these occasions the news and jokes of the community were told and retold. If the mail happened to arrive on that day the postmaster called the mail and handed it out to the owner or to some one who would deliver it to him, the crowd standing round listening to the names. Very little mail was left in the office overnight. This duty performed some one who had received a recent paper might read to the crowd the latest news. In this way our forbears kept reasonably well-posted as to the general happenings of the country and nation.

At these times there might be some simple sport as a game of marbles or a wrestling match or pitching horse-shoes; or on rare occasions a fist-and-skull fight. Religion or rather some of the distinctive doctrines of some particular denomination was apt to be one of the main topics of conversation. These were discussed and Bible references galore given to substantiate the argument. These discussions were of real value to the community and to the citizenship because they fostered a careful study of the Bible which tends to make us all better and happier.

SECESSION CONVENTION. The Secession Convention was held at Milledgeville in January 1861. An election had been held in the county some time before to ascertain the will of the people as to whether the state should secede. The county went against secession by a considerable majority. Accordingly, the delegates to the Convention were instructed to vote against secession which they did. The following gentlemen were the delegates to the convention: Dr. G. G. Gordon, R. B. Dickerson, and Thomas A. Sharpe.

A GEOLOGIST. Mr. Augustus R. McCutcheon, one of the early settlers of Walker county, was for a great number of years connected with various departments of the State, being in 1883 Editing Clerk of the Agricultural Department, in which position he contributed some very fine articles on the geology of the state, which were published in "The Common-Wealth of Georgia." After the Civil War he served as assistant geologist for a number of years, in which position he was tireless in his efforts to examine and make records of the geology of Northwest Georgia. It is to be remarked that later geologists have found little to add to or take from his researches. Patient and painstaking, he was eminently qualified for the work and was the first to examine and make record of the geological formations of Walker county.

FISH TRAP. Some records left by the old Brainerd Mission established by the Moravian missionaries in 1817 at the mouth of the Chickamauga creek some miles above Chattanooga, gives a glimpse of how the country has changed during the past hundred years. The missionaries at that place installed a rude fish trap for the purpose of helping obtain a supply of food. The account says that fish were caught at all times of the year except during high water. They were taken principally at night. A Mr. Evarts visited the mission in October 1820 and describes the mission and the fish trap. On the morning of his arrival he says that forty fish were taken from the trap aggregating 150 pounds. On another morning while there 150 fish were caught weighing from five to ten pounds each. Verily, the Chickamauga a century ago must have been a fisherman's paradise.

In our day if some lucky fisherman should happen to take a five-pounder from that historic stream it would be the talk of the country side for weeks. This writer recalls that fifty years ago there were quite a few fish in this stream—some quite-sizeable ones, now they have practically disappeared, except a few minnows, so to speak. What will be the condition in another century

Truly, we pay a price for our civilization! The Indian was uncivilized—knew little or nothing of its arts—but he enjoyed some advantages that we do not, one of which was his ability to obtain an abundant and easy supply of food from the forest and streams. When civilization entered the country, roads built, forests cleared away, and erosion began to do its work of washing the soil and mud into the streams along with the saw dust and chaff of man's manufacture, the denizens of the streams were choked; and as if to hasten this destruction, civilized man then resorted to the sein and to dynamite.

FAMILY RE-UNIONS. It is a beautiful custom—that of annual family re-unions, and one that is growing in our county. More and more families are growing into the custom and putting it into practice. How delightful it is for all the family and their friends to meet annually and spend a day rehearsing the history of ancestors—telling of their movements, their works, their accomplishments; of their successes and failures, maybe, for who of us is infallible?

Some competent person should be appointed historian, whose duty it is to make and keep a short but concise history of the family. In the course of years this history might be published and handed down to the next and succeeding generations. True, when we are young and life's morn seems so rosy and beautiful, we think and care little for the family history and tradition, but as we grow older in years and become more settled and thoughtful our minds revert to our forbears and we begin to ask about them and their surroundings. Every head of a family should carefully prepare in some permanent form a concise and accurate account of his life and family and leave it to his children with the request that it be preserved for future reference and request all the children to make additions to it from time to time. In this way an accurate and interesting history of the family would grow up in a few generations. Who of us, especially those advanced in years, would not be delighted if we were able to sit down and read some reliable history of ours, back a few generations? It would give us great pleasure. Even though we might, and probably would, run across some dark spots—some black sheep—in some of our forbears (for who of us, I say again, is perfect?), still the history of our parents and grandparents would be welcome to us.

Some of the families in the county who have been holding these reunions for years are the following: The Park Family; The Jones Family; The Jones-Moon Family. Quite a number of families in more recent years have begun the custom. Let the good work continue. Should we not say that family pride should stand next door to national pride—to patriotism?

A rather unique custom and a desirable one has grown up in the Cove by the people who live near the Coulter grave yard. These people meet annually on a stated day at the burying ground and spend the day, scatter flowers over the graves of their ancestors, make addresses and keep up the history of their families. This is a kind of settlement reunion composed of different families. Whatever form it may take the idea of keeping up the family history should not be neglected.

WHEN CLEMENTS BEAT FELTON. In 1880 Judson C. Clements ran for Congress against Doctor Felton, who had been Congressman for a great many years. Doctor Felton was a Republican and had not been defeated for that office though he had had opposition by some of the strongest Democrats in the seventh district, including such able men as Colonel Dabney and others.

It was a most spirited and exciting race, and every one who had kept up with events knew that it was likely to be close with the odds in favor of the Democrats. The Walker County Messenger, whose editor at that time was Mr. E. A. McHan, a staunch Democrat, had boldly championed the Democratic nominee and had predicted his election.

After the contest, when it was known that Mr. Clements was elected, the Messenger came out with a famous and humorous editorial which was substantially as follows, as best I recall it:

First, at the head of the column was the strutting democratic rooster crowing. Then followed something like this:

                HURRAH! HURRAH! HURRAH!
        The Democratic Party to the Fore!
        Judson C. Clements Elected!
        News from all over the District Gives
        The Democrats a Majority.

GLORY!
The Republican Party Takes a Back Seat!
Doctor Felton Retired!
The Seventh District Regained from
RADICALISM!

HALLELUJAH!
The Latest News from over the District
Indicates that the Democrats Won by
A Handsome Majority.
Walker County to have the next Congressman!

HURRAH! HURRAH! HURRAH!
Light your Bon Fires!
Fire off your Old Guns!
Give the Rebel Yell!
We have Met the Enemy and they are ours!
AMEN!

Chapter Thirty-six

MISCELLANEOUS CONTINUED. STRAIGHT GUT VALLEY—TAN YARD—OLD TAX RECEIPTS—RECORD OF BIRTHS OF NEGROES—A FIGHT—GENERAL ASSEMBLY, 1835—A RARE OLD TEACHER—A CIVIL WAR INCIDENT—LOST IN THE MOUNTAINS—LAFAYETTE BAPTIST CHURCH—HOG RIFLE—BUGLE CALL—MORE OLD TAX RECEIPTS—FIRST COURT HOUSE AT CRAYFISH SPRING—A UNIQUE SCHOOL COLLECTION—A HURRICANE—RECALLING SOLOMON'S TEMPLE—AN OLD AUTOGRAPH ALBUM — JOHN INGRAHAM — W. H. C. FREEMAN—INDIAN HOMINY.

HISTORIC STRAIGHT GUT VALLEY. There is a small but beautiful valley lying just across the ridge west of Noble and Rock Spring and running north and south some four or five miles which is a most delightful section of the county. The first part of its nomenclature is quite expressive and descriptive, while the second is somewhat harsh and uncouth. Why so-called? Could it be that Straight Gut was originally Straight Cut, and by careless habit of speech was corrupted into Straight Gut? To the antiquarian there are a number of objects of more than ordinary interest scattered along the entire length of this sequestered valley.

There is a log school house, notched and pegged at the corners, built about 1840, on the William Glass old place, now owned by Dr. J. H. Hammond, and now used as a barn. It is in a perfect state of preservation, the logs showing no signs of decay. The size is 16 by 18 feet and contains, besides one door, three windows or openings on the other three sides. These windows were made by simply sawing out two or three logs to admit the light. No such thing as glass. Mr. Peter Jones, now 90 years of age, says he attended school in this house when he was about six years of age. It was known then as the Glass school house. There is a large never-failing spring of pure, cold water some sixty yards back of the house which furnished water for the school. Mr. Jones remembers the following teachers at that place: Andy Carson (1848), Henry Jones, John James, and Joe Lemocks. After the Civil War, he remembers Liza Campbell, and Tom McCall as teachers there.

Near the school house are two Indian graves, said to be those of Chief "Red Bird" and wife, and some mile or so further west are four Indian graves—Chief "Three-Killer," his wife and two children. There are, also, nearby, the graves of two soldiers who were said to have died there with smallpox during the war. This valley is further noted, according to many old citizens, as being the route taken by Andrew Jackson on his way to fight the Seminole Indians in Florida, and the British at New Orleans, in 1814. It is said that Jackson's army spent a night in camp at the Glass old place where there is an abundance of water flowing from several springs. Tradition says, also, that there was an Indian "Ballplay" ground near the head of this falley, where the Indians were wont at stated periods to gather and engage in that celebrated game of theirs. Old settlers tell of many Indian trails passing through this valley. One such trail came by way of Leet's Spring and passed on through the Warthen Gap and on westward to the Chickamauga Creek. Another came from Cold Weather Spring and went by way of Crawfish Creek to Crawfish Spring, thence to Rossville. These two trails crossed each other in this valley. Many Indian relics have been found hereabout, which taken in connection with the fact that several noted chiefs are known to have had their headquarters in the valley leaves no doubt that this was once an important Indian community.

About one mile west of the Glass Spring lies the Lawrence graveyard, begun in 1846, and containing now probably 150 to 200 graves. This hallowed ground contains the moldering dust of some of Walker's celebrated (and justly so) citizens. The Honorable John B. Wheeler, for many years a member of the Georgia Legislature, and who earned the sobriquet, "Watch Dog of the Treasury," and his wife lie here; as also, Moses Wheeler, Moses Jackson and wife, and Elder Clinging, a Primitive Baptist preacher. Taking all in all, there are few sections of the county richer in historic interest than Straight Gut Valley.

TAN YARD. One of the most important articles of clothing in this climate and in this mountainous section has always been footwear—boots and shoes. In the early days of the county, and up till some forty years ago it was common and quite stylish for men to wear boots. The country being rough and men being much in the woods and on the rough roads, they required substantial footwear. Leather was much in demand. Hence the tan yard; and leather tanning was an important business and was likely to be quite remunerative. There were several tan yards in different sections of the county. Two of these were located at or near Rock Spring. In an old ledger of that pioneer settler, James R. Jones, the oldest date of which is 1844, there are very many entries concerning leather and tan yards.

The hides were placed in a large vat built for the purpose and a layer of tan bark was placed between each hide. Large vats might hold a hundred or more hides. Water was then turned in and allowed to cover the hides and all was kept in this shape for twelve months, when the hides were taken out and the hair removed; and by scraping and working the hides the flesh was also removed. After more scraping and working to produce pliancy, the hide was allowed to dry and was ready for use. These hides were used for making boots and shoes, harness, horse-collars, and many other articles. Every farmer in the old days after killing a beef which he always tried to do in the fall of each year, was sure to carry the hide to the tan yard. The tanner then cut his initials on the hide so as to identify it and put it into the vat where it slept for a year. In this way everybody had leather for shoemaking and repairing.

ANTEBELLUM TAX RECEIPTS. The following old tax receipts are in the possession of Mr. J. R. Tyner of Rock Spring. Each one is written on a small piece of blank paper about one-half inch wide by 5 inches long:

Recd. of Elizabeth Brigman 7 ^{m} her tax for the year 1856. J. T. Deck, T.C.

Recd. of Temperance Brigman 38 $^{c\ m}$ 4 her tax for the year 1857. J. T. Deck, T.C.

Recd. of Harris Brigman $7.76 $^{c\ m}$ 4 his tax for the year 1858. J. T. Deck, T.C.

Recd. of Temperance Brigman 30 ^{c} her tax for the year 1858. J. T. Deck, T.C.

Recd. of Elizabeth Brigman $1.14 ^{c} her tax for the year 1858. J. T. Deck, T.C.

Recd. of Elizabeth Brigman $1.07.6 $^{c\ m}$ her tax for the year 1860. J. T. Deck, T.C.

Recd. of Linsy and Mary Brigman $5.45, their tax for the year 1862. H. T. Gill, T.C.

Recd. of Linsy Brigman $\frac{c\ 44}{100}$ his tax for the year 1866. H. T. Gill, T.C.

Recd. of D. R. S. Baker, $1.86, his tax for 1866. W. D. Lumpkin, T.C.

Recd. of Elizabeth Brigman $2.59, her tax for the year 1872. F. M. Simpson, T.C.

RECORD OF BIRTHS OF NEGROES. The following record of the births of negroes is taken from the record by the owner, Mr. Joshua Brigman, the grandfather of Mr. J. R. Tyner. This record is given along with the births in the family record.

(Written with goose quill).

Negro Joseph was born on the 10th of November 1821.

Negro Jesse was born on the 15th of January 1824.

Negro Charles was born on the 3rd of July 1827.

Negro Nathan was born on the 13th of February 1832.

Negro Ann was born on the 19th of October 1833.

Negro Margaret was born on the 13th of September 1835.

Negro Tom was born on September 1st 1837.

Negro Sarah was born on the 17th of September 1839.

Negro Emeline was born on the 3rd of January A.D. 1842.

Negro Caroline was born on 3rd of January A.D. 1844.

Negro Amanda was born on the 24th of February 1854.

A FIGHT. During the decade immediately preceding the Civil War there was a blacksmith shop not far from what is now the Wallin place west of Chickamauga creek and south of Kensington. There was nearby a doggery or whiskey shop, where one might go to imbibe when thirsty. It was a center for gathering of the rougher element of the community, especially on Saturdays, or other convenient occasions. On a certain occasion, when there was to be a shooting match, there were present three brothers, Jack, Jim and Joe Turner. Also, three other brothers, Abe, Dave, and Jack Woodall, and associated with the Woodalls was West Kinman, a brother-in-law. Prior to this time one of the Turners and one of the Woodalls had had some little disagreement, but had agreed to drop the matter and made up. However, at this time it was renewed by Turner. Woodall was seated on the counter while Turner was standing on the floor fronting him. Turner was mouthing at Woodall while, it seems, Woodall was rather reluctant to renew the difficulty. Suddenly Turner slapped Woodall in the face. Instantly Woodall sprang from the counter and began cutting Turner in the shoulder with a knife. This was a signal for others to take a hand, and the other Turners and Woodalls and Kinman all joined in the fracas, using knives, fists, rocks, and what not. When the affair ended four men were unable to get up, while all the others were more or less wounded. Only one man was able to get home unassisted. However, as by a miracle, all recovered.

FROM ACTS OF GENERAL ASSEMBLY, 1835. Be it further enacted, that the sum of Sixteen dollars and twenty five cents be paid the Justices of the Inferior courts of the county of Walker, the amount paid by them to the Coroner of said county for holding an inquest over the body of Alexander McPherson, a Cherokee Indian, and burial expenses.

A RARE OLD TEACHER. During the decade immediately preceding the Civil War, there was a most remarkable man, resident of McLemore's cove, named Wesley Thurman. He was a local Methodist preacher; he was also a school teacher. Teaching was his principal business. He was one of those old teachers who boarded among his patrons, that is, he stayed about a week with the parents of each pupil in his school. This was the agreement between teacher and patrons. It was agreeable on both sides as it reduced the expenses of the teacher, and was the chief factor for the reason of his meager salary. It was further agreeable to the patrons because of the pleasure they received from his association and entertainment for a week. It was an age of few newspapers, or books, or of communications with other people, and so the patrons were glad to entertain the teacher. This author was once just such a teacher; he once "boarded" among his patrons.

Many old people take a pleasure in telling about the good qualities of this unique old teacher. He was very religious and was not ashamed of it. Always, and everywhere, he called to prayer when visiting at the homes of his pupils. Not a long tedious reading or prayer, but short and earnest were his prayers and devoted in his conversations.

On Sundays, at the local church or school house he was often called on to preach, which he did with power and often with eloquence. He was often happy in his preaching and with clapping of hands and hallelujahs he would pass around the house shaking hands with the congregation. This spirit of his was often contagious and others of the congregation, devoted Christians, would sometimes catch the blessing and join with him.

His was not a Sunday religion only. It pervaded his teaching as well. He was sometimes known to get happy in the school room and go up and down the house with clapping of hands and shouting the praises of God. This old teacher taught at the Payne's Chapel school house, near where the Coulter brothers now live. Alas for his race, they are now extinct!

CIVIL WAR INCIDENT. The author once heard Captain Wood tell the following incident of the Civil War: On one occasion, when the two armies were drawn up in close contact, during the Virginia campaign, there was very acute sharp-shooting between the two armies. Numbers of men were being killed or wounded on each side by this means. There stood immediately in front of the Confederate commander's position a large bushy tree, which he was anxious to have removed as it obstructed, seriously, his vision. Accordingly, he called for volunteers to cut it down. But every man knew that it was a most dangerous undertaking, and no one offered. Finally, the commander offered any man a thirty-day furlough, who would do it, whereupon a young soldier stepped out and offered to undertake it. Securing a sharp ax and discarding all unnecessary clothing, he rushed suddenly out of the breastwork and running to the tree began feverishly his chopping. As he worked in plain view of the Federal army and sharpshooters all eyes were focussed on him, expecting, momentarily, to see him fall from the shots of the Yankees. His comrades looked on in wonder and admiration at his bravery. Finally, as the tree swayed and fell, he rushed back and fell headlong behind the breastworks. Upon examination it was found that he had been seriously, though not fatally, shot. After the surgeons had dressed his wound he was asked why he did not quit when he was shot. His reply was: "I didn't want the d—n Yankees to know they had hit me."

LOST IN THE MOUNTAINS. Mrs. Martha Harp of Cedar Grove, who lived to be 96 years of age, related the following incident to this chronicler some years ago: There were 14 children in the family of her father, and there was scarcely more than a year between their successive ages. They lived in a mountainous section of the county, where the neighbors were few and far between. With so large a family, the father and mother were always busy with the duties of the farm and household, the children assisting in the lighter work. On one occasion one of the boys strayed off into the woods for some purpose, maybe to find an armful of pine knots for the night's fire. The boy got lost and was not able to find his way home by night fall. After wandering about for some time, he finally lay down and slept till morning, when he began again to search for his home. Finally, up in the day, he succeeded in locating himself and was soon at home. Imagine the surprise of the whole family when he reported the matter, for he had not been missed during the whole time.

LAFAYETTE BAPTIST CHURCH. Mrs. John Miller, an old resident, now nearly 90 years of age, who lives near Burnt Mill ford, recalls much old interesting history, among which is the following: She relates how, before the war, the members and attendants of the Baptist church at LaFayette were called together for church services. She says it was done by a bugle call. The bugle, in the hands of an expert, says this authority, could be heard for miles and miles—much farther than our present-day bells. She relates it now, as how it seemed to her as a child that God in heaven must have heard it and come down to the meeting. It had to her a reverent tone and an invitation to come to the house of God and worship the Creator of all things.

This same authority tells of attending a Baptist Association at LaFayette in 1860 when two Indians, preachers, were present and took part in the deliberations. One of them could not speak English and when he spoke the other, who understood English, stood and interpreted his message.

Still another. She tells of how she has often heard her father tell his experiences when carrying the Indians away. He was gone for some months, and would often relate something of the hardships and troubles of these unfortunate people on their journey. There were many thousand, probably 10 or 12 thousand, on the journey, with hundreds of wagons, horses, mules, slaves and other equippage. The line of march extended for many miles. Every able bodied man, woman, and child walked; only the infants and sick rode. There was much sickness and many deaths daily. Every morning before the journey began, there were buryings along the line of march, not just one or two, but often, and almost always, from 10 to 20 funerals along the line of march. The Indians performed their own peculiar services at these funerals, the last of which was to prostrate themselves, face downward, near the new-made mound. Then rising, with tear-dimmed eyes, they pursued their journey.

THE HOG RIFLE. Almost every man owned a Kentucky rifle, sometimes called a hog rifle. The barrel was long and heavy and was a most accurate piece among the early settlers. They were accurate marksmen and prided themselves on it. They could generally hit the bull's eye at a distance of 75 or more yards. These were used at the shooting matches, as well as in hunting for deer, turkey, and other wild animals.

BUGLE CALL. Many old people speak of the bugle call as one of the customs among the early settlers. This was a long tin bugle, some 4 or 5 feet long, with a mouth piece and thence expanding to the large end to about 8 inches in diameter. One of these in the hands of an expert bugler could be heard many miles on a still evening. They were able, by swinging the bugle up and down, and across the ground, while blowing, to produce considerable music. The loneliness and faintness of the sound as it was heard far away, was quite pleasant; and when two or more were blowing in different directions, as they responded to each other's call, there was "music in the air." Some of the old-time negroes were experts with the bugle.

MORE OLD TAX RECEIPTS: Mr. J. B. F. Jones and his sister, Miss Nannie, both now deceased, had in their possession many interesting old documents handed down from their ancestors. Among these are a number of tax receipts. The first one given is the oldest strictly county document that I have run across. It gives the tax collector's name for 1834, which was the first year of the county's life.

Recd. of Nancy Jones $\frac{35}{100}$ tax for 1834—W. K. Bagby, T.C.

Recd. of J. B. Jones, 75c his tax for 1839, A. N. Ross.

Recd. of J. B. Jones, 57½c his tax for 1847. Nathan Anderson, T.C.

Recd. Nancy Jones, 57½c her tax for 1847. Nathan Anderson, T.C.

Recd. of Nancy Jones, 58½c her tax for 1848. N. Anderson, T.C.

Recd. of James B. Jones, $5.51.6, his tax for 1856. J. T. Deck, T.C.
(c m above 51.6)

Recd. of James B. Jones, $4.17.4, his tax for 1858. J. T. Deck, T.C.
(c m above 17.4)

FIRST COURT HOUSE AT CRAWFISH SPRING. White's Historical Collections, published in 1854, says the first court held in the county was at Crawfish Spring, Judge Hooper presiding. In connection with this it might be stated that many old citizens, among whom are Mr. W. C. Bailey, and Mr. C. C. Ransom, both now octogenarians, say that at the court held at that place, according to tradition, two Indians were tried, convicted, and hanged for murder. They killed a man and hid him in a pile of stones near the Orville Henderson place. If true this was the first legal execution in the county.

In the "Cherokee Land Lottery," published in 1838, in the 9th district and 4th section, on lot of land No. 281, are the following words: "Crawfish C.H." and also, "Big Spring." There is also a representation or picture of a house, which evidently means Court House. Inasmuch as the State of Georgia had extended her jurisdiction over Cherokee Georgia some years before the Indians were removed, and even before Walker county was established, it is likely that the court house was built at that place before the county was made a unit, probably sometime in the twenties.

Another explanation is that the court house at Crawfish Spring was built by the Indians. It is known that the Indians had adopted a constitution, established courts, and had in force a regular schedule of court proceedings similar to that of the United States. The territory contiguous to Crawfish Spring was quite populous and it would be more than likely that one of their court centers would be established at that place. When the surfeyors found the court house there they simply marked it "Crawfish C.H."

A UNIQUE SCHOOL COLLECTION. The little house contained a single room, about 12 by 18 feet. It was arranged much as that of a modern ten cent store with counters running through the floor, passageways between, and shelves on the walls. All these counters and shelves were literally loaded with various school-room paraphernalia including specimens of both pupil's and teacher's work and handicraft.

It is impossible after the lapse of a quarter of a century to enumerate these accurately, but as I recall the scene there were various concrete objects by means of which pupils could be taught more easily and quickly the meaning of certain terms in arithmetic, as the inch, foot and yard measure; the square inch, foot and yard; the cubic inch, foot and yard: the cubic foot filled with cubic inches; the cubic yard filled with cubic feet. The various units of dry and liquid measure, as the pint, quart, gallon, peck, bushel. The difference between long, square and cubic measure clearly illustrated by objects representing each.

There was an extensive collection of pupils' work and examinations,

There were sheets of paper folded to illustrate the size of books, as folio, 4to., 8vo., 12 mo.; watch and clock faces; calendars; flags; blackboards; erasers and crayons. There were old-time slates, tablets, pencils, pens and ink. Copies of the various school books in use at that time, making altogether in the collection probably half a hundred text books. There were copy-books, showing the chirography of the various pupils. Numerous dialogue and recitation books for use on Fridays and other stated or special occasions. A small collection of the common coins of the United States and other countries. A collection of minerals, stones, clays and sand, all neatly arranged and labeled. A collection of the common woods, leaves, flowers, insects and nuts.

There was an extensive collection of pupils' work and examinations, all arranged according to subjects so as to give an attractive display. Maps of the county, state, nation and world, made by the pupils. Children's playthings, as balls, bats, marbles, etc. Also, lunch baskets, and buckets.

In one end of this room was the library proper. Here was assembled some of the choice literature of the language, and here he spent much of his leisure giving audience to some of the master minds of ancient and modern times.

All these he had brought together during a long series of years in the school-room, making altogether one of the most unique school collections ever assembled—Professor E. I. F. Cheney, of fragrant memory.

HURRICANE. In the year 1878 a most destructive cyclone passed through the county traveling in an easterly direction. It approached from the west coming across Lookout mountain into McLemore's cove thence crossing Pigeon mountain it swept through the section slightly south of LaFayette, passing near Waterville and crossing Taylor's ridge and on through both Armuchees. On Lookout mountain it blew down the home of Clayton Tatum, killing one child and pinning Mr. Tatum under the timbers till his wife went a great distance to the nearest neighbor for assistance. Houses were destroyed on the Oliver Thurman and the Clarkson places in the Cove; a brick house on the Calhoun place near Waterville and another on the Frank Little place in West Armuchee. There were several other houses and barns destroyed.

The storm passed about 10 o'clock at night. Its path was about half a mile wide. Everything was leveled within this path. Its path was distinctly marked by the destruction wrought for 50 years and can yet be seen in some places (1931).

RECALLING SOLOMON'S TEMPLE. It is reported by old-timers that James Clarkson built before the war on the Clarkson place in the Cove a log house for his own use. It was constructed of large poplar logs. The trees were felled, carefully measured, hewn, and notched in the woods. They were then assembled and when placed in position were found to fit exactly. This calls to mind the Bible account of the building of Solomon's Temple in which every stone was hewn and measured in the quarry under the careful supervision of the Master Builders, and when assembled was found to fit, each piece with its fellow, even to the capstone.

This log house was in the path of the hurricane described above and was so well constructed that it was unhurt—probably the only one escaping. It is still standing.

AN OLD AUTOGRAPH ALBUM. I have been permitted to examine an antebellum autograph album whose owner was Miss Sallie Suttle of West Armuchee, sister of the late James T. Suttle. The proud possessor of this prized memento is Miss Jamie McCullough, Miss Suttle's niece. I was just wondering if our young people take the pride and pleasure in such matters as did our grandmothers in the days of "Auld Lang Syne." It contains many beautiful expressions of friendship, love and esteem. Many of these were written by old citizens of West Armuchee valley during their palmy days, but some were written by men and women who helped to make history for the commonwealth and in so doing made themselves illustrious; as for instance this:

Miss Sallie Suttle:

May your heart, like your album, this day, be free from every stain! May Friendship and Love, alone, be permitted in either to make an impress! May the recollections of Life be all hallowed with sweet memories—and the agonies of Death calmed by bright hopes founded on Faith in a Savior's Love!

Your Friend,

Thos. R. R. Cobb.*

Athens June/17, 1859.

JOHN INGRAHAM. The first and only private marker in the Chickamauga Park, erected long before any park was dreamed of, is said to be that of a Walker county boy who fell in action on September 19, 1863. He was a private in Company K, First Reg. Ga. Vol., commanded by Col. James Clark Gordon. This simple diminutive marker, the oldest and smallest among the thousands that crowd that hallowed spot, is not easily found—the leaves and grass may hide it from the passer-by. It bears this simple inscription: "John Ingraham, Private Company K, First Confederate Regiment, Georgia Volunteers, Killed September 19, 1863." (Z. Armstrong, in Sunny South).

W. H. C. FREEMAN (Uncle Billy) lives some five or six miles north of

---

*Thos. R. R. Cobb was one of the State's most brilliant young men. A member of the Secession Convention, he strongly advocated the course which was finally adopted, and when war broke out he promptly enlisted and had just been promoted to the rank of brigadier-general for bravery and gallantry as well as his ability as a soldier, when he was killed in action at the battle of Fredericksburg, December 13, 1862. Had he been spared to the State he would doubtless have been the peer of any of that illustrious galaxy of eminent statesmen who have embellished many of the conspicuous positions within the gift of the people of the State, and no doubt would have filled some of these positions. He was a devout Christian.

Villanow, in Whitfield county. However, he was born in Walker county and lived in it for many years. The changing of county lines back in the fifties placed him in Whitfield county. He is living on the very farm and in the same house in which he was born. He has lived in two counties and has never moved. He was born in 1839, and is therefore in his 92nd year and still hale and hearty. He fought through the war and surrendered under Johnston in North Carolina.

Mr. Freeman is remarkably active for his years. He talks most interestingly of the days when he was a boy. Among other matters he related how he attended school when he was a boy, near Gordon Springs, where the late John B. Gordon was a pupil. He recalls most vividly a dialogue in which John B. Gordon took part and in which he (Gordon) described how to dress a 'possum, to the great amusement of all present.

John B's father was named Zachariah, a Baptist minister, who had two brothers, Wash and Jim, the latter being Judge. These brothers came to Walker county in the late thirties and settled at Gordon Springs, then in Walker county. The old home at Gordon Springs was much noted in the days before the war.

Mr. Freeman says Dogwood valley took its name from an old Indian chief named Dogwood. (Since writing the above, Mr. Freeman has "Crossed the Bar").

INDIAN HOMINY. An old citizen tells the following story which he had from his father who came to the county before the Indians emigrated: If an Indian invited one to partake of a meal with him, he took it as an affront to be refused. One of the early settlers knowing this and being on one occasion invited to eat with an Indian, sat down around the pot of hominy with the family and pretended to partake. The family dog, of which the Indians were especially fond, was standing by and when permitted would also put his snout into the pot of hominy and help himself. The old citizen only shammed by putting his spoon into the pot and pretending to eat, but really not tasting the food. On another occasion this same authority was present when the pot of hominy was boiling. Two Indian youngsters came in and each slipped a live terrapin into the pot of boiling hominy, which was considered a rare dish, and which in reality it was.

Chapter Thirty-seven

COUNTY NAMES, THEIR MEANING INTERPRETED. A DAY SPENT IN AN "OLD FIELD SCHOOL" AT SYLVAN BOWER.

LOOKOUT MOUNTAIN. Why was this noble mountain so called? Several explanations have been advanced: First, it is said that General Coffee who had charge of one division of General Jackson's army, after crossing the Tennessee river, in 1813, encamped with his division near the foot of the mountain, and that he gave the word "lookout" as the pass-word for the night, from which circumstance it derived its name. Some say it was so-called from an old Indian chief whose home was near the mountain. The following explanation, given by Tennessee historians, is likely the correct one: Following the Revolution many travelers down the Tennessee river came to grief, either by losing their boats and goods in the turbid and dangerous passes so common near the mountain, or by being robbed and killed by the hostile Indians hidden among the overhanging cliffs and bluffs. This continued so long that it got to be a much dreaded locality and parties starting on the trip were carefully warned to be vigilant and on the lookout for trouble at that place. "Lookout for trouble at the big mountain," they were warned. Eventually the mountain was called Lookout. (Note—According to Walker's History of Chattanooga, the Chattanooga creek, which flows through the northern part of Walker county, was called by the Indians, *Tsatanugi,* and the Lookout mountain is several times referred to in Ramsey's Annals of Tennessee as the Chattanuga mountains. Later when the citizens of Ross' Landing were granted a postoffice at that place the postmaster sent in the name Chattanooga which was accepted. Still another explanation by Tennessee historians: Lookout mountain and the Cumberland mountain seem to have been abruptly cut asunder by the Tennessee river, so that each stands up fronting the other. The Cherokees called it O-tullee-ton-tanna-ta-kunna-ee, or "Mountains looking at each other." The English said "Lookout mountain").

PIGEON MOUNTAIN. It seems that the mountain got its name from the fact that when the first settlers came to the county, the mountain was a great feeding place for wild pigeons. They gathered there for the acorns and chestnuts which were so plentiful at that time. Old people and old manuscripts mention how the pigeons gathered in such numbers as to break the limbs from the trees. The early settlers would go there and kill them by the sacks full. In those early days the country was full of the wild pigeon. Old citizens relate how they have seen so many passing through the air that the light of the sun would be obscured; that a gun fired into them would kill many at a shot. At certain seasons of the year thousands upon thousands could be seen all over the country. This pigeon is now extinct.

MISSIONARY RIDGE. Named for the Moravian missionaries who established a mission at Brainerd just east of the ridge from Chattanooga, and some 3 or 4 miles from the Georgia line. This mission was established early in the 19th century—probably as early as 1820.

PEAVINE RIDGE, named from the abundance of wild peavines growing along the creek of the same name.

TAYLOR'S RIDGE, named for the Indian chief Richard Taylor who lived at or near the ridge not far from Ringgold. Richard Taylor signed the treaty at Red Clay, in 1835.

DICK'S RIDGE, named for the old Indian Chief Dick, who lived near the ridge in East Armuchee.

McLemore's Cove, named for John McLemore, an Indian chief who lived in the section. He went to the Indian Territory in 1826, and was still living in 1884.

Broomtown, named for the Indian chief, The Broom, who lived not far from Alpine.

Chickamauga Creek. Tradition says the word means "river of death," that a fatal epidemic once broke out among the Indians who lived along the stretches of this beautiful stream, which virtually depopulated their settlements, very few escaping from its ravages. The early settlers of the county used to speak of the region along that stream as well as about Crawfish Spring as a sickly one, which caused many to shun those fertile lands and seek less desirable locations because of a health consideration. As late as the seventies many people referred to those low lands as unhealthy. No doubt the Indians had a potent reason for calling it "River of Death."

The author of the History of Hamilton County says that this meaning is erroneous, that the name comes from the Cherokee word, "Chucama," meaning good, and a Cherokee word, "Kah," meaning place, therefore meaning "Good place."

Armuchee means the same in the Indian language as Florida in Spanish, viz., "Land of Flowers."

Chestnut Flat was so called because of the abundance of chestnuts that grew in that beautiful valley and on the adjacent ridge when the early settlers arrived.

LaFayette. The town was first known by the name of Chattooga, afterward called Benton, and then named LaFayette in honor of the celebrated and loved general who was the friend of Washington and of America.

Chickamauga was known as Crawfish Spring till about 1890 when it was changed to the present nomenclature. Crawfish, or Crayfish, Spring, so-called from an Indian chief, Crayfish or Crawfish, whose home was there many years ago.

Rossville, named for Chief John Ross, whose home was located there prior to the exile.

Villanow. This is, without doubt, the most beautiful name in the county. It is said to have originated as follows: When it was proposed to establish a postoffice there a name was needed. Constantine Wood's wife, and mother of the late Captain J. Y. Wood, proposed the name, saying: "It is no longer a hamlet, but is now a village, or village now, i.e., Villanow."

Greenbush was first known as Vicksburg. Later, when the postoffice was established, it was so called from a beautiful green bush which stood in the yard of Mr. S. Bomar, the postmaster.

TRICKUM was originally called Graysville from a Mr. Gray who sold goods at that place. It is related that an old resident had some difference with Mr. Gray about an account at his store. He paid the account but was dissatisfied about it and said that it was a place where they love to "trickum." The name stuck.

CASSANDRA. Some years before the war there was a church house near Hiniard's Cross Roads called Payne's Chapel. A physician, Dr. Thornburg, who was also a local Methodist preacher, came into the community. He suggested that the name of the church be changed to Cassandra, which was the name of the ship that brought him to America. The change was made and when the postoffice was established it took the same name. The name, of course, had its origin in Greek mythology.

KENSINGTON. During the land boom at that place about 1895, the gentlemen who were mostly interested in it named the place in honor of the home town where they came from, i.e., Kensington, Pennsylvania.

CENCHAT. The Central of Georgia R. R. crosses the Chattanooga Southern at that place. The first syllable in each name: Cen plus Chat.

PITTSBURG. A popular name for many towns—the original being in Pennsylvania, named for the English soldier Pitt. The railroad station is called Durham.

LYTLE, for General Lytle, a Union soldier, who fell at that place during the Chickamauga Battle.

ASCALON. Postoffice on Lookout mountain, named by Miss Lila Howard for the Bible city of Askelon. See Judges 1:18.

HIGH POINT. Near a high point on Lookout mountain.

NAOMI. Taken from Bible.

TRANS. When Professor E. I. F. Cheney left Everette Springs, where he had been teaching for some years, he engaged to teach in East Armuchee valley, which was *across* the mountain from Everette Springs. He called the new location Trans, meaning "across."

CENTER POST. So called because that postoffice was midway between Bronco and Trion, this being the mail route at that time.

SYLVAN BOWER. Another beautiful name. This was the name of a school house near Bronco. "Boog" Little, and other famous teachers once taught there. What pleasant memories the name suggests! Hidden away among the green trees, near the gurgling brook, on a warm summer day! Let us loiter here for a season, enjoy the scenery, and observe the teacher and his school.

It is mid-summer; the crops have been "laid by" and the children of the community are all in school which will last only two or three months, for every one will be needed to help gather the crops in the fall. These two or three months will be the only opportunity these children will have to attend school during the year. For this reason they are urged to apply themselves to their utmost and make good use of the time. The school day is long. The teacher begins the work of the day about an hour by sun, which means before seven o'clock in the morning in the summer time, and he is seen still teaching his school at five in the afternoon.

Before we enter the house, let us look at the surroundings. The house is an old-fashioned log building, with one door at the end and maybe two or three windows with shutters but no glass. The sandy yard is broad and ample, with here and there a large oak tree whose spreading branches shut out the torrid rays of the noon-day sun. A spring of clear, cold water gurgles up some fifty yards back of the school house, where the pupils are wont to gather at play time to quench their thirst. Several gourds, clean and sweet, with long handles, are kept hanging near by for the use of the children. Some of the larger boys and girls are wont, about the noon hour, to monopolize the shady nooks near the spring where they pretend to discuss the lessons of the day, or other events of the school room; however, that blind little elf, Cupid, is seated near by, and, unobserved, is shooting his darts in various directions. Happily (or shall we say unhappily?), although blind, he rarely misses his mark.

Those were the days when young men and women—not only in their teens, but in the twenties—attended the community school. It was quite common to see young men with beard on their faces in school. Numbers of young men above twenty were often seen in these community schools.

But let us enter the house and see the pupils at work. There are no desks. The children sit on plain hard benches with their books beside them. A single blackboard made of boards and painted black, about 4 by 6 feet stands in one end of the house; and even it is rarely used. No teacher's desk is to be seen, or even a chair, the teacher standing or walking most of the time. A stage is seen in one end of the house where the teacher may sit on a bench and call his classes to recite.

Of the 40 or 50 pupils in his school he has classes from the A B C's to cube root. There were no such things in those days as grades. Most children studied Webster's Blueback for the first three or four years of his school life. This was fundamental; the foundation. Whatever else might be said there was no escaping the Blueback. Many a boy would sit on those hard benches and chew on the corners of his Blueback till he literally ate it up. But what did he care for that, since they only cost ten cents. There was no getting away from that old book. He learned his letters, learned to spell both on the book and by heart, and learned to read in the old Blueback. And what is more, he rarely ever graduated from the Blueback. If he went to school till he had beard on his face he was still studying Webster. The teacher of the "old field school" had his hands full. No wonder he had long hours; he needed them to get around and hear all his classes.

The teacher was often called upon to "work" an example for his pupils. If a boy failed at his first effort to solve his problem, he went to the teacher, slate in hand, for help. The teacher, then, in the midst of his other work must stop and do the sum. This required time, and maybe before he could finish it, another pupil had come with his slate for help, and yet others till several sometimes were waiting for assistance. And, too, these were the days when the arithmetics were full of puzzles. The examples were not practical sums as we have to-day; they were difficult to solve in many cases. For instance, like this:

"If 2 be 3 and 3 be 5 and $6\frac{1}{2}$ be 11
What is the $\frac{1}{2}$ of 26 and the $\frac{1}{4}$ of 27?"

But the teacher must do every one, for, if he failed he had lost his reputation in that community. Not only the children had lost faith in his ability, but the patrons as well. During these hot summer days, especially in the long afternoons, the larger boys were permitted to leave the school room and take up their places on the outside under the shade of the trees and "cipher." With slate and arithmetic in hand they would sit side by side under the trees and work at the last of the three R's. This arrangement relieved the school of much noise and the teacher could do his work much faster and better. But occasionally, some of the boys must come in from out doors, slate in hand, to get the teacher to "work" an example. When the smaller boys got large enough to go out and sit under the trees they thought they had reached the pinnacle of fame—the *ne plus ultra*.

At the noon hour the children gathered under the spreading oaks in small groups to eat their lunches, which had been brought from home in tin buckets early in the morning. These buckets were covered with tight fitting lids to exclude the flies, and when opened the pent up moisture, escaping, and permeating the surrounding atmosphere, and assailing the olfactory nerves, produced a not-very-agreeable odor. However, the children of those days, being robust and hearty, were not very fastidious or overnice about a mere lunch at school, the main point being to dispatch it as quickly as possible and get to the mid-day games. Lunches generally consisted of large, brown-baked biscuits in generous quantities. The word biscuit means baked on two sides; these biscuits were well up to the definition. They were made of whole wheat flour ground at the local mills, and contained all the health-giving and strengh-giving qualities found in the grain. These biscuits were sandwiched with generous pieces of country ham, bacon, or eggs, and were washed down with frequent draughts of butter-milk which had been brought from home in bottles. An apple or other fruit in season completed the lunch and the children, while consuming this latter, gathered in groups ready to inaugurate the game.

Several games might be engaged in and there were often divisions of opinion as to what to play. The smaller children and girls might play "jumping the rope," which was always exciting and full of exercise. Another game which was quite exciting and very vigorous was "Base." The whole school sometimes engaged in playing base, and if the teacher happened to ring the bell while this game was in progress, it would be well for him to give some ten minutes extra to allow them time to cool off and get in some kind of shape for their work. Another game often engaged in was marbles. This game was not so strenuous and was often played by the older boys and sometimes the teacher. It was called seven-up; that is the side winning seven games first, was winner.

Besides these, there were two other games in common use by the children. They were played with balls, and were called "bull pen," and "town ball." Town ball was the favorite, and most of the larger boys were devotees of this game. No one has been able to trace the origin of our national game, baseball. There are those who contend that it has evolved from the old-field-school town-ball. Others claim that it dates from the Indian game called "ball-play." If some antiquarian, delving into some old musty records, should some day resurrect an old musty paper showing just how the game originated, he would at once become famous, and liable to rest eventually in Statuary Hall. It is probable that the Indian play-ball was the nucleus from which baseball has evolved. Its first change was, maybe, to the old-field-school townball, and from that it might easily change to baseball. At any rate the children of our grandfathers' day got a great kick out of townball and bullpen.

During those long summer days the teacher often gave more than an hour for dinner and playtime. However, about 1:15 or 1:30 the signal was given for books. Some of the old teachers had bells for a signal; however, others had other methods to call the children to work. This chronicler remembers one such teacher who used a cane which he vigorously applied to the side of the house or to the door as a signal for books. He might have had a dual purpose for using this method, the other one being to impress his pupils with the possibility of the cane. There was no lining up before the door and marching in. Every child came running, helter skelter, into the house, the noise and confusion of which was something terrible. However, after a time everyone got seated and the teacher was able to maintain tolerable order.

But let us hasten on. Interesting though the whole exercises are, we must pass to some other part. The day of our visit happens to be Friday —the last school day of the week. One part, at least, of the old field school, was like our modern school—they had no school on Saturday. Who invented Saturday as a holiday for schools? How did it get started? Many a boy (and teacher too) has blessed the author of this holiday! But Friday afternoon was an important occasion in the schools of our grandfathers. It was speaking day. Speechmaking! Every pupil, barring, possibly, the very small ones, must have a piece to read or recite. It was an iron-clad rule. True, it sometimes caused some excitement in the school room on Fridays, or maybe on Monday mornings, but "ye" old teachers were usually equal to the occasion and ready to enforce their rules.

There were no lessons after recess. It was a speechmaking occasion.

The teacher took a list of the names of his pupils and called them, and every one called was to be ready at once and respond with a reading or recitation. He usually started off with some of the little fellows so as to "break the ice" so to speak for the larger ones. But by and by he got to them and there was some excitement. "Bill Smith," called the teacher. Bill arose amid confusion, face flushed and blushing, self-conscious, awkward, gangling, and wishing himself in Halifax, took his place on the stage and began:

>"The boy stood on the burning deck,
>Whence all but him had fled;
>The flames that lit the battle's wreck,
>Shown round him o'er the dead.

When he had repeated those lines, he, somehow, gained confidence in himself and with some power and even eloquence, he continued to the close, and took his seat amid the applause of both teacher and pupils; whereupon, the teacher, always ready and anxious to encourage his pupils, took occasion to remark on the fine showing made by Bill, and to hold him up as an example of what a boy could do when he tried. This little speech of the teacher had its effect on the other pupils, as he hoped it might, and when their names were called, came forward promptly and did their very best which in most cases was quite creditable. Following are the first lines of some of the recitations of that afternoon:

>"A soldier of the Legion lay dying in Algiers,
>There was lack of woman's nursing, there was dearth of woman's tears;
>But a comrade stood beside him, while his life blood ebbed away,
>And knelt with pitying glances to hear what he might say."
>
>* * * *
>
>"I remember, I remember, the house where I was born,
>The little window where the sun came peeping in at morn;
>He never came a wink too soon, nor brought too long a day,
>But now I often wish the night had borne my breath away."
>
>* * * *
>
>"When Freedom from her mountain height,
>Unfurled her standard to the air;
>She tore the azure globe of night,
>And set the Stars of Glory there."
>
>* * * *
>
>"I come not here to talk. You know too well
>The story of our thralldom. We are slaves!"
>
>* * * *
>
>"Backward, turn backward, Oh! Time, in your flight!
>Make me a child again, just for to-night."

"Tell me not in mournful numbers,
Life is but an empty dream."

* * * *

"Come, come, come, the summer now is here;
Come out among the flowers, and make some pretty bowers,
Come, come, come, the summer now is here."

* * * *

"Twinkle, twinkle, little star,
How I wonder what you are,
Up above the world so high,
Like a diamond in the sky."

* * * *

"Half a league, half a league,
Half a league onward;
All in the Valley of Death,
Rode the six hundred."

* * * *

"Oh, were you ne'er a school boy,
And did you never train
And feel that swelling of the heart
You ne'er can feel again?"

* * *

"Mary had a little lamb,
Its fleece was white as snow;
And everywhere that Mary went
The lamb was sure to go."

* * * *

"Bob-o'-link, Bob-o'-link, spink, spank, spink."

* * *

"Abou Benadhem. May his tribe increase!"

* * * *

"I met a little cottage girl,
She was six years old, she said,
Her hair was thick with many a curl,
That clustered round her head."

* * *

"Curfew must not ring to-night."

* * *

"How dear to my heart are the scenes of my childhood,
When fond recollection presents them to view."

* * *

"Over the hills to the poorhouse, I'm wending my weary way,
I, a woman of seventy, and only a trifle gray."

* * * *

The casual visitor as he sat observing the exercises and listening with much interest to the effusions of these young minds, was able to envision among them, doctors, lawyers, preachers of the Gospel, judges, legislators and maybe governors; all in embryonic form, it is true, but the signs of power in these young minds were visible, and it was plain that there was only needed encouragement and training to bring those powers to fruition. And let it be observed, that, from such material, amid such surroundings, many men of power have been developed, not only in Walker county, but throughout the State of Georgia.

The day's work ended the school is dismissed and all eagerly wend their way homeward with shouts and jests interminable.

Many other interesting incidents, or descriptions of lessons, pupils, teacher, or scenes might be added, but these will suffice to give a general idea of the day's work in the school of our grandfathers.

BRONCO. Mr. Cicero McWhorter, to whom the author is indebted for information about Sylvan Bower, says that it was proposed to establish a postoffice at or near Sylvan Bower and that name was suggested as the name for the office. But the postal authorities objected to the name for some reason, whereupon the name Broncho, or as it is spelled, Bronco, was proposed and accepted. Broncho, meaning a wild, bucking, western horse, was thought to be next in appropriateness to the name Sylvan Bower, a secluded, or wild location.

EAGLE CLIFF. Near a promontory of cliffs high up on the side of Lookout mountain where eagles once established their aeries.

SHARPE. Named for Thomas A. Sharpe, an early settler and delegate to the Secession Convention in 1860.

Chapter Thirty-eight

SOLDIERS OF THE WORLD WAR—ROSTER OF COUNTY OFFICERS—ULSTER COUNTY GAZETTE.

WORLD WAR VETERANS—WALKER COUNTY.

(This Roster of World War Veterans was Furnished from the Office of the Adjutant General, Georgia National Guards, Atlanta, Georgia).

Abbot, Horton
Abraham, Benjamin L
Adkins, Riley
Akin, Clyde D
Akins, Archie
Akins, George B (col)
Akins, Henry (col)
Allgood, Marshall (col)

Allison, Adolph B
Anderson, Clarence (col)
Anderson, George H
Anderson, James F
Anderson, Linton Jackson
Andrews, Herbert McCullah
Armour, Charles E
Arp, Grover C

Aters, Commodore
Atkins, Grover Cleveland
Atkins, Harry T
Atkins, John W

Bailey, Henry C
Bailey, Jerdie (col)
Bailey, Vance-col-
Baker, Elbert E
Baker, Jeptha C
Baker, Luke
Baker, Paul Hamby
Ballow, Robert F
Barfield, John
Barnes, Robert
Barnett, Sam-col-
Bartlett, Emmett B
Beagles, Mack
Beaird, Elston M
Beard, Tobie
Bearden, William Travis
Bell, Chiel A.
Bennett, Ernest L
Bird, Carl Bradford
Bird, George D
Bird, Haskell D
Bird, James
Bishop, Sanford
Blanton, Charlie
Blaylock, Ben
Blaylock, Fred
Blevins, Kenyon William Riley
Bloxter, Ezekiele-col-
Boggs, George B
Boling, William W
Bolt, George L
Bomar, John Leroy
Bomar, Joseph W
Branan, John
Brannan, Horace B
Brannan, Millard O
Brannon, Charley
Brock, John C
Brooks, Forney F
Brooks, Herbert L
Brown, Claude M
Brown, John Clifton-col-

Brown, James C
Brown, Roy
Brown, William
Browning, Clifford
Brumett, William L
Bryan, Charles C
Bryant, Fate
Bryant, Frank
Burrows, Floyd
Burwick, Joe
Byerly, James W

Cagle, Henry S
Cagle, Homer C
Camp, Avery H
Camp, Charles E
Camp, Clarence
Campbell, Daniel W
Campbell, John R
Campbell, Robert YR
Cantrell, George A
Carlock, Thomas H
Carmon, James A
Carnes, Clifford W
Carroll, Claborne
Carter, Abb
Carter, Charles J
Carter, Clarence-col-
Carter, Joseph Ernest
Carver, William J
Catlett, Richard F(rank)
Catlett, William H
Cauthorne, Eugene
Chaney, Jim -col-
Chaney, Robert-col-
Chandler, Simon S-col-
Chapman, Emette
Chapman, Hewlette M
Chapman, John B.
Chapman, William W
Childres, Maynard A
Christian, John S
Claridy, William R-col-
Clark, Fines E
Clark, Harry E
Clements, James V
Clemenst, Oliver

Clements, William -col-
Collins, Thomas A
Conger, Edgar
Conley, Roy
Cook, Artie
Cook, Edgar M.
Cook, Richard A
Cook, Willis C
Clifford, Angus
Cline, Artie D
Coker, Columbus
Coker, Dennis Solomon
Cooper, Adolph R
Cooper, William E
Cornelison, Elbert W
Cornelison, Walter M
Coulter, Gilbert G
Coulter, Robert S
Coulter, Joe R
Courtney, Oscar D
Couch, Robert I
Covington, DeWitt-col-
Craig, Glenn A
Crawford, Robert Guy
Crisp, Ernest J
Cromer, Robert L
Crouch, James
Crow, Ottie
Crow, Robert L

Daniel, Harrison-col-
Daniel, Shep
Devenport, Edward A
Davis, Earl S
Davis, Floyd E
Davis, Henry-col-
Davis, John Bueton
Davis, Paul-col-
Davis, Willie-col-
DeCicco, Munziante
DeCuir, Nicholas-col-
DeLar, Joseph J
Dent, Arron L -col-
DeRatt, Ambrose E Jr
Dickerson, Henry Grady
Dickson, Walter E
Dilbeck, Clint R

Divine, Samuel W
Dobbs, James Wiley -col-
Dodson, Perry
Doston, Berry
Doty, Mortimer A
Douglas, James S
Dover, Henry
Dover, Millard
Dozier, Jim -col-
Driggers, George T(homas)
Dudley, John H
Duncan, Glenn A
Dunwoody, William H
Dyer, William J

Earwood, Roy L
Eastman, William C -col-
Edmonson, Edd-col-
Eledge, Charles L
Elliot, James C
Ellis, Bascomb F
Ellis Carl
Ellis, Clarence
Ellis, James C
Ellis, John
Elmore, Frank
Ensign, James Lee
Ensign, John E
Evers, Hugo
Evans, Clyde M
Evans, Reece -col-

Fariss, King D
Fillers, Jessie W
Fincher, John M
Fincher, Zack M
Fisher, Fred
Fisher, Ruben
Fisher, Taylor
Flanagan, James William
Fleitz, Bernard L
Flowers, Thomas W
Fouts, Charlie F
Foutz, Samuel C
Fox, Cyrel V
Frady, Gordon
Franklin, Jessie H

Freeman, Bert
Freeman, Scollard F
Fricks, Spurgeon
Fulgum, Herman W

Gaines, William M
Gardner, William L
Garfenflo, Frank G
Garner, Arthur
Gassett, John S
Gates, George E
Gentry, John T
George, Jessie Alex
Gilbert, Josh
Gilreath, Frederick A
Gilstrap, Harrison L
Gladden, Wesley O
Glanton, Elbert -col-
Glenn, Burl
Glenn, Ernest
Glenn, Lawrence
Godfrey, John W
Goodson, Franklin F
Goodson, J. B.
Goodson, Jefferson F
Goodson, Jesse H
Goodson, Joseph
Goodson, Mack
Goree, John Henry-col-
Gore, Jim
Gothard, Samuel
Grace, James W
Gray, Newton E
Gray, William
Green, James M
Griffin, Oakley O
Griffin, Will H
Grogans, Charley M

Hackney, Edward M.
Haddock, Wallace C
Hale, Deforest
Hall, Franklin A
Hamby John
Hames, George R
Hames, Luther
Hamilton, Leonard B

Hammond, Dewey W
Hammontree, Arther W
Hammontree, Deed F
Hammontree, Eugene
Hampton, Lee
Harp, Carl E
Harp, Jessie R
Harper, John W
Harris, Ralph H.-col-
Harrison, Charlie H
Harrison, Lawrence R
Hartline, Jesse W
Harvey, August Mystery
Haslerig, James -col-
Hasty, William D
Hawkins, Arthur A
Hawkins, Paul E(ugene)
Haywood, Barney R
Headrick, Leonard
Headrick, William
Headrick, Will F
Hearn, Clark B
Hearn, Toliver C
Hemphill, Gus -col-
Henry, Homer V
Henry, James T
Henry, John
Henry, Lee R -col-
Herod, Robert L
Heywood, Deforest
Hickey, Joseph E
Hilburn, Thomas D
Hill, Archie C(larence)
Hill, Gordon L
Hill, James R
Hill, Rufus M
Hill, Russell T
Hill, Theodore W
Hilley, Carl
Hinton, Mack -col-
Hinton, Robert Lee -col-
Hinton, Russell James-col-
Hise, John
Hixon, Clark Lee
Hixon, James C
Hobbs, Jesse Cleveland
Holcomb, Frank

Holcomb, Will
Hollingsworth, Ernest H
Horton, Gus -col-
Houston, Thomas W
Houston, Thomas E
Howell, Andrew J Jr
Howell, Paul A
Hughes, Burnon O
Huskey, Olin

Ivie, Marvin K
Ivey, Love E

Jackson, Douglas M
Jackson, Ernest (D)
Jackson, James E
Jackson, Paul R
Jackson, Ralph R(ussell)
Jackson, Thomas E
James, Claude
James, Eugene
Jennings, Ralph W
Jett, Roy L
Jewell, Robert H
Johnson, Charles Carl
Johnson, Ernest
Johnson, Lester, -col-
Johnson, Rufus M
Johnson, Samuel B
Jones, Dewey H
Jones, Daniel W
Jones, Frank H
Jones, Harry Henderson
Jones, Jesse J
Justice, Carl H

Kelly, Elisha
Kemp, William C
Kesley, Ed
Kilgore, Gordon L
Kinsmon, John T
Kingston, James M
Kinsey, Frederick W
King, Richmond -col-
Kirk, John L
Knox, Henry -col-
Knox, James L

Lane, Carl C
Lane, James E
Lawrence, Charley Lord
Lawrence, Daniel W
Lawrence, Fred A
Lawrence, Pearl-col-
Lawrence, Sam -col-
Ledford, Homer H
Ledford, John H
Lee, Gus
Lee, John H
Leigh, Marshall W
Lemons, Earl
Lewallen, Anderson L
Lewis, Clifford W
Liner, Carl H
Little, Paul
Lockman, Newton
Long, Harlar C
Love, Elmer -col-
Lowery, William L
Lumpkin, Virgil
Luttrell, William D

McBride, Gilbert W
McClure, Carl
McClure, Chester F
McClure, Robert D
McClure, Samuel
McClure, Willie Robert
McClure, Freeman C.
McCormack, John W
McCormick, Julius
McCollough, Homer Lee
McCurdy, Windell D
McDougal, Heshel
McDanial, Arthur
McDaniel, Ernest
McDaniel, Frank
McDaniel, Joshua
McDaniel, Olin
McDaniel Wheeler S
McFarland, Buie
McFarland, Robert W
McGaha, Narvy O
McGaha, Roy S
McGinnis, Arthur -col-

McGinnis, Charlie W -col-
McGinnis, John T
McGlothin, Samuel Harmon
McKnight, William Thomas
McKown, William E
McMillen, William R
McWhorter, Arthur M-col-
McWilliams, Will

Madaris, Elmer D
Madaris, James L
Mahan, John L
Marks, John M
Marsh, James M -col-
Marsh, Spencer Douglas -col-
Martin, Ed
Martin, Henry
Martin, John R
Martin, Roscoe F
Martin, Wilburn
Mashburn, Homer
Massey, Earl
Massey, George W
Massey, Jess L
Massey, John William
Mathis, James
Matthews, Benjamin
Mathews, Robert E
Meaps, Henry L
Melton, Gaines
Millard, William J
Millican, Fred L
Millican, Cecil C
Miller, Lonnie
Mills, Clifford -col-
Miras, John L
Mitchel, Jesse
Mityhel, Willis-col-
Mize, Frank A
Montgomery, Hutck -col-
Montgomery William
Montgomery, William T -col-
Moore, Charles, R
Moore, Robert W
Mooreland, Dewey
Moreland, Henry
Morgan, James

Morgan, Rice M
Morrissey, Bernard L
Morrison, Grady H
Morrison, Jacob P
Mosely, William G
Moss, Jessie J
Millis, John B
Mullis, Robert
Mullis, William R(anza)
Murphy, Russell
Myers, Graves T
Myers, Warner -col-

Nations, Robert L
Neal, Henry C -col-
Nichols, Arthur Boss
Nicholson, Dan C
Norman, Deforest
Norman Erbie
Norton, Robert H
Nuckols, Anderson L
Nuchols, Milton F

O'Barr, George K
Ogle, John B
O'Neal, John H -col-
Orton, Leland
Orr, Thomas H. G
Orton, Inman
Osborn, Wade -col-
Osborn, Amos B
Osborn, Gerald L
Osborn, Wallace O(scar)
Osborn, Wallace C
Owens, Brown
Owensby, Melvin R

Palmer, William M
Parker, Wheeler Hamilton
Parris, Charlie
Parris, Hugh Jr
Parris, Ollie
Partin, Tom
Payne, Glen
Peeler, Aron H
Peacock, Edgar L Jr
Peacock, Hugh M

Peacock, Oscar M
Penley, William, A
Peppers, Lee
Perry, James L
Pettigrew, Ira D
Pettigrew, William A
Peterson, James F
Philpot, Albertus E
Phelps, Waldo E
Phillips, James T
Phillips, Marion F Jr
Phillips, Taylor W
Pierce, Herbert J
Pilcher, Aticus
Pilgrim, Joe
Pitts, Bob -col-
Pitts, Solomon T
Pitman, Ross H
Pitman, Walter O
Plaster, Lee H
Pless, Hill
Poindexter, Eliga D
Poindexter, Edd A
Pope, Clay H
Potter, James M
Prescott, Robert L
Price, Braden
Prince, James
Pursley, Robert-col-
Pursley, Alexander
Puryear, Lee

Quarles, Woodie

Rainey, Mack E
Ramsey, Carl J
Ransom, George H
Ransom, Henry
Ransom, William M
Ray, Wren B
Reed, Arch Jr
Reed, Charlie
Reese, yerald Cummins
Reese, Griffin
Rhinehart, George A Jr
Rhudy, William A
Rhyne, John J

Rhyne, Julian T
Rhyne, William Thomas
Ridley, Jack
Roach, George W
Robertson, Henry A
Roddy, Walter S
Robinson, Charley
Robinson, Emmett
Rogers, Kennings B
Rollins, Pink C -col-
Rollins, William Jessie Lee
Roper, Wilburn H
Rosser, James R
Rudicil, Roland Knox
Russell, Claude

Satterfield, Parks P
Schmitt, Charles W
Schmitt, Clarence
Schrimpsher, James S
Schrimpsher, Tom
Schubert, Clarence Alexander
Schubert, Fred A
Scott, Artie E
Scott, Ernest George
Settlemire, John Howard
Sellers, Joseph J
Shankle, Deforest
Shahan, Joe Brown
Shelby, Henry Creed
Shields, Clayton
Shipp, Henry D
Shropshire, John B -col-
Shultz, Clayton
Simmons, Henry
Simmons, Jessie S
Sizemore, John W. A.
Sizemore, Luther A
Slater, Charles
Smartt, Ray A
Smith, Claude Terry
Smith, Daniel -col-
Smith, Ernest G
Smith, George E
Smith, George R
Smith, Gordon F
Smith, Isaiah -col-

Smith, Joseph E
Smith, John M
Smith, Loney L
Smith, Lowe
Smith, Otis -col-
Smith, Russell Vance
Smith, Shirley
Smith, Starling B
Smith, Thomas D
Smith, Walter A
Smith, Walter Andrew
Smith, William C
Smith, Wiley
Sparks, Spencer W
Spencer, Benjamin F
Spencer, Samuel D
Srite, Samuel D
Stallion, Frank
Stamper, Sammie M -col-
Stallings, William
Stansell, Ames C
Steele, Archibald R
Steel, John A
Stele, Luther
Stegall, Phillip H
Stephens, Robert J
Stephens, William Eddie
Stoker, Alexander
Stoker, Oscar L
Stoner, George R
Stoner, Peary J
Strickland, Isaiah Harlan
Strickland, John E
Stump, George F
Suggs, Charlie
Suggs, Otis L
Suttle, Perry -col-
Suttles, Shelly
Sutton, Ernest
Swafford, Jeff F
Swafford, Walter W
Swicegood, Clayton
Swinford, Will

Tarvin, Alvin H
Tallant, James G(lenn)
Tatum, Julius G

Tatum, Webb
Taylor, Bruce
Taylor, Henry S
Thrailkill, Wiley R
Thomas, Arthur
Thomas, Carl R
Thomas, Harvie
Thompson, Bill
Thurman, James R
Thurman, Roy A
Tinsley, Albert -col-
Townsend, Charley
Tracy, A Lanson
Travis, Frank L
Traylor, Charlie B
Tudor, Jesse Andrew
Turner, Clarence
Turner, John O
Turner, Oliver
Turman, Cloves V
Turman, I. B.

Upshaw, Twig -col-

Vanhorn, James
Vaughn, Cleveland -col-
Visage, Roudey L
Vick, Noble J

Waldrop, Hubert H
Waldrup, Sherman
Wallin, Judson T
Wallin, Thomas E.
Walker, Charles Franklin
Wallace, Charlie B
Wallace, Daniel C
Wallace, Judson
Wardlaw, Samuel F
Wardlaw, William O
Warrenfels, Allen P
Warrenfels, Roy F
Ward, Charlie D
Ward, Ira -col-
Warren, Charlie E
Warren, George W
Waterhouse, William Franklin
Waters, Henry

Watkins, Anson
Watkins, Dock
Watson, Luther -col-
Watts, Charlie L
Watts, James E
Webb, Leslie P
Weeks, Miller
Welch, Roger G
Wells, Frank M
West, Harvey E
Westbrook, Winter E
Whitlow, Sylvester -col-
Wheeler, Charles H
Wheeler, Fred D -col-
Wheeler, John T
Wheeler, King D -col-
Wheeler, Richard Jepthia
Wheeler, William M
White, George H
White, Green -col-
White, Louis N or H
White, Shelton
White, William D
White, Willie
Whitmire, Charles A
Wike, Robert L
Wiley, Walter
Willbanks, Sam -col-
Williams, Earnest A

Williams, Joseph F
Williams, Mark
Williams, Paul L
Williams, Robert T
Williams, Thomas
Wimpee, Clarence L
Wimpee, Clyde Stanford
Wise, George H
Wooden, Chester L
Wooden, Monroe
Wolfe, Arthur J
Womack, Arlie D
Woods, Clinton -col-
Wood, Edgar L
Woods, John T -col-
Wood, Orie M
Woods, William W -col-
Wooten, Albert R
Wright, Horace Lee

Yates, Thomas Arthur
Young, Benjamin F -col-
Young, John -col-
Young, Milton J -col-
Young, Robert W
Young, William E -col-
Young, Walter L
Young, William E -col-

DECEASED.

Brown, Alonzo W
Coley, Walter Marion
Davis, McKinley -col-
Durham, Jesse M
Dunn, Samuel
Dowles, Wates P
Eskew, Willard J
Frady, Charles B
Freeman, William L
Graham, Ross Quinn
Green, Crofford F
Harp, Sam G
Hewitt, Alvin

Holbrook, J Daniel
McKinley, Hobart -col-
Mize, Thomas R
Palms, Will L -col-
Steele, John H
Stegall, Jerry Goldsmith
Stewart, John
Thornton, Wallace
Tucker, Lude
Wadkins, Walter
Wheeler, Harrison W -col-
Williams, Fred
Young, Eddie P

OFFICERS.

Andrews, Maurice N
Barker, Hampton M
Blaylock, Charles David
Bryan, Thomas William
Camp, Earl Franklin
Carroll, Edward Grady
Corbly, John B
Coulter, Robert Mitchel
Erickson, Louis
Fisher, Marshall O
Flanagan, James William
Flynn, Mathew A
Gaines, Robert
Hall, Burl F
Henry, Charles Robert
Henry, Roy Oscar
Jenkins, Thomas Grady
Jewell, Daniel A Jr
Jewett, Carl Wooten
Korb, Harry Hames
Peacock, Edgar Lindsay Jr
Peacock, David William Killin
Puryear, Edwin Alfred
Rhyne, John James
Rhyne, Thomas
Stevens, Emmett Finley
Stiltner, Horace Frank
Strimpel, Harry Fred
Turner, Harry Clyde
Wilson, William John
Wood, Marion Eugene

NAVY.

Alverson, Wilson Francis
Baker, Wililam Grady
Baudy, William Wilson
Beagles, Mack
Bell, George Dewey
Bell, Jesse Franklin
Berry, Evert Ernest
Bohannan, Glenn
Bowen, Albert Sidney Jr
Bowman, Charles Wilson
Bradley, Claude Luther
Bryan, James Avery
Buchanan, Louis Clifford
Bullard, Emmett Dewitte
Campbell, James Harrison
Cantrell, James C
Carroll, Edward
Carter, Odes Scott
Chapman, Benjamin James
Cooper, Andrew Stephens
Cordell, James Monroe
Day, John Elmer
Eubanks, Avery Clinton
Gerren, Henry Clay
Glenn, Byron Clifford
Gray, Robert Quillian
Griffith, Porter Hoyt
Harris, Walter Gardner
Harvey, Robert Lawrence
Helms, Cecil Frank
Hughes, Joseph Simpson
Jett, Joseph Archey
Johnson, Clyde Kirklen
Johnson, George Martin
Johnson, Henry Andrew
Johnson, Horace Robert
Johnson, Roy
Hix, William Grady
Landers, Hillard Garmon
Langley, Walker Benson
Loughridge, James Alfred
Lovingood, James Charles Monroe
Lowery, Edward Walton
McBroom, Edward Everette
McCullough, Grayson
McDurmin, Chester Bazzle
McEntire, Claude William
Morgan, Charley Thomas
Morgan, Tate Herman
Parson, Robert Lee
Partridge, Andrew Denham

Peeler, Richard Leeland
Pittman, Robert Carter
Powell, William
Prince, Frank George
Rollins, Joseph Claborn
Rogers, Samuel Marvin
Sartain, Virgil
Scruggs, Thomas Calvin
Shankle, Charles Cain
Sissom, Claude Ernest
Smith, Cecil Douglas
Smith, Colman Hull

Smith, Joseph Sidney
Steverson, Samuel Franklin
Suggs, Ralph Walter
Tabb, David Cunningham
Taylor, Clarence Macon
White, James Foster
White, Mell
White, Willie Julius Jr
Willis, William Warner
Wilson, John Henderson
Worthy, William Thomas
Wright, Relous Irvin

DECEASED.

Henley, John

In addition to the above the following names of ex-service men have been reported as living in the county, or belonging to the county:

Adams, Clint
Anderson, Edmund H.
Anthony, Reed M.

Bryant, Ave
Barton, Robert L.
Bean, Thomas A.
Blaylock, Ed
Blaylock, Sim Monroe
Brannon, James L.
Bullard, Thomas B.
Byrd, Roy Gifford

Campbell, James
Cherry, Walter Lee
Clements, Oscar
Cornett, Albert
Cooper, Edgar
Cooper, John F.
Cory, Basil
Cucksee, A. M.
Carver, John David

Dickerson, James S.
Day, John D.
Donham, Horace A.

Dunwoody, Lewis Wallace
Dunage, Sam T.

Fouts, Jesse C.
Fouts, William R.

Gilbreath, Judson J.
Hill, Will
Hinson, Clark
Hamilton, Clarence
Hammond, James L.
Hampton, Frank
Harris, LaFayette
Hartline, Sidney James
Hays, David M.
Henderson, John O.
Henderson, Cicero
Hise, John
Holcomb, James R.
Howard, A. L.
Hunter, Elmer
Hutcheson, John M.
Hadley, John

Jackson, John Jefferson
Johnson, Ray

HISTORY OF WALKER COUNTY, GEORGIA 297

Justice, Archie B.	Ransom, Samuel L.
Jones, Harry	Rogers, Julius C.
Lawrence, Fred	Scoggins, Leroy
	Scott, Westy G.
Mason, Jasper L.	Smith, Mack
Montgomery, John G.	Singleterry, Alvin R
Moreland, Dewey (Dec'd.)	Sprayberry, Roy
Moreland, Joe	Stansell, James C.
Moreland John	Stephenson, Tren T
Moore, James M.	Smith, Duke
Morse, Neil	
Mosely, William G.	Thomas, Jeff A.
McClure, S. K.	Tracy, Andrew J.
	Trammel, A.
Neal, William W.	Trammel, Capers B.
	Trundle, Vines A.
Owens, C. H.	Vanhorn, Singleterry
Patterson, Conrad C.	Wardlaw, Samuel F.
Pless, Hill	Wheeler, Lee J.
Prince, Frank	Wilson, Robert C.
Prince, Carl	Woodard, J. B.

On the completion of the hard surfaced road from LaFayette to Lee and Gordon's mill, the bridge crossing Chickamauga river was, on June 20, 1931, dedicated to the memory of the ex-service men and women of the county who gave their lives in the World war. The beautiful bronze tablet, a gift to the two Legion posts of the county from Congressman Tarver, placed on the Memorial Bridge, bears the following inscription and names:

"This Bridge Dedicated by Latner Freeman Post No. 123 and Ross Graham Post No. 87 American Legion As A War Memorial To the Men and Women of Walker County, Who Patriotically and Unselfishly Gave Their Lives for Their Country During the World War. Others Gave Much, These Gave All.

"Alonzo Brown, Jesse B. Davis, McKinley Davis, Samuel Dunn, Jesse Monroe Durham, Willard Eskew, Charles Boyce Frady, Gerald Frazier, William Latner Freeman, Geo. Samuel Harp, Ross Quinn Graham, James Harold Helton, Alvin Hewitt, James Elmer Hunter, Bert Hix Kensen, Emil P. Lawson, Francis Arthur Mason, ——— Mitchell, Thomas Rudicil Mize, Delbert Murphy, Garrett Hobart McKinley, William Palm, Marvin H. Smith, Jerry Goldsmith Stegall, Wallace Thornton, Luke Tucker, Linsay Wallin, Fred Williams, Harrison Wheeler, Eddie P. Young, Mrs. Belle Steele Jackson, (Red Cross)."

Roster County Officers.

The author has spent much time and labor in an effort to secure a correct roster of all county officers from the organization of the county. Because of the burning of the court house this has been impossible. A trip to Atlanta where he was permitted to examine the records in the office of the Secretary of State was rewarded with a partial record of the early officers, but not all.

SHERIFF. (Incomplete). William Faulkner, 1834-36; Asa Dickson, 1837-38; William Faulkner, 1839-40; Peter Jackson, 1841-42; Nathaniel Newsome, 1843-44; Hiram M. Shaw, 1845-46; John Rogers, 1847-48; William Thedford, no date; Abner Mize, no date; James Hunt, no date; Abner H. Mize, no date; Thomas Evatt, no date; Abner H. Mize, no date. It is likely that each of these served two years which would bring it to the next name and date, viz. James Bunch, 1861-(?); A. H. Mize, 1863-64; J. B. Rogers, 22 days in 1866; L. Conley, no date; A. A. Simmons, no date; Bill Strange, no date; Joel Withers, no date; Harvey Mize, served one day—killed by Brad Redden; G. W. Patterson, 1879-80; W. M. McClatchey, 1881-84; W. A. Foster, 1885-94; William Riley, 1895-96, 1899-1902; Hugh A. Sims, 1897-98; Robert Garmany, 1903-10; also 15-20; A. G. Catron, 1911-14, also 1921 to June—killed by James Douglas; L. W. Harmon, June 1921-1928; J. C. Keown, 1929-.

CLERK. (Nearly correct). Jesse Clements, 1834-36; John Caldwell, 1836-46; Wm. F. Wright, 1846-48; Hiram M. Shaw, 1848-50; John Dickson, 1850-60; Francis I. Grogan, 1860-(?); J. M. Rogers, 1864-(?); W. R. Neal, 22 days in 1866; James H. Rogers, 1866-68; R. N. Dickerson, Sept. 14, 1868-1914; Q. M. Clemons, 1915-16; J. L. Rowland, 1917-20; T. W. Bryan, 1921-.

ORDINARY. The first ordinary mentioned is James Hogue, 1852-60; T. R. A. Haslerig, 1861-(?). Mr. Haslerig resigned, entered the army and was killed, Mr. Grogan, the clerk, taking over the duties of ordinary. Thomas W. Cobb, 1863-(?); Milton Russell, 1869-84; W. B. Foster, 1885-96; J. L. Rowland, 1897-1904; Jerome Henderson, 1905-March, 1908, died; E. Foster, July, 1908-Oct., 1914, died; W. L. Stansell, Dec., 1914-.

TAX COLLECTOR. (Incomplete). W. K. Bagby, 1834; A. N. Ross, 1839; Noah Meridith, 1844; Nathan Anderson, 1847-54; Wm. P. Sparks, 1855-(?); J. T. Deck, 1856-60; M. Rhodes, 1860-62; L. B. McWhorter, 1863-(?); W. D. Lumpkin, S. D. Roberts, no dates; F. M. Sampson, 1872-(?); G. W. Innman, (?)-1880; Jacob Goodson, Jr., 1881-82; J. C. Hall, 1883-84, 87-88, 97-98; James McCamy, 1885-86; W. G. Conley, 1889-92; G. W. Pierce, 1893-96, 1913-14; J. R. Hunter, 1899-00; W. A. Martin, 1901-02; 1909-10; W. Z. Hayes, 1903-06; W. W. Tucker, 1907-08; Robert Martin, 1911-12; T. M. Coffee, 1915-20; Henry Brown, 1921-24; Claude Clements, 1925-.

TAX RECEIVER. (Incomplete). Hiram T. Gill, 1851-(?) (The record shows that he was both tax receiver and collector in 1864); Frank Neal,

HISTORY OF WALKER COUNTY, GEORGIA

1881-82; George Brigman, 1883-84; T. F. Sims, 1885,86; H. H. Williams, 1887-90; M. S. Baker, 1891-92, 97-98; W. A. Weaver, 1893-96; J. M. Shields, 1899-00; D. T. Scoggins, 1901-04; L. A. Price, 1905-06; W. O. Talley, 1907-10; C. B. Ezell, 1911-14; F. O. Plaster, 1915-18; J. H. Garmany, 1919-20; 1925-28; Edwin Puryear, 1921-24; Bess M. Catron Warrenfels, 1929-32; Ruby Phipps, 1933- (Elected in Democratic Primary, March 5, 1932).

TREASURER. James Culberson, 1862-66; G. W. Clements, (?)-1888 (about 20 years); R. F. Mize, 1889-96; L. A. Price, 1897-00; J. R. Tyner, 1901-04; C. R. Johnson, 1905-08; J. W. Deck, 1909-12; O. L. Forester, 1913-Feb., 14 (died); J. P. Shattuck, Feb., 1914- May, 15; S. G. Hayes, May, 1915-16; Fletcher Parker, 1917-18 (office abolished).

CORONER. James Burress; Aaron Hughes; Parrot N. Poe; Robert Hyde; James Elliot; Constantine Wood; R. W. Cassady; Robert Hyde; V. Thompson; Wm. Duke; Wm. B. Payne; James Hamby; M. S. Cox; I. M. Henn; Wm. Pogue; E. S. Thompson; B. A. McCall; E. M. Simonton; Ray Johnson; M. F. Nuckols; Joe Deck; W. R. Hilton; G. W. Brown; Roy Neeley; L. W. Cagle (Elected in Democratic Primary, March 5, 1932).

CLERK INFERIOR COURT. Daniel A. Baker; Marvel Duncan; Eddy Briers; Jesse P. Freeman; Thomas M. Nash; Richard M. Cassady; Charles F. Bruckner; James H. Rogers; I. S. Martin; R. N. Dickerson. (The Inferior Court was abolished during the sixties).

SURVEYOR. Haley S. Tatum; John B. Davis; John Catlett; James Elliot; B. R. McCutchen; Joseph C. Henderson; Benj. R. McCutchen; B. Woolbright; B. R. McCutchen; Sam Hatcher; B. R. McCutchen; A. R. McCutchen; H. P. Lumpkin; Fletcher Walton; T. W. Haslerig; J. T. Scott; Chester Veach; Julius Rink.

ROSTER BOARD ROADS AND REVENUE.

1883-84—L. K. Dickey, J. B. Rogers, Wm. McWilliams, J. F. Smith, N. G. Warthen (L. K. Dickey, res.).

1887-88—Wm. McWilliams, J. F. Smith, J. B. Rogers, B. L. Glenn, A. J. Caldwell, vice.

1889-90—J. F. Smith, J. B. Rogers, A. J. Caldwell, Wm. McWilliams, B. L. Glenn.

1891-92—J. T. Alsobrook, C. A. Cameron, O. R. Henderson, T. N. Jones, J. T. Suttle.

1893-94—J. F. Smith, R. B. Neal, T. J. Alsobrook, J. F. Bonds, Jasper Love.

1895-96—J. F. Bonds, T. J. Alsobrook, Jasper Love, R. B. Neal, N. C. Napier.

1897-98—R. B. Neal, N. C. Napier, T. J. Alsobrook, C. W. Evitt, Jasper Love.

1899-00—R. B. Neal, James Weaver, J. M. Ransom, R. B. Shaw, Gordon Lee.

1901-02—R. B. Neal, B. F. Thurman, James Weaver, R. B. Shaw, W. A. Horton.

1903-04—J. P. Hall, R. B. Shaw, J. C. Young, W. A. Horton, James Weaver.

1905-06—J. H. Hammond, R. B. Shaw, J. C. Young, T. F. McFarland, James Weaver.

1907-08—James Weaver, R. B. Shaw, J. C. Young, John B. Henderson, T. J. Bandy.

1909-10—John B. Henderson, R. B. Shaw, J. C. Young, T. J. Bandy, J. M. Ransom.

1911-12—John B. Henderson, R. B. Shaw, J. C. Young, J. V. Johnson, J. M. Ransom.

1913-14—R. B. Shaw, J. M. Ransom, J. V. Johnson, J. D. McConnell, J. C. Young.

1915-16—J. C. Young, J. M. Ransom, J. D. McConnell, A. J. Wheeler (R. B. Shaw, Res.), S. P. Hall.

1917-20—S. T. Carson, Claude Clements, R. V. Thurman, T. C. Coulter J. B. Henderson, Res.), James R. McFarland.

1921-24—Claude Clements, M. A. McConnell, S. P. Hall, W. S. Abercrombie, J. R. McFarland.

1925-28—J. H. Kilgore, C. M. Thurman, Clark Tucker, L. P. Keith, G. R. Morgan.

1929-32—J. H. Kilgore, C. A. Chambers, L. P. Keith, Frank Shaw, G. R. Morgan.

1933-( )—W. A. Loach, W. P. Blackwell, J. M. Baker, W. L. Johnson, J. H. Williams (Elected in Democratic Primary, March 5, 1932).

ROSTER REPRESENTATIVES WALKER COUNTY SINCE ITS ERECTION.

1834—Xanders G. McFarland
1835—Thomas S. Tanner
1836—Miles Davis
1837—Xanders G. McFarland
1838—Robert Cross
1839—Asa Dickson
    Stephen Smith
1840—Asa Dickson
    Stephen Smith
1841—Stephen Smith
    Henry H. Armstrong
1842—Stephen Smith
    Henry H. Armstrong

1843—Lawson Black
    Peter Jackson
1845—Lawson Black
1847—E. R. Harden
1849-50—James Gordon
1851-52—X. G. McFarland
1853-54—Adam Clements
1855-56—J. Caldwell
1857-58—F. M. Young
1859-60—Charles C. Patton
1861-62-63 Ex.
    A. B. Culberson
    Adam Clements

1863-64 Ex.-64-65 Ex.
   John Y. Wood
   A. Cooper
1865-66-66—M. E. Rhodes
   J. Dixon
1868 Ex.-69-70 Ex.
   W. B. Gray
1871-72-72 Adj.
   John Y. Wood
1873-74—Judson C. Clements
1875-76—Judson C. Clements
1877—J. M. Shaw
1878-79 Adj.
   John B. Wheeler
1880-81 Adj.
   John B. Wheeler
1882-83 Ex.-83 Ann. Adj.
   John G. Wood
1884-85 Adj.
   John B. Wheeler
1886-87 Adj.
   John B. Wheeler
1888-89 Adj.—B. F. Thurman
1890-91 Adj.—John B. Wheeler
1892-93—John B. Wheeler
1894-95—Gordon Lee
1896-97 Adj.-97
   Francis Wall Copeland
1898-99—Francis Wall Copeland
1900-01—Francis Wall Copeland

1902-03-04—B. F. Thurman
1905-06—H. P. Lumpkin
1907-08-08 Ex.
   B. F. Thurman
1909-10—James E. Rosser
1911-12 Ex.-12
   B. F. Thurman
1913-14—S. W. Fariss
1915-15 Ex.-16-17 Ex.
   Don Harris
1917-18—Don Harris
1919-20—James Robert McFarland
1921-22—Freeman C. McClure
   Charles Robert Jones
   (Aug. 4, 1921)
1923-23 Ex.-24
   Freeman C. McClure
   David F. Pope
1925-26-26 Ex.—Freeman McClure
   J. R. Rosser
1927-28—J. M. Hutcheson
   D. F. Pope
1929-30—J. M. Hutcheson
   J. R. Rosser
1931-31 Ex.-32—J. M. Hutcheson
   J. R. Rosser
1933—E. A. Leonard, J. A. Sartain
   (Elec. Dem. Pri. Sept. 14, 1932)

ROSTER OF SENATORS OF WALKER COUNTY AND 44TH SENATORIAL DISTRICT FROM 1834 TO DATE.

Samuel Fariss, 1834-35-36-37, 43, 47, 51-52.
Thomas G. McFarland, 1838.
William Huff, 1839.
James Thompson (died Nov., 1840)
   Spencer Marsh (seated Dec. 15)
William K. Briers, 1841-42.
Stephen Smith, 1845.
Samuel McBee, 1849-50.
M. Dickson, 1853-54.
James Gordon, 1855-56.
G. G. Gordon, 1857-58.
James M. Bond, 1859-60.

R. A. Lane, 1861-62-63 Ex.
H. J. Sprayberry, 1863-64 Ex.-1864-65 Ex.
R. M. Paris, 1865-66-66.
B. R. McCutchen, 1868 Ex.-69-70 (ineligible '70; died '70).
William Henry, 1871 (seat declared vacant 11/10/71).
T. Y. Parks, 1872-72 Adj.
W. H. Payne, 1873-74.
Payne, 1875-76.
James W. Cureton, 1877.
Judson Claudius Clements, 1878-79.

A. T. Hacket, 1880-81 Adj., 1892-93.
M. A. B. Tatum, 1882-83 Ex. 83 Ann. Adj.
Robert Marion Wallace Glenn, 1884-85 Adj. 1890-91 Adj.
Ezekiel Foster, 1886-87 Adj.
J. B. McCollum, 1888-89 Adj.
G. W. M. Tatum, 1894-95, 1900-01.
T. F. McFarland, 1896-97 Adj. 97.
William E. Mann, 1898-99.
Gordon Lee, 1902-03-04.
W. H. Yates, 1905-06 (died 1905; member elect, J. S. Alsobrook).
J. R. Brock, 1907-08-08 Ex.
J. Y. Wood, 1909-10.
W. C. Hullender, 1911-12 Ex., 12, 17-18, 23-23 Ex.-24.
Le Pope, 1913-14.
J. R. McFarland, 1915-15 Ex.-16-17 Ex.
Walter W. Cureton, 1919-20.
David F. Pope, 1921-22.
Daniel Spencer Middleton, 1925-26 Ex. 26 2d Ex.
James Ralph Rosser, 1927-28.
B. F. Harris, 1929-1930.
B. T. Brock, 1931-1932.
John M. Hutchison, 1933 (Elec. Dem. Pri. Sept. 14, 1932).

CONGRESSIONAL DISTRICTS—WALKER COUNTY.

5th—Dec. 23, 1843-Mch. 23, 1861.
10th—Mch. 23, 1861-Oct. 26, 1865.
7th—Oct. 26, 1865-date.

SENATORIAL DISTRICTS—WALKER COUNTY.

46th—Dec. 23, 1843-Jan. 19, 1852.
44th—July 2, 1861-date.

SUPERIOR COURT TRANSFERS—WALKER COUNTY.

Cherokee Circuit, 1833-1869.
Rome Circuit, 1869-date.

ROSTER JUDGES SUPERIOR COURT.

CHEROKEE CIRCUIT. John W. Hooper, 1832-35; Owen H. Kennon, 1835-38; Turner H. Tripp, 1838-42, also 1854-56; George B. Anderson, 1842-43; John A. Janes, 1843-43; Augustus R. Wright, 1843-50; John B. Hooper, 1850-50; John H. Lumpkin, 1850-54; Dawson A. Walker, James A. Milner and Josiah R. Parrot served from 1856 to 1869, exact terms of each unknown.

ROME CIRCUIT. Francis A. Kirby, 1869-70; R. D. Harvey, 1870-73; J. W. H. Underwood, 1873-1882; J. Branham, 1882-87; John W. Maddox, 1887-92, also 1910-13; W. M. Henry, 1892-95, also 1896-05; W. T. Turnbull, 1895-96; Moses Wright, 1905-10, also 1913-25; James Maddox, 1925.

The following have served as Solicitors-General, dates unknown: J. A. W. Johnson of Dalton; C. D. Forsythe of Rome; C. T. Clements of Walker county; J. L. Wright of Rome; Charles G. Janes of Cedartown;

A. Richardson of Cedartown; W. J. Nunnally of Rome; Moses Wright, Rome; Wm. H. Ennis, Rome; John W. Bale, Rome; Claude H. Porter, Rome, E. S. Taylor, Summerville; J. F. Kelly, Rome; M. Neil Andrews, LaFayette.

JUDGES OF INFERIOR COURT. Official records show that the following were judges of the Inferior Court of Walker County: Daniel Gartman, John Catlett; A. L. Barry; L. C. Graddy. In addition the following are said to have served in that capacity; Judge Easterling; James R. Jones; B. R. McCutchen; James Bonds; and M. E. Rhodes.

ULSTER COUNTY GAZETTE.

Mr. W. C. Bailey, of Pond Spring, now in his 85th year (since deceased), has in his possession a copy of the Ulster County Gazette, of Kingston, New York, published by Samuel Freer and Son, and dated Saturday, January 4, 1800. This is the issue containing the announcement of the death of General Washington, who had died on December 14, 1799, about 20 days previous. The following extract is taken from it for the purpose of showing with what reverence and love Washington was held in the hearts of his contemporaries. Other extracts are given for their general interest and historical value. Notice the occasional use of the old form of s, which the printer endeavors to represent by the use of the letter f:

WASHINGTON ENTOMBED.

Georgetown Dec. 20.

On Wednesday laft, the mortal part of Washington the Great—the father of his Country and the Friend of man; was confined to the tomb, with solemn honors and funeral pomp.

A multitude of persons assembled, from many miles around, at Mount Vernon, the choice and laft refidence of the illuftrious chief. There were the groves—the spacious avenues, the beautiful and sublime scenes, the noble manfion—but, alas! the auguft inhabitant *was now no more*. The great soul was *gone*. His mortal part was there indeed; but ah! how affecting! how awful the spectacle of such worth and greatness, thus to mortal eyes, fallen!—Yes! fallen! fallen!

In the long and lofty *portico*, where oft the Hero walked in all his glory, *now* lay the fhrouded corpse. The countenance ftill, composed, and serene, seemed to depress the dignity of the spirit, which lately dwelt in that lifeless form. There those who paid the laft sad honors to the benefactor of his country, took an impressive—a farewell view.

On the ornament, at the head of the coffin was inscribed SURGE AD JUDICIUM—about the middle of the coffin GLORIA DEO—and on the silver plate,

GENERAL GEORGE WASHINGTON

Departed this life on 14th December, 1799. AEt 68.

Between three and four o'clock, the sound of artillery from a veffel in the river, firing minute guns, awoke afrefh our solemn sorrow—the corpse was moved—a band of mufick with mournful melody melted the soul into all the tenderness of woe.

The proceffion was formed & moved on the following order:

CAVALRY

INFANTRY
(With arms reversed)

GUARD

MUSIC

CLERGY

The General's horse with his saddle, holsters, and pistols.

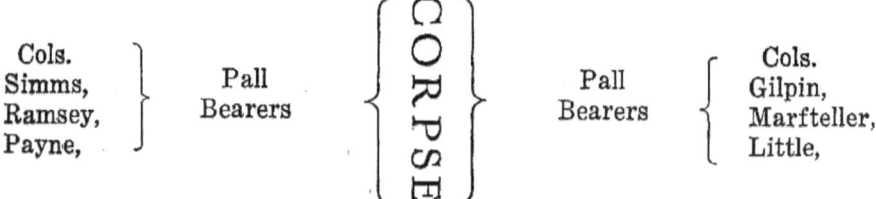

| Cols. Simms, Ramsey, Payne, | Pall Bearers | CORPSE | Pall Bearers | Cols. Gilpin, Marfteller, Little, |

MOURNERS
MASONIC BRETHREN
CITIZENS

When the proceffion had arrived at the bottom of the elevated lawn, on the banks of the Potomac, where the family vault is placed, the cavalry halted, the infantry marched toward the Mount and formed their lines—the Clergy, the Masonic Brothers, and the Citizens, descended to the vault, and funeral service of the Church was performed.—The firing was repeated from the veffel in the river, and the sounds echoed from the woods and hills around.

Three general discharges from the infantry—the cavalry, and 11 pieces of artillery, which lined the banks of the Potomac back of the Vault, paid the laft tribute to the entombed Commander-in-Chief of the United States and to the departed hero.

The sun was now setting. Alas! the SUN OF GLORY was set forever. No—the name of WASHINGTON—the American President and General—will triumph over DEATH! The unclouded brightness of his glory will illuminate future ages!

ON THE DEATH OF
GENERAL WASHINGTON.
(By a Young Lady)

What means that solemn dirge that strikes my ear?
What means those mournful sounds—why shines the tear?
Why toll the bells the awful knell of fate?
Ah! why those sighs that do my fancy sate!

Where'er I turn, the general gloom appears,
Those mourning badges fill my soul with fears;
Hark!—Yonder rueful noise!—'tis done!—'tis done!
The filent tomb invades our WASHINGTON.

Muft virtues so exalted yield their breath?
Muft bright perfection find relief in death?
Muft mortal greatness fall?—a glorious name?—
What then is riches, honor and true fame?

The Auguft chief, the father and the friend,
The generous patriot,—let the Muse commend;
Columbia's glory, and Mount Vernon's pride,
There lies enshrined with numbers at his side!

Weep—kindred mortals—weep—no more you'll find,
A man so just, so pure, so firm in mind;
Rejoicing Angels, hail the heavenly Sage!
Celestial Spirits greet the wonder of the AGE!

(From Ulster County Gazette).
LUTHER ANDRES & Co. have this day
Been opening goods both fresh and gay.
He has received near every kind,
That you in any Store can find,
As I purchase by the Bale,
I am determined to retail
For READY PAY a little *lower*
Than ever have been had before.

I with my brethren mean to live,
But as for credit shall not give.
I would not live to rouse your paffions,
For credit here is out of fafhion,
My friends and buyers one and all,
It will pay you well to give a call.
You may always find me at my sign,
A few rods from the house divine.

The following articles will be received in payment: Wheat, Rye, Buckwheat, Oats, Corn, Butter, Flax, Afhes and Rawhides. The articles will be taken in at Esopus prices, CASH will not be refused.
Warwick, Dec. 24, 1799.

FOR SALE—The one-half of a saw mill, with a convenient place for building, lying in the town of Rochester. By the mill is an inexhaustible quantity of PINEWOOD.—And also, A Stout, Healthy, Active NEGRO WENCH. Any person inclined to purchase, may know the particulars by applying to JOHN SCHOONMAKER, Jun. at Rochester.
November 23, 1799.

Second Notice, of my wife HANNA H, is hereby given, forbidding all persons whatever, from harboring or keeping her, and from trusting her on my account, as I am determined to pay no debts of her contracting.
MATYS VAN STEENBERG.
Nov. 18, 1799.

Chapter Thirty-nine

OLD HISTORY BY: FRANK COPELAND: T. B. SIMMONS—OLD DOCUMENTS—LAFAYETTE'S EARLY HISTORY—LEGAL EXECUTIONS—LONGEVITY—GOLDEN WEDDINGS—ANTEBELLUM HOUSES—HEIRLOOMS—SENTENCES—LARGE FAMILIES.

SOME ANCIENT COUNTY HISTORY
As Told by Frank W. Copeland.

IN 1826 an Indian named Swayback murdered his wife at the breakfast table. He was tried at ten o'clock A.M. the same day by the medicine men and chief; found guilty and sentenced to death at 12 noon, or two hours after his trial, and was executed promptly. A wagon was drawn under a limb containing a barrel on which stood Swayback with a rope around his neck. When the end of the rope was securely tied to the limb the wagon was moved from underneath and the fall broke his neck. This occurred at Crayfish (Crawfish) Spring, now Chickamauga. A few minutes before Swayback went to his death he asked to be allowed to go to the spring near by and take one more drink of water before dying. His request was granted; and true to the Indian's stoic nature he went unattended and returned and met his death without showing the least fear.

This story was related to me by Mrs. Hixon, forty-two years ago, on Lookout mountain. She said she was thirteen years old at the time. She also stated that she went to school with the Indian children at the old mission school (Brainerd). Mrs. Hixon, I think, was the mother of William P. Hixon of Lookout mountain who was present when she related these and many other Indian stories to me.

Two Indians were hanged at Crayfish Spring about 1833-34. They had murdered two white men whom they found asleep in the entry of their house and killed them while asleep. Judge Hooper presided at the trial and (as I remember) a lawyer by name of Hansel was solicitor-general. The murderers were brought from jail at Canton, Georgia, by the militia. I have seen the framework of the gallows used on this occasion at the foot of the hill near the home of the late Hon. Gordon Lee.

Jonathan McWilliams, father of Mrs. Spencer Bomar, Mrs. Hugh McClure and Mrs. William Burgess, migrated from Ireland early in the 19th century. One of his three daughters was born in Ireland, one on the Atlantic ocean and one in America. All these came to West Armuchee valley about 1841.

The first permanent white settler in West Armuchee was a Mr. Vick. He lived at Greenbush. For a number of years Greenbush post office bore the name Vicksburg. This was told to me by Mr. George W. Clements fifty years ago. He said that he and an Indian neighbor were deer hunting in West Armuchee valley and took dinner with Mr. Vick. G. W. Clements was treasurer of Walker county for a great many years. The Indian word Armuchee in English is said to mean "much gold."

Not one of the following early settlers of West Armuchee, or their descendants, now resides in the valley: Prior Keeling; Robert Patterson; Hugh McClure; William Burgess; Thomas Manning; William Little; Jackson; Story; Lyles; Bennett; Chapman Baker; Mosteller; Cargall; Samuel Saxon; Alex Copeland; Dr. Bailey; Gore; Evans; Esterling; Foster; Kilpatrick; Keclin.

Young men killed in battle from West Armuchee: Lieut. James McWilliams; Calvin McWilliams; Bud Esterling; Ed Esterling; Pink Chapman; James Kilpatrick; Benj. Chapman; Lieut. Robert Little; _____ Bennett; _____ Lawrence; Edward Glazner; _____ Oliver.

Col. F. H. Little of West Armuchee was commissioned Brigadier-General a few days before Lee's surrender.

As late as eighty years ago Indian arrow heads could be seen in trees where Indian hunters had shot at turkeys, deer and other wild game.

BRIEF HISTORY OF MCLEMORE'S COVE, AND SOME OF THE MEN WHO MADE IT.

By T. B. Simmons.

McLemore's was a rich section with both limestone and freestone land

—the limestone predominating, and was covered by as fine forest of white oak, red oak, popular and pine as could be found in Georgia at the time of its settlement. It was just such a place as suited strong, able, brave, fearless men; and in the beginning that was the class of men that settled the Cove. McLemore's Cove was honored by two soldiers of the War of 1812, who selected it as their home, Robert A. Anderson and George W. Reid, both of whose bones rest in its soil.

While the Cove was yet in its virgin state a noted lawyer from Athens, Georgia, William Dougherty, bought most of the valley land from the head of the Cove to Cedar Grove—all in fact except the lot owned by Jefferson Coulter, pioneer. This he later sold to settlers coming into the Cove, reserving to himself the extensive farm in the head of the Cove, since known as the Dougherty place. The early settlers were mainly of the Methodist and Baptist persuasion, and since that time each of these churches has maintained strong organizations.

But the men who probably did most for the Cove came in immediately before, and soon after the War of the Rebellion. These came from Virginia, the Carolinas, Tennessee, other Georgia counties as well as from other parts of Walker county. Few of these early settlers had any worldly possessions when they arrived; but were men of iron will and nerve; men of character with a will to work and build for the future. They were men who stood for the things that build up a country—roads, churches, schools, masonry and a noble manhood and womanhood. Arriving here they began to strengthen the churches, establish better schools, organize masonic lodges and help to bring a superior civilization in the Cove.

These men were Captain John Y. Wood, W. B. Gray, Dr. Wm. B. Simmons, J. F. Smith, Hyram Smith, E. White, W. P. Frazier, Tom Rowland, Dr. G. W. Cochran. A. Andrews and many others. All honor to these pioneer citizens! They have builded well. A man who deserves to be spoken of highly was E. White. When he married he could neither read nor write. His wife taught him both and he became a power for good in the community. He was a great churchman and one of the brightest masons in the county. Mr. White was a poor man—probably worth less than $500.00; but he told Antioch Baptist church if they would build a brick church he would furnish the brick, and he did it. He made them. But there were other men who labored and sacrificed for the new church—Frank Bell and his father, Johnathan Bell, brick masons, were valuable in erecting the academy and church. Frank, the son and upright citizen, and the father, Johnathan, a Baptist minister. G. W. Harp, Wm. Denton, E. G. Francis were all high-toned Christian gentlemen, always standing four-square for the right. We honor their memory.

MUSTER ROLL OF CAPTAIN AYCOCK'S COMPANY OF CAVALRY OF WALKER COUNTY, GA.

Captain, R. M. Aycock; 1st Lieut., Samuel Hoge; 2nd Lieut., S.

Marsh; Ord-Sergt., S. N. Barns.

Privates: Thompson Allman; Bird Anderson (served two days); William Cupp; John C. Johnson; William Hamilton; George Hartland (served but one day); James Kirkes; Joseph N. Live; Joseph H. Rogers.

Subsistence and forage furnished by each man two days at $1.50 per day, entire amount $37.50. One pound of powder at 37 cents; 13 pounds of shot at 18¾c, $2.62½ (?), $3.37½.

The foregoing list represents the statement of a small company of cavalry raised by voluntary enlistment at Walker C.H., Geo., from the circumstance of the Creek Indians reported to be passing into the county, and the danger apprehended therefrom to the citizens during the difficulties with that tribe the past year.

After scouring the county two days the company returned, dispersed and retired to their homes, having for the time quieted the fears of the inhabitants. These men were not mustered into the service of the U. S., neither were they paid by the U. S. for the time mentioned.

The nature of the expedition made it necessary that each man furnish himself with subsistence and forage, which they did from their homes or paid for it at public houses (the latter, I believe, was the case).

Myself and the two lieutenants were called to command by the voice of the company—the orderly sergeant was appointed by myself.

All of which is respectfully submitted.

* * * * *

County of Walker, State of Georgia: I hereby certify on honor that the above muster roll of volunteer cavalry of this state commanded by myself in the county of Walker during the year 1836 exhibits the true state of said company for the period therein mentioned; that the remarks opposite the names of each officer and soldier are accurate and just.

Given under my hand this 7 day of Feby. 1837.

R. M. Aycock.

Copies of some old war-time letters on file in the office of Secretary of State, Atlanta:

LaFayette, Ga., Walker County, May 27, 1861.

Major-General H. C. Wayne,
    Milledgeville, Ga.

Sir: We have a cavalry company made up and organized and we wish to know on what terms we can get arms and, on what terms we can be received and for what time we would have to serve. We will be glad to hear from you as soon as possible. Address us at Frick's Gap, Geo.

Yours truly,   E. L. Cooper, Capt.
F. J. Fricks, Sec.

Cedar Grove, Walker County, Geo. May 24, 1862.
To His Excellency, Joseph E. Brown, Governor.

Sir: In response to your proclamation of the 8th inst., I report myself captain of the 971st District G.M. of Walker County, Georgia, bearing commission under your hand of May 11, 1861.

I have in my company 75 rifles; 4 muskets; 32 shot guns and 20 pistols. My address is Cedar Grove postoffice, Walker county, Geo.

Respectfully, your obedient servant,

James W. Head, Capt. 971st Dist. G.M.

The following subpoena is in possession of J. B. F. Jones. It was issued to his father and seems to be an echo from the attempt to build a railroad in this county during the fifties. The actual construction of the road was begun and later abandoned. Some of the embankments of this construction are still pointed out near the location of the Union Cotton Mills at LaFayette:

State of Georgia, Walker County:

Coosa & R. R. R. Co., Vs Complaint, Constantine Wood.

To James B. Jones—Greeting:

You are hereby commanded that laying all other business aside, you personally be and appear at a Superior Court to be held in the County of Walker on the fourth Monday in August 1860, then and there to testify and the truth say on the part and behalf of the defendant. Herein fail not on pain of Three Hundred Dollars.

Witness the Honorable James A. Walker, Judge of said Superior Court, this 21, day of August, in year etc. 1860.

Francis I. Grogan, C.S.C.

Endorsement:

Ga. Walker Co. Personally came before me the undersigned, J. B. Jones, the witness in said writ mentioned, who, being sworn, says that he attended court four days in obedience to this subpoena. Sworn to and subscribed before me, March 1, 1861.   J. B. Jones.

John M. Catlett, J.P.

A REVOLUTIONARY BILL. Mrs. Myers, relict of the late W. W. S. Myers of fragrant memory, is the proud possessor of two revolutionary bills described as follows:

Obverse side.

This Bill entitles the Bearer to receive Fifty Spanish milled DOLLARS, or the value thereof in GOLD or SILVER, according to Resolution passed by CONGRESS at Philadelphia, September 26th, 1778.

50 DOLLARS   SNODEN N. Donnel

Reverse side.

Three flying arrows crossing each other in a field of gray, with the words: "FIFTY DOLLARS," Printed by Hall and Sellers.

Confederate Bond issued to J. B. Jones, father of J. B. F. Jones:
Confederate States of America, Depositary Office.

Center, Ala., Mch. 22, 1864.

This will certify that J. B. Jones has paid in at this office One Thousand Eight Hundred ($1800) Dollars, for which amount, Registered Bonds, of the Confederate States of America, bearing interest from this date, at the rate of four percent, per annum, will be issued to him, under the "act to reduce the currency and to authorize a new issue of notes and bonds," approved February 17, 1864, upon the surrender of this certificate at this office.

J. C. Cunningham, Depositary.

LaFayette's Early History.

By an act of the Legislature of 1835 the town of Chattooga was made the county seat and the following were named as commissioners: John Caldwell, Daniel Gartman, Lawson Black, Haley S. Tatum, John Allen. This same Legislature appropriated $800 for building an academy for the county. According to old citizens the name Chattooga was soon superceded by that of Benton, and soon afterward it adopted its present name —LaFayette. Some old documents, still extant, dated in the latter thirties, are headed, "Walker C.H."

This writer, when a boy, once heard an old citizen say that the location of the town was due to an Indian ball-play location at that place before the county was organized—probably soon after the Revolution. The first court was held at Crawfish Spring in an old Indian Court-House, pending the election of one at the county seat, which was built of hewn logs and served for some years till a more commodious building could be established—probably in the forties.

LaFayette was a modest, but aristocratic village for half a century after its establishment. The population was small, probably from 300 to 500 during these years, but it was composed of families of culture, education and refinement. A splendid school was maintained for the education of the young which was patronized by the surrounding country. A few lawyers, doctors, merchants and numerous artizans formed the nucleus of the town which was surrounded by many well-to-do farmers, many of whom had slaves to do the work of the farm.

The building of the Chattanooga, Rome and Carrollton railroad about 1888 gave the little town its first vision of prosperity. This was followed two years later by the establishment of the first big enterprise, the Union Cotton Mills. Mr. A. R. Steele was the genius who engineered this by raising a subscription of $100,000 for the purpose. Later this was doubled and thus added materially to the prosperity of the town.

The following data concerning the Walker County Hosiery Mills will be of increasing interest as the years pass: Organized in 1906. Capital stock, $100,000. Manufactures mens' cotton hosiery. Officers: W. A.

Enloe, Pres., J. M. Patton, V. Pres., W. B. Shaw, Secy., A. S. Fortune, Treas. The company started with 80 machines which has been increased to 400 now in operation. The daily output of men's cotton hosiery is the largest of any similar plant in the country, being 2,400 dozen pairs, and uses 750,000 pounds of carded yarns annually. The annual payroll is approximately $200,000.00. Number of employees 300.

BRIEF HISTORY OF RICHMOND HOSIERY MILLS.

In 1898 the Chattanooga Knitting Mills decided to remove to Rossville, Georgia, and enlarge their plant. The name was changed to Richmond Hosiery Mills, and was chartered at $75,000. The business now has a capital of $1,000,000 common stock, and the same amount preferred stock. The plant covers a city block at Rossville, including a spinning mill of 6,000 spindles, dye house, knitting, boarding, finishing and shipping departments, together with main office. Number of knitting machines, 1,500; full-fashioned machines, 30; number of employees in normal times, about 2,000; value of raw silk consumed per annum, about $1,000,000.00, and approximately the same amount of rayon; wool yarn, about $100,000.00; number bales of cotton about 5,000. The annual payroll reaches beyond $1,000,000.00. Manufactures knit goods and hosiery which is shipped to every part of the world.

Maintains a mill hospital with trained nurse in charge; gives assistance to community service, churches, educational and charitable institutions; maintains a school of its own for half-time pupils.

President, Garnett Andrews; V-Pres., Alex W. Chambliss; Treas., J. Harvey Wilson.

LEGAL EXECUTIONS IN WALKER COUNTY.

The first legal execution in the county is said to have been that of a man by the name of Hog Smith who was executed at Crawfish Spring for killing an Indian. This was while the sessions of the Superior Court were held at that place, and was probably in the early thirties. This was told the author by the late W. C. Bailey and other old citizens who heard it from older citizens of the county.

Pocket-Book and Cush, Indians, robbed and killed a man and his wife by the name of Burk on the Napier old place, near Harrisburg, many years before the war. They were tried and sentenced to be hanged and were executed at LaFayette. The field where the victims were buried is still known as the Burk field.

William Mitchel, a white man, was hanged by Abner Mize, sheriff, for slaying John Cole near Pond Spring, about 1859. Two negroes named Cunningham and Barks were hanged by Sheriff McClatchey in 1883 for killing an old man by the name of Rudd near Mission Ridge.

A negro named Roscoe Marible was hanged by Sheriff Foster for slaying Mira Evitt near the tunnel on Pigeon mountain about 1895. George Baker was hanged by Sheriff Harmon for killing Deputy Sheriff Joe Morton in 1924 on Lookout mountain.

EXAMPLES OF EXTREME LONGEVITY.

Probably no county in the state can show a greater percentage of its citizens living to the ripe old age of 80 years and over than our county. These examples of longevity have been gathered, many of them at least, by first hand as I have talked to the older people. Some have been taken from old Bible records and some from markers in cemeteries. Many of these are still living, but the greater number have "Crossed the Bar."

LAFAYETTE. Mrs. M. A. Borders 86; Mrs. M. E. Bidding 91; T. P. Norman 91; W. P. Jackson 85; George Patterson 88; Joe Phipps 88; J. D. McConnell 81; J. T. Ashworth and wife, each 83; W. H. Neeley 80; E. L. Culberson 92; Miss Orpha Center 90; A. J. Caldwell 87; Rebecca Goree 88; Clarentine Kelly Johnson 82; Susan Johnson 81; Rev. Joe Wardlaw 83; R. H. Johnson 81; B. F. Loughridge 85, his wife 84; Alexander Stoker 80; G. S. Martin 80; Joshua Martin 88; Mary Marsh Allgood 94; Addie Marsh Warthen 90; Edwin W. Marsh 89; Jacob Srite 81; Mrs. Hugh B. Johnson 83; Richard Baker 80; J. E. Thompson 80; Wm. Fariss 85; Capt. J. C. Wardlaw 89; Mary A. Allgood 93; Alice Allgood 86; Ruth Terrell Marsh 82; R. R. Turner Senr. 88; Rev. W. T. Russell 81; Andrew Lawson 87; James Park 81; C. C. Bryan 83; James Andrew Park 84; J. F. Shaw 79; Nannie Foster 82; Dr. J. W. Nash 82; Capt. J. M. Jackson 79; Betty Ezell 87; R. A. Watson 78; J. W. Harmon 80; Dr. S. A. McArthur 81; Mrs. Laura G. Snow 80; T. P. Henry 83; Martha J. Phillips 87; Parks Mashburn 80; J. H. Reed 82.

CHICKAMAUGA. Sarah Roberts McWhorter 81; Andy Osborn 83; Joe Weathers 83; J. R. Horton 81, his wife 81; Z. C. Conger 84; John Bradley 86; George Hixon 84; John J. Moore 90; L. W. Myers 83; Polly Myers 84; Hartwell Weathers 93; Mary E. Mullis 87; Reuben Couch 87; "Granny" Parcilla(?) Osborn 93; Victoria Thedford 81; W. A. Horton 84; James Lewis 80; Mary E. Osborn 85; Mrs. Susie Jane Osborn 80; Temperance McWhorter 85; Charles Moore 93; John Lecroy 82; W. D. West 84, his wife 82; W. M. Ireland 81; T. M. Ireland 80; Sallie Hall Blaylock 80; Samuel Hall 81; Etha Moore 87; Daniel Prince 85; Mary Harris 82; L. F. Coker 82; Rachel Schmitt 85; H. M. Thompson 83; Susan Glass 84; Eliza Nations 84.

POND SPRING. W. C. Bailey 84; Elizabeth Bailey Owings 81; J. N. Wilson 85; Martha Hollingsworth 96; J. M. Madaris 83; Susan Cameron 83; Caroline Smith 92; Nancy Pilgrim 83; Joe Floyd 88; W. H. H. Simmons 84; Nancy Parker 84; Elvira Roark 81; Joe Henry 87; Duncan Bryan 82; F. T. Ellison 82, his wife 92; John Parish 80.

EAST ARMUCHEE. Lucy Puryear 88; Sarah Tate 86; R. M. Pitman 84; John A. Tate 80, his wife 84; J. A. Shahan 83, his wife 83; Miss

Fannie Price 88; Wash Kinsey 89; Jesse Kinsey 85; John Puryear 86; Mrs. J. N. Myers 80; Dr. Wilson Clements 90; George Heffner 86; Joseph Travillian 82; Tuma Tarvin 86; Jane Jones 86; Priestly G. White 80; J. E. White 82; Newton White 91; Nannie E. Clements 79; Elizabeth Keith 79; W. P. Tate 87; Sallie M. Tate 86; Nathan Keown 80; Ellen Travillian 80; Thomas Griffin 80, his wife 80; B. F. Elsberry 90; W. E. Elsberry 82; James Boastwick 90.

WEST ARMUCHEE. J. T. Suttle 82; Susan Bomar McWilliams 85; Mrs. Mary A. Lawrence 86; Mrs. Elizabeth Lawrence 82; B. J. Huggins 86; Jane Bomar 82; S. E. McWilliams 84; John Liles 79; Margaret McClure 84; Artemus Shattuck 81; William Little 81; Capt. William McWilliams 81, his wife, Nancy Neal, 88; Thomas Manning 87; A. H. Neal 79; W. M. Potts 85, his wife 82; Rebecca Moore 86; J. F. Evans 81; J. H. Chapman 83; Elizabeth Hewatt 83; Jane McKnight 79; Mrs. W. J. Chapman 80; J. C. McWilliams 79; Frank McWilliams 87.

CHATTANOOGA residents from Walker county. Mrs. B. M. Garrett 84; John C. Abercrombie 81; Temperance Kirkes 98.

LISBON. I. B. Kendrick 80.

LOOKOUT MOUNTAIN. Catherine Massey 89; Nerve Drennon 91; Terrell Brown 83; Melvina Ellison 84; Susan Elvira Strickland 80; Frances Hixon 82; Sallie M. Prothro 81; Nathan T. Massey 90.

WILSON. Sarah Wall 83; Jane Mitchel 83; B. L. Richardson 79; Jeremiah G. Blackwell 81; J. G. Lumpkin 86; Henry Wilson Boss 80; John A. Woods 82; Wilburn Wall 79; Lecil Day 86; R. H. Mahan 89; F. B. McWhorter 80; Rev. John Boyles 87; Theron Crowder 89; John P. Long 90; Sarah Adeline Long 88; John Stoker 83; Sarah Chapman 86; Mrs. Ann Harper 81.

CHATTANOOGA VALLEY. T. H. Fowler 84; Miss Mary Ellis 82; H. G. Mallicoat 93; A. M. Martin 88, his wife 82, sons, E. C. and W. R., 80 and 77 respectively.

The following have been reported as having lived more than a century: Dr. Anderson 101; James Coulter 106; John Heffner 114.

KENSINGTON. Wm. Voiles 83; W. H. Martin 80; Ary Stephens 85; Emeline Shepherd 81; Billy Free 82; Washington Ransom 84, his wife 84; Mrs. Margaret L. Agnew 96; S. B. Phillips 88; Henry Bowers 88; R. L. Wallin 80, his wife 88; Mrs. James Parks Hall 84; Robert Johnson 79, his wife 87; Martha Wallin 88; R. H. Ellis 81; Ples Clark 79.

CEDAR GROVE. Mrs. G. W. Harp 95; Kitty Simmons 87; Wm. Taylor 92; Margaret Srite Morgan 80; J. F. Smith 90, his wife 85; C. C. Ransom 85; Tom Hensley 92; H. M. C. Johnson 82; Elender Rawlings 80; Sally Catlett 89; George W. Reed 81; Elexanna Evitt 83; Martha Bemberton 84; Capt. J. Y. Wood 85, his wife 83; Alexander Andrews 82; Wesley Hobbs 85; W. M. Hunter 86; Ellen Hunter 86; W. C. Millican 86; Mrs. E. E. Bell 81; Henry Hise 82; Catherine Forester 79.

ROCK SPRING. Peter Jones 90; Nancy Middleton Jones 83; Harriet

Brigman 84; Catherine Tyner 85; George Brigman 80; J. R. Tyner 81; Elizabeth Brigman 80; J. W. McClure 84; Reese Jones 81; James Weaver 80; W. A. Weaver 79; Ansel Massey 79; Moses Jackson 84; Rebecca Jackson 93; Elizabeth Lawrence 82; L. A. Conley 85; Celia Shields 85; Thomas S. Tapp 82; B. L. Chastain 81; William Conley 88; S. T. Brice 82; James M. Wellborn 87; W. T. S. Adams 84; F. A. Thedford 80.

CHESTNUT FLAT. Edom G. W. Moon 93; Mary Jones 91; Revis Jones 80; Mary Lowery 86; Marry Ann Moon 80; T. B. Cooper 86; W. J. Arnold 81; Alexander Arnold 91, his wife 87.

CANE CREEK. Nancy Alexander 86; Marilla Lowery Myers 87; Mrs. Fletcher 85; W. M. Ramey 87; J. A. McConkey 80.

ROSSVILLE. Joseph Au 81; Ersula Au 81; Angeline Brown 82; Wiley Wall 81; R. B. Stegall 89; John Hawkins 80, his wife 80; Alex. Martin 85, hise wife 88; T. H. Fowler 83; Nancy Pearce 80; Xanders G. McFarland 85; T. G. McFarland 84; Sallie McFarland Thompson 81; John Buie McFarland 81; Martha Pearce 80; John McClain 88; John B. Henderson 89; Nancy Clayton 88; J. P. Hixon 84; Mrs. "Granny" Miller 89; C. E. Cooper 77.

GOLDEN WEDDINGS.

The following have been reported as having celebrated the fiftieth anniversary of their weddings. No doubt there are many others in the county who might have been thus recorded. For the sake of brevity only the names of the husbands are given.

In eastern part of county: R. M. Pitman, E. F. Boman, J. A. Shahan, Cape White, Thomas White, J. M. Roper, W. M. Bowen, John A. Tate, Dan Kinsey, Alex Copeland, E. R. Hamilton, George Heffner, A. H. Cooper, Andrew Cooper, John Cook, T. A. Cooper, Frank McWilliams, Gus White, Newton KiKnsey, John Hall, Alex Arnold, W. W. Kinsey.

In central and southern part: G. S. Martin, R. A. Watson, J. T. Ashworth (66 yrs.), J. T. Renfro, Andrew Hicks, James R. Jones, B. F. Loughridge (62 yrs.), Wm. Glass, Calvin Wheeler, George Brigman, Johnny Jones, A. J. Caldwell, Jacob Srite, John Miller (60 yrs.), A. E. Rogers, G. W. Brown, John Ware, J. W. McClure, W. M. Ramey, John Higgins, Maj. James M. Shields, Joel K. Landers.

In western part: J. Y. Wood, Noah Meridith (60 yrs.), J. M. Ransom, J. R. Hunter, Alex. Hunter, R. J. Glenn, M. M. Whitlow, J. A. Ridley, Wash Harp, James Kirkes, Wm. Linzie Connally, W. H. Singleterry, John Edwards, Harvey Rogers, Dr. Jim Lee, Dr. Thornberg, S. B. Phillips, C. W. Smith, H. M. C. Johnson, James A. Coulter.

In northern part: J. A. R. Walker, J. C. Campbell, Hartwell Weathers, Ed. Howard, J. H. Weathers, Hiram Mallicoat, L. C. Davis, Joseph Au, B. M. Garrett, J. R. Horton, T. J. Parish, Charles Moore, B. F. Morgan, S. B. Dyer, John Bonds, W. M. Ireland, Samuel Hall, T. H. Fowler, John C. Abercrombie, F. T. Ellison, W. W. Ireland, J. H. Carlock.

ANTEBELLUM HOUSES. One mile south of Chickamauga is the old Couch house built in 1840 by John Couch, now owned by Peter Lewis. It has an interesting history. It was a haven of refuge for many women and children as well as wounded soldiers during and following the Chickamauga battle. It is said that "Uncle Dick" Glenn carried his sick "missus" wrapped in a blanket to this house during the battle. It is of log construction containing two rooms about 20 feet square with a hallway between.

Other antebellum houses are the following: On the Park—Kelly, Dyer, Snodgrass, Viniard, Poe, Brotherton and McDonald houses; in Cove—Lane, Sam Smith, Burl Hall, Floyd Stephens, John Phillips, and Las Strickland houses; LaFayette—Cooper, Fortune, Dr. Shields, Dickerson, Culberson, Borders, Cromer, Warthen, Roland, Street, Enloe, Neeley, Spencer, Rea houses; East Armuchee—John Cavender, Pope, Keith, Goodson, Shahan, Newton White, Dr. Clements houses; West Armuchee—Capt. McWilliams, William McWilliams, Frank McWilliams, Robertson, McClure, Suttle, Neal, Copeland, Easterling, Blackwell (2 rooms), log house on the Story place, and others. The dining room and kitchen of John R. Tyner, in rear of his home, was built probably in the thirties—certainly in the early forties. It is of hewn logs and is one of the most substantial log houses in the county.

HEIRLOOMS. Miss Mary Jones, granddaughter of James R. Jones, who lives in Wood Station valley, has a much-prized heirloom in the old "secretary" in which her ancestor kept the postoffice at Rock Spring during the forties. Also, an old ledger.—Mrs. J. F. Stanfield has a teaspoon carried through the war by her father, engraved as follows: "J. A. Eaton, Co. C, 23 Regt., Ga. Vol."—Mrs. Lucy Hammond has a platter handed down by her forbears said to have come over in the Mayflower.—Mr. Pelly Blackwell has three old ledgers used by his ancestors in keeping accounts, dating back to 1845.—J. B. F. Jones has a razor once used by his great-grandfather, who died in 1832, also a quill pen used by his father before the war, still serviceable.—Miss Nannie Jones (died 1931) has a beautiful pitcher on which is the likeness of General Lafayette, inscribed thus: "Welcome, Lafayette, the Nation's Guest, and the Country's Glory." It has been in the family more than a century.—'Squire J. C. Myers of Chickamauga has fifty cents in paper money, greenback, given to him by a veteran of the Union Army, an old soldier who was visiting the Park in 1892, for which he has refused $75 by collectors.

HISTORICAL ITEMS IN SINGLE SENTENCES. The city of Nashville, Tennessee, was named for the father of the late Thomas M. Nash, of LaFayette, who came from that state, near Nashville, many years ago.—Mr. James A. Coulter of McLemore's Cove has planted and propagated the Georgia rattlesnake watermelon continuously for more than fifty years. —H. B. Colquit built the old Gordon mill, afterward called the Lee and Gordon mill.—Crawfish Spring was called by the Indians, "Spring of Dead-Man's-Land," because of so many Indians dying at that place of

HISTORY OF WALKER COUNTY, GEORGIA 317

typhoid fever.—A man by name of Andrew Kline built Shiloh church about 1850.—Dr. Clendennon once had an office at the southeast corner of the square. He died in Texas during the seventies. He was the maternal ancestor of the Wardlaws.—Noah Meridith was the first mail carrier from Cedar Grove to Chattanooga.—J. V. Little, oldest of 13 children, is said to have been the first white child born in West Armuchee valley.—The county's tax returns for the year 1874 was $1921100.—It is claimed that B. F. Hunt, Sr., was one of the first, if not the very first Confederate soldier to fall in the Chickamauga battle, being killed on Saturday morning, the first day of the battle by Yankee sharpshooters. He was carried to his old home in Armuchee and buried after the battle. He was the father of the two well-known and much beloved Baptist ministers, Revs. B. F. and J. G. Hunt.—It is said that General Bragg planned the battle of Chickamauga while under the old oak tree, afterwards called the Bragg Oak, which stood till a few years ago in front of the John B. Gordon Hall. It was killed by lightning.—Miss Jamie McCullough of West Armuchee has three old letters, heirlooms in the Suttle family, received from relatives in Virginia and North Carolina, dated 1824, 1826, and 1831, showing cost of postage, which was 25c, 25c and 10c respectively.—A small pocket Testament such as was carried by the soldiers of the sixties shows that it was struck by a Minnie ball and perforated two-thirds of the leaves. Tearing them out and glancing upward it was deflected and doubtless saved the life of the owner. This is in possession of Mr. A. A. Gentry whose mother's first husband was carrying it in his knapsack when shot. It is inscribed thus: "Shot in my knapsack on the 27th of Nov. 1863. W. H. Dillahunty."—Robert Dickerson carried the mail from LaFayette to Calhoun before the war.—Prof. Charles M. Conley in a letter to the author says: "My great-grandfather was in the war of the Revolution, my grandfather in the war of 1812, my father in the Seminole Indian war and the Civil war, also three brothers and three brothers-in-law in the Civil War and I had one son in the World war"—a record hard to beat.

LARGE FAMILIES. What would be a reasonable estimate of the cost of rearing a family of say ten children to maturity? How much actual expense would it incur? What would be the outlay for clothes, food, medicines, doctor bills, books, schooling, recreation, travel and various other necessary expenses? The cost necessarily will vary according to the income of the family and their station in life. Taking the average farmer of the county as a median what may be expected to be spent on a child till he is 18 years of age? This writer used to hear the opinion expressed, when living was much lower than at present, that $1,000.00 would be a low estimate for each child. $10,000.00 for ten children! But in recent years when the cost of living has been so high, this estimate is certainly far too low.

This does not take into account the multitude of little attentions necessary for every child and which is freely given by the mother and other members of the family—the vigils at the sick bed, the careful attentions while baby is young or convalescing, the clothes-making, the cooking, the washing, mending and ironing and such like attentions for which no money outlay is seen, but which if performed by a hired servant would amount to a large sum for each child.

What have parents done, therefore, who have reared a large family to maturity? Certainly they have performed no insignificant work. The outlay in money has been considerable, the expense in work and anxiety has been more. Those parents, therefore, who have reared, cared for and educated a large family have performed no small task. This writer has been interested in making a record of large families in the county. The following is some indication of the results:

James R. Jones, 11 children, 10 boys, 1 girl. All lived to have families. R. M. Pitman, 12 children, 5 boys, 7 girls. All living but one (1932). H. A. (Tip) Blaylock, 10 children, 8 boys, 2 girls, all lived to be grown. S. B. Dyer, 15 children, 4 boys, 11 girls, 11 of these raised families of their own. R. B. Stegall, 17 children, 6 boys and 6 girls still living (1932). L. C. Davis, 10 children, 2 boys, 10 girls, all to maturity. Dr. M. M. Crowder, 10 children, 6 boys, 4 girls. All grown and living. Charles McClure, 6 boys, 4 girls. L. A. Conley, 6 boys, 6 girls. D. B. Baker, who settled in the county in 1855 near Cedar Grove, was the father of 14 children, all lived to a ripe old age, one of these was Macajah Baker at one time tax collector of the county. Another, George Baker, reared 9 children to maturity. A. E. Rogers, 6 boys, 6 girls. J. J. Davis, 9 boys, 3 girls. George Glenn, 8 boys, 4 girls. Thomas N. Jones, 7 boys, 5 girls. Robert Patterson, 7 boys, 3 girls. Reese Jones, 5 boys, 7 girls. John B. Suttle, 1 boy, 8 girls. Orran W. Jones, 4 boys, 5 girls. William Little, 9 boys, 5 girls—13 to maturity. Abraham Neal, 8 boys, 2 girls.

Webster Lawrence, 7 boys, 5 girls. (Some years ago, Mr. Lawrence was given a prize of a bolt of cloth at the county fair for having present the largest family—14). J. M. Goodson, 7 boys, 5 girls. Arch Reed, 7 boys, 2 girls. W. A. Weaver, 8 boys, 5 girls—10 living. George Hixon, 4 boys, 7 girls. Rev. James Drinnon, 5 boys, 7 girls. 10 lived to raise families—wife lived to be 92 years old. Mr. Allgood, Chattanooga Valley, 7 boys, 6 girls. J. M. Clarkson, 8 boys, 2 girls. John Mahan, 7 boys, 3 girls. Andrew Cooper, 9 boys, 3 girls. Amos Welborn, married twice, 12 children by each marriage. George Hise, 5 boys, 4 girls. Nathan Hise, 4 boys, 7 girls. Billy Hise, 9 boys, 2 girls. J. M. Henry, 6 boys, 3 girls. Jacob R. Brooks, 8 boys, 2 girls. Hiram Malicoat, 6 boys, 4 girls. James Kirkes, 4 boys, 5 girls. James Voiles, 10 boys. H. G. Fuller, 8 boys, 3 girls. William Brooks, married twice, 15 children. Anthony Voils, 7 boys, 5 girls. Rev. L. H. Stephens, 8 boys, 4 girls. Dr. J. C. Lee, 5 boys, 8 girls. William Andrews, 14 children, all sat down around table when grown. Henry Steverson, 9 boys grown and married. W. M. Pettigrew, 10 boys, 2 girls. J. N. Steverson, 2 boys, 7 girls. Thomas

Cooper, 7 boys, 2 girls. P. B. Steverson, 4 boys, 6 girls. W. S. Parker, 2 boys, 7 girls. P. W. Stanfield, 4 boys, 7 girls. R. A. Jennings, 4 boys, 4 girls. Andy Ford, 8 boys, 2 girls. Jacob Goodson, 6 boys, 6 girls. J. C. Campbell, 5 boys, 5 girls. T. J. Parish, 3 boys, 7 girls. M. M. Whitlow, 2 boys, 8 girls, all to maturity and living. James Young, 6 boys, 6 girls. J. A. R. Walker, 12 children, 9 to maturity, 5 boys, 4 girls. Parks Mashburn, 8 boys, 1 girl. A. M. Martin, pioneer, 14 children, 10 to maturity—two sons, E. C. and W. R., now living at Rossville. Lewis Watkins, 9 boys, 2 girls. Fred Stansell, 6 boys, 4 girls. P. H. Goodson, 6 boys, 4 girls. W. A. Vanhorn, 7 boys, 5 girls; 11 to maturity. W. A. Chambers, 8 boys, 3 girls.

Chapter Forty

"BILL ARP'S" HUMOR—WALKER COUNTY MESSENGER—ROSSVILLE NEW AGE—ROSSVILLE OPEN GATE—MEDICAL PROFESSION —LEGAL PROFESSION.

BECAUSE of its local history as well as the quaint humor involved, the following bit of State history is, by permission, taken from "Knight's Reminiscences of Famous Georgians," vol. 1, page 477:

Mr. Knight says: Quite a dainty morsel of State history is humorously served by Major Smith (Bill Arp) in the story which he tells of how the Georgia Colonels originated. "We used to have musters all over the State," says he, "twice a year. The militia were ordered out to be reviewed by the commander-in-chief, which was the Governor. The Constitution required him to review 'em, and as he couldn't travel all around in person, he had to do it by proxy, and so he had his proxy in every county, and he was called the Governor's aide-de-camp with the rank of colonel. This gave the Governor over a hundred aides-de-camp, and they all took it as a compliment and wore cockade hats with red plumes, and epaulets, and long brass swords, and big brass spurs, and pistols in their holsters, and rode up and down the line at a gallop, reviewing the meelish. The meelish were in a double crooked straight line in a great big field, and were armed with shot guns and rifles, and muskets, and sticks, and corn stalks, and thrash-poles, and umbrellas, and they were standing up or sitting down, or on the squat, or playing mumble peg, and they hollered for water half their time, and whiskey the other; and when the colonel and his personal staff got through reviewing he halted about the middle of the line and said: 'Shoulder arms—right face—march,' and then the kettle drums rattled and the fife squeaked, and some guns went off half cocked, and the meelish shouted awhile and were disbanded by the captains of their several companies.

"These colonels held rank and title as long as the Governor held office, and they were expected to holler hurrah for the Governor on all proper occasions, and they did it. If the Governor ran again and was defeated, the next Governor appointed another set from among the faithful, and the old set had to retire from the field, but they held on to the title. For a great many years the old Whigs and Democrats had it up and down, in and out, and so new colonels were made by the score until the State was chock full again.

"They had a general muster and grand review once up at LaFayette. Bob Barry lived up there and was the mischief maker of the town. Bob never wore shoes or hat and hardly anything else in those days, and he had petted and tamed a great big long razor-backed hog, and could ride him with a rope bridle, and so as the colonel and his staff came galloping down the line with his cockades and plumes and glittering swords, Bob suddenly came out from behind a house, mounted on his razor-back hog, and a paper cap with a turkey feather in it on his head, and a pair of old tongs swinging from his suspenders, and some spurs on his barefooted heels, and he fell in just behind the cavalcade, and got the hog on a run, and scared their horses, and the whole concern ran away and the hog after 'em, and such a yell and such an uproar was never heard in those parts or anywhere else. The hog never stopped running till he got home, when Bob dismounted and took to the woods for fear of consequences. Bob is running a Sunday school now, and I'm glad of it, for it will take a good deal of missionary work in him to make up for those things the LaFayette people tell about.

"But these militia musters got to be such farces that the Legislature abolished 'em about thirty-five years ago, though they couldn't abolish the colonels. When the war broke loose most of 'em went into the army and got reduced. Many a peace colonel got to be a war major or a captain, or even a high private, and in that way their ranks were thinned. Our Governors, however, still make a few new ones as often as they are elected, and so the peace colonel is still destined to live and illustrate the good old State."

WALKER COUNTY MESSENGER.

Captain Augustus McHan of Carrollton, Georgia, soldier, educator, gentleman, and man of affairs, established the Walker County Messenger at LaFayette, in 1877. Much interesting history is associated with the first efforts to launch the infant as a member of the State Press. Mr. McHan had just passed through the great panic of 1873 in which he lost all save a determination to succeed in life, and after various discouraging efforts he succeeded in purchasing a small hand press and with his family came to LaFayette, where, with his small son, E. A., who had previously learned the printer's trade, issued the first paper on July 27, 1877. It was christened "Walker County Messenger" by its founder—a most happy appellation.

The young son, E. A., who afterward became foreman, says of the first issue: "The first issue of the Messenger, a six column, four-page paper, was issued on the 27th day of July, 1877. The paper was housed upstairs, over John Shaw's store, on the corner where the Foster House now stands (now the Pan-Am Station). How well do I remember the first paper taken from that old Washington hand press late in the afternoon of that day. The room was full of people, so full, that we actually became fearful of a cave-in of the floor. I was only a boy, 16 years old, weighing only nine-nine pounds, but as that first issue of the Messenger was spread out before that waiting crowd, I would not have exchanged places with the President of the United States."

The paper filled a long-felt want and became the official organ of the county, as well as, also, of Chattooga, Catoosa and Dade counties till papers were established in those counties. In the founder's account of those trying days, grateful reference is made to Hon. Judson C. Clements and Mr. McCutchen, who each advanced $25 to pay for necessary supplies with which to start the paper. During the first year these loans were repaid together with the initial cost of the press while the paper was also enlarged to seven columns. About this time the New York World carried a write-up in its columns that Adolph Ochs of Chattanooga, was the youngest publisher of a daily paper, and that E. A. McHan of LaFayette was the youngest publisher of a weekly paper in the South.

In 1880, Captain N. C. Napier bought the paper from the founder and became owner and publisher, but retained young McHan as foreman. Later the young foreman and George M. Napier, son of the owner, leased the paper and ran it till 1886, when the owner again assumed the editorship, in which position he continued till his death in 1902. After his death the paper was run by his estate, N. C. Napier, Jr., being editor.

In October, 1915, Mr. E. P. Hall, Jr., a Walker county boy who had recently finished his education at the University of North Carolina and had traveled extensively in Europe and Asia, purchased the paper from the Napier Estate and became the editor and publisher. Mr. Hall had previously been associated with the paper as assistant editor and contributor. He had thus shown not only his sk'll, aptitude and ability for the work, but incidentally had become aware that it was a work to his liking, and seeing an opportunity to launch out into an agreeable, if responsible, avocation, he negotiated the deal and so became sole owner.

Mr. Hall put the paper on a cash-in-advance basis which has operated so well that the paper is now on a firm financ'al standing. The young editor is an outstanding advocate of all matters for the progress of the town and county. Too, he is on the right side of all moral questions and does not fail to say so. The paper is widely read throughout the county and circulates largely in many other counties and states.

The Walker County Messenger is one of the outstanding weeklies of the state.

ROSSVILLE NEW AGE. In 1906 Mr. W. D. B. Chambers established at Rossville the "Rossville New Age," a weekly newspaper of the Democratic faith, which was continued till 1917 when the plant was destroyed by fire. The loss was so great to the owner that he was never able to obtain another printing outfit.

During its life the New Age was a staunch friend of Rossville and Walker county and contributed much toward the upbuilding of the community.

ROSSVILLE OPEN GATE. The progressive citizens of Rossville often speak of their town as the first city of the State, and this is literally true to travelers going south. It is as if the city was a gateway to the state. Taking cognizance of this happy thought the promoters of the new paper established at Rossville on April 10, 1925, named the infant, "Rossville Open Gate."

The editor is Mr. J. M. Bryan, while the business manager is Mr. C. E. Carter, and these two gentlemen are owners and publishers of the paper. It is a weekly Democratic paper.

At first it had a struggle to exist—and this is true of most young enterprises, but to-day the business is on firm ground and the investment is earning fair dividends.

Because of its situation, no community in the county has a brighter future than the city of Rossville. It takes no prophet to predict a great city at that place within the next few decades. The Open Gate, therefore, with proper business management, is likely to enjoy much prosperity as the years come on. The management is progressive and stands four-square for any and every movement that will make the town and county a bigger, better and happier place to live.

THE MEDICAL PROFESSION.

The doctor from time immemorial has been held in high esteem. Anciently, especially among primitive peoples, he was regarded with more or less reverence, and superstition, vestiges of which still adhere to him in some communities. The history of medicine dates back to the dawn of recorded history among the Egyptians. Those mysterious characters used by the doctor in his prescriptions to the druggist which resemble a bug's track after crawling through ink were used by the Egyptian apothecary and have been handed down to us from that remote age.

The pioneer practitioners of the county were not unlike those of other sections of that early time. Many of them were not graduates of medicine, probably, but were what were called botanic or "yarb" doctors. Even so, they were generally men of wide experience and good common sense and by dint of study and hard work learned much about the treatment of most of our common diseases. One of these doctors once related the following to this writer: He was hurriedly called to attend a patient who had been wounded and was bleeding severely and was feared he would bleed to death. He hurried off with the messenger without time to consult any medical authority on the subject, wondering what he should do when he arrived as he knew nothing to do. As he trotted along the narrow rough road he spied in front of him some green persimmons hanging from a tree. Without stopping he tore off a branch and when he arrived made a strong solution of the juice, which when applied to the wound was efficacious in stopping the flow of blood.

But many of these old doctors were graduates of medical colleges and as such were well up on medical treatment. The old-time doctor was no fool as shown by the following incident: The story is told that Doctor Barry, a Walker county practitioner, had a patient, a lady of wealth and refinement, who had lost her voice. After thorough, careful examination that no mistake be made, he called for a bucket of cold water. The cover was turned down and the bucket of cold water was quickly emptied on the lady from her face downward. Instantly, as soon as a deep beath could be drawn, her voice was restored to its pristine beauty and power. The author had this story from Dr. J. H. Hammond.

DR. J. H. HAMMOND

The late J. P. Hall, an eye witness, once related the following incident: A patient was suffering from a dislocated jaw bone. Two of Walker's good doctors after some two hours of hard work and worry had failed to reduce the dislocation. A lady present, noting their exhaustion and despair, said: "Gentlemen, I am not a doctor and don't like to butt in, but I have always heard that steaming oats is a good remedy." The suggestion was at once acted upon; a bundle of oats tied over head and face and hot water poured on. Immediately the bone slipped into place.

An old custom in Walker, now rapidly passing, was the neighborly attentions given to a sick neighbor. When a case of serious sickness which continued for weeks occurred, the neighborhood divided itself into shifts to watch by the bedside in order to relieve the family, each knowing his appointed night. No lack of help then. Most of this, like many other old customs is now history, since we now have the trained nurse, so helpful in serious sickness.

DR. D. C. FARISS

DR. G. G. GORDON

DR. R. B. DICKERSON

A century ago there were few roads throughout Cherokee Georgia, and those few scarcely more than bridle paths. The doctor was often called far away from home, almost a hundred miles in extreme cases. This journey he made horseback, traveling for days—almost day and night, being away from home probably a week. Dr. Barry, mentioned above, was occasionally called as far as the Coosa River and further to attend severe cases of sickness, three days or more being consumed in making the trip, and most of this time spent in the saddle; strenuous work, this. Dr. Hammond relates this circumstance concerning one of Dr. Barry's trips to see a patient whose home was on the Coosa river. The patient was suffering from rheumatism, which the doctor after thorough and careful examination was convinced was more or less feigned. Spending the night at the patient's home the doctor by morning had decided on the treatment. It was a beautiful morning in June. The doctor walked up and down the bank of the river to select a suitabel location. Returning he had the patient placed on a stretcher and ordered four servants to take him up and follow him. Arriving at the location selected he had him suddenly plunged into the river. The treatment was efficacious, but the doctor, fearing consequences, letf prematurely. (Dr. Hammond says this story was vouched for by the late Dr. Glenn, as also, by Dr. Barry's daughter, Mrs. W. A. Moore).

DR. P. S. ANDERSON

The old-time country doctor carried a supply of drugs in his saddle bags. No writing of prescriptions with him. When he had arrived at his patient's bedside and diagnosed the case he opened his "pill box" and carefully measured out and labelled each medicine, and in case of serious sickness, to carefully write down full directions till his return. With what awe and amazement the younger members of the family would look on as the doctor opened his medicine chest and began to take out the contents! To them he was almost super-human.

The following list comprises some of the pioneer doctors of the county: Dr. Adam Clements, Dr. Bailey, Dr. Joseph Marsh, Dr. Tarvin (Indian), Dr. Lee, Dr. Jarnigan, Dr. Cole, Dr. Catlett, Dr. Hogan, Dr. R. H. Dyer, Sr., Dr. T. Y. Park, Dr. Asa Fricks, Dr. Barry, Dr. Whit McGuffey,

Dr. D. C. Fariss, Dr. Daniel Abbey (Rock Spring), Dr. Charles H. Holland, Dr. G. G. Gordon, Dr. Glenn, Dr. Thornburg, Dr. Anderson, Dr. Story, Dr. Simmons, Dr. W. H. Wilbanks, Dr. Blackwell, Dr. J. W. Clement, Dr. G. W. Cochran, Dr. A. Hawkins.

Other later doctors are the following: Dr. Julius Broyles, Dr. G. W. Jones, Dr. Fricks, Dr. Jenkins, Dr. Bolen, Dr. Stillson, Dr. Bush, Dr. Cunningham, Dr. L. M. Mitchel, Dr. C. C. L. Rudicil, Dr. Dan Alsobrook, Dr. T. D. McKeown, Dr. S. W. Fariss, Dr. J. P. McWilliams, Dr. J. M. Underwood, Dr. Hunt, Dr. S. V. Price

Present doctors practicing in the county:

LaFayette: Dr. J. H. Hammond, Health Commissioner; Dr. J. A. Shields, Dr. R. M. Coulter, Dr. Dewey Hammond, Dr. S. B. Kitchens.

Villanow: Dr. J. J. Johnson.

Cedar Grove: Dr. M. M. Crowder, Dr. J. P. Wood.

Kensington: Dr. J. P. Hunter.

Chickamauga: Dr. H. F. Shields, Dr. W. M. Spearmen, Dr. D. G. Elder.

Rossville: Dr. Sam Alsobrook, Dr. B. C. Hale, Dr. G. P. Wilbanks.

Rock Springs: Dr. E. H. Hice.

In 1927 Dr. W. A. Loach, druggist, erected at LaFayette an up-to-date sanitarium, complete in all respects. It is in charge of Dr. R. M. Coulter, while all other physicians of the county have access to it as practitioners. It was erected at a cost of approximately $50,000.00.

THE LEGAL PROFESSION.

When the county was organized it was placed in the Cherokee circuit, and continued there till the amount of business made it necessary to form a new circuit when it was placed in the Rome circuit. This was about 1869.

In those early days before the time of railroads the judge generally traveled by horse-back, and was likely to be accompanied by a bevy of lawyers who followed him to the various courts where they engaged in the legal practice of law. They put up at the public inn or tavern and this became the headquarters for court attaches when court was not in session. Here for days or weeks they remained and to beguile the time it was spent in story-telling, everyone during this time becoming familiar with the new stock of "yarns." When court was dismissed the judge with the lawyers departed for the next court in another county.

The census of 1850 lists the following as among the early lawyers of the county: William Daugherty, Vines Harwell, A. L. Borders, James R. Gambell, C. D. McCutchen, A. F. Burk, Augustus Culberson, Thomas P. Aycock, H. B. Johnson, Lawson Black, M. N. B. J. H. Alley, Andrew G. Gordon, Henry L. Sims.

Other lawyers of more recent date, as well as the present are: D. C. Sutton, William Wright, H. P. Lumpkin, R. M. W. Glenn, James P. Shattuck, John W. Bale, O. N. Chambers, John D. Pope, D. F. Pope, W. M. Henry, T. W. Lee, W. J. Nunnally, James E. Rosser, Earl Jackson, Walter B. Shaw, S. W. Fariss, Julius Rink, Norman Shattuck, J. R. Rosser, Horace Shattuck, Neil Andrews, J. M. Hutcheson, Charles Robert Jones, F. M. Gleeson, G. W. Lankford, J. E. Ensign. (R. F. and W. A. McClure, Tennessee attorneys, practice much in the Walker Superior Court).

Chapter Forty-one

POST OFFICE RECORDS.

The Post Office—"Messenger of sympathy and love—servant of parted friends—consoler of the lonely—bond of the scattered family—enlarger of the common life. Carrier of news and knowledge—instrument of trade and industry—promoter of mutual acquaintance of peace and good-will among men and nations." (Engraved in marble on the walls of the national postoffice at Washington).

AS a matter of general interest the author has tried to collect information concerning the postoffices of the county, both present and past. Reliable data about these, as about many other matters has been hard to assemble. Records in most of the older postoffices were destroyed during the war and only by talking with very old persons has it been possible to learn even the postmasters at that time.

The James R. Jones ledger, mentioned elsewhere, is interesting as giving much information regarding postoffice rules and regulations sixty years ago. It appears that Mr. Jones was the postmaster during the sixties and seventies. He kept records in this old ledger. One page devoted to the cancellation of stamps gives the daily cancellation and makes note of the arrival and departure of mail. The following entries are seen:

1867: Feb. 25, "No mail, horse gave out." Feb. 27, "No mail, horse gave out." Mar. 4, "No mail, high water, Chickamauga." Mar. 6, "No mail, high water, Chickamauga." Same entry for the following dates: March 7, 9, 11, 14, 16. On March 18, is the single entry, "Mail," which means that the mail came that day.

The number of letters received at this office during the week ending June 30, 1867, was 34. The number leaving for the same date was 24. This entry: "There was a package of postage stamps passed here for P. M. Trion Factory June 3, 1867. No. 10075." Also this: "Received at this office one package of postage stamps, 600, $18, from New York, No. 4343, July 25."

This entry: "James Gray takes Southern Recorder, the first came to this office April, 1845. Moses Park takes the Christian Index, Penfield, Ga., the first came to this office June first, 1845."

The following entry is noted: The Cincinnati Weekly Times taken by the following persons. The first came to this office Jan. 7; J. R. Jones, 5c paid; Oda Castleberry, 5c paid; D. W. Jones, 5c paid; George Brigman, 20c paid for the year; R. M. Jones, 5c paid for the quarter; J. R. Gladdon, 5c paid for 1 qr.; J. H. Smith, paid 20c; Levi Bird, paid 5c; Philip Bird paid 5c; Wm. James paid 5c; A. Swicegood paid 5c.

Another entry: Names of persons taking papers at Rock Springs, Walker County, Ga., the last quarter in 1866: "New York Ledger, taken by Miss C. Shields once a week, paid 5c; Saturday Evening Post, taken by 18 Subscribers. Paid." "The names below take the Jolly Joker: W. R. Cooper; J. M. Cooper; W. W. Gladden; A. Cooper; Jacob Arnold; ——— Rutherford; J. Thomas; S. M. McDaniel." All marked 5c paid.

There are numerous other entries similar to the above giving the names of many of the old citizens of the Rock Spring section back in the forties and on to the seventies, showing that they were patrons of the postoffice at that place and showing too how postal affairs were conducted in those early times. It is seen that a subscriber for a paper not only must pay for the paper but must also pay the postage on it; and this was done at the office where he got his mail. The postage seems to have been 5 cents per quarter, or 20 cents a year. The postmaster kept a record of all these transactions.

Other names in this old ledger given as taking various other papers and paying for them are: Milton Lawrence; J. A. Bowman; G. W. Brewer; Elizabeth Brigman; Thomas Lawrence; A. Hicks; G. W. Jackson; F. D. Brigman; Wm. Glass; J. M. Shields and many others.

Most of these transactions occurred after the surrender. Looking back we may see these old citizens trying to get in touch with the country after the bloody conflict. They were reaching out for knowledge and for information. They were not content to isolate themselves and to live to themselves and become hermits, so to speak. They had lost the war and no doubt they were discouraged and blue. Times were hard and money scarce, but with all this they wanted to recover and assume their proper places in life. They did it.

In our imagination we may see these hardy folk going once a week to the postoffice for the mail. The paper is carried home and read and re-read, and then probably exchanged with his neighbor for one of another kind. On Sundays as they visit each other, or at church, the latest news from the papers is discussed and passed on to others. It took men of iron wills and muscles of steel to overcome the inconveniences and hardships through which our ancestors passed. All honor to their memory!

CRAWFISH SPRING, afterward changed to Chickamauga. It is not known just when this office was established, probably in the latter sixties or early seventies. Mr. James M. Lee was the postmaster till his death in 1889. Other postmasters are the following: J. T. Blaylock 1889-92; M. T. Bonds 1893-97; Paul J. Murphy 1897-01; Beatrice Henry Myers 1901-03; C. W. Richter 1903-05; James H. Blaylock 1905-08; E. H. Wyatt 1908-12; S. D. Blaylock 1912 (May to August); J. L. Moore 1912-14; Jesse H. Hicks 1915-16; George L. Bonds 1916-18; Jesse H. Hicks 1918-

R.F.D. Route No. 1, established 1904. Gordan Wallace carrier June to September. J. D. Welch 1904-date. Route No. 2, established 1905. W. W. Ireland was first carrier to June, 1921. Clark B. Hearn, 1921-date.

CEDAR GROVE. Established before the war. There have been only three post masters at that office all these years as follows: Aaron Smith; J. F. Smith; O. T. Simmons. This office was supplied from Chattanooga once a week, later twice a week, then three times a week. After the T. A. G. railroad was built the mail came daily. Noah Meridith was carrier to and from Chattanooga.

POND SPRING. Established in the fifties. As far as can be ascertained the following have served as postmasters: Joe Limmocks; Pony Mathis; Samuel Hall; Dave Hall; Ave Glenn; J. P. Hall; Charley Glenn. Discontinued about 1905.

HIGH, on Lookout Mountain, established 1895. Postmasters: Mrs. Charley Taylor; Delia Howard. After it was discontinued another office was established at

LOOKOUT in the same community. Charley Henry P.M.

NAOMI. Established about 1875. Postmasters: Johnny McDonald and Barney Edge. Discontinued about 1905.

DUCK CREEK. White's Statistics mentions this office in 1849. The following are remembered as postmasters: A. B. McWhorter; Asa Lumpkin; Tom Blackwell; J. D. McConnell; Rev. T. B. Dodd; W. A. Wardlaw.

CENTER POST. Postmasters: T. J. Lumpkin; M. A. McConnell; C. C. Bryan.

BRONCO. (First kept at Hendricks place). Postmasters: W. P. Blackwell; L. B. McWhorter; J. R. Wardlaw.

SHARPE. J. A. Williams, P.M.

GUILD. Established about 1888. Postmasters: W. O. Alexander; Sam Edmonson; Rube Underwood; W. C. McWhorter.

ASCALON. Established in the early eighties: Postmasters: J. L. Moore; Otto Bostrom; W. A. Chambers; C. A. Chambers; J. W. Oliver.

DILLON. Established in the eighties. Postmasters: Miss Lila Howard; Mrs. J. W. Bryan; Thomas Stephens. Discontinued 1927.

SALEM. Established about 1884. J. T. Renfro P. M.

MANCO. Established 1884. W. C. Blackwell P. M.

CATLETT. Established 1898. Postmasters: B. Catlett; Tom Sims.

SCOTT. About 1881 this office was established one-half mile west of Lee and Gordon's mill. Jesse Ireland was postmaster. Its life was short.

SNOW HILL. This office was operated about one mile south of Lee and Gordon's mill before the war. It is not known who the postmaster was.

ZONE. Named in honor of Zone Fowler, daughter of Doc Fowler. Established 1903. Postmasters: Doc Fowler; Mr. Lockeby; Lula Puryear; Bertha Warnock.

"Uncle" Billy Hixon says there was no postoffice on the mountain before the war. The inhabitants got their mail from Eagle Cliff. About 1885 a star route was established to supply the offices at Dillon, Ascalon and Gerber. A few years later an office was established at Guerry. When the latter was discontinued Hinkle was established and operated for 25 years with T. M. Massey as postmaster. This office was discontinued in 1930 when the rural route was started from Rising Fawn. A postoffice at Pittsburg has been in existence for probably 40 years. No record of postmasters at hand.

ROSSVILLE. The first office was established in 1819, when the Federal star route ran from Nashville to Augusta. The early inhabitants of Ross' Landing (Chattanooga), got their mail at Rossville. This office was in existence for many years, but eventually was discontinued. During a part of this discontinuance an office was established on the Tennessee side, called Divine, which in turn was abolished and Rossville again took its place.

As far as records are available the following have served as postmasters: Mr. Taylor, I. M. Flegall, Charles Robert Jones, 1906-14; 1922-1932, J. S. Alsobrook, 1914-22; G. W. Bryan, 1932-.

The rural route service was begun about 1905, displacing the following offices: Mission Ridge, Lytle, Hargraves, Dodge. Earlier carriers were: Larkin A. Brown, W. H. Frazier, C. V. Henderson, J. W. Terrell, F. G. Shambaugh, Ed Veazey, J. J. Rhyne. Present carriers: Luke E. Williams, Gordon H. Gilbert. City carriers: James F. Ireland, Russell R. Shaver, Lester C. Teeters, Subst.

Office Help: Miles T. Gilbert, Asst. P.M., Gaith D. Lamb, John C. McDaniel, Charles W. Schmitt, Thomas Velton Williams, John R. Williams. A branch of the office at Ft. Oglethorpe is in charge of J. W. White.

LAFAYETTE. Miss Orpha Center says that Miss Gene Kelly was postmistress for a time during the war; that during a part of the war there was no office and no mail. Miss Kelly succeeded Boud Johnston. Others were: Doc Kelley, Jim Rogers, Esther M. Waters, Ock Rogers, Wm. Carroll, Mr. Snow, Mrs. Snow, A. S. Sparks, Frank Farris, James A. Allen.

Present R.F.D. carriers: T. A. O'Neal, route No. 1; W. M. Hammond, route No. 2; J. R. McCurdy, route No. 3; W. R. Neely, route No. 4; W. C. Smith, route No. 5; B. F. Lawrence, route No. 6. Other carriers have been: R L. Powell, W. J. Farrow, J. J. Mattox, Oliver H. Linn.

Office Help: J. J. Mattox and John Craig, clerks; E. E. Baker, city carrier, Neal Watts, subst.

An old copy of Minutes of the Coosa Baptist Association for 1854

HISTORY OF WALKER COUNTY, GEORGIA

mentions the following post offices then in the county: Chestnut Flat, Wood Station, Frix Gap.

SOME MASONIC HISTORY OF WALKER COUNTY.

WESTERN LODGE NO. 91, F. & A. M.
Chartered October 31, 1849.
Ebenezer Stockbridge, W.M.
Richard A. Lane, S.W.
Archibald T. Burke, J.W.

Wm. C. Dawson, Grand Master
Jas. F. Cooper, Dep. Grand Master
A. A. Gaulding, S.G.W.

Wm. R. Kitchen, J.G.W.
Peter Solomon, Grand Treasurer
Simri Rose, Grand Secretary

MEMBERS ON ROLL FIRST RETURN, 1849.

Ebenezer Stockbridge, W.M.
Richard A. Lane, S.W.
Archibald T. Burke, J.W.
Jas. R. Gamble, Treas.
John Caldwell, Secty.
Andrew J. Healan, S.D.
Thos. P. Kelly, J.D.
A. W. T. Clendenen, Chaplain
Edw. R. Sasseen ⎫
John Dickson ⎬ Stewards
Jas. H. Rogers ⎭

Madison E. Rhodes
Augustus B. Culverson
Edwin E. Marsh
Thomas M. Nash

Wm. A. Moore
John McWhorter
William Simmons
Jos. M. Wardlaw
John M. Gregory
Horace Lindsey
Benj. W. Keaton
Richard O. Gordon
Calvin W. Simmons
Saml. W. Thomas
Greenbury G. Gordon
Abraham Martin
Adam Clements
James Gray
Cicero D. McCutchen
Thomas D. Kelly

WORSHIPFUL MASTERS.

1850-62—Richard A. Lane
1863-65—No return
1866-67—M. E. Rhodes
1868-69—G. W. Holden
1870-71—D. C. Fariss
1872 —John Dickson
1873 —Benj. L. Chastain
1874 —M. E. Rhodes
1875 —J. H. McWhorter
1876 —John Dickson
1877 —A. A. Simmons
1878-82—Jas. H. McWhorter
1883-84—H. P. Lumpkin

1885 —Wm. A. Foster
1886 —Jas. H. McWhorter
1887-88—B. F. Thurmond
1889 —J. H. McWhorter
1890-94—H. P. Lumpkin
1895-96—John R. Steele
1897 —Jas. P. Shattuck
1898-00—John R. Steele
1901 —Jas. P. Shattuck
1902 —W. A. Nickols
1903-04—J. E. Patton
1905 —J. H. Hammond
1906-07—W. E. Withers

1908	—S. W. Fariss	1922	—D. W. Herndon
1909	—J. P. Hall	1923	—J. W. Massey
1910	—W. J. Shattuck	1924	—Thos. W. Bryan
1911-12	—Jno. W. Bale	1925	—Frederick Moore
1913	—J. P. Hall	1926	—J. M. Patton
1914	—R. A. Whatley	1927-28	—J. R. Rosser
1915	—O. W. Bledsoe	1929	—Roy R. Neely
1916-17	—E. P. Hall, Jr.	1930	—John V. Craig—
1918	—J. P. Hall		J. B. Freeman
1919	—Jas. P. Shattuck	1931	—R. H. Pittman
1920-21	—J. P. Hall	1932	—O. W. Bledsoe

EASTERN STAR CHAPTER.

LaFayette Chapter No. 107 was organized July 1, 1914, with O. W. Bledsoe, Worthy Patron; Mrs. E. A. Jackson, Worthy Matron. The following were charter members: O. W. Bledsoe, Mrs. O. W. Bledsoe, R. A. Whatley, Mrs. R. A. Whatley, E. A. Jackson, Mrs. E. A. Jackson, J. E. Patton, Mrs. J. E. Patton, Dr. J. A. Shields, Mrs. J. A. Shields, Miss Carrie McCall, Dr. R. M. Coulter, Mrs. R. M. Coulter, Dr. J. H. Hammond, R. D. Love, Henry Ball, Mrs. Henry Ball, J. M. Coley, C. M. Conley, Mrs. C. M. Conley, J. R. Greene, J. P. Hall, J. W. Holland, D. W. Herndon, Miss Nannie Jones, Miss Emma Jones, J. C. Knox, Mrs. J. C. Knox, J. W. Murray, Mrs. J. W. Murray, Mrs. Susie Robinson.

The following have served as Worthy Matron: Mrs. E. A. Jackson, Mrs. R. A. Whatley, Miss Madge Conley, Mrs. H. J. Spencer, Mrs. O. W. Bledsoe, Mrs. G. W. Ashworth, Mrs. Mollie Scrugs, Mrs. J. C. Keown, Mrs. Grace Burney, Mrs. D. C. R. Myers, Miss Mary Johnston, Miss Johnnie Williams; and the following as Worthy Patron: O. W. Bledsoe, R. A. Whatley, D. T. Cooper, D. M. Cornett, and R. D. Love.

The present officers are: Johnnie Williams, W.M.; O. W. Bledsoe, W.P.; Willie Craig, Associate Matron; G. W. Ashworth, Asso. P.; Mrs. O. W. Bledsoe, Sec.; Mrs. W. C. Burney, Treas.; Mrs. R. V. Thurman, Cond.; Mrs. J. L. Rowland, Asso. Cond.; Mrs. H. D. Scruggs, Chap.; Mrs. H. V. Henry, Org.; Mrs. D. M. Cornett, War.; Dr. J. H. Hammond, Sen.; Mrs. W. R. Neeley, Adah; Mrs. H. P. Burney, Ruth; Mrs. T. A. Cochran, Esther; Mrs. H. J. Spencer, Martha; Mrs. G. W. Ashworth, Electa.

Number of active members at present, 48; number initiated since organization, 141. The Chapter clothes and cares for a little orphan boy, Wade Martin, eight years old, at the Masonic Home, Macon, Georgia, whom all the members love dearly.

CRAWFISH SPRINGS LODGE No. 300, F. & A. M.
Chickamauga, Ga.

Crawfish Springs Lodge, No. 300, F. & A. M., was instituted December 25, 1874, by the following:

E. R. White (P. M. Meigs Lodge No. 266), Grand Master Pro Tem.
J. H. Gardner (P. M.), Grand Senior Warden Pro Tem.
J. H. McWhorter (W. M.), Grand Junior Warden Pro Tem.
J. F. Smith, Grand Secretary Pro Tem.

The following officers were elected:

    Worshipful Master—A. I. Leet (P. M.)
    Senior Warden—J. J. Jones
    Junior Warden—L. K. Dickey
    Treasurer—J. M. Lee
    Secretary—J. C. Gordon
    Senior Deacon—W. M. Foster
    Junior Deacon—B. M. Garrett
    Senior Steward—J. D. Strange
    Junior Steward—Wm. Burke
    Tyler—J. T. Bilbo
    Chaplain—W. T. Park

The charter members were:

A. I. Leet	J. M. Bird
J. C. Gordon	T. Y. Park
Allen Thedford	J. B. Donegan
J. M. Lee	C. G. Smith
J. C. Hall	G. W. Jones
W. T. Park	W. H. Garmany
D. C. Payne	J. J. Jones
B. M. Garrett	J. T. Bilbo
W. A. Foster	H. J. Conley
A. Woods	L. K. Dickey
G. W. H. Anderson	A. Mitchell
M. W. Owings	J. D. Strange
M. M. Phillips	Wm. Strange
T. S. Phillips	H. P. Tierce
Thos. Harris	J. R. Cravens
Wm. Burke	J. M. Head
D. B. Baker	H. C. Christian

ROSTER OF MASTERS WHO HAVE SERVED THE LODGE.
1875-1932.

1875-76—A. I. Leet	1885 —J. J. Jones
1877 —L. K. Dickey	1886 —L. K. Dickey
1878 —A. I. Leet	1887 —J. B. Henderson
1879 —J. J. Jones	1888 —J. J. Jones
1880 —A. I. Leet	1889 —O. R. Henderson
1881-82—L. K. Dickey	1890 —J. J. Jones
1883 —A. I. Leet	1891-92—E. P. Hall
1884 —L. K. Dickey	1893 —J. J. Jones

1894	—E. P. Hall	1913	—W. H. Henderson
1895	—O. R. Henderson	1914	—Don Harris
1896	—J. J. Jones	1915	—W. M. Housch
1897	—R. L. Catlett	1916	—J. F. Henderson
1898	—J. P. Hall	1917	—Lee H. Dyer
1899	—W. A. Horton	1918	—T. H. Hunt
1900	—W. J. Nunnelly	1919	—R. U. Harper
1901	—J. J. Jones	1920	—Lee H. Dyer
1902	—J. T. Kirkpatrick	1921	—Frank L. Burnside
1903-04	—T. W. Lee	1922	—D. A. Jewell, Jr.
1905	—C. C. L. Rudicil	1923-24	—R. H. Jewell
1906	—R. B. Bagwell	1925	—E. G. Glenn
1907	—T. W. Lee	1926	—F. H. Henderson
1908	—E. P. Hall	1927-28	—E. B. Osborn
1909	—Lee H. Dyer	1929	—C. R. Ireland
1910	—O. R. Henderson	1930	—B. R. Stogsdill
1911	—J. A. Sartain	1931	—R. R. Shaver
1912	—T. W. Lee	1932	—Joe Reed

The officers serving the lodge at present are:

Worshipful Master—J. D. Reed
Senior Warden—C. G. Murdock
Junior Warden—W. H. Edwards
Secretary—R. U. Harper
Treasurer—J. B. Mason
Senior Deacon—Roy E. Parrish
Junior Deacon—Connie Tate
Senior Steward—H. M. Holsomback
Junior Steward—Geo. M. Parsons
Tyler—W. H. Wilmot
Chaplain—J. M. Baker

The present membership of the lodge is about 200.

Approximately 500 men have been made masons by this lodge.

The first Masonic Hall was over the old Methodist Church which was built about 1874. About 1907 the City of Chickamauga and the Masonic Lodge built a new frame school building, the upper story of which was used for a lodge hall. Then in 1914 or 1915 a new brick school house was erected and the lodge hall was moved to the upper story of this building. In 1925 the Masonic lodge sold their interest in the school property and purchased a corner lot on the main street in Chickamauga where the present 3-story Masonic Temple was erected at a cost of $45,000.00, by the Blue Lodge, Chapter and Knights Templar.

A Short History of Chickamauga Chapter No. 99, Royal Arch Masons.

On April 27, 1897, Chickamauga Chapter No. 99, Royal Arch Masons, was chartered with Companions J. J. Jones, High Priest; J. R. McFarland, King; and W. A. Horton, Scribe.

Below is given a record of the High Priests of the Chapter from its organization to the present time.

1898-03	—J. J. Jones	1920	—R. U. Harper
1904	—T. F. McFarland	1921	—E. F. Camp
1905-06	—J. J. Jones	1922	—James M. Troutt
1907	—C. C. L. Rudicil	1923	—Joseph E. Mansfield
1908	—T. W. Lee	1924	—Burl F. Hall
1909-10	—J. J. Jones	1925-26	—R. H. Jewell
1911-12	—Don Harris	1927	—L. S. Burgess
1913	—B. F. Quigley	1928	—J. N. Freeman
1914	—Arthur T. Hayes	1929	—F. H. Henderson
1915	—J. F. Henderson	1930	—W. A. Shaw
1916	—W. H. Housch	1931	—E. B. Osborn
1917	—H. V. Henry	1932	—Carl C. Hearn
1918-19	—D. A. Jewell, Jr.		

Chapter Forty-two

Some Efforts at Composition by Walker County Citizens.

THE following efforts at composition were not intended for publication in the county history. They were jotted down at odd times many years ago. Almost accidentally the author ran across them and decided to give them a place in the history. They were written by Walker County boys.

It's Not Too Late.
By J. E. Rosser

Had I lived in the long ago,
   Too late it might have been
For Time to rap at my door,
   Or in turn, to enter in.

I know there's wisdom in my time,
    No matter when I may live;
Human kindness much I'll find
    If I human kindness give.

I know I've missed the House of Fame;
    In it I've had no fixed abode;
Heard no applaud, heard no acclaim
    For my deeds along life's road.

I've not been termed great or strong,
    But, I know my heart is warm.
I have plodded slow, along—
    I have lived the mild reform.

It seems not an age that spirits me
    To reach dazzling, bewildering heights,
But nature grants the same old key
    To unlock the vast stores of right.

I confess the age has extended plain
    Where—oft, it seems, by accidental birth
One may find this Hall of Fame,
    But 'tis only answer to his worth.

The same old wheel today will turn
    And roll to the end of time—
To follow in the track man may learn
    The way yet to things sublime.

So, it matters not when I was born;
    The sun's bright rays are given me;
There's, alike, shelter from the storm—
    The same old haven will always be.

Any time in which I'm given
    A chance to solve my fate—
The same old path leads to heaven
    And no one is born too late.

This may be the very time—the age,
    For me to find the better way—
To indite good deeds on history's page,
    For with endeavor, now's the time—the day.

Another by the same author:

YOUTH DOES NOT KNOW.

When I was a youth I was told
    Of trials I'd meet at every turn;
That long before I was termed old,
    Many serious lessons I would learn.

That even while young I would see
    That many perils lay out ahead;
That hardships, many, awaited me
    To be early snows upon my head.

But being a youth I wanted to try
    To clear—traverse fields of my own;
I wanted the endeavor; and to apply
    The seeds that I have sown.

Some of the way has weary been—
    Heavy laden, long seemed the lane,
For many tilts have intervened—
    Clouds have clustered o'er my main.

How sad would be youth if it knew
    The truth as older ones do know—
How real the pain ere we older grew,
    However well the trips we may go.

It is best to treat with each new sun,
    Its light and its shade and its heat;
Endeavor each task to be better begun,
    Strive harder each foe to defeat.

If I had to worry with what's to be.
    Knowing that sorrow with pleasures blend;
Knowing it once I would not be free
    Till I found the shadow's end.

When I reach the new hill's top
    And see those vales extending there,
May my fruition never stop
    Till I the victor's laurel wear.

May I find at the end of each day
    A brighter light for my wandering feet,
That I may from evil hie me away
    And lesser obstruction meet.

The odes in this column were written by Hon. John B. Henderson of Chickamauga, Ga., a Confederate veteran, now in his 88th year. (Died soon after).

We love our friends all through life,
Through pathos, humor and strife;
Across the Sea of Life from shore to shore
They die; why mourn, they've only gone before.

If you want to live a consecrated, righteous life—
Avoid intemperance, excess and strife;
Don't worry—pay your debts and bridle your tongue
That your good example may appeal to the young.

When the well-springs of youth dry up,
The door to bodily pleasures has been shut,
And the animal passions have been slain—
After growing old our thoughts of sex are not the same.

I have moved because I had no good neighbors,
I have lived and striven with other laborers—
At last I've had a vision—my moving is done;
If I expect to have good neighbors, I myself must be one.

"I've had my ups and downs," said the Miser,
"With the fair sex who think they are wiser,
But old age brings on my confession,
That pursuit is greater than possession."

These simple little cards only say,
What we should think and practice every day;
We think it great to receive—'tis greater to give,
For Christ is our example to give and to live.

I think when we reach the sunset of life,
We will be free from sickness, sorrow and strife;
For this is true as truth can be,
"As man thinketh, so is he."

Of immortality we all want to know,
But it is safe to believe in eternal kindness before we go,
And to do unto your fellow men as you would they do unto you,
For this is what Christ taught us to do.

THE VICTORS.

By C. A. Chambers

(Nov. 12, 1918)

The bravery of the Belgians
    First halted the haughty Hun;
The fearless, fighting Frenchmen
    Were first to make him run.

The brilliant bull-dog British
    Stood like a wall of steel,
And saved the allied nations
    From the Hohenzollern heel.

Courageous, cool Canadians
    All gave and asked no quarter,
They took the greatest strongholds,
    Inflicting awful slaughter.

Audacious, bold Australians
    Were fearless of the foe;
They charged and swept the enemy
    Like an avalanche of snow.

The nervy, brave New Zealanders,
    When brought to rigid test,
Were found to be the equal
    Of the bravest and the best.

The invincible Italians,
    With desperate, stern resolve,
Hurled back the hateful, heartless Huns
    At the battle of Piave.

The irresistible Irish,
    The plucky Portuguese,
The gallant Greeks and Serbians,
    The gingery Japanese.

The irrepressible Indians,
    Reliable Russians, true,
The mighty Montenegrins,
    Arabs, Albanians too;

Redoubtable Roumanians,
    And other nations, all
Have done their part to bring about
    Autocracy's downfall.

But amazing-all, Americans,
    Made good in every case,
Defeating all the Boches' plans
    With the valor of their race.

And when the Huns in their great might,
    Drove hard against "Paree,"
They turned the tide of that great fight
    Which brought the victory.

Honor the boys who faced the storm,
    Honor the boys who trained,
Honor the workers in every form,
    Whose aid the victory gained.

V-ain was the fight of German ghouls
I-n their mad lust for power;
C-hrist's law of right from this day rules
T-o the world's remotest hour.
O-n earth sweet peace, good will to men,
R-ejoice, for war shall ne'er again
Y-ield bitter woe. Amen! Amen!

OLD GEORGIA LAND.

By C. A. Chambers.

Old Georgia is a goodly land
    From highlands to the sea,
Her products fill the full demand
    Of man's necessity.

More zones of climate belt her breast
    Than any other state;
Here Nature did her very best
    And made her grand and great.

I love her mountains' splendid scene,
    I love her southern plains;
I love her hills that lie between
    And all her vast domains.

She formed an altruistic rule,
    And built first orphan's home;
She gave us our first Sunday school
    And female college dome.

She showed the world a simple means
    To make its sufferings easier,
Abolished awful surgery scenes
    With gentle anaesthesia.

Her heroes and her heroines
    Have made a brilliant story,
Their names are writ in golden lines
    To their eternal glory.

Her citizens of every class
    The world's attention claim,
And many think that none surpass
    The greatness of their fame.

This noble state's my native land,
    I deem it my good fortune;
My warmest love she'll e'er command,
    I'm proud that I'm a Georgian.

THAT'S GEORGIA.

By C. A. Chambers.

A land of mountains and of plain,
Of golden sunshine and of rain,
Of peanuts, rice and sugar cane,
Potatoes, cotton, peas and grain,
A land of talent and of brain—
    That's Georgia.

A land of marble and of gold,
Of bubbling springs, both clear and cold,
Whose hills and mountains in their hold,
Have mineral wealth that is untold,
Whose rivers are both slow and bold—
    That's Georgia.

Land of the famous red old hills,
Of cotton, saw and shingle mills,
A land of odious wild-cat stills,
A land whose glorious history thrills,
And whose nobility instills—
    That's Georgia.

A land of live oak and of pine,
Magnolia and of jessamine,
Of rosin and of turpentine,
A land of poultry and of swine,
O, glorious land, I call thee mine!—
　　That's Georgia.

A land of the paper-shell pecan,
Of flowers fair to look upon,
A land of muscle and of brawn,
A land where hope is never gone,
A land of beauty on and on—
　　That's Georgia.

A land of churches and of schools,
Of ball-grounds and of swimming pools,
A land of wise folk and of fools,
A land of Christians and of ghouls,
Where moral sentiment always rules—
　　That's Georgia.

Land of the fiddle and the bow,
Where sunny smiles and warm hearts glow,
Where choicest fruits and melons grow,
Where mountain and sea breezes blow,
Where honey, milk and moonshine flow—
　　That's Georgia.

Land of the hunter and his pack,
Land of the skillful and the quack,
Land of the white race and the black,
Who travel each a separate track,
Where both go forward, never back—
　　That's Georgia.

Land of the fish-fry, oyster-stew,
Land of the picnic, barbecue,
Land whose people are brave and true,
Loyal to country through and through,
Ninety-nine per cent are natives too—
　　That's Georgia.

Old "Wisdom, Justice, Moderation,"
The fairest land in all creation,
In many things she takes first station,
A balance wheel for all the nation,
That stands upon a true foundation,—
　　That's Georgia.

These three exquisite poems are by Caroline Arnold of LaFayette.

To a Robin.

Wake, robin, wake,
Too long a nap you take,
The world has waited long
To hear your cheer-up song
For love's sweet sake.

Sing, robin, sing,
Some note of joy to bring
To drooping heart.
There're souls that are oppressed,
And wrongs to be redressed,
And you must do your part.

Fly, robin, fly,
Fly up into the sky
And sing your strain;
Some may forget their fears,—
Make rainbows of their tears—
And live again.

There's naught for you to fear,—
So sing your song of cheer
From day to day.
Who marks the sparrow's fall
Will hear your welcome call
And guide your trackless way.

Trees.

Oh trees! with leaves all gone and branches bare,
Art thou forlorn?
Thy roots are deep, thy limbs are strong;
Thy leaves will come again,
Oh trees!

Oh heart! with mem'ries sweet, but friends all gone,
Art thou forlorn?
Thy faith is deep, thy love is strong;
Thy joys will come again,
Oh heart!

Oh soul! deem not earth's loss a heavy cross,
Thou art divine!
Faith breathes thy prayers, love sings thy songs,
Oh! soul of mine!

NATURE POEM.

Wild flowers are Nature's alphabet,
Written on field and wood
Mysterious truths for us to learn,
If rightly understood.

Wild sounds are Nature's orchestra,
Bringing from far and near
The most mysterious harmonies,
If we could rightly hear.

Wild scenes are Nature's gallery,
Of sky and sea and land;
Of most exquisite coloring
Wrought by Nature's hand.

Wild thoughts are Nature's garden,
Where flowers and weeds are grown;
Flowers that God has planted,
Weeds that man has sown.

And all is one vast problem,
Ages and ages old,
Hinting at Nature's secret,
Which never can be told.

THE PERMANENT SMILE.

By J. T. Kirkpatrick, Jr.

It's the person who smiles we are happy to meet;
   That's the face which we all like to see;
The one who smiles at Success or Defeat,
   He's the fellow we'd all like to be.

It's quite easy to smile when all's going well—
   When things are just coming our way;
But the permanent smile—it will always tell,
   For it shows that it's on there to stay.

Smiles aid us in finding success we're told—
  Keep us healthy and happy and gay;
They make us look young when really we're old,
  For they help to keep wrinkles away.

Then smile when awake, and smile when asleep,
  Keep smiling, whatever you do;
For the PERMANENT smile will help you to keep
  New courage to carry you through.

Chorus:
Then *smile*, Smile, SMILE,
  As you scatter bright sunshine and song;
It will lighten the load and make smoother the road
  And help the other fellow along.

WHEN JESUS WALKS WITH ME.
By J. T. Kirkpatrick, Jr.

Though the pathway may seem dreary
  As I tread life's dusty way,
And my heart is faint and weary
  At the burden of to-day;
Still I know there's naught can sever
  From the love that makes me free,
And that keeps me—keeps me ever—
  When my Saviour walks with me.

When the howling tempest rages—
  Hope and courage sorely tried,
I shall 'neath the Rock of Ages
  From the fury safely hide.
I shall have no fear, no anguish,
  As I sail life's fitful sea,
For—unlike the souls that languish—
  Jesus, Saviour, pilots me.

In life's sunshine, in life's sorrow,
  I shall strive to keep Him near;
Trusting Him to-day, to-morrow,
  I shall have no thought of fear;
And at last if death o'ertake me
  As I watch for Him to come
I am sure he'll not forsake me,
  But will gently lead me home.

Help me, Lord, to lead some other
    Soul to Thee while yet 'tis day;
May my life attract some brother,
    And help him to find the way.
Step by step, dear Saviour, guide me,
    Let me never go astray:
Walk each day, O Lord, beside me—
    Be thou with me all the way.

SMILE AND LOOK UP.

By J. T. Kirkpatrick, Jr.

(The author of these beautiful lines was stricken with flu in 1920, from which he never fully recovered, and which finally brought his death. He has given us a lesson of how to "smile and look up.")

The constant thinking of your ills,
    Your trials and your woes,
Will help to make more steep the hills
    O'er which your pathway goes.
No use to always nurse your grief:
    Nor should you burden friends
With tales which do not bring relief—
    Which cannot make amends.

Why not push back the thought of pain,
    Of sickness, and of fear?
There's nothing you may hope to gain
    By bringing trouble near.
You'd better say that you are well—
    Or, all is well with you—
And look to God to break the spell,
    And make your words come true.

Instead of thinking of dark days,
    Help bring the sunshine in;
Just let your face reflect the rays—
    The cheerful heart will win.
Your smile will help some other soul,
    Your friendly greeting save
Some one who's fallen short the goal,
    Perchance, who's not so brave.

You'll find that as you speak to-day
   So will you soon believe:
Say, "All is well,"—help drive away
   The thoughts which so deceive.
Thank God afresh each new-born day
   For His sustaining care:
For blessings found along the way—
   Yes, blessings everywhere.

Then, if we must drink deep the cup
   Before we wear the crown,
Let's cling to hope, smile and look up,
   As faith our doubts shall drown.
And when in need of new supplies
   We'll go to Him, and rest
Assured that He will hear our cries,
   And give that which is best.

"NOBODY BUT TOM."

(In loving memory of my brother, J. T. Kirkpatrick, Jr., who departed this life July 2, 1927.—Earl Kirkpatrick.)

When Pa and Ma started their journey through life
To meet the world's pleasure as well as its strife;
E'er many years passed, so tedious and long,
Who came to greet with a coo and a song?
And to make their lives happy and full of joy?—
Their first-born child, a bouncing boy,
   Nobody but Tom.

As the years rolled by, and other babies came,
And the job got hard for Master and Dame,
Who, yet but a child, took a grown man's place
With a brave young heart, full of vim and grace—
Cooked and kept house when Ma was sick—
Helped Pa in the field when the grass was thick?
   Nobody but Tom.

Who blazed the trail for the rest of us boys,
To the field, to the school, with its tears and its joys?
To the little brown church that stood in the dale,
Where we started our journey on the heavenly trail?
Who carried us there, who was it I said?
While Pa stayed with Ma who was sick in bed?
   Nobody but Tom.

And who carried sunshine all through his life,
To his folks, to his neighbors, to his friends, to his wife
And who with a zeal withstood suffering and pain,
When a dreadful disease was wrecking his frame?
And looked straight ahead when the last hour came,
With nothing to lose and with Heaven to gain?
   Nobody but Tom.

When through the gift of God's infinite love,
My soul takes its flight to that mansion above,
And I meet the loved ones who have gone on before,
And are safely at rest on that beautiful shore—
As I enter the gate and join them there,
I wonder who, with forethought and care,
Will spring to his feet and give me a chair?
   Nobody but Tom.

RESPITE.

(A Shut-in's Meditation.)

By Frank G. Prince

Far up on the mountain side,
   'Mid chestnuts, oaks and pines,
Beside a rippling trout-filled stream,
   'Neath honey-suckle vines;
Above the smoke, among the clouds,
   Away from care and toil,
I go to rest my weary soul
   From the city's mad turmoil.

Far up on the mountain side
   I built my humble shack;
'Tis here I hunt and fish and dream,—
   Dream of time turned back,—
Dream of care-free childhood days,—
   The days of yester-year;
Ah! Here I live in quiet peace
   And God seems very near.

SOME SELECTIONS FROM SARTAIN'S NOTE-BOOK.
THE ROBIN.

In May, 1927, while resting under the shade of a peach tree from a spell of digging in the garden, a robin suddenly flitted into the tree above. Instantly he saw me and was off, lighting in another tree not far away. Here he sat for a time the while casting suspicious glances in my direction, till bethinking himself, he dropped down into a strawberry bed and began to sample the ripest berries, hopping from one to another scarcely tasting each but perforating the skin and destroying it. Thus engaged for a time I observed his movements till I decided to disturb him before he destroyed all the berries. I was not so stingy as to wish to deprive him of a few berries if only he would finish each one before he tackled another. So standing upright I moved slowly in his direction when he lifted himself atop a high fence post and stood there with that jaunty glance for which he is noted.

His eye was on me but it was likewise on other objects that came within his field of vision, for of a sudden I saw him fall to the ground beyond the fence in a pasture and begin manfully to peck and pull at something. Several efforts at this were required before I saw him succeed in extricating a large fat cut-worm which he seemed to exhibit with lordly pride. He strutted around on the ground with worm in bill for maybe a minute before he finally dispatched it, when he darted away in search of new adventures.

On another occasion I was interested in the movements of a robin as he hopped about in a pasture, when I saw him stop with his head turned sidewise as if listening. Suddenly he seemed to place his ear closer to the ground for an instant, then he began his pecking in a tuft of grass and after several efforts was rewarded by a toothsome cut-worm.

The robin seems especially partial to the cut-worm. I see him often hopping around in the pasture grass with that quick little series of hops, stopping for a few seconds, and on again. He is, I think, looking for his favorite menu, the cut-worm. However, he will, during these raids on that delicacy, devour almost any insect that comes his way.

Birds are not over-fastidious about their food. Anything that comes to hand is readily eaten by a hungry bird. This is true of most animals. Man, alone, from his long years of training and environment as well as heredity is squeamish about his victuals. Since the days of savagery and cannibalism his forbears have learned, more and more, as the ages came and went, the exercise of foresight in laying up supplies for the future. Man is provident, frugal—perhaps too much so. If he has an overabundance of food for the present, he lays some of it up for future use. Very few animals do this.

The bushmen of Australia subsist much on bugs and worms—food that the system of civilized man would rebel at. If eaten for any considerable time it would produce a breakdown of health in our bodies.

There may have been a day when our ancestors could live and thrive on such food, but for us who have been so long used to better food it would not agree.

The system—constitution—of birds and animals has not been thus refined. Their ancestors from time immemorial have subsisted on bugs and worms. Their being is inured to that kind of food. For this reason it is not so necessary for them to lay by food for the future. Their food is ever-present, so to speak, except when there is an abnormal season as a severe drought or a prolonged freeze, at which time bird-life and animals may suffer for food.

I saw a mother robin collecting material for her nest. She was just under my window where I could observe her movements. She hopped about and collected small straws till her bill was overflowing, and even after it was loaded she continued to try to collect more, losing, I fancied, as much as she gathered. Cock robin was near-by and took cognizance of her work and movements, but did not assist. Where he does so at times, I do not know. When she finally flew away he followed.

Once I observed a robin making love to a female. Suddenly another robin appeared on the scene and attacked the first one, and there was an old-fashioned fist-and-skull fight as robins go. Almost instantly they were so completely mixed that I was unable to tell which was the legal husband and which the interloper. It was a nip-and-tuck fight for some minutes—the while the female stood with head erect looking on. It was evident that she was interested in the outcome, but on which side her preferences lay I could not determine. She hardly moved while the tussle continued. At last the two hurriedly left, the one savagely following the other, soon followed by Mrs. Robin.

Presently Mrs. Robin returned accompanied by one of the twain which I conjectured was the legal spouse. Instantly he was all attention to her, exhibiting, apparently, no animus because of her late indiscretion.

The Mocking Bird.

One of the happiest of our songsters is the mocking bird. He is the prince of singers and he seems to know it. He will perch himself in an apple tree, near his mate, who is brooding near by, and sing his happy anthems for hours on end, occasionally flitting away but is soon back again. He is probably the most graceful of all our birds. Notice him as he sits and sings on the topmost twig of a tree. Active, agile, mobile, his slender body is so nimble as to appear always in motion. I have observed him while singing thus, suddenly fly aloft some distance, catch a gnat or fly and back again without losing a note of his song.

He is always on the alert for an enemy, especially if the wife is brooding near by. And when the enemy appears the happy song changes to a quarrel. A dog, cat, snake, boy—in fact almost anything coming toward his little family is sure to receive his imprecations. He comes nearer saying "scat" than any of the birds, unless it be his first cousin, the cat bird—the latter so called because of her ability to say "scat."

In the summer of 1928 a mocking bird built her nest in a cluster of grape vines a few feet away from my back porch. I discovered the nest just before the young were hatched, and I felt some solicitude for the hatch because of the family cat, so that I kept an eye on the nest when possible. Within a few days I noticed with pleasure that the young fledglings were prospering and growing. Daily the parents were doing their full duties bringing food to the nestlings.

During this period I observed two things that I had not before seen. One day a sudden shower came up. I soon saw the mother bird come hurrying home and perching herself above the young with wings outspread she shielded them securely from the falling rain. When the shower had passed she hurried away in search of food. I saw her on several occasions perch herself above the nest to shield them from the torrid rays of the July sun.

The Wren.

The house wren is one of the most welcome birds about the homestead. She is always friendly and pleasing. Quiet and gentle, she examines every nook and corner, every crack and crevice in search of a worm or spider. The wood-shed is her favorite place of rendezvous. Here, if conditions are propitious, she is apt to find a snug little box, or suchlike receptacle in which to build and raise her young. This is a good location, too, she thinks, to secure food for the babies later on. I have observed the female busy looking for a suitable place to build her nest, with that happy, jaunty little husband of hers, Mr. Joree, encouraging her and looking on and talking to her as only lovers can.

One morning in early May, I awoke to find the rain coming down in torrents. It was one of those early morning rains with heavy thunder and lightning for which the springtime is noted, and withal a delightful time to steal an extra half-hour to snooze. As I lay there enjoying the rain and the semi-sleep, suddenly there came through an upraised window, like a bugle blast, the merry note of Mr. Joree. He sang as if he might split his little throat. He was very near the open window, but whether ensconced beneath a friendly leaf to shield him from the rain I do not know; but I thought I never heard him sing so merrily as on that occasion, Joree! Joree! Joree! Joree! Then after a short pause the note was repeated and so on for some minutes, the while the rain was coming down in torrents. No doubt he felt as Mr. Loveman did when he sang:

"It isn't raining rain to me,
  It's raining daffodils,
In every dimpled drop I see
  Wild flowers on the hills.
The clouds of gray engulf the day,
  And overwhelm the town,
It isn't raining rain to me,
  It's raining roses down.

"It isn't raining rain to me,
  But fields of clover bloom,
Where any buccaneering bee
  May find a bed and room;
Health unto the happy,
  A fig to him who frets,
It isn't raining rain to me,
  It's raining violets."

The young of the wren—and all young birds so far as I have observed—have a ravenous appetite. It is almost incredible the number of caterpillars, worms, flies, and spiders one mite of a wren will consume during a day. As soon as the little fellows emerge from the shell, the parents begin to find and bring food to them. Now, if ever, Mr. Joree must lay aside his holiday robe and show himself equal to the demands. If carefully observed it will be seen that he is as diligent as the mother in feeding the babies. As soon as the day is begun they are abroad to catch the early worm, and until quite dark they are coming and going with solicitous attention to the birdlings.

In the spring of 1906, I had the pleasure of calling on the late Dr. Anderson, who lived then near Rock Spring. I found him seated on his porch reading. The porch was shielded by many vines and much shrubbery. The doctor related to me how, a few minutes before my arrival, a wren had flown and lit on his shoulder, where it remained for some seconds before leaving. He called his wife to see it which may have been the cause of its flight. He was very gentle and kind toward birds and this one which had a nest near by had, no doubt, noted his harmlessness and had become unafraid of him.

Once I was watching a mother wren feeding her young, coming and going almost with the regularity of the clock, when she appeared in the neighborhood of her nest with a large cut-worm in her bill. It must have been an inch and a half in length and large in proportion. Her instinct told her it was too large for the birdlings to gulp down. She knew too that the cut-worm has a rather leathery covering and would not be safe for a small bird to consume so large a one. What could be done in the circumstances? Why, cut it into pieces, of course; and this is what she did. She lighted on the ground and began with sledge-hammer blows to kill and cut it to pieces. How she would raise her slender body aloft and come down with all her little might on that worm was a caution! Blow upon blow she gave it and so continued till it was parted in two. Then she selected a dainty bit from the interior of the worm and carried it to the nestlings, soon returning for other parts and made several trips till all was consumed.

Many of our native birds delight to build their nests and live around the homestead. This may be because they enjoy the company of man and domestic animals to be found there, but it is more likely because of the greater ease with which food is found about the home of man. Some of our native birds, however, seem to prefer to live far from any human habitation. The mocking bird, cat bird, house wren, robin, and some others nearly always build near the home of man. All these, if kindly treated are susceptible of becoming almost tame, as in the case referred to above.

Birds have a greater understanding than we sometimes give them credit for—at least most of them. Their apprehension is very acute. In my yard I have about a dozen fowls of the Rhode Island variety. They are so much alike that I am never able to distinguish one from another. If one of my neighbor's hens happens to get into my yard I never know the difference—they all look alike to me. Not so with Biddy. She not only knows the members of her own flock, but she instantly recognizes any interloper that happens into the yard. This acute sense of perception applies not only to her own race but also to other animals. A strange dog, cat, cow, man or other animal is at once recognized and generally given a wide berth.

It is remarkable, too, how quick a hen will know her own brood from another. It happened once that I set off two hens with young broods about the same time. They were at once jealous of each other and before the day was spent they had a severe spat. Their chicks were completely mixed and they were quarrelling and scolding at each other, with wings and feathers flushed, when one gave a savage peck at a little chick, almost finishing it. Instantly the other hen sprang at the offender and there was one of the most savage fights I ever beheld. They said not a word but with bill and feet and wings each was intent only on flogging, not to say killing the other. The show continued for some minutes before one of them seemed to have the worst of it and decided to call it off. In the meantime the chicks of each were grouped in bunches as if to await the outcome. As soon as it was called off the victor walked over to her chicks and began her familiar cluck, cluck, cluck. I never saw them try it again. It seems to have been decisive.

But how did the one know she was pecking the other's chick? And how did the other know it was hers? They were all alike to me. Within a day each seems to have been able to recognize her babes from others. A wonderful sense of perception—maybe we should say intuition!

On the farmyard every bird assumes a distinct and definite place. Every chicken, large and small, is circumscribed by his fellows. The cock alone is lord of all. Careful observation will generally reveal that every hen is pecked at and imposed on by some other hen. In a group of three hens it often happens that number one pecks at number two, number two fights number three, and number three imposes on number one. Once this relation is established it is rarely ever afterward questioned. Only the direst necessity or the grossest provocation, as that mentioned above, will impel number two to attack number one, or number three, number two.

These positions of master and servant are generally assumed and maintained as the young flock grows to maturity, and when so established, is rarely ever reversed, even to old age and death. A fowl who thus dominates others will continue to do so even when sick unto death. Her appearance upon the scene is sufficient to dispel those who have so long been subject to her, even though they may be in the best of condition for a masterful fight and could easily give her a fearful flogging.

If another fowl, a stranger, is introduced into the farmyard, this position of master and servant must be decided by all parties. The newcomer must meet all the others and make some kind of acquaintance with each. In doing so she assumes a subordinate or a master's position. Sometimes this is done by a hard fight, sometimes by a mere sham, or a few motions may decide their respective positions. This, however, is not true of the male bird. He assumes, generally, a lordly position without question, unless there is another male in the flock, in which case there will be a prolonged pugnacious battle to decide the question of superiority. But in the case of the male this position is often questioned afterward and sometimes entirely reversed.

This applies also to most other domestic animals, especially the cow, dog and pig. If conditions are propitious these animals are apt to decide the question of superiority—of master and servant—at their first meeting. I have often observed two cows, strangers to each other, meet. They are quite apt to show fight while yet some distance apart, and within a few seconds their respective positions are established, which is quite apt to be maintained ever afterward. This is one remarkable thing about animals.

An Object Lesson in Sanitation.

Many of our native birds are experts in sanitation. It is pleasing to note with what exacting wholesomeness their sanitary life is directed. The bowel discharge is never allowed to pollute and render unsightly the home and surroundings, being carefully disposed of from time to time by the parent. The discharge is made immediately after consuming food and while the parent is still present, who quickly seizes it in bill and carries it far afield where it is cast away. When the parent arrives at the nest with food, immediately the several mouths are opened wide and extended upward, each eager for the morsel; and the parent has only to deposit it in that extended cavern. Having done so, she pauses for an instant and immediately the ends of the birdling, who has received the food, are reversed and there appears a bowel discharge which is seized by the parent's bill and carried away from the nest. At the next return with food this operation is likely to be repeated with other members of the family. These discharges do not always occur after taking food, but the parent pauses for an instant after each feed to see and look out for necessary cleanliness.

Just after sundown one misty evening in the latter part of May, I heard out in my orchard what seemed to be the squealing of a rabbit. I failed to make investigation, however, and early the following morning it was repeated with great emphasis; so I decided to investigate. I discovered that the commotion was caused by some jay birds. I soon found a young jay hidden in the weeds and a cat near by. The parents were intensely occupied with pussy trying to detract her attention from the young jay, and which they were doing in fine shape.

Flitting from post to post, and from limb to limb, just above her head, they had her attention securely directed on themselves. While she was eyeing one of the twain on one side, the other was likely to skim just above her head and nip at her ears which would cause her to change her position, soon to be repeated by the other bird. During this performance, the rabbit squealing that had attracted my attention the evening previous was much in evidence. To the parents it was a tragic circumstance, no doubt, as the life of their offspring was severely in jeopardy. The situation was too much for pussy. She soon gave up the bird hunt and vamoosed for other parts.

A LESSON LEARNED. (By Paul Chambers). "Several years ago I had quite an unusual outdoor experience which taught me one of the greatest lessons of my life. In the hope others may benefit as I have I am telling it through the Voices From the Wilds page of the Denver Post:

"One spring day I was out in the fields shooting blackbirds near my old home by the little mining town of Pittsburg, Georgia. I saw a large flock flying toward an adjoining farm and, loading my gun, set off in that direction. Up to this time I had always been fond of guns and hunting and had an almost insatiable desire to kill anything that was classed as game, either animal or fowl.

"I had gone down the road about half a mile when I located the birds in an open field. I crept up to the old-fashioned rail fence and watched them. The ground seemed fairly alive with birds. I poked my shotgun through an opening in the fence, aimed at the thickest part of the flock and pulled the trigger.

"At the discharge the greater part of the flock rose swiftly and flew away. I could see the fluttering forms of wounded birds and the still bodies of those killed by the shot. I sprang over the fence and started to pick up the birds and was nearly ready to leave the scene of slaughter when I saw an injured bird struggling to reach a nearby brush pile. I hurried over and captured it.

"I held the wounded bird in my hand. It did not try to escape even though its wing was broken and its life blood trickled from other wounds. The bird, one of God's most perfect creatures, rested from its struggles for a moment and then suddenly began to sing. At first I thought I was dreaming, but when I realized the wonder of what was happening I experienced the most bitter remorse and I saw my hunting in another light. The lesson of humanitarianism was driven home to me and to this day I have not killed another bird or animal."

Chapter Forty-three

CHURCH HISTORY.

(Note: In gathering a history of the churches of the county I have consulted many old members of most of the churches, as well as old minute books and other records. Some of the oldest churches in the county still have records of the organization of the church, now about 100 years old. I regret that I have been unable to secure a history of every church. The Author.)

PRESBYTERIAN CHURCH. The LaFayette Presbyterian church was organized on August 12, 1836, under the name of Ebenezer; this was while the town of LaFayette was called Chattooga. In 1841 the church took the name of the town. The account of its organization is as follows:

"We, the undersigned, being members of the Presbyterian church in good and regular standing, but having removed from our respective congregations and located in this village and its vicinity, feeling the importance of having the means of grace and the ordinances of the church regularly administered to us according to the constitution of our church, do agree to associate ourselves together to be organized into a church to be known by the name of Ebenezer. We do further promise and covenant to endeavor to live together in Christian fellowship and love—to watch over each other and admonish, when necessary, with tenderness and Christian regard. We also desire that this church be taken under the care and supervision of Hopewell Presbytery." This first entry in the sessional record is dated Chattooga, Walker County, Georgia, August 12, 1836, and it is further stated that the church was duly organized at the time and place stated. John McWhorter and Johnathan Fielding were elected elders. The following were the charter members: John McWhorter; Johnathan Fielding; William Henry; Sarah Henry; Andrew L. Barry; Margaret I. Barry; James McWhorter; Temperance McWhorter; Sarah McWhorter; Lidia Dickson; Elizabeth Fielding; Abner H. Mize; Mary Mize; Mary H. Smith; Elizabeth Beaty; Isaac N. Swan; Amanda Love; Filis—colored, (Henry's), and Susan—colored, (Fielding's).

Previous to the erection of a church building the congregation worshipped in the old Baptist church and at another time in the Methodist church. For several years prayer meetings and Sunday school were held in the old academy. In 1848 during the pastorate of Rev. William H.

PRESBYTERIAN CHURCH AT LAFAYETTE

Johnson the present church was built. The pastor gave several years' services to the congregation without remuneration in order to assist the congregation in paying for their house of worship. The building was erected by Mr. Billy Duke and the brick used were made by Mr. James Wellborn and his father, Mr. Amos Wellborn, who donated 5,000 brick for the work. Originally there was a gallery for the use of slaves, but this was removed many years ago. In 1922 the church was repaired and refurnished and is now one of the most beautiful edifices of its kind in this section of the state. At that time a memorial window was installed by the family of Rev. W. H. Johnston to his memory.

According to the best information available the following pastors have served the church: Rev. Wm. Quillin, 1836-38; Rev. James Gambel, 1841-45; Rev. Wm. H. Johnston, 1846-52; Rev. A. Y. Lockridge served in 1850 while Mr. Johnston was incapacitated by ill health; Rev. H. C. Carter, 1853; Rev. R. M. Baker, 1854; Rev. J. W. Baker, 1856; Rev. T. F. Montgomery, 1857; Rev. R. M. Baker, 1857-58, also 1863-70. The dates of service of the later pastors are not obtainable but those who have served since 1870 are J. G. Lane; J. W. Baker; J. L. King; W. A. Milner; Scott Johnston; Chalmers Fraser; C. Z. Berryhill; H. E. McClure; W. R. McCalla; W. N. Scholl; J. H. Clark; B. F. Guille; J. P. Anderson and Taylor Morton. Of these godly men perhaps the most notable were Rev. Wm. Quillin and Rev. James Gamble, both of whom did great service in this field—they being noted educators. The two Bakers, Richard and John, also deserve special mention as having been among the outstanding characters in this list. J. W. Baker was at one time professor of ancient languages in old Oglethorpe University, then in South Carolina, now at Atlanta. His daughter, Ophelia, married Dr. Woodrow, who was an uncle of our late beloved President Woodrow Wilson, for whom he was named. Mr. Wilson in his writings often spoke of his visits to the home of "Aunt 'Felie." (As a girl she lived at what is now known as the Loughridge place on Warthen street).

Besides the original elders already mentioned the following have served as such: David Stewart; A. L. Barry; James Hoge; Charles I. Hooper; T. E. Patton; James Shumate; J. M. McSpadden; W. F. McWhorter; Ezekiel McWhorter; Lloyd Neal; J. E. Patton; A. R. Steele; J. M. Jackson; W. H. Steele; P. D. Fortune; J. R. Killian; R. S. Steele; and J. E. Shuford. Three of these, viz. Thomas E. Patton, James Hoge and John McWhorter deserve special mention for their long and faithful service as elders, having served 27, 23, and 38 years respectively.

Of the many families deserving special mention in connection with the history of the church some of the most notable are: Patton; Hoge; Johnston; Dickerson; McWhorter and Henry. Some of these names are still to be found on the roll of the church book, and all of these families have borne a large part in the development of the church.

The sessional records reveal some amusing incidents and show that church members were often taken to task for misconduct and sometimes expelled from the church for various offences. In one case in the year 1844, a brother was brought before the session for trial on the charge that he had failed to give in his taxable property correctly and that he had sold a lot of land to be paid for when Henry Clay was elected President of the United States. Mr. Clay not having been elected, the brother brought suit to recover the price of his land in violation of his contract. He was tried and sentenced to expulsion from the church. Later upon a proper showing of repentance, he was reinstated. Perhaps if our present day sessions were not so busy making money and giving in their taxable property at the lowest possible figure, we might have more spirituality in our churches and church membership might mean more than it often does at the present day.

The war history of the church is most interesting. An account of the Battle of LaFayette as given in a paper by Judge W. M. Henry on the occasion of the homecoming exercises in the church in 1923, is partly reproduced in another part of this history to which the reader is kindly referred.

OTHER PIONEER PRESBYTERIAN CHURCHES OF THE COUNTY.

CHICKAMAUGA—1837. At the time this church was organized it was located in the northern part of the county. Later that part of the county was cut off to form Catoosa county, thus placing that church in Catoosa county and leaving only LaFayette and Peavine. Many years ago Peavine was dissolved, and later a church was organized at Chickamauga. This was in 1908. At the present time the LaFayette and Chickamauga churches are the only ones in the county. There was once a small band of Presbyterians in McLemore's Cove, perhaps organized, but without a house of worship. However, Presbyterian ministers went sometimes and preached for them. Dr. Burkhead, a famous evangelist, of the Synod of Georgia, held a meeting there at one time. There was, also, at one time many years ago, a church building in West Armuchee, with a very small membership, most if not all of whom are now dead.

* * * * *

Rev. William Quillan, who organized the two Presbyterian churches of early days in Walker county, was a native of Tennessee. He came to Georgia soon after being licensed to preach and married here. He located in LaFayette and lived there till his death in 1842, while still a young man. His widow lived for some years in LaFayette but moved to middle Georgia during the Civil War. This zealous and faithful minister left as a memorial to his memory four churches which he was instrumental in organizing. He also assisted in the organization of a church in Chattooga county as well as the First Presbyterian church in Chattanooga, Tennessee. His name is listed as one of the trustees of the LaFayette Female Academy, chartered in 1837. He is buried in the LaFayette cemetery.

Rev. A. Y. Lockridge was another pioneer preacher of the Presbyterian church. He supplied the LaFayette church in 1850 during the illness of the pastor. He was a native of North Carolina, and a man of great strength of character. He did much to establish Presbyterianism in this section of North Georgia in the early days.

Rev. Wm. Hall Johnson, third pastor of the LaFayette church and under whose ministry it was built, was born in 1819 in Rowan county, North Carolina, of godly Scotch-Irish parents. He graduated from Davidson college in 1840. Having decided to enter the ministry, he entered the Theological Seminary at Princeton, in 1841, graduating therefrom in 1845. He came to Georgia as a home missionary in 1845 or 46. The courageous spirit of this young missionary had to battle continuously with ill health. His period of service only covered ten years, but in that time he made lasting impressions on his flock and did much good for the master whom he served. Two years after giving up active work he returned to his native state and died at the age of 40, thus cutting short a most promising career.

Hugh Boudinot Johnston, pioneer lawyer, brother of Wm. H. Johnston, was a young lawyer of much promise. He received his education at Davidson college and Princeton. He graduated from Chief Justice Pierson's Law School at Mocksville, North Carolina. He was a pioneer citizen of LaFayette, Walker county, Georgia. Broken in health, he soon retired from his profession and took up stock farming; also ran a tannery in the early years of the Civil War; also postmaster in the early sixties. He refugeed to Covington, Georgia, in the fall of 1863, where he died soon after. Mr. Johnson was considered a very eloquent speaker.

UNIVERSALIST CHURCH. The first Universalist church in Walker county was established in the summer of 1898 by Dr. Q. H. Shinn, an evangelist from Maine. For some years previous meetings had been held at the Abercrombie school house some three miles south of Chickamauga, and as the number of believers in Universalism increased the erection of a church was agitated by the itinerant preachers, who had been holding the meetings at the school house. Among the itinerant preachers who did good work was Rev. James Park, a descendant of the pioneer Park family of North Georgia.

For many years—in fact from the very first settlement of the county in 1833 or before, there had been quite a number of citizens in this part of the county who had believed and clung to this faith. Among these might be mentioned the Abercrombies, Hendersons, Bosses, Gentrys, Joneses, Parks, Butlers, Buchannans, Hunts and many others. As their descendants increased and grew up in the faith of their fathers it was seen that an organization was needed to shepherd this band.

About this time Dr. Shinn, a man of deep intellectual power and a great Bible student, visited the community and became interested in the work. Those who recall Dr. Shinn will remember how he always read his Bible in the pulpit from memory. Selecting his morning lesson he could ready every word from memory; and this applied to a very large part of the Bible—especially the New Testament.

Having selected a location about half a mile west of beautiful Crawfish Spring, at Chickamauga, the property was acquired and a beautiful church building was erected. The late L. A. (Bud) Boss was a most ardent worker for the new church. He was a carpenter and gladly donated his services in the erection of the house, and when completed, was one of the handsomest churches in that section. Mr. Boss loved his faith and as long as the church held services at that place he rarely ever missed.

The story of the First Universalist church of Chickamauga is an eventful one. The charter members were composed of some of the most substantial citizens of the community, many of whom had been solicited by pastors and members of other faiths to abandon their beliefs that there was no endless punishment, and unite with other faiths; but they were faithful to their first love and stood by it to the last.

One of the first ministers of the church was the Rev. James Rasnake from South Carolina, who had been reared in another faith but having satisfied his mind that he was a believer in Universalism he united with that church and became pastor at Chickamauga. Rev. Chapman, from near Atlanta, was another pastor who did a good work and assisted in building up the work. During these years Dr. Shinn often visited the church, always bringing a great message and furnishing an inspiration to the struggling band.

This church flourished from 1898 to 1907 and many happy meetings were held there. It was the custom of the church to hold all-day services at each meeting and a basket dinner was spread under the large oak trees in the church yard. On these occasions many visitors were always present and enjoyed the bountiful spread. These church days were always full of good fellowship.

Following the death of the beloved evangelist, Dr. Q. H. Shinn, a movement was started to build the "Shinn Memorial Church," in Chattanooga, and as the membership of the Chickamauga church had become scattered, a number of families having moved to Chattanooga, it was decided to consolidate the church with the new church in Chattanooga. The building was sold to the Presbyterian people at Chickamauga who removed it to its present site and it stands to-day without change from former years. The membership was transferred to the new church at Chattanooga.

Among the charter members of the Chickamauga church were Mr. and Mrs. John B. Henderson, M. C. Butler, Dr. and Mrs. G. W. Jones, Mr. and Mrs. S. R. Thurman, Mr. and Mrs. A. T. Park, Mr and Mrs. John Abercrombie, Mrs. John Morgan, L. A. Boss, A. J. (Uncle Jackie) Boss, Miss Julia Carlock and Mrs. Missouri Hunt. Members of the families of these charter members were added to the church from time to time and a number of these are active members of the Shinn Memorial Church in Chattanooga.

Additional information from Mr. S. A. Buchanan of Chickamauga is to the effect that a church of this faith was in existence before the war, located near High Point. This was in the fifties. Some of the members of that church were the following: Rev. James Park and wife, Walker Masson and wife, S. A. Buchanan and wife, Mrs. Mary Carlock, Jackie Boss and wife and M. C. Butler.

CORINTH BAPTIST CHURCH. Organized September 16, 1899, in a small tenant house on J. M. Foster's farm where it worshiped for 9 months while a house was being erected. The following were the first members: Rev. H. W. Head and wife; Misses Frances and Ellen Head; Mrs. J. B. Wheeler; Houston Wheeler; James Bomar and wife; S. D. Carter and wife; Miss Lizzie Carter; Mrs. Dora Hegwood; E. D. Cremer and wife; Lee Greene; Mrs. N. A. Scott.

The first house was built in 1900. In 1916 an addition was made to it and in 1923 because of the growing community a larger and more handsome house was erected at a cost of about $4,500.00 Also at this time a Delco light plant was installed at a cost of $350.00.

Roster of pastors: H. W. Head, 1899-1905. 1909-1910; T. D. Cooper, 1905-1908; J. M. Mathis, 1908-1909; T. E. Ezell, 1910-1915; O. G. Lewis, 1915-1916; J. A. Ezell, 1916-1918; B. H. Howard, 1918-1922; W. L. Mavity, 1922-1926, 1928-1929; J. F. Scott, 1926-1928, 1929.

Present membership about 191. In the church's short history there have been 244 baptisms—a splendid record. 24 deaths have occurred. The present pastor, Rev. J. F. Scott, was licensed and ordained by this church. Few churches in the county have a better record than Corinth.

VALLEY HEAD BAPTIST CHURCH. Organized 1876 by Rev. T. C. Tucker and others, Rev. Tucker serving as pastor for a number of years. The early records have been lost and it is impossible to give a correct roster of charter members. The following were either charter members or were among the early members: Mercer Shaw, Algy Careathers, Wm. Beaird, George Shaw and wife, S. R. Andrews, Angeline Andrews, Margaret, Adeline and Susan Beaird, David Fricks, and others.

The church was organized in Poplar school house, and later moved to its present location. George Shaw deeded two acres with a right of way 30 feet wide to the public road and another twelve feet wide to the spring. The present house was built in 1878.

The following pastors have served this church: T. C. Tucker, 1876-81; W. L. Shattuck, 1882-83, 1888-91; J. A. Mathis, 1886; T. D. Cooper, 1892-98, 1907; J. M. Mathis, 1900-04; H. W. Head, 1905-06; T. J. Ratliff, 1908-14; J. A. Ezell, 1915-16; H. S. Cordell, 1917; B. H. Howard, 1919; Lee Lecroy, 1920-21; S. R. Tucker, 1922. Besides these other pastors without dates were: Rev. Griffin, J. J. Sizemore and probably others. This church is beautifully located at Dug Gap on top of Pigeon mountain and is one of the leading churches in that part of the county.

EAST ARMUCHEE BAPTIST CHURCH. Established in 1886, mostly from the Macedonia church. The following were charter members: J. C. Clement and wife; Rev. B. F. Hunt; Dr. R. E. Talley; Mr. and Mrs. W. H. Talley; Mrs. J. T. Griffith; Mr. and Mrs. J. A. Hames; Mr. and Mrs. J. F. Green; Mrs. Elizabeth Hames; Miss Annie Keith; Mrs. Mary Cheyne; Mr. and Mrs. G. L. Keith; Mr. and Mrs. J. R. Richardson; Mr. and Mrs. J. M. Rives; J. H. Hames; J. W. Keown; Mr. and Mrs. Abe Richardson; Mrs Sarah Roper; G. W. Sims and wife. The present membership is 103.

The following pastors have served this church: B. F. Hunt; John Head; P. C. Deason; John Seymore; J. M. Barnett; D. A. Barrett; T. A. Burgess; J. L. Burk; J. E. Hudson; J. M. Cargall; J. A. Smith.

WALNUT GROVE BAPTIST CHURCH. Organized January 29, 1922, with twenty members. Rev. J. M. Coley preached the organization sermon. Rev. B. H. Howard was elected pastor, D. A. Houston clerk and W. A.

Houston treasurer. A commodious, convenient building was immediately erected which seats about 500 people.

The church maintains an evergreen Sunday school and is attended by the community generally. Rev. W. L. Mavity served as pastor two years, from July, 1925, to July, 1927. Rev. B. H. Howard was then re-called as pastor and is still serving the church as such. Present membership 79.

WATERVILLE BAPTIST CHURCH. Established 1840. Among the charter members were B. M. Powell and wife, Ann Powell. The first pastor was Rev. Artemus Shattuck. Following him came William Newton, Nathan Percell, Edwin Dyer, Henlett Moon, A. C. Dayton, John Young, W. L. Shattuck, T. C. Tucker, Mose Jackson, W. C. Luther, B. F. Hunt, and J. M. Coley. Brother Coley was pastor 18 years.

During the ministry of W. L. Shattuck, T. C. Tucker and Mose Jackson some of the leading members were A. G. Bryan, A. C. Hovis, Mr. Garner, John Partain, Ben, John, and Taylor Powell, and W. M. Martin, who was clerk.

The first church was built of logs with a huge fireplace and seats made of slabs. A Doctor Jones bought the land on which this church stood and converted it into a dwelling which is still used and well-preserved. The second church was a frame and rather frail affair which soon began to need repairs. Then A. C. Hovis bought the Jones farm and became one of the leading members of the church. About 1890 J. G. Sims bought the Hovis farm and wishing to raise the mill-dam near by which would interfere with the road leading to the church the members gladly consented to build a new church on the east side of that farm where the present church now stands. This church was built in 1891. Brother Coley was pastor at this time and was a moving spirit in the erection of the new church and did much work in person on the building. It cost about $1,000.00.

Since Brother Coley's ministry the church has been served by the following pastors: H. W. Head, T. J. Ratliff, J. L. Reeves, Alfred Ezell, W. L. Mavity, J. H. Bowman, Rev. Lord, W. R. Veach and C. D. Gilreath.

Occupying as it does one of the most lovely vales in the county and being surrounded by a prosperous community, this church is most favorably located, and is one of the leading churches of the Baptist denomination in the county. Present membership 110.

WOOD STATION CHURCH. The early minute book of this church has been lost or destroyed and there is no record as to the exact date of its organization. It is one of the older churches of the county—some say the very oldest. It was probably established a century ago. That pioneer Baptist missionary, Humphrey Posey, who labored among the Cherokee Indians, helped to organize it, being one of the presbytery—Edwin Dyer being the other. The church was organized near the William Hullender place in what was Walker, now Catoosa county. Rev. Posey's wife died and was buried at that place, a small stone still stands at the grave.

Soon after the Civil War the church was moved to a new location near Catlett where it has a splendid house of worship built in 1918. There is no record of the older houses of worship. The following were probably charter members—at least they were among the very first members: Isaac Kilgore, E. Cooper, R. Marlow, Martin Camp, H. M. Shaw, J. M. Bryant, J. C. Cain, Thomas McEntire, Amos Williams, J. M. Cain, Thomas R. Davis, J. W. Williams, A. C. Whittle, J. Q. Barber, Andy Cooper.

The following pastors have served this church: J. Tate, 1854; A. Fitzgerald, 1855; J. Young, 1869; Z. D. Clark, 1871; W. L. Shattuck, 1872-73; J. C. Cain, 1874-79, 1882-85; M. C. Jackson, 1880; J. M. Mathis, 1886; T. D. Cooper, 1888-91, 1893; J. G. Hunt, 1892-; W. H. Boyd, 1894-96; H. W. Head, 1897-99, 1907-09; J. L. Burk, 1900-01; J. M. Coley, 1903-06; (No pastor reported from 1910 to 1917); B. H. Howard, 1918-24, 1927; J. W. McClan, 1925; Charles Lane, 1928; W. H. Cumming, 1929; J. F. Scott, 1931.

MACEDONIA CHURCH. Organized 1844. The present church building was erected before the war by William Clements. Two of the charter members were Newton Keown and James Keown. Because of a want of old records it is impossible to secure anything like a connected account. It is known that this was for many years one of the strong churches of the county.

The following have been some of the pastors in charge: A. E. Vandivere, 1854-55; H. Stout, 1858; J. J. S. Caloway, 1869, 1872; J. B. Blitch, 1871; J. M. Robertson, 1873-74; W. C. Wilks, 1875; H. S. Moore, 1879-80; W. M. Bridges, 1882-86; W. L. Shattuck, 1888-93; B. F. Hunt, 1894-97, 1909-22, 1924-25; H. W. Head, 1900-04; J. M. Barnett, 1906-08; W. L. Mavity, 1923; L. B. Arvin, 1927-28; J. H. Cargle, 1929.

BRUNER'S CHAPEL METHODIST CHURCH, SOUTH. This church was located some 3 miles south of Rossville in Dry valley. It was organized soon after the war and for many years was a prosperous and influential church of the North Georgia Conference. After Rossville began to assume liberal proportions it began to decline and was finally dissolved about 1912, most of the members going to Rossville. During its palmy days the membership was composed of probably 100 members and were served by some of the leading pastors of those days, of whom may be mentioned the following: Revs. Bui McFarland; Hughes; Dubose; Stewart; Christian; Roberts; Williams and Quillian, all of the North Georgia Conference.

PEAVINE BAPTIST CHURCH. This church was organized in 1836, and is, perhaps, the second oldest Baptist church in the county. Since most of the records prior to 1874 have been destroyed or lost and the older members have all passed on, it is impossible to give a connected history from the beginning.

Thirteen acres of land was bought from Mr. Jake Buffington for $29.00. Of this amount David Trundell, a Baptist, paid $10.00, Johnnie Henderson, a Presbyterian, paid $10.00, the rest being paid in corn and potatoes. The land was purchased for four objects: Baptist church, Presbyterian church, cemetery and school. The Presbyterians never built a church house—worshiped mostly under a brush arbor. Finally their interest was all sold in a way that it fell to the Baptists, cemetery and school. The old school building—a two-story frame structure—was destroyed by fire during the war. It was replaced by a one-room log house.

The church is now worshiping in the third house of its history, which was dedicated in 1906 at an approximate cost of $1,000.

It is impossible to give the charter members. David Trundell, Jake Buffington, and Mr. Brigman who died in 1892 and who had served as clerk for more than 40 years, were very likely charter members.

The old Minute Book of the Coosa Association, mentioned elsewhere, gives a glimpse at the history of this church in the fifties and early sixties. It was in those early days one of the leading churches of the county.

Since 1874 the church has had 16 different pastors, some of them serving at different times as follows: W. T. Park, 4 years; T. C. Tucker, 4 years; L. N. Brock, 1 year; H. S. Moore, 1 year; T. R. Hardin, 17 years; J. L. Burk, 1 year; J. M. Coley, 3 years; S. L. Barrett, 1 year; L. H. Sylar, 9 years; W. C. Tallent, 4 years; J. B. Tallent, 1 year; R. L. Auston, 1 year; E. C. Harris, 6 years; E. G. Epperson and Carl McGinnis, 1 year. Rev. L. H. Sylar is present pastor. Membership 225.

FRIENDSHIP BAPTIST CHURCH. Established 1854. Charter members: Harris Hammontree, Mr. Sampson and wife, R. A. Jones, Arthur Davis, S. W. Dobson, Sam Serratt, Polly Hammontree and Wm. Hammontree, Sr.

The first house was built of logs and stood near the graveyard. The present house was erected in 1919 at a cost of approximately $2,000 and is in good condition. This is one of the substantial churches of the county, being situated in a beautiful fertile section and is supported by a prosperous membership. This church is affiliated with the North Georgia Baptist Association, being the only church in the county maintaining membership with that body. Present membership 150.

Pastors who have served this church are: Zacariah Gordon (father of Gen. John B.), Jake Tate, V. A. Bell, Britt Williams, Z. D. Clark, M. L. Clouts, Artemus Shattuck, W. L. Shattuck, John Head, W. C. Luther, J. J. S. Calloway, Billy Foster, Jake Ponder, J. H. Blaylock, J. A. Mathis, H. S. Cordell, J. L. Burke, B. F. Hunt, W. L. Mavity, W. R. Veach, James Cargle.

LAFAYETTE BAPTIST CHURCH is one of the oldest churches in the county, having been organized on June 7, 1835. The present clerk, Mr. E. L. Culberson, has the first book of records used by the church, giving the Organization, Charter Members, Presbytery, Constitution, Rules of

Decorum, etc. These old records were written with a goose quill and show with what pains and exactness the early church officers were imbued. This record is a model of neatness in arrangement, chirography, and spelling.

Charter members: R. M. Aycock, Ann W. Aycock, William Catlett, Sally Catlett, B. F. Davis, John Criswell, Nancy Criswell, Partheny Criswell, Nancy Davis, Phoebe, a servant of Jonathan Davis. The presbytery was composed of Elders Hugh Quinn and Evan Pearson. The church was organized at B. F. Davis' school house, near Burnt Mill bridge.

William Catlett was chosen pastor and served till 1840. Edwin Dyer was then chosen and served till 1855. Other pastors were as follows: William Newton, 1855-1856; Edwin Dyer, 1857-1862; A. C. Gayton, January to July, 1863; during 1865 Brother Warren preached on Sundays but no record of conferences; I. Percell, 1866; Brother Blitch, 1867; W. T. Russell, 1868-1872; H. S. Moore, 1872-1884; J. J. S. Calloway, 1884-1890; B. F. Hunt, 1890-1895; C. E. Wright, 1895-1902; Jesse M. Dodd, 1902-1907; C. B. Wright, 1907-1911; I. S. Leonard, 1912-1925; L. B. Arvin, 1926-1929; Ira Dance, 1929-1932.

The following have served as church clerks: B. F. Davis, R. M. Aycock, Jas. H. Culberson, S. Marsh, Thomas A. Seals, A. N. Careathers, E. L. Culberson.

HOUSES OF WORSHIP. The congregation worshiped in a log house near Burnt Mill from 1835 to 1842, at which time a building committee was appointed and a new house of worship was erected near the present high school building, which served as a place of worship till 1891. The building committee for this house was George Shaw, S. Marsh, Lindsay Edwards, Jas. H. Culberson, and R. M. Aycock. Building committee for the present house of worship were: E. L. Culberson, J. H. Hammond, F. W. Copeland, J. C. Clements, and R. F. Shaw. This house, a handsome brick, was erected in 1898.

Spencer Marsh gave $1250.00 to the church the interest of which goes annually to the support of the pastor. Likewise, the sum of $5,000.00 was derived from the estate of the late James P. Shattuck, the interest from which is used for the support of the church. A pastorium was built in 1904, at a cost of about $1300.00.

SUNDAY SCHOOL RECORD. R. H. Dyer, Supt.; J. G. Walraven, Asst.; Addie Augusta Wert, Secy.; Mrs. Troy Scoggins, Superintendent Pri. Dept.; Mrs. O. L. Stansell, Asst. The teachers are: Rev. Ira Dance; Miss Sara Hackney; Mrs. I. S. Leonard; H. D. Shattuck; W. J. Shattuck; Mrs. Troy Scoggins; Mrs. Oliver Stansell; Mrs. J. W. Massey; Mrs. H. D. Shattuck; Mrs. Ben Loughridge; Mrs. Roy Neeley; Mrs. Homer Hill; Miss Grace Bowen.

DEACONS: W. A. Enloe, Chm.; Dr. J. A. Shields; W. J. Shattuck; Hill Hammond; J. W. Massey; J. A. Sartain; J. G. Walraven; H. D. Shattuck; R. H. Dyer; W. C. Smith; E. A. Leonard.

B Y. P. U. This department is doing splendid work under Mrs. A. M. Martin, Director.

The Woman's Missionary Society was organized in 1880. Mrs. R. S. Neeley, Mrs. N. G. Warthen; Miss Orpha Center; Mrs. T. C. Hackney; Mrs. Polly Mize were among the first members. Some of the presidents have been: Mrs. J. M. Dodd, Miss Emma Pickle, Miss Mattie Clements, Mrs. Emma Hammond, Mrs. I. S. Leonard, Miss Sara Hackney, Mrs. W. H. McDaniel, Mrs. Quillian Clemons, Mrs. W. A. Wardlaw, Mrs. C. C. Gilbert. The Society has always co-operated in the work outlined by the State Officials, and holds high rank in the Coosa Association. Miss Sara Hackney has been both Superintendent and Young People's Leader in the Association. She is now President of the Society, and Mrs. Ben Loughridge is Vice-President. The organization is now divided into three circles: The Orpha Center Circle named for one of the first members; the A. Y. Napier Circle named for the only missionary that has gone from this church to a foreign field, Rev. A. Y. Napier; the third circle was named for Mary Crawford, a Georgia missionary in the foreign field. The Y. W. A., G. A., R. A., and Sunbeam Auxiliaries are presided over by Mrs. Ira Dance as Young People Leader.

The oldest members of the church are E. L. Culberson, now in his 93rd year, and Miss Orpha Center, in her 92nd year. Mr. Culberson is active clerk of the church, a position he has held for more than fifty years, thus probably breaking the record as a church clerk. He is also treasurer. Because of a fall several years ago Miss Center is now confined to her bed, but no one is more interested in every phase of church life than she.

LOOKOUT BAPTIST CHURCH was organized in 1849 near High Point on the property belonging to the Widow Dickey. A good many years later a deed to the property was executed. The first church, a small log cabin, was erected on the east side of the road; later, about 1873, another hewed log house was built on the west side of the road, costing about $150. The present handsome building was erected in 1927 at a cost of about $2500.

The charter members were: Rev. David Dickey, first pastor; John Sammons; Lemuel Carter, deacon; Aaron Fitzgerald, second pastor; Moses Morrison, Tom Dickey; J. R. Chambers; John Phillips, deacon; Van Bell, third pastor; John Bell, fourth pastor. Other pastors have been: T. C. Tucker, 1875; J. W. King, 1883; J. A. Mathis, 1886-88, and 1892-97; L. C. Burk, 1900; H. S. Howard, 1903; T. D. Cooper, 1904; H. W. Head, 1907-08; Tom Smith, 1909; J. A. Ezell, 1911; J. W. C. Oliver, 1914; J. C. Kington, 1916-19; J. L. Smith, 1921; Lee Lecroy, 1922-23; J. H. Hisey, 1924-28; Charles Dunn, 1929.

CENTER POINT CHURCH. Organized Feb. 24, 1878, in an old log building on Willis Dunn's place, by the following presbytery: W. T. Park, J. C. Cain, J. A. Mathis and John Shaw. The following were some of the charter members: J. T. Renfroe and wife, W. E. Colquit and wife, Willis Dunn and wife, Henry Glass and wife, Rev. and Mrs. T. D. Cooper, Rev.

and Mrs. John Shaw, Green Dunn and wife, Sarah Glass, Savannah Glass, Melvina Glass, George Brigman, Mrs. W. H. Bayless, Mrs. Beckie Culberson, Mrs. Cealy Smith.

The present church house was erected in 1914 at a cost of about $3,000. Seating capacity 400. The Association met with this church in 1908 and in 1927. The following pastors have served the church: T. D. Cooper, L. N. Brock, J. A. Mathis, S. F. Akin, D. T. Murdock, John Shaw, H. W. Head, L. H. Stephens, J. A. Ezell, J. A. Clemons, T. J. Ratliff, W. C. Tallent, Rev. Hudlow, G. W. McClure, C. W. Howard, E. C. Harris, G. T. King, K. C. Baker, S. R. Tucker.

MISSION RIDGE CHURCH was organized in 1895. Later it was dormant for some years and again in 1921 was re-organized, since which time it has prospered and is now one of the progressive churches of the county. Three of the early pastors were J. M. Mathis, T. D. Cooper and J. S. Kinsey. Recent pastors are C. R. Jones, C. W. Howard, D. W. Crawford, H. M. Linkous, and W. L. Mavity. There are 140 members and the building is valued at $2,000.00.

TRINITY METHODIST CHURCH. Many years before the Civil War, probably in the late thirties or early forties, a Methodist church was established about half a mile east of the present site of Trinity church. The old church was near the ancient burying ground just east of Duck Creek. The building was of log construction as were most buildings of that day and served for a house of worship for many years and probably, also, for school purposes at times. In the decade preceding the war this old house was abandoned and a frame building was erected at the present site, the name being changed from Bird's Chapel to Trinity. This is one of the very old churches of the county, having been established near its organization.

The original deed to the church land is still held by the trustees. It is dated February 3, 1852, and recites that for "divers good causes" this parcel of land is granted to "Thomas Sharp, John S. Shields, Enoc Boils, Joseph M. Wardlaw, and Benjamin W. Maddux, Trustees in trust," etc., and is signed by E. Mabry, being witnessed by H. W. Mabry and Enos Martin, J. P. It was recorded in the Clerk's office on August 23, 1852, by John Dickson, Clerk. In 1904 this church was destroyed by fire and the present handsome and commodious church was erected.

An interesting old record and minute book of the quarterly conferences held at Trinity has been brought to light, which gives the names of pastors for the period from 1870 to 1878. The following pastors were in charge during those years: A. Edom; Hayden C. Christian; B. G. Reynolds; W. W. Lumpkin; C. G. Pearce; T. H. Timmons. One pastor makes this report at a quarterly conference: "Traveled 620 miles, made 110 visits, and preached 44 times," which is pretty good for a quarter's work in that day. Another report of the Sunday school lists 5 McGuffey's readers as a part of the literature used in the Sunday school.

MT. CARMEL METHODIST CHURCH. This is another very old church, being organized long before the Civil War. The first house was a log building. Later two other frame buildings were constructed and used for many years. In 1929 the present handsome building was erected at a cost of approximately $3,000.00. This is one of the progressive churches of the county, maintaining a lively Sunday school and other organizations for the young people. The following are supposed to be some of the charter members: John Miller; Alex. Coulter; William McCurdy and wife; Andrew H. Caldwell and wife. The present membership is 155.

Trinity and Mount Carmel churches, being on the same circuit, have been supplied with the same pastors. The following is believed to be a correct roster of pastors:

William Brady (pastor before the war; raised a large company, went to the war, was made captain and later regimental chaplain. Killed). Wiley Hamilton, first pastor after the war; Rev. Lupo; Rev. Odum; Rev. Lambkin; Haden C. Christian; Rev. Duvall; A. J. Hughes; Rev. Timmons; T. J. Edwards; E. W. Ballenger; Rev. Moon; G. W. Thomas; J. L. Perryman; R. R. Johnson; J. F. Davis; A. S. Harris; J. J. Ansley; A. B. Weaver; Neal A. White; A. F. Ward; J. A. Sprayberry; H. O. Green; R. A. Cliett; T. L. Rutland; N. A. Parsons; W. S. Norton; J. G. Lupo; J. E. Statham; Van B. Harrison; R. A. Coleman; J. R. McCurdy; H. L. Byrd; Rembert Sisson; Barrett Barton; McLowery Elrod.

NAOMI BAPTIST CHURCH. Organized in 1898 in the old Rennold's Chapel, an abandoned Methodist church on the property of W. B. Edge. The presbytery was composed of Revs. H. W. Head, J. M. Coley, and Deacons John Edge and J. E. Headrick. The following were charter members: D. N. Keown and wife; Georgia and Emma Keown; W. W. Robertson and wife; C. A. West; R. F. Delay and wife; W. L. Cameron and wife; J. R. Greene and wife; W. C. and A. J. Greene; W. B. Brown; T. J. Edge and wife.

One year after its organization the church erected the present splendid commodious building at a cost of approximately $1500.00. Since the organization 346 names have been enrolled as members, there being now some 140 on roll. Approximately 170 persons have been led to accept Christ through the instrumentality of this organization since its beginning.

The following pastors have served the church in the order named: J. M. Coley, W. L. Shattuck, H. W. Head, T. D. Cooper, J. M. Mathis, J. L. Burk, I. S. Leonard, T. J. Ratliff, T. R. Hardin, H. S. Cordell, W. L. Mavity, S. W. Lord, J. W. McClannahan, B. H. Howard, S. R. Tucker, and W. L. Head. W. C. Green was elected clerk at the first meeting and is still serving in that capacity—34 years.

THE CHURCH OF GOD. The Church of God is a distinct movement whose faith, doctrine and practice is claimed to be apostolic. Its discipline and standard of conduct are the Bible. Its mission is the salvation of the world from sin, and the unity of all believers into the one body of Christ. Its operative headquarters is Anderson, Ind., U. S. A.

This church has two congregations in the county, one white and one colored. The white congregation is located at Catlett, Ga., and the colored congregation is located at LaFayette, Ga.

The church at Catlett was organized, or set in order, in 1911, and was the result of the labors of W. M. Pettigrew and others. They now have an up-to-date chapel with a seating capacity of about 300. The pastors since its organization have been H. L. Hackler, N. E. Setser, J. Lee Collins, W. M. Pettigrew, and W. P. Long.

Its membership has consisted of some of the best citizens of the county, which are as follows: Mr. and Mrs. J. A. Pettigrew, Mr. and Mrs. S. M. Carnes, Mr. and Mrs. J. A. Howard, Mr. and Mrs. W. E. Cooper, Mr. and Mrs. W. M. Pettigrew, Mr. and Mrs. J. J. Arnold, Mr. and Mrs. G. W. Cranmore, Mr. and Mrs. C. W. Lail, Mr. and Mrs. Henry Williams, J. D. Cook, W. C. Thompson, P. B. Stephenson, Mrs. J. C. Pettigrew, Mrs. S. P. Mattox, Mrs. W. B. Carroll, Mrs. W. H. Carroll, Mrs. C. F. Spencer, Mrs. T. E. Chapman, Mrs. J. L. Lawrence, Mrs. J. F. White, Mrs. T. A. Johnson, Miss Addie Arnold, and many others.

CHATTOOGA. Organized 1838. Present membership 147. The first house of worship was of log construction and stood near the present building. It was built about the time the church was organized and served the congregation till about 1870 when a frame building was erected which in turn was used till 1906 when the present commodious house was built at a cost of several thousand dollars.

Mr. J. D. McConnell, one of the oldest living members, recalls that when he was a mere lad in the fifties he often heard people refer to the church as a "hardshell Baptist church." The fact is that many of the older Baptist churches of eighty or ninety years ago were what we would now call hardshell churches. Many of them believed in and practised foot-washing. There was little thought of missions and Sunday schools and many others of the present day practises and beliefs of our Baptist churches. During the fifties and sixties an agitation and discussion of these subjects began to take place and gradually sentiment crystallized in favor of Sunday schools, missions and other reforms. Hence it was that there was a division among many Baptist churches because of these discussions, some adopting the newer ideas and others holding out for the old landmarks. In this way many churches were divided, each forming a distinct organization. In most cases those holding for the newer plans and beliefs were called "Missionary Baptists," because they believed in missions, while the others retained the name Baptist, or Primitive Baptist, and were often called "Hardshell Baptists."

It is not known who were the charter members, but the following were some of the very early members and may have been at the organization: Johnathan Wall; Wilburn Wall; J. C. Lumpkin; John Williams; Dr. Joseph Underwood; Bob Blackwell; A. J. Price; Lecil Day, and John Day.

It is impossible to give a complete roster of the pastors who have served the church, however, the following are among the former pastors: Zachariah H. Gordon; Artemus Shattuck; David B. Dickey; Wm. Burk; Rev. Glazener. These served during the early years of the church's history, some of them before the war. Later pastors were: W. L. Shattuck, 1889-90, 1898-99, 1907-08; D. T. Espy, 1890-94; J. M. Coley, 1894-95; W. L. Head, 1895-96; S. F. Akin, 1896-97; A. J. Weaver, 1899-00; H. W. Head, 1900-01; J. L. Burk, 1901-07; W. M. Griffith, 1908-1913; I. S. Leonard, 1913-14; Charles R. Lee, 1914-15; A. J. Coalson, 1915-16; B. F. Hunt, 1916-20; W. L. Mavity, 1920-22; B. H. Howard, 1922-27; E. C. Harris, 1927-28; K. C. Baker, 1928-30; W. R. Veach, 1930.

ELIZABETH GORDON LEE MEMORIAL CHURCH.

In 1874 a brush arbor meeting was held near the spot where the present church now stands, conducted by Rev. A. I. Leet and Rev. Grafton. At this meeting a church was organized. The late J. M. Lee donated a lot for the church building and was the moving spirit in the erection of a handsome church building near where the D. A. Jewell home now stands. Above this building was a Masonic Hall built by the Masons of the community.

Among the original members were: Mr. and Mrs. James M. Lee; Mrs. E. K. Roberts; Mrs. S. T. McWhorter; Mr. and Mrs. L. W. Myers; Mrs. Emma Roberts Brotherton; Mr. and Mrs. R. R. Couch, Mr. Alec Jackson; Mr. and Mrs. Jason Conley; Mr. and Mrs. James A. Park, parents of Hector Park, medical missionary to China; Rev. A. I. Leet; J. T. Bilbo; Mrs. Jim Henderson. The present membership is about 340.

In 1910 the heirs of J. M. Lee donated the lot on which the Houston Jewell house stands for a site on which a new church was to be built in 1913. After T. W. Lee resigned, the Board of Trustees traded this original lot to the Jewells for a plot of ground south of the springs and the church building was moved there. Later this was sold for a store building when the present church was built. The trustees traded the Jewells a 50-foot lot south of the spring for a 45-foot lot on which the present church stands. The old church was utilized as a store for some time and finally destroyed by fire.

At the Annual Conference in the fall of 1928 Rev. Wilson J. Culpepper was sent to Chickamauga as pastor. Soon after arriving he began to inquire into the possibility of erecting a Religious Educational Building. By the spring of 1929 a building committee was at work and plans for such a plant were in process of formation. The plans were worked out under the supervision of the architect of the Central Board of Church Extension of our church and approved by him. In November, 1929, actual construction began on this new plant. In March,

1930, the Sunday school was occupying the new building. Since then the Sunday school has more than doubled and keeps growing. The building committee was as follows: R. S. Wheeler, Chm.; C. R. Street, V-Chm.; A. S. Bowen, Sec.; C. Caloway, Jr., Treas.; Mrs. T. W. Lee; Mrs. R. H. Jewell; George Parish.

When Hon. Gordon Lee died in 1927 he left an endowment of $10,-000.00 to the Elizabeth Gordon Lee Memorial Episcopal Church, South. This fund has been invested through the Hamilton National Bank of Chattanooga, Tennessee, as trustee. Dividends are now available every six months. These amounts are to be spent for the upkeep of the church building. At present certain repairs on the church building and certain improvements on the church yard are being effected by income from this endowment. The outlook for the church is splendid.

GORDON LEE

A Walker countian who represented the 7th District in Congress for twenty years.

Hon. Gordon Lee also donated to the Elizabeth Gordon Lee Memorial Church before he died the lot on the south side of the church building on which the religious educational building now stands. This donation was made during the pastorate of the Rev. S. D. Cherry.

The following Christian workers have gone out from this church: Rev. George Matthews taught school in Chickamauga (then called Crawfish Spring) and was a member of this church. While here he heard the call to the Gospel Ministry and decided to preach. Later he became a member of the South Georgia Conference and served there till his death.

Dr. Hector Park joined the church while his parents were living here. Later he was sent out by the Southern Methodist Church as a missionary and served for many years in China as such. He became one of the outstanding missionaries to that country and won the love and esteem of the heart of China.

Mr. J. B. Horton joined this church when a boy. Later he entered the Y. M. C. A. work as a secretary and is now General Secretary of the Y. M. C. A. at Columbia, S. C. He has served at other places and is one of the most useful men this church has blessed.

The present pastor is Rev. W. J. Culpepper. The following roster of former pastors is given, though the list is incomplete: N. E. McBrayer, 1882-83; R. Toombs Dubose, 1891; R. R. Johnson, 1892-93-94-95; A. B. Weaver, 1896; J. A. Thurman, 1897-98; J. F. Balis, 1899; W. G. Crawley, 1900-01; Olin King, 1902-03; H. M. Strozier, 1904-05; W. O. Butler, 1906; W. K. Patillo, 1907-08; C. S. Martin, 1909; O. M. Ponder, 1910-11; H. L. Hendrix, 1912; C. A. Hall, 1913-14-15; W. J. Culpepper, 1916; F. G. Spearman, 1917-18; L. L. Landrum, 1919; C. P. Harris, 1920-21-22-23; J. M. Radford, 1924-25; S. D. Cherry, 1926-27-28; W. J. Culpepper, 1929-30-31.

The Dalton District Conference was held with this church in 1916.

HISTORY OF THE LAFAYETTE METHODIST CHURCH.

By Mrs. O. W. Bledsoe.

Having been requested to give the history of the Methodist church I have gathered the following authentic facts:

In talking with the late beloved Mrs. W. A. Foster, she told about attending services in the old log cabin church that stood where the Fortune home now stands and was called New Town District, that Clement A. Evans and other such famous ministers preached there.

I have been unable to find out in what year the next church was built, but it stood in front of the present courthouse. Mrs. Foster and the late Miss Rebecca Goree told me about how during the War Between the States, the Union soldiers used this church for a livery stable, turning two benches together to form troughs to feed the horses in. All song books, Bibles and church records were destroyed. They related how they with others went and cleaned out the house with scouring mops and brooms so they could hold services there.

Brother Cotter of Newnan, a noted Methodist preacher, wrote me about the Annual Conference being entertained in LaFayette in 1836, he being present at the meeting. At that time there was no railroad at LaFayette so the delegates came on horseback and in buggies. At this conference Bishop Morris presided, D. R. Cumming was presiding elder and W. H. Rogers preacher in charge. Also at this conference the name was changed from New Town to LaFayette Circuit and the mission was called Cherokee. It was later changed to LaFayette-Rock Springs charge and then to LaFayette Methodist Church.

The first preacher in charge here was Christopher Stump in 1835 and W. H. Rogers in 1836. It is with the deepest regret that I must skip for several years as I have stated before our church records were destroyed. I would like to give a brief sketch of each preacher but limited knowledge prevents. In 1856-57 W. D. Bond was pastor; James L. Lupo and Rev. Odum served the church in the latter sixties. 1870, F. F. Reynolds; 1871, T. H. Timmons; 1872, H. C. Christian; 1877, G. W. Duvall; 1878, A. J. Hughes; 1880, O. C. Simmons; 1881-82, Thomas J. Edwards; 1883-84-85, E. W. Ballenger; 1886, J. L. Moon; 1887-88,

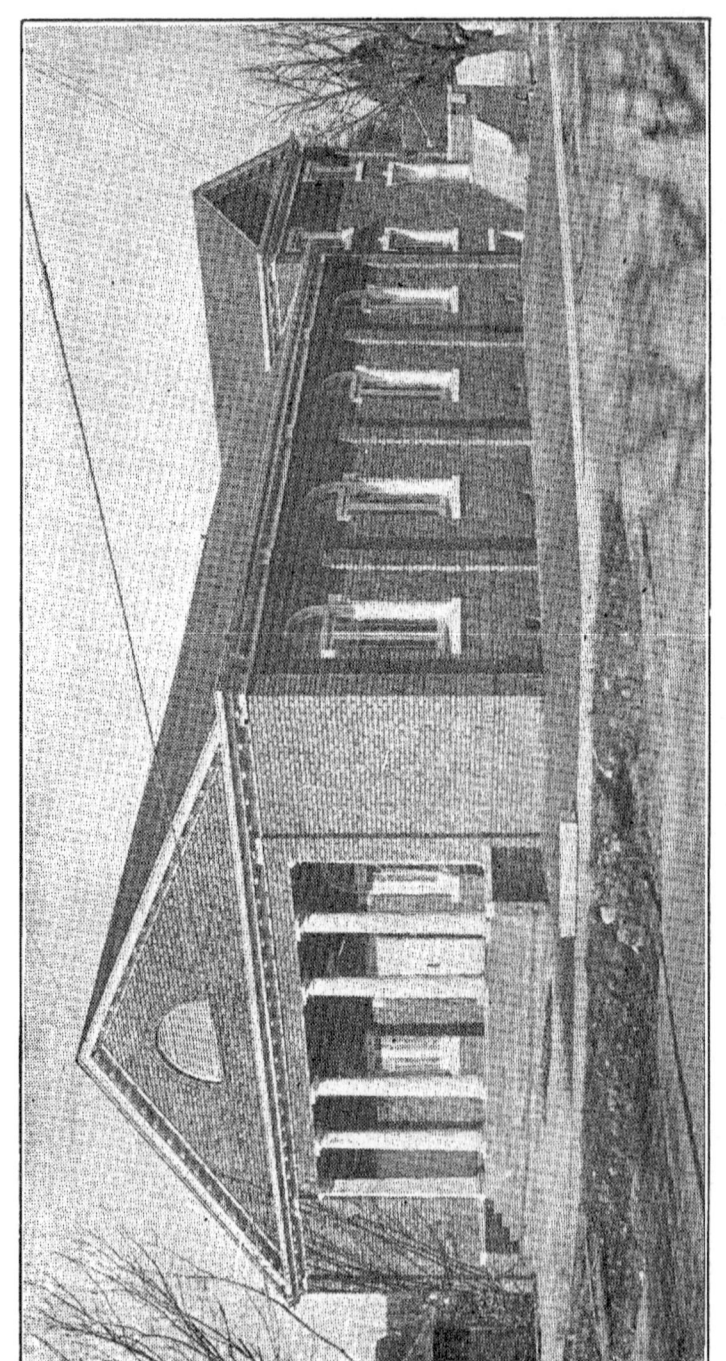

LA FAYETTE M. E. CHURCH, SOUTH.

G. W. Thomas; 1889-90, J. L. Perryman; 1891-92, Fletcher Walton; 1893-94-95, R. R. Johnson; 1896, A. B. Weaver; 1897-98-99, J. F. Davis; 1900-01, S. P. Wiggins; 1902, J. J. Ansley; 1903-04, A. S. Harris; 1905-06, C. M. Verdell; 1907-08-09-10, H. S. Smith; 1911, C. K. Henderson; 1912-13, A. S. Hutcheson; 1914, J. R. Jordan; 1915, T. M. Elliott; 1916, Neal White; 1917-18, J. A. Partridge; 1919-20, A. E. Scott; 1921-22-23-24, J. W. Brinsfield; 1925, W. O. McMullen and C. B. Hughes; 1926-27-28-29, H. L. Byrd; 1930, T. H. Williams; 1931, E. W. Jones.

The following presiding elders have served this district: 1867, W. P. Hamilton; 1868, Atticus Haygood; 1869, W. P. Harrison; 1870, H. J. Adams; 1871-72, G. J. Pearce; 1873-74, R. W. Bigham; 1875-76, B. J. Myrick; 1877-78-79, A. M. Thigpen; 1880-81, W. A. Parks; 1882-83-84, J. F. Mixon; 1885-86-87, W. F. Quillian; 1888-89, J. M. Lowery; 1890, A. G. Worley; 1891, J. B. Robbins; 1892, W. C. Dunlap; 1893-94-95-96, H. J. Adams; 1897-98-99, A. M. Williams; 1900-01-02, P. B. Allen; 1903-04-05-06, Ford McRea; 1907-08-09, W. T. Lovejoy; 1910, T. J. Christian; 1911-12-13-14, W. T. Ervine; 1915-16-17-18, S. B. Ledbetter; 1919-20-21-22, J. F. Yarbrough; 1923-24-25-26, S. A. Harris; 1927-28-29-30, Frank Quillian; 1931, J. R. Turner.

During the pastorate of S. P. Wiggins a new church was built on the lot where the present church now stands. The following composed the building committee: T. A. Jackson, H. P. Lumpkin, and J. D. Fariss. In 1924 this church was torn away and a handsome building was erected, valued at $22,000.00. This building is modern in every respect, has Sunday school rooms, kitchenette and dining room in the basement. The building committee was: O. W. Bledsoe, Chm.; E. P. Hall, Jr., I. H. Holleman, T. M. Quillian, and T. A. Jackson.

The Sunday school is fully organized under the efficient leadership of W. E. McKeown, assisted by W. D. Dunwoody, O. W. Bledsoe, Mrs. Max Wallace, Mrs. George Ransom, Jr., and Mrs. C. C. McConnell as superintendents of the different departments, who in turn are assisted by an efficient corps of teachers.

The church trustees are I. H. Holleman, T. M. Quillian, E. P. Hall, Jr., W. D. Dunwoody and O. W. Bledsoe. The beautiful parsonage is located on South Main street and is kept supplied by the ladies of the church. The parsonage trustees are T. M. Quillian, W. B. Shaw, H. S. Lovern, W. D. Dunwoody and A. F. Gilreath.

Dr. Hector Park went as a medical missionary to China from this church in 1882 and served till 1927, when he returned to his native land broken in health. He died in Florida in 1928. He was dearly beloved by the Chinese. Mrs. Park and her family are yet in China. Dr. Park's work among these people was an inspiration to all who came under his influence and the good he did will ever stand out as a monument to his memory.

The Woman's Missionary Society is fully organized and doing splendid work in every department. Mrs. W. L. Stansell is president and under her Christian leadership the society is doing fine work. Mrs. J. A. Shaw is teacher of one of the most interesting Bible classes; and Mrs. E. P. Hall, Jr., is leader of the Mission Bible class. Too much cannot be said of this class. We have just completed the book, "The Turn Toward Peace." All who availed themselves of this opportunity felt blest from having been fortunate enough to have attended these lectures. Mrs. J. C. Cavender is leader of the Belle Bennett Circle, and Mrs. J. C. Keown leader of the Dorcas Circle. The following are the officers for 1931: Pres., Mrs. W. L. Stansell; Vice Pres., Mrs. J. C. Keown; Rec. Sec., Mrs. R. H. Pitman; Cor. Sec., Mrs. J. C. Cavender; Treas., Miss Mary L. Patton; Asst. Treas., Mrs. W. D. Dunwoody; Christian Relation Chrm., Mrs. Max Wallace; Supplies, Mrs. Fletcher Hegwood; Pub. Chrm., Mrs. W. M. Hammond; Program Leader, Mrs. O. W. Bledsoe.

Mrs. Laura G. Snow has been a member of this society for 45 years, and has always taken an active part and still does so. Miss Mary Lizzie Patton has been the treasurer for 40 years. Mrs. W. M. Hammond has been pianist for six years and has not missed a meeting. Mrs. J. H. Hammond helped to organize the society in 1883 and except for the few years she resided in another town has been a continuous member and has held prominent offices.

The society was organized in 1883, the first president being Mrs. McWhorter. I was unable to secure all the presidents' names but the following have served the past twenty years: 1911, Mrs. S. J. Shaw; 1912, Mrs. H. P. Lumpkin; 1913-14, Mrs. J. H. Hammond; 1915-16-17, Mrs. J. A. Shaw; 1918-19-20-21, Mrs. S. J. Shaw; 1922-23, Mrs. J. A. Shaw; 1924-25, Mrs. D. R. Thurman and Mrs. J. C. Cavender; 1926-27, Mrs. J. A. Shaw; 1928-29, Mrs. E. P. Hall, Jr.; 1930-31, Mrs. W. L. Stansell.

The following stewards are serving now. Some of them have been in this office for several years while others have been gradually added: I. H. Holleman, Chrm.; E. P. Hall, Jr., Treas.; W. E. McKeown, Sec.; O. W. Bledsoe, D. W. Stiles, A. F. Gilreath, R. C. Wilson, T. M. Quillian, R. H. Pitman, John Dodson, R. A. Wardlaw, Sr., Tom Rhyne, R. V. Thurman, W. D. Dunwoody, Max Wallis, M. M. McCord, Gus Martin, and T. A. Jackson, honorary steward.

METHODIST EPISCOPAL CHURCH. Several churches of this denomination are located in the county, as follows: South Rossville, Wallaceville, Garrett's Chapel, Bethel and Harrisburg. A church of this denomination once existed near Center Post, called Mt. Zion, but it was discontinued about 1888. There was also, in the eighties, an organization on Pigeon mountain called Mt. Nebo which was later discontinued.

South Rossville is, perhaps, the leading and strongest of these churches. It was organized in 1910 in the home of S. F. Blaylock with the following charter members: S. F. Blaylock and wife, J. A. Allen, Ernest Cook, G. B. Miner, Dora Hixon, Rev. P. R. Broyles, Henry Stanley, Harbert Cook, Anna Stanley, Stella Miner, and Ruth Wright. The present house of worship is of brick and is modern in every respect, having an annex for Sunday school classes and other church activities. This is one of the leading churches of Rossville. In 1920 it entertained the Georgia Conference, also again in 1928.

The other churches mentioned are scattered throughout the county and are composed of some of the leading citizens of the county. They are worshiping in good houses and are surrounded and supported by a strong membership. These churches were organized soon after the Civil War and have been served by many excellent pastors. The following may not be charter members but were among the older members of this denomination in the county: B. F. Loughridge, John T. Thurman, H. A. (Tip) Blaylock, Peter Wallace, Philip Schmitt, Rev. Broyles and many others.

Among the pastors who have served these various churches may be mentioned Revs. D. W. Cook and B. F. Allen, both of whom are aging fast and are now honored citizens of our county.

The following have at different times served these churches as pastors: H. Boyd; Henry Mitchel; D. W. Cook; P. P. Carroll; W. D. Allen; T. J. Turner; David Boyles; J. H. Hurley; J. H. King; W. A. Styles; B. F. Allen; J. D. Harris; W. F. Pitts; J. L. Anderson; W. A. Martin; L. D. Ellington; P. R. Broyles; F. F. Frisbie; E. J. Williams; T. A. Morgan; T. N. Crumpton; W. W. Adcock; E. E. Caveleri; E. B. Aycock; H. H. Bowen; J. W. May; M. D. Perry; F. L. Waid; J. A. King; Dr. Ashe; G. O. Mulkey; O. B. White; Rev. Freeman; Arthur Chastain.

CHICKAMAUGA BAPTIST CHURCH. Organized at the home of Marcus Johnson on August 31, 1850, being constituted by John Burk, Wm. P. Burk and Brother Williams as a presbytery. The following were charter members, or, were among the very early members: Edward Baldwin, Margarett Baldwin, Zedakiah Myers, Mary Myers, Hiram Lemmons, Rebecca Lemmons, Mary Higgins, Mary Turner, James Moad, John Gray, John Turner, Jane Malicoat, Wm. Mayfield, Jefferson Dyer, John Dyer, Aneel Patrick, Burrell Dalton, S. B. Dyer, Marcus Johnson and wife, Avis Camp and wife, H. Weathers and wife, Wash Harp and wife, Susie Glenn, Samantha Lewallen, Levy Weathers, Elizabeth Gordon, Rebecca Lard, Mary Lard, Ellen Shamblin, Gabriel Cooper, Daniel Murdock, Wilson Partin, and Miss Morgan. Aaron Fitzgerald was the first pastor. Marcus Johnson donated five acres of land for the church and burial ground. The first building was a small log house which was burned during the War Between the States. The second building, a small frame structure, was erected in 1862 which was succeeded by a larger house in 1883 which cost $434.24. The following were the building committee: John C. Greene, J. T. Scott, John T. Blaylock, and S. B. Dyer. Rev. T. C. Tucker was pastor at this time.

In April, 1912, the name was changed to First Baptist church of Chickamauga, and the present handsome building was erected at a cost of $3,500.00. The building committee being J. T. Troutman, W. M. Prince, J. A. Hearn, C. R. Phillips, E. V. Pless, S. C. Tarver and G. W. Lindsay; W. M. Griffitt being pastor. The present membership is 226.

The first minute book of this church has recently been located and is a most interesting relic of church matters of antebellum days. It recites with remarkable clearness and exactness the actions and operations of the church during its first few years of existence. During a large part of this time there was one or more charges against various members for some actual or imaginary misconduct and for which the member was cited to the next conference for trial, some being excluded and others exonerated. At all these conferences one item was to "call for acknowledgments," and it is noted that often some member offered his acknowledgments for some infraction of conduct,—at one time as many as four doing this. After passing this item the moderator always called for the "peace and fellowship" of the church, and under this head they who had failed to make acknowledgments, where due, were generally brought up and a charge preferred against them, a committee appointed to see them and cite to trial at the next conference. Most of this has passed away. It is now history. It is more or less familiar to some of our older brethren but the younger membership of the church knows nothing of it. This writer has not heard these items called in a church conference in more than a quarter of a century. Verily, we are moving!

This old book recites that a petition was made to the State Line Association for membership on August 23, 1852, the delegates being Wm. P. Burke, Wm. L. Gordon and Samuel Carson.

The Crawfish Spring church does not appear in the minutes of the Coosa Baptist Association till 1869, so far as this writer has been able to obtain old copies of minutes. Evidently the church was at first a member of the State Line Association, later joining the Coosa.

Marcus Johnson was licensed to preach on October 16, 1852. At the conference held on September 26, 1868, a motion was carried that "we keep up the ordinance of washing feet." There are many other interesting records in the old minute book. This church has had a remarkable history and is now one of the leading churches in the county.

A roster of pastors, which is believed to be nearly correct, is as follows: A. Fitzgerald; Wm. P. Burk, 1852-56; R. Ware, 1856-(?); John Burk, 1865-(?); W. T. Russell, 1869-71; W. T. Park, 1872; J. H. Blaylock, 1873; D. Scruggs, 1874-(?); J. M. Robertson (?)-1881; T. C. Tucker 1882-88; W. A. Howard, 1889; R. L. Trotter, 1890-93; T. R. Harden, 1894-(about 1901); J. L. Burk, about 1902; L. H. Sylar (?)-1911, also 1914-15; W. M. Griffitt, 1912-13; W. C. Tallent, 1916; S. N. Hamic, 1917-18; R. M. Brooks, 1919-20; R. L. Austin, 1921; G. W. McClure, 1922-24; U. S. Thomas, 1927-28; Carl McGinnis, 1929-.

KIRBY CHAPEL. Second Christian Adventist. This church was organized in 1915 with 11 charter members. Present membership about 70. It is located one mile east of Sharpe and is composed of a loyal membership of some of our best citizens. They have a neat house of worship of necessary size where they have regular preaching and other services.

The following ministers have acted as pastors of the congregation: J. W. Gilbreath; C. D. Gilbreath; F. M. Powell; L. B. Allmon; J. M. Allmon; and Cleve Weston, the present pastor.

Some 25 years ago a church of this faith was established near High on Lookout mountain which was later discontinued because of many members moving away. Recently, however, it has been reorganized with some 15 members and L. B. Allmon, pastor.

CAMP MEETINGS, CONCORD, CEDAR GROVE AND PEAVINE.

There were, according to the best information obtainable at this time, three Camp Grounds in Walker County before the War. These were Concord in the eastern part of the county, Cedar Grove in the western part and Peavine in the central part. Since they were operated on the same plan, a description of the Concord meetings will suffice for all.

The Methodist church at Concord was organized about the year 1844, and is, therefore, among the oldest churches in the county. The first building was of logs which was about 20 by 24 feet. In 1851, Rev. Henry Casper gave to the church a deed to two acres of land on which the log house stood at that time. The deed recites that for "good considerations" the land is granted "to have and to hold in trust for the ministers and members of the Methodist Episcopal Church, South, as a place of worship". Later, in 1855, the trustees of the church bought 12 more acres from the administrators of the Rev. Casper, making 14 acres in all.

About 1851 or 52, the congregation erected a large two-story building to be used as a church, and Masonic hall above. In 1882, the two-story building was torn down and a new building erected in its place, which was in turn remodeled in 1907 and is still used for worship—a handsome and convenient house. The first and original log house was used for school purposes for many years.

Soon after the establishment of the church—probably in the late forties—a camp ground was laid out, and, annually, till the days of the Civil War, a camp meeting was held at this place. It is related by old settlers, who have heard it from still older citizens that immense crowds of people attended these meetings. They came for many miles, —from Summerville, Rome, Dalton, Calhoun, Resaca, and from points in Alabama and Tennessee to attend these meetings. The crowds were often estimated at from 1500 to 2000 people. An immense brush arbor was erected in which the meetings were held. Houses and tents were built to accomodate those who came to camp. These houses contained sleeping rooms, porches and passageways, and were quite comfortable. Long rows of these houses were erected, mostly of logs, but some of lumber. Cooking and eating was done, mostly, in the open. The occasional visitor, or stranger who happened at these meetings, was made to feel at home, and solicited by every body to partake of the viands which were present in abundance. Great numbers of horses, wagons and buggies were present on the grounds, and the whole scene was a most animated one.

The camp-meetings were discontinued during the War, but after peace was established, they were again inaugurated and continued till about the year 1893.

Many of the old-time, Gospel preachers attended these meetings. Among them may be mentioned such characters as, Tom Simmons, Joe Ab Louis, Dickey Harwell, Presiding Elder Thigpen, Dr. Felton and others. These old preachers spoke with such force and power, and with such heart-felt unction that, not only were Christians made to rejoice, but many sinners were made repentant and converted from their evil ways. There were usually three sermons each day—morning, afternoon and night—with grove meetings between. At these latter, the people would gather in the adjacent groves and sing and pray, and often there were praises and hallelujahs at these simple services. The spiritual awakening from powerful sermons, leading to a renewal of consecration in the Christian lives of the people, the daily Bible readings, the holy conversations, and the delightful associations and fellowships of these Camp Meetings were sources of great religious power in the very early history of the county.

These meetings were usually held in the month of August, when there was little work to do on the farm. Having spent a week or ten days thus, everybody would break away and return home to talk of the wonderful experiences of the occasion, and to long for the next annual meeting.

The meetings at Concord and at Cedar Grove were run by the Methodist churches at those places. The meeting at Peavine was a Baptist Camp-Meeting and was run by that denomination as noted elsewhere.

PLEASANT HILL CHURCH. Organized 1847. The first house, erected from poplar logs, stood on the hill-side north of the spring. Miss Sue Gore, who lived at that time near where the Marsh-Horn residence now stands, in looking across the little hollow toward the church noting the beautiful environment of the situation on the hill-side suggested that it be called Pleasant Hill, a name most happily suggested and adopted. It is believed that the log house was torn away about 1858 or 1859 and a small frame house erected which in turn was replaced by the present house in 1871. The present house has just recently (1931) had an annex added which improves much its usefulness and appearance.

It is not known certainly who were the charter members. Abraham Belton Neal and his wife Rebecca it is believed were charter members, certainly they were among the very first members. An old minute book of the quarterly meeting held March 11, 1870, now in possession of Mr. George Morton of near Subligna, gives R. P. Neal, R. B. Neal, Wm. Gore, and A. W. H. Tweedle as official members of the church.

Abraham B. Neal was of the old fashioned type of Methodist exhorters and did a lot of religious work and was followed by some of his boys and grandchildren in religious teaching. He deeded the land on which the church is built. Services were held in his home for several years before the first house of worship was built. During the spring and summer the audience would sit in the yard, the preacher standing in the hall-way between the two log rooms. At protracted meetings they erected a brush harbor for services. Mr. Neal came into the valley about 1839.

According to the old record book of Mr. Morton mentioned above the following have served this church and Concord church as pastors: Samuel Price 1870; J. B. Moreland 1871; W. R. Branham 1872; S. D. Evans 1873; G. W. Thomas 1874; J. B. McFarland 1875; W. T. Yarbrough 1876; E. B. Reece 1877-78; R. P. Martin 1879; Rev. Shackleford 1880; Mark Edwards 1881-82; J. T. Edwards 1883; George King 1884-85; S. B. Ledbetter 1886; S. N. Snow 1887; T. S. Edwards 1888; F. L. R. Smith 1889; Fletcher Walton 1890; F. L. R. Smith 1891; L. D. Coggins 1892-93; W. R. Kennedy 1894-95; J. N. Myers 1896-97; C. H. Hartman 1898-99; J. E. Russell 1900; Walter Millican 1901-02; J. A. Sprayberry 1904-05-06; J. S. Ralls 1907-08 (Died in May 1908 and C. S. Martin finished out the year); J. T. Pendley 1909; J. T. Lovern 1910; L. B. Hughes 1911; W. S. Norton 1912-13; T. T. Thurman 1914; A. E. Silvey 1915-16; J. B. Gresham 1917; Wilson Hensley 1918; J. B. Legg 1919; J. H. Couch 1920-21-22; V. A. Roark 1923-24; R. J. Johnson 1925-26; Odum Clark 1927-28-29; V. H. Taylor 1930; Barrett Barton 1931. (For Presiding Elders, see roster elsewhere).

PRIMITIVE BAPTISTS. So far as the author is aware there is no church of this distinctive faith now in the county, the last one having disbanded some years ago. This was located near Cooper Heights and was the Mecca for the gathering of all the members of that faith during the last quarter-century of its existence. This church had its origin, it is claimed, near Pond Spring where there was a building and congregation before the war and after. Finally it was decided to remove farther west near the center of the greater number of the membership. There was also a church of this denomination at or near Warren and here for many years the congregation had regular services and stated meetings. There were probably others in the county many years ago.

While there is no organization now in the county there are still quite a number of the old members among us. They are and always were among the most upright, reliable and honest citizens of the county. Much should be said in favor of and in honor of the old-time Hardshell Baptists. They were great believers in honesty and truthfulness. It is said that if a stranger came into the community and wanted to buy on a credit it was an easy matter for him to do so when it was known that he was a Primitive Baptist. It is generally agreed that no distinctive set of people have ever been known who were more scrupulous, ardent and zealous in meeting their obligations—which is saying something in their honor in this Year of Our Lord One Thousand Nine Hundred Thirty and One.

The author recalls an incident that made a deep impression on him when a mere lad back in the early eighties. He lived as an orphan boy with an old gentleman, his benefactor, near what was then Crawfish Spring. It happened that the Honorable John B. Wheeler, then and for many years afterward Representative from this county, on his way to Chattanooga, stopped to spend the night with his benefactor, they being old acquaintances and friends. Mr. Wheeler was a Primitive Baptist, my benefactor a Missionary Baptist and his wife a Methodist. After supper the conversation easily turned to religious and church matters. Well do I recall how I sat there a very attentive listener to the conversation. Much was said that I fail to remember, but I recall that the lady asked Mr. Wheeler if he were not afraid of the devil. "Afraid of the devil?" he said. "I am no more afraid of the devil than I am of that house cat." The lady (and myself) who had always been taught to fear the devil, looked aghast at this reply; but as I have grown older and learned more I have come to be very much of Mr. Wheeler's mind.

Foot-washing was one of the distinctive doctrines that differentiated the Primitive Baptists from most other denominations. This is described in the thirteenth chapter of John. Our primitive brethren accepted this as one of the ordinances of the church to be observed and practised equally with other ordinances—the ordinance of baptism and the Lord's supper. At least once annually, generally in the spring, the ordinance of foot-washing was observed by the church. Many of our older citizens have been present and witnessed the procedure. It was always entered into with great reverence and humility. Not only the pastor who officiated but those who took part showed by their actions and movements that they felt the deep humility that must have permeated the Master when he washed the feet of his disciples. Many times it happened that the moist eyes bore mute testimony to the heart-felt happiness that pervaded those taking part in the exercises.

It used to be, also, that many Missionary churches occasionally observed this ordinance. It is probable that we have a few churches even yet that practise it. Foot-washing was not the cause of the decline of the Primitive church. Far from it. The reason was deeper seated. There was a want of vision among the leaders as to missionary endeavor, Sunday schools and other religious movements of the day and time. Had the leaders been more progressive and led the membership to take part in the great missionary movement inaugurated by Paul; had they embraced the opportunity to educate and train the younger generation by means of Sunday schools and other church auxiliaries it is likely that the great Primitive church would be thriving among us to-day. (These observations are made in the very kindest feeling and with no intention to criticise. They are given here as an honest opinion on a historical matter).

The following are some of the older members of this famous old denomination as it existed years ago in the county. The bare mention of many of these names recalls the rugged honesty and manly virtue with which their lives were associated: John B. Wheeler; Calvin Wheeler; James Boman; Elder Ansel Massey; Reuben Childress; Elder William Shaw; Arby Shaw; John Childress; Webster Lawrence; Elder Thad Scoggins; Elder Clingling; Thomas Blackwell; J. P. Johnson; L. J. Scroggins; Simeon Brymer; Jack Adcock; Hamp Young; Adam Davis; John Fisher; Rev. Rambo.

SHILOH BAPTIST CHURCH. Organized Saturday, June 29, 1839, by presbytery composed of E. Dyer and Wm. Catlett. Charter members: John McWilliams, Thomas Whitlow, John Amos, Constantine Wood, Maiden Wood, Mary Liles, Mary Young, Jane Suttle, Elvina Robertson, Elizabeth McWilliams, Omey, a servant of J. Young. The following day, Sunday, Elizabeth Little was received as a member. Wm. Catlett was called as pastor.

Humphrey Posey was one of the early pastors of this church. He was a missionary to the Cherokee Indians, and after their removal he labored among the early settlers of this region, establishing many churches. His wife died in 1842 and was buried in Wood Station valley, near Temperance Hall in Walker, now Catoosa county. The Baptists of this section owe a great debt to this faithful minister of pioneer days.

The present church house was built by Andrew Kline during the latter fifties and is one of the largest and most commodious church houses in the county—possibly the very largest. This is, and has been, one of the very strong Baptist churches of the county. Here the Suttles, McWilliamses, Youngs, Bomars, Easterlings, Jacksons, Littles, Cleckler's, McClures, Ponders, Woods, and many others—all old aristocratic families from the Old South State, met on stated occasions for worship. During those palmy days that lovely valley was teeming with a busy population of prosperous people who rarely failed to attend church services. A section of the church was set apart for the use of slaves, many of whom were members of the church. Most of the old settlers of the valley owned slaves. Often during those prosperous days did the Association meet with this church.

The minute for Oct. 21, 1843, has this entry: "Took up the reference of the last conference, (viz), whether this church will in the future take up the duty of foot washing, which was agreed to." Also, this in the minute for conference held on Sept. 14, 1850: "Agreed to wash feet on Saturday night of our next meeting."

Roster of Pastors: Wm. Catlett, Z. H. Gordon, S. M. Pile, H. Posey, E. Dyer, A. Shattuck, Hillman Williams, Jacob Tate, James Adams, Wm.

Newton, G. W. Selvage, D. B. Dickey, A. C. Dayton, J. J. S. Caloway, D. K. Moreland, H. Stout, F. W. Cheyne, W. C. Wilks, H. S. Moore, J. G. Hunt, B. F. Hunt, C. E. Wright, J. M. Dodd, C. B. Wright, E. B. Farrar, I. S. Leonard, C. W. Howard, Wilburn Head.

Page 110 of the Minute Book tells a tragic story. It says: "July, 1863, no meeting. July 2, C. W. McWilliams killed at Gettysburg, Pa. Aug. 15, 1863, no meeting. Sept., no meeting. Sept. 19, 1863, Robert M. Little killed in the battle of Chickamauga. Oct. 63, no meeting; Nov. 63, no meeting; Dec., ditto; Jan., 64, no meeting; Feb., 64, no meeting. March, April, May, June, July, Aug., Sept., we had no meeting. Oct., 64, Brother Shattuck preached for us and agreed to serve us if the church wished."

CHURCH OF CHRIST, OR CHRISTIAN CHURCH. The first organization of this denomination in the county was established on Monday, May 8, 1848, near Waterville, by Evangelist Rees Jones, and was called Philadelphia. It is not clear just how many names were enrolled on that date, but from that time till September 7, 1863, the number of members was 156. Among the early members at that place were the Halls and Mills and their descendants, as well as Bryan S. Rutledge and others. Some of these old church records are still extant and are interesting as showing how the fathers lived and acted in the long ago. After some of the names on the church record it is written: "Took the sop and went out," which means they forsook the faith or backslid.

Some years after the Civil War the place of worship was changed to Hall school house, then to Pleasant Grove near Trion. The Hall's Valley church was organized in 1901, and is a prosperous thriving congregation at this date. The following were charter members: J. G. Holland and wife; J. T. Hendrix and wife; Mary Rutledge; Catherine and Elizabeth Hall; Sallie Rutledge; R. T. Hall and wife; Flavil Hall; Mary Ocie Hall; Johnnie F. Hollis and wife; W. T. Westbrook and wife.

Among the preachers who did service for the Philadelphia church before and after the war were: Rees Jones, Gilbert Randolph, T. A. Witherspoon, M. Love, George W. Bacon, and Joe Wheeler. At Pleasant Grove the following have served as pastors: Nathan W. Smith, Charlie Jones, J. K. Walling, W. T. Kidwill, N. J. Tumlin, R. N. Moody, W. H. Bird, J. D. Jones, T. B. Larimore, A. B. Lipscomb, Granville Lipscomb, S. H. Hall, S. R. Logue, W. C. Philips, Charles Holder, H. W. Banks, L. H. Reavis, Flavil Hall and his son, Gardner.

About the time of the organization of the Philadelphia church, a traveling preacher stopped at William Jones', near Rock Spring, and preached there one night. Part of the family obeyed the Gospel and repaired to the creek after the service and were baptised. Later a church was established near by on what was known as the Peacock place where the congregation worshiped till the Civil War when the house was destroyed by fire. After the war, for many years, Gilbert Randolph, Nathan Smith,

Charles Jones and others preached in the grove on Mrs. Willoughby's place near the site of the old church.

A church was established at Mission Ridge about 1885. The membership was small. C. Clements was one of the leading members there. Brother Avery preached there about 25 years. It was finally disbanded and the church property went into the hands of the Baptists.

The LaFayette church was established in 1913 at the present site. The first members were: J. J. Williams, G. S. Ramey, John Hollis, E. M. Colbert, Mace Rutledge, Clark Thompson and others, being organized by Rev. Charles Holder. The church has a handsome and convenient house of worship and is in a prosperous condition. Some of the pastors have been: Charles Holder, Aruna Clark, R. E. Wright, S. H. Proffitt, Sam Connally, L. H. Reavis, Flavil Hall, L. E. Pryor, E. G. Collins, E. A. Lowery, Paul Buchanan, W. C. Philips, R. A. Zahn.

The church at Chickamauga was established in 1920 and is in a prosperous condition. They have a suitable and convenient house of worship situated in a central part of the town. Elder Sam Connally is the pastor. Other pastors have been: Paul Buchanan, Aruna Clark and others.

A church of this faith was organized near the Furnace in East Armuchee Valley in 1882 by Rev. Charley Jones who served as pastor for a number of years. Following him John Jones was pastor till 1915 when his health broke, since which time no regular services have been held. Some of the older members here were Adam Davis, Jesse Davis, and Rial Stansell.

CEDAR GROVE METHODIST CHURCH. This is one of the county's antebellum churches. Here during the fifties an annual Camp Meeting was held for many years. This meeting was attended by everybody in that part of the county, as also by many people from Tennessee, especially from Sequatchie valley. For the accommodation of the Camp Meeting a large barn-like structure was erected with no sides and no floor. Lumber was placed for seats between which was a liberal application of straw and saw dust. This substantial building was used for years for meeting purposes.

For the use of the church William Daugherty deeded three acres of land to James Bunch, Laden T. Rogers, Vines Harwell, Charles G. Holland, James H. Clarkson, Thomas Jones and Jefferson J. Coulter, trustees. It is dated 1851. The first house served the congregation till 1883 when a better building was erected. This house was used for 48 years, or till 1923 when it was destroyed by fire. The present handsome house was immediately built.

Mr. J. A. Coulter, one of the older members of the church, recalls most vividly some of the old incidents of the early life of the church. He tells of one of the old Gospel preachers who used to preach with such unction and power that often not a dry eye might be seen in the audience. He recalls how this old servant of God, himself aged and infirm, in his public devotions and prayers would sometimes say, "Oh Lord bless us old people; we who have already lived out our three-score years and ten and now living on borrowed time; we who have traveled the King's Highway for half a century, and not tired of it yet, although we may weary because of the roughness of the road and the infirmity of the flesh; we who, like Christian, have, at times, passed through the Valley of the Shadow of Death, and at other times have mounted the Delectable Mountains; Oh Lord bless us old people." The peculiar manner, trembling voice, solemn and humble, of this old servant of God in his devotions and prayers was a benediction in itself.

ROSTER OF PASTORS of the Methodist churches, Cedar Grove, Kensington and the Cove. In the early years Chickamauga was served by these same pastors. The author is indebted to Rev. Geo. W. Barrett, Secretary of the North Georgia Conference, for a list of the names of pastors of that denomination serving the various churches of the county. This list only reaches back to about 1888. A few of the older pastors are remembered by some of the older members. Mrs. Lottie Hunter gives the first.

Samuel W. McWhorter, 1871-72; J. B. McFarland, 1873; A. O. Steward, 1874; H. C. Christian, 1875-76; P. G. Reynolds, 1877-78; J. N. Myers, 1879; A. J. Hughes, 1880; R. L. Campbell, 1881; N. E. McBrayer, 1882-83; William Dunbar (no date); Wililam Shea (no date); R. B. O. England, 1888; W. C. Dunlap, 1890; J. R. Speck, 1891; W. R. Kennedy, 1892-93; G. C. Andrews, 1894; J. A. Quillian, 1895-96; J. A. Thurman, 1897-98; J. F. Balis, 1899; W. G. Crawley, 1900-01; Olin King, 1902-03; H. M. Strozier, 1904-05; W. O. Butler, 1906; M. K. Patillo, 1907-08; C. S. Martin, 1909; O. M. Ponder, 1910-11; H. L. Hendrix, 1912; C. A. Hall, 1913-14-15; W. J. Culpepper, 1916; F. G. Spearman, 1917-18; L. L. Landrum, 1919; C. P. Harris, 1920.

Other pastors' names without dates are as follows: B. Jones; W. B. Taylor; H. O. Green; T. L. Rutland; J. A. Sprayberry; Henry Harden; W. F. Powell; J. R. McCurdy; H. A. King.

The author does not flatter himself to believe that this roster is correct in all respects. Charges and circuits often change names and because of this it is difficult to know just what churches are included.

PRESIDING ELDERS of the Dalton District from 1870 to date: H. J. Adams, 1870; G. J. Pierce, 1871-72; R. G. Bigham, 1873-74; J. D. Myrick, 1875-76; A. M. Thigpen, 1877-78-79; W. A. Parks, 1880-81; J. F. Mixon, 1882-83-84; W. F. Quillian, 1885-86-87; J. M. Lowery, 1888-89; A. G. Worley, 1890; J. B. Robins, 1891; W. C. Dunlap, 1892; H. J. Adams, 1893-94-95-96; A. W. Williams, 1897-98-99; B. P. Allen, 1900-01-02; Ford McRee, 1904-05-06; W. P. Lovejoy, 1907-08-09-10; J. T. Christian, 1911; W. T. Ervine, 1912-13-14-15; S. B. Ledbetter, 1916-17-18-19 (died in March, 1919, and J. F. Yarbrough filled out the term); J. F. Yarbrough, 1920-21-22; A. S. Harris, 1923-24-25-26; Frank Quillian, 1927-28-29-30; J. R. Turner, 1931-.

KENSINGTON METHODIST Church. This church was organized near Hiniard's Cross Roads, later known as Bailey's Cross Roads, and now called Coulter's Cross Roads. It was organized long before the War Between the States, and was known as Payne's Chapel. Later, at the suggestion of Dr. Thornburg, one of the early members and a local preacher, it was re-named Cassandra, and the postoffice of that name took its name from the church. About 1890 it was moved to its present location and the name again changed.

This is one of the substantial churches of the county, being located in the beautiful and fruitful valley of McLemore's Cove, and surrounded by and composed of many of the prosperous people of that fertile valley. It stands well to the front among the leading rural churches of the county.

A roster of the pastors who have served this church are the same, in the main as those serving the Cedar Grove church, both being on the same charge. The present pastor is Rev. H. A. King.

ROCK SPRINGS METHODIST CHURCH.

The following information regarding this church is furnished by Mr. J. R. Tyner.

The church was organized about 1838 or 1840. The land was given by Wm. Satterfield and was deeded the 22 day of April, 1844, to William Conley, Thomas Evitt, Daniel Evans, Samuel Brice and Wm. Satterfield, Commissioners, and their successors in office so long as used for church purposes. The brethren named were some of the early members of the church. Others of the old members were: William Conley, L.P., H. J. Evans, L.P., Wm. W. Tyner, L.P., Samuel Brice, L.P., Riley Payne, Exhorter, William Smith, C.L., H. J. Conley, Steward. There were others whose names are forgotten at this time.

It should be recorded here that many of the old sisters of the church were very zealous as workers in the church and were always on hand and ready to lend a helping hand in any way possible. Old Grandma Brice was one of these, as were also, Aunt Margaret Conley, Aunt Sarah Conley, Adlaid Brice and many others now forgotten. To the honor and to the memory of these saintly old ladies whether named here or not, who have been sleeping in the adjacent burying ground now for many years, it is desired to say a word of praise for their beautiful lives of unselfish devotion to the cause of the church and for the good of the community.

The first house of worship was a log cabin which was used as such for a number of years. During the late fifties a good sized frame building was erected and used for worship, but was not ceiled till after the war, when it was also painted and new benches placed into it. This house served the community for many years during which the church prospered. In 1907 the present house was erected by the following building committee: C. M. Conley, Z. W. Jones, R. G. Wellborn and Dr. Lee Bird. Mrs. Jack Jones, nee Maggie Conley, now residing in Chattanooga, was active and instrumental in procuring and furnishing seats for the church and furniture for the pulpit, this being her childhood home and church. After completion it was dedicated by Rev. Ford McRea, Presiding Elder of the Dalton district.

A roster of pastors of the church will be the same in the main as that for the LaFayette Methodist church, since the two churches were served by the same pastors till a few years back.

THE COOSA BAPTIST ASSOCIATION.

The Coosa Baptist Association was organized in 1837. Most of the churches going into the organization of the body had formerly belonged to the Cave Spring Association. Originally the Coosa covered a large part of northwest Georgia as well as large parts of Alabama and Tennessee. Churches composing this association were scattered from Rome to Chattanooga and from Dalton to Fort Payne, Alabama. As late as 1905 several churches in Tennessee and Alabama held membership in the Coosa. From the territory of the original Coosa Association have sprung the following associations: North Georgia, Chattooga, Lookout Valley, Catoosa, Floyd and possibly others.

A generation ago, and for many years previous, the annual meeting of the association was one of the principal events of the summer season. The association usually met on Thursday evening and continued in session till Sunday noon—three full days. It was considered quite an honor in those days to be sent as a delegate to the association, and there was, sometimes, in some of the churches, a friendly rivalry as to who the messengers should be. They were generally selected a month in advance and preparations were immediately begun to attend. The old buggy was repaired, or horse shod; a new hat or pair of shoes was purchased, and a little money carefully laid by for missions.

The church and community entertaining the association was active for weeks in advance getting ready for the meeting. The church house might be repaired or painted, or a large brush arbor might be erected to be used in lieu of the church; the grounds were to clean off and long tables to be built; homes were to be secured to entertain the delegates and visitors; a beef or two, sheep, kids and pigs were to be killed and divided among the members to feed the throngs.

The people came in wagons, buggies, mounted or afoot. And such crowds as might be seen at these meetings! Conveyances and animals were crowded together for several hundreds of yards, maybe; and there was a constant movement out doors of people attending to horses and other matters.

These meetings were great spiritual feasts, for there were present some of the great old-time preachers who were full of the Holy Ghost and when they spoke or preached it carried conviction and there was hardly a dry eye in the vast audience. There were always at least two sermons a day, at eleven and at night—maybe in the afternoon. There were reports and discussions on Missions, Education, Publications and some other subjects, but the program was not filled to overflowing with reports as we have it today. There was time for preaching, singing and prayer and for old-time Christian fellowship—a spiritual feast.

At these meetings a collection was always taken for missions or other such objects, usually after the Missionary sermon was preached. Also, the delegates were called upon to make pledges in the name of their churches for money to be paid during the year for missions or other worthy cause. The Finance committee was one of the important committees at that time. Its report was a kind of balance sheet for the year, showing collections and disbursements of funds.

In those days every delegate spent at least two nights, sometimes three. Instances have occurred when fifty or more people have been entertained by one household. The beds and every available space on the floor being occupied by the ladies, the men sleeping at the barn in the hay. An improvised table out doors under the trees was generally used on these occasions on which to serve meals, especially where there was a large number being entertained. Breakfast over, everybody repaired to the church—all except the good lady and her daughters, who must now get the mid-day meal ready to take to the church to feed the crowds at noon. And such dinners! Everything cooked at home, fresh and good. No ready-bought loaf bread in those days; no canned goods. Everything prepared at home. Beef, mutton or pork, ham or chicken, eggs and bacon, with a heaping platter of beans or other vegetables; old-fashioned corn light-bread, fresh biscuits, pies, cakes, fruits and often hot coffee made up the noon-day meal.

In that early day of moderation, slow travel and leisure, it often happened that a delegate went almost a hundred miles to the Association—quite frequently sixty. He started the day before and spent the night with some friend on the way, continuing his journey with his friend the following day, this procedure being reversed when returning home. Although the roads were rough, the weather hot and travel slow, the journey was thoroughly enjoyed by our forefathers because of the friendly association and delightful conversation along the way. They were as "Pilgrims bound for Canaan's Land."

An Old Minute Book—Coosa Association.

"A Book Containing the Proceedings of Annual General Meetings for the Third District of the Coosa Association, Commencing with the Meeting held at Union Peavine Church, Walker County, Ga., the 6th & 7th of September, 1850." Z. A. Gordon, Modr., Moses Park, Clk.

The above is on the title page of an old blank book which has weathered the passage of time for more than eighty years, and is still in fair condition. Having read and pondered the contents carefully, I have reached the conclusion that this was not the annual meeting of the Coosa Association itself, but was one of the divisions of that body, which seems to have met annually. The following churches seem to have composed this district: Concord Tenn., Wood Station, Ringgold, Union Peavine (or what we call Peavine), Rocky Creek, (or Rock Creek), Medicinal Springs, (Gordon Springs), Antioch, Lookout, LaFayette, New Providence, Sulphur Springs, Ebenezer, Pleasant Grove.

The records show that these General Meetings were held annually at Peavine for a number of years. At the meeting held in 1853, it was resolved to hold the meetings with the Peavine church for the next five years. It was likewise decided at this meeting to build tents and hold a Camp-Meeting in connection with the General Meetings. Accordingly the following churches agreed to build tents, being vouched for by their delegates: LaFayette, two tents; Wood Station, one; Medicinal Springs, one; Antioch, one; Lookout, one; Ringgold, one. "Resolved, that the meetings be fixed permanently for the Friday before the first Sabbath in August." It appears that these meetings were held annually at Peavine for about eight years, or till 1857. The meeting for 1858 was voted to LaFayette, but there is no record of the meeting for that year. The meeting in 1859 was held at Wood Station. The meeting for 1860 was voted for Antioch but no record of the meeting. 1861 was again at Peavine, as was that of 1862 which was the last one of record.

The following delegates to these meetings are mentioned from year to year, which indicates that they were, many of them at least, ministers and deacons: Medicinal Springs, (Gordon Springs),—Z. A. Gordon (father of General John B.); L. Williams, T. Cooper, M. R. Moore, A. G. Whittle. Wood Station,—E. Cooper, R. Marlow, Hiram M. Shaw, Martin Camp, Amos Williams, Thomas R. Davis, J. W. Williams, A. C. Whittle, Jesse Bryant. Peavine,—T. H. Jones, M. Park, G. Brigham, A. Thedford, J. T. Renfro, D. Major, R. Tierce, E. E. White, G. Ward, Eli Cox. Rock Creek,—T. R. Davis, J. Smith, J. Turner, G. W. Ellis, G. W. Harp, Isaac Newton, Pohn Pearce, F. M. Harp, James Ellis, — Hartsfield, —Miller. Antioch,—B. W. Cordell, Jason Isbell, J. H. Lathrum, John Mahan, William Fowler, Thomas Davis, S. Andrews, C. M. Blair, J. B. Bell, Wm. Mahan. Lookout,—John Sammons, David B. Dickey, M. Dickey, L. Carter, Moses Morrison, Thomas Smith, John Phillips, John R. Chambers, Thos. W. Dickey, Josiah Vernon. LaFayette,—E. Dyer, L. Edwards, N. M. Mathews, George Shaw, J. H. Culberson, Turner Andrews, J. Pullen.

Among a great many other interesting matters the following shows how these old brethren looked at and discharged their duties: "Resolved; That this Union Meeting believe that brother William Burk—a Baptist minister of our Association has acted in disorder in aiding—under the circumstances in the case—in constituting a church at Crawfish Spring, and by receiving into the said church, John Turner, an ex-communicated Baptist minister, who, to the knowledge of the said Brother William Burk—had denounced the faith of the Coosa Baptist Association." "And Resolved, further that we advise the church at

Lookout to call brother Burk to account for said disorder."

The following querry was sent from the Medicinal Springs church: "Is it right, or is it Gospel order to deal with and turn out a member for making or vending ardent spirits?" This question was discussed fully and the following resolution was unanimously adopted: "Resolved, That in the opinion of this meeting the making and vending of ardent spirits as a beverage is inconsistent with Gosped order, and that every church should use all proper means to put the evil from among them. And further Resolved that the clerk furnish every church, through the delegates, a copy of this querry with this resolution." Also, this one: "Has the church the right to deal with her minister and to exclude him from the church without the aid of a presbytery?" Answer: -"Re solved, That in the opinion of this body the church has the right and should never yield it."

In 1852 this querry was sent in by Lookout church: "Doth the 4th and 6th article of the Coosa Baptist Association hold forth a limited atonement, so that a part of the human family is, and has forever been excluded from the grace and glory according to the covenant agreement and that the Spirit doth not strive with them to bring them to repentance, so that a part of the human family are entirely left out of the covenant?" The record shows that this query was discussed by Elders E. Dyer, and A. Fitzgerald and the following was unanimously agreed: "That neither the Bible nor the 4th and 6th article referred to, hold forth a limited atonement so that a part of the human family is and has been forever excluded from grace and glory, according to the covenant agreement; so that they could not be saved, if they would: But that all who will may participate of the benefits of the atonement, according to Gospel requisitions."

"Resolved, That we recommend that the churches of this district revive and keep up a correspondence with each other."

At the meeting in 1855 the following brethren were appointed to discuss the subjects named:

E. Dyer—Final Perseverance of the Saints.
Wm. Fowler—Church Government.
M. W. Vandivere—Duties of Pastors to their Churches
J. R. Chambers—Subject of Missions
A. E. Vandivere—Duties of Deacons
D. B. Dickey—On Prayer
J. T. Renfro—On Sunday Schools
J. H. Park—On Temperance

"Union Peavine, Sept. 12th, 1856.

"The Ministers and Brethren composing the General Meeting of the third district of the Coosa Baptist Association convened at the harbor and after preaching by Brother William Fowler met pursuant to adjournment to attend to the meeting of the General Meeting. Brother

Lindsay Edwards was elected Moderator after which proceeded to business." These are the exact words of the minutes of the session for the year 1856, showing that there was a harbor erected and that a Camp-meeting was being held in connection with these General Meetings. It is interesting to note, also, that no business meetings were held on Sundays. The business meetings were always dismissed on Saturdays till Monday morning.

At this meeting the following brethren were appointed to discuss the subjects assigned at the next regular meeting:

J. H. Park—Duties of Church Member to attend Conference
James Mann—Duties of Members to Pastors
Elder Wm. Fowler—On Ordinance of Baptism
Daniel Major—On Predestination
Lindsay Edwards—On Best Means of Promoting Revivals
James Pullen—On Benefit of a Religious Paper
Dr. A. S. Barry—On Communion
A. Shamblin—Duties of Brethren to Keep up Prayer Meetings in their Churches
O. H. P. Gardner—Duties of Church Members to Each Other.
T. H. Stout—Millinneal Reign of Christ
Wm. Henry—Duties of Deacons
Elder Robert Ware—On Subject of Missions
Elder Pursley—On Kingdom of Christ
Elder Morgan—On Promotion of Piety
Elder A. Fitzgerald—Atonement of Christ

Session of 1857:

At this meeting there is this entry: "Received letter of correspondence from Waterville Church by the hands of Brother B. M. Powell, requesting a correspondence with them who, with other visiting brethren were invited to seats." At this meeting the following querry was received and discussed: "Has the Church the right to require her members to attend her regular conferences?" Which was unanimously decided in the affirmative. Also, this querry: "Should any kind of gambling or of frequenting billiard rooms or other gambling establishments, or going or sending to dancing schools, be tolerated in church members?" Decided unanimously: "It should not."

At this meeting it was decided to hold the next General Meeting at LaFayette, but there is no record of the meeting at that place. The session for 1859 was held at Wood Station. However, there seems to have been a small attendance and very little discussion. The following querry was offered: "Was Judus Iscariot at the Lord's Supper, or not?" There is no record of the decision. At this meeting it was voted to hold the next meeting with the church at Antioch, but there is no record of the meeting at that place.

The two last meetings were held at Peavine, 1861 and 1862. The last page of the minute for the last session reads as follows: "By motion agreed to take up a collection on Sabbath for the Cherokee Indian Missions. By motion a preacher was appointed to preach a missionary sermon to-morrow; appointed Brother Hill, and Brother Dyer to follow him in some appropriate remarks. By motion agreed that the next General Meeting be held on Friday before the fourth Sabbath in September 1863."

"General Business: Agreed to appoint a minister and attempt to preach the introductory sermon for the next General Meeting. Brother Bell to preach, Brother Dyer alternate.

"Adjourned to time and place appointed. Prayer by Brother Park."

J. B. Bell, Modr.   George Brigman, Clk.

Is it surprising that these General Meetings were not held in 1863? Less than a week before the time appointed for the session, and for several weeks previous a seething mass of soldiers in Blue and Gray had paraded the surrounding country and finally met in a death struggle a few miles away. If ever there was a potent reason for a failure to meet in a religious gathering surely this was one. The shock was so great and lasting that it was never possible to reorganize these General Meetings. These old records accidentally brought to light, should be an impelling incentive to all right thinking persons to "go and do likewise." "There were Giants in those days."

Records of annual meetings of Coosa Baptist Association as gathered from old Minutes. The association was organized in 1837.

Year	Place	Moderator	Clerk	Treasurer
1839	Mt. Harmony			
1854	Summerville	Edwin Dyer	C. H. Stilwell	C. W. Sparks
1855	Union Peavine	Edwin Dyer	A. B. Ross	C. W. Sparks
1856	Cave Spring			
1858	LaFayette	Edwin Dyer	A. B. Ross	C. W. Sparks
1859	Pisgah			
1869	Sardis	W. T. Russell	C. H. Stilwell	J. Y. Wood
1870	Ringgold			
1871	Shiloh	W. T. Russell	J. Y. Wood	Joel Withers
1872	New Liberty	J. J. S. Caloway	J. C. Clements	Joel Withers
1873	Macedonia	D. Scruggs	J. C. Clements	Joel Withers
1874	Summerville	D. Scruggs	J. Y. Wood	J. M. Shaw
1875	Chattooga	W. T. Russell	J. Y. Wood	J. C. Clements
1876	Pleasant Gr.			
1879	Mt. Harmony	W. L. Shattuck	J. Y. Wood	E. L. Culberson
1880	Antioch	W. L. Shattuck	J. Y. Wood	E. L. Culberson
1881	LaFayette	H. S. Moore	J. Y. Wood	E. L. Culberson
1882	Shiloh	H. S. Moore	L. N. Brock	E. L. Culberson
1883	Crawfish Sprg.	T. C. Tucker	L. N. Brock	E. L. Culberson
1884	New Liberty	H. S. Moore	W. C. Luther	E. L. Culberson
1885	New Hope	T. C. Tucker	W. C. Luther	E. L. Culberson
1886	Trion Factory	T. C. Tucker	J. Y. Wood	E. L. Culberson
1887	Macedonia	H. S. Moore(?)	J. Y. Wood(?)	F. W. Copeland(?)
1888	Chatta. Valley	H. S. Moore	J. Y. Wood	F. W. Copeland
1889	Chattooga	H. S. Moore	J. Y. Wood	F. W. Copeland

Year	Place	Moderator	Clerk	Treasurer
1890	New Prospect	R. L. Trotter	J. Y. Wood	F. W. Copeland
1891	Shiloh	W. L. Shattuck	J. Y. Wood	B. F. Hunt
1892	Peavine	W. L. Shattuck	J. G. Hunt	J. T. Suttle
1893	LaFayette	W. L. Shattuck	J. Y. Wood	F. W. Copeland
1894	New England	W. L. Shattuck	J. Y. Wood	F. W. Copeland
1895	Wood Station	W. L. Shattuck	J. Y. Wood	F. W. Copeland
1896	Antioch	W. H. Head	J. Y. Wood	Jas. P. Shattuck
1897	Pleasant Hill	T. R. Harden	J. Y. Wood	Jas. P. Shattuck
1898	Chickamauga	W. L. Shattuck	J. Y. Wood	Jas. P. Shattuck
1899	East Armuchee	W. L. Shattuck(?)	J. Y. Wood(?)	J. P. Shattuck(?)
1900	Peavine	W. L. Shattuck	J. Y. Wood	Jas. P. Shattuck
1901	LaFayette	W. L. Shattuck	J. Y. Wood	
1902	New Prospect	J. P. Shattuck	J. Y. Wood	C. C. Childs
1903	Chatta. Valley	J. P. Shattuck	J. Y. Wood	L. S. Barrett
1904	Rossville	W. L. Shattuck	J. Y. Wood	C. R. Jones
1905	Valley Head	J. M. Dodd	C. R. Jones	J. P. Shattuck
1906	Burning Bush	J. M. Dodd	C. R. Jones	Jas. P. Shattuck
1907	Macedonia	W. L. Shattuck	J. Y. Wood	Jas. P. Shattuck
1908	Center Point	W. L. Shattuck	J. Y. Wood	Jas. P. Shattuck
1909	Bethel	W. L. Shattuck	J. A. Sartain	Jas. P. Shattuck
1910	Chattooga	W. M. Dyer	J. A. Sartain	Jas. P. Shattuck
1911	Boynton	Jas. P. Shattuck	J. A. Sartain	Jas. P. Shattuck
1912	Shiloh	B. F. Hunt	J. A. Sartain	Jas. P. Shattuck
1913	Chickamauga	Jas. P. Shattuck	J. A. Sartain	Jas. P. Shattuck
1914	East Armuchee	Jas. P. Shattuck	J. A. Sartain	Jas. P. Shattuck
1915	LaFayette	Lee H. Dyer	Norman Shattuck	Jas. P. Shattuck
1916	Rossville	Lee H. Dyer	Alton Fox	Jas. P. Shattuck
1917	Waterville	Lee H. Dyer	I. S. Leonard	Jas. P. Shattuck
1918	Rising Fawn	Lee H. Dyer	I. S. Leonard	Jas. P. Shattuck
1919	Naomi	Lee H. Dyer	I. S. Leonard	Jas. P. Shattuck
1920	Bethel	Lee H. Dyer	I. S. Leonard	Jas. P. Shattuck
1921	Peavine	Lee H. Dyer	I. S. Leonard	Jas. P. Shattuck
1922	New Prospect	Lee H. Dyer	I. S. Leonard	Jas. P. Shattuck
1923	Antioch	Lee H. Dyer	I. S. Leonard	Norman Shattuck
1924	Shiloh	Lee H. Dyer	I. S. Leonard	Norman Shattuck
1925	Macedonia	L. B. Arvin	Lee H. Dyer	Frank Weaver
1926	Chattooga	L. B. Arvin	Lee H. Dyer	Frank Weaver
1927	Center Point	S. R. Tucker	C. R. Jones	Carl Hearn
1928	LaFayette	S. R. Tucker	C. R. Jones	Carl Hearn
1929	Rossville	S. R. Tucker	C. R. Jones	Carl Hearn
1930	Center Grove	S. R. Tucker	C. R. Jones	Carl Hearn
1931	East Armuchee	S. R. Tucker	C. R. Jones	Carl Hearn
1932	Bethel	S. R. Tucker	C. R. Jones	Carl Hearn
1933	Flintstone			

Chapter Forty-four

FAMILY REVIEWS.

(NOTE—The author has prepared most of these sketches from data furnished and assumes responsibility for the few words of praise. He has been personally acquainted with most of these for many years—has known their lives and characters—and feels, as he believes his readers will feel, that these words of commendation are well-deserved.)

JAMES R. JONES, PIONEER

By Mary Jones Rosser and Laura Jones Whelchel

James Roland Jones, one of Walker County's pioneers, was born November 7th, 1805 in White County, Tennessee, and was of Welsh descent. He was the son of Roland Jones, one of the early settlers of Tennessee. After the death of Roland Jones, his widow and children moved to Coweta County, Georgia, where James R. received such education as the times afforded, learning much in the school of experience as an orphan boy.

He was married January 8th, 1828 to Temperance Velvin (born March 18th, 1812), daughter of Robert Velvin of Coweta County.

James R. and his wife remained in Coweta County until September 1835 when they re-moved to Walker County, and settled what has since been known as the James R. Jones place about one mile South of Rock Spring Church on the Chattanooga and LaFayette road.

This trip was made in an ox cart, which carried his wife and their three children, Martha, Willis, and Russell, and the few belongings. The journey was a slow one and full of dangers. When he arrived on the scene of his future activities, he found not a board, a road nor anything suggesting civilization. He unloaded his ox cart, in the wilderness, felled some "saplings," placed them in the fork of trees, fastened others at the side for rafters, cut down a board tree, rived his boards, and covered his shelters, built his fire out in front, and this was his home until he had time to build a pine lob cabin. This picturesque home was not without its attractions, in its sylvan retreat. A clear cool spring was invitingly near. His table was daintily supplied with venison, wild turkey, and other luxuries of the forest, at his will.

The Cherokee Indians were also natives of this forest, and James R.'s adventures with them were many and interesting though his dealings with them were conscientious. His nearest neighbor was three miles to the North. At this time there was no jail or calaboose, so the sheriff had the whole responsibility of holding prisoners, which he did by chaining them to trees by day. For a long time James R. had to go to Ross' Landing (Chattanooga) to get corn. What is known as the Chattanooga and LaFayette pike was a mere Indian trail, consequently three or four days were spent to make the trip.

JONES FAMILY GROUP: Front row, left to right: Mrs. Martha Jones Rogers, D. Willis Jones, Russell J. Jones, William P. Jones, Thomas N. Jones, J. Robert Jones, Rees Jones. Back row: R. F. (Bud) Jones, R. C. (Doc) Jones, Orran W. Jones, A. J. (Jack) Jones.

Roving Indians were everywhere, so let us pause just here and pay a tribute to brave stouthearted Temperance, the pioneer wife. Was she not a heroine? That memorable old grandmother, whose life jewelled with good deeds has hurried down the years to bless posterity, and whose example has given stamina, courage, and character, to fit

JAMES R. JONES, PIONEER, AND HIS WIFE,
TEMPERANCE VELVIN JONES

us the better to face every turn life assumes. Less than a mile north of his crude home, was erected in 1839, the first Methodist Church of Rock Spring. James R. was not a member of this Church, but attended almost its every service, and kept wide his doors for its every preacher.

In 1840, James R. with his neighbors organized a school in a little house just North of his home. Five of his sons, Russell, William, Thomas, Robert, and Rees, claim old Rock Spring as their "Alma Mater". The Jones school house was also used as a court house. James R. was at one time, one of the three Judges of the Inferior Court of Walker County.

The first post office at Rock Spring was in the home of James R. Jones. He was the first postmaster and gave the place its name. The office has remained in the Jones family almost continuously since first established in 1844.

As to the convictions of James R. Jones in the 60's, he never seceded. Though he had five sons, Russell, Willis, Rees, William and Robert in the Confederate Army, he was heart and soul against secession, and remained so until the end. Allow me to pause here, and say that he had two grandsons (Harry H. Jones, son of Robert, and Willis Jones, son of William) and one great grandson, Capt. Thomas Jones—grandson of Willis who were soldiers in the World War, all living at this time 1930.

During the reconstruction period James R. aided in the upbuilding of his County in every way possible, contributing liberally to every cause which was for the good of his section, and remained as he had ever been, an uprght, honorable, progressve citizen until his death February 20th, 1886.

The quality of his truth and honesty is best shown by an act of his during the Civil War. In March of '64, his son Robert, who was orderly of the staff of Gen. William T. Wofford, had been sent home on furlough from New Market, Tenn., by Gen. Wofford, to carry some money ($800.00) to Cartersville, Ga., to his (Wofford's) wife. On his way back to the front, he stopped at Rock Spring to see his father and mother. Not long after he arrived at home, federal scouts were seen approaching the house. There was no chance for escape it seemed, and Robert ran upstairs. Two or three of the Yankees came into the house and told James R. they understood he had a son home from the Army. "Yes", he replied. "Where is he?" was asked. "Upstairs'; come down, Bob", he said. The son's surprise and consternation at his father's replies can better be imagined than expressed. Robert was captured and sent to Federal Prison at Nashville, Tenn., where he was kept until the war closed.

It is probable that the house would have been searched, but there are few fathers who would not have directed the Yankees' attention elsewhere in hope that all might be well with his boy, but with this grand old man his truth and honor were almost his religion, and were to him above boy or his freedom and liberty.

The history of James R. Jones, is but the history of all pioneers. It was a continual battle with Indians, as long as they were here, wild animals and the cruel hardships incident to pioneer life, but with it all, there was health and happiness. By energy and perseverance he acquired some property, besides rearing his large family of one daughter and ten sons, Martha (Mrs. A. E. Rogers), Willis, Capt. Russell J., William P., Thomas N., J. Robert, (Bob), Reese, R. F., (Bud), R. C., (Doc), Oran W., and A. J., (Jack), all of whom lived to mature years, but are now dead.

His most notable characteristics, were his firmness of purpose and his rugged honesty. Richly does he merit the inscription placed on his monument in Rock Spring Cemetery. "He was an honest man the noblest work of God".

Temperance, his wife whose prowess braved with him those early and dangerous days of the 30's, in December, 1891, became weary and, leaving behind her a beautiful life spent in doing good, was united with him in celestial reward.

Though the entire immediate family of James R. Jones has passed into the great beyond, a host of his descendants gather every year, at Rock Springs, Georgia, in family reunion, to do honor to his memory.

Descendants of James R. Jones and Temperance Velvin Jones:

(1) Martha A. Jones, (Apr. 14, 1830), wife of A. E. Rogers. Their children: Elizabeth Jones Rogers, Jan. 10, 1849; Caldonia Rogers, July 8, 1850; James Edward Rogers, July 7, 1852; Russell Jasper Rogers, Aug. 11, 1855; Andrew Erwin Rogers, Jan. 10, 1857; Temperance Rogers, Sept. 4, 1859; John Robert Rogers, July 18, 1861; Mattie Rogers, Jan. 5, 1864; Mollie Rogers, Jan. 5, 1864; George Washington Rogers, Apr. 30, 1866; Josephine Alice Rogers, July 20, 1868; Oliver Glenn Rogers, Jan. 4, 1871.

(2) David Willis Jones, Sept. 12, 1831. His wife, Martha Park Jones, Jan. 11, 1835. Their children: Julia S. Jones, Nov. 4, 1863; Susan Temperance Jones, Mar. 24, 1855; James Anderson Jones, Mar. 20, 1856; Mary Antionette Jones, Feb. 11, 1858; Thomas Willis Jones, Apr. 14, 1860; Mattie Estelle Jones, July 17, 1866; Infant, Feb. 27, 1868; Cora May Jones, Apr. 26, 1871.

(3) Russel J. Jones, July 11, 1834. His wife, Sarah Camp Jones. Their Children: Aaron C. Jones, Sept. 3, 1857; Lola O. Jones, 1859; James R. Jones, June 26, 1865; Annie L. Jones, Mar. 31, 1867; William A. Jones, May 22, 1869; Robert O. Jones, Apr. 13, 1872; Frank C. Jones, Oct. 8, 1874; Paul G. Jones, Dec. 16, 1878.

(4) William P. Jones, Feb. 1, 1837. His wife, Mary A. E. Smith, Jones, Mar. 8, 1841. Their children: Susan M. Jones, Oct. 28, 1859; Julia Jones, Aug. 4, 1861; William Robert Jones, Dec. 28, 1863.

Second wife, Jane Williams Jones, June 4, 1846. Their children: James A. Jones, Mar. 29, 1873; Thomas Felton Jones, Apr. 16, 1875; Mary Jones Aug. 4, 1877; Sarah Jones, Oct. 9, 1879; Jack Jones, Apr. 29, 1881; Sam Jones, Feb. 2, 1884; Edward Jones, Jan. 10, 1887; Willis Jones, Aug. 18, 1890.

(5) Thomas N. Jones, Apr. 18, 1839; his wife, Margaret Henderson Jones, Nov. 22, 1841. Their children: Charles Willis Jones, Aug. 18, 1860; Thomas Jerome Jones, Feb. 8, 1862; James Robert Jones, Mar. 6, 1864; John Henderson Jones, Sept. 8, 1866; Rees Jones, Aug. 26, 1868; Laura Augusta Jones, Oct. 12, 1870; Alice Temperance Jones, Nov. 21, 1872; Margaret Elizabeth Jones, June 12, 1875; Susie Viola Jones, Oct. 2, 1877; Ruth Winifred Jones, Apr. 26, 1879; William Jackson Jones, Nov. 23, 1882; Orville Roland Jones, Apr. 24, 1887.

(6) James Robert Jones, July 7, 1842; His wife, Mary A. Henderson, Sept. 19, 1855. Their children: Mary Leet Jones, July 23, 1875; Laura Virginia Jones, Sept 30, 1878; Maude Temperance Jones, Jan. 12, 1881; James Marsh Jones, Jan. 3, 1883; Fannie Winifred Jones, May 1, 1885; Harry Henderson Jones, July 4, 1887; Calvin Quay Jones, July 17, 1890.

(7) Rees Jones, Oct. 24, 1844; His wife Susan Smith Jones, May 16, 1847. Their children; William Edward Jones, May 16, 1867; Mary S. Jones, July 1, 1869; Eudora T. Jones, Aug. 15, 1871; Nathan S. Jones, Mar. 1, 1874, and Martha W. Jones, Mar. 1, 1874; Margaret Emma Jones, Mar. 9, 1876; Zachariah Willis Jones, Oct. 4, 1878; Henry Jones, Aug. 1, 1881; Roland Jones, Oct. 4, 1883; Lola Jones, Jan. 28, 1886; Pearl Jones, Aug. 21, 1887; Susie Jones, Nov. 19, 1893.

(8) Randolph Franklin Jones, Mar. 26, 1847; His wife Lula Clark Jones.

(9) Rufus C. Jones, (Doc), July 21, 1849; His wife Theressa Pope Jones, Dec. 7, 1869. Their child: Anna Jones, June 8, 1889.

(10) Orran W. Jones, Oct. 11, 1852; His wife Mary Ellis Jones, June 25, 1857. Their children: Susan Tennessee Jones, Oct. 12, 1876; Maggie Florence Jones, Feb. 11, 1878; James Randolph Jones, June 14, 1879; Orran Franklin Jones, Mar. 29, 1881; Mattie Temperance Jones, Mar. 14, 1883; Andrew Jackson Jones, Jan. 3, 1885; William Chester Jones, Feb. 27, 1887; Nora Malinda Jones, Dec. 1, 1889; Theressa Pope Jones, Dec. 18, 1893.

(11) Andrew Jackson Jones, June 11, 1855; His wife, Margaret Conley Jones, Oct. 5, 1858. (Son died in infancy).

CHARLES W. JONES (b. 1860), son of Thomas N. and Margaret E. Jones, married Paralee, (b. 1868), dau. of Anderson, and granddaughter of Abbott Smith of Tennessee. Anderson moved to the Cove before the war. Mr. and Mrs. Jones have lived in the Cove all their lives where, by industry, economy and frugality they have accumulated considerable property and are possessed of a competence to give them respite and leisure during their declining days, now rapidly passing on. He has recently erected a handsome cottage near the public highway where he and his wife expect to spend their remaining days. The five girls have been residing for a number of years in Chattanooga, while the boys are substantial farmers. Right often the children make their way back to visit their parents and the old home.

FAMILY RECORD: Rufus, (b. 1889), married Hettie Johnson. Children: Daphne, Morris, Willis, Bernard and Bernice (twins), J. D., Dan, Paul, Virginia. John (b. 1890), married Lucile Logan. Ch: Ralph, Billy, Wynnelle, Louise. Pauline (b. 1892), married A. T. Column. Ch: Thomas, Hubert. Margaret, (b. 1893), Single. Robert, (b. 1895), married Mary Banks. Ch: Roberta, Catherine, Leroy. Lillian, (b. 1898), married J. M. Payne. Gussie, (b. 1900), married W. A. Johnson. One child: Mary Catherine. Susie, (b. 1903), married C. E. Coleman. One child: Barbara Jean.

JAMES ERVIN PATTON.

When the splendid ideals of a people were epitomized in an individual, and that individual was a true son of the Old South, and one who was a man of large vision, standing unflinchingly for the development of the highest standard of citizenship and a supporter of all movements for the progress of his county—it is eminently fitting that James Ervin Patton, benefactor to this section, should be featured in the History of Walker county.

Mr. Patton was born in Transylvania county, North Carolina, July 5, 1855. He was the son of James and Louisa Cynthia (Lowry) Patton, grandson of Joseph Ervin and Jane (Orr) Patton, of Scotch-Irish descent —the immigrant ancestor having settled in Pennsylvania with his wife, Margaret Patton.

His father was a plantation owner and slave holder impoverished by the War Between the States, while his mother was a daugther of Colonel James Lowry, wealthy planter and a member of the North Carolina Legislature. His sisters were Ella Swain, deceased, Mary Elizabeth of LaFayette and Jessie Adelaide, now Mrs. John E. Shuford of Chattanooga, Tenn.

JAMES ERWIN PATTON

He was educated in the public schools of Walker county, and in his younger days taught for some years.

In partnership with Joseph A. Miller, he entered the mercantile business at LaFayette, Ga. When he retired in 1897 he had acquired a small fortune.

After two years of rest and travel, he with James P. Shattuck organized the Bank of LaFayette, the first bank in Walker county. Mr. Patton was cashier 1899-1921; not only was he cashier, but he assumed the entire responsibility of the bank management with the advice of the president and directors.

His integrity of character was so high, and his rare executive ability so great, that he enjoyed a wide circle of business associates who depended upon his sound judgment and conservative advice. His bank connection also brought him in contact with the industrial enterprises of LaFayette.

He was one of the organizers, in 1891, of the Union Cotton Mills, of which he was a director. He was foremost in establishing, in 1903, the LaFayette Cotton Mills, and in 1904, the Walker County Hosiery Mills. Of the LaFayette Cotton Mills he was president and of the Walker County Hosiery Mills he was director until Mr. Shattuck's death when he succeeded him as president.

Mr. Patton was also interested in the local telephone company and the LaFayette Roller Mills. He served the city as mayor and as member of the council several terms.

Mr. Patton was well informed on many subjects, being a great reader of the best current and standard literature; also a close Bible student: herein lay the strength of his mental, moral and spiritual development.

He was a prominent Mason, a Knight Templar, a Shriner, an Odd Fellow and a member of the Improved Order of Redmen.

He was an active member of the Presbyterian church. An elder for more than forty years, teacher of the men's Bible class, he was a loyal churchman and vitally interested in its welfare and progress. He was particularly interested in the young men of the county, many of whom came to him for advice and assistance. Always easy of approach, once his word was given it was to be depended upon.

He possessed great initiative, organizing ability and persistent perseverance; and his active influence was felt in almost every phase of his city's life. His love for his county and hometown, LaFayette, and his confidence in their future progress was unbounded. No standard was regarded as too high by which to measure his interest in his community. His deep concern for those in his employment was evinced by his providing community centers equipped with facilities for physical, social and spiritual uplift. These people were also encouraged to beautify their yards and gardens by the awards given each year by Mr. Patton for the one adjudged most beautiful.

Mr. Patton was the promoter of almost every progressive movement in LaFayette and Walker county during his life; yet in his modest and retiring nature he kept his personality in the background, thinking only of the success of the enterprise and the welfare of the people—giving credit to others for the work he did himself. He would have spent every cent of his fortune, had it been necessary, to carry forward to success his plans and ideals.

He was married three times; first, October 23, 1883, to Fannie Jackson, daughter of Z. W. and Eliza Anne Hill Jackson of Cartersville, Ga., who died in 1887, leaving a daughter, Mary Lou, wife of A. C. Whitehead of Atlanta, Ga. Mrs. Whitehead, by her first husband, N. C. Napier, 2nd, of LaFayette, Ga., had three children, James Patton, Frances Jackson, and Nathan Campbell, 3rd.

His second marriage was on August 8, 1889, to Eliza Venable, daughter of Sanford and Harriet Hill Venable of Cartersville, Ga., who died in 1897, leaving a son, Thomas Venable Patton of Norfolk, Virginia, who married Jessie Mae Smith of Atlanta, Ga. Their children are Thomas Venable, Jr., and Betty Jane.

On September 20, 1899, Mr. Patton married Mrs. Margaret Moore Sherrill, daughter of Colonel Williams Hamilton Moore and Mary Gudger Moore of West Ashville, N. C., by whom he had two children, James Moore Patton, banker, and Margaret Elizabeth, wife of Arthur Allen Paty, Jr., of Chattanooga, Tenn. They have two children, Margaret Paty, and Arthur Allen, 3rd.

Mr. Patton died at Newell's Sanitarium, Chattanooga, Tenn., June 28, 1926. Here ended a life which had been faithful in detail, honest in purpose, sincere in love for humanity with the prosperity which he visioned standing as a permanent testimony to his wisdom and foresight. He always threw himself into the breach at the crucial moment which decided whether a thing is to be or not to be. J. E. Patton has gone from us but his work lives.

THE THURMAN FAMILY.

By Lillian Thurman King.

The Thurman name is a very old one and the derivation, as given in a Dictionary of English Surnames, is Thorman, Thurman, Thormund, Thormond, Bapt. "The Son of Thormond," indicating that it is an Anglo-Saxon name.

As early as the twelfth century, Thurmans were living in England, whence came the founder of the American branch, John Thurman, who left England and came to Virginia some time prior to 1638. John Thurman and his son, John, are the first male members of the American Thurman family of which we have authentic record, living in James county, Virginia, in 1638. This family consisted of John Thurman, his wife, Anne (Morecraft) Thurman, and three children, John, Jr., Elizabeth and Joan.

As the new counties in Virginia were erected and population spread toward the Alleghenies and the Blue Ridge, Thurmans followed the westward march of civilization as Government records show them in a number of counties, some going down into the Carolinas. One family settled in Anson County, North Carolina, where Philip Thurman was born November 15, 1757. Other children were born there. Later, this family is found in Cheraw District, South Carolina, and Philip, just 18, is a Revolutionary soldier, and his brother, Benjamin, is furnishing supplies for Continental and Militia use. Benjamin furnished money to the Government in 1780-1781 and 1782. ("Salley's Revolutionary Claims of South Carolina and Pension Records.") Both the South Carolina and Virginia families took prominent part in the Revolutionary War, as we have records of soldiers in almost every branch.

The first census of United States, 1790, shows both Philip and Benjamin Thurman as heads of families in Cheraw District, South Carolina. Philip remained there for some years, finally coming to Anderson county, East Tennessee, and a few years later to Bledsoe county, Tennessee, together with his wife, Kesiah, and their eleven children. Some years later Joe and Wesley Thurman (the former marrying Eliza Smith and the latter Malinda Hicks) sons of Ephriam (7th child of Philip and Kesiah) and Rosa Rodgers Thurman, moved to Walker county, Georgia, from Sequatchie county, Tennessee. They have descendants now living in Walker county. The late Oliver M. Thurman was a son of Joe Thurman.

Benjamin Thurman and his wife, Julia Shumate, daughter of William Shumate, Revolutionary soldier and descendant of French Hugenots, together with their seventeen children, remained in South Carolina at the home built prior to the Revolution. This home burned a few years ago, but the farm is still in a good state of preservation and the old mill and other marks can be located. Near this home is the family cemetery where both Benjamin and Julia are buried. Benjamin died in 1840, Julia in 1846.

David Thurman, son of Benjamin, was educated at Yanceyville, North Carolina, after which he joined the South Carolina Methodist Conference. There were many preachers in the different branches and generations of the family and we find Thurmans always taking a leading part in church affairs. The first Sunday school in the state of Virginia was established in 1817 by John Thurman, son of Richard. John's brother, Richard, Jr., known in Lynchburg as "Uncle Thurman," was said to have had as much influence as a minister and he, with other officials of the Methodist church, always sat inside the altar.

In 1826 three sons of Benjamin Thurman, John, William and David, together with David's wife, Lavina, and three children, David, Jr., (b) November 8, 1819; Lucy, (b) 1821; Jane, (b) 1823, came to Georgia and David located where the city of Atlanta now stands. John settled somewhere in what is now Fulton county. William established a home near Fort Walker, then in Henry county. He lived here until his death at the age of ninety-two years. He was the father of seven sons and six daughters, all of the sons having served as soldiers of the Confederacy in the War Between the States.

David Thurman, Sr., died in 1831. Lavina reared her five children—two more having been born after the family moved to Georgia—and lived in Atlanta until her death in 1864.

David Thurman, Jr., eldest son of David and Lavina, married Margaret Boyles, born in North Carolina February 24, 1824, daughter of Enoch and Nancy Boyles, and lived in Marthasville (now Atlanta) until 1855, when they sold their home there and moved to Walker county, Georgia, where they purchased a farm in Shinbone Valley from Mr. Joshua Martin. David Thurman lived here until his death, with the exception of a short time spent at Athens, Tennessee, where he moved to send the children to school. David Thurman, Jr., like his father, was a Methodist preacher. He was licensed to preach in 1849. He then took work from the Conference serving as supply on circuits. He was ordained a deacon in 1863 by Bishop James O. Andre and an elder by Bishop Levi Scott. He was a man of strong individuality and sterling qualities. He was a well rounded man. He had a great soul; a good mind; a big heart. He was a kind father, interested in the temporal and spiritual welfare of his children to the last. He was always ready to help any good cause to promote the best interest of the community. His home was considered the home of Methodist preachers. Many an itinerant's heart was cheered by his bright fireside.

David Thurman died August 16, 1889. Margaret Thurman died March, 1902.

Following are the names of children and grandchildren of David and Margaret Thurman: Nancy Elizabeth, (b) December 1, 1844, married Jack Bankston; children: Margaret and Edward. Mary Emma, (b) August 5, 1860, (m) Reverend Hugh Boyd September 5, 1878, died in Olean, New York, February, 1928; children: Florence, Clark, Anna and Hugh. Lucy Alice, (b) July 1, 1864, (m) Jerome Clarkson November 12, 1879, died in Chattanooga, Tennessee, August 10, 1898; children: William, Eula, Fanny, Ethel, Deforest and Pluma Lee. Fanny Carrington, (b) September 10, 1868, (m) Alonzo Agnew January 30, 1889; children: Eva, Lena, Margaret, Isabel, James and Robert. Benjamin Franklin, (b) January 10, 1844, (m) Martha McConnell December 24, 1865; children: Stella, Julia and Annie. William Melville, (b) August 17, 1845, (m) 1st, Ann Day; 2nd, Josie Shields; children: Betty, Alice and Deforest; 3rd, Amanda Boyles; children: James and Emma; 4th, Florrie Smith; children: Fred, Duke and Julia. David Clark, (b) August 21, 1851, (m) Adelia MeShaw; children: Lois, Judson, Blanche and Emmett. John Thomas, (b) June 5, 1856, (m) Sallie Martin, November 11. 1879; children: Leola, Pauline and Eugene. Enoch Lewis, (b) September 21, 1858, (m) Lula Cassidy August 3, 1882; children: David Russell, Ray Vaughn, Lillian, Amanda Lee, Lucile, Roy, Edna and Maude.

Lula Cassidy Thurman is a descendant of early Walker county families, she being a daughter of Russell M. and Amanda Wall Cassidy. The Cassidy family, originally from Virginia, came to Walker county from

Tennessee. Russell Cassidy was a Confederate soldier, serving in Company G, Ninth Georgia Regiment.

Amanda Wall was a daughter of Wilburn and Clarissa Wall, who came to Walker county in 1837 from Spartanburg, South Carolina. Wilburn was a son of Robert Wall, born in Wilkes county, North Carolina, in 1777. Wilburn's mother was a sister of Colonel Clark. Robert Wall was a son of Jonathan, Revolutionary soldier, born in Prince Georges county, Maryland, in 1744. The Wall family was of Scotch descent, but Jonathan's wife, whose maiden name was Kilbee, came from Germany.

On her maternal side Lula Cassidy Thurman is a descendant of John Blackwell, Revolutionary soldier and an early settler in Walker county. The early American ancestor of John Blackwell came from Gloucester, England, in 1656 and settled with land patent for 4000 acres in Northumberland and Westmoreland counties, Virginia.

Enoch Lewis Thurman died August 7, 1906.

John Thurman, who lives at the old home, and Fanny Thurman Agnew, also a resident of Walker county, are the only living children of David and Margaret Thurman.

Benjamin Franklin Thurman.

Benjamin Franklin Thurman, eldest son of the Rev. David and Mrs. Margaret Thurman, was born in Marthasville (now Atlanta), Georgia, January 10, 1844. On his father's side he was descended from a prominent South Carolina family of Hugenot extraction.

In 1855, the Reverend Mr. Thurman purchased a farm in Shinbone valley, Walker county, and for more than three quarters of a century that has been the family home. Theirs was a godly home; the family altar was always maintained; the Word of God was loved and honored, and was taught to the children. Years after when making speeches, whether Sunday school, fraternal, or political, words of Scripture seemed always upon Frank Thurman's lips.

In this environment, Frank Thurman grew up. He attended such schools as those times afforded, gaining what knowledge he could; although his education continued throughout his life, for he was always a student. He possessed unusual mentality, and many natural gifts. These combined with broad sympathies and deep sincerity made him a most helpful citizen.

Though but a youth of seventeen and a half years, in 1861 he volunteered as a soldier with the army of the Confederacy, and he "gallantly wore the gray" until 1865 when, with Lee at Appomattox, arms were laid down, and he turned his steps homeward.

His none too robust constitution had been weakened by the hardships and exposure of war; but with undaunted spirit he labored, tilling the soil for several years.

December 24th, 1865, he was married to Miss Martha McConnell, daughter of Joshua and Caroline McConnell, who was his devoted companion for thirty-eight years until death separated them.

From this union were born four daughters, three of whom lived to maturity. The eldest, Stella Leona, was married to Edward L. Jackson, son of a prominent Bartow county family. Dying in early young womanhood, Mrs. Jackson left two sons who grew into splendid young manhood; the elder, Zimri Thurman Jackson, is a successful furniture dealer of Tampa, Florida. The other, Carl Southard Jackson, is a leading citizen and business man of Calhoun, Georgia.

Mr. Thurman's third daughter, Julia Edna, was married to Frank O. Fariss, son of the beloved and honored Dr. D. C. Fariss of LaFayette, Ga.

The youngest daughter, Annie Frank, who is her father's namesake, is a Bible teacher in the public schools of Chattanooga, Tennessee.

In the early eighties, Mr. Thurman moved with his family to LaFayette, Georgia, where for many years he was a successful and popular merchant.

Frank Thurman was a statesman. His political career was noteworthy. He served in the Georgia Legislature in 1888-89-90; 1903-4. For his labor in the introduction, and passage, of the "Ten Trustee Bill," for the State Insane Asylum, Mr. Thurman was presented by the Legislature with a handsome gold headed cane. In 1908 he was re-elected by his friends of the county without solicitation. In 1911-12 he was again in legislative halls, but after this, failing health forbade further public service.

Mr. Thurman also served on the board of County Commissioners in Walker for a number of years; and on the board of Education for twenty years.

Equally brilliant was Mr. Thurman's career as a Mason. Besides serving as Master of Western Lodge for several years he held the office of Grand Junior Deacon for fifteen years and Grand Chaplain of the Grand Lodge of Georgia for three years.

His mind was keenly alert, and his knowledge and interest in world affairs was wide and varied.

Best of all, Mr. Thurman was a Christian. Although for many years he struggled against a hopeless disease, his invincible spirit never failed. When the evening shadows lengthened, with living faith in the finished work of Christ, his Saviour, he calmly awaited the home call. This came December 17, 1916—then his brave spirit took its flight. The battle was over: He had "Fought a good fight, had finished his course, had kept the Faith."

Quoting from a very beautiful tribute written by his esteemed friend, Attorney-General George M. Napier, and published in the Masonic Herald, after Mr. Thurman's death: "As a youth he enlisted in the armies of the 'Lost Cause' and was in the regiments of men who wore the gray on many a crimson field of battle. To him was given the distinction of being with that matchless commander of modern times, Robert E. Lee, when he surrendered the remnant of his unconquered heroes.

"Taking up the peaceful pursuits of life, Brother Thurman endeared himself to all by his kindness, courtliness, and genuine sincerity. He established a name for probity and virtue which was his crowning achievement.

"As citizen, churchman, legislator, and Mason, he won many honors, and he held the esteem of all men."

BLACKWELL.

"For more than 500 years the Blackwell family have been among the first gentry of Cloucester county, England. Our American ancestor, Joseph Blackwell, came to America and located with a land patent for 4,000 acres in Westmoreland and Cumberland Counties, Virginia, in 1656. Their coat of arms was one of the most distinguished in the Book of Heraldry.

The children of Joseph Blackwell were, Samuel, born 1680. Samuel's son Samuel, born 1710, William b. 1713, (He was first sheriff of Tanquire County, Virginia), Joseph b. 1715, Elizabeth b. 1717, Hannah b. 1721. (Record from St. Stephen's parish register, North Cumberland County.) Samuel built the mansion in 1788 on a branch of Potomac River—the old building burned about 1907. The farm (not the 4,000 acres), has passed from father to son without a break, and Edward resides there now.

The will of Joseph Blackwell, recorded in Tanquire county, in 1787, names nine children, among them Captain John Blackwell, b. 1755, who was captain in Revolutionary War, and was General Washington's chief quartermaster. His sons, James and John, moved to Lewisburg and Halifax county, Va., at the close of the Revolutionary War, later moving to Greenville and Rutherford county, North Carolina."—*From History of Blackwell Family.*

Rev. John Blackwell of Rutherford County, N. C., a Baptist minister and Revolutionary soldier, who fought at the battle of King's Mountain, married a Glenn, and reared a large family in Rutherford County, later moving to Walker county, Georgia, he became one of the first settlers in beautiful Broomtown valley. He preached his last sermon in 1839 at the Coosa Baptist Association at Mount Harmony church, now Menlo, Georgia. Several of his children came to Georgia with him, viz., Thomas, who lived and died at his old home place after rearing a large family. Another son, Jeremiah Glenn, born in North Carolina in 1803, died 1884, who married Peggy Ann McWilliams, sister to some of the pioneer McWilliams of West Armuchee. To this union were born three sons, (1), George W. Blackwell who enlisted in the Confederate Army from Chattooga County, and served in Company F. 8th Reg. 3rd Brig., Ga. State

Troops, being first Lieutenant of his Company, later promoted to Captain of Company D, 34th Ga. Inf. He was killed in 1865 while returning home from war and within three miles of his father's home, being killed by some unknown party, (A note attached to his person, when found, stated that he was killed through misapprehension, he being supposed to be another person, and killed by mistake).

(2). James M. Blackwell (1831-1878), married (1) Susan E. Campbell (1846-1871). Children: William Pelham, b. 1869; James (1870-1871). (2) Georgia Ann McWilliams, dau. of William McWilliams. One child, Carl Glenn (1877-1927).

James M. Blackwell, subject of this sketch, merchant, teacher, and Confederate soldier, was one of the early teachers of the county, having taught at Pleasant Hill in West Armuchee in the early fifties. Many of the children of that beautiful and fertile valley were taught by him the rudiments of an education. Some specimens of his handwriting and spelling show him to have been no mean scholar. During the latter fifties he was engaged in merchandising at Greenbush, and was thus employed when the toxin of war sounded. Enlisting in the Confederate States Army, he served throughout that bloody conflict, and at its close was employed as manager of the store of the Trion Manufacturing Company for ten years, after which he again took up merchandising at Greenbush where he remained till his death, after which his two sons, W. P. and Carl, continued in business till the latter's death, leaving the former the only surviving child.

William P., married (1), Dora, (1871-1921), dau. of A. H. and Amanda (McWilliams) Neal. (2), Rebecca, dau. of Edward A. and Mary (Neal) Bomar. Later he sold his interest in the merchandising business and has for some years devoted his time and energy to farming, being one of the progressive growers of his section, as also, prominently identified with county affairs, being jury commissioner for a number of years, and recently nominated as a member of the Board of Roads and Revenue.

To his first marriage one child, William P. Jr., was born (1903). W. P. Jr., received his early training in the common schools of the county, later attending the Berry schools at Rome and finally graduated from the Georgia School of Technology, class 1924. He has for several years held a responsible position with the Illinois Power and Light Corporation, Chicago, Ill.

(3). William Pinkney Blackwell, youngest son of Jeremiah Glenn Blackwell, born 1836, died 1921 at Mineola, Texas, at the age of 85 years, was a sterling citizen and true Confederate soldier. He served in Company D. 34th Ga. Inf. of which his brother George W. was captain.

At the age of 19 this sturdy son of the Old South made his way to San Francisco, going by way of New York, thence to Panama, he crossed the Isthmus and took vessel again to the gold fields where he remained for two years, working in the gold mines, and bringing home several nuggets of gold which are prized possessions of his descendants to this day. Returning from California on horse-back with two companions, James Ponder and Marion McWilliams, after untold hardships, being menaced on all sides by hostile Indians and wild beasts of the Rockies and Plains, suffering from hunger and thirst much of the time, they finally reached home safe and sound. He married Delilah Jane Caldwell and settled on Duck Creek in Walker county, Georgia, where he remained one of the first citizens of the county till 1894 when the old Western urge conquered him again and he moved to Wood county, Texas, where he died in 1921. He reared seven children, the oldest, Dr. W. M. Blackwell, was a prominent physician of Walker and Chattooga counties for many years.

ROBERT McGRADY PITTMAN.

Robert McGrady Pittman was born in Gordon County, Georgia, in 1846 and died at his home near Villanow in Walker County in 1930. He was of French, English and Scotch-Irish lineage. His Pittman ancestry is traceable to Denmark from which they left in the fourteenth century and settled in England in Monmouthshire on the Welsh border where some of them later held high official and military positions.

The Pittmans were divided in opinion in England during the Puritan Revolution. Some were followers of the ill-fated Charles; others were with Cromwell. When King Charles was be-headed three Pittman brothers came to America with a cavalier emigration and landed at Jamestown, Virginia. One of these went to the northern colonies, one remained in Virginia and one came to the far south. R. M. Pittman is a descendant of the one who remained in Virginia.

R. M. Pittman was the son of Henry Hardin Pittman who was the son of Jeffrey Pittman who was the son of John Pittman, Jr., who was the son of John Pittman who with his wife, Mary Rowe Pittman, moved from Amelia County, Virginia, to South Carolina and then moved from Edgefield District, South Carolina, in 1771, and joined the Baptist Colony headed by the celebrated Reverend Daniel Marshall and settled on the Kiokee creek, St. Paul's Parish, afterwards Richmond County, Georgia, and still later cut off into Columbia County, Georgia. John Pittman, Jr., married a daughter of Reverend Daniel Marshall. Among his other descendants was Judge Daniel Pittman, Ordinary of Fulton County for twenty years.

R. M. Pittman's grandmother Pittman was a Hardin of French descent, her parents having come to America as a result of the persecution of the French Huguenots. Mr. Pittman's mother, Nancy Barnwell Pittman, was a daughter of R. M. Barnwell, a direct descendant of Lord O'Barnwell of Ireland, and Judith Byrd. Judith Byrd was a direct descendant of William Byrd who inherited, by will, the site of Richmond, Virginia, from his paternal grandfather, Captain Stagg. Among the other descendants of William Byrd of Richmond, Virginia, are the famous Governor Byrd of Virginia and the renowned explorer Richard Byrd. Among the well known descendants of the emigrant Pittman who remained in Virginia is Senator Key Pittman of Nevada.

R. M. Pittman had twelve brothers and sisters, some of whom died young. Mr. Pittman grew to manhood in Gordon County and became a farmer.

Too young for military duty at the beginning of hostilities during the Civil War, Mr. Pittman later enlisted in service as a volunteer messenger under orders of General Wofford to carry dispatches throughout northwest Georgia. This was a very delicate and dangerous undertaking because of the presence of Federal troops throughout the section through which he travelled as messenger, and the fact that, if apprehended, he might have been taken as a spy and summarily dealt with. After the Civil War he returned to Gordon County where he found the savings and the property of his people to have been swept away in Sherman's march to the sea.

In 1879 he married Leila Thomas, daughter of Phillip and Mary Dickerson Thomas who were both natives of Danville, Virginia, and of Welsh descent. Phillip Thomas belonged to the famous Thomas family of Virginia which claims, as one of its offsprings, General Thomas, commonly known as "The Rock of Chickamauga". The Dickinson, or Dickerson, family is also famous in Virginia history. Mrs. Pittman is also connected with the celebrated Jefferson and Carter families of Virginia. Mrs. R. M. Pittman now resides at LaFayette, Georgia.

To the union between Robert McGrady Pittman and Leila Thomas were born twelve children, all of whom grew to maturity and eleven of whom are still in life. In 1902 this large family moved from Gordon County to Walker County and located in East Armuchee Valley where, by arduous labor and skillful management, the education of all his children was completed.

Mr. Pittman was a member of the Methodist Church and a Mason. He was quiet, unassuming and modest, and a man of rare fine character. The character and spirit of both parents is reflected in the achievements of their children, for whom they struggled and to whom all the labor of their lives was dedicated.

The record of the children is as follows:

Annie, educated at Fairmount High School; LaGrange College and Georgia State College for teachers. Married Professor W. D. Greene (1875-1915). Teacher for many years; now principal of Linwood School, LaFayette, Georgia. Mother of two children.

Sudie, (1881-1931), educated Fairmount High School; LaGrange Female College. Married Doctor J. A. Shields, a practicing physician of Walker county for many years, and who now resides in LaFayette. Mother of four children.

Rufus Willard, educated Berry School and Draughan's Business College. Married Ione Miller of Seminole, Texas. He served one or more terms as County Judge of Gaines County, Texas, and is now County School Superintendent and a ranchman of Seminole, Texas. He is the father of eight children.

Claude Cleveland, educated at Reinhardt College Waleska, Georgia; Emory University, Ph.B. 1912; University of Georgia, B.L. 1915. Served as State Senator from Bartow County; Solicitor General of the Cherokee Circuit 1924-1927. Judge of the Cherokee Judicial Circuit, to which he was appointed in 1927 as a successor of Judge M. C. Tarver who left that office for Congress, and after filling the unexpired term of Judge M. C. Tarver he was elected to the same position which he retains now. Married Emily Daves of Cartersville, Georgia. Father of three children.

Griff Edward, educated at Reinhardt College, and Berry School at Rome. Cashier of the First National Bank of Ocilla, Georgia. Married Chester Wilbanks. He is the father of two children.

Rena, educated at Reinhardt College; single; lives with mother in LaFayette.

Floy, educated Reinhardt College; Georgia State College for Teachers; Peabody College of Nashville, and University of Chattanooga; married Charles Henry Hillhouse of Sylvester, Georgia, (1890-1928). She has one living child. She is now principal of Fairyland School on Lookout Mountain.

Mary, educated Reinhardt College; Columbia University; University of Tennessee; University of Georgia, and Birmingham-Southern A. B. Married Carl Franklin of Adairsville, Georgia. She is now principal of Miramar Public Schools, one of the largest and most modern public schools of Miami, Florida.

Ross Henry, educated Seminole High School, Seminole, Texas, and Young Harris College, Young Harris, Georgia. Married Nannie Rainey of Villanow, Georgia. He is in business in LaFayette with Shields-Hawkins-Pittman Chevrolet Company.

Robert Carter, educated Reinhardt College; Emory University; of Georgia, A. B. (1922), and Columbia University, New York City, B. L. (1927), single. Practicing Attorney-at-Law, of Dalton, Georgia. Ross and Carter are Veterans of the World War.

Helen and Lucile, (twins), educated LaFayette High School, Reinhardt College, and Edmonson Business College, Chattanooga, Tennessee. Helen married Nelson Ward of Miami, Florida, and has one child. Lucile married Harry Sheldon of Bridgeton, New Jersey.

The combined school-years represented in the education of these children is one hundred and fifty-three years. When Mr. Pittman died he left no assets save his investments in the education of his children, which represented quite a large fortune, and a good name. Of the twelve children, eight have been teachers at different times, some of them for many years. Many of them have materially aided in their own education and in the education of others. This is a brief story of a family that is remarkable in many respects.

McFARLAND.

The American people have always been more concerned about the present and future than the past, therefore family records have been neglected. This sketch begins with an epitaph on a tombstone in the McFarland graveyard, as follows: "John Buie MacFarland born of Scotch parentage January 11th, 1765, in Cumberland County, N. C., died January 19th, 1846."

John Buie remained in his native state following the avocations of farming and school teaching till about the year 1804, when he with his wife, Sally Ann Gorden, and their four small children moved to Tatnall County, Georgia. Here he reared a large family.

In the year 1832 his second and third sons, Xanders Gorden McFarland and Thomas Gorden McFarland came to what is now Rossville, which was then in Cherokee county, to survey and did survey the ninth district and fourth section, now in Walker and Catoosa counties. Being pleased with the country and having the hereditary Scottish trait on finding a good thing, "to set down by it," they returned in 1835 to settle. Here they engaged in the mercantile business, selling goods to the Indians and the few white settlers. They also conducted the postoffice known as Rossville, the said office antedating the Chattanooga office. In a few years their father with the remainder of the family consisting of the younger son, Columbus, and five daughters came to settle in this "garden spot."

The elder of the two brothers, X. G. McFarland, married Lucy A. Boyle of Chattooga County in the year 1839 to which union were born ten children, nine living to maturity. The eldest son, Chappell, lost his life in the battle of Missionary Ridge. The next son, Buie, was wounded in the battle of Atlanta. After the war he took advantage of his limited educational opportunities and in the year 1870 joined the North Georgia Conference of the M. E. Church South in which he remained till his death in 1885. Of the remaining three sons, two were ministers.

The younger brother, T. G. McFarland, about the year 1846 married Elizabeth Anderson of Sequatchie Valley, Tennessee. To this union were born six children, five of whom lived to years of maturity. The eldest son, Anderson, saw service for a short time in the Confederate Army. He engaged in the mercantile business in Chattanooga for a number of years; was the first mayor of Rossville; the other two sons, Foster and John, afterward held the same position besides other responsible offices,—John being N. P. & J. P. for a quarter of a century till his untimely death in 1911.

The two pioneer brothers, X. G. and T. G. both represented their county in the General Assembly, as also did one each of their sons, James and Foster, respectively.

The McFarlands were opposed to secession and voted against it, but when their state seceeded they espoused the cause of the South wholeheartedly, every member of the CLAN from 16 to 55 joining the "STARS AND BARS." As captain of a company, Columbus McFarland served until the fall of Fort Donaldson.

The two brothers, main characters in this sketch, deserve much cred't for their careful, painstaking work in surveying and marking the ninth district and fourth section. Though opposite in a number of ways, they lived and worked in cordial relationship for over half a century, serving their community, their county and state, until the autumn of 1887 at the ripe old age of 85 and 84, they were gathered to their fathers. It is the sincere desire of the writer of this article, that their posterity may forget their faults emulate their virtues, and with upright living and honorable dealing serve God and mankind.

(Note—This sketch was prepared and submitted by William Crawford McFarland, one of the five sons of X. G. McFarland. A few weeks later he passed to his reward—(July 1932).

Matthew Whitfield Spearman, M.D.

Dr. M. W. Spearman, physician and surgeon, was born Feb. 6, 1881, on a farm three miles north of Shady Dale, Jasper County, Ga. He received his early education in the schools of Shady Dale, and afterward attended the State Normal School at Athens, Georgia, receiving from that institution his L. I. degree in 1900. He taught for the next five years and having an ambition for the field of medicine entered Emory University, where he was graduated in 1911 as Doctor of Medicine and for the next year was an interne in Grady Hospital in Atlanta, and then took location at Dexter, Georgia, in 1914.

Dr. Spearman successfully practiced his chosen profession in these until the year 1918, when he removed to his present address at Chickamauga, Georgia, where he enjoys a lucrative practice and is also associated with the physicians of Chattanooga, having access to the hospitals of that city; thus enabling him to enlarge his usefulness to his community and patients.

Dr. Spearman has been signally honored by the medical fraternity of his state, being chosen president of Walker County Medical Society, vice president of the Chattanooga District Medical Society and in addition is a member of the Georgia State Medical Society and the Southern and American Medical Association. He is a member of the Masonic fraternity and the Methodist Episcopal church, South.

Matthew Whitfield Spearman, Sr., father of Dr. Spearman, was born in Shady Dale, Jasper County, Georgia, in 1843. When he was of military age he enlisted in the cause of the Confederacy, joining the 44th

Regiment of Georgia Infantry and fought with distinction for the cause of the South until captured in 1864, being sent to prison at Fort Delaware where he remained as a prisoner till the close of the war. M. W. Spearman, sr., was a man of sterling qualities, abstaining through life from intox:cating liquors and never allowing profanity to pass his lips. He was at all times worthy of the name of one of Georgia's best citizens and devoted his life to farming at the old home. He died in 1917, age seventy-four.

Dr. M. W. Spearman was the son of Matthew Whitfield Spearman and Julia Lavinia (Geiger) Spearman. The mother was born in Cuthbert, Georgia, in 1859, and is now residing in Shady Dale, at the old home so long owned by the family.

Gabriel Toombs Spearman, father of Matthew Whitfield Spearman, sr., was born in Heard County, Georgia, in 1853. Gabriel Toombs Spearman was a minister of the Methodist Church, South, and preached in Jasper County until his death in 1868. His wife was Martha Ledbetter a native of Georgia. Gabriel was a son of Thomas Spearman, a native of Virginia, and his father, John Spearman, in company with his brother to the new world, settling in the Old Dominion prior to the Revolutionary War.

BLAYLOCK.

While the name is often spelled Blalock, this is not the correct spelling according to the etymology of the word. It comes from an obsolete adjective—blay—meaning ash-colored, and the noun, lock, referring to hair, and means "ash-colored hair." Thus it comes down to us who bear it from Anglo-Saxon days.

Just when the Blaylocks first crossed the ocean to America is problematical, but was likely about the middle of the eighteenth century along with that great movement of people from the north of Ireland, settling first in Pennsylvania and a generation or so later moving southward into Virginia and the Carolinas, seeking greater freedom, and a land where they might worship God according to the dictates of their conscience.

Arriving in the Old North State, the first Blaylock to purchase land in Lincoln county was David Blaylock, who bought land, according to old records, on July 21. 1777. He was the father of John Blaylock who came to Georgia with his wife, Mary Eaton, about 1822, and settled in what is now Fulton county, but was at that time a part of Fayette county. John and Mary's home was located where the city of Atlanta now stands. The records show that J. L. (John) Blaylock, who was a son of John and Mary Eaton Blaylock, was a pioneer citizen of Fayette county and was a representative from that county to the Secession Convention at Milledgeville.

The children of John and Mary numbered eight, but all their names are not known. Those we do know were Henry, who was ancestor of the

Blaylocks living in and around Chickamauga, Georgia, and other sections of Walker county, and David, who was born in North Carolina, February 14, 1818, coming with his parents to Georgia about 1822. He married Caroline Beatty in 1824 to which union were born 11 children. One daughter, Mary, married William Tucker; Jane married a Thornton and went West, and a son, William, was living in Walker county in 1850.

Henry, who was born about 1825, grew to manhood and became a blacksmith. About 1847 he married Annie Tucker, to which union were born John T., William, Martha Jane, Matilda, Henry A. (Tip), Robert, and three who died in infancy. Like a great many other citizens of the county Henry Blaylock was opposed to secession and this opposition often brought him into conflict with those who favored it. Thus it happened that he became allied with that group of citizens who supported the Union. Because of this he was taken by the Gatewood raiders and carried some miles from his home and shot to death.

H. A. (TIP) BLAYLOCK

His son, Henry A. (Tip), grew to manhood near Crawfish Spring and became a farmer. In early life he was converted and allied himself with the Methodist Episcopal church, which alliance he maintained to his death. For more than half a century he was devoted to his church, supporting it by his presence and influence as well as his means as far as he was able, and even sometimes beyond his ability. During most of this time he was a tenant farmer and on Sunday morning he made it his duty to take his family and repair to church for the worship of God. With his large family he might be seen in a two-horse wagon on his way to church. His home was the minister's home, and he was always delighted to entertain his friends and neighbors. He became a local minister of his church and was very acceptable as a minister on any occasion. He was powerful in prayer and a constant reader of God's word.

In 1879 he married Corrie, daughter of Gilford and Margaret (Scarborough) Sartain, their children being ten; viz., Sidney F. (1881); Sallie (1882); Henry (1885-1906); Sim Monroe (1886); Charles D. (1891); Paul (1893); Edward (1896); Allen (1898); Edith (1900); Earl (1906).

Henry A. (Tip) died in 1927 and was buried at Chickamauga. His widow, though growing feeble, still remains, and is the idol of all the children.

Charles David Blaylock, son of H. A. and Corrie Blaylock, was born on Easter Sunday, March 29, 1891, near Chickamauga, Ga. Attended the public schools of Walker county and the high school at Chickamauga; taught at Pond Spring 1910, and principal of the Plainville, Ga., school 1911-12.

Appointed clerk in the Rossville, Ga., post office under Civil Service May 27, 1912, and was connected with that work till Feb. 6, 1918, being secretary of the Civil Service Board of Examiners. Feb. 6, 1917, was granted leave of absence to enter military service during World War. He entered as a private but was promoted to the commissioned ranks Oct. 18, 1918, and assigned to duty as Q.M. of General Hospital No. 19, Azalia, N. C., (later changed to Oteen), where he served till his discharge Oct. 19, 1919. He was then employed as custodian of supplies of the construction division of the army, as a civilian at Oteen, N. C., which position terminated in July, 1920. Following this he held various positions as auditor, and as general manager for Swift and Company in the Greenwood, S. C., territory till June, 1922, when he accepted a position with the Greenwood Creamery Company as sales and service manager, which position he now holds.

Mr. Blaylock is active as a citizen in all that tends to progress, and is an ardent church worker in the M. E. Church, South.

CHARLES D. BLAYLOCK

After the Armistic he married Gertrude Tretter Koons, a Red Cross nurse, who was on duty at Oteen. They have two children; Charles Sidney, born Nov. 9, 1919, and Gertrude Louise, born June 1, 1921.

He was discharged from the Army with a permanent disability and since then Congress has enacted legislation that has retired him as an Emergency Retired Army officer.

MILES R. HAMMOND.

The Hammonds came from England about the middle of the 17th century. The family tradition says there were three brothers who fought under Cromwell and who fled for their lives when royalty was restored following some years the death of the Lord Proprietor who died in 1658, sailing for America from Ireland soon after. Arrived in the new world the descendants of these brothers took part in the American Revolution, the grandfather of the subject of this sketch having fought under General Marion, according to family tradition.

Miles R. Hammond was born in 1823, in what was at the time the Indian Nation, afterward organized into Forsythe county. His father, Elijah, came from South Carolina. His mother was a Gentry. He was one of twelve children and was brought up amid the frontier conditions prevailing throughout Cherokee Georgia a century ago. These conditions we are prone to look upon as severe and uncouth, and compared with our present mode of life they may be so; but there were elements in them that tended to develop stamina, fortitude and character in our forbears.

There were two outstanding traits in the character of Miles Hammond: Piety and Honesty. He was devotedly a Christian. A deacon in the Baptist church till his death, he was faithful to his church both in attendance and support as far as he was able. This he inherited from his father. He often related how his father, after spreading his homely fare on the ground for the mid-day meal in the field or woods where he was laboring with his children, would call the boys around the viands and return thanks to the good All-Father for the food, often with tears in his eyes. His honesty. He not only met his own obligations but insisted on his employees, of whom during his life he had numerous, paying their debts; and if they failed to do so usually lost their places as workmen with him. Profanity and drunkenness were other vices with which he had no patience, and which, if persisted in, meant dismissal from his employ.

In 1844 he married Catherine Currie (1819-1893), who was of Scotch descent and was of staunch Presbyterian stock. To this union were born nine children, namely: Mary Jane, M. M., died in infancy, D. J., Sarah C., I. Rebecca, E. A., J. H., A. N., and C. J. Of these J. H. and C. J. have lived practically all their lives in Walker county. These two brothers are, as brothers should be, quite chummy. They are often, as occasion permits, seen walking, or riding or conversing together.

Miles R. Hammond was a carpenter-contractor. From a mere boy he was engaged in carpentering and later in life employed many workmen in building bridges, jails, mills, and other public constructions. Thus it was when the Civil war came on he was exempt from military service since he was interested in milling, and during the latter part of the war he often worked day and night grinding to supply the needs of the people as well as for the Confederacy.

(1). Dr. J. H. Hammond was born in 1856, in Chattooga county. He was trained under his father's tutelage as a carpenter, meanwhile attending the community schools when in session till he was of age, when he took a course in medicine. He first attended the medical department of the State University, later going to the Jefferson Medical College at Philadelphia, where he received his degree in 1883. Returning to Walker county he began practise at LaFayette, where he remained two years, going thence to Monroe, Georgia, for two years, after which he returned to LaFayette where he has since lived, spending his life as a practising physician throughout Walker and adjoining counties. In 1912 he took a post graduate course at Polyclinic, Philadelphia. In 1921, he was named Health Commissioner for the county under the Ellis Health Law, and for ten years he has served in that capacity most acceptably to all concerned.

Dr. Hammond is a Baptist, Mason, Knight-Templar and Shriner. Also, member of the Eastern Star Chapter—a full-fledged Mason. He has the respect and confidence of all who know him.

In 1886 he married R. Loudie Fariss, born 1856; daughter of Dr. D. C. Fariss and Eliza Ann (Moore) Fariss, to which union were born Annie Moore, Susan Dewitt and Loudie who died in infancy. Annie Moore married E. P. Hall, Jr., of LaFayette. They have two children, Joe Hill and Bettie Lou. Susan Dewitt married W. E. Gray of Swainsboro, Ga. They have two children, W. E., Jr., and Mary Louise.

(2). C. J. Hammond was born in 1861 in Chattooga county. Like his brother he received such schooling as the times afforded, learning much in the rough school of experience. He is a Baptist, deacon in his church, and a Mason. For many years he served his church as clerk and his lodge as secretary. Always a student, he has during his life acquired a general knowledge of most subjects taught in our best schools and colleges. Charley Hammond is one of the substantial citizens of the county. Friendly and jovial, liberal and honest, he is liked and honored by all who know him.

In 1887 he married Mary H. Wardlaw, b. 1868, dau. of John and Mary C. (Clendennen) Wardlaw. They have the following children: Paul Lee, Maude K., Dewey W., Mary Ruth, and Eloise. Paul Lee (M.D.) married Ruth Height, two children, William and Charles J., Jr.; Dewey W. (M.D.) married Minnie Ruth Shattuck; Maude K. married W. E. McKeown, children, Helen, and W. E., Jr.; Mary Ruth, graduate of Bessie Tift college, is a teacher in the LaFayette High Schools; Eloise, now senior in LaFayette High Schools.

Hill and Bee, brothers, sons of Volentine Hammond, who was a son of Joseph, whose father, "Buck" Hammond, was first cousin to Miles R. Hammond, live at LaFayette.

Other grandchildren in Walker county of Miles R. Hammond are: W. M., son of E. A. Hammond; Mrs. M. A. McConnell, daughter of D. J. Hammond, as well as a number of great-grandchildren not named above. Also, a number of more distant relatives scattered throughout Walker and adjoining counties.

SAMUEL PARKS HALL.

The Halls originated near Dublin Ireland, whence they migrated to

America before the Revolution, in which famous struggle they served, many of their descendants being members of the D. A. R. Three brothers, Samuel Parks, Calvin, and Joe, whose homes were in Blount county, Tennessee, where they were born early in the 19th century, were traders, buying and selling and transporting merchandise. They were among those early, hardy pioneers who often traveled down the Tennessee river with goods and produce for the markets at Memphis and New Orleans where they sold both goods and boat and made their way back to their homes through the country as best they might, often gone from home 90 to 100 days or more. No doubt they often had encounters with the Chickamauga Indians as described in the early chapters in this work. Too, these brothers used to relate some very exciting experiences they had with Indians and other pioneer settlers at Ross' Landing where they generally stopped on their trips down the river.

Later, these brothers carried horses and mules to South Georgia for sale and in so doing passed through and became acquainted with the fertile valleys and beautiful scenery of Walker county; and so, finally, during the decade immediately preceding the Civil War, they migrated to the county and settled in McLemore's Cove.

One of these brothers, Samuel Parks (1813-1889), a native of East Tennessee, came to the county about 1855, settling in the Cove where he became a prosperous farmer. In his younger days he had been in the Indian wars, serving as quartermaster most of the time. His wife was Susan Badgett, whose mother was a Burwell, which name has been perpetuated among the descendants. One son, Burwell (1847-1879), married Mellville Connally (1849-1881), daughter of Thomas W. (1809) and Temperance (Arnold) Connally (1818), to which union were born: S. P., Thomas, Susan, and Burwell.

S. P. (1872) married (1) Lula Garmany (1870-1919), daughter of Newton and Addie (Knox) Garmany. Children: William Roy, Burwell (shortened to Burl), Susan, Mellville, Mary Lula, and Samuel Parks, Jr.

In 1920 he married (2) Emma Pickle, daughter of W. F. and Josephine (Glazner) Pickle. Mr. Hall is a prosperous farmer and merchant, living on a fertile farm in a beautiful section of the Cove. He served for some years as a member of the Board of Roads and Revenue, being a member when the new Court House and the Almshouse were built. Also a member of the Board of Jury Revisors. He is a Baptist and Mason.

FAMILY RECORD. Roy (1894-1922) was killed by a stroke of lightning.

Burl (1896) married Mary Elizabeth Elder, daughter of Dr. D. G. and Ella (Glenn) Elder, and they have two children. He is an R. F. D. carrier at Kensington, Ga. He is a World war veteran, served overseas; enlisted with the 82nd division and commissioned as 2nd lieutenant in France, later transferred to 33rd division, in which outfit he was in several important battles in two of the major offensives.

Susie (1898) married Charley Owings, two children.

Mary (1902) married Martin Clements, three children.
Sam (1908), single.

WILLIAM F. PICKLE.

William Franklin (1856-1920), son of Franklin and Nettie (Daugherty) Pickle, was born in Cherokee county, Alabama. His wife was Josephine (1855-1923), daughter of Rev. James Hasletine (1833-1906) and Millie Ann (Harris) Glazner (1834-1884).

The Reverend Mr. Glazner was one of the most prominent and beloved Baptist ministers of his day throughout Northwest Georgia and Northeast Alabama, serving as pastor and holding evangelistic services in both states. Born in Buncomb county, North Carolina, he was of Dutch descent, his ancestors coming to America before the Revolution. His grandmother's maiden name was Kitchen, relative of the late Senator Kitchen of North Carolina. When a small lad he came with his father to DeKalb county, Alabama, where he was brought up, attending the schools of that day, but receiving much instruction from his parents. In early life he felt the call to the ministry and being ordained began his long and eminently successful life as a pastor and evangelist. He was pastor of Sardis church in Chattooga county for 25 years, Mt. Bethel, 23 years, and at Summerville, Mt. Harmony and Menlo he held long pastorates; also serving churches in Walker county and under the Home Mission Board in Dade county. He died in the Lyerly Baptist church, of which he was pastor at the time, on August 8, 1906. Mr. Glazner was also a staunch Mason—a Mason of the old school, one who lived and practised its precepts.

W. F. Pickle, the subject of this sketch, was the only child of his parents. For a number of years he lived at Cedar Grove where his children were fortunate to attend the school taught by that Prince of Teachers, Captain Wood. His children were: Emma, Alice, Bess, and James.

Emma, or Miss Emma as she is familiarly and affectionately known, taught for many years throughout Walker county, and her pupils, now grown to maturity, and many of them with families, often refer to her with great reverence and respect as being a model teacher and woman of beautiful character and rare accomplishments. For a number of years she was employed in the Civil Service Department at Washington in the Census Bureau. She, like her honored father, is a Baptist, and one of the most faithful laborers in church and missionary movements in her denomination. She has served for a number of years as Superintendent of the Woman's Missionary Union of the Coosa Association. In 1920 she married S. P. Hall, and their home is at Kensington, Ga.

W. F. Pickle, after leaving Cedar Grove community, settled in Dade county at Rising Fawn, where he became a charter member of the Baptist church at that place, and one of its most faithful supporters. He loved his church and denomination and gave of his energy, time and substance to its support. Mr. Pickle was likewise an ardent Mason and never tired of preaching and teaching its doctrines and precepts. Friendly, jolly and jovial, Mr. Pickle was greatly admired by all who knew him.

THE PARK FAMILY OF WALKER COUNTY, GEORGIA.
By Mrs. Frances Park Stiles.

The Park family is said to have originated in Eastern France, and the name is of English-French origin, meaning "he who lives at or near the park." The family is of French-Huguenot extraction and existed in the days before surnames were formed. Some of these Huguenots who lived in the villages assumed the name "Parcs," others "Pack."

When the Edict of Nantes, which had insured religious freedom to Protestants in France, was revoked in 1685, many of the Protestants who lived in the mountain valleys of Southern France left for various other and safer parts of the world—some to England, some to Scotland and the north of Ireland and from them the Park family of Pennsylvania and the South are descended.

The Park family of Walker county are the direct descendants of Moses Park, born in Virginia, but later of Mecklenburg county, North Carolina. He was born Nov. 28, 1738, and his wife, Mary Hill, was born in 1749. They were married about 1770. He was in the battle of Ramseur's Mill, which occurred June 20, 1780. A certificate was secured in 1922 by a member of the Park family of Walker county, stating principal and interest paid him for services.

In the latter part of the seventeenth century, Thomas and James Park, sons of Moses Park, emigrated to Putnam county, Georgia. Thomas Park was born in North Carolina, Feb. 27, 1772. In 1797 he married Elizabeth Phelps, who was born Oct. 18, 1778. He left a will dated July 25, 1823, bequeathing a large plantation and cotton gin to his wife and sons, Thomas, Doctor Andrew, William, Moses, James and George.

James Park (son of Thomas, 1772) married Winnie Lane Nov. 15, 1825. In 1837 James Park and his brother-in-law, Dick Lane, moved to Walker county and bought land in the Cove. One week from that date, James Park died at LaGrange, Georgia; later his widow and four small children moved with her brother, Dick Lane, to the new home in Walker county. Dick Lane was a man of wealth, owning great tracts of land and numbers of slaves. The Lane home still stands and is one of the rare old antebellum mansions of Walker county—a beautiful home.

James Andrew Park of LaFayette was born near LaGrange, Georgia, Jan. 30, 1834, and died Feb. 22, 1918. His wife, Ann E. Smith, born July 28, 1838, died Nov. 28, 1912. They were married Oct. 10, 1857. He was the son of James Park (1802) and Winnie Lane; was a Confederate soldier, first lieutenant Co. F., 39th Ga. Vol., a man of devout faith and a prominent citizen. Eleven children were born to him and his wife, the eldest being the late Doctor Hector Park, a medical missionary to China for forty-seven years under the M. E. Church, South; he had charge of the Soocho Hospital—a great man. No man helped to build up and modernize the great nation of China more than Dr. Park. While on a visit to his home in Georgia and Florida in 1927, he died in Hawthorn, Florida. His ashes were carried back to China by his wife, Nora Lambuth Park, and their daughter, Mrs. D. L. Sherertz, who with her husband are now missionaries in China.

The remaining sons and daughters of James Andrew Park, and their descendants are scattered throughout the Southern States.

James Park (son of Moses, 1738) was born in North Carolina, June 7, 1785. He married Martha Yandell in 1804, from which union there were seven children, all of whom were born in Putnam county, but were all eventually among the pioneers of Walker county; notably, of these, was Moses Park, son of James and Martha (Yandell) Park, and father of Rev. James H. Park, who was the first minister of the Universalist church of Walker county.

In a letter addressed to his children in 1860, James Park (Rev. Park's grandfather) commented happily on the honor of his grandson being chosen the pastor of the new church and how pleased he would be for all to hear him preach the Gospel.

There was a daughter (Mary) of the pioneer James Park who moved to Walker county in 1838, settling near the point of John's mountain. She had married Dr. Adam Clements in Muscogee county, in 1833. Among their children was a son, Judson Claudius, who rose to considerable distinction, representing the Seventh (Georgia) Congressional District for many years, later appointed a member of the Interstate Commerce Commission in which position he served for a time as chairman. He was first lieutenant of his regiment in the War Between the States and was wounded in Atlanta, July 22, 1864.

One of his daughters is a member of the faculty of the National Cathedral School for Girls, on Mt. St. Albans, Washington, D. C., and has recently been accorded an ecclesiastical honor rarely received by American women. She has been awarded the Lambuth Diploma of Student of Theology, first class, by the Archbishop of Canterbury. Judge Clements' family are at present comfortably located in Washington City.

Eugene Culberson of LaFayette, Georgia, Confederate soldier, faithful member of the Baptist church, now in his ninety-third year, is a grandson of James Park (1785), and remembers distinctly being told by his grandfather that the family came to America from Donegal, Ireland.

The lineal descendants of Thomas and James Park have held an annual reunion at Rock Springs, Georgia, for many years. The first officers appointed by the Association were the following: A. T. Park, pres.; Albert Bird, v-pres.; J. L. Park, secy.; Laura Campfield, treas.; Mrs. Frances Park Stiles, historian. Many heirlooms and documents of priceless value belong to many members. The coat of arms of the family is the same as the one carried by the Parks of Scotland. A memorial service is held annually for the members who have died during the year.

A monument has been placed by the Association over the graves in the LaFayette cemetery, of James Park (1785) and his wife, Martha Yandell.

JACKSON-MYERS.

Edward Jackson, soldier of the Revolution, was born in South Carolina and died in Walker county, Georgia, and was buried in the Poe graveyard near Trion, Georgia. His grave cannot be definitely located as his grandsons, the late G. B., W. W. S. and J. M. F. Myers, a few years before their deaths, made an effort to locate it to have marker placed there but failed. There is not the slightest doubt about his burial place.

His name appears on the papers in the Revolutionary war claim W.2119. He enlisted in 1775 and served at various times till the close of the Revolution, amounting in all to about two years. He was in the battle of Coosabatchie. Senate Document, Pension Roll, First Session of the 23rd Congress, page 40, gives his name as a Revolutionary pensioner, placed on the roll July 1, 1833, on his application executed October 5, 1832, at which time he was a resident of Gwinnett county, Georgia. He received a bounty grant as a Revolutionary soldier in the lottery of 1827—Lot 52, tract 14, Muscogee county, Georgia. He is mentioned in White's Historical Collections, page 483, as one of the old men of Gwinnett county, his age being given as 87 years. He came to Walker county to live with his children and grandchildren a few years before his death in 1845. He was living near Waterville at his death.

MYERS COAT-OF-ARMS

The children of Edward Jackson were: David, Benjamin, Booker, Mahaley and Sarah. He had other children but their names are unknown. David married Rachel Bracken; children: William, James, Isaac, Edward, John, Nancy, Lydia, Judy and Elizabeth. Mahaley married Carna Myers of Anson county, North Carolina, to which union were born one son, William, and one daughter. Carna Myers died when his son William was only a few years old. After his father's death, William was taken by his mother's people (Jacksons) and reared in Georgia; his mother, Mahaley Myers, later married David Rutherford.*

William Myers, grandson of Edward Jackson, married Lydia Jackson, daughter of David Jackson. She was a granddaughter of Edward Jackson. To this union were born the following children: Edward J., David C., Greene B., W. W. S., Alexander S., James M., John M. F., Jane, Parthena, Charity, Sarah. William Myers was a pioneer is the county, coming while the Cherokee Indians were here. Mr. Myers was one of those rare old characters whose "word was his bond." He was noted for his truthfulness, honesty and uprightness; and those who know his descendants intimately say that those traits are found throughout all his generations. William Myers was a model citizen and one who imparted to his children a like heritage.

Edward J. married Mary Ann Clements; David C., single; Greene B. married (1) Tabitha Campbell, (2) Nancy Greene Campbell, (3) Murilla Lowry; W. W. S. married (1) Sarah Ann Calhoun, (2) Sarah Lydia Roane; Alexander S. married Betty Hicks of Texas; James M. married Dora Hicks of Texas; John M. F., a physician, married (1) Fannie Mariah Calhoun, (2) Tennie Pursley, (3) Beulah Hammond; Jane married Wililam J. Martin, Esq.; Charity married Dr. W. H. Wilbanks; Sarah married James E. Lansford; Parthena passed in childhood.

Greene B. Myers (1837-1910), one of the eleven children of William Myers, was born in Walker county, May 12, 1837—on the farm still owned by the Myers family—Land Lot Number 202, 7th District and 4th Section, Cane Creek Militia District. He served as private and later as sergeant-major in Company C, 4th Georgia battalion, afterwards 60th Georgia Regiment, C. S. A.

In 1868 he accepted a position as bookkeeper with Marsh and Allgood, founders and owners of the Cotton Factory at Trion, Chattooga county, Georgia. In April, 1875, the mill was destroyed by fire, after which a stock company was organized and the mill rebuilt and he was elected secretary of the company and continued as such till his death in 1910. He was a quiet, unassuming Christian gentleman, holding the confidence and esteem of his employers and a multitude of friends all his years, and died in the supreme knowledge of a faithful servant well-rewarded. He was positive in his convictions as a Christian and citizen. He was an ardent Baptist and always attended the services of his church as long as health permitted, being clerk of his church more than forty years. Prominent in fraternal circles, he was secretary of his Lodge of F. & A. Masons from its organization at Trion till his death; also, treasurer, each, of the Odd Fellows and Red Men from their organization till his death.

---

*The late W. C. McFarland of Rossville, Georgia, says that David Rutherford and his wife, Mahaley, died within an hour of each other and were buried in the same grave.

His first wife was Tabitha Ann Campbell, of which union one son was born who died in infancy. His second wife was Nancy Greene Campbell, a sister of his first wife. Their children were eight, to-wit:—Graves Trenholm, who married Clara Hutchens; David Rudicil married Lula Lowe; A. McMillan married Hattie Hawkins; Kate Tibatha Ann married Charles Gore; Alice married H. W. Stegall; Fred O. married Daisey Kellett; Hill Clements married Eva Osment; Nannie Greene, unmarried.

His third wife was Murilla C. Lowry, who survives and is at this writing, June, 1932, 91 years of age.

Another son was W. W. S. (Scott) Myers (1847-1921). He was for probably half a century one of the most prominent citizens of Walker county. He was born, lived and died in the Waterville community, but his popularity was not confined to his immediate neighborhood; he was known and admired throughout the county for his honesty, integrity and his many sterling qualities of character. In his young manhood he enlisted in the ranks of "the lost cause," and served with distinction in Company K, 4th Georgia Cavalry. For twenty years he was County School Commissioner during which time he gave the county splendid service as head of the public school system. He was County Guardian and County Administrator for a long number of years; also Jury Revisor, and Cotton Statistician for the Federal Government. In all these positions he showed the sound judgment, worth and integrity of the true gentleman and honest official that he was.

Mr. Myers was prominent as a churchman. Being a member of the Baptist church, he was a faithful supporter and served in various official capacities. Mr. Myers was for many years one of the outstanding citizens of the county.

Mr. Myers' first wife was Sarah A. Calhoun, cousin of that famous statesman and orator, John C. Calhoun. Of this union were born eight children, viz: W. E. A. married Addie Hackney; J. M. S. married Carmi Stegall; R. W. C. married Jessie Coley; D. J. D. married Susie McCoy; Mary J. passed in infancy; Fannie B. married Bell Willbanks; P. H. married Mary Robeson; Z. V. married Sammie Askew. His second wife was Sarah Lydia Roane of Tennessee. The Roanes are related by blood to George Washington, James K. Polk and Dr. Ephrain Brevard, author of the Mecklenburg Declaration of Independence, and other notables of American history. By this marriage there were four children: Sarah Ruth married Dr. A. T. Cline of Cherokee county; Virginia Bell married Dr. F. L. Rountree of Emanuel county; Carmie Lydia passed in young womanhood; James Dennis passed in infancy.

Jane, oldest daughter of William Myers, married Esquire William Martin, and their children were: Edward, Abraham, John, Daniel, Greene, Deed, Gordon and Samuel. One daughter passed in childhood; the other two are: Mrs. Will Landers of Rome, and Mrs. Will Lowe of Chattanooga. This large family of eight boys and two girls all grew to manhood and womanhood and all made honest, reliable, dependable men and women of usefulness. No doubt they inherited some of these qualities from the grandfather, William Myers. Many of the Martins of the county are descendants of this family.

Nancy Jackson, daughter of David Jackson, married Alston Mills; children: Hugh, John, Harrison, Graw, Margaret, Rachel, Doliska, Lizzie, Mattie, Vicey and Malinday. Hugh married Mary E. Hall; John, Harrison and Graw were soldiers in the Confederate army and were killed in action. Margaret married William Roberts; Rachel married J. M. (Dote) Hall; Doliska married Robert T. Hall; Lizzie married D. J. (Bud) Hammond; Mattie married J. Wash Lowry; Vicey married John Poe.

There are approximately 200 descendants of Edward Jackson now living in Walker and Chattooga counties not to mention those in other sections of the country; and for lack of space it is impossible to give their names. Among these are the children, grandchildren and great-grandchildren of the late Greene B. Myers, W. W. S. Myers, John M. F. Myers, William J. Martin, William Roberts, J. M. Hall, Robert T. Hall, D. J. (Bud) Hammond, J. Wash Lowry, Volentine Hammond and George Justice.

The Myers coat-of-arms, shown above, dates back many centuries, and is a relic of those early days when every clan had its individual banner and delighted to follow and fight for its principles. The Myers coat-of-arms may be traced back to the Middle Ages when it had its origin among their early English ancestors.

THOMAS CALVIN HACKNEY.

A picturesque and well-known citizen of Walker county more than half a century ago, and especially during the eighties and early nineties, was Thomas Calvin Hackney. He was then robust, energetic, high spirited and of an adventurous disposition, bold in assertion of opinion and impetuous in action—yet so jovial, kind, generous, sympathetic, altogether friendly and neighborly, with a spirit of boyish buoyancy and wholesomeness that he was a fair type of the perfectly likeable and companionable man. His early life was colorful and adventurous. From his boyhood on his grandfather's plantation in North Carolina, through his exploits during the War Between the States with Lee's army in Virginia; his experiences in the wilds of Florida immediately after the war, and later in a pioneering section of West Tennessee. These years of stirring action gave him a store of interesting experiences which he could relate with the gift of narrative that he possessed most effectively and interestingly. He loved the Old South, revered the "Lost Cause"—but he believed in progress and always looked hopefully and expectantly to the future. He was the typical Confederate veteran, and when he came to Walker county most men of mature years in the county had been soldiers in the Confederate army. Like most of those who had worn the gray he no sooner met an old soldier of the Confederacy than they were at once acquainted—and friends. But he was naturally a friend to man—interested in and loved all classes of people. He often said that for a number of years he was acquainted with, and on friendly terms with practically every man in the county. He was the soul of honesty, integrity, fidelity to duty, purity of life and lofty patriotism.

A student of the basic industry, agriculture, Mr. Hackney passed his entire career as a planter, being remarkably alert and active until the last few weeks of his life. Soon after his arrival in Walker county in 1878, Mr. Hackney purchased the then interesting, highly developed and well-equipped McCutchen farm in Dry Creek valley about two miles west of LaFayette. He became a friend and neighbor of the McCutchen, Henry, Lumpkin, McWhorter, Miller, Chastain, Shattuck and other families of that unusually fine neighborhood. The farm was still further developed, additional acreage was brought into cultivation and a program of general farming, stock and poultry raising was entered upon. The place was an outstanding one of that time—far in advance of the period. The abundance of the choice fruits, the beauty and variety of flowers, the well-kept gardens and the conveniences added much to the attractiveness and comfort of the home. A school in the home, arranged by Mr. Hackney for his own small children and those of a neighbor, completed the ideal life of that time on a farm.

After some years Mr. Hackney sold his farm and moved into LaFayette, where his talent for development was again strikingly illustrated, spending his last days quietly experimenting in horticulture and floriculture, the results of which were most satisfactory and valuable.

Mr. Hackney was of English descent. The Hackney estate was in Middlesex, England, now a part of the city of London. "It was at one time the favorite suburban residence of the Hackney family." This family in the New World was identified with the early history of North Carolina, being leaders in civic, social and religious life. Daniel Hackney, great-grandfather of Thomas of this sketch, was a soldier of the American Revolution. He was one of the first deacons and trustees of the Rock River Baptist church, in Chatham county, N. C., and resigned in 1825, having served fifty years. His son, Daniel II, served this church as pastor twenty-five years. Robert, son of Daniel, followed in his father's footsteps and served this church throughout his life. He married Sarah Jones and their son, Thomas Calvin, of this review, married Mary Marsh, daughter of James Gray Marsh, September 6, 1866, at Hackney, Chatham county, N. C. Their children are Misses Sara and Mamie Hackney, who live in the parental home at LaFayette; James Brantley, official Court Reporter, of Dothan, Alabama, who married Blanche Murphee of Troy, Alabama; Addie of Memphis, Tennessee, who married W. E. A. Myers of Walker county—her sons are Edward and Eugene; Edwin Marsh of Washington, D. C., for sixteen years in the Valuation Department, Interstate Commerce Commission, except eighteen months in World War—twelve of which were spent in France. He married Mary

Wade, daughter of Rev. J. T. Wade, who was pastor of the Presbyterian church at Calhoun. Their only child is Mary Marsh.

Through successive generations the Marsh, Brooks, Hackney, Brantley and Jones families, who were closely allied, have been numbered among the representative men of affairs and influential citizens, being ministers, teachers, doctors, statesmen and planters. Mrs. Hackney, of English-French descent, was the great-granddaughter of William Marsh and Isaac Brooks on her paternal and maternal sides, respectively, whose coat-of-arms are now in the family; both ancestors gave valuable service in the American Revolution. Her father, husband, two brothers and five uncles served in the Confederate army. One son, Edwin Marsh, served in the World War. Fourteen descendants of William Marsh have united with the D. A. R. Chapter at LaFayette, which was named for him. Mrs. Hackney was also a member of Chickamauga Chapter U. D. C., and Ross Graham Unit, American Legion Auxiliary. She was a charter member of the Woman's Missionary Union of the First Baptist church, organized more than fifty years ago. She was always interested in her church and its welfare. Her home and her family received her untiring devotion. By her charming gentle manner, her love and her gracious hospitality, she won and held many friends—a typical woman of the Old South. She passed away May 9, 1929.

Mr. Hackney was an enthusiastic member of Chickamauga Camp, Confederate Veterans, a representative of Company E, of the famous 26th North Carolina Regiment. He saw four years of service and was present when General Lee surrendered at Appomattox Court House. As a Mason he was loyal to its high principles; he gave his hearty support to the Democratic cause; was a member of the Baptist church for fifty years and gave it his ardent support. He died at his home in LaFayette, September 21, 1914.

JOHN SCOTT HENDERSON.
By Miss Mattie Henderson

The name Henderson is old in Scotland, the family having lived there since the fifteenth century. Many authentic and traditional stories are current portraying the valor and dexterity of the earlier generations in peace and war. The subject of this sketch, John Scott Henderson, was the son of John Henderson of Rock Ridge county, Virginia, who emigrated with his family to Greene county, Tennessee, about 1800. In 1849 his son, John Scott Henderson, and wife, Winnifred Brickey Davis Henderson, emigrated to Georgia and located near Crawfish Spring, now known as Chickamauga, Georgia.

Realizing the richness of a virgin soil and the advantageous location, he interested his younger brother, William, and together they bought large tracts of land and established their homes in what is now known as the Red Belt section.

Before the Civil war a stage route from Knoxville via Chattanooga to Rome, Georgia, was in operation carrying passengers and mail by stage coaches. A relay station and a post office called Snow Hill was operated by John S. Henderson. It was in this house that a council of war was held by high Confederate officers where the great battle of Chickamauga was planned and mapped out. Such notable men as Bragg, Longstreet, Wheeler, Leonidas Polk, Horton and others were there. Among the papers of the late Mrs. Augusta Henderson Jones was found a contract for supplies for fifty men and all animals for G. F. Bailey & Company circus, dated September 14, 1855. This circus was staged in a big field across the road from the old Henderson dwelling, and was chosen because the circus could be adequately cared for by Mr. Henderson. This circus later became the famous Barnum & Bailey Shows.

Mrs. Henderson was a daughter of Rev. William Davis and Elizabeth Brickey Davis, who were natives of Virginia, and moved to Tennessee. He joined the state militia of Tennessee, and was one of that noble company who followed Andrew Jackson in his brilliant victories in the war of 1812. This grand old man's grave in Peavine cemetery near Rock Springs, Georgia, was the first grave in Georgia to be honored with a marker, being erected by the Atlanta Chapter U. S. D. 1812.

The children of John Scott Henderson and his wife were as follows: Jerome Bonaparte, unmarried; Margaret Elizabeth married Thomas N. Jones; John Washington married Addie Jackson; Laura Virginia passed in infancy; Orrville Rice married Lou Anderson; William Horace married Fannie Moore; Mary Augusta married James R. (Bob) Jones; Robert Lee married Lillie Napier; Joseph Eugene married Nettie Lee Dunagan.

True to the customs of that day among the better class of settlers, John S. Henderson was able to have his children tutored in his home, later sending them to college; and as each son or daughter married they were given a large bounty of land for a home.

Mrs. Henderson, herself the daughter of a soldier. was thoroughly patriotic. When the tocsin of war sounded in '61. she. Spartan mother-like, courageously sent two boys to the front. The oldest son. Jerome B., born 1840, received his early education at LaFayette High School, later taking a law course at Lebanon, Tennessee, and still later a theological course at Mercer University, then located at Penfield, Georgia. He forsook the class-room, came home and volunteered, being among the first to enlist and go to the front. At Crawfish Spring he made a speech urging others to join the colors. He was mustered into service July 8th. 1861, Company H, 26th Tennessee. He served in the Western Army of Tennessee as first sergeant. He was captured and confined in the Federal prison at Camp Douglas (Chicago), where he died from exposure and was given a Christian funeral. A comrade has said of him that no man's moral character was brighter. As a soldier he was always at his post—calm, cool and brave. For fifty-two years the final resting place of this "Hero in Gray" was unknown.

His diploma from Mercer University, sent to his parents after the war, is a grim reminder of the fact that he had spent great effort to prepare for a useful normal life, but that war robbed him of the opportunity to do other than to lay down his life for his country.

John W., the second son, born 1844, enlisted in Company G, 4th Georgia Cavalry, and was in many hard-fought battles, notably Chickamauga, Perryville, and the siege of Knoxville. He belonged for a time to the bodyguard of General Buckner. At the close of the war he returned to his home and faced conditions all southerners had to face—want, poverty and broken family circles. He died in 1909 at his home in Calhoun, Georgia. He was an upright and useful citizen and left his family the heritage of a blameless life.

The four younger sons—Orville, William, Robert and Joseph Eugene ("Buddie") were too young to go into the army. They all grew to manhood and made their homes in Georgia with the exception of William, who lived in Missouri. They were honorable, law-abiding, God-fearing men and outstanding citizens of their respective communities.

Two daughters, Margaret and Augusta ("Gussie"), grew to womanhood and married brothers, Thomas N. and James R. (Bob) Jones respectively, sons of a neighboring pioneer, James Roland Jones. The last member of the John Scott Henderson family to die was Mary Augusta Henderson Jones, who died August 11, 1930, age 74 years.

The family is now represented by numerous descendants, some of whom live in the ancestral home of their parents. They cherish with pride the memory of those grand old forbears—John Scott Henderson and his courageous wife, Winnifred Brickey Davis Henderson. Together they struggled valiantly through those perilous pioneer times, the devastating years of the War Between the States, the reconstruction period—years of soul-trying experiences.

The old Henderson home, rich in history of war-time activities, is a veritable monument slowly succumbing to the elements; but the memory of its builders, John and Winnifred, comes to their children's children like a benediction that follows after prayer. So goes the history of the ages. One generation after another passes off the stage of action and "goes to join that innumerable caravan which moves to that mysterious realm, where each shall take his place in the silent halls of death." So mote it be.

CAPTAIN NATHAN CAMPBELL NAPIER.

Capt. Nathan Campbell Napier, a gallant Confederate officer, widely known in North Georgia, was born in Troup county, Dec. 22, 1834, the son of Leroy and Matilda Moultrie Napier. His youth was spent in Macon. He attended Franklin College and Yale, and spent a year at

Dresden University in Germany. In 1859 he was given Woodside plantation in South Walker. The spring of 1860 saw his fortunate and happy marriage to Julia Sharpe, daughter of Thomas and Harriet Young Sharpe.

With the gathering of war clouds, he volunteered for service, and, in '62, after four months with the Fourth Ga. battalion, was elected to a first lieutenancy in the Third Ga. Cavalry under Col. Martin J. Crawford. As part of Bragg's advance under Gen. Joe Wheeler, in a scouting skirmish on the battle of Perryville at Bigg Hill was severely wounded, losing his right eye. Though captured he was soon exchanged. Raising a company later, it was put into the Sixth Ga. Cavalry, Col. John R. Hart, which under Forrest, was in the first fierce clash at Chickamauga on the extreme right of the Southern line. His command saw hard service in the Tennessee campaigns, the fighting under Hood and Forrest and, after the rush into North Carolina, surrendered at Kingston in the spring of 1865.

His first pedagogic venture was in '73 with the school at the Chattooga Baptist church. The years of '74 and '75 saw him a citizen of LaFayette as principal of the old academy. In '75 and '76 he taught in Forsyth's school for boys, the Millard Institute. His living pupils are honored women and men in all walks of life. In 1880 he bought the Walker County Messenger from its founder, Capt. Gus McHan, and thereafter for over twenty years, until his sudden death Jan. 21, 1902, devoted every energy of mind and heart to the advancement and development of the best interests of his home section. It was his joy to see two railroads built through the county and the construction of the Union Cotton Mill and the Hosiery Mill. He served the county as a commissioner and as a member of the Board of Education.

He urged the organization of the Chickamauga Chapter U. D. C., but did not live to see its labor of love in the beautiful Confederate monument. A Master Mason since 1874, a tribute from Western Lodge says: "Brother Napier was qualified intellectually for any position and might have attained distinction in any station, but preferred a private career, possessing a spotless moral character, valued as a teacher, recognized extensively as a man of rare culture, loved and respected by those near him as a sympathetic and generous neighbor, ready at all times to do a full share in the establishment and maintenance of every common and charitable enterprise. No one surpassed his record as a brave and patriotic soldier, distinguished as a public character in our county, and more than all, widely known as a courteous gentleman." The Masonic resolutions were signed by Hon. B. F. Thurman, Dr. J. H. Hammond and Col. J. P. Shattuck.

One of his sons survives, Augustus Young, for twenty-one years a Baptist missionary in China. The youngest, Nathan C., Jr., editor of the Vidalia Advance, died in 1923, and Leroy, an able and beloved physician, died at Lumber City in 1930. His eldest son, George M., past

Grand Master of Georgia Masons and eleven years attorney-general of the state, died May 4th, 1932, at his home in Decatur.

The four daughters, all of whom are living, are as follows: Miss Caroline Napier, who lives at LaFayette, Ga.; Miss Alice Napier, who occupies the chair of mathematics at the State College for Women at Milledgeville, where she has had a long and creditable service in this position; Mrs. Early W. Adams (Julia Sharpe Napier), of Philadelphia, Pa., and Mrs. Emma N. Ledbetter, of Decatur, widow of Rev. Samuel B. Ledbetter, who died in the service of the Methodist Episcopal Church, South, as presiding elder of the Dalton District.

ROBERT BLACKWELL STEGALL.

Robert Blackwell Stegall was born near Cartersville, Bartow county, Ga., in 1842. He was educated in the "Old Field Schools" of those antebellum days, later attending high school at Cartersville, where he made rapid progress in his studies, so much so that he began teaching himself before he was 20 years of age, and was thus engaged when his country sounded the bugle-blast calling young men to arms—to the defense of the young nation. Dismissing his classes he promptly enlisted in the 14th Ga. Inf., on the 15th day of June, being his 20th birthday.

He was sent to Virginia where he saw service on numerous hard-fought battlefields, being in the Seven Days Battle Around Richmond. Because of organic trouble he was discharged from further army service from a Richmond hospital.

In the fall of 1863 he took service as a brakeman with the old Western and Atlantic R. R. until Sherman neared Atlanta in July, 1864. He then went to Columbus, Ga., and took service with the Muscogee R. R., now a part of the Central of Georgia system, being conductor of freight trains until the latter part of May, 1865, when the news of Lee's surrender reached Southwest Georgia. When the U. S. Government quit operating the W. & A. R. R., turning it back to the State, he was one of the first conductors running a train out of Atlanta to Chattanooga. During his 14 years of service on that road, he filled all the arms of service in train and freight yard operation, his last service being general yard master at Chattanooga terminating on November 6, 1878.

Four days later he took service with the Alabama Great Southern, and remained with that line, through many changes in management, in various capacities till December 31, 1925, when he was retired by the Southern Railway on account of age, being then 15 years past old age limit. He had then given over 47 years of continuous service to the line. Since then he has been living on his little farm one mile south of the Tennessee line at Rossville, Ga.

While working out of Columbus he married Mrs. Carrie Murphy, December 25, 1864, to which union were born two children, one of whom, Emsley D., survives and lives at Valentine, Texas, who, having lost his first wife and baby, married Miss Adelaid Graffing and they have a son.

Mr. Stegall's first wife died September 2, 1871. On November 23rd, 1872, he married Miss Mary Jefferson, daughter of James Jefferson, a farmer near Cartersville, Georgia, who died June 2, 1911, having given birth to fifteen children, eleven of whom are in life, to-wit:

James Blackwell, conductor on the Texas Pacific for twenty years, living at Mineola, Texas, has two children; Nannie J. Mason, living at Ferguson, Missouri, has three children; Hugh W., has five children by a former marriage, he later married Miss Nell Rhodes and they live at Jonesboro, East Tennessee; Mamie R., single, lives with her father; Pauline Alberta Hudgens, Wenonah, New Jersey, one child, and her twin brother, Paul Albert, at Everett, Washington, has two; Carroll R. is a Presbyterian minister at Montreat, North Carolina, has three children; Carmi Myers and Ruth Veatch, near LaFayette, Georgia, and Philip, Chattanooga, Tennessee, have no children. One son by first wife, Robert J., died in 1915. His widow has two children, which makes 25 grandchildren. Another son, Jerry Goldsmith Stegall, lost his life in the World war; his name is engraved on the bronze memorial tablet at the Memorial Bridge crossing Chickamauga creek on the Dixie Highway. On October 15, 1916, Mr. Stegall married Miss Bessie Lowry. They have no children.

Mr. Stegall was elected secretary and treasurer of Division 148, Order of Railway Conductors, when it was organized at Chattanooga in September, 1884, and he has been elected every year since without an opponent. He has been remarkably healthy all his life; cannot remember having missed a meal in 50 years—does not use glasses except when reading or writing, although he lost the sight of one eye when ten years of age. If he lives till June 15, 1933, he will be 91 years of age.

Mr. Stegall's father's name was Emsley, grandfather, Blackwell, and great-grandfather, Richard, who moved from North Carolina to South Carolina and died in 1834. He had 12 children.

Mr. Stegall has not yet been able to connect genealogically with James Stegall, who was a soldier in the 4th Va. Regiment, Revolutionary War, but is following a clue now which he believes will connect him with revolutionary soldiers. He knows but little of his maternal ancestors except his mother whose name was Sarah Lackey and her mother was a Ward.

REV. WILLIAM L. SHATTUCK.

Rev. William L. Shattuck, the subject of this review, was the son of Artemus Shattuck (1795-1876). Artemus Shattuck was a native of Connecticut, later moving to New York state where he was engaged in farming. While thus occupied it happened that one very cold winter day he was at work in the woods felling trees, when one tree in falling lodged on another. Climbing the fallen tree to cut away some limbs it happened that one of his feet was caught in a split limb in such a way that he found it impossible to extricate his foot, and release himself; and knowing that he must soon freeze to death in that condition, he, with the aid of a pocket knife, hacked his foot from his leg at the ankle, and thus released himself. Binding up the wound as best he might, he made his way, with almost superhuman endurance, to his cabin, where, by careful nursing, he finally recovered.

Later he moved South, living at different times in North Carolina and Mississippi, and finally, about 1846, he arrived in Walker county and settled in West Armuchee. Artemus Shattuck was an ordained Baptist minister and was for a numbers of years pastor of Shiloh church as well as other churches in the county. Many old citizens still recall his actions and movements as he stood in the pulpit with his wooden leg. He was a man true and tried, steadfast and immovable in his convictions —a man of character. His wife was Mary Cadwell and they had two sons, Alvin, who moved to Texas and served in the Confederacy, and died in 1912. The other son was:

Rev. William L. Shattuck (1839-1915), was born in North Carolina and came with his father to Walker county in 1846, being a lad of seven years. His home was in West Armuchee valley where he attended such schools as were prevalent in his day, learning much from his home life and the rough experiences of a pioneer farmer, and altogether, with his later experiences as a soldier and citizen, rounding out a most beautiful character and life spent in doing good among his fellow men. When the war clouds gathered in the sixties, he enlisted in Company I, Ninth Georgia Infantry, and served four years, participating in many of the hard-fought battles, including Bull Run, Seven Pines, Richmond and Chickamauga; and while he was never seriously wounded, he was several times burned with powder and had two bullets pass through his clothing. Like his father he was an ordained minister of the Baptist church, and following the war was, for more than forty years, a popular pastor and an acceptable minister, serving many churches in this and adjoining counties. He was pastor for seventeen years at Trion, Georgia. Rev. W. L. Shattuck labored long and well among an appreciative people who learned to love and admire him for his sterling qualities as a man, citizen and minister.

In 1859 he married Martha, daughter of William McWilliams and his wife whose maiden name was Wall. They were the parents of seven children, viz.: Annie, who married T. E. Shaw; James P.; Sarah, who married G. W. Ransom; John A., who was for nine years before his death a Baptist minister; George C.; William Judson; Francis J.

William Judson married Mary Lou, daughter of Captain Sanford and Harriett (Hill) Venable, and they have four children, viz.: Horace, William, Annie Laurie, and Mary Hill. Francis J. married May, daughter of James and Mary Ann (Bonds) Hall. They have five children: Annie, Ruth, Frank, Minnie Lee, and Edmond.

Perhaps more than passing reference should be made to James P., second child in Rev. Mr. Shattuck's family. James P. Shattuck (1863-1922) received his grammar school education in the schools of the county, later attending the University of Georgia where he was graduated in law in 1889. For more than a quarter of a century he was one of the leading attorneys of the LaFayette bar and during that time participated in much important litigation. Aside from his law practise, he was instrumental in developing in the county many improvements and bringing many industries to LaFayette. Chief among these may be mentioned the Bank of LaFayette, the first bank in the county, of which he was president till his death. He was also interested in the organization of the Walker County Hosiery Mills and the Union Cotton Mills, in which he served as president and secretary respectively. He was for a time mayor of the city of LaFayette and also treasurer of the county.

Mr. Shattuck was a prominent leader in church and fraternal affairs. He was a devoted member of the Baptist church from whose services he never allowed his business to prevent his attendance. He was for many years a constant attendant at the meetings of the Association, where he often served as moderator or other officer. He was likewise a prominent Mason.

Joshua D. McConnell.

Joshua D. McConnell, the subject of this review, was born in 1851, died 1932. He was the son of Joseph N. (b. 1826) and Melissa (Lumpkin) McConnell (b. 1833), dau. of A. J. Lumpkin. His grandfather was Joshua, b. 1806, and his great-grandfather came from Ireland in the latter part of the 18th century. In 1871 he married Francis B. Price, to which union were born, Burl L. (1872-1925); Maurice A. (b. 1874); Claudius D. (1876-1898); Lula (b.   ); and Maude (b.   ).

During his active years Mr. McConnell was one of the most prominent citizens of the county. He was a very successful business man. Because of his keen business foresight and good judgment he was able to accumulate considerable property, and because of his ability he was made a member of the Board of Commissioners in which place he served with distinction. He also served his county as a member of Jury Revisors as well as serving on the Board of Tax Equalizers. He was ever an advocate of good schools and through his efforts his community was able to secure the services of such outstanding teachers as Captain John Y. Wood, A. R. McCutchen, and other fine instructors. By this means he succeeded in giving his children a good education in the days when there were few good schools in the county. Mr. McConnell was a life-long member of the Chattooga Baptist church, which he regularly attended and supported.

Maurice A. married Fannie Mae, dau. of D. J. and May Elizabeth (Mills) Hammond. They have one son, J. D., Jr., now in the senior class of the LaFayette high school. Another son, Edward, died in infancy.

Maurice, like his father, is a man of keen business foresight and good judgment. He is interested in various successful business enterprises, and is a director in the Bank of LaFayette. Also member of the Board of Education for the city of LaFayette, and councilman from his ward. He served for some years as a member of the Board of Roads and Revenues. He is a Baptist.

Lula married W. A. Wardlaw. They have four children and live at LaFayette.

Maude D. married W. O. Davenport. They have two children and live at Rome.

HEARN.

There is a record of the Hearn family reaching back as far as the Battle of Hastings in 1066, and can be traced down through English history for more than 600 years. In those early days there were various spellings of the name, as, Harin, Herron, Hearne, and Hern. In the course of time it assumed the form of either Hearne or Hearn.

In 1660, William Hearne, who had been an officer in the army of Cromwell, left London and came to St. Christopher's in the West Indies, and there opened up a large mercantile trade with London and also along the coasts of Maryland and Delaware. In 1681, two of his brothers, Derby and Ebenezer, crossed with him from England and settled in Delaware. William joined them there in 1689 where he lived on a farm till his death. From there the descendants became scattered along the coast southward.

Joshua Hearn, born 1800 in North Carolina, with his wife, Jane, came into Walker county very early in its history, as shown by old records. He lived in the region about Round Pond and here he reared a large family of children, viz.: William B., George D., John C., Sarah E., Liddie, Noah, Make, and Stephen Toliver. Five of his sons took part in the War Between the States. Joshua lived to the unusual age of 97, dying at Chickamauga in 1897.

William B. Hearn, born in 1838, served four entire years in the war and was wounded four times. The most serious one was received in the Battle of Gettysburg when a bullet struck him just below the right breast and emerged just left of the spine. After his recovery he fought for another year before the surrender. At the time of the Battle of Chickamauga he was in prison in Chattanooga, having been captured together with other soldiers. His wife, formerly Mary E. Deck from east of Rock Springs, whom he had married just before the war, heard that he was there and made the trip to see him on foot through the battlefield. She said that she had never experienced such a horror as walking over and around dead men strewn as thickly as rocks upon the ground. Some of the living had not been moved and these lay on the ground groaning and moaning. She wore a new pair of home-made shoes which blistered her feet and made the return journey a great trial. Soon after this William was exchanged and returned to service and remained until the war ended. He signed the Oath of Allegiance at LaFayette, was released, and returned home to his family. To them were born two children, James A. and William Lem Hearn.

Sarah E. Hearn married Allison Blaylock and is living in Alton Park, Tenn., at the present time. She is in good health for one at the advanced age of eighty-nine. She has one daughter, Daisy, who married Charlie Joiner and is now living in Chattanooga, Tenn.

Liddie Hearn married George W. Brotherton of Ringgold, Catoosa county, Georgia, and has several children: Thomas and Napoleon Brotherton of Burning Bush; Maud, who married Robert Benton of Boynton; Lizzie, who married a Mr. Simms, and Ruby, who married Thomas A. Horton and who is now living at the old home place with Liddie.

Stephen T. Hearn, now living near High Point, Georgia, married Julie Hollingsworth and has four children: Frank, Farmer, Thomas, and Jessie Hearn.

James A. Hearn, the oldest son of William B. Hearn, married Caldonia Parrish in 1889 and reared the children: Carl C., Clark B., Lucy E., Gertrude, and Walter. He was a resident of Chickamauga all his life, being a farmer there, and died Feb. 22, 1928. Carl C. Hearn married Ora Lee Boss and has two sons, James Charles and Harold Hearn. Clark B. Hearn married Annie Maude Smith on Dec. 25, 1931. Lucy E. and Gertrude Hearn are not married. Walter Hearn married Elizabeth Welch and is living at the old homestead with his mother.

JAMES PONDER, JUNIOR.

James Ponder (1831), of South Carolina, son of Jacob Ponder (1807), of South Carolina, son of James Ponder (1786), son of Thomas Ponder, who was born on the Delaware river in 1765; a soldier of the Revolution, who rose to the rank of sergeant, was honorably discharged at the end of the war, and who drew pension number 21906, granted Oct. 10, 1832.

James, the younger, following the excitement incident to the discovery of gold in California, went thither in 1831, making the seven weeks journey via the Isthmus of Panama. He was gone five years. After returning he married Elizabeth, daughter of Constantine and Maiden (Young) Wood and settled in Chattooga county in 1858. Enlisting in the Confederate army, he served throughout as a brave and highly honored soldier in the 6th Ga. Cav. under General Joe Wheeler.

In 1885 he moved to Walker county and settled in West Armuchee valley. Here he became a prosperous and substantial settler of that beautiful section, and made an honorable citizen. Here he had extensive holdings in real estate and was one of the outstanding farmers of the county. Because of his early travels he was a man of extensive information and was always welcomed and given attention in any company. Because of his early experiences as a traveler in a strange and sparsely settled country, he had much sympathy for a wayfaring man, and his home was always open to a stranger. He was given to hospitality. He died June 6, 1904.

In his home were born the following children: (1) Laura (1858), Compton, Cal. Married Richard Doak. Children: Sam, Lillie, Rose, Winnifred, Anna. (2) Jefferson D. (1860), Cadix, Texas. Married Mary Tindall. One child, Nell, a nurse at Baptist Hospital, Dallas, Texas. (3) Maiden V. (1862), Edinburg, Texas. Single. (4) James Robert (1864), Walker county. Married Julia Justice. Children: John Y. (1910-1919). Russell, Robbie Nell. (5) C. A. (1866), Sherman, Texas. Married Martha Arnold. One child, Arnold. (6) J. A. (1868), Sanford, Texas. Married Maggie Moore. One child, James Hewlett. (7) Mary (1872-1910). (8) Russell (1874-1877). (9) Frank (1876-1928), Wichita Falls, Texas. Married Nannie Brown. Children: Lowell, Russell, Mildred, Grace. (10) Sonora (1881), single, connected with schools at Edinburg, Texas.

Sonora served overseas during World war as a nurse. Returning she was with the Red Cross as nurse at Mission, Texas, and is now connected with the Public Health Department of the schools at Edinburg, Texas. Sam Doak, grandson of James Ponder, served with the American Army overseas during the World War.

The Ransom Family.

James Ransom (1782-1854) was a native of the old North State, where he was born during the closing days of the Revolution. His wife, Nancy, was born the same year in South Carolina, and died in McLemore's Cove in 1854. His wife was a Randolph and according to family tradition was a descendant of Pocahontas. James Ransom first settled in Dogwood valley, Whitfield county, later moving to McLemore's Cove about 1848. The census of 1850 gives his name as a resident of the Cove. There were seven children in this family, namely: John, Milton, Washington, Reuben, Elizabeth, Eliza and Permelia. Two of these, Washington and Reuben, came with their father to the Cove and the numerous Ransoms of this section are descended from these two brothers.

(1). In 1841 Washington (1817-1901) married Annie Dobson (1819-1904) to which union were born: Adaline, Syrena, Cicero, Caldonia, Palestine, Joe, Olive and Blucher. Of these, Cicero, born 1846, married Martha (1851-1928) daughter of George and Elizabeth (Foster) Hunter, and their children are as follows: Volney, Virgil, Ettie, Hattie, James, Gussie, Bruce, Lonnie, George and Henry. George and Henry were each in the World War and saw service overseas.

Cicero Ransom is now in his 86th year and is hale, hearty and active. He takes much interest in the affairs of life and bids fair to round out a century. He was for many years notary public of his district and his records were kept with care and precision. He makes his home with his son, George, in the Cove. He is a highly respected and honored citizen.

(2). Reuben (1826-1873) married Caroline Owings (1828-1867). Children: Permelia, J. M., Ocena, George W., James B., W. M., and Cora A.

J. M., born 1852, married Josephine (1853-1831), daughter of George Clements, for many years treasurer of the county. Their children are: George, Charles, Reuben, W. O., and Belma. John Ransom was for many years a member of the Board of Roads and Revenue and is one of our best citizens. Eleven years of age during the Chickamauga battle, and living in that immediate vicinity, he recalls most vividly many of the scenes and circumstances of those never-to-be-forgotten days. He lives on his fertile and beautiful farm in the Cove.

George W., born 1859, married Sallie Shattuck, daughter of Rev. William L. Shattuck, a soldier of the Confederacy and for half a century one of the leading Baptist ministers of the county. Mr. Ransom has extensive farming interests throughout the county and is one of our most substantial citizens. His home is at LaFayette.

James B. (1862-1917) married Gussie (1860-1922), daughter of George Clements. Children: Lillie, William, Sam, George. Lillie married Lee Parker (decd.); William married Helen Stansell; Sam married Fannie Rea; George married Nelle Loughridge. William and Sam served overseas during the World War.

Another son of Reuben Ransom, well known throughout Northwest Georgia, was Professor W. M. Ransom (1866-1914), who was for many years a leading educator of this section, and was at one time State Senator from Chattooga county. His wife was Belle Wyatt, who lives at Menlo, Georgia. Children: Wyatt, Max, Daphne, Ruby (recd.), and W. M., Jr.

CAPTAIN JOHN Y. WOOD.

In any discussion of the Wood family the center of interest, necessarily gravitates about Captain John Young Wood. His father, Constantine Wood, and his mother, Maiden Young Wood, were both born in South Carolina in 1806. Constantine's father is said to have served in the Revolutionary war under General Marion; but of this there is now no direct proof, however an effort is being made to establish it for the sake of the only grandchild of the subject of this sketch, Mrs. Mary Lou Kell Camp.

Constantine Wood immigrated to Georgia probably in the early thirties and settled first in DeKalb county near Atlanta, where his first born son, John Y., first saw the light in 1834. Two years later he removed to Walker county, settling in East Armuchee valley, where he engaged in farming and assumed a prominent place among the early settlers of that beautiful section. His other children besides John Y. were: Ann, Elizabeth, Edward, James P., Maiden, Robert C., and Constantine A.

Constantine was too old for service in the War Between the States. Following the battle of Chickamauga, and when the Federal troops were over-running the county, his home was burned by them and he with his family were compelled to take refuge in an old cotton house on the farm. Because of exposure he and his wife each contracted pneumonia and died during two successive days.

Both Constantine and his wife, Maiden, were college-bred. Coming, as they did, of old established families, from among one of the most aristocratic states of the Union, they had imbibed deeply of refinement and culture. The young mother, Maiden, especially was educated and refined—an accomplished woman of the old school. A teacher before her marriage, she was now able to realize the importance of training to her own children. It was from her therefore, that John Y. and the other children received so much sympathy and love, and by her were taught the rudiments of an English education. There were few schools at that early day and they very indifferently taught in most cases. Knowing this, and being very solicitous about her children, the young mother, Maiden Wood, never allowed the years to slip away and leave her offspring in ignorance. They were constantly employed with their books when not engaged in farm activities.

CAPTAIN J. Y. WOOD

John Y. often related that he only attended school three months before he reached his majority. Do you suppose he was an ignoramus at that time? By no means. He was a fine reader, had mastered English grammar and higher arithmetic, and had made a fair beginning in higher mathematics and Latin. Beyond and above all this, he had read and steeped his soul in some of the principal literature of the English language, including Shakespeare and the great poets. In fact he was so well prepared that he was able to enter the Junior class at the University of Georgia, where he graduated with honors in the class of 1859, being second honor man. Some of his classmates were: John D. Pope (1st honor), also of Walker county, afterward Chief Justice of Supreme Court of Cal.; Dr. W. J. Nunnally, president Mercer University; A. O. Bacon, U. S. Senator, and others.

Following his graduation, John Y. began teaching at Pleasant Hill in

West Armuchee valley, and was thus engaged in 1861 when the tocsin of war sounded calling the sons of the South to the defense of the young nation. He promptly dismissed his classes and organized a company of volunteers, many of his former pupils enlisting under his banner, and at once offered his services to his country. He was sent to Virginia where he served under General Longstreet, taking part in most of the hard-fought battles of the war—First and Second Manassas, Antietam, Gettysburg, Fredericksburg, Chancellorsville, Seven Days Fight Around Richmond, and was with Longstreet at Chickamauga, arriving there on Sunday morning after a hard all-night march from Ringgold.

He was severely wounded at Malvern Hill and at Gettysburg, and desperately wounded at the Wilderness, being shot through the right lung. Because of this disability he was mustered out of service and returned home. His wound was slow in healing, so much so that he was never able to take up the practice of law which he had planned to do after leaving the University. And this may, in a way, have been providential; he could hardly have impressed himself for good on the community and county as a lawyer as he did as a teacher. "God moves in a mysterious way."

After the surrender he again took up teaching, first at Pleasant Hill where his work had been so rudely broken off at the beginning of hostilities; then at LaFayette where he taught for some time; and finally moving to McLemore's Cove he established at that place the only high school in the county at that time. Here for many years—a quarter of a century —he taught young Americans the duty of citizenship. For this work he was eminently qualified, not only because of training, but because of his experiences as a soldier, patriot, statesman and Christian. Here for many years was the Mecca to which many of the ambitious young men of the county and of other counties came to receive instruction at the hands of a Master-Teacher.

Captain Wood was proficient as a teacher of the higher branches. He was fine in Literature, Latin, Greek, Mathematics, Philosophy and Astronomy. Pupils attending his classes were able, in the old days, to enter the Junior class at the University. It is said that at one time he had as many as 75 pupils in his school studying the higher branches.

Perhaps as a churchman John Wood impressed himself on the county in equally as favorable manner as he did as a teacher. Joining the Baptist Church in 1860 he at once assumed a leading place as a layman, which place he continued to occupy to the end. As deacon of his church or superintendent of the Sunday school he was always on hand. He could, upon occasion, when the pastor was absent, occupy the pulpit to the great satisfaction and pleasure of the audience. He was a constant attendant of the Association. For more than half a century he could be seen at these annual gatherings. For many, many years he acted as clerk of that body, filling the place to everybody's satisfaction. He also served as moderator.

One of the first advocates of prohibition—even before that word was in popular use—he was instrumental in the passage of the three mile law which prohibited the sale of liquor within three miles of a church or school. He not only fought intemperance but lived a temperate life himself. His labors and teaching on this subject together with others finally brought a change of opinion as to the use and sale of ardent spirits.

Captain Wood was a poet. True he never wrote poetry but he was a great reader of poetry, loved it; he had a poetic nature—a poetic soul. "The next best thing to being a poet is to be a lover of poetry." He read it voraciously; and what is better he remembered it—could recall upon occasion any striking poetic gem to emphasize, embellish and beautify his argument. Burns, Pope and Shakespeare were three of his favorites whom he delighted to so aptly quote. Many are able to recall some of his beautiful and impressive quotations, as Pope's

> "Eat and sleep, and sleep and eat,
> And die and rot, and be forgot."

Once after listening to a rather tiresome address by a man who had ignorantly murdered the King's English, he whispered to this writer:

> "Oh, wad some power the Giftie gie us,
> To see ourselves as ithers see us."

Those who were associated with him in Sunday school and church work recall some of his beautiful poetic prayers—full of praise and honor to Jehovah for his wonderful goodness and blessings to man. They reminded one of some of the psalms of King David.

John Y. Wood held various offices during his eventful career. He was, during the latter years of the war, a member of the lower house of the state Legislature. Again he served in this capacity in 1871-72 during the reconstruction period; and again in 1882-83. In 1909-10 he was a member of the State Senate. In 1899-00 he was County School Commissioner. In all these positions he served with distinction and honor to himself and to his constituency. He was also a prominent Mason.

In the heyday of his maturer years Captain Wood was much in demand on all proper occasions as a public speaker. Because of his knowledge of subjects in a wide range of human experiences and activities, his logical reasoning, his known honesty and piety, he was welcomed in any public gathering and listened to with rapt attention. During the latter part of his life, Captain Wood was, beyond doubt, the first citizen of the county. All honor to his memory!

In 1865 John Y. Wood married Miss Mary Underwood, daughter of William M. Underwood, who had migrated to this section from South Carolina about 1830. Mr. Underwood first settled in the Armuchees, later moving to Chattooga county in the vicinity of what was afterward, in honor of himself, called Subligna, which is Latin for Underwood. To this union were born the following children: Roberta Lee, 1866-1901; Frank, 1868-1919; James P., 1870-( ); Mary Lou, 1872-1898; Mattie (Kell), 1877-1931; John, 1879-1899. Of these, five have passed on, leaving only James P. The only grandchild is Mrs. Kell's daughter, Mrs. Mary Lou Kell Camp, a teacher in the Cedar Grove Consolidated school.

In old Antioch burying ground may be seen an unpretentious, though rather heavy, bulky stone with this engraving:

"John Y. Wood, 1834-1919."   "Mary, His Wife, 1836-1919."

DR. JAMES P. WOOD   DR. FRANK WOOD

DR. JAMES P. WOOD.

Dr. James P. Wood, son of Captain and Mrs. J. Y. Wood, was born at LaFayette, Georgia, in 1870. In early childhood his parents moved to Cedar Grove where he was educated under the tutelage of his father, after which he taught for some years in the county. He obtained his medical education at the Atlanta Medical College and at the Suwanee Medical College where he graduated in 1901, since which time he has practiced his profession in Walker county and in Chattanooga, being located at present in McLemore's cove.

In 1915 he married Miss Belle Wallin of Kensington, Georgia. Dr. Wood is a Mason and member of the Eastern Star Chapter; also of the Baptist church.

DR. FRANK WOOD.

Dr. Frank L. Wood, son of Captain and Mrs. J. Y. Wood, was born in 1868 at Cedar Grove, Georgia. He was educated at St. Mary's Institute of which his father was principal, later attending the University of Georgia and the Atlanta Medical College from which he graduated. Returning home he practiced for a number of years in the county.

In 1900 he entered the New York Medical College from which he was graduated, serving also a term as an interne at the Belleview Hospital, New York City, where he specialized in genito-urinary diseases as an associate professor in his alma mater after his graduation.

In 1915, in Jacksonville, Florida, he married Miss Ella Griffith, an Iowa teacher, and the following year, because of declining health, he gave up his practice.

He died at Johns Hopkins Hospital January 14, 1919, following a serious operation. He was for many years one of Chattanooga's best loved physicians and had many warm friends and admirers among the medical profession and people of that city.

DR. ROBERT DICKERSON.

Dr. Robert Dickerson was born in Rutherfordton, North Carolina. He was the son of Garland and Elizabeth Revis Dickerson. His grandparents were Nathaniel and Rebecca Terry Dickerson, and his great-grandfather was Griffith Dickerson of Surrey county, North Carolina.

In his young manhood Dr. Dickerson was a teacher. Later he studied medicine, graduating from the Medical Department of Transylvania University, Lexington, Kentucky. For nearly forty years he was engaged in the practice of his profession.

Soon after his graduation he came to Georgia, and lived for a few years at Lawrenceville, Gwinnett county. Later he moved to Marietta. In 1847 he became a citizen of LaFayette, Walker county, where the remainder of his life was spent. His practice covered a wide territory.

Dr. Dickerson was elected a delegate to the Secession Convention. Believing that the South could secure her rights in the Union, he opposed secession, but after the state seceded no one was more loyal to the Confederacy. He was past the age for military service, but two of his sons were in the Confederate Army, Robert N. enlisting at sixteen and Marcus at the age of fourteen. Dr. Dickerson was twice married, first to Miss Sophia Tate, a member of a prominent Gwinnett county family. Her mother was a Verdell of French ancestry. By this marriage there were five sons, two dying in childhood.

The second son, Robert, was clerk of the Superior Court of Walker county for forty-eight years. The third son, Marcus, settled in Texas in early manhood. David, the youngest, made his home in Mississippi.

After the death of his wife, Dr. Dickerson married Miss Lydia Dickson, of LaFayette.

By this marriage there were two daughters, Florence, who became Mrs. George Jackson, and Miss Mary. The Dicksons were of Scotch-Irish descent. William Dickson, father of Major Michael Dickson, came to America about 1738, settling in Duplin county, North Carolina. Major Michael moved to Pendleton, S. C.

Mrs. Dickerson's parents were Colonel John Dickson, colonel of State Militia, and Lydia Tourtelotte, who was a native of Providence, Rhode Island. When Mrs. Dickerson was a child her parents moved to Coweta county, and were among the first settlers of that county, and charter members of the First Presbyterian church of Newnan.

R. N. DICKERSON
For 48 years Clerk Superior Court

Mrs. Dickerson's paternal grandfather was Michael Dickson, who served as major during the Revolutionary War. He also furnished the government with wagons, teams, and provisions. He lived to the age of ninety-five years. Her paternal grandmother was Sara Neely. Her maternal grandparents were Asa Tourtelotte and Avis Hines, of Providence, Rhode Island. Asa Tourtelotte was a lineal descendant of Roger Williams.

After the death of Colonel Dickson, Mrs. Dickson moved to Walker county. She was a charter member of the Presbyterian church of LaFayette. Her oldest son, Asa, was the first sheriff of the county. Her second son represented the county in the legislature. Her third son was clerk of the Superior Court.

JOHNSTON.

Noel Johnston came to America from Ireland about the middle of the

18th century and settled in North Carolina, where he married El'zabeth Park. Among other children he had a son, Joshua, born 1779, who came to Georgia during the thirties while the Indians still occupied this region. Joshua's wife was Frances Barnett, and they settled in Dirttown Walker county, afterward made a part of Chattooga. Joshua had six children, two boys and four girls. One of these boys, Joshua P., born 1820, grew to manhood and married Elizabeth Hood, born 1821, to which union were born thirteen children, nine boys and four girls, namely: Joshua P., for 24 years Ordinary of Chattooga county; Matthew Noel died 1899; Randolph B. died 1913; Mrs. A. F. Shaw died 1920; Mrs. R. C. Boss died 1928; John M. died 1880; James H. died 1901; Mrs. G. W. Shaw; Mrs. D. W. Lawrence died 1880; Joseph F. died 1922; Benjamin died 1882; and J. J.

Joshua P's wife, Elizabeth, died in 1869, and in 1871 he married Elmina Quinn to which union was born one child, Mary, who married Jerome H. Spencer of LaFayette.

Joshua P., the elder, was a Primitive Baptist minister and as such was one of the best known and most lovable characters throughout Northwest Georgia. For fifty years he traveled over Walker and Chattooga counties and in Alabama, preaching in churches, school houses and in private homes, and serving as pastor. He was for 23 years pastor of Union church, near Warren; and most of the time for nearly fifty years served his home church at Mt. Paron, near Subligna. Traveling throughout this section for half a century as minister and pastor he was greatly loved and admired by all who knew him.

DR. J. J. JOHNSTON

The youngest son J. J. born 1867 because of a lame foot in his youth was unable to do manual labor. Realizing his situation and being ambitious to succeed he cast about to find something to do, finally deciding to study medicine. Without funds or means this was no small undertaking, but with a vim and determination he went at it and continued till he received his diploma from the Atlanta Medical College in 1895. Returning home he practised in Chattooga county t'll 1904 when he located at LaFayette where he remained till 1928 when he settled at Villanow where he now resides and enjoys an extensive practise.

In 1898 he married Catherine Dawson (b. 1875), dau. of James and

Martha (Millican) Dawson. They have two children, Mary and Virgil.

Joshua Johnston, son of Noel, was a soldier of the War of 1812, serving in Captain G. W. Bennerman's Company of Infantry, Local Militia of North Carolina. He is buried in the Johnston family plot near Subligna in an unmarked grave.

THOMAS PICKENS HENRY.

William Henry was born in North Carolina about the close of the Revolution. His wife's name was Sarah Pickens, niece of General Andrew Pickens of Revolutionary fame. Among other children he had a son, John Pickens, born 1808 in South Carolina, whither his father had migrated. William and his son, John, came to Georgia about 1830 while the Cherokee Indians were occupying North Georgia. They settled first in Henry county for whom it was named, later moving to Walker county and still later to Chattooga county. John P. married Mary Patience Powell, daughter of John Powell of Newnan, Georgia, to which union were born nine children, one of whom was Thomas Pickens, the subject of this sketch.

Thomas Pickens Henry was born in 1848 in Chattooga county, Georgia. At the age of fifteen, just before the Chickamauga battle, he joined the Confederate army at Calhoun, being assigned to Co. H, 3rd Ga. Cavalry, and served under that gallant commander, General Wheeler. Although there were but two days of the Chickamauga battle, Mr. Henry often insisted that he fought three days, being in several severe skirmishes on Friday before the battle closed on Saturday. Happily he escaped without a scratch. Following this engagement, with his doughty commander, he saw service in almost every part of the South, especially in Tennessee, Alabama, Mississippi, Georgia, North and South Carolina, traveling through those states probably 10,000 miles and was in North Carolina at the time of the surrender.

After the surrender he returned home and engaged in farming, merchandising and various other enterprises. In 1868 he married Sallie Harper, daughter of James and Cloyie (Majors) Harper. They had the following children: John, Charles, Oscar, Beulah, Minnie, Catherine, and Harper. His second wife was Fannie J. Bryant with whom he lived forty-two years. In 1930 he married Mrs. Mary (Bomar) Little of LaFayette, Georgia.

Mr. Henry was widely known throughout Northwest Georgia. Being a man of sound judgment and keen foresight he was, during his long life, very successful in business. He was ever devoted to the interests of the soldiers of the "lost cause," and delighted to talk in reminiscent mood of those never-to-be-forgotten days. He died May 15, 1932, in the 84th year of his age.

T. B. ARNOLD

Thomas Arnold, son of Elias Arnold, son of Jacob Arnold, son of John Arnold, son of Mark Arnold of Jamestown, who migrated from England during the early part of the seventeenth century. This, in a nutshell, is the history of a man who has lived 83 years in the eastern part of the county and is still "carrying on." Probably no other citizen of the county is able to trace so accurately, his lineage back for five generations, and boast of a nobler heritage than Thomas B. Arnold.

It is not known exactly when Mark Arnold came to Jamestown from England. Here he reared a family of children, one of whom, John, moved to Fairfax where he resided for a time, later going on into North Carolina where Jacob, his son, was born in 1773. Jacob, following the general movement of the population southward and westward, migrated into South Carolina where he married Elizabeth Hughes about 1805. To this union were born William, Elias, Butler, Eldridge, Nancy, Betsy, Polly and Mealy. With this large family he continued his movement westward and during the exciting days of the thirties while the Indians were still occupying this immediate section, he arrived in the eastern part of Walker county where he bought land, built a cabin and began to clear fields for farming. His eight children, now grown, were soon married and had families of their own. Elias, the second son (born 1807), married Amelia Cooper. Children: James, 1841-1876; Jacob, 1843-1891; Margaret, 1845-1927; Emily, 1846-1926; Thomas B., 1848-( ); Frances, 1851-1870; Harrison, 1856-( ).

Thomas B. Arnold, the subject of this sketch, grew to manhood in the Chestnut Flat section of the county. He was ten years of age before he attended school, but when he started he learned very fast. He only went to two terms of school, his teachers being John Arnold and Carey Jackson. While his school opportunities were limited, he was a student of nature and learned much from experience and observation. The old Blue Back and Davies arithmetic were his text books.

In 1863, when the Confederacy was in dire need of more man power, just a few days before the Chickamauga battle, he enlisted in Co. K, 4th Ga. Cav., Cruse's Brig. Here for two days without any experience as a soldier, not even having an opportunity to learn the tactics of the routine of the soldier, he was lined up along with veteran soldiers and vied with them for the honors of war. Happily he escaped from this fierce battle without a scar. He was in that prolonged march and hard fought series of battles from Dalton to Atlanta, especially at New Hope church, Kennesaw Mountain, and Jonesboro. In one of these he was wounded in the leg. Retreating with Hood from Atlanta, he was present at the hard-fought battle of Franklin near Nashville. In June, 1864, he was prisoner in the hands of the Yankees and was lodged in the Alex Simmons old home in LaFayette, where he had lain as a prisoner for some days. This was his situation when General Pillow appeared at that place on the morning of June 24. When the fighting began the Yankees departed without giving him orders and rushed for the Court House for safety. He secured a good horse and at once joined the Confederate forces and with them escaped at the close of that engagement.

He was paroled at Salisbury in May, 1865. Returning home, he went to LaFayette, took the oath of allegiance, returned home and went to work to make a crop and to bear his part in the re-habilitation of the country.

Mr. Arnold has served 24 years as a Justice of the Peace in the county. During all these years his decisions as judge have been generally accepted as full of common sense and justice and have been pleasing to his fellow citizens. During this time he has performed many marriage ceremonies—reaching into the hundreds.

In 1867 he married (1) Margaret Prim (1848-1881). Children: Jennie and Nannie (twins, 1868-1930-1906 respectively); Charles (1870); Martina (1873); Susie (1880). (2) Refina Coffman (1849-1924). Child: Etna (1883).

Mr. Arnold has six children, 74 grandchildren, and 102 great-grandchildren, 16 great-great-grandchildren, as well as a number of lateral relatives.

Although his educational opportunities were limited in youth, still, because of his alert, active mind, his acute sense of observation, he has, by intensive reading and thoughtful meditation acquired a general knowledge of many of his subjects taught in our best schools. He is a most interesting conversationalist on any common topics of the day, and what is better his conclusions are apt to be found correct. Mr. Arnold is hale and hearty, now in his 84th year. Beloved by his neighbors and friends, he is the idol of his children and grandchildren, and as he descends, now rapidly it may be, toward the going down of the sun, his features are composed and serene, and without a fear he awaits the

"CROSSING OF THE BAR."

HISTORY OF YOUNG FAMILY.

By John C. Young, Jr.

James Young, b. 1775, d. 1850; moved to West Armuchee from Spartanburg, South Carolina, in 1837; married Anna Foster, b. 1782, d. 1840. There were 12 children, six boys and six girls: James, William, John Calvin, Robert, Hamilton, Frank, Mary Ann, Margaret, Maiden, Jane, Betsy, and Polly. James and William went to Texas. John died in young manhood. Robert was a colonel in Civil War, later a merchant in Calhoun. Hamilton married Louisa Fariss. Their daughter, Rebecca, married a Mr. Russell near Dalton. Robert's daughters were Mary, Nannie, Sallie, Mattie. Nannie married Dr. Miller, and Sallie married a Mr. Williams of Lawrenceville.

Frank married Martha Ann Green of Mississippi. Children: George, James, Sallie, Sarah, Francis Marion, John Calvin, Robert Hudson. All died young except Frank who went to Texas when nineteen and John who has remained at the home place in West Armuchee. Frank married Lizzie Fry who died when their three children, Henry, Sallie and Johnnie, were young. He later married Jennie Thompson. Johnnie and Sallie are married and live near Canadian, Texas.

In 1900, John Calvin married Lula, daughter of Nannie Neal McWilliams and Capt. McWilliams. Their children are: Frank, John, Robert, Jimmie, Martha, George, Sarah, Eugenia (deceased). Frank married Daisy Hudson of Elberton. He graduated from State University and is Superintendent of Nancy Hart Memorial School. John Calvin graduated at Mercer and Peabody and is Superintendent Menlo Schools. Robert attended University but is at home. Jimmie finished Georgia in 1932. George and Martha are in college at Berry and Sarah in high school at home. All but Sarah attended and finished Berry. Mr. Young is one of the best known citizens in the county, having served on Board Roads and Revenue for fourteen years. He was chairman of the Board when the present Court House was built. He is a very successful farmer and business man and one of the foremost citizens of the county. He is a prominent member of the Baptist church.

Mary Ann died in young womanhood. Margaret married Jackson in Calhoun. Maiden married Constantine Wood. His son, Capt. J. Y. Wood, organized the first company of volunteers from Walker. Jane married John B. Suttle. Children: Dora, Sarah, Georgia, Susie, Emma, James, Louisa, Margaret. Dora married a Mr. Tittle and Georgia married Dr. Hunt. They are the only ones living. Emma married McCulolugh and Jamie, their daughter, still lives at the Suttle homestead. Louise married John Clements, with four children: Nannie, Jannie, Mattie and Rosa. Nannie married Frank Shaw and Jannie married George Little.

Betsy married William Little. Children: Robert, Frank, James, Tabor, Rannel, Pierce, Nora, Joe, Walter, William, Betty, Sallie. Bob was killed at twenty-one, youngest officer in Confederate Army, the only one of the generation killed in the Civil War. The four who married and lived in Walker county were: Rannel, who married Addie Esterling; children: Ernest, Beulah, Carl, Lester, Maude, Dixie, Jessie. Bettie, who married Rev. Mose Jackson. Sallie, who married Captain William McWilliams; their child is Dr. J. B. McWilliams, Ada, Ohio, who has ten children. Pierce married Mary Bomar, and their son, Frank, lives at LaFayette.

Polly married William Puryear: Children: Hamp, Clay, John, Frank, Charley, Jennie, Lou, George. Hamp married Nancy Ward; Clay married Elizabeth Calloway; John, Mary Jackson; Jennie, Sam Hamilton; Lou, John Ward; George, Neely Fry.

MCCUTCHEN.

Benjamin Reeves, son of William McCutchen, a Revolutionary soldier, was born in Hall county, Ga., in 1797. His father, William, came from Augusta county., Va., shortly after the Revolution and settled in Hall county. Benjamin R. married Jane Bell in 1821, coming to Cherokee county, Georgia, very soon after this section was taken over by the State. He owned a large tract of land near LaFayette and the old McCutchen home was one of the early landmarks of that section. He was one of the early representatives in the Georgia Legislature.

The children: (1) Ira William (1822-1876), married in 1844, Juliet A. McCulloh. His home was in Chattanooga Valley where he practiced medicine and had large farming interests. (2) Cicero Decatur (1824-1905), married Frances Kelley, studied law and moved to Dalton, Georgia, where he became one of the foremost members of the North Georgia bar, serving several terms as Judge of the Superior Court of his district. (3) Wyatt Socrates (1827-1879), married, (a) Scott Stuart, (b) Sarah Geraldine McCulloh, was a merchant in Dalton, Ga. (4) Augustus Raymond (1836-1886), married Mattie McCulloh, was a geologist and surveyor—for many years was State Geologist of Georgia. (5) Cynesca Jane, was never married (1841-   ).

Cicero D, Wyatt S., and Augustus R. all served the Confederacy. Cicero was a colonel, Augustus R. a captain and Wyatt S. a ward master in Confederate hospital. The McCutchen family were direct descendants of John McCutchen, one of the earliest settlers of Shenandoah valley, Virginia, and many representatives of this Scotch-Irish family are found in the Southern States. Benjamin Reeves McCutchen and his wife, Jane Bell McCutchen, are buried in the LaFayette cemetery.

MCCULLOH.

Joseph Portlock McCulloh (1803-1880) was the son of John and Nancy Butt McCulloh. John was of Scotch descent, a soldier of the Revolution, and one of the early school teachers of Savannah, Ga., moving later to Hancock county, Ga.

Joseph Portlock married Elizabeth Raiford Daniel of Edgefield District, South Carolina, in 1827 and came to North Georgia in 1830-36, buying a large tract of land in Cherokee, later Walker county, Ga. His old home still stands in Chattanooga Valley near the village of Flintstone. He was one of the Commissioners of Georgia for the removal of the Indians from this section, and a successful planter. At one time he made a venture in the silk business, planting a considerable acreage in mulberry trees, importing silk worms and machinery for weaving silk. This was no doubt the first plant for weaving dress materials in North Georgia —but it proved unprofitable.

Having a family of eight daughters and one son, he was interested in securing educational advantages for them and was a promoter of one of the earliest schools in this section, the Aderhoff school on Lookout Mountain. These children were: Caroline, married Dr. Thomas Y. Park; Juliet A., married Dr. Ira Wm. McCutchen; Katherine, married Wm. Branham; Martha Cook, married I. P. Russell; John, married Jane Bennett; Sarah Geraldine, married Wyatt S. McCutchen; Mary Elizabeth, married John T. Burkhalter; Florence, and Johanna.

A Methodist church was recently built on land given for this purpose by Mrs. M. E. Burkhalter. The McCulloh family burying ground adjoins this picturesque stone church. Many descendants of Joseph and Elizabeth McCulloh live in this section.

WILLIAM B. MOORE.

The English name Moor or Moore, and the Scottish Muir, are from the Saxon word meaning heathy ground, and has risen from residence at a boggy heath or moor. It also means Great, Tall. A careful examination of the various censuses and war records of the nation reveals a multitude of Moores who have diffused themselves throughout the nation from its earliest conception. A large number of these have been famous as governors, senators, congressmen, physicians, lawyers, ministers, etc.

Jacob Moore was born in 1817 in South Carolina, whence he migrated into Alabama where he died in 1859. His wife's name was Looney Ann Sweatman. They had two sons, William B. and Allen J., who came into McLemore's Cove soon after their mother's death in 1847, and lived some years in the home of Theron Crowder.

William B., while still a mere boy, enlisted in the Confederate Army and served as a courier, being wounded in some of the many battles. Following the surrender, he grew to manhood in the Cove, and during these years attended school at St. Mary's Institute, taught by Captain J. Y. Wood. Here under that model teacher he made rapid progress in his studies, so much so that he began teaching himself, and for a number of years he taught in the county.

In 1877 he married Sarah E. Wells, daughter of Daniel C. and Lydia Wells. Daniel C. Wells was a soldier of the Confederacy, serving throughout the war, and was killed about its close near Macon, Georgia. His father was Andrew Wells, born 1803, in Kentucky. After his marriage William B. Moore bought a farm in McLemore's Cove, later known as the Moore farm, where he lived till his death in 1901. He was a Mason and member of St. Mary's Lodge.

In this home were born the following children: Laura, George, Arthur, Luther, Tenia, Albert, Sallie, Rufus, Fannie, Charles, Mary. Laura, b. 1879, d. 1902, married Charles L. Evitt, three children; George, lives in Arizona; Arthur married Lizzie Garrett and they have four children. He lives at Cedar Grove; Luther (1884-1905); (Tenia (1886-1887); Albert (1887-1905); Sallie (1898-1899); Rufus lives in Chattanooga; Fannie married Augustus F. Edwards. They have nine children and live at Marietta, Georgia; Charles (1893-1911); Mary lives with her brother, Rufus, and is a teacher in the public schools of Chattanooga, Tennessee, where she has been teaching for eleven years. Mary Evitt, daughter of Laura, lives with Rufus and Mary. She holds a responsible position in the purchasing department of the Tennessee Electric Power Company, where she has been for several years.

JESSE MERCER SHAW.

Jesse Mercer Shaw (1824-1903) was the son of Amos Shaw and Sara Wagner Shaw. Amos Shaw was born 1789 in Oglethorpe county, Georgia, where also his wife was born in 1793. They were married in 1812, and to this union were born eleven children. With this large family he came to Walker county about 1838. The first night of his arrival he camped on a small hill, where afterward he established his home and spent the remainder of his life. His grandson, Frank M., now resides in the old home on the hill where the first camp was made. Amos Shaw acquired quite an acreage of that fine fertile land for which the Cove is justly famous. Some of the old deeds are in possession of the present owner, Frank M., and show dates of 1838. Amos died in 1859, his wife in 1873.

Jesse Mercer, one of the younger sons of Amos, bought the home place and spent the remainder of his life on the ancestral homestead. In 1847 he married Mary Camp (1831-1881). They had eleven children, all of whom lived to maturity, as follows: Nancy E. (1848-1867); Robert B. (1851-1927); Sara E. (1843-1909); George W. (1856-1929); Mary F. (1858-1918); Houston A. (1862-1888); Estelle P. (1864-1882); Jesse E. (1871-1913). James M., born 1867; Minnie E., born 1869, and Frank M., born 1875, are the only ones left of the family. James M. lives in Chattanooga where he has been a successful merchant for many years. Minnie E. (Freeman) and Frank M. are residents of the county.

Jesse Mercer Shaw was named for the Rev. Jesse Mercer, famous Baptist minister of Georgia and founder of the Mercer Institute, now known as Mercer University. He was, during his day, one of the outstanding citizens of the county. He stood for good schools, churches and for progressive methods in farming. On his farm he developed the variety of corn known by his name and which often won prizes at county and state fairs, including also first prize at the World's Fair, in 1892, at Chicago. He was a Confederate soldier. In 1877 he represented the county in the Lower House of the General Assembly.

Frank M. Shaw, the youngest child of his father's family, lives at the old Shaw home, being the third generation who has lived where the first pioneer, Amos Shaw, camped when he arrived in the county. Frank M. married Nannie Clements, daughter of John and Louisa (Suttle) Clements, two families who were pioneers in the county. They have three children, Frank Clements, Mary Louise, Martha Camp.

Frank M. Shaw is a farmer and one of the leading citizens of the county. He is now a member of the Commissioners Board of Roads and Revenue, and is one of our most progressive citizens. He is a Mason and a Baptist.

ROBERTS.

K. B. Roberts (1854-1931) was the son of Champion Roberts and Elenor Catherine (McWhorter) Roberts. Champion Roberts was born in 1832 in Tennessee. His wife, born 1833, was the daughter of Temperance McWhorter, who was a native of South Carolina. In this home were born three children, viz.: Emma, who married Lemuel Brotherton; Sade, who married David Dalton; and K. B., who married Millie Jane Bird. Children: Charley, Clinton, Cora, Carl, Hattie, Tempie, Myrtle, and Joe. Millie Jane Bird Roberts (1859-1926) was the daughter of John and Lucinda Bird, who were natives of Tennessee. Their children were: Sallie, who married John Hall; Millie Jane, who married K. B. Roberts, in 1883; Catherine married J. J. Fletcher; and Lee married Addie Dyer.

John Bird came to Georgia before the Civil War, settling near Crawfish Spring where he died in 1873, his wife surviving till 1900. John Bird was a blacksmith by profession, because of which he was exempt from military duty and did not serve in the Civil War.

Of the eight children born to Mr. and Mrs. K. B. Roberts, Charley married Grace Boling; Clinton married Hattie Bridges; Carl married Jewel Bridgeman and they have six children: Evelyn, Edwin, Earl, Elizabeth, Eloise, and Etheridge; Joe (1900-1932) married Lucile Bowman; children: Joe, Jr., Jack, and Roy Lamar.

The girls are all single and live at the old home, "The Twin Poplars," near Chickamauga. Cora, Tempie and Myrtle are teachers, having taught 23, 17 and 11 years respectively. All have permanent State Certificates, Class A. They have made good in the school room and proved to be excellent instructors. Cora has the honor of being the first teacher in the county to bring her school up to the state standard, receiving for her school the first certificate for a standard school in North Georgia.

All the children are doing well in their several fields of endeavor. Charley and Clinton live at Lyons, Georgia, Carl in Chattanooga, and Joe at Lyons till his death April 15, 1932.

It is delightful to observe the beautiful spirit of loyalty and affection pervading these sisters and brothers. They are sincerely devoted to one another and to each other's welfare.

VEATCH.

John David Veatch was born in Cherokee county, Ala., in 1851. He was the son of John and Rebecca (Chapman) Veatch, natives of Whitley county, Ky. John was born in 1805. His father came into the "Dark and Bloody Ground" soon after the Revolution and was associated with Daniel Boone and his followers as hunters and Indian fighters. John often related not only his own, but many of his father's exciting and dangerous encounters with the fierce natives of the forests which occurred during the half century following the Revolution. He often related how those red-blooded Kentucky mountaineers often, on the least provocation, would challenge each other to fight a duel; he, himself, once engaged in one, but, happily, escaped unhurt. The mode of procedure was substantially as follows: The course being measured off the principals with their seconds standing at each end with firearms ready. The umpire called: "Ready, one, two, three, stop." The firing must be done between the words "ready" and "stop." After this each considered his honor saved whether his life was or not. John died in 1892 at the age of 87. He lived first in Kentucky, afterward in Alabama and finally in Georgia.

Among other children, John had a son, John David, who married Sarah Frances Lowery, dau. of William and Sarah (Ray) Lowery. John David came with his father to Walker county during the latter part of the Civil War, being at that time a lad of some 14 years. Here he grew to manhood and reared a large family of children, six boys and two girls, all living, as follows: A. C. married Lula Wilson, one child, Mary Frances, now at Wesleyan College, Macon, Ga. K. A. married Minnie Skates. C. N. married Glennie Lewis, eight children. C. L., graduated Powder Springs and State University, four years at each; now editor Commerce News, Commerce, Ga.; married Romelle Sudduth, three children. W. R., a Baptist minister and pastor, married Allie Lawrence and they have eight children. F. B. is in the United States Army and is stationed at present in the Philippine Islands. Allie married James P. Skates, four children. Gussie married J. W. Burnes, one child.

A. C. Veatch, the oldest of these children, was educated at Piedmont college, later attending the State University where he took courses in Agriculture and in Engineering, later returning for other short courses. He was in his early days one of the country's successful teachers. He served five years as County Agent, the first the county had, afterward appointed county engineer which he held for three years. In 1925 he was appointed Warden of Chain Gang which position he now occupies.

John David Veatch is still in life, now in his 82nd year, is reasonably active and in good health, and bids fair to remain for many years.

LEE H. DYER.

R. H. Dyer was born in 1808 in Tennessee, his wife, Kevern, was born in the same year in South Carolina. They came to Walker county in 1847 and settled where not many years later the bloody battle of Chickamauga was fought. The eldest son, Spill B., was born in 1828, coming to Walker county with his father where he became a prosperous farmer and possessed of one of the finest farms in the county. When the tocsin of war sounded in sixty-one, he promptly enlisted and served throughout that bloody conflict. He was in the Chickamauga battle and because of his familiarity with the territory he became General Bragg's personal courier. After the war he settled down to his farm life and to raise and educate his large family. In 1890 he disposed of his farm to the U. S. government and bought another in the Cove near Pond Spring where he lived till his death in 1905. In 1851 he married Ellen Parker, to which union were born fifteen children, eleven of whom raised families.

Lee H. Dyer (1858-1931), the sixth child of Spill B. and Ellen Parker Dyer, grew to manhood on his father's farm near Lytle where he received his education in the local schools, later attending school at Sumac, Ga., taught by that famous educator, Prof. E. I. F. Cheyne. For some years he was a teacher rendering excellent service in that field; however, he spent the greater portion of his life as a farmer. For many years he served as a member of the Board of Education of the county.

Mr. Dyer was a prominent Mason. He served his lodge as master many times and was always intensely interested in Masonry and its teachings. For many years he was a member of the Grand Lodge and at times was one of its officers. He loved the principles of the order and lived up to its precents.

LEE H. DYER

Perhaps as a churchman he was most favorably known. He became a member of the Baptist church early in life and continued till the end a devotee of Christianity. He loved his church and all its activities. He gave of his energy and his substance to its advancement. For ten years he was moderator of the Coosa Baptist Association, and for perhaps fifty years a member of that body.

Being a man of positive convictions and always standing for those convictions, he stood four-square for the right as he saw the right. He would never compromise with wrong in order to make or keep a friend, but stood out, clear and distinct, a beacon light, for what he regarded as truth and right. On all moral questions his acquaintances knew where he stood—he possessed the backbone of his convictions.

In 1883 he married Alice, daughter of William J. and Myra (Chapman) Greene, granddaughter of James K. and Ann (Underwood) Greene, and great-granddaughter of John Greene, soldier of the Revolution. To this union were born: (1), R. H., married Belle Glenn, one child, Ruby Lee. (2), Minnie Lee (1887-1888). (3), Edgar H. (1888-1904). (4), Irene (1892), married Napoleon Abbercrombie. (5), John Greene (1896), married Ruth Goodson; children: E. Roland, B. Frank, Gussie, Georgia Mae, Joe Alice.

PARKER.

W. S. Parker, son of Joel Parker, son of Benjamin Parker, son of George Parker. George was born in 1755, probably in Virginia or North Carolina. Crossing the Blue Ridge he became a resident among those early settlers who organized the State of Franklin, later Tennessee. Benjamin, born 1779 in Monroe county, Tenn., married Catherine Gray (b. 1783). Their children were nine in number. One of these was Joel (b. 1820), who married Margaret Sherk in 1847. They had 11 children, 9 living to maturity; one of these was W. S. (Billy) Parker. Joel lived during the war in Bradley county, Tenn. He was the community blacksmith and because of his occupation was exempt from military duty. In consequence of the panic of 1873 he lost all his worldly goods and to begin anew he migrated to Georgia, settling first at Trion, later moving to Walker county where he died and was buried at Trinity. He was coroner at the time Sheriff Mize was killed by Brad Redden and held the inquest.

W. S. Parker was born 1861 in Bradley county, Tenn., coming to Georgia at 12 years of age where he has since resided. He grew up on the farm under his father's tutelage, attending such schools as the county afforded at that time. Much of his education was secured at home where he was able by close application and "burning the midnight lamp" to acquire a considerable knowledge of most of the subjects taught in our common schools. Later he had the good fortune to attend the school taught by that Master Teacher, Captain John Y. Wood, as also, R. W. Blackwell, Boog Little, A. R. McCutchen and M. H. Edwards, because of which he was able to begin teaching himself and for nearly 20 years he taught in Walker, Chattooga and Catoosa counties, giving general satisfaction wherever he taught. He has been, always, a stanch believer in education; so much so that he has by hard work, economy and careful living—sometimes depriving himself of the comforts of life—been able to give all his nine children a splendid education, going through high school. Reared and educated nine children—some accomplishment! He is a member of the Methodist church and has always taken a keen interest in church, Sunday school and civic affairs. He is also a member of the Masonic fraternity. A Christian gentleman, upright, honorable, reliable, Billy Parker stands well to the front among the county's citizens.

In 1886 he married Laura, daughter of D. C. and Mary Brewer of Catoosa county, to which union were born the following children: Eula (1888), married Max Wallis, they have two children and live at LaFayette; Cleveland (1890), married Mary Harris, two children, home, Macon, Ga., general agent for Royal Typewriter Co.; Joel C., married Ruby Hogue, three children, in business near Ft. Oglethorpe; Belle (1894), single; Margaret (1897), married J. F. Hampton, two children; Thelma (1900), married A. E. Harrington, three children; Rose (1902), single; Denver (1905), single; Mary (1911), single.

The girls have all held desirable and responsible positions in business at Chattanooga for a number of years, where by close application and attention to duties they have made good, and are among some of Walker's splendid girls who have located in our neighboring city. The older ones located there first and by economy they were able to assist their father in educating the younger girls, later helping them to secure a business education and a position. Happy, thrice happy, is that parent who has such children! Ever and anon, the girls make it their duty as it is a pleasure to go back to the old home to see father and mother, never forgetting to carry some memento or other reminder of filial love. The mother, especially, is growing feeble and the girls have arranged for a helper in the home so as to conserve her strength, and maybe prolong her life.

Joel Parker was closely related to many noted East Tennessee families, as the McSpaddens, Trims, McCaslins, Spraggins, Carters, Mosiers, etc. He was first cousin to David M. Key, Postmaster-General in Hayes' Administration, many of whose descendants now live in and around Chattanooga.

The Wheeler Family.

The descendants of Benjamin Neeley Wheeler constitute one of the pioneer families of Walker county. He and his wife, Rebecca Bridgeman, were each born in England, according to family records, he in 1793 and she in 1797. Settling first in Virginia, they came later into Tennessee. Two brothers came over with him, one going to Arkansas and the other to Alabama. There is a tradition that General "Fighting Joe" Wheeler is in the line of one of these families.

Benjamin Wheeler finally made a settlement at the spot where is now East Lake Park, near Chattanooga, using the family drinking water from the spring at that place. About 1830 he removed to Walker county, settling this time at Crawfish Spring, moving later to LaFayette where he lived till his death in 1841. He was taken to Chattanooga for burial, perhaps because there was no well-established burying ground in the county at that time.

This family divides into three major branches according to the three sons, Calvin C., William M., and John B., all of whom spent most of their lives in the county. Harriet, a daughter, married Benjamin Burns, no children, and Elizabeth, another daughter, married James Walker, moving early to Texas. Catherine and Nimrod, two other children of Benjamin, died young, thus leaving in the county the three sons named above. They and their children make up this sketch principally.

(1). Calvin Wheeler, oldest of these three brothers, was born in Tennessee in 1822 and was a faithful upright citizen of those early days; he lived for many years on the farm still known by his name north of LaFayette, where he died and was buried at the Lawrence graveyard near Rock Springs. His wife was Elizabeth Posey, and they reared a large family, as follows: Henry, Martha, Rebecca, John, Harriet, Jack, Mary, James and Richard (Dick). Henry, Green and Jack all went to Texas in early manhood, where they married and reared families. The names of their children we have been unable to get correctly. Martha, James and Rebecca died in youth. Harriet married George Young and they had a son, Louis, who lives now in Savannah, Ga. Mary married Mack Hartline, and they moved to Texas. Richard (Dick) married Amazone Bowman and they live at McKinney, Texas. Their children are known here by the names, Jim, John, Frank, Tom, Blanche and Dora. Of their immediate families there is no record at hand.

JOHN B. WHEELER
For many years representative in the General Assembly of Georgia. He won the sobriquet, "Watch Dog of the Treasury."

Those in the family who have carried the family line down to the present are the children mainly of John, who married Dei Adams and are living now, most of them, in the vicinity of Rossville, Ga. They are known as Marvin, Etta, now Mrs. McCall, Jessie, now Mrs. George Turner, Dona, now Mrs. Charles Roth, Willie Belle and Richard now a prominent merchant of Rossville and a religious leader. Elmer died some years ago. Most of these have families of splendid young people who value highly their connection with this wing of the Wheeler family.

(2). William M. Wheeler was born in Tennessee in 1827. Coming with his parents to Georgia, he married Lucretia Shipp and they had the following children: Kitty, Susie, Harriet, Nancy, John, Charlie and Mattie. Of these Susie and Kitty died in young womanhood. Nancy married Elijah Thompson, who dying left two children, Laura and Florence. John married Zoe Fielding and they had a son, William M.

Wheeler, now of Dallas, Texas. Harriet married Bob Floyd, they have no children.

Charlie married Isabell Strange to which union were born two children, Luther and Estella. Losing his first wife, Charlie married Lucy Davis and they had the following children: Lee, Maggie, Henry, Clark, Carl, Roy, Grady and Albert. Clark and Carl died when small. Luther, a machinist of Chattanooga, married Ethel Bowman and they have three children, Evelyn, Melba and Margaret. Estella married John Mashburn, lives at LaFayette, and they have seven children, Irene, J. C., Hill, Annie Joe, Alvin, Alma Lucy and Martha (twins). Lee, a contractor, lives at Rossville, married Fannie Fox, two children, Quilla and Leon. Maggie married M. B. Loughridge of LaFayette. They have a son, Ross, and three daughters, Doris, Avis and Genelle. Henry, a Chattanooga merchant, married Florence Hill, two children, Edna Ruth and Anita. Grady married Lorena Jones of Rock Springs and lives at the William Wheeler home place, his mother living with him. He has two little daughters, Mary Frances and Mayree Pope. Albert, a commercial worker of Atlanta, married Norma Torbett. Roy is still single and is one of the business men of LaFayette.

Mattie, the youngest and only living of William Wheeler's immediate family, married James Bowman, who did not live long, leaving with her a daughter, Claudia, now Mrs. R. C. Martin of Celina, Texas, who also has the following children: Scott, Newell, Herman, Augusta, Weldon, Mary Kathryn, Dunaway, and Bobbie Ray. After the death of James Bowman, Mattie married J. H. Moreland, to which union were born Jessie, Isabell, Della, Fred and Nellie. Jessie married Effie Leath, and they had two children, Samuel and Mary Frances. Isabell married C. B. Ezell, and they had three children, Bernice, Genevia, and Duffie. Della married Charlie Floyd and four children were born to them, Robert, Daphnee, Hazel and Marguerite. Nellie married Clyde Estes, no children; Fred married Ruth Robinson, one son. He later married Freda Taylor.

William Wheeler, of whom these are the descendants, was an excellent, substantial citizen, living for years at the place that now bears his name, about four miles north of LaFayette, where Grady now lives. The record shows that he was a Confederate soldier and saw gallant service; he was in the battle of Chickamauga. This entire branch of the Wheeler family have held together with strong family ties through the years. Most of the present generation are now living in the county or not far removed. The old homestead has been kept in the family name since the "fifties", Charlie Wheeler having spent his entire life there.

(3) John B. Wheeler, pioneer, farmer, landowner, statesman, was an acknowledged leader among his fellowmen. Born October 12, 1829 in Tennessee, Campbell county, he came with his parents to Walker county in 1833. Because of the death of his father in early life he was

left with little educational advantages, but being a man of great native ability and full of energy he educated himself along practical lines and was a student throughout life, his motto being, "Live and Learn".

In 1852 he married Catherine J. Jackson, to which union were born one daughter, Rebecca, and seven sons, Henry F., Moses C., Andrew J., Benjamin N., Richard, Oscar, and Sylvester, who died in boyhood.

Rebecca married D. T. Scoggins, pioneer educator of Walker county, and to this union were born one daughter, Cora, and three sons, John, Thomas and Arthur. Cora, now Mrs. S. D. Mullinax of Atlanta, has two daughters, Donnie and Muriel. John Scoggins, who died some years ago, married Dora Adams, who lives with her son Troy of LaFayette. Thomas S., for a long time manager of Georgia Baptist Orphanage at Hapeville, Ga., married Margaret Jones of Rock Springs. They live in Atlanta and have a son Billie. Arthur married Sus'e Leath and they have a daughter, Aubrey.

Henry, John, Benjamin and Oscar all moved some years since. Oscar lives at Ada, Okla., where he is engaged in commercial work. Henry, now deceased, made his home at Colorado City, Texas, as a prominent farmer. John W., now a wealthy ranchmen, resides at Merkel, Texas, and Benjamin also a farmer lives there. These have all married and have families. Oscar married Lulu Butts of Thomaston, Ga. They have no children, having lost two little boys in death. Henry F. married Hass Morgan of Walker county before leaving for the west and they have three sons, Edgar, Omas and Ulric, all of whom have families and live in Texas. John W. married Hattie Killen of Texas and have two children, John W. Jr., and Alva. Benjamin married Drucilla Hall of Texas and their children are Katie, Araminta, Rosa and Ruby; also two sons, Paul and Andrew. All these are adults now and reside in Texas.

Andrew J. Wheeler, prominent farmer of Walker county, now deceased, married Mary Smith of Walker county and removed to Texas with his brothers, returning to this county in the early nineties, where he made his home till his death in 1917. For a number of years he was a member of the Board of Roads and Revenues. His children are as follows: Ulric R., construction worker and contractor, married Pearl Loughridge and their children are Russell, John, Elizabeth, Cecil, Ruth and Frank. Clint M., business man of LaFayette, married Louise Blaylock and their children are Clint, Jr., Frances, Mary Catherine and Sidney Ann. John Paul, banker and insurance man, married Adelia McClure and lives in Chattanooga, having recently moved there from Macon, Ga. Archie Jackson, traveling salesman, married Mary Catherine Fleming and lives in Chattanooga. Mary married Lester C. Larson and lives in Chattanooga. Vera lives with her mother in that city and is single.

Moses Wheeler, successful farmer and live-stock man, having lived at the same place he settled when he married and being the only one of the adult children who never moved away from the county, died at the meridian of life and was buried at the Lawrence cemetery. His widow, Minnie Renfroe Wheeler, lives at the home-place still near LaFayette. Their children are Margaret Edna, married Rev. Julia J. Sizemore, with two sons, Lamar Wheeler and Julian Jr. Edwin Oscar was married to Tex Steverson, one little son, Marvin.

At the time of the death of Moses Wheeler, Jan. 4, 1901, aged 43, the Walker County Messenger among other things had this to say of him: "If he had a fault speak it softly, for it was not veiled in a garment of hypocrisy. If living for others instead of one's self is living like a true philosopher, then Moses Wheeler knew what true life is".

The foregoing are the descendants of John B. Wheeler, and they honor, with many others, the public services of the man, as well as to revere his name as kinsman and family head. Aside from duties performed in the county, he served with distinction for a dozen years or more at three different times in the Georgia Legislature. Of his record there is an old Atlanta paper, perhaps the words of Henry Grady, has this to say:—

Mr. Wheeler is a man of untiring industry and excellent business qualities. He is no politician, although he held several county offices before coming to the Legislature. With his sound views of public honesty and economy, there is nothing attractive to him in official station, yet he shirks from no duty imposed upon him by his people of Walker county. During the years he has served in the House, he has pursued but one course, that marked by a consistent desire to suppress useless legislation; to cut off extravagant expenditures; to defeat all schemes to rob the treasury through doubtful appropriation, and to put good and true men into all offices. He has been very properly called the 'Watch Dog' of the treasury; and he is very often the cutter-off of useless debate by calling the previous question. For these valuable offices, condemned by some of course, and praised by others, the House has complimented him with a vote of thanks. Even those who feel the power of his retrenchment and reform policies must acknowledge his honesty and integrity of character".

He died amid such services, surrounded by his family and many friends, at his home north of LaFayette, November 18, 1895, and was buried at the Lawrence cemetery. At the time of his death the Walker County Messenger among other words of praise and evaluation had this to say: "In his hands the interest of the commonwealth was safe. Many a raid on the treasury he has defeated. In all relations and duties of life he was found faithful. Among all her sons Walker county has had none more worthy of the high regard in which he was held. His loss is one that cannot be replaced".

GARNETT ANDREWS.

Garnett Andrews, the subject of this sketch, was born in Washington,

Wilkes county, Georgia, September 15, 1870, the son of Col. Garnett Andrews, of Washington, Ga., and Rosalie Champe Beirne, of Union, Monroe county, W. Va. Garnett Andrews' grandfather was Judge Garnett Andrews, who was Judge of the Superior Court in the district surrounding Wilkes county, for twenty-eight years. Judge Garnett Andrews ran for Governor of Georgia on the old "Know Nothing" ticket. Judge Andrews' father, John Andrews, having come from Essex county, Virginia, to Wilkes county settlement shortly after the Revolutionary War. Garnett Andrews spent his early boyhood in Yazoo City, Miss., where his father was the partner of John Sharpe Williams who afterwards became United States Senator from Mississippi. Col. Garnett Andrews moved with his family to Chattanooga, Tenn., in January, 1882, though he had previously made investments in that city several years before and it is quite a coincidence that his father, Judge Garnett Andrews, also invested in real estate in Chattanooga back in 1836 and 1837 and was one of the contributors to the fund for the surveying and laying out of the city of Chattanooga when it was incorporated in 1837.

Garnett Andrews was educated in the public schools of Chattanooga, in the Virginia Military Institute of Lexington, Virginia, Class of 1890, and the Worcester Polytechnic Institute, Worcester, Mass., Class of 1892. Leaving college he was teller in the old City Savings Bank of Chattanooga and afterwards went into the steamboat and warehouse business at the foot of Pine Street in Chattanooga, but in 1896 he established the Chattanooga Knitting Mills, which in 1898 was moved out to Rossville, Georgia, and the name changed to the Richmond Hosiery Mills. These mills have grown until they now employ around 1700 people and have become one of the foremost industrial institutions of Walker county. Garnett Andrews in 1895 married Miss Elizabeth Lenoir Key, daughter of the late Judge David M. Key, of Chattanooga, Tenn., who was United States Senator, afterwards Postmaster General under Hayes' Administration and later United States District Judge for East Tennessee. Their children were Betty Beirne, who married J. B. Waters of Rumson, N. J., and New York; Katharine Lenoir, who married Samuel C. Hutcheson, of Chattanooga; Garnett Andrews, Jr., the Superintendent of the Arrowhead Fashion Mills at Rossville, Ga., and David Key Andrews, who is connected with the National City Bank of New York. Mr. and Mrs. Andrews were unfortunate enough to lose their oldest son, who was named Garnett, when this boy was three and a half years of age, and their youngest daughter, Margaret Avery, who was burned to death in Chattanooga in 1917 at the age of ten.

For eight or ten years Mr. Andrews resided on his farm, known as Arrowhead Farm, south of Chickamauga Park on the LaFayette Road, which farm is considered to be one of the show places of Walker county. He is a member of the Mountain City Club, of Chattanooga, and of various other public organizations of that city and last year moved his residence from his farm to Chattanooga, Tenn., where he resides on Cameron Hill.

DAVID NEWTON KEOWN.

James Keown (b. 1810), and his wife, Rebecca (b. 1812), grandparents of the subject of this sketch, were natives of South Carolina. They were married about 1831. They removed to Alabama where their second son, William Jasper, father of D. N., was born 1835. Returning to Georgia with his family, James settled in East Armuchee Valley where he spent the remainder of his days. He was in the county when the Indians were removed from the county and was familiar with those exciting days of turmoil. James was one of three brothers who settled in the county and from whom the numerous citizens of the county spelling their names thus, have descended.

When he grew to manhood, William Jasper, in 1856, married Sallie Davis, to which union were born three sons, viz., David Newton, Harvey and Walter.

D. N. Keown was born in Walker county Nov. 8, 1857, and on Dec. 14, 1876, was married to Martha A., dau. of Chapman Baker, who through her mother was descended from the McWilliams family of West Armuchee. To this union were born ten children, all of whom grew to maturity, the oldest son, alone, being now dead, viz., Georgia Keown Smith, 1877; Emma, 1882; Harvey, 1884-1901; Ola Keown Coulter, 1887; J. C., 1889; B. D., 1890; W. E., 1892; Nannie Lee Keown Bomar, 1894; P. D., 1897; D. H., 1900.

A mere lad during that horrible war of the sixties, he nevertheless was able to recall during his last years most vividly many of the scenes of those troublous times when his part of the county was for months over-run by the troops of the two armies. His father having died early, much of the labor necessary to support his mother's family devolved upon his shoulders. For this reason, and because of the unsettled condition of the country at that time and for years afterward, he was deprived of an opportunity to secure an education. He, however, by dint of hard work during the few weeks he was permitted to attend school, gained a passable knowledge of the few books used in the schools of that early time. He possessed as a natural gift a fund of good common sense and accurate judgment. With this he gained a much broader and more effective education in the rough and tumble of experience. Along with his struggles he acquired habits of industry, tenacity and pertinacity. He was a tireless worker, never left off when he had begun and never ceased effort until the thing attempted became an accomplished fact.

He was a man of honor. The spirit of honor dominated his conduct. Sincerity and integrity characterized his life. It can be said of him— and was often said—that his word was his bond. No need of a written agreement with him; death alone could prevent the fulfillment of his promise. For his convictions of matters of vital concern to him, he stood like a stone-wall. No half-way ground for him; no compromise where character, honor or justice were involved. He had decided views on vital subjects, and having the courage of his convictions, he never failed to give expression to them regardless of whether his position met with popular favor. Criticised at times for his pertinacious stand in the face of vital issues, he was ready to acknowledge himself in error if his position were found untenable. He championed the right side of all moral issues. Everybody knew where to find him.

In early life he became a Christian and united with the Macedonia Baptist church, later moving his membership to the Waterville church, and still later he joined the Naomi church, being a charter member there. He was a zealous Christian and a staunch Baptist. Called to the office of deacon, he filled it to the entire satisfaction of the church; was regular in his attendance upon the church services and supported it by his means as far as his ability permitted. The members learned to rely much on his wise judgment in church matters, and his opinion was always sought when questions were to be decided. He was a constant attendant at the sessions of the Association. For many, many years, his was one of the familiar faces to be seen at those annual gatherings. He enjoyed meeting and shaking hands with his brethren and that pleasure was reciprocated. Often at these meetings might be seen the tear of joy fall from his eyes under the power of some of the good old songs, or prayers, or sermons. He believed in heart-felt religion.

He was pious in his home. His wife being a devout Christian, his home was an ideal place for the rearing of children. He labored and prayed for the salvation of his own children and had the great pleasure to see them all happily united with the church before his passing.

When, on February 23, 1930, David Newton Keown died, it could be said "Truly, a good man has gone."

STANSELL.

Levi Stansell was born in South Carolina in 1832 whence he came to Georgia as an orphan boy about the year 1840. There were 13 boys and 4 girls in his father's family. William Stansell, his father, lived to be 104 years of age. He came as a small lad to Roswell, in Cobb county, where he wrought in the now famous Roswell Cotton Mills. Later he moved to Atlanta where he served an apprenticeship as a brick mason, which occupation he followed ever afterward. In 1868 he moved with his family to Walker county, settling in East Armuchee valley where Ryal and Elijah, two older brothers, had previously settled. He died in 1910 in Cullman, Ala., at the age of 78 years.

In 1859 in Atlanta, Ga., he married Harriet Boutell (1830-1901), who was born in New Salem, Mass., to which union was born one son, William L.

William L. Stansell, the subject of this sketch, was born in Atlanta, Ga., on December 12, 1860. In 1868, when a lad of seven years, he came with his parents to Walker County, where he grew to manhood near Villanow, attending the community schools when there happened to be one. Two of his teachers were Sam P. Maddux and John C. Stokes. However, his first learning and the most important part was received from his mother, who was careful to instill in his youthful mind principles of truthfulness, honesty and right-living. Growing to manhood he became a farmer till about 1898 when he removed to LaFayette and was for many years employed in the stores of the Union Cotton Mills.

In 1915 he was elected Ordinary of the county and has served in that capacity since, having been recently re-elected for another term (1932). Mr. Stansell has proved to be one of the most efficient of our county officers. Strictly attentive to the business of the office, accurate and obliging, he is greatly admired by the citizenry of the county. He is a member and constant attendant of the Baptist church.

On November 2, 1879, he married (1) Permelia, (1859-1918), daughter of M. G. and Emily (Robbs) Clements, to which union were born the following children: Clemmie, Oliver, Hattie, Sadie, Perry, Maybel, J. C., and Helen, (2) Ethel Tyner, daughter of J. R. and Mary (Conley) Tyner. One child died in infancy.

H. S. SIMMONS.

W. H. H. Simmons, the father of the subject of this sketch, was born in 1842 in Forsyth county, Georgia, where he grew to manhood and in 1861 enlisted in the Confederate Army, serving throughout that fateful struggle, seeing service in the Virginia campaign together with his brother, James. In 1865 he married Loucinda N. Jones, to which union were born three children, viz., Martha (Mrs. J. R. Walker), H. S., and Charley. With his family he came to Walker county in 1885, having resided for some years in Tennessee. Both he and his wife are buried at Chickamauga.

H. S. Simmons (1867-1930) married Beulah Pirkle in 1893. Miss Pirkle was likewise a native of Forsyth county, having come to this county when a child. To this union were born six children, as follows: Mae (Mrs. Olin Pitman); Ray, who married Venice Wilson; Paul married Madge Dangler; Freda married Luther W. Cagle; Hansel and Thelma both single.

Few people in the northern part of the county were better or more favorably known to more people than 'Squire H. S. Simmons. Elected Justice of the Peace in 1900, he served continuously for 30 years, except for a short interim when his district was declared abolished in consequence of the operation of the no fence law; but as soon as the district was restored all minds reverted to H. S. Simmons and he was re-elected. Mr. Simmons was an officer of the old type—one who labored to keep the peace among his people, and to settle disputes out of court. Many a man with his ire up because of some actual or fancied grievance has gone to him for some action in his court and after a conversation with the justice has changed his mind, dropped the matter and gone home.

Probably more people sought his advice on ordinary legal matters than any man in his section—and sought it with confidence in his knowledge of course, but especially in his honesty and probity. He was not an officer for the little fee simply,—for his nobleness of mind reached above a mere matter of money—but if he could serve his neighbors by acting as peacemaker—by preventing an action at law—he felt that he had performed an act greater than that of a judge. "Blessed are the peacemakers for they shall be called the sons of God."

In his decisions as judge, Mr. Simmons has exemplified to a remarkable degree the motto of the Constitution of the State of Georgia, "Wisdom, Justice, Moderation."

Mr. Simmons became a member of the Baptist church in 1894 and continued an acceptable and devoted member till his death. Regular in his attendance at its services when possible, liberal as far as his ability extended in its support, his presence and genial smiles are missed by the congregation.

WHITLOW

Miles W. Whitlow, (1811-1885), was the son of Bolden Whitlow. His first wife Emily Gholston, died in 1846 leaving five children, Eleanor, Alima, Nency, Martha Jane, and John, his second wife being Elizabeth A. Woods (1821-1898). He had six sisters, who married, respectively, James Bonds, Archie Bonds, Henry Boss, Avery Camp, Billy Mathis, and William Bailey, all of whom lived, at that time, in the Cove, and whose descendants are, many of them, still residents of that section. Miles Whitlow was one of those early hardy pioneer settlers whose religion was not averse to labor. In work season it was his custom to be standing by the plow handles when day light dawned, that he might see how to follow the plow; and the darkness of twilight was his signal for "taking out." There was no stopping for water, this being brought by his wife or children. If a neighbor happened to pass through or by the field and wished to stop for a chat, he must follow Mr. Whitlow's plow or there was no chatting. This was the situation during work season; at other times when the rush was over his life was not quite so strenuous. However, he was always busy with his farm work. At his death he left a handsome home and property to his heirs.

M. M. Whitlow, (1855), was the oldest of four children, the others dying young. They all died within a space of less than 25 days (See Thurman Graveyard). In 1875 he married Ella T., daughter of Robert F. and Mary Frances (McWhorter) Shaw, and granddaughter of George Shaw, pioneer settler. Mr. and Mrs. Whitlow owned and lived on a beautiful fertile farm near Davis Cross Roads. Here their home was blessed with 12 children, 10 of whom grew to maturity and are still living—eight girls and two boys. All these he educated and trained for life's work. Ten healthy children reared to maturity! Mr. Whitlow was never sent to Congress or the Legislature, but he has done a greater work than many who went there. He is now in his 77th year and has never had a lawsuit.

In 1907 he sold his holdings in the Cove and went to Arizona where he remained till 1910 when he returned to the county, settling near Kensington where he resides with his wife on the farm, greatly beloved by all the children and grandchildren who often visit at the old home.

FAMILY RECORD: Willie (1876), married Charley Kaylor. Children: Estelle, Frank, Erwin. Effie (1878), married Martin Davis. Children: Harold, Miles. Lela (1879), married J. C. Wyatt. Children: Jack, Whitlow, Harold, Eleanor, Virginia. Virgie (1881), married Knox Brooks. No children. Mary (1883), married H. B. Hankinson. Children: Wood, Morris. Ethel (1885), Single. Frank (1887), married Fannie Nelson. Children: Frank, John, Fletcher. Kate (1890), married Elmer Messer. Children: Anna, Peggy. Ruth (1892), died in infancy. John (1893), married Kate Ellis. Children: Franklin, Ralph, Mary Elizabeth. Fay (1895), married Charley Evitt. Children: Mary Frances, Betty Jane, Billy. Dewey (1898-1900).

VOILES BROTHERS.

Anthony Voiles, born in South Carolina in 1819; his wife, Priscilla, was born in same state in 1826. It is not known when they migrated to this state but they were in Georgia when their first child was born in 1845. The census of 1850 gives his name as a resident of the eastern part of the county, now included in Whitfield county. His home at that time was near Gordon Springs and his occupation was given as a miller. A few years later, 1852, he removed to McLemore's Cove and settled near Harden Springs, afterward called Kensington. Here he bought a small farm and by industry, frugality and economy, he lived for many years, paid for the farm, reared and educated one of the largest families in the county.

In 1892, when land prices were inflated, he sold his little farm and bought the Shamblin old farm where the family has since resided. He died during the year 1892, his wife surviving till 1901. Mr. Voiles and wife were each members of the Antioch Baptist church. For many years he operated the Dr. Lee old mill near Kensington and labored as a carpenter. His principal business, however, was farming. The children were as follows:

Annie (1845-1908); Martin (1846-1919); William (1847-1931); Emeline (1849-1926); John (1851-1862); James (1852-1923); Charles (1855-1857); Mollie (1865-1928); Price (1867-   ); Edward (1869-   ).

Martin married Josephine Collins in 1875. Children: Ida, Samuel, Addie, Price, and Grace. Annie, Frank, James and Joseph also had families. The three boys, William, Price and Edward, and the girls, Emeline, and Sallie, also, Grace, dau. of Martin, have lived at the old home since the death of the parents, and have built up and maintained one of the very best farms in McLemore's Cove. They have devoted their attention to stock raising, grain and hay during all these years, not a seed of cotton being allowed to grow on the farm. They have probably the largest and most commodious barn in all that section. The story is told that after the barn was completed and as they were looking over and through it, Price remarked to Ed, that 'we didn't need all this dog-gone big barn." But the large crops of hay and forage annually gathered sometimes taxes its capacity.

The principal crop raised annually is corn. Without exaggeration, it may be said that more corn is raised here each year than on any other farm of equal size in the county. Three very large cribs of shucked corn are filled each year, with an overflow stowed in the barn or other convenient place. More than 100 large two-horse wagon loads are harvested almost every year. This corn is fed to horses, mules, hogs and cattle, much also, being sold for bread purposes. Almost daily, during the spring and summer, one or more buyers come for bread corn.

Milk cows, beef cattle, hogs, both for home consumption and for market, fine heavy mules, an abundance of poultry are some of the things that are sure to attract the attention of visitors.

Rotation of crops is a part of their religion. Rarely is corn ever allowed to follow corn, or wheat follow wheat. It is usually corn, small grain, pasture,—taking three years for rotation. Very little commercial fertilizer is used—perhaps none. There is practically no hired help, all labor being performed by themselves. There is a sufficient supply of all farming tools needed; and tools up-to-date are kept. They do their own smithing, and this mostly at idle times.

No car is kept. Perhaps as well able to own an ordinary car as any farmer in the county, certainly more so than the average farmer, they have not been led away by the craze for quick transportation, which has beyond doubt brought havoc to many of our farming population.

This home is given to hospitality. Perhaps more people, both well-to-do and the lowly, are entertained here annually than at most farm homes in the county. It is pleasing, especially to the voluptuary, to happen at the home about the noon-day hour and be invited, which is sure to happen, to take dinner. Seated at the table the visitor soon discovers that he is lord of all he surveys, which is likely to include two or three dishes of different vegetables in season, with their appurtenances; a dish of ham and gravy; a large cobbler pie made of some fruit in season with maybe a dish of pan pies. Then there will be corn bread "baked to a turn" as Uncle Remus would say, with a plate of fresh biscuits, butter, eggs, pickles and the various other little necessaries.

Neighborly, friendly, helpful,—always willing and ready to lend assistance to any in need, these boys and their sisters have walked along the quiet, sequestered way of life and are now rapidly descending toward the setting sun,—two or three having departed during very recent years. If a neighbor is sick, a grave to be dug, or any other service needed in the community, they will be on hand. Mr. Ed has probably assisted in digging more graves than any man in the county. The boys are familiarly and affectionately known in the community as Mr. Bill, Mr. Price and Mr. Ed; the sisters as Miss Em, Miss Sallie, Miss Grace, etc. It is a pleasure to visit at the Voiles home.

W. A. (DOCK) WEAVER.

Isaac W. Weaver, of Irish descent, was born in East Tennessee in 1814, his father having moved into the Holston region from Virginia or the Carolinas following the Revolution. In 1838, in Monroe County, Tenn., he was married to Harriet Allen to which union were born the following children: John, W. A., Nancy, James, Bradley, Randall and Charlotte. John and W. A. moved into Walker County before the War Between the States; the others arriving after the war. All these, except W. A. and James, later emigrating westward.

W. A. (Dock), enlisted in the Confederate army in Co. K. 39th Ga., serving throughout that fratricidal strife till the surrender. He was with Kirby Smith and Joseph E. Johnston in many hard-fought battles and forced marches. Was at the siege of Vicksburg, at Missionary Ridge, and in that long series of engagements from Dalton to Atlanta, where he did valient service in the trenches. He was not present at the Chickamauga battle, being still on parole from the Vicksburg siege. He was severely wounded in the neck at the battle of Resaca. After the fall of Atlanta he retreated under General Hood toward Nashville and so continued his service till the surrender.

Returning home he laid aside his soldier uniform, if it could be so-called, and took up the duties of the citizen and made a model one. Here in the Rock Spring community he lived for many years till his death, honored and respected as a friend, neighbor and citizen. He was a devoted member of the Baptist church and was always found at its services unless providentially hindered. He was for a number of years Tax Receiver of the county.

In 1868 he married Lois, dau. of Edward L. and Adeline (Evatt) White, granddaughter of Thomas Evatt, once sheriff of the county. To this union were born thirteen children, viz., C. D., single; James, married Rena Flack, one child; Lela, married W. D. Chapman, two children; Bessie, married Sam Williams, six children; Isaac, married Kate Bird, three children; Laura, married J. A. Howard, two children; W. J., married Ella Johnson, seven children; Annie, married Ed Johnson, one child; Susie, married Augustus Peters, five children; Frank, married Nora Bird, no children; Dera, married Burrell Stanfield, three children; Mary, married Emmet Hawkins, three children; Bertie, died in infancy.

SUTTLE.

George Suttle, who was a soldier of the Revolution during his early teens, and fought in the Continental Army for American Independence, was born in 1766 in Shenandoah Valley, Va. The Suttles were of German descent, coming to America, probably, early in the 18th century. In 1787

HOME OF JOHN B. SUTTLE
A typical Southern Mansion, in West Armuchee valley, built during the fifties. Below is seen the slave quarters, grim reminders of a past civilization, still standing and in fair condition, now nearly a hundred years old. Before the war there were many such scenes throughout the county but they have all disappeared save the one shown here.

he married Nancy Bias and settled in Rutherford county, N. C., where he reared a large family of children.

John Bias Suttle, youngest son of nine children, was born 1810, and in 1836 married Jane Young. In 1838, with their first born, and negroes, household goods and stock they launched forth on a journey to North Georgia, recently vacated by the Cherokee Indians, to carve a new home in the wilderness, setting in West Armuchee Valley where they lived the first year in an Indian hut, near where the Suttle homestead was afterward located. Courageous, honest and godly, John B. Suttle was a man of vision. Although making his home in a new country with no conveniences, no refinements and little civilization, he went to work to bring these things out of chaos, and order to his new surroundings. To this end he was the first to advocate schools and churches, both of which soon sprang up in the beautiful valley. Later he sent his children to LaFayette, Rome and Athens for a finished education.

Possessed of broad acres of fertile, virgin lands and with many carefree, happy negroes to do the farm work, Mr. Suttle established here one of the most typical and attractive old Southern mansions in Walker county. This old homestead is situated on an eminence in the eastern part of the beautiful valley. Here are still to be seen the ancient slave-quarters still in good repair, grim reminders of a past civilization.

A more prosperous, happier family could hardly have been imagined when in the fateful year, sixty-one, the war-clouds burst over the Southland. John B. Suttle, because of deafness, was ineligible for military duty, but his only son, that cavalier, the gallant James T. Suttle, then only 16 years of age, together with his bodyguard, "Rude" Suttle, as attendant, marched forth, to give his life, if necessary, in the defense of his country, serving till the war-clouds lifted, when he returned home and once more the family circle was re-united.

This beautiful story of slavery is typical of John B. Suttle: When he left North Carolina he brought among other slaves a woman whose husband belonged to another slave-owner, Mr. McDowell. Arrived in Georgia, Mr. Suttle wrote Mr. McDowell in North Carolina that he did not wish to separate a man and his wife, and asked what he would take for the woman's husband. "Fifteen hundred dollars in gold," was the reply. Mr. Suttle sent the money and the husband was brought to Georgia and a family was re-united, and made happy, and 22 children were born in this home. Rude, mentioned above, was one of these and proved an invaluable friend and companion to J. T. Suttle both in war and peace.

To John B. Suttle and his wife were born ten children, all living to mature years except the second child, Calvin. There were eight daughters, viz.: Margaret, Mary, Sarah, Sue, Lou, Dora, Emma and Georgia, and one son, James T. All the children, except the oldest daughter, have spent their lives in Walker and adjoining counties. Margaret married Gideon Walker and moved to Texas in 1860. One daughter, Blance, has been a missionary in China for 25 years. A son, Young, was a Baptist minister, passing to his reward in 1931. Dora Suttle did a great work as teacher in Walker county for many years. James T. was a splendidly educated man, having attended Athens and the University of Virginia. After completing his education he taught for a number of years, but the passing of his father compelled him to forsake the school room and devote his time and energy to his father's estate. From early manhood till he answered the last call, Nov. 2, 1925, he devoted his life to his sisters and their families, two of them having been left widows in early life. His was indeed a noble example of self sacrifice.

This happy homestead, once pregnant with its happy inmates, the prosperous, refined, joyous Suttle family, is now deserted of them all—all save one grandchild of the original owner, Miss Jamie McCullough, who lives in and cares for the old home. Few families of the county have a more interesting history than that of the Suttles.

Abraham B. Sizemore.

In the death of Rev. Abraham B. Sizemore, at his home near Rock Springs, June 14, 1925, age 72 years, Walker lost a splendid citizen, he having lived in the county over forty years, in Upper Cove, Mt. Carmel and Warren communities, and at the present home.

The Sizemore family connects back to Northeast Georgia and the Carolinas, Abraham's father, Allen Grant, having been born at Cornelia, Ga., and Richard L., the grandfather, in the territory of Greenville, South Carolina. The subject of this sketch was born near Valley Head, Alabama, May 22, 1853, and was given his name from his maternal grandfather, Abraham Horton, of Habersham county, the Sizemores having moved to Alabama just prior to the War Between the States.

The older family was sadly divided over the issues of this struggle. Allen Grant was an ardent non-secessionist, later won to the support of the Confederacy. William went North, joined the Federal armies and was killed in service. John F. and James H. were officers in the Southern army, while John W. of the immediate family, eldest son, enlisted as private in the Southern cause.

Abraham came of a large family and had the following brothers: John W., Richard L., Allen G., Jr., Wofford A., and Geo. W.; while the sisters, by married names, are Mrs. Mary Bennett, Mrs. R. R. Turner, Mrs. Bettie Lovelace, Mrs. John Martin, Mrs. Hiram Dodd, as well as Miss Annie Sizemore. All of these are now dead, except Mrs. Dodd, of Valley Head, Ala., and, perhaps, Mrs. Bennett, of Arkansas.

Of large family, suported only by a small farm, naturally his material advantages were few, but heroically he accepted his place amid the Reconstruction days. With little money but with the good wishes of his father, Abraham came to McLemore's Cove, still a minor, having a sister, Mrs. Shankles, later Mrs. Turner, living there, and he took up residence with her, working with others also, and there in the Cedar Grove community grew into mature manhood. In the memory of this early struggle for a foothold of material things, he always spoke kindly of the aid and encouragement given by such outstanding citizens as John Y. Wood, with whom he lived a year; Washington Head, also with whom he worked;

and Nelson Smith, who gave him his first industrial opportunities, and many others also.

Under the preaching of the Rev. Joe Harwood he was converted, in Alabama, and joined Town Creek Baptist Church, but on coming to the Cove he sustained a regular attendance upon the Cedar Grove Method'st Church, where he met Melissa McCarty to whom he was married in 1876, they living in that community for some years.

Mrs. Sizemore was the daughter of Floyd L. and Catherine Acree McCarty, the McCartys and Acrees being wholly of Scotch and Irish descent respectively, the McCartys moving from Monroe, Georgia, into the county at the close of the war, Floyd L., broken in the service, dying just a few months later. Of this family, as brothers, there were two sons, Isaac, of large family, some residing in county still, and Starling, educated at Calhoun by the Acrees, taught two terms of school, was smitten of typhoid fever and died in youth. The other daughters were: Nancy, dying young also; Mrs. Thomas Wood, moved to Texas; Mrs. John W. Sizemore, Sr., and Mrs. Robert Mahan, Sr., all now dead, and most of them buried at the Cedar Grove Cemetery, near the church of their youth.

With family responsibilities a reality and with two or three children born to this union, Abraham felt distinctly that it was his duty to enter the ministry. He realized that his education was limited, for he had had only the advantages of a few short term schools, having "gone through" Smith's Grammar, Davies' Arithmetic, with some Geography, History, and Penmanship. After an intense struggle he confided the matter to Capt. John Y. Wood, the educational and spiritual leader of that section, and to Rev. Mr. Morgan, the pastor of the local Baptist Church. These good men encouraged him to enter Union University, Jackson, Tenn., but he had a family and was from a family of strong antipathy to Baptist Mission Boards and Baptist schools, no doubt; though he became an ardent supporter of missions. He was confronted with dangerous discouragement, and Capt. Wood assured him that he could do much good, and that academic limitations would not count heavily in the rural churches.

He became a close student of a few books, Bunyan's, a few classics, histories, dictionaries, commentaries, and, most of all, the English Bible. He "steeped his soul" in the language of the New Testament. He quoted it fluently and freely, with good meaning if not literally. Dr. Jameson, then president of Mercer University, said that he was one of the most proficient in chapter and verse references from memory. Not considered by all a profound preacher, he however, had a fine evangelistic gift, knew always how to fit in well to serve where churches were supplied with pastors, and had an accomplishment, without compromise, in effectively working with other denominations, his fervor, heart power, and prayer causing him to render a large service even where no churches were or church pivileges prevailed.

Reorganizing and reviving the Mentone (Ala.) Church, where the

Baptist Assembly Ground is now, they called for his ordination, where he baptized, in Little River, his wife into this church. Following this pastorate, he was pastor for some years, of the Head River Church, baptizing into this church his eldest son, Julian, in the same river. It was in this, the Lookout Valley Association, that he had the help and the encouragement of such laymen as James M. Forrester, G. A. R. Bible, W. F. Pickle, the Hamics and others, whom he loved greatly. He was pastor and leader at Oak Hill and Fairview churches, now disbanded, in the Coosa Association.

Hard work and frugal living made him and his wife able to rear eight children and give them all some measure of education, some attending college. He lived within his means, hated artificiality, feared debt, eschewed all manner of evil, and was punctual in all obligations. The late James E. Patton, prominent banker, said of him that he was as sure as the calendar.

The accidental death of his wife, May 25, 1911, whose genuine life, frugal ways, practical idealism, and unfailing faith had been his stay, gave him a blow from which he never recovered. Then, a few years later, he sensed keenly the horrors of the World War, and with declining years he broke completely, lingering till his death referred to above. The newspaper notices of his passing used these fitting words: "His life has been simple with the best of simplicity, beautiful and sacrificial, genuinely devoted to his home, his country, and his God."

The surviving members of this immediate family are eight in number, four sons and four daughters, Ada dying in infancy. We offer this brief sketch of them at this time. Vesta Lula married J. Monroe Kirby, of Valley Head, Ala., and lives on a farm home near Fort Payne, Alabama; Mary Catherine, ardent Christian worker from youth, married J. B. Lowry, of Valley Head, Ala., and resides now on a portion of the Sizemore home place; Janie never married, administor of maternal love, however, to the younger children and to her father, after the untimely death of her mother, lives now with Mrs. Lowry; Julian J., teacher-minister, graduated from Mercer University, studied with Southwestern Seminary, has held important school positions and church connections in East Tennessee and Southwest Georgia, married Margaret Wheeler, this county, resides at Perry, Georgia, pastor of First Baptist Church; John W. attended the Berry School, Rome, Ga., had short term agricultural courses also, veteran World War, rehabilitation courses after return from same, married Willie Powell, this county, and lives on farm near Rock Springs; Omer L. was for some years mechanic for the Atlantic Line Railroad, living at Waycross, Georgia, married Ollie Johnson, also of this county, lives at Rossville, Georgia, and does clerical work, was recently set apart as a licensed Baptist minister by one of the Rossville Churches; Ethel Mae graduated from the LaFayette High School, taught in the county some time and at Lakeview, married Alton Fox, Warren Community, and lives now in Rossville; Luther A., finishing high school in class with Ethel, the World War defeated his college education, saw gallant and continued service in the Eighty-Second Division, married Myrtle Moon, Holland, Ga., high school principal Chickamauga and Calhoun some years, lives in Chattanooga and does commercial work.

THE COULTERS.

Alexander Coulter was born in Tenn. about the close of the Revolutionary war. His father was prbably one of the early immigrants who followed Daniel Boone into the western wilderness. He was a saddler and silversmith and traded much with the Indians till his death soon after their removal, having died about 1850. James J. Coulter, son of Alex was born in 1816, in Tennessee, coming to Georgia with his father during the thirties. He married Mary A., dau. of Vines Harwell, an attorney, who lived in the Cove, and whose wife was sister of Richard Lane. James J. assisted in the removal of the Indians in 1838. He was one of those early, hardy pioneer settlers who were able and willing to face the unsettled condition of the country a century ago—to fell the forests, build roads, establish schools and churches and do his part in wresting the land from its primal stage of inactivity. He was a man of iron nerve and indomitable will-power, as most of those early settlers were. There were seven children in this home, viz. R. A., Mary Ann, T. S., W. H., J. A., O. L., W. M. These six boys all had families, the total number of children being about 31; the sister never married.

The combined height of these six brothers was 33 feet 7 inches, or an average of more than 6 feet 8 inches. The tallest was 6 feet 11 inches, the lowest 6 feet 4 inches. To see these six brothers together was not unlike seeing six giants.

James A., the fifth child, was born 1855 and in 1881 married Elizabeth Looney (born 1862), daughter of J. H. Looney. This home has never been blessed with children, but Mr. and Mrs. Coulter have always been friends of children, having kept and cared for orpans for a number of years. Mr. Coulter is one of the most substantial citizens of the uper Cove. Industrious, honest, friendly, neighborly and jovial he stands well to the front among the first citizens of McLemore's Cove.

HASLERIG.

Richard Haslerig and his wife Mary came to America from Scotland about 1790 and settled in Washington county, Virginia. Tradition says that Richard was descended from that most heroic of Scottish kings, Robert Bruce. Among other children, Richard had a son, Thomas Jefferson, who married Delilah J. Coulter, daughter of Alexander and Margaret McReynolds Coulter; and who, following the trail blazed by Daniel Boone and his followers, moved into the Cumberland region and settled in Tennessee where he died in 1830 at Jasper. His wife, Delilah with her two children, Thomas Richard and Margaret, came to Walker county about 1835.

Thomas Richard (T. R. A.) married Anne McConnell, 1857, daughter of William and Martha Dixon McConnell and granddaughter of David Dixon, a Revolutionary soldier. She had a brother, Major Joe McConnell, who was killed in the battle of Missionary Ridge. Richard (T. R. A.) Haslerig enlisted in Company H. 23rd Regiment Georgia Infantry, Confederate States Army, and was appointed 1st Lieutenant August 31, 1861, in Walker County, and promoted to captain in June 1862. He was killed in the battle of Sharpesburg, Maryland. Mr. Haslerig was Ordinary of Walker county at the time of his enlistment, and as such was exempt from military service; but his sense of patriotism was so strong that he waived his right of exemption and offered his services to his country. He early showed his ability and was promoted to a captaincy; had he been spared he doubtless would have advanced much farther in official ranks before the close of the conflict.

His only son, Thomas W., (b. 1858), married Cora A. Ransom, (b. 1869), in 1892 to which union were born four children, to wit:—Ludye, Roy, Bess and Lucile. Few men in the county are better or more favorably known than T. W. Haslerig. For twenty-four years he served as chairman of the Board of Education of Walker county, and at various times has been county surveyor. A man of broad information, sound judgment and of a jovial nature, he is admired and respected by all who know him.

Alexander Hunter.

Alexander Hunter (1831-1914) came to McLemore's Cove from Tennessee. His wife was Emeline Wheeler (1832-1917), also a Tennesseean. His father was William Hunter (1792-1870) and mother Ellen Walker (1794-1880). They migrated from Virginia and settled in the Cumberland region before the Cherokee Indians were removed West. Alexander came into the Cove before the war and settled near Cedar Grove. He enlisted in the Confederacy and served throughout that fratricidal conflict. Returning to his family and home after the surrender he took up the duties of the citizen and made a model one. Six children were born in his home, as follows: Sarah, Nancy, J. R., Martha, William G., and Mary Lou.

William G., born in 1867, married Lottie Looney (1868), dau. of John (1833-1907) and Martha (Smith) Looney (1840-1922), who also came to the Cove from Tennessee soon after the war. The Looneys are of Irish descent, coming to America before the Revolution. One maternal ancestor was born on the Atlantic while making the passage.

W. G. Hunter has one of the most attractive homes in the county, and what makes it doubly so is the hearty welcome awaiting any visitor who chances that way. He and Mrs. Hunter are devoted members of the Methodist church at which they are very apt to be seen on church days and at Sunday school. The greatest sorrow of their lives was the loss of their eldest son, Elmer, who gave his life in the World War. Hanging over the front door is a small banner containing a gold star with the words "Over There." No, he is not "over there" in Flanders Field", but is "Over there" in Canaan's Land.

Children: Elmer, (1892-1918); Fay, (1898); Ray, (1913).

The War Department furnishes the following record:

"James Elmer Hunter enlisted in the service April 2, 1918. Embarked for overseas service in May 1918, attached to Co. K. 80th Div. Was killed in action Sept. 29, 1918. His company was the first to cross the Hindenburg lines. He was killed in that battle."

"UNITED STATES ARMY. (IN MEMORY OF)

James Elmer Hunter, Sgn. Dept. 120th Infantry, 30th Div., who died September 29th 1918. He bravely laid down his life for the cause of his country. His name will ever remain fresh in the hearts of his friends and comrades. The record of his honorable service will be preserved in the archives of the American Expeditionary Forces.

John J. Pershing"

Commander-in-chief".

G. W. BROWN.

G. W. Brown was the son of W. M. Brown who was born in W lton County about 1825 and died in 1862. His mother was Nancy, daughter of Geary Davis, a Methodist minister of Cobb County. G. W. Brown was born in Paulding County in 1857 where he was brought up amid the hardships incident to an orphan boy during and following the lean years of the Civil war. In 1877 he married Ollie C., daughter of W. A. J. Freeman, a veteran of the Confederacy. He came to Walker County in 1890, living one year in East Armuchee, then moving to the Chestnut Flat district where he bought a farm and settled near Catlett and resided there 24 years. Here he labored industriously and paid for the little farm, reared and educated his children and became one of the leading citizens of his section.

In 1915 he sold his farm and moved to LaFayette where he has since resided. Since coming to LaFayette he has served 12 years as an officer of the law,—eight years as Notary Public and four as Justice of the Peace. During his term of service much business has passed through his hands, both of a civil and criminal nature and he has always rendered judicial decisions that have met with popular and legal approval. Squire Brown is known and recognized by all as an honest and impartial judge.

Mr. Brown is much given to music, and during his younger days and in middle life was a teacher of music classes. For 30 years he taught in Walker, Catoosa and Polk counties. He is the author of a number of pieces of music, several of which have been published by the A. J. Showalter Music Company, notably that popular piece, "O Who Shall Be Able to Stand," and "I am on my Journey Home."

There were four children born in this home, namely: Eula, Nancy, G. Mark, and Fonnie Lee. Although rapidly aging, Mr. Brown and his wife are quite active and take great interest in the affairs of life. Mr. Brown has the respect and confidence of all who know him.

DUNN.

Samuel H. Dunn was born in Walker County, Georgia, March 20, 1857. Here he has lived a highly respected citizen and prominent farmer and has reared an honorable family. He gave to his children a beautiful and useful home training, and provided for them ample school advantages. In their younger days they were among the county's most popular and successful teachers.

His father was the late Willis Dunn and his grandfather Dunn was a pioneer of Walker County, who was descended from the Irish colonies of the Carolinas. His Grandmother Dunn before her marriage was Miss Hurst, and his mother's maiden name was Narcissa Hill. His grandmother Hill before her marriage was Miss Bates.

After a long life of useful service, he is spending his declining years in quietude, in varied recollections of the past and in dispensing hospitality to his friends and neighbors. He recalls the horrors of the battle of Chickamauga, and the sorrow felt at the loss of an older brother who fell under the Southern flag at the battle of Savannah. In viewing the beautiful modern highways of Walker County, he recalls how, more than fifty years ago, he worked the crude roads of the county beginning at the age of sixteen and often working for fifteen days in order to make the roads passable.

His wife before her marriage was Miss Amanda Pettigrew, and was born in Wayne County Mississippi, but has lived in Walker County, near LaFayette, since 1876, where she was occupied in teaching before her marriage. Her father, William Pettigrew, was of Scotch parentage, and his mother before her marriage was Miss Filyaw, and his grandmother was Miss McPherson. Her mother's maiden name was Jemima Robinson, and her grandmother before her marriage was Ellen Preslar. Her father served in the Civil War and many of her relatives fell in battle under the Confederate flag.

In this family were born three children, namely: Gussie, who married M. E. Arnold; Maude, who married H. V. Henry; and Samuel. There are three grandchildren, Eugenia Arnold, who married D. A. Snow; Eloise Arnold and John Arnold; one grandchild, Mary Alice Snow.

Of these all survive except Samuel who died in the service of the World War, and in loving memory the following tribute is inscribed and dedicated to him.

SAMUEL DUNN

Samuel Dunn who was a son of Samuel H. Dunn was born in Walker County, Georgia, December 4, 1894. He was reared on his father's farm where he had access to farm culture. He received his early education in the schools of his town and county, and his college training at Mercer University, Macon, Georgia.

He applied himself well in these schools of learning and was an efficient young man of an outstanding influence for good. His usefulness, his high ideals of morality and his integrity combined to make of him a young man of unblemished character. His life was filled with beautiful examples of helpfulness to those around him. He was an obedient son, a kind brother, a generous friend and held the respect and confidence of all who knew him.

He enlisted for World war service at Camp Gordon, June 27, 1918, and was assigned to book keeping in the information office at General Headquarters. His ability, accuracy and trustworthiness made for him a high record in his war service. He was gentle and unassuming and was loved and admired by the personnel of his office and by the General Headquarters Staff. His loss was felt and mourned there and in his sorrowing home and county. He died in the service of the World war at Camp Gordon October 11, 1918.

"BY COLUMBIA."
"Columbia gives to her son
the accolade of the new
chivalry of humanity.

Samuel Dunn pvt. Co. D, 1st Div. Bn 157th D. B. served with honor in the World War and died in the service of his country."

Woodrow Wilson."

GRAHAM.

JOHN A. GRAHAM

John Adam Graham, the subject of this sketch was the son of Joseph R. Graham. Joseph R. Graham (1819-1855) was born in South Carolina but settled in Walker county about 1840. He built and operated the first tan-yard in LaFayette, afterwards known as the Phipps tan-yard. He married Melissa, daughter of Anthony Story, another pioneer who settled in West Armuchee Valley. The Storys were great friends with the James R. Jones family with whom they often visited in pioneer days.

John Adam Graham (1854-1927) of Scotch-Irish descent, was born at LaFayette, but lived most of his early life in West Armuchee Valley, where he was a successful farmer. Later moving to LaFayette, he was made superintendent of the county Almshouse where he remained for a dozen years. Moving later to the Rock Springs community, he purchased the farm originally owned by that pioneer, James R. Jones. Here for the remainder of his life he was a successful farmer and fruit grower, having, perhaps, the most extensive commercial peach orchard in the county.

In 1880 he married Catherine, daughter of Adam and Matilda (Eslinger) Stroup. Adam Stroup, of German descent, was born in South Carolina in 1800. He ran a stage line from Gordon Springs to Catoosa Springs before the Civil War. He also drove a wagon that helped carry the Indians from this country. His brother, Andrew Stroup, operated the old Furnace in East Armuchee Valley before the Civil War.

To this union were born seven children—Hattie (1883-1900), single; Jesse (1885), married Ida Lawrence, two children; Ruth (1889) marrid Chester Deck, three children; Walter (1891), married Exie Adams, four children; Ross (1894-1918), single; Ima (1900) married Frank Stevenson, four children; Beatrice (1903), single.

ROSS QUINN GRAHAM enlisted in the World War in Chattanooga, Tennessee, December 12, 1917. He was trained at Paris Island, South Carolina, and Quantico, Virginia, where he was made corporal, sailing for France April 22, 1918. While serving in 78th Company, 2nd Division, U. S. Marines, he was gassed in action at Chateau Thierry, France, June 14, and died June 16, 1918, in a field hospital at Luzancy, France. Here he was buried, later removed to National Cemetery, France, and in 1921

ROSS GRAHAM

his body was brought to his native soil and laid to rest with military honors in the Rock Springs cemetery.

Ross Graham Post American Legion, No. 87, LaFayette, Georgia, is named in his honor, he being the first Walker county boy to give his life in the World War.

"UNITED STATES MARINE CORPS"

"In grateful memory of Corporal Ross Quinn Graham, who, on June 16, 1918, gave his life that others might enjoy the blessings of liberty throughout the world. His supreme sacrifice in devotion to duty upheld the finest traditions of his Corps and its motto 'Semper Fidelis.'

"Given under my hand and seal at Washington, D. C., this twenty-eighth day of February, 1919.

George Barnett,
Major-General Commandant."

JAMES M. FREEMAN.

James M. Freeman, (1856-1924), was the son of John and Malinda Freeman of South Carolina. John came to Dawson County, Georgia, about 1850, where he was engaged in farming till the War Between the States. He enlisted at the beginning of hostilities and saw service in many hard-fought battles, being killed at the battle of Winchester.

James M. married Theoria Redd, daughter of Thomas and Malinda (Nix) Redd in 1887. In 1904 he moved with his family to Walker County, settling in McLemore's Cove, where he was interested in farming. Here his children labored with him on the farm, attended school, grew to maturity and assumed an enviable place among the young people of the community. Mr. and Mrs. Freeman were either model parents, or there was something in heredity that made good children—perhaps both. Later the family removed to Chickamauga and engaged in merchandising, where they still reside. The children were:

Maggie, born 1888, married Homer Millican. They have six children, Evelyn, Lillian and Leon (twins), Leslie (Decd.), Dorsey, Thomas Latner.

Redden, born, 1891, married Bessie Gracy. Latner, 1894-1918). Needham, born 1900, lives with his mother.

William Latner Freeman was born September 18, 1894, in Forsythe county, Georgia. He left Walker county for Camp Gordon December 17, 1917. Left Camp Gordon May 9, 1918, for New York. Left New York for France May 19, 1918. Was killed in action near the front in a motorcycle accident at Berhecourt, France, June 24, 1918. 82nd Division, 307th Field Signal Battalion, Co. C. Latner Freeman Post No. 123, Chickamauga, Ga., was named in his honor.

"UNITED STATES ARMY."

"In memory of William Latner Freeman, Co. C., 307th F. Signal BN, who died June 24, 1918. He bravely laid down his life for the cause of his country. His name will ever remain fresh in the hearts of his friends and comrades. The record of his honorable service will be preserved in the archives of the American Expeditionary Forces.

LATNER FREEMAN

John J. Pershing, Commander-in-Chief."

ROBERT ANDERSON.

Robert Anderson (1796-1887) was born in South Carolina. His father was Samuel Anderson who died in 1828. His mother, Mary Hinton, died in Augusta, Georgia, in 1826. In 1825, Robert Anderson married Eliza Sullivan (1803-1881), who died in McLemore's Cove. She was a daughter of John and Sarah (Pierce) Sullivan. To this union were born three children, viz: Elizabeth, John and Caroline, the first two dying young. Caroline married Wm. C. Kilgore in 1856. They had ten children, four of whom are now living in Utah.

In 1883, Robert Anderson married Irminia I. Catlett, daughter of Peggy Catlett, to which union was born one son, Robert, Jr. He was a soldier of the war of 1812, being only 16 when he enlisted. He was a fifer and his service was confined to the Atlantic coast. Following the war he moved westward into Tennessee and was living in Chattanooga during the fifties where he served as Justice of the Peace for a number of years. About 1859 he purchased a large tract of fertile land near the head of McLemore's Cove where he settled, his son-in-law joining him there after the war. Here he lived till his death. He is buried in the Anderson family plot near his old home.

In consequence of his service as a soldier in the war of 1812, Mr. Anderson was a Federal pensioner till his death, and since then his widow has been a pensioner and is the only one such in the State of Georgia, there being only three in the United States at the present time (1932). In 1931, a marker in memory of, and in honor of, Robert Anderson was unveiled at his grave by the Daughters of the War of 1812. Mr. Anderson was a Mason.

Robert Anderson, Jr., (S.R.H.), born 1855, lives with his mother at the old home and is a substantial farmer. He has a lovely home on the foothills of Pigeon Mountain near a fine cave spring which furnishes water to the home by means of a hydraulic ram. In 1909 he married Elizabeth Carroll, born 1886. Robert, Jr., is a Mason and takes a great interest in the order. The Andersons are Methodists.

Sartain.

The name is of French derivation and means "tailor." The Sartains were wool carders, weavers, fullers, tailors, living some fifty miles northeast from Paris, France, in the town of Maux. After, and in consequence of the invention of the art of printing, because of the persecutions aimed at those convicted of reading the Bible, the Sartains were among others who fled from France to England, settling at Trowbridge, in Wiltshire. This exodus took place at least as early as 1557 and most likely earlier.

Because the English kings had long been anxious to introduce manufacturing into the country, as also, because King Henry VIII had separated the Church of England from the Roman Church, and denied the authority of the Pope, and for other reasons the French immigrants were welcomed.

The records of the Sartains in this little English town, as they were kept in the parish church, have been carefully examined and tabulated by John Sartain (1808-1900), of Philadelphia, who, himself, was born in Trowbridge. He gives tables of baptisms, marriages and deaths from 1557 to 1886, as shown in these old records—earlier records being lost. Some of the early spellings of the name were: Serton, Sarton, Sartaine, Sartayne, Certen, Sartin, etc. (Paraphrased from "Annals of the Sartain Tribe," by John Sartain).

John, James and Sier Sartain, brothers, migrated from Virginia to Madison county, Georgia, soon after the Revolution. There can be little doubt that either they or their forbears came over from England and were a part of the colony of Sartains at Trowbridge. John settled in Madison county where he had among others a son, Elisha (1797-1881). Elisha married Fanny Bonds, to which union were born several sons and daughters. One of these, Gilford (1838-1869), married Margaret Scarboro (1844-1881).

Gilford served in the Civil War, and after that bloody conflict was ended, he returned to his home and engaged in farming. He was a robust man of unusual physical strength, and at the community log-rollings he was sure to carry the heaviest load. On one occasion he was placed at the heavy end of a large log and although he managed to carry it, he ruptured a blood vessel in doing so and before leaving the field had a hemorrhage. He never recovered, but gradually declining, he died a few years later, leaving six small children to be reared by his widow. How that mother worked, lived in penury, suffered for the necessities of life, but still clung doggedly to the little ones, would be a long story. In 1879 the little family came to Walker county, settling at Crawfish Spring, where she died and is buried, leaving the little fellows to face the world alone.

FAMILY RECORD. David A., b. 1859, married Arminda Bagwell. Children: Mack, decd.; Ola; Corrie; Virgil and Virgie (twins); Ruth. Corrie, b. 1861, married H. A. (Tip) Blaylock (see sketch). Gilford (1864-1881). James A., b. 1866, married (1), Nannie Glenn (1866-1915), (2), Sallie Shankle (1881-1925), one child, James Shankle. Elizabeth (1868-1888). John W. (1869-1901).

WILLIAM H. BAYLESS.

R. B. Bayless, father of the subject of this sketch, was born in Tennessee about 1823. In 1853 he married Mary M. Reed and was living near Ringgold, Ga., when the war-clouds were lowering in sixty-one. Promptly he enlisted in the service of his country and gave his all to the "lost cause." After the siege of Vicksburg he was permitted to return to his home on furlough, where he found to his great sorrow that his wife was dead, leaving three small children. Sorrowfully he again started to the front, this time to the Virginia battlefields, where he took part in some of the hard-fought battles under the Peerless Leader. Here he was mortally wounded and died in one of the many hospitals. While in the army he wrote home some pathetic letters and sent to his loved ones some mementoes as keepsakes if he should never return—perhaps unconsciously prophesying a fact to come, for he never saw his loved ones again. One small card, still lovingly preserved, says: "Be a good boy, my little son." Another, "If I should never return, keep this in memory of me." No doubt this instance is only one in ten thousand of such that occurred in those never-to-be-forgotten days.

William H. Bayless was born in 1854 near Ringgold, whence he came to Walker county and settled in the Warren community, living a number of years with his uncle, Webber Spears. In 1879 he was married to Malinda, dau. of Willis and Freshie Dunn. This home was never blessed with children, but in 1900 there was received into the home a beautiful little orphan girl, Anine R. Head, who thus came into the home to be trained and educated and incidentally to bring sunshine and joy therein. She grew to lovely womanhood and became a teacher, later marrying a scion of one of the county's leading families, Henry Shahan. They have five children, Margaret, J. D., Catherine, Pauline, and Willie Maude.

Mr. Bayless is known as an upright, honorable, Christian gentleman. An industrious hard worker, sociable, neighborly, friendly, he is beloved and respected by all who know him. Careful in making an obligation when once made he is most punctual in discharging it. He and his wife are now aging fast but still take much interest in the affairs of life. As they contemplate the closing scene they are content. Happy are they who can do so!

REV. T. C. TUCKER.

REV. T. C. TUCKER

"Rev. Thomas C. Tucker was born in Jackson county, Georgia, July 14, 1847. His father, Richard O. Tucker, and his mother, whose maiden name was Virginia Moore, were natives of Virginia. They were irreligious, but did not fail to instill into his youthful mind right moral principles. The spirit of religion, however, was wanting, and he was reared without that Christian example in the household which is so often made effectual to the salvation of the young. Being a mere boy when the late war commenced, his opportunities for education were very restricted. For a short time he was sent to school in Walton county, and that rudimentary training was all he enjoyed until after his marriage to Miss Martha Kilgore of the same county, in October, 1866. Soon after this event he removed to Walker county. Here the Lord was pleased to bless him in the conversion of his soul and he was baptised into the fellowship of the Crawfish Spring church, by Rev. Mr. Higgins. His admission into the church was soon followed by his election as deacon, which office he filled with honor to himself and profit to the church. Not long after his ordination as deacon, he was licensed to preach and called to supply High Point church. He was ordained June 1874, at Antioch church, Walker county. Feeling deeply the importance of a more thorough education he entered St. Mary's Institute, Walker county, and enjoyed the instruction of Rev. J. M. Robertson and Captain J. Y. Wood for eight months, at the same time filling regularly four appointments to preach each month.

"He has had the care of several churches during his brief career as a minister and has constituted three, Bethel, Valley Head and New Prospect. He is now pastor of Waterville and Bethel and has been for four years. He has, also, been appointed to the mission work in Dade county, by the Georgia Baptist State Mission Board. As a minister he is deeply pious and zealous and a bold defender of the truth as it is in Jesus. He warns sinners with great faithfulness, and does not forget to tell Christians of their responsibilities. He is ever ready to minister to the poor and comfort them. His exhortations to sinners are often very touching, particularly, when recounting the love and sufferings of our saviour, and bring tears to the eyes of old and young. He is an earnest, unflinching advocate of Baptist views, but his manner is so kind that he rarely offends, and has baptised a number of Methodists, Presbyterians and Campbellites. He is of fine, robust form, with heavy beard and grey eyes and always wears a pleasant smile when you meet him. He entered into the vineyard early and being an earnest worker has accomplished as much good perhaps as any man in the Coosa Association for his age and opportunities. He has been peculiarly successful in building up churches, arousing Christians to a sense of their duty, and awakening an interest in Sabbah schools. The church at Waterville has been wonderfully revived under his ministry."

The above sketch is taken from the Georgia Baptist History published in 1881. It describes the life and labors of one of Walker County's most outstanding and beloved ministers. Rev. T. C. Tucker impressed himself on the people among whom he labored as few ministers are able to do. His intense earnestness, his zeal, his logical reasoning and his uncompromising attitude toward sin and worldliness—all these together with his knowledge of the Word made him a powerful ambassador. He died in 1889 at the age of 42 years. Had he been spared to the denomination he would in all probability have become the outstanding Baptist minister in Northwest Georgia. He was buried at Chickamauga where a handsome shaft marks his grave, placed there by the Crawfish Spring church of which he was pastor at his death.

There were born to Rev. and Mrs. Tucker the following children: W. M., (1867), who served the county as tax collector 1907-08, married Abbie Ingle. They live in Dade County. Lula (1871), married Dr. E. H. Hise. Samuel R. (1873), married Ella Johnson. J. Clark (1876), married Florence Boss. Served for a number of years as member Board Roads and Revenue; also Commissioner of Jury Revisors. Naomi (1878), married M. K. Hise. Electra (1881), married O. A. Woods.

The writer of this sketch feels impelled to say a brief word concerning one of these boys, Rev. S. R. Tucker, upon whose shoulders his father's mantle seems to have fallen. A mere lad at the time of his father's death, he grew to manhood in the same community and has to a very remarkable degree come to fill his father's place. He was converted in 1904 and joined the New Prospect church. For some years he worked in his quiet way as layman. In 1920 he was licensed to preach and a month later was ordained to the full work of the Gospel ministry and

REV. S. R. TUCKER

was immediately called to the pastorate of his home church and ever since has served it to the complete satisfaction and joy of both church and community, now eleven years. In addition he has served Bethel, Valley Head and Mt. Hermon each the same number of years besides serving other churches several years.

Mr. Tucker has served for a number of years as moderator of the Coosa Baptist Association, which position he fills to the entire satisfaction of that body, exhibiting fairness, kindness and impartiality to every one. He is modest and retiring, qualities that always prompt admiration. His judgement is eagerly sought on all matters pertaining to denominational, educational or civic matters. Coupled with his other qualities he is an earnest convincing Gospel minister. Perhaps no preacher of the county enjoys a greater influence for good among all people than Sam Tucker. A leading Presbyterian layman once remarked that Sam Tucker seems to contradict Christ's words that "A prophet is not without honor save in his own country and among his own people."

DR. ADAM CLEMENTS.

Dr. Adam Clements, one of the pioneer residents of Walker county, was born in Jackson county, Georgia, on the 15th day of August, 1804. His parents, with their family, moved from Jackson county to Fayette county, Georgia, in the year 1820.

On the 13th day of September, 1833, in Muscogee county, Georgia, Dr. Clements was united in marriage to Mary Wilson Hill Park, who was born in Putnam county, Georgia, on May 18, 1810, the daughter of James Park and Martha Yandell Park. Miss Enid Yandell, of Boston, the well-known sculptor, is descended from a brother of Martha Yandell.

In the year 1838 Dr. Clements, with his family, moved to Walker county, Georgia, locating in the southeastern part of the county, in which section he passed the remainder of his life, engaged in the practice of his profession.

Dr. Clements served as a member of the Georgia Legislature 1853-54. He was a consistent member of the Christian church, and in the year 1824 commenced to preach the gospel, two years later being ordained to the full work of the ministry. This work he continued for eighteen or nineteen years, when he was forced to give it up on account of bronchial trouble.

Dr. Clements was the father of ten children, two of whom died in infancy. The others grew to maturity, married, and became parents. The eldest, William Flavius Josephus, was born July 31, 1834. He was a captain in the Confederate army, a physician, and a resident of Greene county, Arkansas, having located there when a young man. He married Miss Dovie Rhea, of Arkansas.

The second son was Julius Park Clements, born September 12, 1837. He was assistant surgeon of the Twenty-third Georgia Regiment. Married Miss Ann Wood, a sister of Capt. John Y. Wood, a prominent educator and much loved citizen. His wife died soon after marriage, without leaving an heir. He practiced medicine at Villanow for about a year, then located at Tunnel Hill, in Whitfield county, and represented his county in the legislature. He married a second time, his wife's maiden name being Mary Howell. With his wife and family he finally moved to Atlanta, where he passed away about the year 1920.

Adolphus Charles, the third son, born February 7, 1839; died November 23, 1912. He married Nannie Elvira Phillips. Was a farmer, living at Villanow, near his fathers' old home place.

James Wilson Hill, born February 11, 1841. Married Ludie Lowe. Was assistant surgeon of the Twenty-third Georgia Regiment. Is a physician, lives at Subligna, in Chattooga county, and is the only one of Dr. Adam Clements' children surviving. He recently celebrated his 91st birthday.

Cicero Thomas, the next son, was born May 2, 1842. He practiced law at Rome, Ga., where he was married to Sallie Wardlaw. He was sergeant-major in the Eighth Georgia Battalion, and was Solicitor-General for the Rome Circuit for twelve years.

John Adam, born March 14, 1844; a farmer. Was wounded in the Confederate service in the First Regiment, Georgia, S. L. Stovall's Brigade, July 22, 1864, and endured the hardships of prison life at Camp Chase, Columbus, Ohio. He married Louisa Suttle and lived for many years near his father's old homestead near Villanow, where he was engaged in farming. The later years of his life, however, were passed at LaFayette, where he died on October 1, 1908.

Judson Claudius, born February 12, 1846; married Bettie Wardlaw, who died about a year afterward. After the lapse of many years he was married a second time, to Lizzie Dulaney, of Louisville, Ky., who survives him, and is a resident of Washington, D. C. He, also, saw military service, having been First Lieutenant in the First Regiment, S. L. Stovall's Brigade.

Martha Almina, the youngest child (being the only daughter who survived), was born November 11, 1849; married Joseph Warren Cevender and lived at Villanow, where she died November 15, 1882.

Mention should be made here of the political career of one of Walker's most distinguished citizens,—Judson Claudius, the youngest son of Dr. Adam Clements. He was elected to the legislature at the age of 26, serving for two terms, and one term in the state senate. He was, in the year 1880, elected to Congress, which honor he won in four succeeding elections. In March, 1892, he was appointed by the president to a place on the interstate commerce commission to fill the unexpired term of Commissioner Bragg, of Alabama, who had died. He subsequently received similar appointments at the hands of three other presidents, being reappointed by President Cleveland in 1895, by President McKinley in 1901, and finally by President Roosevelt. On the occasion of completing his twenty-five years of continuous service on the commission (part of the time as its chairman) Judge Clements was the recipient of an unusual testimonial of esteem and affection from his colleagues and all the employees of the commission. Those who knew him best loved him most, and all who came in contact with him learned to revere and honor him.

The children of Adolphus C. Clements and Nannie E. Phillips were as follows: May, single, lives in Atlanta. Ella, married J. W. Sweeny (deceased); children: Ella May, Julia, Clements, Ruth. Ruby, passed in infancy. Charley, married Etheldred Clement; children: Charles, James, May Nanella. Claude, married Fannie Reed; children: Ruby, Claudius A., Russell A., Harold, Charlie Reed. Mr. Clements is one of the county's most popular officers, having served two terms as a member of the Board of Roads and Revenues and two terms as tax collector, and recently nominated for another term. Nannie, married W. A. Price (deceased).

The children of John A. and Lou Suttle were: Nannie, married F. M. Shaw; children: Louise, Frank Clements, Martha Camp. Jennie May, married G. W. Little; children: Georgia May, Lucile, Samuel. Mattie Lou, single.

The children of Mattie and Joseph W. Cavender were the following: Minnie, married W. H. Warrenfels; child: Melville. Murtis, married Lee N. Shahan; children: Martha, Maxwell. Georgia married Ben Beck; children: Clementine, Adelaide. Clemmie, married Charlie McGill; children: Warren, Lillian, Jane. Judson C. married Flora Collins; children: Ben Warren, Martha, Joe, Robert.

The other children of Dr. Clements left the county early in life and were not closely identified with the county's history. However, J. W. (Wilson), a physician, located in Chattooga county, near Subligna, where he has spent his life as a physician, being still in life, now nearing the century mark. His children are Ernest Yandell, Lillian, Iula. Of the others, Julius lived in Atlanta, Cicero in Floyd county, William in Arkansas and Judson in Washington, D. C.

FARISS.

The Fariss family is closely identified with the very earliest history of Walker County. However, the different ways of spelling their names, including Ferrers, Farriars, Ferris, Farris, Faris and Fariss, has made it somewhat difficult to trace the family associated with this county's history.

The Fariss family of Kent, England, have armorial bearings of the Ferrers, an ancient family of England, tracing to the time of William the Conqueror. One branch found residence in Ireland and became Faris or Fariss in the course of time. The records show that John Faris was born in County Cavan, Ireland, and his profession is given as "gentleman". He married Louisa Edison and reared four children— Louisa, John, James and David. From the similarity of Christian names, it is reasonably certain that this is the branch from which the Fariss' of Walker County descended, the family coming first to South Carolina and Tennessee.

William Fariss and family lived in Rabun County, Georgia prior to 1834, records at the State Capitol having the name of his son, Samuel Fariss as Legislator and Senator from Rabun County from 1825—1832.

He was also a member of the State Convention from Rabun in 1833. Then his name appears as Representative from Walker County from

DR. SAMUEL WILLIAM FARISS
1914, during service House Representatives, with first grandchild, William Mercer Glenn, Jr., born in LaFayette (both deceased). Mother this child being first grandchild in family of Dr. D. C. Fariss.

1834 to 1843, and as State Senator from the 46th. Senatorial District, which included Walker County, 1847 and 1851-52. This record further shows that he married Rebecca Pinson, and was the son of William

Fariss, a Revolutionary Soldier, and that graves of father and son are at LaFayette, Walker County.

Samuel Fariss and family, together with his father's family, settled in Walker County in 1833 or early 1834, just after the formation of the county, and before the town of LaFayette was named. These families, with several others made homes near the Northern boundary of the present city, and probably intended the main part of the town to be about a mile North of the present location. A marker, hewn from native stone, showed the grave of Wm. Fariss, whose remains were brought in 1925 from its resting place North of town, to the family lot in the LaFayette cemetery. It bears this inscription: "Wm. Fariss died in 1835 in the 85th year of his age. A soldier of the Revolution." "Through the efforts of the Wm. Marsh Chapter Daughters of the American Revolution, a government marker was obtained and unveiled with appropriate ceremonies.

There appears to be no records of any children of Wm. Fariss, except Samuel, but he (Samuel) spent his life here and was known as an upright man and patriotic citizen. He married Rebecca Pinson in 1822 in Habersham County, and their children were Clarissa Jane, born in Habersham County, who married T. E. Patton of Walker County: Louisa Ann, born in Rabun County, who became the wife of Hamilton Young; Adeline, born in Rabun County, who became the wife of T. E. Patton, after the death of Clarissa; DeWitt Clinton, born in Rabun County in 1829; John Curtis, born in 1831 in Rabun County; Benjamin Franklin, born in 1833 in Rabun County, and later a well-known minister of the North Georgia Conference; Margaret, born in Walker County in 1836, became the wife of Reverend T. A. Seals, a Methodist minister; and William Albert, born in Walker county in 1840, and served as itinerant Methodist preacher for a long number of years.

Captain Samuel Fariss was given command of the Indians in this section when they were transferred to the West in 1838, and a handsome bronze tablet marks the spot near LaFayette of the Cherokee Indian Stockade, where he and a company of Georgia Volunteers kept them until their removal. He served his generation well in capacity of lawmaker, private citizen and soldier in trying times. When legislator and senator, he went on horse back to the State Capitol, a perilous journey, especially since he carried the county taxes on his person. At the outbreak of the War Between the States, although beyond the age for service, he organized a company that he might further serve his state, and marched away with several of his sons. He died in a hospital in Savannah in 1862 while in active service, and was later buried in LaFayette cemetery. Among the most grief-stricken at his bier were numbers of his former slaves, most of whom he had already set free, for he was indeed a good master.

Of the sons, only DeWitt C. cast his fortunes with Walker County, and remained here throughout his unusually useful and fruitful life.

After graduating in medicine in New York, he began practicing here about 1850. Perhaps no man ever did a larger practice or was more beloved as a physician. He had other interests also, owning and operating the only drug store on the corner where Rhyne Brothers' Drug Store now is; held much real estate, almost the entire town south of the Courthouse belonging to his estate. He was also a local Methodist preacher, and occupied the pulpit somewhere every Sunday. He married Eliza Ann Moore, of Tennessee in 1854. She was the sister of William Moore, who was one of the pioneer merchants here. They reared five children, who took their places in the town's history. They were Dr. S. W. Fariss, who in turn was one of the county's most beloved physicians until his death in 1923; Rebecca Lou (Loudie) who was married to Dr. J. H. Hammond, and now resides in LaFayette; Susan Eliza (Dovie), wife of Rev. J. G. Hunt, of College Park, Ga.; J. D. (Duke), much-loved druggist, who died in 1907; and Frank O. Fariss, former merchant and Post Master of LaFayette, who died in 1927.

Dr. Samuel William Fariss married Miss Annie King, and to this union five children were born as follows: Calla Eliza, King DeWitt, Derelle, Samuel William Jr., and Loraine. Calla Eliza married William Mercer Glenn, and their children are: William (deceased), Fariss Lanier, Mary Ann, Sam Frank and Alice LaFayette. The children of King DeWitt are: Jack, Carl Frank and Robert E. Lee. Derelle married J. H. Cherry, and have no children. Samuel William married Carrie Ingle and their two children are: Samuel William, III, and Anna Mae. Loraine married George Dickson Jackson, the names of their children being: Samuel Fariss, George Dickson and Derelle.

Mrs. Rebecca Lou (Loudie) married Dr. John Hill Hammond and their two children are Mrs. Annie Moore Hall and Mrs. Susan DeWitt Grey. Annie Moore married Edmund P. Hall, Jr., and their children are Jo Hill and Elizabeth Louise (Betty Lou). Susan DeWitt married William Ernest Grey, their children being William Ernest, Jr., and Mary Louise.

Mrs. Susan Eliza (Dovie) married Rev. Jesse G. Hunt and their children are: Jessie Fariss, DeWitt Clinton and Frank Fariss. DeWitt Clinton married Miss O'Neil Lindsey and their two children are DeWitt, Jr., and Lindsey. Frank Fariss married Miss Mary Adams and they have one child, William Jerry.

J. D. (Duke) married Miss Sarah Batts and to this union four children were born: Louise, Eliza, DeWitt and MacAllen. Louise married a Mr. Ware and have no children. Eliza married a Mr. Luttrell and they have two children, Barbara Jean, and Sally. DeWitt and McAllen are married but have no children.

Frank Osmond was first married to Miss Julia Thurman. They had no children. His second wife was Miss Fannie Barnett, of Whitfield County and to this union two sons were born, Hammond DeWitt and James Franklin.

There is, perhaps, no more honorable name in the county's history than that of Fariss. From the days when the county was erected to the present the Fariss's have been prominent as soldiers, statesmen, ministers, physicians, lawyers, teachers, citizens and successful business men. The record shows six serving as soldiers in the various wars dating from the Revolution to the World war. There have been two statesmen, two physicians, two lawyers, three ministers, a druggist, and others successful business men,—and all excellent citizens.

The late Dr. Samuel W. Fariss I spent his early life in Northwest Georgia as a practicing physician. He was for many years one of the county's most prominent and best loved practitioners. In his capacity as doctor he did much charity work, never failing to respond to a call for the relief of suffering among the poor. In 1913-14 he was a member of the Legislature, thus following in the steps of his grandfather, Colonel Samuel Fariss, who was in the Senate for a number of years in the early days of the county's history. In 1921 Dr. Fariss suffered a stroke of paralysis from which he never fully recovered. He died in 1923 at the age of sixty-eight.

Samuel W. (Rock) Fariss II, the only one of his father's family remaining in the county and closely identified with its history, is a lawyer and is one of the foremost and most successful attorney's in the county. He is also an ex-soldier of the World war.

HUGH JASON CONLEY.

Hugh Jason Conley, son of John and Diana Moore Conley of Burke county, North Carolina, migrated to Walker county with his parents and one brother, John F. Conley, in the early thirties, while the Cherokee Indians were still roaming the forests. He settled near Rock Springs, where so many of the early immigrants made their homes and became integral parts of the new county. Jason Conley was not a strong man physically, but was always active in church work—interested in all developments pertaining to civic and religious improvements in his community. He was a charter member of the Rock Springs Methodist church.

Jason Conley married Margaret, daughter of Aaron and Sarah Suttle Camp, of Rutherford county, S. C., who was a member of the famous "Camp family of 5000." Her mother, Sarah, was sister to John B. Suttle, pioneer citizen of Walker county. Her father, Aaron Camp, was one of a family of 24 children, 21 sons and 3 daughters. Margaret Camp was, at the time of her marriage to Jason Conley, a member of the Baptist church, and retained her membership in that church until several years later, when she, with the eldest daughter, united with the Methodist church, and remained a faitful member of it till her death.

Jason Conley bought land and built a home one mile north of Rock Spring, where he lived till his death, in 1883. The following children were born in the home: John Randolph (1847-1925); Sarah Elizabeth

CONLEY FAMILY GROUP. Left to right, standing, Napoleon Charles, Margaret Susan, Minnie Electa, Lula Camp, Rufus William; seated, Octavia Mary, John Randolph, Margaret Camp (mother), Nancy Cornelia.

(1849-1868); Nancy Cornelia (1852-1920); Octavia Mary (1854-   );
Rufus William (1856-   ); Margaret Susan (Maggie) (1858-   );
Napoleon Charles (1860-   ); Lula Camp (1866-1924); Minnie Electa
(1867-   ).

John Randolph married (1) Sarah McFarland, two children, Chapell and Hugh Jason; (2), Sarah Hicks, five children, Ruth, Mabel, Claude, Frank and Joe; Sarah Elizabeth, unmarried; Nancy Cornelia married

HUGH JASON CONLEY AND WIFE, MARGARET CAMP

John Fletcher (Doc) Conley, who died in 1892. Their children are Pearl, Rex and Erin; Octavia married Louis Taylor Walker who died in 1920. They had a son who died in infancy. Rufus William married Maggie Henry of Rock Springs and moved to Texas, where they now reside. Children. Paul, Nora and Earl. Margaret Susan (Maggie) married Jack Jones who died in 1918. They had a son who died in infancy. Napoleon Charles married (1) Tennie Arp who died 1922. Children: James W., Walter and Gordon; (2), Venie Jenkins. This family also lives in Texas. Lula married James I. Arp, who died in 1927; children, Bernice, Conley and Ruth. Minnie married Frank Crawford Stovall, who died in 1916; children, Lyle and Margaret.

At the time of the battle of Chickamauga, Mrs. Jason Conley and her family were living in their home about three miles south of Lee and Gordon Mills. She was ordered to vacate as she was too near the lines for safety. Gathering her little ones and a few necessities together she left her home and crossed Taylor's Ridge, into West Armuchee, where she remained till after the battle. On her return home she found that the home had been used as a hospital, quite a number of wounded soldiers being still cared for in the home. Six or seven soldiers had died and were buried in the garden where their graves may still be seen.

In 1890 Mrs. Conley and three daughters, Maggie, Lula and Minnie moved to Chattanooga, Tenn., to make their home, which place is now the home of many of the descendants of this pioneer family of Walker county, Georgia.

Frank W. Copeland.

Alexander Copeland left Ireland about 1760; settled in Spartanburg, South Carolina, near Pacolet river. He was a soldier of the Revolution. A brother, William, came over at the same time, who was a captain in the war of the Revolution. His company fought in the battle of the Cowpens in January, 1781.

Alexander reared a large family. Four of his sons married four sisters by name of Chapman; one of these sons was Joseph G. Copeland, father of Alexander Copeland who settled in Walker county in 1845. Joseph G. moved to McMinn county, Tennessee, in 1819. Alexander, son of Joseph G., married Melissa Sartain in 1848. Of this union were born eight children, viz., Sarah L., F. W., James M., Elsie A., Penelope C., J. D., Fannie R., and W. P., five of whom are yet in life.

Melissa (Sartain) Copeland's mother's maiden name was Wall. Her father, John Sartain, came from Virginia to South Carolina, and was originally from north England. He settled in Chattooga county in 1845 and he and wife died during an epidemic of fever in 1848.

Frank W. Copeland, born 1851, married Carrie M., daughter of B. F. Hunt, in 1883. Mr. Hunt was killed in Chickamauga battle. Of this union six children were born, to-wit: John A., of Atlanta; B. F., Rome; Susan M. (Copeland) Peacock, Rome; Hunt, Menlo; F. W., Jr., deceased; Lois Ruth (Copeland) LeFevre, Atlanta.

Mr. Copeland was reared on his father's farm in West Armuchee valley. After his marriage he moved to LaFayette and began the practice of law, later locating in Rome, Georgia, where he still practices, though now an octogenarian. From 1896 to 1901 he represented Walker county in the lower house of the General Assembly. Mr. Copeland, during his almost half century before the bar, has handled much important litigation.

Eli Center

Eli, son of William Center, was born in S. C., in 1811, came to Walker County in 1850 and settled at LaFayette. William had two brothers, noted ministers, one a Baptist who served one church as pastor for more than 50 years; the other a presiding elder in the Methodist church, preaching for a number of years in Charleston.

Eli married Elizabeth, dau. of Berry and Mary (Little) Holcomb of Cherokee County, Ga. Mary Little had a brother who was a member of the State Senate.

Children: Jane, married Robert Wilson; Winchester, married Sallie Horton; Lee served in the Confederate army; never married; Orpha, single; Linn, single; Ruth married Emanuel Gerber; W. W. married Molly Park; Harriet, single. His wife dying, Eli married Mrs. Nancy Hill. Children: Augusta married E. A. McHan, for many years editor and manager of the Walker County Messenger; also a prominent and noted Mason; Lydia, single.

W. W. Center's children: Molly, invalid; Harry, married Beth Rhyne; Eli, single.

Miss Orpha, as she is familiarly and affectionately called, is one of the historic characters of LaFayette. As a small lass she came into the town with her father in 1850, and from that day, now 82 years, she has been intimately acquainted with, and associated with the life of the town. She is able to recall much of our antebellum history, but on the exciting and distressing times of the Civil War her recollection is most accurate and acute. Naturally possessed of an alert and receptive intellect, she is able to recall many historic occurrences of her long life and discuss them with great intelligence. For almost half a century she and her sister, Miss Linn, presided as hostesses at the "Center House," a hostlery, noted for its home-like surroundings and its culinary attractions. During these many years, Miss Orpha, the gracious hostess that she was, probably entertained more court officials, high and low, as well as travelling men than any other person in the county.

In 1925 she had the misfortune to fall from her steps and sustained a broken hip. Being at that time about 85 years of age and of heavy build, it was feared that she might not survive the accident; but while she has been confined to her bed for these seven years she is still hale and hearty and bids fair to reach the century mark, as all her admirers and well-wishers pray may be the case. As an example of the love and esteem in which she is held the ladies of the Baptist church of which she is a member named one of their missionary societies in her honor, The Orpha Center Circle.

GEORGE LANE CHASTAIN.

George Lane, son of Benjamin LaFayette and Eliza Harwell Chastain, was born in Walker county, Ga., May 16, 1859. Attended the schools of LaFayette and Sumac Seminary, in Murray county. Taught school at Snodgrass Hill (Chickamauga battlefield) and at Floyd Springs, near Rome. Entered the Atlanta Medical College 1880 and graduated with the class of 1882. Practiced at Plainville for two years.

In June 25, 1884, Dr. Chastain married Miss Mattie Kiker, of Calhoun, where he practiced his profession until called to preach the gospel in the spring of 1893. Admitted into the North Georgia Conference, the session of 1893, and appointed to Spring Place, thence to Tunnel Hill, Everett Springs and Hamilton Street, Dalton, where Mrs. Chastain passed away on January 14, 1902. Children: Irene (Mrs. E. L. Blackwood, Atlanta), and Eddie Mae (Mrs. T. H. Lang, of Calhoun).

After his apointment to North Rome, at the conference of 1903, Dr. Chastain married Miss Nina Oxford, of Dalton, on Nov. 25. In 1906 he was sent to St. John, LaGrange, 1907-08-09-10; Woodbury, 1911; Center Street, Atlanta, 1912-13-14-15; North Rome, 1916-17-18-19-20-21; Third Church and Kincaid, Griffin, 1922-23; South LaGrange, 1924; St. John, LaGrange, 1925-26-27-28; Warm Springs, 1929-30-31.

Dr. Chastain passed away on the morning of May 20, 1931, and was laid to rest in beautiful Fain cemetery, Calhoun, on May 22.

GARMANY.

Hamilton Garmany was one of three brothers who migrated from Scotland about the year 1800. Hamilton settled in Gwinnette county, Georgia, where he reared a family of five children, one of whom, William Newton, later came with his father, Hamilton, to Walker county and settled in McLemore's Cove before the Civil War. Wash, another son, also came with his father to the county.

William Newton, born 1828, married Addie Knox, to which union were born ten children, as follows: Mary Brooks; Maggie Scudder; Emma Wyatt; Ida Connally; Lula Hall; Hampton, married Nola Bonds; Knox, married Eula Jennings; Robert married Julia Jones; Clark married Splint Davis; John, died young. For more than fifty years, William Newton Garmany lived in the Cove, reared and educated this large family, and was one of the most influential and prominent farmers of that section. He owned one of the finest farms in the Cove, still known as the Garmany farm. He died in 1912 at the age of 84.

Robert Garmany, born 1861, married Julia (born 1861), daughter of L. W. and Mary (McCleary) Jones. In this home were born the following children: Perry, married Margaret Betts. They have three children and live in Chattanooga. Robert died young. John, married Mary Wilks. Four children, home Pensacola, Florida. Wirt, married Martha Hutcheson. They have three children and live at Ashville, N. C. Jennie May, single.

Robert Garmany was reared on his father's farm in McLemore's Cove where he received his education in the common schools of the county. His early days were spent as a farmer. In 1902 he was elected sheriff of the county and moved to LaFayette where he has since resided, reared and educated his family. For 14 years he served the county as sheriff, longer by several years than any other officer has held that important position, since the organization of the county. Mr. Garmany, now rapidly advancing in years, is still quite active and takes great interest in l'fe's affairs. He is one of the county's loyal and much respected citizens.

JOHN M. CLARKSON.

It is not known when John Clarkson came from England to America. Among other children he had a son, Joseph, born 1792 in North Carolina, who married Nancy Gober, born 1794. Their children were John, William, James, Wesley, Martha, Mary, Nancy, Harriet, Dan, and Green. With this large family Joseph came into McLemore's Cove in the early thirties while the Indians were still occupying this region.

James H. (1819-1884), married Jane Hammond (1821-1884), and their children were William, John M., Elizabeth, July A., Sarah A., Cicero, Roxanna, Jerome, Albina, and Ova. Of these, John M., born 1842, married Amanda Lawrence (1850-1928) to which union were born M. E. (dcd.), Lela, James (dcd.), William, Arthur, Minnie and Byron (decd.), Reno, Luck, Lee.

John M. grew to manhood on his father's farm and when about 19 years of age enlisted in the Southern Confederacy and followed the "Stars and Bars" to the surrender. He had a brother, William, and an uncle, Dan, who met death at the hands of the Gatewood raiders. After the war he settled in Duck Creek valley and reared and educated a large family of children.

J. M. CLARKSON

Mr. Clarkson is now hale and hearty at the age of 90 years. He is a worthy and highly respected citizen and bids fair to round out a century which all his friends devoutly wish he may do. He makes his home with his son, Lee, near Chickamauga.

NEWTON WHITE.

William White, a soldier of the Revolution, lies buried at the White cemetery one mile east of Villanow. His grave was marked by the D. A. R. some twenty years ago. It is said that following the Revolution, in some forgotten manner, Mr. White received a blow on the head with a blunt instrument or weapon which caused a pressure on the brain and which was never relieved, causing him, to the end of his days, to be wanting in mentality. The official marker erected by the D. A. R. bears the single name "Wm. White."

Newton White was a son of William White. He was born in South Carolina August 11, 1798. His first wife was Edna Cooper, who died in 1848. His second wife was Sarah A. Bolt, who died in 1890. Newton died 1889 and is buried in the White cemetery. He was one of the pioneer settlers of the county.

Augustus P. White, son of Newton, was born near Villanow July 30, 1851, and is now in his 81st year. His first wife was Sereptia Harris, who died in 1873; his second wife was Cordelia Harmon who is still in life.

THE CHAMBERS FAMILY.

This family lived in England during the political and religious disturbances of the 17th century. Dissenting from the Church of England, they emigrated to Scotland, thence to Ireland about 1700. Being protestants they did not like the catholicism of the Irish, and longing for religious freedom they migrated to America and settled at Chambersburgh, Penn., and after a time branches of the family scattered to the South and West.

Early in the 19th century Elihu Chambers and son William removed from Haywood county, N. C., to Habersham county, Ga. Elihu had fought through the Revolutionary war including the battle of King's Mountain. William served as a soldier of the War of 1812, later in the Mexican War, and assisted General Winfield Scott in the removal of the Cherokees from North Georgia. William was born in Haywood county, N. C., in 1792. He married an excellent young woman named Jane Hughes, to which union were born the following: Samuel H., Joseph W., Gabriel J., William A., Albert and Margaret.

William owned and operated gold mines in Habersham county, later moving to Whitfield county, and thence to Walker county, where he settled near Villanow immediately preceding the War Between the States. Here the family lived during that fratricidal strife and for several years afterward. He was living with his son Gabriel when he died at Morganville, Dade county, in 1882, in his 91st year.

Samuel, Joseph and Albert sacrificed their lives for the Southern Confederacy. Gabriel was most severely wounded while making a charge to take Little Round Top at Gettysburg. Samuel, Albert and Margaret never married. Margaret died at her brother Gabriel's, at Morganville, in 1878. Joseph had a daughter, Mary, who married John Hill at Subligna, Ga., who went to Oklahoma.

Gabriel married Miss Fannie Tittle, daughter of George Tittle of Dade county. Their family consists of Prentice C., Custer L., Roscoe D., Sadie, Monta, and Blande, all living in California except Sadie who married Hal Patton, a mechanical draughtsman, who lives in Cleveland, Ohio. Blande is also married. Gabriel was an exemplary citizen, whose memory is sacred to this writer. He died in Chattanooga in 1909.

William Adams Chambers was born in Habersham county, Ga., January 26, 1832. He was living at Villanow, Walker county, when the War Between the States broke out, where he volunteered, joining Co. C. 8th Ga. Bat. Inf. He served as first sergeant of his company through the war, acting at times as captain. He was in the numerous campaigns of Joseph E. Johnston in Mississippi, Alabama and Georgia, and with General Bragg at Missionary Ridge and other battles. Sixty-four of his company went into the Chickamauga battle and thirty-two came out,—a fifty per cent loss. He and his comrades and close personal friend, Cicero T. Clements, brother of Hon. Judson C. Clements, were captured near Atlanta during the fighting of that campaign and were carried to Indiana by their captors. Near the end of the war William A. taught school near Jeffersonville, Indiana, in a community of Southern sympathisers, or copperheads, as they were called.

WILLIAM A. CHAMBERS

Shortly after the war he returned to Georgia and taught school at Morganville, Dade county, where he was married to Miss Sarah Queen Tittle, daughter of George and Sallie Hale Tittle, whose family consisted of Mary, Didama, Bettie, Charles, Martha, Kizziah, Sarah, Annie, David, Fannie, Susannah, Nannie, and George Washington and Andrew Jackson, twins, who died in infancy. George Tittle emigrated from Virginia and Sallie Hale, his wife, from Tennessee. He was owner of a large plantation in Dade county which he cultivated with slave labor, being a most successful farmer in his day. He was somewhat deaf and was killed by an A. G. S. train near his home in 1866. His wife passed in 1877.

William A. Chambers was teacher, farmer, merchant, postmaster, and Justice of the Peace. He belonged to the Masonic fraternity. He was the only master of his local Grange, and only president of his local Farmer's Alliance Lodge. He was a typical Southern gentleman. His wife, Sarah Tittle (1847-1913), was a woman of rare personality and attainments, who, in the language of a friend, was "every inch a lady." William A. and his wife were married in 1868; his death occurred in 1913. His children were as follows: Charles A., Oscar N., W. D. B., Colquitt, Paul, Joseph E., James B., Philip, Nellie, Grace and Lily.

Charles A., like his father has followed various occupations,—farmer, teacher, merchant, postmaster, Notary Public, and is now member of the Board of Roads and Revenue of Walker county. He married Miss Kittie McInness of near Valdosta, Ga., April 14, 1904. She was the daughter of John and Margaret McIntyre McInness. John McInness was a Confederate soldier, serving under General Joseph Wheeler, and a successful farmer. His wife was a teacher and active in church and club work. The family of Charles A. and his wife consists of J. W., Trudeau G., Queen Madge, Iva J., and Elsie G.

Oscar N. married Miss Dora Ingle, daughter of John and Mollie Morrison Ingle. Their children are: Bee, Ennis, Glenn, Foy and Jamie. Oscar was a teacher and successful lawyer, having graduated with first honors in the University of Chattanooga Law School. He died 1928.

W. D. B. was teacher and merchant. He founded and published for a number of years "The Dade County Sentinel," Later he founded and published "The Rossville New Age," for a number of years. He married Miss Daisy Tatum, daughter of Hon. and Mrs. M. A. B. Tatum of Trenton, Ga. He has two daughters, Josephine and Evelyn.

Colquitt was teacher and merchant. He died in 1930; single. Paul was merchant and artisan. Died 1932; single. Joseph E. was clerk in the Chattanooga postoffice when he died in 1916; single. James B. was connected with the Chattanooga postoffice when he died in 1909; single. Philip was telegrapher and printer. His death occurred in 1911; single.

Nellie is one of the county's popular and successful teachers. Grace has been teacher. She is married; has a daughter, Beryl. Lily was teacher, also prose and poetry author, writing much for the press. She married George V. Kern of Adamsville, Ohio. She has a daughter, Valerie.

MILLICAN.

Thomas J. Millican was born in Alabama in 1850. He was left an orphan when a small lad, being cared for by his grandfather, Wm. Millican, till his death during the Civil war. He came to the county during the fifties and during the war and for many years afterward he endured the many hardships incident to those times of deprivation, especially for an orphan boy. During these lean and distressing years Thomas knew what it meant to go without wholesome food at times as well as without sufficient clothing, probably, for this was the common experience of most orphan children of his age and day. By dint of hard study he gained a smattering knowledge of reading and arithmetic which later in life he was able to augment by careful study, so that he became well-informed on general subjects. Early in life he became a member of the Antioch Baptist church which he was faithful to attend and support.

In 1875 he married Mary Savannah, dau. of Alvin and Martha Ann (Hawkins) Leslie. Mr. Leslie came to the county from Hall county and became one of the well-known and well-to-do citizens of the Cove. He was a prominent Mason and Baptist. His death brought sadness to his host of friends by its tragic circumstances—being burned to death in a building in 1911.

FAMILY RECORD. Children: The first two, Della and Oliver, died young. Homer married Maggie Freeman, and they have five children. Freeman married Stella Mitchel, they have five. Bert married Vesta Laster, two children. James married Maude Mason, two children. Leroy, single. Clyde married Mary Lou Mathis, two children.

Chapter Forty-five

(The following blank pages have been inserted in the county history with the earnest wish of the author that they may be utilized from year to year to make additional records of historical matters as they occur, and thus keep the history up-to-date. Any interesting events in the community life—school, church, graveyard, roads, etc., should be recorded. Likewise, county affairs, as records of county officers, courts, and various other matters. These records should be neatly and correctly made with pen-and-ink. If utilized with care, sufficient space is here to make records for many years).

Chapter Forty-six

GRAVEYARDS.

Tombstone Inscriptions.

HAVING visited practically all the graveyards in the county and examined the graves and markers, I hope I may be pardoned for making these observations, not in a spirit of criticism, but from a sincere desire to be of aid in keeping these hallowed spots beautified.

I note that almost every graveyard has cedar trees growing among the graves. So far as I know there is no objection to this tree as a shade or beautifier, except for its influence on the markers. I have noticed almost without exception that markers near a cedar are discolored and rusty and dark; moss growing on many of them. This is true to some extent with other trees, but the cedar seems to be especially detrimental to the appearance of marble. I would suggest that some other tree be made to take the place of the cedar. How would the apple tree do? I have found one cemetery with a number of large apple trees growing among the graves. I thought they looked well. They are clean and beautiful and seem to affect the markers less than other trees.

Most of the cemeteries are in good to fair condition. Occasionally one is found that is not well-kept. Erosion has been at work there as elsewhere and some stones have been undermined and toppled over, some being broken thereby. Some graves are sunken and present an unsightly appearance.

It is interesting, too, to note the changes in the style of markers. Half a century ago the markers were of two or three kinds—the tall slender monument, the thin head slab, or the horizontal slab covering the grave. Most of these are frail and poorly adapted to withstand the changes incident to the passage of time. The tendency now is toward low, heavy or bulky stones. These are much less liable to topple or fall and if once placed with care will remain in position indefinitely.

The custom of erecting a double marker for husband and wife is a beautiful one. This is often done when one of the partners dies, all names and dates being engraved except the date of the death of the one surviving. It is noted that in very many cases this last date is never placed on the marker, which is to be regretted.

LaFayette Cemetery.—Tombstone Inscriptions.

Established about 1833. Number of graves about 2500.

Matilda Johnson 1827-1897. "Erected by the devoted pupils and friends of Walker and Chattooga counties to their beloved teacher. She labored long and well.—Her works follow her and many rise and call her blessed. 'He giveth His beloved sleep'." (This is a handsome stone and is most appropriately placed at the resting place of this faithful old teacher. During her life of seventy years, most of them spent in the school room, she wielded a power for good in the young lives of her pupils that lives on and on. Though dead she still speaks through their lives.)

The following inscription is copied from an old rough lime-stone marker exactly as it appears: "Sacred to the Memory of WILLIAM FARISS who died in the year 18 Hundred & 35 in the 85 year of his Age. A Soldier of the American REVOLUTION, A faithful Friend, & an Honest Man." At the foot is a marker erected by the D. A. R. with this inscription: Wm. Fariss, Ga. Mil. Rev. War.

"In memory of Col. Samuel Fariss 1797-1862. God grant that his children in all their generations may meet him with our beloved mother in heaven." By his side lies his wife Rebecca 1799-1848.

Benjamin Franklin Thurman 1844-1916; T. E. Patton D. 1880 A. 71; James Erwin Patton 1855-1926; John R. Wardlaw 1829-1883; Mary C. Wardlaw 1840-1910; Joseph Jackson Patton, Born in Buncomb Co. N. C., 1815, Died in LaFayette, Ga. 1879; R. N. Dickerson 1845-1915. "48 years Clerk Superior Court Walker County." Dr. Peter S. Anderson 1823-1924 (101 yrs.); Captain J. C. Wardlaw 1827-1916; P. D. Fortune 1854-1926; Wife 1856-1927; John A. Shaw 1856-1927; Alexander A. Simmons 1823-1894; Andrew P. Allgood 1816-1882; Wife Mary A. 1827-1920 (93 yrs.); D. F. Allgood 1787—Age 90 yrs.; Wife, Alice Lawson 1797—Age 86 yrs.

Spencer Marsh born Chattham Co. N. C. 1799—Died LaFayette, Ga. 1875. Ruth Terrell Marsh Born Chattham Co. N. C. 1799. D. LaFayette Ga. 1881; Dr. J. J. Marsh b. Chattham, N. C. 1830. D. Walker Co. Ga. 1885; Florida, wife of J. J. Marsh, b. Winchester, Tenn. 1835. D. La-Fayette, Ga. 1888. Rev. Wm. T. Russell 1830-1911; Wife, Mary L. 1831-1894; Amos Wellborn 1776-1854; Rev. Alexander Robeson of Buncomb Co. N. C. 1792-1868; George Innman 1836-1906, Wife 1859-1916; T. B. Lawrence 1856-1904; Wife 1859-1916; H. A. Sims 1863-1914 (Mizpah); Andrew Lawson Barry 1805-1892 (87 yrs.); John Dickson, died 1896, Age 75 yrs.; James Park 1785-1866 (81 yrs.). Wife Martha 1785-1851; C. C. Bryan 1840-1923 (83 yrs.); Thomas Foster M. D. Died 1847, age 45; Rev. William Quillin, 1799-1842. JOHN T. WOODS pvt. Med. Dept. March 14, 1921; Dr. Dewitt C. Fariss 1829-1891; James Herbert Hill 1864-1917; James P. Shattuck, 1862-1921; Claude W. Route 1876-1923; James Andrews Park 1834-1918 (84 yrs.); Ann E. Park 1838-1912; Hugh P. Lumpkin 1846-1915; J. F. Shaw 1850-1929; W. A. Foster 1841-1912; Wife Nannie 1843-1925 (82 yrs.); D. W. Stewart 1876-1918; Wife Jewell 1881-1921; Pierce B. Little 1856-1926; E. Foster 1839-1914; Joseph Parks Hall 1853-1928; Wife Martha Conley 1855-1883; Dr. James W. Nash 1841-1923 (82 yrs.); Wife Elizabeth 1841-1918; J. S. Tate 1855-1928; J. M. Moreland 1861-1923; William Robert Craig 1855-1929; Wife

Geneva 1862-1926; W. C. Moreland 1860-1927; Samuel J. Shaw 1855-1924; Oliver Thurman 1856-1924; Wife Albena 1857-1923; George Erastus Walraven 1876-1922.

Captain JAMES MARION JACKSON 1841-1920, Capt. Co. G, 11 Ga. Vol. C. S. A. Soldier, Scholar, Educator, Christian Gentleman. Good Night Great Heart. Laura Anderson, wife J. M. Jackson 1848-(?).

Isabella Steele, wife of Earl Jackson 1864-1920. "Loving, loyal and true to her people, her country and her God, she gave her life in sacrificial service."

NATHAN CAMPBELL NAPIER 1834-1902. Capt. Co. K, 6 Ga. Cav. C. S. A. "One of the many soldiers of the Lost Cause, who, though grievously wounded in battle continued to the last to hazard life and sacrifice fortune in support of their convictions, which devotion defied despair and challenged the admiration of mankind."

"Journalist, Scholar, Patriot, Churchman, his relations in life were manifold, to his family, his associates, his country—in them all he was an ideal of love and loyalty."

Wife, Julia Sharpe Napier, 1840-1906.

Sergeant ERNEST W. BARRON, 1897-1925; HERMAN R. HUGHES, 1894-1922. Pvt. DEWEY MORELAND, Co. D. 16th Inf. and 2nd M. G. Battalion 1899-1920. Died of G. S. W. received in France.

ROBERT W. MOORE, Pvt. 101st Engineers 26th Div. 1893-1920. St. Mihiel—Meus—Argonne—Defensive Sector.

Mrs. Mary Nicholson Chastain, daughter of a Revolutionary soldier, is buried here.

BRYAN GRAVEYARD. Established about 1863. Number graves 130. Emaline Helton 1834-1919; J. F. Bryan, Sr., 1843-1925. Confederate Veteran, Co. D. 39 Ga. Wife F. D. Bryan 1846-1925; H. G. Keown 1845-1899, wife Martha 1846-1918; Dr. J. M. Fulmer 1859-1891; Martha P. Brown 1847-1916; Elizabeth Foster 1852-1904; Willie A. Lowery, wife J. D. Martin 1853-1888; Martha M. Mills, wife J. W. Lowery 1853-1890; D. A. Martin 1856-1914, Mrs. D. A. Martin 1861-1927; Andrew Tyner, C. S. A. Wm. Johnston C. S. A. Thomas Bryan 1793-1878 (85), Thomasin Bryan 1824-1918 (94); Andrew Jackson Sims 1849-1922, Wife Margaret Shamblin 1849-1901; Joseph A. Williams 1855-1900, Wife Emma 1855-1895; L. C. Bryan 1848-1923; W. A. Martin 1851-1924; Wife, Mollie E. 1853-1925; W. J. Martin 1828-1888, Wives (1) Jane 1832-1874, (2) Nancy 1832-1883, (3) Rebecca 1846-1894; Mary Jane Fulmer 1836-1878. J. W. Fulmer, died about 1922, age about 74 is buried here, grave unmarked; also, his second wife. Also, E. D. Mitchel 1849-1928, grave unmarked.

SINGLETERRY CEMETERY. About 200 graves. Laid out (?). Drury D. Singleterry 1822-1897, First wife, Elizabeth 1820-1863, Second wife, Rachel 1820-1890; Mary J. Singleterry 1847-1863; Aunt Eliza Singleterry 1810-1894; Francis M. Singleterry 1857-1900, wife, Sallie M. 1858-

1893; Flora Singleterry Bridges 1875-1890; T. J. Johnson 1840-1904, Wife, (1), Susan 1842-1881, Wife, (2), Sarah 1849-1902; James R. Shaw 1850-1908; Columbus C. Boss 1853-1913, wife, Rhoda A. 1854-1923; Mary M. Mallicoat 1859-1916; Jerry M. Leath 1869-1927; Arba F. Shaw 1844-1909, Wife, Rebecca 1852-1920; G. W. Shaw 1854-1913; Martha A. Broom 1842-1917; J. V. Johnson 1857-1924, Wife, Sarah Hartman, 1855-1918; Mamie Ramsey Smith 1822-1893; Wm. H. Fricks 1866-1897; Ramsey Fricks 1860-1922; J. H. Wyatt 1853-1928, Wife, Emma O. 1852-1926; H. L. Cambron 1825-1909 (84); Mary E. Shook 1854-1930; N. G. Johnson 1855-1923, Wife Annie Ellison 1855-1928; Frances Ann Johnson 1849-1904; Zillie Johnson Sterns 1875-1901; Aunt Ann Weathers 1845-1900; George W. Johnson 1837-1909.

PAYNE'S CHAPEL CEMETERY (Lookout Mountain).

Number of graves about 113. George Hixon gave the ground for the cemetery and was the first one buried there in 1894.

John C. Hinkle 1846-1907; William F. McCallie 1863-1921; John Scarborough 1849-1916; Francis Hixon 1815-1897 (85); W. M. Hixon 1816 (80); J. W. Morton 1857-1922; His wife 1865-1926; Rev. W. J. Drennon 1831-1903; R. V. Hinkle 1842-1917; Catherine S. Massey 1842-1929 (87); George Hixon 1820-1894; W. W. Hixon 1850-1921; Sallie M. Prothro 1829-1910 (81); Mary A. Hixon 1856-1926; J. R. Hixon 1860-1926; Mary Miller 1844-1909; W. F. Miller 1828-1904; Leah Massey 1835-1903; Nathan T. Massey 1835-1925; Sarah F. Gossett 1842; John W. Gray 1862-1916.

WESLEY CHAPEL. Estab. 1861.

Andy Grier 1767-1869 (102); Mrs. Jane McDonald Died 1861, first person buried here. Elizabeth Harris 1801-1881 (80); Wm. Lowery 1809-1869; John Wilbanks 1847-1929; B. F. Roberts 1819-1888; Miss Jane Dowdy 1825-1904; Mrs. Jane Poe 1825-1894; Mrs. George W. Wilson 1865-1920; Benjamin C. Wilson 1845-1914; C. P. Allen 1843-1916; Mrs. C. P. Allen 1845-1908; David P. Allen (?)-1869; Robert A. Robinson 1856-1929; Jeremiah Burns 1842-1920, wife 1845-1929; Mary Eliza Allen 1839-1911; Mary E. Hovis 1858-1881; Overton Harris 1830-1908; Mary E. Lowery 1839-1922; Julia A. Lowery 1857-1919; John T. Lewis 1847-1921; W. M. Allen 1813-1907 (94); J. W. Hill 1815-1899 (84); R. A. Hill 1842-1928 (86).

GARRETT'S CHAPEL. Number graves 100. Established 1884. Joseph McClure 1856-1920; J. M. Duncan 1838-1920 (82). R. E. Madaris 1864-1918; Frank Garrett is buried in family plot near by, died in 1883, age about 75.

FRIENDSHIP CEMETERY. Estab. about 1850. Number of graves 180. Mrs. Starrett Dobson was the first person buried here. Died 1850. Age about 40. Mrs. Arthur Davis died about 1860 age 50. Harris Hammontree died 1861 age 75. His wife died 1861 age 73. Mandy Shahan died

1872 age 60. Marion Hammontree died 1865 age 35. W. C. Self died 1910 age 77. His wife died 1916 age 79. Harden Moreland died 1899 age 82. His wife died 1895 age 80. None of these have markers.

THURMAN GRAVEYARD, near Cedar Grove. Number graves about 223. Est. 1850. Nancy C. Corgim 1861-1888; Wm. Rawlings 1859-1883; Elendar Rawlings 1800-1880 (80); Henry H. Stone 1852-1887; C. A. Hise and M. J. Hise (No dates); E. E. Hale 1863-1921; Amanda, wife M. Massey 1870-1904; Wheeler Sams 1868-1916; Alice Sams, Year 1813; William A. Woods 1858-1922; Peggy D. Catlett 1881-1913; Sally Catlett 1789-1876 (87); George W. Catlett, No date; the following is graved on an old rough lime rock marking a grave: "Henry Hise was Bourned February 9, 1812 and died July 6, 1894"; Laura Roberts 1877-1908; Miles Whitlow 1812-1885; Elizabeth A. Whitlow 1821-1898. On the north side of this handsome marker is this: Ida 1857-1863 (Jan. 23); George W. 1859-1863 (Jan. 28); Jefferson D. 1862-1863 (Feb. 15). Showing that Mr. Whitlow lost three children within less than a month—a tragedy.

Martin Fralix 1795-1870; Anthony Voiles 1819-1893; Pricilla Voiles 1826-1901; Susan G. Voiles 1861-1898; Emeline Voiles 1849-1926; Anna G. Colquitt 1845-1906; Elizabeth Wallin 1831-1866; W. D. Bailey 1829-1891; George W. Reed 1790-1873 (81).

ANTIOCH. Number of graves 242. Laid out 1882.

E. W. White 1830-1882 (First person buried); Fannie Forester, wife S. R. Smith 1868-1894; Nannie Lou Smith 1866-1893; Preston B. Smith 1859-1889; Roxanna Hunt 1834-1905; J. F. Smith 1830-1920 (90); N. Evitt 1836-1891; W. L. Owings 1837-1900; Wife Sarah 1848-1909; Mrs. Avilla Colquitt 1858-1906; R. J. Morgan 1846-1889; Elizabeth, wife Wm. Morgan 1811-1887; Elexanna wife C. W. Evatt 1838-1921 (83); Wesley A. Kenman, 1832-1898; James V. Bell 1875-1910; Robert Berry Camp 1857-1922; Julia Camp 1863-1928; Caswell Camp 1828-1897; J. W. Head 1828-1899; wife Sarah 1823-1884; W. H. Tatum 1855-1923; Wife Mary C. 1854-1929; Mary Pearl Tatum 1890-1907; J. I. Head 1852-1896; Wife Donnie Shields 1856-1896; James R. Shankle 1856-1924; Rebecca Shankle 1859-1908; Vesta Wheeler Shankle 1857-1929; BURL E. TURNER 1897-1919 (World War Soldier); Emma, wife C. L. Evitt 1865-1904; J. L. Bullard 1849-1906; Alvin T. Leslie 1836-1911; Wife Martha 1838-1906; T. J. Millican 1850-1919; Martha Bemberton 1822-1906 (84); Captain J. Y. Wood 1834-1919 (85); Wife Mary E. 1836-1919 (83); Roberta Wood wife Rev. D. P. Lee 1866-1901; Dr. Frank L. Wood 1868-1919; Mary Lou Wood 1872-1898; John Wood 1879-1899; W. C. Evitt 1868-1920; John Sidney Fincannon 1828-1902; Alexander Andrews 1823-1905; Wife Sarah E. 1839-1912; Archie Steele Andrews 1903-1928; H. H. Glenn 1861-1914; Charles W. Evitt 1838-1909; Wife Mary Shaw 1828-1901; James Oveys 1855-1923; Mary E. wife W. A. Hatfield 1843-1914; W. A. Hatfield Age 77 (No marker); Wm. R. Fowler 1866-1898; Thomas M. Rowland Died 1907, Age 74; Nancy Evitt, wife T. M. Rowland 1833-1898; J. L. Evitt 1822-1900; S. A. Weathers 1840-1900; Wife Rachel 1833-1895;

Julia Akins 1852-1927; Thomas Akins 1849-1918; Clayton Tatum 1852-1924; Wife Lucy 1855-1926; John V. Pearce 1873-1926; Hardy L. Tatum born in N. C. 1831, Married Miss Mary Foster 1851, Died 1905; Wife Mary Foster 1834-1903; Pleasant Loyd 1817-1892; Wife Margaret L. 1811-1887; John B. Bell 1819-1884; wife Elizabeth 1817-1885; William B. Simmons, M. D., Born Floyd Co. Va. 1829-1889; Corrie Wallin 1857-1897; G. W. Harp 1826-1904; Wife Martha 1826-1922 (96); Martha Leona Hise 1878-1895; T. M. Hensley, Con. Vet. buried here. Died 1931, age about 92. (No marker).

CHATTOOGA. Number graves about 360. Est. about 1840.

Martha O. Day 1834-1891; N. H. Day 1832-1912 (80); E. F. Day 1857-1906; J. L. Day 1855-1897; George Nations 1850-1903; M. J. Cordle 1861-1921; James A., son of T. J. and Americus Blackwell 1821-1891; Jane Littlejohn 1841-1907; Abram Littlejohn 1837-1914; T. K. Purcell 1833-1909; M. Purcell 1833-1902; Nancy E. Roach 1859-1898; W. M. Nix 1865-1906; Eliza I. Gore 1860-1885; Sophia Jackson 1820-1883; Mary Ann Mitchel 1858-1915; J. G. Milligan 1886-1907; Charles Milligan 1854-1928; Rebecca Keith Milligan 1860-(?); Rev. Abraham B. Sizemore 1853-1925; Melissa Sizemore 1856-1911, "I have fought a good fight, I have finished my course, I have kept the faith."

Elizabeth, wife of W. B. Williams 1844-1883; Sallie Vann died 1896, age 72. Mary E. wife D. J. Hammond 1851-1904; Daniel J. Hammond 1849-1888; B. L. RICHARDSON Co. B. Phillips Ga. Leg. C.S.A. 1841-1920; Sarah E., wife of J. L. Haas 1853-1895; Mary Emma Haas wife J. L. Shamblin 1874-1894; Lina E. Strickland 1847-1903; Simon Y. Strickland 1822-1895; Jeremiah G. Blackwell 1803-1884 (81); Peggy Ann Blackwell 1809-1885; Sarah Wall 1812-1895 (83); Jonathan Wall 1809-1885; Sarah A. Wall 1832-1904; Reuben A. Jennings 1851-1904; Sarah Ann Jennings 1852-1914; S. R. Williams 1843-1895; Martha J., wife L. R. Williams 1850-1886; Nancy, wife J. G. Lumpkin 1850-1886; J. G. Lumpkin 1806-1892 (86); Thomas H. Lumpkin 1847-1896; Martha Ella Underwood 1864-1899; J. A. Hale 1852-1908; Joseph Hale 1857-1897; B. L. McConnell son of J. D. and F. B. McConnell 1872-1924; J. D. McConnell 1851-(?); Frances R. McConnell wife J. D. McConnell 1854-1910; A. J. Price 1831-1886; Nancy Price 1831-1900; Mary Lucindy Boss 1842-1900; Henry Wilson Boss 1844-1924; John Atwood 1829-1999; L. C. wife John A. Woods 1845-1927; Joseph Underwood M.D. 1826-1891; Sarah G. Phillips, wife of Joseph Underwood 1832-1858; Eliza F. Alexander, wife R. W. Blackwell 1832-1896.

"Joseph Price, son of Joseph and Nicy Price, born in Spartanburg Dist. S. C., Oct. 30, 1804; joined the Baptist Church in 1825, Married Feb. 14, 1826 and died Sept. 11, 1872." "Elizabeth Price, Dau. of Thomas and Sarah Liles, Consort of John Price, was born in Rutherford Co., N. C., Dec. 28, 1800, Married Feb. 14, 1826, joined the Baptist Church in 1848, and died Dec. 16, 1870."

"Asleep in Jesus, Oh how sweet,
From which none ever wake to weep."

The above, neatly graven on the markers of Mr. and Mrs. Price, is an epitome of what they doubtless believed, and are, the four important events of life—birth, church connection, marriage, death.

Mrs. T. A. Cassady 1844-1902; Wilburn Wall 1812-1891; Clarrissa Wall 1821-1897; W. M. Curtis 1862-1895; Mrs. Caroline M. Blackwell, consort of Robert W. Blackwell and Dau. of James A. and Mary Turnley, 1827-1851; Nancy Ann, wife of G. W. Lumpkin 1814-1867; G. W. Lumpkin 1804-1876; Lecil Day 1821-1907 (86); Lehelia Day 1834-(?).

COULTER GRAVEYARD. Number of graves 232.

W. F. Turnley 1852-1912; Nettie Brooks, wife James M. Turnley 1886-1915; Alma Lee Hall 1885-1920; Wesley Parks Lee 1879-1910 (His last words: "How sweet to be at home."); Leila P. Wallin, wife of R. D. and Dau. of J. W. Lee 1876-1897; Martha, wife R. L. Wallin 1829-1917 (88); Robert L. Wallin 1822-1902; James H. Hunter 1854-1913; Wife Lucy 1857-1930; Mrs. James Parks Hall 1823-1907 (84); Robert Johnson 1846-1925, Wife Nelia 1843-(?); Lindsay Wallin 1885-1918; Stephen B. Phillips 1810-1898 (88); Julia Phillips 1813-1891; Mattie A. Fricks 1829-1876; Edgar M. Coulter 1849-1917; Wm. Coulter 1823-1879; M. L. Coulter 1824-1895; Mrs. N. E. Wallin 1864-1888; Wm. J. Wallin 1859-1924; Gertrude Bryden 1877-1895; Amos Thornburg 1835-1902, "Fell asleep in Birmingham Ala."; Martha A. Thornburg 1842-1889; J. W. Thornburg Died 1877 Aged 49; D. R. Fricks, (Other words illegible on stone); Captain A. L. CULBERSON Co. E. 39 Ga. C.S.A.; Mary Elizabeth Mitchell 1848-1898; Jesse Carter Morgan 1837-1913; Wife Henrietta N. Morgan 1835-1896; William Morgan 1812-1883; D. M. Guthery 1846-1919; Wife Sallie 1850-1892; Dr. J. C. Lee Died 1876 age 58; Wife Sarah Died 1863, age 42; M. I. Lee, (Mother) 1826-1898; William C. Lee 1855-1878; Mrs. J. A. Lee 1847-1902; James W. Lee 1848-1919; John D. Fricks 1842-1882; S. C. Camp 1853-1891; G. C. Baker 1842-1914, Wife L. J. Baker 1844-1914; J. H. Baker 1873-1904; Mollie E. Baker 1868-1891; Effey May Baker 1873-1899; William B. Guthery 1836-1894; P. H. G. McGuffey 1827-1900; Mary E. McGuffey 1839-1912; Mickey McCarty 1860-1923; A. J. Jarman 1845-1917; Martha McGuffey wife A. J. Jarman 1861-1920; Wm. A. Coulter 1856-1930.

DAVIS FAMILY PLOT. Davis Cross Road. Number Graves 12.

John Davis 1813-1892; Jane Davis 1830-1904; Julia Davis 1860-1861; Susannah Davis 1852-1872; Martin Davis 1809-1859; Julia Davis 1832-1882; Martin Jr. 1856-1871; Bessie Perry, Parks Hall, and Martin Luther, children of J. R. Davis, each about 1 yr. old.

PLEASANT HILL. Estab. about 1850. Number Graves 173.

Margaret Anderson 1842-1918; Mrs. R. S. Anderson 1876-1912; Reece Neal 1831-1904; Wife 1840-1905; Rebecca Neal 1808-1875; A. B. Neal

1809-1853; A. H. Neal 1840-1919 (79); Wife 1853-1923; W. M. Potts 1844-1929 (85); Wife 1846-1928 (82); William A. Yother 1885-1908; Rosena Franklin 1873-1908; Rebecca Moore 1841-1927 (86); W. G. Hewatt 1842-1882; Elizabeth Hewatt 1838-1921; W. H. Nemmett 1856-1906; R. W. Maloney 1844-1904; S. G. Maloney 1833-1910; Wife 1842-1910; B. P. Chapman 1861-1928; Blanch Chapman 1892-1919; Ellen Chapman 1888-1903; Manay Woodruff (?)-1855; Sarah Morton 1839-1870; Lewis Huggins 1848-1926; Malinda Huggins 1851-1922; James Huggins 1844-1903; Georgia Huggins 1879-1894; Octavia Bailey 1860-1923; Martha Coulter West 1858-1894; Mahalic Kearns 1826-1904; Ella McGill 1875-1898; Adaline McGill 1846-1897; R. B. McGill 1852-1901; Samuel McGill 1850-1909; Selican McGill 1853-1902; John McGill 1880-1895; Mary Jane McGill 1852-1893; J. M. Easterling 1856-1874; J. F. Evans 1818-1899 (81); Wife 1821-1892; Jane McKnight 1820-1899 (79); Henry McKnight 1856-1911; Betty Lee Karns 1853-1906; Vina Hargraves 1866-1899; Dora Hampton 1881-1909; Lillie Mae Gossett 1897-1917.

CHAPMAN FAMILY BURYING GROUND. Estab. 1863.

J. T. Chapman 1857-1900; W. J. Chapman 1825-1896; His Wife 1827-1907; J. H. Chapman 1779-1863 (83); His Wife 1808-1886; Robert Chapman 1827-1853; Jesse Chapman 1835-1854; John Chapman 1831-1856; Josephine 1865-1883; Mrs. C. F. Chapman 1855-1922; J. S. Chapman 1865-1928; Selettee Maloney 1852-1889; Drucilla Scoggins 1859-1922; Annie Lee Scoggins 1886-1904; Elender Grigsby 1832-1862; Wilson Lawrence 1880-1914.

PEAVINE CEMETERY. Estab. 1834. Number Graves about 1200.

Robert Patton 1834-1856; William Davis, Pioneer-Patriot-Soldier, 1786-1869, (83), (U.S.—U.S.D. 1812). Dr. Charles W. Shields 1876-1920; Maj. C. W. Simmons 1849-1876; D. W. Jones 1831-1900, Wife Martha Park 1835-1924; THOMAS WILLIAMS Co. B. 9th Inf. 2nd Division. Born 1895. Killed in Action Oct. 3, 1918. JAMES F. HILL Co. E. 6th Inf. Dec. 6, 1892. Wounded in service Nov. 4, 1918. Aug. 20, 1926. William A. Crow 1867-1918; Frank Cook 1863-1911; John Bird, 1834-1908, Wife Margaret 1842-1922; W. M. Cochran 1830-1911, Wife Jane 1837-1913; Louis J. Lupo 1853-1925; Wesley T. Lupo 1848-1906; W. T. S. Adams 1808-1892 (84); wife J. G. Adams 1806-1886 (80); Warren H. Lansford 1850-1905, Wife Millie J. 1851-1923; F. A. Thedford 1846-1926; Robert R. Shields 1852-1895, 1792-1867, (U.S.—U.S.D. 1812); James C. Cartwright Co. G. 12th Ga. Cav. C.S.A.; James A. Smith 1843-1925, Wife Carrie E. 1844-1930; M. D. Lansford 1836-1924; Rev. J. G. Cain 1826-1892; T. V. Williams 1825-1899, Wife, Mary A. 1826-1887; John S. Henderson 1805-1871, Wife Winifred B. 1818-1893; Daniel Bolton 1833-1901, Wife Martha 1839-1913; Richard Ward 1833-1904, Wife Rebecca L. Harwell 1831-1892; Mrs. David L. Trundell 1824-1890; Moses Park 1803-1863, Wife Susan 1807-1891; Mrs. A. Q. Simmons 1798-1850; William Glass 1822-1906, Wife Margaret 1825-1903; R. M. Catlett 1841-

1906, Wife Thursa G. 1845-1910; David C. Blaylock 1818-1903, Wife Caroline Beaty 1826-1909; Allen Thedford 1808-1882; Wife M. C. 1812-1898; George W. Cavender 1813-1889, Wife Nancy 1820-1884; J. W. Scott 1798-1889 (91).

MORGAN BURYING GROUND, near Pond Spring.

J. J. Morgan 1839-1909; Richard A. Fisher 1877-1909; Thomas A. Fisher 1849-1901; H. W. Boss 1809-1896 (87); Wife Susan 1824-1889; Susan A. Boss wife T. A. Fisher 1853-1919; R. J. Shaw wife J. J. Morgan, Born 1852, Married 1870, Died 1896.

THE COVE GRAVEYARD. 283 graves.

J. C. Hall 1820-1901; Martha A. Kilgore 1840-1917; Margaret L. Kilgore 1849-(?); Robert D. Kilgore 1842-1917; J. W. Clark 1863-1896; John G. Pierce 1826-1902; Lydia G. Pierce 1833-1900; Missouria, wife J. R. Camp 1858-1891; B. B. Cumpton 1867-1882; Eliza Camp 1840-1880, Married J. M. Glenn, 1858, W. B. Cumpton 1866; W. B. Cumpton 1821-1892; Lucian Strange 1858-1926; C. M. Hall 1811-1897 (86); Lavinia Tipton Hall 1821-1913 (92); Reuben Massey 1833-1863; Sarah Alexander 1848-1822; Tennie A., wife J. B. Bonds, Dau. J. C. and S. W. Hall, 1857-1880; Sarah, wife Rev. H. H. Porter 1826-1895; Rev. H. H. Porter 1818-1895; Dennis B. Baker 1801-1876; Mary J. wife J. G. Blackwell 1846-1894; H. G. Bonds 1853-1885; Mrs. Mary A. Hall 1842-1877; Eliza Ann 1820-1882; Peter W. Kilgore 1819-1893; Nargissa Adaline Garmany 1832-1883; Robert Lee (——)-1880; James M. Bonds 1803-1889 (86); T. A. Eubank 1832-1895; J. G. Hall 1843-1912; Mahanna wife Richard Morgan 1817-1882; "Sacred to the Memory of Susank, Consort of Richard A. Lane, who departed this life Oct. 24, 1841, Age 29"; Amanda Baker 1808-1885; Mrs. Jeremiah G. Blackwell 1830-1904; James B. Bonds 1851-1899; Millard F. Bonds 1853- 1929; Archibald Bonds 1807-1872; Sarah E. Kilgore 1817-1899; John Winters 1821-1885; Tahetha Bonds 1808-1874; Mrs. Martha Eubanks 1841-1891; Richard Morgan 1815-1880; Elizabeth Massey 1840-1919; Dr. J. L. Selman 1859-1896; Ruth Augusta Selman 1859-1887.

ANDERSON FAMILY PLOT. Number of graves about 20. ROBERT ANDERSON, born 1796, died 1887 (91). "Served in War of 1812."

MOON GRAVEYARD. Laid out about 1840. Number graves about 75. Wm. A. Vanhorn 1858-?; His wife Sophronia 1858-1927; Revis Marion Jones 1830-1912, His wife, Mary Moon, 1825-1918 (93); Edom Moon 1782-1879 (97); His wife, Obidince 1789-1863; Edom G. W. Moon 1831-1925, Mary A. Moon 1850-(?); W. M. Lail 1846-1922, Wife, Slena, 1848-1920. Here also is buried Louis Williams and wife, pioneers of the county who settled in the valley in the early thirties. Other old settlers also are resting here.

SUTTLE FAMILY PLOT, West Armuchee. John B. Suttle 1810-1875; Jane Young, wife John B. Suttle 1813-1878; Mary A. Suttle 1840-1873;

Sarah Suttle 1842-1919; Susan M. Suttle 1844-1918; JAMES THOMAS SUTTLE 1848-1925. Co. F. 1 Ga. Reg. Gen. Wheeler's Cav.; Emily Beautie McCullough 1853-1925; James Lawrence McCullough 1851-1884; Robert J. Young 1869-1894.

CATLETT FAMILY PLOT, near Noble. No. Graves about 30. Laid out 1870. H. M. Jones 1829-1887; Lewis Jones 1829-1913 (84); M. J. Boyles Jones D. 1902, A. 56; Frances M. Neyman 1846-1893; John M. Catlett 1825-1894; Eliza Jane Catlett 1833-1911; Miss M. A. Catlett 1849-1918; Peter Jones, D. 1930 Age 90, Wife Dicey. No markers. Billy Jones and wife buried here, no markers.

CLARKSON FAMILY PLOT, upper Cove. 7 graves. Roxanna Clarkson 1854-1866; William W. Clarkson 1840-1864; James H. Clarkson (?)-1883; Mrs. Jane Clarkson 1821-1882.

SMITH FAMILY PLOT, upper Cove. 16 graves. Mrs. Melisse Smith 1862-1922; Anderson Smith 1831-1896; Mrs. Anderson Smith 1837-1895.

BROWN GRAVEYARD in Cove. 9 graves. No markers.

LONG'S FAMILY PLOT, near Harrisburg. Margaret Emily Jones 1819-1898; Elizabeth Long 1818-1897; John P. Long 1805-1895 (90); Sarah Adaline Long 1811-1899 (88).

WILSON GRAVEYARD, near Rossville. Ground donated by Booker Wilson who is buried here. Number graves about 100. Very few markers. Edwin Graves died 1881; Mrs. Sarah Graves died 1880; Caleb Reynolds 1823-1898; Mrs. Mary Reynolds died 1893; Mrs. Parmelia Foster 1828-1888.

CHATTANOOGA VALLEY CEMETERY. Est. 1890. No. Graves about 450, many without markers, especially the early ones. Mattie Long 1873-1917; Nancy Precilla Long 1845-1913; John Deakins 1842-1900; Ollie Thurman 1862-1903; Elizabeth Allison 1837-1904; Mattie Rogers 1878-1903; Albert J. Allison 1842-1902; W. F. Allison 1832-1907; Minerva Allison 1836-1904; Margaret Long 1832-1908; H. W. Talley 1827-1900.

LAWRENCE BURYING GROUND, 3 miles west Rock Spring. No. graves 130. Est. 1845. Moses Jackson 1773-1857 (84); Rebecca Jackson 1773-1866 (93); Elizabeth Lawrence 1805-1887 (82); H. S. Loyd 1826-1892; Thomas Lawrence 1812-1873; Lucy Ware 1806-1877; Susannah Bowman 1846-1886; H. F. Wheeler 1818-1877; Susannah Bowman 1846-1886; Ansel Massey 1800-1879 (79); C. J. Wheeler 1832-1897; J. B. Wheeler 1829-1895; William Faulkner 1834-1866; E. N. Wheeler 1827-1898; C. C. Wheeler 1820-1901 (81); W. M. Wheeler 1827-1904.

TENNESSEE-GEORGIA MEMORIAL PARK, INC. Est. 1929. On Hogan Road 2 miles south of Rossville. Room for 156,000 graves. As yet only a few buried there but the convenience of location as well as the beautiful situation together with the dense and growing population in that part of the county combine to assure it as a popular and populous burying place for the future.

CEDAR GROVE GRAVEYARD. Number graves about 200. Est. about

1840. Most of the graves are unmarked. Bertha Hixon 1876-1924; Rebecca Hixon 1825-1888; Wesley Hobbs 1829-1814 (85); Mrs. E. J. Hobbs 1844-1922; A. J. Holland 1842-(?); Barbary Holland 1843-1914; Kittie E. Holland 1882-1900; W. M. Hunter 1794-1880 (86); Ellen Hunter 1794-1880 (86); W. R. Jackson 1850-1888; A. Sevier Jackson 1873-1898; R. E. Jackson 1855-(?); Margaret E. Jones 1841-1890; T. N. Jones 1839-1900; Mary A. Kell 1839-1888; Nimrod I. Kell 1837-1910; Mary S. Kerr 1862-1917; W. C. Millican 1777-1863 (86); Delilah Millican 1830-1894; W. P. Millican 1833-1906; Elizabeth Millican 1844-1882; James M. Millican 1836-1912; Mrs. Mary Millican 1862-1931; G. B. Rogers (dates illegible); Lizzie Rogers 1847-1912; H. W. Rogers 1822-1896; S. H. Rogers 1821-1891; Harvey W. Rogers 1863-1917; Mary Ann Smith 1841-1873; Rev. Rauswell Rogers 1789-1866; James Robinson 1875-1915; John L. Evitt 1873-1909; Lorena Evitt 1875-1909; Robert Marion Durham 1861-1931; William P. Frazier 1835-1911; Emma his wife 1861-1916; Catherine Forester 1806-1885; Galendar Forester 1807-1861; James Hixon 1832-1910; Rebecca Hixon 1825-1888; W. R. Henson 1859-1900; Nancy E. Henson 1831-1908; James Henson 1834-1889.

WHITE CEMETERY. one mile east of Villanow. Number graves 208. S. S. Phillips 1850-(?), Julian Phillips 1850-1924; Bartow Warnock 1861-1924; L. W. Bailey 1850-1911; Julia Ann Tudor, wife of Rev. Jesse W. Kinsey 1844-1919; Salena E. wife of F. A. Stansell 1858-1908; Mary, wife of Rial Stansell 1814-1886; Isabella White 1839-1904; Priestly G. White 1832-1912; J. W. Stansell 1840-1925; Elizabeth Williams, wife of Jesse Griffin 1845-1916; Jesse D. Griffin 1843-1915; Susannah Stancil wife of J. W. Bolt 1842-1911; Mary E. Warnock 1836-1909; Mary A. Love, wife of J. H. White 1846-1910; JOHN N. WHITE, Co. C. 23 Ga. Inf.

J. E. White, 1828-1910 (82). This stone is graved as follows:

> "Stranger, as you now are, so once was I;
> As I now am, so you must be,
> Prepare your self to follow me."

Martha B., wife J. E. White 1830-1905; Mary O. Bailey, 1864-1895; Rebecca E. Harmon 1850-1899; John Harmon 1844-1886; Newton White 1798-1889 (91); Edna, wife of Newton White, Died 1848, A. 46; THOMAS N. WHITE Co. K. 39 Ga. C.S.A. 1838-1861. WM. WHITE, Rev. War.

There is a rare, if solemn, fascination in visiting alone an ancient burying ground and spending some time in serious meditation as one looks at and reads the names and epitaphs graven on the markers. It is easy to imagine one's self as living a century back and acting in the long ago. Surrounded thus by the dead, one may recall some of the beautiful verses of Gray's Elegy so fittingly descriptive of such scenes:

"Oft did the harvest to their sickle yield,
  Their furrow oft the stubborn glebe has broke:
How jocund did they drive their team afield!
How bowed the woods beneath their sturdy stroke!

"Perhaps, in this neglected spot is laid
  Some heart once pregnant with celestial fire;
Hands, that the rod of empire might have swayed,
  Or waked to ecstacy the living lyre:

"Full many a gem of purest ray serene,
  The dark, unfathomed caves of ocean bear:
Full many a flower is born to blush unseen,
  And waste its fragrance on the desert air.

THE EPITAPH.

"Here rests his head upon the lap of Earth,
  A youth, to Fortune and to Fame unknown:
Fair Science frowned not at his humble birth,
  And Melancholy marked him for her own.

"Large was his bounty, and his soul sincere,
  Heaven did a recompense as largely send:
He gave to Misery (all he had) a tear:
He gained from Heaven ('twas all he wished) a Friend."

VILLANOW CEMETERY. Number of graves about 175. Est. about 1840. Tinnie Watkins 1868-1915; Matilda Cuma Tarvin 1843-1929 (82); Harriet Stancil 1830-1890; Amanda Clements 1841-1911; M. G. Clements 1823-1901.

James A. Shahan 1846-1929; His wife Martha J. Keown 1846-1929. Mr. and Mrs. Shahan died within 38 hours of each other and were buried at the same hour and in the same grave. Each 83 years of age. Mrs. Shahan was born, married and died in the same house.

Sarah S. Rea Keown 1853-1927; N. A. Keown 1831-1901; James A. Keown 1811-1887; Lela Goodson, wife J. M. Shahan 1874-1912; Basheba Ann, wife Robert Story 1839-1900; W. B. Buckalew Died 1915, A. 69; Mary, wife of W. B. Buckalew, Married 1866, Died 1911, A. 68; John L. Clements 1872-1895; William Fuller Tarvin 1853-1925; His wife Martha Elizabeth Love 1862-1923; Adolphus C. Clements 1839-1912; Nannie E. Clements 1842-1921; C. T. Townsend 1847-1908; Samuel Henry Love 1882-1911; Jasper Love 1851-1907; Rebecca J. wife of J. Love 1852-1895; Rebecca G. Stokes 1828-1899; G. Gordon Bowen 1888-1911; Maggie T., dau. Mr. and Mrs. W. M. Bowen 1876-1911; W. M. Bowen 1842-1918; Martha M. Bowen 1848-1923; L. Denton Bowen 1887-

1922; Richard Lanier 1811-1880; Annie E. Keith 1835-1886; Matthew Keith 1805-1862; Elizabeth Keith 1806-1885.

CONCORD. About 1200 graves. Est. about 1840.

Pvt. ALVERN HEWITT, Troop C. 15 Cav. 1896-1919. Died in France; Martha A. Roper 1845-1926; Rufus E. Cantrell 1879-1922; Fromey Morman, wife W. P. Young 1834- 1928; Zima Brock 1832-1914; Wm. E. Brock 1832-1909; John T. Cleghorn 1878-1927; D. L. Kennemer 1834-1917; Prof. W. D. Greene 1875-1915; Mary E. wife of Dr. C. T. I. Giles 1872-1900; Amanda, wife A. D. Wilson 1857-1910; Annie E. Keown wife W. M. Morgan 1865-1909; C. E. Cleghorn 1857-1927; Mrs. C. E. Cleghorn 1854-(?); M. F. Pope 1849-1925; Martha A. Pope 1850-1919; Media Hegwood, 1862-1923; Alfred L. Hegwood 1859-1902; Katie J. Hegwood 1860-1896; G. W. Wyatt 1862-1931; Emma J. wife G. W. Wyatt 1869-1908; James W. Norton 1874-1899; J. B. Norton 1848-1912; M. E. Norton 1850-(?); Thomas King 1840-1919; Callie F. wife W. H. Gray 1858-1909; Octie, wife of J. M. Gray 1886-1923; Joseph M. Travillian 1836-1917; Lucy, wife of J. M. Travillian 1847-1920; W. B. Hewitt 1855-1901; J. C. Bohanon 1842-1894; Four neat little markers in a row giving the names of Lillie, Clarence, Marvin, and Infant Peterson, all died in infancy.

Rev. J. S. Rawls 1870-1908; Fanny Jane Rhudy 1874-1901; Mrs. N. T. Shaw 1829-1902; John F. Shaw 1859-1921; Gaines Shaw 1849-1921; J. L. McKin, J. R. McKin, and Mollie McKin, wife of Sam Carpenter (No dates); Mrs. Mattie White 1836-1911; D. P. White 1822-1893; Mary E. wife J. E. Woodall 1843-1906; Arra Belle, wife G. W. Smith 1874-1893; M. B. James Martain and Mrs. Thompsy Martain (No dates).

D. N. Price 1846- (no marker); Rebecca C. wife D. N. Price 1851-1903; Emma Eaton Holcomb 1868-1894; Hugh Hampton 1833-1910; Isaac Newton Keown 1822-1895; Sarah Jane Harris, wife Isaac Newton Keown 1833-1913; J. M. Jolly 1845-1921; Anna, wife J. M. Jolly 1856-(?); Rev. J. A. Clemons 1862-1910; Mrs. Fannie A. Clemons 1867-1893; Milly Tate, wife Milton Keown 1837-1858; Columbus H. Tate 1844-1877; David Tate Sr. 1829-1862; David Tate Jr. 1831-1867; Nancy O. wife W. P. Tate 1830-1878; W. P. Tate 1827-1914; Sallie M. Tate 1842-1828; John A. Tate 1804-1884; Elizabeth Tate 1830-1894; Sarah M. Duncan, wife John A. Tate 1804-1898 (94); Mary A. Eaton, Nee Harris, wife J. E. Eaton 1845-1905; C. P. Harris 1815-1862; Major J. Harris 1841-1862; Margaret, wife C. P. Harris 1816-1894; Jesse Amos Griffin 1858-1921; Mary Griffin 1852-1886; Martha Griffin 1843-1885; P. L. Jane Cosper, wife of James T. Rainey 1826-1849; Rev. Henry Cosper 1803-1852; Mary C. Smith 1844-1922.

The following old citizens are buried at Concord but have no markers: Nathan Keown, age 80; Ellen Travillian, age 83; Mr. and Mrs. Ault, ages about 80 each; Mrs. T. E. Hall, Nee Travillian 1885-1927.

Family plot near Concord contains four graves with two markers: Macajah Pope 1808-1867; Harriet Pope 1810-1874.

TRINITY. Established about 1875. Number Graves about 250.

Julia C. Cannon 1845-1922; James M. Cannon 1843-1905; Frances Elizabeth McWhorter, wife of A. J. Boyles 1838-1899; F. B. McWhorter 1816-1896; A. B. McWhorter 1815-1895; Ada M. wife R. L. McWhorter 1859-1892; Our Father, D. Thurman, was born in S. C. 1819-1889; Our Mother, Margaret Thurman 1824-1902; Eddie Taylor, 1872-1905; Emma, wife J. W. Brice 1887-1929; Alice Agnew 1869-1897; J. H. McWhorter 1844-1908; Emelia Edwards, wife J. H. McWhorter 1837-(?); Dora Williams Camron Dyer 1875-1915; Georgia Day 1872-1910; Ulsa Day 1869-1902; Sarah E. wile Jesse Williams 1836-1890; Jesse Williams 1833-1904; Mary B. wife J. S. Cannon 1879-1908; Ellen Hampton 1873-1909; Zeb Vance Ledford 1881-1906; Luella Perkins 1877-1909; N. B. Rutledge 1871-1911; Alice L. wife W. H. Harper, Nee Gleeson, 1880-1903; Mrs. E. J. Wall 1825-1903.

M. E., son of Mr. and Mrs. J. M. Clarkson 1876-1908; J. B., son Mr. and Mrs. J. M. Clarkson 1881-1903; Hattie, wife M. E. Clarkson 1880-1904; W. A. Simmons 1849-1923; H. M. Simmons, wife W. A. Simmons 1848-1814; H. A. Rogers 1859-1926; Laura A. Rodgers 1863-1898; Tuler Rogers 1857-1917; Perry Rodgers 1885-1905; Rev. John Boyles "Preached the Gospel 54 years," 1818-1905 (87); E. L. Thurman 1858-1906; Robert L. Boyles 1885-1901; Caldona Boyles 1854-1916; William P. Boyles 1853-1901; Enoch Boyles 1832-1899; Minerva E. Boyles 1835-1900; John D. Crowder 1869-1925; Theron Crowder 1828-1917 (89); Sarah A. wife Theron Crowder 1828-1902; Haden Hale 1879-1904; Florence Virginia Boyles, wife C. W. Junkin 1866-1892; S. L. Parker 1886-1822.; Joel Parker 1820-1886; Lulian M. Parker 1871-1888; Rachel E. Crowder 1856-1880; Melvin D. Orr 1890-1925; H. C. Weaver, Died 1899. Age 64 yrs.; Amanda, wife J. B. Parker 1861-1910; Arvelin M. wife J. L. Frady 1870-1906; Margaret, wife J. J. Howell 1835-1897; John Agnew 1833-1899; Celottie G. wife Samuel Ware 1846-1901; William M. Shields 1855-1901; Jane E. Shields 1828-1901; S. P. Shields 1825-1900; Mrs. W. J. Hillburn 1867-1915; O. J. Cranmore 1885-1926; Ralph Mitchel 1908-1925; R. H. Mahan 1826-1915 (89); Leah H. wife W. M. Shields 1863-1917; Mary Bell, wife J. H. Holmes 1885-1922; C. D. Gilbreath 1873-1920; J. G. Smith 1862-(?); Martha M. Smith 1867-1927; Miller P. Groover 1850-1822; Mary D. Groover 1859-1931; B. H. Groover 1878-1916.

The old cemetery across the creek where the old Payne's chapel stood contains about 56 graves. It was established probably about 1840. J. S. Jackson 1834-1888; A. D. Lumpkin 1812-1870; John Shields 1800-1876; M. P. Rodgers 1815-1876.

CENTER POINT. Laid out 1878. Number of graves about 350. A. L. Fillers 1838-1878, first one buried here; John Moreland D. about 1915, age about 75, No marker; J. W. Dunn 1817-1890; His wife 1822-1906 (84); Thomas J. Tipton 1836-1892; His wife Millie 1843-1907; Wm. B. Bird 1836-1900; His wife Mary 1834-1898; J. T. Renfro 1819-1899 (80); L. R. Renfro 1822-1902 (80); G. W. F. Newsome 1843-1900; M. S. Newsome 1854-1912; Caswell C. Tipton 1830-1893; Milligent Tipton 1830-1900; J. A. Bowman 1824-1904 (80); Benjamin F. Loughridge 1845-1930 (85), His wife Georgia Poe 1845-1927 (84); W. R. Nave 1845-1901; Zachary T. Ashley 1850-1902; E. S. Thompson 1832-1897; Mrs. J. C. Pettigrew 1829-1906 (77).

ALLEN PETTIGREW 1893-1924. Priv. Co. A. 4th Inf. M.D. Camp Gordon. Margaret, wife of D. W. Cook 1858-1909; Martha E. wife of J. W. Elrod 1864-1905; Mrs. Sarah L. Cook 1820-1901 (80), Mother of Rev. D. W. Cook; James W. Bird 1859-?; Wife Sarah E. 1861-1910; Mrs. A. L. Fillers 1831-1912; Othniel Bird 1854-1924; Wife Margaret V. 1858-1928; Amanda Noblitt 1845-1903; Lucinda Rice, Died 1910, Age 80; Mrs. R. E. Culberson 1839-1901; Charles A. Wheeler 1866-1911; Wilburn Spear 1825-1906 (81); Wife Amanda 1828-1898; S. M. Bird 1831-1907; Wife Susan 1830-1899; A. G. Dunn 1845-1914; Wife Jennie Tipton 1848-1921; J. F. Catlett 1851-1921; M. E. Catlett 1852-1907; G. F. Spencer 1847-1914; Elizabeth Spencer 1817-1896 (79); G. W. Spencer 1812-1892 (80); J. W. Jay 1862-?; Wife 1866-1918; Hannah Jane, wife of J. B. Johnson 1861-1918; W. M. Free 1829-1913 (84); Wm. H. Rutledge 1836-1908; Wife Emiline 1842-1924 (82); J. L. Pendley 1835-1906; Charles White 1844-1924; His wife 1845-1921; James M. Quinn 1854-1924; Wife Mary 1860-1926.

ANDERSON CRASHMAN, Co. B. 1 Tenn. Inf. C. F. Edwards 1851-1921; Wife L. J. 1853-1920; A. J. Wheeler 1860-1917; L. J. Stanfield 1856-1919; Sarah M. Reed 1837-1918; Sarah E. Barrett 1861-1924; Joseph B. Aters 1860-1922; Wife Lydia A. 1855-1924; John A. Bird 1833-1916; Sarah Amanda Wife of Dan Bird 1851-1918.

SAMUEL, Son of S. H. and A. J. Dunn 1894-1918. 23 Co. 157th Dept. Brigade, Camp Gordon, Ga.

JONES FAMILY PLOT. Number of graves about 23. James B. Jones 1815-1883, wife, Harriet Brigman 1827-1911 (84); Susan Emma Jones 1868-1922; E. M. Willoughby 1821-1882; M. N. Willoughby 1828-1897; R. J. Glenn 1829-1908; wife Susan C. Jones 1828-1905; Nancy Jones 1804-1876; Nannie Glenn, wife of J. A. Sartain 1866-1915; Joel J. Jones 1845-1913; wife Brittanna, 1853-1885; Samantha C., wife of Joel J. Jones 1851-?

ROCK SPRINGS CEMETERY. No. Graves about 600.

Mabel E. Conley 1882-1925; John Higgins 1818-1897, Wife Rebecca 1820-1905 (85 yrs.); George Higgins 1849-1921; Martha L. wife H. P. Mashburn 1853-1915; Samuel H. Brice 1843-1903. Myra A. Brice 1844-1901; Robert Wesley Brice 1832-1900; W. D. Jenkins, M.D., 1856-1895; Rev. James Cole 1875-1917; W. H. SMITH Co. D. 1st Ga. Inf. C.S.A.;

Mary, wife W. P. Jones 1841-1866; Susan, wife Joe H. Smith 1808-1878; Joe H. Smith 1810-1879; H. B. Little 1850-1926; E. L. wife M. V. Boyd 1857-1913; W. E. Evatt 1850-1912; B. L. Chastain 1825-1906 (81 yrs.); E. P. Chastain 1834-(?); Jessie Chastain 1871-1902; Eliza McAlister 1819-1883 (Erected by Mary E. Conley); Maj. J. M. Shields 1818-1893, Wife Alice E. 1813-1898 (85 yrs.); P. H. Bird 1806-1894 (88 yrs.); Mary, wife P. H. Bird 1808-1888 (80 yrs.); J. F. Adkins 1860-1923; Lena, wife P. H. McDermott 1868-1891; Rev. Samuel Brice 1809-1879, Wife Ann Brice 1810-1873; W. E. McCall 1848-1895; B. A. McCall 1856-1904; Mrs. S. T. Brice 1837-1918 (81 yrs.); L. A. Conley 1812-1897; S. M. E. Conley 1822-1899; J. F. Conley 1846-1892; Isaac W. Hill 1817-1915 (98 yrs.); Wm. H. Ellis 1788-18g8; Wm. Conley 1780-1869 (89); James H. Chambers 1808-1864; Adaline N. Foster wife James H. Chambers 1818-1892; Reese Jones 1844-1924, Wife Susan E. Smith 1847-1893; William L. Davis 1873-1896, Lena L. Davis 1871-1891. On this stone is graved this beautiful verse:

> "Every year the Father calleth
> Some loved one to endless rest,
> And the heart, though filled with anguish,
> Can but cry, 'He knoweth best.'
> But a year not distant, cometh;
> When we tread the vast unknown,
> We shall find our ransomed loved ones,
> Seated round the great white throne."

Rev. Arthur Irwin Leet 1812-1892 (80); Ida, wife W. R. Conley 1863-1899; J. E. Conley 1827-1917 (90), Wife, Sarah E. 1829-1928 (99); John Randolph Conley 1847-1924; Sallie Hix Conley 1847-1920; H. J. Conley 1818-1883; Margaret R. Conley 1825-1903; James Weaver 1843-1929; Mattie Weaver 1849-1901; Thomas L. Tapp 1837-1919, Mary Fielding Tapp 1847-1922; W. B. Carroll 1843-1902; Thomas L. Jones D. 1913, A. 52; L. C. Rosser 1859-1899; William D. Rosser 1835-1901, Lucy J. Rosser 1837-1900; Mary Leet Jones, wife James E. Rosser 1875-1925. "One of her favorite verses:

> 'I know not where His islands lift,
> Their fronded palms in air,
> I only know I cannot drift,
> Beyond His love and care.'"

Joseph Deck 1858-1919, Wife Hattie 1855-(?); J. J. Foster 1872-1919, Wife Alice 1868-(?); A. E. Rogers, Senr., 1818-1898, Wife Martha A. 1830-1911 (81); R. C. Jones 1849-1930; Theressa Pope 1869-1918; William W. Shields 1842-1901, Wife, Rebecca 1847-1912; Robert Ramey 1836-1909, Susan L. Ramey 1839-1917; John Wallis 1845-1893, Manerva

Wallis 1845-1918; J. H. Bird 1839-1905, Mrs. A. M. Bird 1846-1922; J. C. Baker 1847-(?), Jane Baker 1841-1897; Dr. R. L. Bird 1869-1899; Phoebe T. Baker 1811-1892 (81); Mary L. Conley, wife J. R. Tyner 1859-1911; Mr. J. W. Keys 1841-1919; Mrs. Adelia Keys 1851-1893; Jane Catherine Tyner 1855-1919; W. H. Bowman 1844-1898; S. E. Bowman 1845-1902; James W. Hunt 1858-1923; Wife Mary K. 1863-1909; Jacob Deck 1850-1912, Alice Anderson Deck 1852-(?); E. C. Ducket 1845-( ); E. A. Ducket 1840-1907; W. A. Weaver 1839-1917; Lois White, wife W. A. Weaver 1853-1923; C. D. Weaver 1868-1918; G. E. D. Williams 1850-1911, Wife M. H. 1849-1915; Malissa, wife W. H. Spencer 1844-1911; Ida, wife A. J. Wellborn 1871-1906; James Madison Wellborn 1826-1916 (90); D. N. Pursley 1829-1904; N. E. Rosser Pursley 1842-1911; J. W. McClure 1847-(?); Wife Elizabeth 1850-1926; James Knox Forester 1843-1911; Margaret Ann Potts 1838-1913; James M. McClure 1852-1920, Minerva E. 1854-1926; L. F. Coker 1843-1925 (82); Sidney Potts 1853-1920, Nellie Potts 1847-1925; Laura B., wife C. M. Conley 1875-1915; WILLIAM R. SWICEGOOD Co. H. 12th Tenn. Cav.; Andrew J. Hicks 1853-1917, Martha L. Hicks 1856-1924; John A. Graham 1854-1927, Catherine S. Graham 1863-(?).

Corpl. ROSS GRAHAM, son of J. A. and C. S. Graham, 1894-1918, 76 Co. 2nd Division, U. S. Marine Corps. Gassed in Action at Chateau Thiery, France.

Lula V. Tucker, wife Dr. E. H. Hice 1871-1921; Martha J. Ross 1853-1928; Richard Boss 1848-1924; DANIEL C. WALLACE 1893-1928, Ga. Pvt. Army Service Corps. At Rest.; Leonard J. Shields 1868-1929, Lillie Wallace Shields 1878-(?); Sanford Leake 1835-1923 (88), Wife Nannie Smith 1849-1923; Bertha L. Tyner, wife C. H. Howard 1888-1926; James J. Blackmon 1849-1926; Ossie E. Blackmon 1889-1930; Wm. T. Cooper 1858-1920; Sergt JERRY DOTY 1899-1925; FRED LAWRENCE Ga. Pvt. 6 Prov. Ord. Depot Batln. 1892-1927; D. R. Iley 1854-1919; G. D. Hays 1849-1920; Thomas J. Smith 1837-1913; Emma J. Smith 1852-(?); J. F. Loyd 1858-(?); Sarah S. Loyd 1857-1926; Elijah J. Rosser 1854-1910; Robert J. Williams 1851-1921; Wife Susan M. 1859-1927; Z. H. Cannon 1852-1918. Lula Cannon D. 1925, A. 59; Harriet Wheeler wife G. E. Young 1856-1920; T. C. Coffman 1837-1908; T. B. ARNOLD, A Confederate Veteran (No dates); Wife Refenia 1849-1924.

CHILDRESS GRAVEYARD, near Pond Spring. No. graves, white 60; colored 36. Established 1853. R. B. Childress 1818-1853; Abraham Childress 1809-1856; Susan Childress 1816-1869; Mary, wife R. B. Childress 1817-1878; Richard Childress 1788-1879 (91).

FAIRVIEW CEMETERY. About 350 graves. Date unknown.

Berry Atwood 1852-1890; Elizabeth Ann Atwood 1829-1901; G. B. Atwood 1826-1896; Berry Atwood, Sr., 1799-1853; Ann Atwood 1799-1858; Nancy R. Bradley 1831-1854; Sergt JOHN T. VISAGE, Co. H. 11 Tenn. Cav.; Georgia Ann Echols 1827-1854; Mary J. McWhorter 1853-

1904; William Jacob Pettyjohn 1837-1892; High Dickson 1852-1928; Judia Dickson 1850-1916; Sarah Echols Dickson 1823-1892; Virginia Dickson 1848-1915; A. G. Dickson 1819-1892; John B. Rodgers 1823-89; Elizabeth A. Rodgers 1827-1896; Millie D. Shields 1848-1926; Tululu J. Chastain 1857-1885; G. W. Jones 1837-1894; Wm. McBryan 1819-1892; Jane E. McBryan 1824-1897; R. M. Bryan 1848-1891; M. D. Little 1843-1906; Jane Cargle Little 1851-1928; William H. Chafin 1841-1912; Julia G. Chafin 1838-1912; William Barnes 1839-1900; Mary E. Visage 1850-1929; Harriet E. Sharpe 1808-1850; Jacob Srite 1793-1885 (92); Mary N. Srite 1802-1880; Austin H. Bradley 1853-1912.

EAST ARMUCHEE. Number graves 140. Established 1887.

First person buried, George F., son of George L. and Sophia Keith, 1886-1887; George L. Keith 1831-1903, Wife Sophia 1847-1924; Lilla Keith 1879-1926; Charles McClure 1856-1914; E. F. Bowman 1845-1923; Wife Winnie 1845-1927; Rev. B. F. Hunt 1853-1926, Wife Laura 1866-1913. This handsome marker bears the inscription, "In loving memory of B. F. Hunt and wife. Erected by his churches and friends." Francis R. Carender 1817-1906 (89); Wm. H. Talley 1836-1898; W. T. Roper 1858-1914; Rev. J. L. Burk 1872-1914; Mary Jane Phillips 1826-1908 (82); W. H. Parsons 1865-1911; Susan Richard Davis 1840-1917; James R. Richardson 1841-1908; E. M. Tate 1832-1916 (84); Martha Robins Tate 1858-1912; Frances Elizabeth, Wife of J. W. Smith 1869-1901; Frank W. Ward 1849-1910; Delilah Ward 1825-1903; Malindy Ann, wife of Henry Alsberry 1840-1912; J. J. Walraven 1844-1898; Mrs. P. V. Walraven 1844-1926; W. H. Walraven 1867-1894; Mary Bohannon 1816-1893 (77); B. F. ELSBERRY, Co. L. 4 Ga. Cav. C.S.A. Elizabeth Hames 1827-1910 (83); Sara A. Richardson 1835-1902; Frances E. Alverson 1842-1925; Georgia Hames 1848-1917; Precious Owens D. 1895, Age 80; Reuben A. Keith 1848-1915, Sallie E. Keith 1844-1910; Joel M. Keith 1839-1910; E. I. F. Cheyne 1837-1905; Mary A. Cheyne 1843-1920; Wm. A. Price 1873-1915; John A. Griffith 1861-(?); Sallie J. Griffith 1869-1915; James Claude Keown, Senr., 1874-1927; N. M. Fouts 1858-1922; Mary A. Fouts 1859-(?); John F. Fouts 1877-1919; J. C. Clement 1852-(?); wife Emily 1852-1917; J. A. J. Hames (No marker), died 1923, Age 70.

SHILOH CEMETERY. Estab. about 1840.

John McWilliams 1794-1857, Born in Ireland; Wife Elizabeth 1776-1840, Born in Ireland; Spencer Bomar 1810-1884; Wife Mary J. 1815-1898 (83), Born on the Atlantic Ocean; Dr. W. P. Bomar 1838-1874; Margaret L. P. Bomar 1847-1882; Jane Bomar 1836-1918 (82); Edward A. Bomar 1840-1895; Wife Mary E. Neal 1846-1921; Thomas Neal Bomar 1890-1912; Lelia Bomar 1870-1895; Robert Bomar 1892-1925; Alice E. Bomar 1903-1923; James W. Storey 1851-1914; Wife Martha 1851-1926; J. Robertson 1831-1904; Wife Mary M. 1843-1915; George W. McWilliams 1815-1884; Wife Nancy 1809-1887; Dr. W. G. McWilliams 1853-1913; Wife H. C. McWilliams 1847-1919; S. E. McWilliams 1845-

1929; Dr. J. P. McWilliams 1849-1924; Wife Helen H. 1850-1925; Henry H. McWilliams 1885-1928; George B. McWilliams 1879-1920; L. Addie McWilliams 1846-1892; Georgia Mae McWilliams 1879-1908; Armanda McWilliams Neal 1848-1871; William McWilliams 1818-1878; Wife Martha Batey 1815-1891; William Francis McWilliams 1856-(——); Georgia A. Jackson 1846-1903; J. M. Blackwell 1831-1878; Carl G. Blackwell 1877-1927; Dora Blackwell 1871-1920; Sally Lee Talley 1870-1919; John Liles 1830-1899 (79); Elizabeth J. Liles 1826-1867; Hugh McClure 1812-1882; Margaret McClure 1813-1897 (84); George W. Sims 1843-1907; Wife Margaret A. 1857-1878; Susie B. McWilliams 1881-1927; James Ponder 1831-1904; Elizabeth Ponder 1837-1890; Mary S. Ponder 1872-1910; Elizabeth A. Orr 1826-1893; Kate L. Walton 1857-1891; Artemus Shattuck 1795-1876 (81); Sallie McWilliams Neal 1852-1890; Chapman Baker 1820-1874; Wife Caroline 1827-1903; Emma Baker 1860-1882; Katie Norman 1857-1915; Lenora Sellers 1887-1921; Magie Wortham Neal 1855-1896.

THE YOUNG FAMILY BURYING GROUND. Estab. about 1840.

James Young 1775-1858; Wife Sarah Anna 1782-1857; Captain F. M. Young 1823-1895; Wife Martha 1835-1870; Sarah Ann Young 1859-1883; George T. Young 1853-1884; William Little 1801-1882 (81); Wife 1815-1884; Bettie Jackson 1849-1877; J. R. Little 1847-1919; Wife M. A. Little 1853-1826; Captain William McWilliams 1836-1915; Wife Nancy Neal 1844-1922; Wife Sarah 1842-1862; R. P. McWilliams 1881-1907; Thomas Manning 1802-1889 (87); Wife Jane 1807-1885; John S. Manning 1830-1860; Robert Patterson, Died 1864. Age about 65.

SHAW FAMILY PLOT. 7 graves. Rev. Wm. Shaw 1821-1890; His wife, Harriet, 1824-1893; Amanda M., wife of A. F. Shaw, 1841-1878.

SHAW GRAVEYARD. Number of graves, about 350. Established about 1840. Mary A. Jolly 1878-1916; Emma J. Stepherson 1869-1929; Emeline Shaw 1847-1907; G. W. Shaw, 1837-1907; Sarah Lena, wife J. F. Andrews 1878-1904; "Old Confederate." (This is probably the last resting place of some unnamed Confederate solder, as the marker bears no name). T. E. Shaw 1854-?; M. J. Shaw 1854-1915; Clara Shaw Hamilton 1885-1925; A. J. Shaw 1856-1884; J. A. Shaw 1822-1861; Sarah M. Shaw 1830-1898.

Two small, neat markers standing side by side are graved "Amos Shaw," and "His Wife." There are no dates. Rev. W. L. Shattuck 1839-1915; A faithful minister of the Gospel, a loving father and a noble man has gone to his reward; Martha, wife of Rev. W. L. Shattuck, 1836-1917 (81); Rev. J. A. Shattuck 1868-1898; George Shattuck 1870-1896; Tom Shaw 1860-1927; Wife, Amelia Shaw, 1860-1890; Georgia F. wife of E. M. Marks 1861-1927; J. H. Miller 1840-1926 (86); Emmer Lee Taylor 1870-1914; Elizabeth, wife of Joseph Wallin, 1854-1902; Cora, wife of W. R. Williams, 1870-1904; M. L. Stallings 1858-1895; N. A. Shaw 1831-1894; Archibald Beaird 1797-1884 (87); Louisa Patterson, wife of A.

B. Patterson 1802-1859; S. R. Andrews 1846-1904; Amanda M, wife of S. R. Andrews, 1846-1912; George Shaw 1796-1877 (81); Jane Shaw 1792-1873 (81); James E. Shaw 1832-1914 (82); Nancy A. Careathers, wife of James E. Shaw, 1831-1894; R. F. Shaw 1824-1902; Mary F. McWhorter, wife of R. F. Shaw, 1833-1890; Benjamin Gilbreath 1849-1892.

"A. P. ELLISON, Color Bearer Co. F. 18 Ga. Vol. C.S.A." Mary Wallin 1833-1907; Joseph Wallin 1840-1913; Mrs. H. A. Lindsey 1867-1906; W. R. Lindsey 1845-1916; Chanie Wallin 1849-1911; Maggie, wife of J. M. Walden 1862-1907; W. F. Glenn 1855-1915; Mary E., wife of G. W. Beaird, 1857-1894; Lela Dell Howard 1880-1905; Charley Wallin, 1876-?; His wife, Alice, 1877-1927; Sallie, wife of T. J. Lawrence, 1861-1917; Mrs. H. A. Brown 1853-1913; J. J. Gilbreath 1850-1917; N. A. Gilbreath 1855-1924; J. R. Howard 1872-1922. Jonathan Miller, pioneer settler of the county is buried here. No marker. D. B. Cornelison 1866-1927. No Marker.

ESTELLE GRAVEYARD. Number of graves about 250. Jesse M. Shaw 1824-1903 (79); His wife, Mary Camp, 1831-1881; Sallie C. Shaw 1858-1909; Houston Shaw 1862-1888; ALBERT FRANKLIN. Texas. Pat. 1CL. 18 Field Art. 3 Div. March 30, 1925. S. J. Nelson 1879-1916; W. S. NELSON, Co. E. 10 Ga. State Troops, C.S.A. 1844-1927; His wife, 1844-1916; Joseph Ray 1841-1927; Thomas W. Neeley 1869-1912.

NAOMI CEMETERY. Estab. about 1890.

Arlean Thompson 1858-1920; Mary E. Cooper 1863-1929; J. A. Cooper 1859-1916; J. V. Cameron 1862-1905; Delia E. Burns 1856-1923; Mrs. Jane Hillburn 1846-1892; Susannah P. Mattox 1848-1928 (80); T. J. Edge 1864-1917; Wm. Know Chapman 1877-1929; Mrs. G. O. Clark 1859-1907; Lewis H. Dunwoody 1853-1922; Wm. A. Heartsill 1840-1926 (86).

OSBORN BURYING GROUND. Contains approximately 50 graves. Estab. about 1864. The first person buried there was James Osborn Humphrey, who was wounded in the Chickamauga battle and died a year later. Old citizens relate that he was brought there on a stretcher and placed in the first grave by his uncle and cousin. No marker at his grave. A number of old citizens have been buried here but I have been unable to get their names.

PHILLIPS FAMILY PLOT. East Armuchee. Several graves. One marker, Phally Myers Phillips 1812-1902 (90).

GOODSON FAMILY PLOT. East Armuchee.

Jacob Goodson 1805-1883; Barbary Goodson 1813-1893 (80).

CLEMENTS AND CAVENDER FAMILY PLOT.

Dr. Adam Clements 1807-1887 (80); Mrs. Mary Park Clements 1810-1892 (82); Mrs. Martha Cavender 1849-1882; Lula Belle Cavender 1869-1910.

DUNCAN GRAVEYARD. John Partain 1840-1896; Mrs. Larsinda Partain 1853-1912; A. Underwood 1834-1911; Velero Patton Underwood 1844-1920; Nancy Lee Hovis 1810-1871; Henry Hovis 1802-1879; Marvel Duncan 1795-1883; Mary Duncan 1804-1884 (80); Mrs. Hettie G. Duncan 1849-1926; Hugh L. Duncan 1836-1909; James Partain D. 1883, Age about 78; His wife D. about 1882, Age about 75 (No markers).

WALNUT GROVE. Established 1929. 3 graves.

COULTER, near George A. Langley's Home. About 50 graves. Not known when established, but very old. Only three markers. Andrew H. Caldwell 1805-1879; Deliah J. Caldwell 1809-1876; Margrete Haslerig 1880-1900.

ARNOLD GRAVEYARD. Laid out about 1840. Number graves about 100. Nancy H. Arnold 1846-1899; David Hall, died 1880, age 77; Elias Arnold 1807-1899 (82); Amelia Arnold 1811-1886 Jacob Arnold 1770-1856; Narcissa, Wife J. B. Headrick, 1832-1910; J. B. Headrick 1825-1875; Winnie Arnold died 1893, age 55 years. John Arnold 1833-1892.

TALLEY GRAVEYARD. 25 graves. Established about 1850.

Robert D. Talley 1799-1856; His wife 1809-1884; Son of R. D. 1829-1895; J. C. Cannon 1832-(?); James Shahan 1813-1854.

LOOKOUT GRAVEYARD. (New), Estab. about 1890. Number graves about 325. C. C. Parish 1851-1923, Wife Mary 1847-1906; Rachel Keys 1814-1895; H. V. Bird 1865-1920; J. F. Patterson 1869-( ), Wife Julia Howard 1866-1929; Wm. B. Parish 1834-1901, wife, Sallie, 1839-1894; T. J. Parish 1853-1930, Wife Minerva 1857-( ); W. N. Meridith 1855-( ), Wife, Mollie 1865-1918; R. M. Parish 1836-1909, Wife Lucy 1845-1899; Oliver Hambright 1833-1898, Mary E. Hambright 1833-1906.

Nine graves neatly enclosed with a concrete wall have the following names in concrete at the heads, without dates: Amous Kendrick, I. B. Kendrick, L. K. Pitts, Wallace Kendrick, A. L. Kendrick, E. H. Pitts, Burn Pitts, Blonnie Pitts, M. J. Oliver.

LOOKOUT GRAVEYARD. (Old). Estab. about 1850. Number of graves 150. William H. Burk 1846-1910; Mrs. A. D. Burk 1821-1893; R. P. Burk 1848-1919; J. N. Oliver 1859-1900; W. A. Oliver 1855-1891; John Long 1799-1885 (86); Elizabeth Long, died 1882; Gabriel W. Moore 1832-1896; Virginia More 1836-1900; Moses A. Morrison 1832-1890; John Mitchel 1841-1916; Sarah A. Mitchel 1850-1928; J. B. Carlock 1856-1910; Mrs. M. J. Carlock 1850-1902; James Carlock 1800-1865; Elizabeth Carlock 1825-1890; Elbert Kerstison Carlock 1852-1927; Matilda E. Boss 1855-1892; John B. Phillips 1797-1866; Martha Phillips 1817-1907 (93); Jane Roberts Mallicoat 1863-1921; Elizabeth J. Moore 1839-1889; William Oliver 1825-1897; Lucinda Ann Oliver 1826-1920 (94); Mary Jane Phillips 1844-1931 (87); L. P. Boss 1852-1928; Lemuel Carter 1818-1884; Mary Ann Carter 1837-1895.

CHICKAMAUGA CEMETERY.

A plot of five acres of land was donated in 1850 by Marcus Johnston for church and burial purposes. Later the late J. M. Lee gave another plot lying on the western side of the original five acres. This is a well-kept burying ground and is a pride to the citizens of that excellent community. It contains many beautiful markers and is probably the handsomest cemetery in the county. There are probably 3000 graves here.

Rev. Thomas C. Tucker 1847-1889, His wife Susan 1844-1897; M. A. Holcomb 1852-(?), His wife A. M. 1857-1925; John S. Holcomb 1875-1910; Aunt Mary Suttle 1823-1910; R. B. Bagwell 1846-1915; Louisa, wife of R. B. Bagwell died 1889 A. 39; J. T. Kirkpatrick, Jr. 1867-1927; Ianna, wife of J. T. Kirkpatrick 1845-1890; Maggie A. M. wife of J. T. Kirkpatrick 1852-1910; William Lemuel Hearn 1870-1919; E. L. Stoner 1858-(?); I. C. Stoner 1854-1922; L. C. Davis 1845-1910; Margaret J. Davis 1843-1930; Sarah C. wife of James H. Lewis 1835-1890; Amanda Couch 1840-1891; J. M. Harp 1854-1891; Amanda J. wife of J. M. Harp 1853-1920; Hortense, wife of C. C. Clements 1870-1892; Lucy R. wife of J. A. Mullis 1863-1886; C. A. Clements 1820-1886; J. A. Clements 1827-1888; Sarah Jane Heady 1844-1907; J. H. Heady 1873-1918; George A. Woods 1858-1929; His wife Elizabeth P. Evans 1858-1927; A. J. Liner 1845-1927; Wife Josephine West 1856-1906; Rev. L. H. Stephens 1851-1927; Wife Katherine E. 1854-1900; J. T. Trotman 1859-1928; His wife Ella C. 1864-1899; Mary Amanda, dau. D. B. and Amanda Baker 1825-1903; John T. Parker 1819-1894; Aunt Nancy R. wife Jno. T. Parker 1836-1922; Sarah V. Woody 1873-1912; Ida Woody 1876-1903; Lillian N. wife J. L. Baker 1886-1914; Mary A. Mullis 1834-1888; Wiley Mullis 1829-1904; Grandmother Myers 1804-1894 (84 yrs.); H. Weathers 1810-1891; Mary wife H. Weathers 1820-1894; Five neat little stones in a row marking the resting places of five infants of J. W. and N. M. Middleton; Adaline Weathers 1835-1911; James M. O'Leary 1871-1909; Susan C. Todd 1821-1884; Wirt Gordon 1869-1895; George P. Glenn 1852-1905; Wife Hannah C. 1861-1921; Rachel Winery 1818-1870; T. B. Killingsworth 1854-1830; wife Caroline 1847-1894; John F. Harp 1832-1897; Frances, wife John F. Harp 1833-1911; Frances E. wife Z. Lewis 1854-1915; Martha, wife J. J. Hixon 1865-1899; Mrs. W. J. Davis, nee Vina Eller 1855-1909; George E. Broyles 1834-1893; Mrs. C. C. Broyles 1812-1883; Major John T. Broyles 1806-1898 (92 yrs.); Buried at the feet of his parents facing south lies Dr. Julius J. Broyles 1831-1898; Captain A. G. Reynaud, Born at Martinique 1836-1902; William Lard Gordon 1828-1872; Sarah J. wife W. L. Gordon 1828-1903; James C. Gordon 1834-1911; Frances B. Gordon, wife Col. Jas. C. 1845-1892; James Gordon 1801-1863; Sarah A. Gordon 1804-1868; Joseph H. Fletcher 1836-1861; John C. Devoti, Served the Confederate States throughout the Civil War; Annie C. Devoti D. 1821 A. 85; Catarina Devoti 1810-1887; Romenico Devoti 1808-1883; John Boggiano 1808-1878; Macajah S. Baker 1830-1911; wife Arametha A. 1829-1905; Sister Mary Ann, wife J. J. Pearce 1852-1890; Brother James T. Baker 1851-1885; Mary E. wife J. J. Dyer 1847-1895; D. A. Reese 1860-1919; Two are buried in the Abercrombie Mausoleum, viz. H. C. Abercrombie 1851-1917; and Martha, wife Avery

Camp 1822-1903; B. M. Garrett 1833-1919; Walter A. Garrett 1871-1925, wife Lucy Russell 1875-1912; Willie Abercrombie 1817-1897; Thomas Ober 1818-1889; Ella, wife W. M. Prince 1867-1911; The handsome Scott stone contains the following names and dates: Joseph LaFayette Scott 1810-1882; Matilda Scott 1817-1900 (83 yrs.); John Hamilton Scott 1845-1892; Emma Scott 1849-1899; Joe Thomas Scott 1853-1901; Charles Davis Scott 1859-1862; Emma Scott 1887-1895; Another stone has Sidney Evan Scott 1859-1918.

"Erected by Crawfish Baptist Church in memory of Marcus Johnson for the Donation of 5 Acres of Land for Church and Burial Purposes. Died about 1867, Age about 70 Years."

David L. Dalton 1852-1885; Rev. Samuel W. McWhorter D. 1910; E. K. Roberts 1829-1908; Temperance Roberts 1798-1885 (87 yrs.); James C. Bird 1863-1926; John L. Garrett 1845-1911; Nancy Garrett 1857-1910; Harrison Dalton 1825-1884; Lucinda Brown 1848-1887; W. H. H. Simmons 1842-1926; wife Lucinda 1845-1905; Berry May 1845-1911; Eliza May 1830-1913 (83 yrs.); H. S. Simmons 1867-1930, wife Josie 1876-(?); E. N. Broom 1864-1913; J. B. Moore 1826-1916 (90 yrs.); M. C. Moore 1868-1922, wife Josie 1858-1911; J. W. Turner 1854-1913; Mamie Turner 1869-(?); C. H. Boss 1818-1909 (91 yrs.); Joseph Conley 1850-1877; Caleb Conley 1814-1889; Martha Conley 1827-1889; Julia A. Conley 1869-1892; W. A. Horton, Co. K. 43 Tenn. Inf. C.S.A.; George W. Brotherton 1812-1890; George Brotherton D. 1869 Age 63; G. W. Cook 1852-1896; Pauline Cook 1853-1918; David Childress (No date); Susannah Childress (No date); W. T. Childress 1867-1895; R. A. Childress 1879-1893; C. R. Childress 1845-1912, wife Mary Ann 1843-1899; R. E. Green 1855-1896; W. C. McDonald 1840-1929 (89 yrs.); Nancy A. McDonald 1840-1930 (90 yrs.); Thomas L. Pirkle 1851-1892; T. P. Pirkle 1874-1898; J. C. Broom 1857-(?), wife Mary L. 1855-1926; H. M. Thomason 1836-1919 (83 yrs.); Mae Thomason 1855-1919; Henry L. Madaris 1872-1927; wife Ella M. 1876-(?) Joseph N. Wilson 1837-1923 (86 yrs.), wife Sarah E. Schmitt 1848-1927; Margaret Dean 1828-1922 (94 yrs.).

Carl E. son of Mr. and Mrs. J. H. Harp 1894-1921, Bat. F. 129 F.A., A.F.E.; Reuben Couch Co. I. 60 Ga. Inf. C.S.A.; James Harp 1859-1826; Sallie Couch 1872-1919; James L. Brotherton 1842-1921; W. M. Milwee 1833-1917 (84 yrs.); Dorcas, wife W. M. Milwee 1843-1892; R. M. Jackson D. 1907 A. 77; E. J. Boss 1825-1903, wife M. A. 1823-1894; Margaret Sartain-Ginn 1844-1879, Elizabeth Sartain 1868-1888; John W. Sartain, 1869-1901; F. O. Plaster 1878-1919; Wm. B. Hearn 1838-1880, wife Mary E. Deck 1844-1896; Mark Bradley 1839-1913, wife Mary, D. 1913 A. 60; Nancy J. wife John Broom 1819-1897; Mary Williams 1814-1884; Thomas J. Manly 1839-1813; Lucrittie Manly 1842-1911; Oscar Martin 1867-1913; T. M. Jones 1868-1930, wife Sallie 1870-1930; J. R. Cagle 1874-1918; Mary Jane Thompson 1833-1810; G. W. Ellis 1847-1918, His wife 1847-(?); Nancy Ellis 1846-1893; Jane C. Ellis 1819-1890; James H. Ellis 1817-1903 (86 yrs.); J. M. Madaris 1839-1924 (85 yrs.); Sarah

Madaris 1844-1894; Wiley Wall 1831-1913; Harriet Wall 1840-1892; Mary Elizabeth Hall D. 1911 A. 86; Aunt Jane Hall 1826-1902; Samuel Hall 1808-1892 (84 yrs.); Annie M. Hall 1815-1892; J. Z. Miller 1856-1919, wife Emma 1860-1892, wife Ola F. 1873-1915; Liza A. Miller 1835-1899; Julia Ann, wife H. S. Davis 1832-1916 (84 yrs.); Wm. M. Ireland 1817-1903 (85 yrs.); wife Elizabeth 1819-1889; R. F. Parish 1860-1925, Mary L. Parish 1877-1919; R. L. Meredith 1850-1898, wife Sarah 1859-1926; Anna Clements 1878-1900; Rufus Bohanon 1868-1915; Sarah Jane Bohanon 1846-1898; Janie, wife H. C. Bohanon 1876-1914; Edgar H. son L. H. and A. M. Dyer 1888-1904; J. L. Plaster 1871-1902; A. T. Wooten 1845-(?); Charles M. Stoner 1852-1927, Sarah M. Stoner 1852-1912; Millie Jane Roberts 1859-1926; W. H. Liles 1856-1918; Janes A. Liles 1856-1926; Mary J. Merciers 1848-1914; W. H. Carroll 1860-1914; Lydia Carroll 1834-1918 (84 yrs.); W. O. Sholl 1873-1915; W. C. Davis 1867-1930; W. K. Shott 1859-1913, wife Sarah 1852-(?); W. D. West 1826-1910, R. A. West 1832-(?); H. S. Davis 1830-1910; Patsy P. wife T. S. Shaver 1848-1913; Thomas S. Shaver D. 1930 A. 72 (No marker); Nancy M. Miller 1850-1917; J. J. Davis 1848-1909, His wife 1849-(?); Thomas B. Akins 1835-1909; J. P. Million 1846-1895; Wm. K. Weathers 1872-1906; Eli Myers 1838-1908; Louisa Susan Myers 1835-1908; James Monroe Dyer 1852-1900; Eugene Dyer Osborn 1873-1918; Auguston, wife Henry Russell 1867-1893; Spill B. Dyer 1891-1917; Joseph W. Osborn 1854-1910, wife Florence Park 1868-1917; Spill B. Dyer 1828-1905, wife P. E. Parker 1833-1908; Susan, wife A. P. Boss 1861-1924; Lucinda Bird 1830-1900; Jessie Lee, J. L. and Addie Bird 1899-1910; Virginia Victoria Park, wife W. P. Park 1879-1914; Azalia Pierce 1870-1904; W. B. Pierce 1866-1915; Mary J. Ellison 1873-1923; Susan M. Ellison 1848-1889; Minerva A. Ellison 1846-1912; Mrs. W. M. Mullis 1870-1916; Their three children, Bertha Lawrence, Redie Rebecca, and Robert Daniel; N. B. Massey 1861-1909, Irene Massey 1855-(?); Paul A. Hearon 1882-1929, His wife Lillie Baker 1882-(?); Wm. D. Baker 1857-1925, His wife Lillie Ann Boss 1858-(?); R. B. Evatt 1858-1923, M. L. Evatt 1869-(?); H. D. Broom 1867-1930; Samuel Pickard 1879-1910; Flora wife J. L. Wallace 1872-1908; Kizah Hixon D. 1907 A. 73; Amanda Hixon 1838-1918; Wm. E. Hixon 1865-1904; Missouri Hunt 1854-1926; E. A. Goode 1824-1910; Allie Lewis 1862-1920; James K. Jackson 1853-1919; Mary C. Jackson 1875-1919; Sarah M. wife E. J. Robinson 1848-1914; Minerva, wife Rev. J. C. Kington 1869-1928; Paul Raymond Kington 1906-1930; Laura Hall Rogers 1868-1929; Virgil Abercrombie 1875-1925; Ida Mae Abercrombie 1881-1925; S. V. Abercrombie 1873-1924; J. C. Abercrombie 1849-(?), wife Tilihal 1854-1924; W. R. Henry 1851-1921; Mamie Lee, wife O. B. Glenn 1879-1914; Wiley M. McClatchey D. 1908 A. 68; James C. Erwin 1855-1928; William A. Wiley 1868-1922; Jefferson W. Lovinggood 1861-1923, Mary Lovinggood 1856-(?); Joanno H. Butler 1845-1910; Sarah A. wife S. R. Buchanan 1848-1905; Susannah Jones 1844-1903; Wm. A. Goza 1846-1908; Noah B. Hearn 1855-1881; Jane, wife J. B. Hearn 1813-1882; Joshua B. Hearn 1807-1897 (90 yrs.); Mary

Jane Knox 1848-1886; Addie Florence Carlock 1868-1896; Jefferson Carlock 1861-1900; G. W. Carlock 1834-1902; Mary, wife G. W. Carlock 1832-1891; M. C. Butler 1825-1900; W. C. Dedmon 1858-1929; Julius B. Dedmon 1884-1918; Sara J. Weathers 1852-1927; LUKE BAKER, Tennessee —Pvt. 157 Depot Brig. Mch. 31, 1921; James A. Hearn 1866-1928; James C. Ware 1862-1918; Wm. W. Ware 1857-1917; Rebecca S. Ware 1834-1915; Mary Josephine Sims 1860-1922; Vera Lee Camp Henderson, dau. Mr. and Mrs. M. A. Camp 1885-1918; Homer A. Davis 1877-1918, wife Octavia Strain 1879-1926; Lucinda, wife W. G. Davis 1844-1899; Robert Sparger 1838-1905; Mary Sparger 1847-1911; Mary, wife Z. T. Broom 1845-1919; John T. Broom 1880-1903, Annie, wife John T. Broom 1880-1918; Marion B. Broom 1855-1930; Susan R. Broom 1859-(?); W. T. Hasty 1862-1919; Sarah Hasty 1869-(?); O. R. Henderson 1849-1912; Louisa Henderson 1849-1910; Jerome G. Henderson 1876-1908; John Scott Henderson 1874-1899; W. F. Park, M.D. 1851-1903; Rev. J. H. Park 1829-1903; Susan R. Park 1828-1900; G. D. Price 1872-(?); Minnie Price 1875-1929; D. M. Sartain 1884-1899; Mary A. Miller, wife George Hixon 1847-1921; Emily A. Sparger 1851-1930; G. W. Sparger 1847-1912; Minerva, wife J. N. Parker 1848-1916; Benjamin B. Freeman 1856-1914; A. Smith 1854-1917, Mrs. A. Smith 1856-(?); Charley Davis 1864-1911; Mary Matilda Broom 1872-1917; AARON M. TAYLOR Co. I. 59 Tenn. Mtd. Inf. C.S.A.; John J. Taylor 1887-1925; A. L. Bagwell 1875-1925; J. T. Mashburn 1826-1910 (84 yrs.); Robert J. Mashburn 1861-1915; S. A. D. Mashburn D. 1905 A. 84; JAMES F. WYATT Co. M. 36 U. S. Vol. Inf.; Elizabeth E. wife B. L. Glenn 1839-1904; A. J. Glenn 1874-1908; Benjamin L. Glenn 1835-1917 (82 yrs.); Mrs. Elizabeth H. wife J. T. Bryan 1834-1905; James T. Bryan 1817-1906 (89 yrs.); W. R. Gilstrap 1865-1928; James M. Freeman 1855-1924, wife Theoria 1871-(?); WILLIAM LATNER FREEMAN son Mr. and Mrs. J. M. Freeman, Killed in France, June 24, 1918. Co. C. 307 Field Signal Bat. 32 Div.; Etha A. Moore 1829-1910 (81 yrs.); J. J. Moore 1841-1931 (90 yrs.); M. C. Moore 1836-1921 (85 yrs.); S. T. Osborn 1855-1912; wife Union V. 1851-1916; Giles G. Spencer 1852-1908; Rev. J. M. Moore, 1827-1906 (79 yrs.); wife Elizabeth 1840-1919 (79 yrs.); Joseph E. Henderson 1849-1910; Fannie Gabrella wife J. E. Henderson 1871-1909; James R. Camp 1850-1924; Ida Bonds 1870-1897; Elizabeth Bonds 1851-1919; John F. Bonds 1845-1924; G. H. Garmany 1856-1919; Mrs. Lou Smith, wife J. N. Pursley 1866-1903; Julia A. Wife Nelson Smith 1846-1915; Nelson Duke Smith 1836-1926 (90 yrs.); Kate Ireland Bagwell 1853-1825; Mary, wife T. M. Ireland 1855-1904; Jesse M. Ireland and wife (No dates); Martha J. Conger 1843-1894; J. C. Schmitt 1859-1911; Florence, wife Philip Schmitt 1860-1888; Ida V., wife Philip Schmitt 1874-1900; Elizabeth Ray 1847-1904; Reuben Moore Ray 1844-1906; Philip Schmitt, Born in Germany 1831-1906; Wife Christina, Born in Germany 1833-1912; Mary Suggs 1834-1912; W. L. Bradley 1864-1926; Robert B. Shaw 1851-1927; Wife Elizabeth Anderson 1862-1925.

M. A. Ellia 1872-1930; M. E. Ellia 1876-(?); Roxie C. Stotts 1857-

HISTORY OF WALKER COUNTY, GEORGIA 545

1920; Wife Mary Ann Smith 1870-(?); A. J. Shaver 1814-1898 (84 yrs.);
Mary C. Ward 1842-1919; Henry Slater 1823-1900; W. S. Abercrombie
1852-1925; Richard J. Abercrombie 1883-1919; Jesse S. Henderson 1847-
1930 (83 yrs.); Victoria Henderson 1853-1928; M. J. Ireland 1858-1919;
J. D. Ireland 1859-1918; Herman C. Gilstrap 1889-1910; John R. Hall
1820-1906; Mary A. Hall 1823-1896; James Gordon 1868-(?); Lular Gordon 1868-1911; Mrs. Mary Lou Gordon 1850-1923; Cicero N. Gordon
1836-1891; Clark Gordon 1879-1928; W. T. Bartlett 1845-1912; Nettie
Gilstrap 1871-1911; D. C. Smith 1874-1904; Wm. Littlejohn 1839-1899;
Pollyanna Littlejohn D. 1902 A. 60; Charles H. Roark 1843-1912; Elvira
Roark 1847-(?); Z. M. Tussey, 1875-1918; T. D. Brock 1862-1925; Martha A. Reed 1851-1926; F. T. Ellison 1841-1922 (81 yrs.); Wife Mary A.
1836-(?); Jack Harris 1828-1915 (87 yrs.); Mary, wife Jack Harris
1841-1924; Don Harris 1872-1928; David Mack Dalton 1884-1919; Samuel Travis 1853-1924; Alice, wife W. H. Sanders 1861-1920; John B.
Henderson 1843-1932; Cornelia V. Henderson 1846-1910; Major Thomas
H. Lyman 1830-1905; Cynthia A. Lyman 1839-1910; Emily M. Lyman
1872-1898; L. W. Myers 1837-1919; Amanda Louise Myers 1844-1916;
Harry David Myers 1871-1893; Dewitt Talmadge Myers 1876-1927; T. H.
Satterfield 1865-1908; Ella N. wife Dr. D. G. Elder 1861-1895; G. W.
Snodgrass 1811-1890 (79 yrs.); Elizabeth Snodgrass 1823-1895; J. T.
Byron 1837-1906; Rev. W. M. Monroe 1834-1898; James Morga Lee,
Born in Athens, Georgia, 1825-1889; Clarke Lee Nunnally 1865-1904;
Sallie Lee, wife C. R. Gaskill 1860-1896; The Hon. Gordon Lee, and
his mother, Mrs. Elizabeth Gordon Lee, are also buried here but their
graves are, as yet, unmarked.

Appendix

The following historical matters were discovered too late for insertion in their proper place in the body of this work, and being important items in the county's history are herewith appended.

INCOMPLETE ROSTER CO. C, 8TH GA. BATTALION, GIST-WALKER BRIGADE, ARMY OF TENNESSEE, GENERALS BRAGG AND JOHNSTON, COMMANDING.

Aikin, Stephen
Anderson, Dr., Sergt.
Barton, James
Berry, Charles
Brown, Frank
Butler, Jack
Butler, Bayless
Butler, George
Burch, William
Brogden, G. N.
Brogden, Ellsworth
Camp, T. J.
Carpenter, Calvin
Chambers, William A., 1st Sergt.
Chambers, Joseph W.
Clements, Cicero
Cooper, Seaborn
Davenport, Dr. H. S., Surgeon
Davis, P. R.
Dugger, J. A.
Eaves, Foss
Finley, W. V.
Finley, John
Fowler, James
Fowler, George
Fuller, Spivey, Sr.
Fuller, Spivey, Jr.
Fuller, J. B.
Fox, J. H.
Gales, James
Graham, Joseph
Gresham, Thomas
Green, Jesse
Hall, W. J., 2nd Lieut.
Holsomback, W. M., 3rd Lieut.
Hollins, M. L.
Harlan, J. M.
Hoover, George
Hoover, A. M.
Hendrix, John
Hunt, B. F., Major
Hudgins, R. C.
Jones, S. M., 1st Lieut.
Jones, L. N.
Jones, R. F.
Jones, T. G.
Keith, George
Keith, Joel
Kiker, Wills
King, A. J.
King, J. D.
King, John
Lay, John
Lanier, John
Lazenby, Press
McEntyre, William
McLain, Larkin
Miller, John
Mitchel, R. M.
Mitchel, J. B.
Miller, Oliver
Miller, Marvin

Miller, Bud
Murphy, James
McMullen, William
Moore, Creed
Mabley, T. B.
Owens, R. D.
Owens, John
Owens, ——
Owens, ——
Oxford, William
Oxford, ——
Pass, John
Putnam, Monroe
Rider, Hampton
Rogers, Joe
Roberson, J. W.
Scott, William
Scott, W. J., Jr.
Scott, Abe
Scott, Spencer
Stagg, James
Sutton, James

Sutton, Dick
Simpson, William
Stone, Arris
Stone, Henry
Thorubrough, J. B., Capt.
Thorubrough, J. H., Sergt.
Talley, Till
Talley, Bird
Talley, Starling
Talley, Carp, Corp.
Thompson, ——
Tomlin, William
Terry, ——
Wells, Dr. W. F.
Westbrook, F. M.
Walker, Henry
Walraven, David
Walraven, Buck
Williamson, William, Sergt.
White, Andrew
White, Leander

Justices of the Inferior Court, Walker County.

John T. Story	Mch. 3, 1834-Jan. 20, 1837
Robert Boyle	Mch. 3, 1834-1836
William S. McGuire	Mch. 3, 1834-1835
Colby Wheeler	Mch. 3, 1834-Jan. 20, 1837
Benjamin Wheeler	Mch. 3, 1834-Jan. 20, 1837
Samuel Fariss	Jan. 1, 1835-Jan. 20, 1837
Miles Davis	Jan. 16, 1836-Jan. 20, 1837
Samuel Fariss	Jan. 20, 1837-1838
Miles Davis	Jan. 20, 1837-1840
William G. Harris	Jan. 20, 1837-1839
Spencer Marsh	Jan. 20, 1837-Jan. 14, 1841
Alexander H. Dobkins	Jan. 20, 1837-1838
Eldridge J. Jones	Feb. 19, 1838-
Edwin G. Rogers	Mch. 17, 1838-
Constantine Wood	Mch. 18, 1839-Jan. 14, 1841
James Hoge	July 15, 1889-Jan. 14, 1841
Benjamin R. McCutchen	Mch. 30, 1840-Jan. 14, 1841
A. M. Sloan	Jan. 14, 1841-Jan. 15, 1845
Abel Crow	Jan. 14, 1841-Jan. 15, 1845
David Stewart	Jan. 14, 1841-Jan. 15, 1845
Spencer Marsh	Jan. 14, 1841-Jan. 15, 1845
John Wicker	Jan. 14, 1841-Jan. 15, 1845
John Wicker	Jan. 15, 1845-1846
John Catlett	Jan. 15, 1845-Jan. 6, 1849
Andrew L. Barry	Jan. 15, 1845-Jan. 6, 1849
William K. Briers	Jan. 15, 1845-1846
William Satterfield	Jan. 15, 1845-Jan. 6, 1849
Samuel Fariss	July 3, 1846-Jan. 6, 1849
Lindsay Edwards	July 3, 1846-1846
Daniel Gartman	July 23, 1846-Jan. 6, 1849
Samuel Fariss	Jan. 6, 1849-Jan. 8, 1853
John Catlett	Jan. 6, 1849-Jan. 8, 1853
Daniel Gartman	Jan. 6, 1849-1852
David Stewart	Jan. 6, 1849-Jan. 8, 1853
Andrew L. Barry	Jan. 6, 1849-Jan. 8, 1853
Jeremiah C. Culberson	Apr. 21, 1852-Jan. 8, 1853
Thomas E. Patton	Jan. 8, 1853-Jan. 12, 1857

Jeremiah C. Culberson .... Jan. 8, 1853-1855
John Caldwell .... Jan. 8, 1853-1855
Lewis C. Graddy .... Jan. 8, 1853-
Edley Bevert .... Jan. 8, 1853-
William T. S. Adams .... May 12, 1853-
Davis Fricks .... Feb. 13, 1854-Jan. 12, 1857
George Brigman .... Feb. 13, 1854-Jan. 12, 1857
Hugh B. Johnston .... Aug. 31, 1855-Jan. 12, 1857
Daniel M. Harris .... Dec. 6, 1855-Jan. 12, 1857
Thomas M. Phipps .... Jan. 12, 1857-Jan. 10, 1861
Thomas Richard A. Haslerig .... Jan. 12, 1857-1860
Hugh B. Johnston .... Jan. 12, 1857-1859
Spencer Marsh .... Jan. 12, 1857-Jan. 10, 1861
Robert B. Dickerson .... Jan. 12, 1857-Jan. 10, 1861
Thomas J. Warthen .... Feb. 9, 1859-Jan. 10, 1861
John F. Evans .... Mch. 2, 1860-Jan. 10, 1861
John McWhorter .... Jan. 10, 1861-1862
Thomas M. Phipps .... Jan. 10, 1861-Jan. 26, 1866
James T. Bryan .... Jan. 10, 1861-Jan. 26, 1866
Samuel Fariss .... Jan. 10, 1861-1862
Lindsay Edwards .... Jan. 10, 1861-1862
Spencer Marsh .... Mch. 15, 1862-Jan. 26, 1866
Dewitt C. Fariss .... Sept. 2, 1862-Jan. 26, 1866
John Catlett .... Dec. 29, 1862-Jan. 26, 1866
James M. Bonds .... Jan. 26, 1866-1868
Benjamin R. McCutchen .... Jan. 26, 1866-1868
Dewitt C. Fariss .... Jan. 26, 1866-1868
Madison E. Rhodes .... Jan. 26, 1866-1868
James R. Jones .... Jan. 26, 1866-1868

Bibliography

White's Historical Collections.
Stephens' History of Georgia.
Smith's Story of Georgia.
Avery's and Evan's Histories of Georgia.
Ramsey's Annals of Tennessee.
Walker's History of Chattanooga.
Knight's Georgia's Landmarks, Memorials and Legends.
Knight's Reminiscences of Famous Georgians.
War of the Rebellion—Official Records of the Union and Confederate Armies.
General Gordon's Reminiscences.
Census Bureau, Washington, D. C.
42nd Annual Report, Bureau of American Ethnology.
Records in the Office of the Secretary of State.
Acts of the General Assembly of Georgia.
Various Newspaper Articles and Clippings.
Many Old Settlers and Citizens of the County.
Court Records. Files of the Walker County Messenger.
Many communications from Former Citizens of the County, or their descendants, now living in other Counties or States, giving interesting information and incidents concerning Early History of the County.
Etc., etc.

Index*

Ab Wisdom 213; Agriculture 181; Acts General Assembly 1835, 271; A Judicial Community 262; A Geologist 264; A Fight 270; Alabama Road 33, 209; Allen, Davie 118; Allgood, A. P. 216; Allgood Wagons 260; American Revolution 5, 10, 13, 14; Amusements and Entertainments 200; Anderson, Robert 308; Anderson, S. R. H. 254; Antebellum Houses 316; Antebellum Homestead 245; Andrews' Raiders 246; Appendix 546; A Pottery Plant 245; Antebellum Picture 238; Anderson Spring 254; A Rare Old Teacher 271; Armuchees 24, 279, 307; Ash Hopper 202, 216; Ashworth, J. T. 120; A Subterranean Village 39; At the Battle of Sweetwater 229; Attorneys 326; A Unique School Collection 274; Autos 189; Autograph Album 276; Ascalon 280.

Ball-play 207, 268, 283, 311; Bailey, W. C. 274; Barbary Powers 7; Bauxite 187; Battle of LaFayette 111 (Number engaged 117, Casualties 117, Notes on the Battle 117;) Battle Above the Clouds 112; Battle of Missionary Ridge 112; Bill Arp's Humor 319; Big Shanty 246; Birth of Negroes 270; Bill Stallings 239; Big Fool 5; Bills of Sale 130; Blackwell Ledger 247; Blacksmith Shop 263; "Blueback" 280; Blackwell, W. P. 193, 200; Blaylock, Miss Susie 216; Blank Pages 508-519; Blue Bird 24, 25; Blue Bird Spring or Gap 24; Boone, Daniel 3, 14; Boudenout, Elias 16, 33; Boundary, Ga.-Tenn. 49; Boss, W. H. 187; Bonds 189; Born at Sea 257, 307; Board Roads and Revenue 299; Board of Education 177; Bragg's Hdqrs. at LaFayette 57; (Original Purpose 59); Brainerd Road 32; Brainerd 10, 29, 31, 32; Bronco 286; Brothertons, The 102; Broomtown Valley 23, 279; Brown, Col. James 8; Brown, Joseph 8; Brown, Terrell 30;

---

*No attempt has been made to present an exhaustive index,—only the more salient items being recorded.

INDEX—Continued

Brocks, The 105;   Bryan Family 249;   Bruner's Chapel 364; Buffalo 23;   Bugle Call 272, 273.

"Camac's Rock" 50;   Camp Chickamauga 149;   Camp Meetings 379;   Carson, S. B. 248;   Cassandra 280;   Center, Miss Orpha 114, 118, 237;   Center Point 367;   Cedar Grove Church 58, 385; Cenchat 280;   Center Post 280;   Cherokees 3, 4, 15, 16, 258; Cherokee Alphabet 15;   Cherokee Country Surveyed 26;   Cherokee Land Lottery 26, 32, 74;   Cherokee Romances 33;   Cherokee Rose 40;   Chestnut Town 206;   Chattooga Church 113;   Chattooga Town 207;   Chastain, Mrs. G. L. 229, 230;   Chattooga Bap. Church 370;   Charles 20;   Chattanooga Times 13, 98;   Chattanooga 4, 7, 20, 24;   Chestnut Flat 22, 279;   Che-nah-wah 24;   Cemeteries 520;   Chickamaugas 4, 5, 6, 7, 8;   Chickamauga Creek 4, 5, 6, 7, 25, 28;   Chickamauga Town 6, 7, 8, 29, 207;   Chickamauga Path 29; Chickamauga Battle 55;   Chickamauga, Poem by Walker, 55; Chickamauga Battlefield 29;   Chickamauga Battle, Judge Lusk's Article, 98;   Chickamauga Bap. Church 377;   Civil War Terrorists (Guerrillas, "Bushwhackers," Raiders, Tories, etc.) 120;   Civil War Incident 271;   Church History 356;   Church of God 369; Church of Christ 384;   Clark, George Rogers 4, 5, 6;   Clinton Dangerfield 249;   Clements, Judson 256, 266;   Clerk Superior Court 298;   Clerk Inferior Court 299;   Clouds, The 108;   Clothes 200;   Cooper, Alonzo 29, 208, 257;   Cooper, T. A. 33, 208, 257; Cooper, Joel and Thos. 211;   Coosa Bap. Association 388;   Country Young People 194;   County Organized 41;   Coal 185;   Cotton 184;   Conley, Jason 184;   Confederate Soldier Muster Rolls 134, 546;   Confed. Mon. at LaFayette 155;   Confed. Bonds 311; Confed. Veteran's Picture 136;   Contributions 204;   Court House 252, 258, 263, 274;   Connally, Sheriff 256;   Cobb, Thos. R. R. 276; County Officers 298;   County Names, Their Meaning 277;   Coroner 299;   Copeland, F. W. 306;   County Sch. Supt. 177;   Corn, King 182;   Corn Clubs 183;   Conveniences 201;   Country Social Life 196;   Corinth Bap. Church 361;   Crawfish Spring, 7, 25, 27, 205,

INDEX—Continued

215; Creek Indians 8, 13, 16, 28; Crayfish Town 206; Crow Town 6; Crawfish Spring Masonic Lodge 331; Culberson, E. L. 68, 117; Cummings, Rev. David B. 54; Dahlonega 16; Daugherty, William 26, 308; D.A.R. 52, 158; De Soto 3; Debating Society 195; "Devil-and-Tom Walker" 257; Dick's Ridge 29, 278; Districts and Sections 47; Dickerson, R. N. 258; Dickerson R. B. 264; Doctors 322; Dogwood 206; Doc Morse Band 124; "Doc" McWhorter 23; Dogwood Valley 22, 120; Dragging Canoe 5, 8; Dr. Tarvin, Indian 258; Duck Creek Valley 23, 30; Dyers, The 105.

Eagle Cliff 29, 280; Early School Records 164; Early Teachers 173; Early Customs 179; Early Days in Walker, by Captain Wood 212; East Armuchee Bap. Church 362; Edwards, Cyrus 119; Economical 188; Eminent Domain 26; Elizabeth Gordon Lee Memorial Church 370; Examples of Extreme Longevity 313; Executions 312.

Family Reviews 395; Family Reunions 365; Fariss, Captain Samuel and Dr. Samuel 51; Felton, Dr. 256; Federal Road 33; Five Lower Towns 6, 7, 8; Five Spring Trail 23; First Court House at Crawfish Spring 25, 27, 48; Fire Clay 187; First Cotton Gin 243; Filched a Church 250; Fish Trap 265; Fields, Jim 208; Flag of Truce 115; "Flint-and-Steele" 264; Fleecy Staple 184; Fort Cummings 17, 51; Foster, Mrs. W. A. 236; Foster, W. A. 249, 262; Friendship Bap. Church 365; Furnace 29, 186, 187; Fuller, H. G. 211.

Gatewood, John 120, 233; General Gordon's Description of Battle 60; Gander Pulling 253; Georgia Crackers 193; Glenns, The 109; Geological History 1; Georgia Counties Analyzed 42; Georgia-Tennessee Boundary 49; Gold, Harriet 33, 34; Gordon, General John B. 67, 212, 277, 242; Gordon Brothers, Charles, James and Thomas 215; Gordon Hall 57, 114, 159; Gordon, Dr. 264;

INDEX—Continued

Gordon, Mrs. Mary 230; Golden Wheat 183; Golden Weddings 315; Great Chickamauga War Path 6, 28; Greenbush 279; Guerrillas 113; Great Crossing (Hales Bar) 6; Graveyards 520; Governor Hamilton 6, 10.

Hackney, J. B. 221, 256; Hackney, T. C. 221; Hat Factory 242; Harks Back to Declaration 257; Harden, Miss 13; Hales' Bar 6; Hall, J. P. 323; Hammond, Dr. J. H. 268, 323, 325; Hawk, Bill 52; Hamilton, Governor 6, 10; Hayes, Roland 126; Henderson, John Scott 196, 217; Henry, Judge W. M. 118, 262, 358; Hicks, Charley 206; Hicks, Elijah 209; Hiawassee 20; Hooper, Judge 25, 206, 213, 215, 309; "Home Sweet Home" 12, 34, 259; Horse Racing 217; Hog Rifle 273; House Raising 192; "Hoe-Cake" 202; Horse Swapping 253; Hog Smith 215; Hunt, Thomas Gordon 215; Hixon-Miller Family 249; High Point 280; Heirlooms 316; Hinniard's Cross Roads 280; Hunter's Paradise 257; Hurricane 275; Historical Items in Single Sentences 316.

Indian Mounds 2, 7; Indian Graves 3, 21, 27, 31, 32; Indian Territory 21; Indian Trail 22, 23, 27, 28, 30; Indian Settlement 23, 24, 30; Indian Titles 25; Indian Farming 30; Indian Names 30; Indian Romances and Stories 33; Indian Play-ball 206; Indian Rock Mound 247; Indian Hominy 277; Indian's Valedictory 260; Inferior Court Justices 548; In-conveniences 203; "In Memoriam" 550; Iron Ore 186; Island Town 6; Irregular Southern Boundary Line 245; Ingraham, John 276.

Jackson, Andrew 9, 30, 33, 209; "Jim Fields" 208; Johnston, Reed 256; "Johnny Cake" 202; Jones, Benjamin, Dr. G. W. and Olmsted 26, 31; Jones, J. J. 184; Jones, James R. Ledger 255; Justices Inferior Court 303, 548.

Kaskaskia 4, 5; Kaolin 187; Kelleys, The 104; Kenyan, Judge 212; Kensington 280; Kensington Meth. Church 387;

Kingsbury, Rev. Cyrus 35;   Kirby Chapel 378;   King Corn 182.

LaFayette, Battle of 112;   LaFayette Volunteers 225;   LaFayette Before the War 230;   LaFayette's Public Square 263;   LaFayette, Early History 311, 320;   LaFayette Bap. Church 272, 365; LaFayette Meth. Church 373;   Land Districts and Sections 49; Lane Home 248;   Lane, Richard 248;   Langley, G. A. 237;   Large Families 317;   Lawyers 326;   Leath, Ben 183;   Lee, Gordon 215; Lee, Mrs. Ruth M. 215;   Legal Executions 312;   Legal Profession 326;   Leslie, Alvin 256;   Legend of Nacoochee 38;   Legend of Cherokee Rose 40;   Liberty 251;   "Little Bob Dickerson" 257; Local Trails 29;   Longfellow 17;   Long-Roberts Band 123, 124, 257;   Log-rollings 192;   Lookout Town 6;   Lookout Mountain 3, 4, 8, 13, 28 (How Named 209, 277);   Lower Towns 7, 8;   Lost in Mountains 272;   Lytle 280;   Lowery, George 206;   Lookout Bap. Church 367;   Lumpkin, Judge H. P. 234, 262;   Lusk, Judge Charles W. 98.

Macedonia Bap. Church 364;   Maddox, Judge John W. 125, 232; Marsh, Spencer 213;   Masonic History 331;   Members Board of Education 177;   Methodist Episcopal Church 376;   Medical Profession 322;   Menu in Revolutionary War 245;   McCall, Asbury 249, 262;   McCutchen, Augustus 256, 264;   McCutchen, B. R. and C. D. 262;   McFarland, Thomas and X. G. 211, 214;   McFarland T. F. 214;   McCulloh, Joseph 26;   McLemore's Cove 7, 30, 279, 307, (Union Soldiers Encamped in 57);   McLemore, John 25;   McDonald, John 10, 214;   McDonalds, The 103, (John 104, 106);   McWhorter, Cicero 286;   McWilliams, Dr. J. C. 32;   Militia Districts, How Formed and Named 47, Boundaries 48;   Mission Ridge Bap. Church 368;   Mineral 185;   Milk Sickness 218;   Minutes Board Roads and Revenue 258;   Missionary Ridge 278;   Mountain Rifles 243; Moon, Edom 249;   Morse, Dock 124;   Moravian Missionaries 27; Mother's Gift to Her Soldier Boy 221;   Mount Carmel Church 369; Mound Builders 2;   Montgomery, John 5;   Myers, William 29;

INDEX—CONTINUED

Mullisses, The 105; Murder of the McSpaddens 237; Muster Rolls, Confederate Soldiers 134, 546; Muster Roll, Captain Aycock's Company of Cavalry 308.

Nickojack 7, 9, 29 (How Named 50); Nickojack Trail 29; Napier, Captain 245; "Narrows" 4, 6; Nacoochee 38; Naomi 280; Naomi Bap. Church 369; New Echota 15, 16, 29; Negro, The 125 (Longevity 129); Newnan, General Daniel 206; Northwest Georgia 208; Note of a Partridge 227.

Old Field School 170, 280; Old Singers 249; Ordinary 298; Other In-conveniences 203; Original Settlers 43, Roster of 45, Emigrated 47; Old Blueback Speller 280.

Patton, Thomas, "Secesh" 248; Parker, J. B. 246; Payne, John Howard 12, 259; Patton, Mrs. M. E. 225; Pension Rolls 151; Peavine Creek 210; Perry, William, First Merchant at LaFayette 212; Peavine Bap. Church 364; Peavine Ridge 278; Pittsburgh 280; Pillow, General 9, 113, 114; Pillow, William 9; Pigeon Mountain 24, How Named 209, 278; Phoenix 34; Phipps, Thomas 117; Play-ball 207, 268, 283, 311; Pleasant Hill Meth. Church 380; Pocketbook and Crush 213, 216; Poes, The 99 (Picture 106); Poor School Fund 160; Posey, Humphrey 213; Post Office Records 327; Primitive Baptist Church 380; Presbyterian Church 356; Presiding Elders, Dalton District 386; Puryear, John 245,—S.W. 31.

Quilting 192.

Raccoon Roughs 242; Race Track 253; Ramey, W. M. 261; Ransey Sniffle 239; Ransom, J. M. 58, C. C. 124, 274; Revolutionary Bill 310; Refugees in Ravine (Chick. Bat.) 100; Recent Teachers 174; Revolutionary Soldiers 157; Reminiscences of a Refugee 218; Reid G. W. 308; "Red Bird" 268; Richmond Hosiery Mills 312; Ridge, John 12; Ridge Major, 12; Rhodes, Madison 245,

INDEX—CONTINUED

262; Rossville 10, 211; Ross, John 10, 211, 214, 250, 259, House 12, 214, 259, Picture 11, Landing 19, 209, 211; Ross, Daniel 10, 12, 14; Rossville Postoffice 33, 214; Roberts-Long Band 123, 237; Round Pond 205; ROSTERS: (County Officers 298, 548; Board Roads and Revenue 299; Representatives 300; Senators 301; Judges Superior Court 302; Judges Inferior Court 303, 548); Lawyers 326; Doctors 325; Rosser, J. E. 262; Rossville New Age 322; Rossville Open Gate 322; Royal Arch Masons 335; Rock Spring Meth. Church 387; Running Water 6, 28.

Schools 160; School Trustees 162; Scott, General 17, 53; School Teachers 173-177; Sevier, John 6, 9; Sequoya 15; Seminoles 17, 28, 211; Secession Convention 264; Senators 301; Shaw, Hyram 211; Shaw, Seab 121; Shaw, Mrs. Sam 235; Simmons, Tom 49, 307; Singing Convention 262; Skirmish at LaFayette 119, 232; Shiloh Bap. Church 383; Shelby, Col. Evans 5, 6; Shooting Match 243; Schmitt Family 250; Sheriff 298; Sharpe 280; Sharpe, Thomas 264; Signal Point 255; Slaves, prices 127; Smith, Hog 215; Smith, Major W. B. 4; Smith, C. W. 30; Smith, Nelson 31; Snodgrass House 100, 101, Picture 106; Soldiers of 1812 158; Soldiers of Indian Wars 158; Soil, Types 182; Solomon's Temple 275; Soldiers, World War 286; Spelling Bee 195; Spinning in Old Fashioned Way 241; Some Efforts at Composition 335; Stood Guard While Rebels Dined 236; Stansell, Fred 29, 187, Rev. Levi, 53; Strawberries 184; Strawberry Town 206; Straight Gut Valley 29, 267; Suttle, John B. 222; Sunnyside 244; Stony Point 251; Surveyor 299; Swayback 306; Sylvan Bower 280.

Tamar Escapes from the Indians 40; Tarteechee Pond 29; Taylor's Ridge 22, 29; Tennessee River 3, 4, 5, 7, 8, 11, 19, 29; Tatum, J. G. 254; Tax Receipts 269, 273; Tax Receiver 298; Tax Collector 298; Tan Yard 268; Tennessee Company 13; "The Broom" 23, 279; Three Notch Trail 30; Thrash, Doc 130;

INDEX—CONTINUED

Tittle, Mrs. Dora Suttle 222; Thorny Hall 251; "Three Killer" 268; The Old Field School 170; The Negro 125; "The General" 246; The Poes 99; The Snodgrasses 100; The Brothertons 102; The McDonalds 103; The Kellys 104; The Brocks 105; The Mullisses 105; The Dyers 105; The Viniards 108; The Winfreys 108; The Vittetoes 108; The Clouds 108; The Glenns 109; Teachers 173-177; Tombstone Inscriptions 520; Trickum 31, 280; Types of Soil 182; Tripolite 187; Treasure Trove 263; Trans 280; Treasure 299; Tradition, What Is It? 239, 250, 268; Trinity Meth. Church 368; Tyner, J. R. 269, 270.

Upper Towns 7, 15, 28, 31; U.D.C. 155; Universalist Church 360; Ulster County Gazette 303.

Valley Head Bap. Church 362; Venable, Captain 262; Vincinese 4, 6; Villanow 29, 213, 279; Vicksburg 279, 307; Viniards, The 108; Vittetoes, The 108; Veterans World War 286.

Watts, John 8; Walker, Robert Sparks 27, 35, 55, 98; Ward, J. A. 31; Walker, Major Freeman 42; "Wax-and-Tallow" Deeds 47; Warthen, Mrs. N. G. 218; Washington Entombed 303; Walker County Hosiery Mills 311; Walker County Messenger 320; Warthen, Spencer 263; Walnut Grove Bap. Church 361; Waterville Bap. Church 361; White-Man-Killer 8; Whirlpool 4; Wheeler, Benjamin 212; White's Historical Collections 204; When Husband Went to War 235; White's Statistics 252; When Clements Beat Felton 266; Wheeler, John B. 268; A West Armuchee Family Refugees 222; Whipping Post 256; "Witch" Spring 254; Winepress 250; Wool Rolls 240; Wooten, James 249, 260; Wood, J. Y. 191, 212, 271; Wood, Constantine 212; Weathers, Hartwell 185; Williams, Louis and Amos 210; Wood Station Bap. Church 361; Wheat, Golden 183; Winfreys, The 108; William Marsh Chapter, D.A.R. 52; Wisdom, Ab 213; Western Lodge F. & A. M.

331; Walker County: Organized 41, Position 180, Topography 180, Drainage 181, Climate 181, Wealth 188, Autos 189, Bonds 189, Miscellaneous 189; World War Veterans, Roster 286.

Yazoo Fraud 13; Young J. C. 32.

www.ingramcontent.com/pod-product-compliance
Lightning Source LLC
Chambersburg PA
CBHW020632300426
44112CB00007B/88